Historic Events *for Students*

The Great Depression

Historic Events for Students

The Great Depression

Volume 1: A-E

Richard C. Hanes, Editor
Sharon M. Hanes, Associate Editor

Detroit • New York • San Diego • San Francisco • Cleveland • New Haven, Conn. • Waterville, Maine • London • Munich

Historic Events for Students: The Great Depression

Richard C. Hanes and Sharon M. Hanes

Project Editor
Nancy Matuszak

Editorial
Jason M. Everett, Rachel J. Kain

Permissions
Debra J. Freitas, Lori Hines

Imaging and Multimedia
Dean Dauphinais, Christine O'Bryan

Product Design
Pamela A. E. Galbreath

Composition and Electronic Capture
Evi Seoud

Manufacturing
Rita Wimberley

For more information, contact
The Gale Group, Inc.
27500 Drake Rd.
Farmington Hills, MI 48331-3535
Or you can visit our Internet site at
http://www.gale.com

LIBRARY OF CONGRESS CATALOGING-IN-PUBLICATION DATA

The Great Depression / Richard C. Hanes, editor; Sharon Hanes, associate editor.
p. cm. — (Historic events for students)
Includes bibliographical references and index.
ISBN 0-7876-5701-8 (set)—ISBN 0-7876-5702-6 (v. 1)—ISBN 0-7876-5703-4 (v. 2)—ISBN 0-7876-5704-2 (v. 3)
1. United States—History—1933-1945. 2. United States—History—1919-1933.
3. Depressions—1929—United States. 4. New Deal, 1933-1939.
5. United States—History—1933-1945—Sources.
6. United States—History—1919-1933—Sources.
7. Depressions—1929—United States—Sources.
8. New Deal, 1933-1939—Sources. I. Hanes, Richard Clay, 1946- II. Series.

E806 .G827 2002
973.917—dc21
2001007712

Printed in the United States of America
10 9 8 7 6 5 4 3 2 1

Table of Contents

E

F

G

H

I

J

L

N

P

R

S

T

W

Chronological Table of Contents

1920–1929

1929–1941

1930–1941

1932–1939

1932–1941

March 1933–June 1934

1933–1941

March 1933

May 1933

June 1933

June 1933–1941

December 1933

1934–1939

1934–1941

April 1935–June 1938

April 1935–1941

May 1935

August 1935

1935–1939

1936–1968

1940–1944

1964–1968

Advisory Board

A seven-member board consisting of teachers, librarians, and other experts was consulted to help determine the contents of Historic Events for Students: The Great Depression.

The members of the board for this set include:

Glen Bessemer: Department of History, Wayne State University, Detroit, Michigan

Monica Cornille: Reference Librarian, Adlai E. Stevenson High School, Lincolnshire, Illinois

Professor Charles K. Hyde: Department of History, Wayne State University, Detroit, Michigan

Joel L. Jones, M.L.S.: Kansas City Public Library, Kansas City, Missouri

Ann Marie LaPrise: Junior High/Elementary Media Specialist, Huron School District, New Boston, Michigan.

Margaret Lincoln: Library Media Specialist, Lakeview High School, Battle Creek, Michigan

Scott Durham: Lakeview High School, Battle Creek, Michigan

Credits

Copyrighted excerpts in *Historic Events for Students: The Great Depression,* were reproduced from the following periodicals:

American Heritage, v. 40, May-June, 1989 for "The Other Fair," by Richard Reinhardt. Reproduced by permission of the author.

American Quarterly, v. 46, September, 1994. © 1994 American Studies Association. Reproduced by permission.

Chicago Tribune, October 17, 2000 for "Gus Hall, 1910–2000: Longtime U. S. Communist Party Chief." (Obituary). All rights reserved. Reproduced by permission.

Harpers Magazine, v. 172, December, 1935. Copyright © 1935 by Harper's Magazine. All rights reserved. Reproduced from the December issue by special permission.

Indian Magazine of History, v. XC, December, 1994. Copyright 1994, Trustees of Indiana University. Reproduced by permission.

The International News Service, 1938 for "Louis Knocks Out Schmeling," by Bob Considine. © 1938 by The Hearst Corp. Reproduced by permission.

The Nation, v. 136, March 1, 1933. © 1933 The Nation magazine/ The Nation Company, Inc. Reproduced by permission.

The New Republic, v. 102, May 2, 1940. Reproduced by permission.

The New York Times, June 7, 1932 in a letter by John D. Rockefeller, Jr. Copyright © 1932 by The New York Times Company. Reproduced by permission.

The New Yorker, January 31, 1931, for "The Talk of the Town," by Franklin P. Adams. Reproduced by permission.

The Reader's Digest, v. 19, June, 1931. Reproduced by permission.

Reelclassics.com, October 26, 1999 for "How I Came to Love the Classics" by Al Cunningham. © Al Cunningham. Reproduced by permission of the author.

The Saturday Evening Post, April 20, 1935; December 4, 1937; December 14, 1963. Reproduced by permission.

Science, v. 77, January 27, 1933. © 1933 The American Association for the Advancement of Science. Reproduced by permission.

Time, March 6, 1939; June 12, 1939. © 1939 Time Inc. Reprinted by permission.

Copywrited excerpts in *Historic Events for Students: The Great Depression,* were reproduced from the following books:

A., G. From **Recipes & Remembrances of the Great Depression** by Emily Thacker. Tresco Publishers, 1993. Copyright 1993 Tresco Publishers. All rights reserved. Reproduced by permission.

Adamic, Louis. From **My America: 1928–1938.** Harper & Brothers Publishers, 1938. Copyright, 1938, by Louis Adamic. All rights reserved. Reproduced by permission.

Agee, James and Walker Evans. From **Let Us Now Praise Famous Men.** Ballantine Books, 1960. © 1941 by James Agee and Walker Evans. © renewed 1969 by Mia Fritsch Agee and Walker Evans. All rights reserved. Reprinted by permission of Houghton Mifflin Company.

Asbury, Herbert. From **The Great Illusion: An Informal History of Prohibition.** Doubleday & Company, Inc., 1950. Copyright, 1950, by Herbert Asbury. All rights reserved. Reproduced by permission.

B., Mildred. From **Recipes & Remembrances of the Great Depression** by Emily Thacker. Tresco Publishers, 1993. Copyright 1993 Tresco Publishers. All rights reserved. Reproduced by permission.

Balderrama, Francisco E. and Raymond Rodriguez. From *Decade of Betrayal: Mexican Repatriation in the 1930s.* University of New Mexico Press, 1995. © 1995 by the University of New Mexico Press. All rights reserved. Reproduced by permission.

Baldwin, C. B. (Beanie). From "Concerning the New Deal," in **Hard Times: An Oral History of the Great Depression** by Studs Terkel. Pantheon Books, 1986. © 1970, 1986 by Studs Terkel. All rights reserved. Reproduced by permission.

Bolino, August C. From **From Depression to War: American Society in Transition—1939.** Praeger Publishers, 1998. © 1998 by August C. Bolino. All rights reserved.

Bonnifield, Paul. From **The Dust Bowl: Men, Dirt, and Depression.** University of New Mexico Press, 1979. © 1979 by the University of New Mexico Press. All rights reserved. Reproduced by permission.

Brown, D. Clayton. From **Electricity for Rural America: The Fight for REA.** Greenwood Press, 1980. All rights reserved.

Brown, Josephine Chapin. From **Public Relief 1929–1939. Henry Holt and Company, 1940.** Copyright, 1940, by Henry Holt and Company, Inc.

Burke, Clifford. From "Man and Boy," in **Hard Times: An Oral History of the Great Depression** by Studs Terkel. Pantheon Books, 1986. © 1970, 1986 by Studs Terkel. All rights reserved. Reproduced by permission.

Burns, Helen M. From **The American Banking Community and New Deal Banking Reforms, 1933–1935.** Greenwood Press, 1974. © 1974 by Helen M. Burns. All rights reserved.

Colbert, David. From "Crash," in **We Saw It Happen.** Simon and Schuster, 1938. Reproduced by permission.

Daniels, Roger. From **Asian America: Chinese and Japanese in the United States since 1850.** University of Washington Press, 1988. © 1988 by the University of Washington Press. All rights reserved. Reproduced by permission.

Deutsch, Sarah Jane. From "From Ballots to Breadlines, 1920–1940," in **No Small Courage: A History of Women in the United States.** Edited by Nancy F. Cott. Oxford University Press, 2000.

Deutsch, Sarah Jane. From "From Ballots to Breadlines: Taking Matters into Their Own Hands," in **No Small Courage: A History of Women in the United States.** Edited by Nancy F. Cott. Oxford University Press, 2000.

Edsforth, Ronald. From **The New Deal: America's Response to the Great Depression.** Blackwell Publishers, 2000.

Farrell, James T. From "Introduction," in **Studs Lonigan: A Trilogy.** The Modern Library, 1938.

Introduction copyright, 1938, by Random House, Inc. Reproduced by permission.

From "Grease Monkey to Knitter," in **These Are Our Lives** as told by the people and written by members of the Federal Writer's Project. The University of North Carolina Press, 1939. © 1939 by the University of North Carolina Press, renewed 1967. Used by permission of the publisher.

From "Preface" in **These Are Our Lives** as told by the people and written by members of the Federal Writer's Project. The University of North Carolina Press, 1939. © 1939 by the University of North Carolina Press, renewed 1967. Used by permission of the publisher.

From "Till the River Rises," in **These Are Our Lives** as told by the people and written by members of the Federal Writer's Project. The University of North Carolina Press, 1939. Copyright © 1939 by the University of North Carolina Press, renewed 1967. All rights reserved. Used by permission of the publisher.

Flynn, George Q. From **American Catholics & the Roosevelt Presidency, 1932–1936.** University of Kentucky Press, 1968. Copyright © 1968 by the University of Kentucky Press, Lexington.

Gelfand, Mark I. From **A Nation of Cities: The Federal Government and Urban America, 1933–1965.** Oxford University Press, 1975. © 1975 by Oxford University Press, Inc.

Glaab, Charles N. and A. Theodore Brown. From **A History of Urban America.** The Macmillan Company, 1967. © The Macmillan Company, 1967. All rights reserved.

Golby, John et al. From **Between Two Wars.** Open University Press, 1990. © 1990 The Open University. All rights reserved. Reproduced by permission.

Hansberger, Billie. From "Mother Burned the Midnight Oil To Keep the Pantry Stocked," in **Dining During the Depression.** Edited by Karen Thibodeau. Reminisce Books, 1996. © 1996, Reiman Publications, L. P. All rights reserved. Reproduced by permission.

Haworth, Norman "Yanky". From "A Pram, A Baby and Bottles of Booze," in **The Rumrunners: A Prohibition Scrapbook** by C. H. Gervais. Firefly Books, 1980.

Hays, Will. From "Conclusions," in **We're in the Money: Depression America and Its Films** by Andrew Bergman. New York University Press, 1971. Copyright © 1971 by New York University.

Healey, Dorothy. From **Dorothy Healey Remembers: A Life in the American Communist Party** by Dorothy Healey and Maurice Isserman. Oxford University Press, 1990. © 1990 by Oxford University Press, Inc. All rights reserved.

Heline, Oscar. From "The Farmer is the Man," in **Hard Times: An Oral History of the Great Depression** by Studs Terkel. Pantheon Books, 1986. © 1970, 1986 by Studs Terkel. All rights reserved. Reproduced by permission.

Hemingway, Ernest. From "Dispatch from Spain," in **Years of Protest: A Collection of American Writings of the 1930's.** Edited by Jack Salzman. Pegasus, 1967. © 1967 by Western Publishing Company, Inc. All rights reserved.

Hersch, John. From "The Big Money," in **Hard Times: An Oral History of the Great Depression** by Studs Terkel. Pantheon Books, 1986. © 1970, 1986 by Studs Terkel. All rights reserved. Reproduced by permission.

Hooker, Robert J. From **Food and Drink in America: A History.** The Bobbs-Merrill Company, Inc., 1981. © 1981 by Richard James Hooker. All rights reserved.

Jackson, Kenneth T. From **Crabgrass Frontier: The Suburbanization of the United States.** Oxford University Press, 1985. © 1985 by Oxford University Press, Inc. All rights reserved.

Kearns, Doris. From **Lyndon Johnson and the American Dream.** New American Library, 1976. © 1976 by Doris Kearns. All rights reserved.

Leuchtenburg, William E. From **Franklin D. Roosevelt and the New Deal: 1932–1940.** Harper Torchbooks, 1963. © 1963 by William E. Leuchtenburg.

Lippmann, Walter. From "President Roosevelt's Leadership: The First Roosevelt Year (February 27, 1934)," in **Interpretations: 1933–1935.** Edited by Allan Nevins. The Macmillan Company, 1936. Copyright, 1936, by Walter Lippmann. All rights reserved. Reproduced by permission.

Low, Ann Marie. From **Dust Bowl Diary.** University of Nebraska Press, 1984. Copyright 1984 by the University of Nebraska Press. All rights reserved. Reproduced by permission.

McCraw, Thomas K. From **TVA and the Power Fight, 1933–1939.** J. B. Lippincott Company, 1971.

McElvaine, Robert S. From **The Great Depression: America, 1929–1941.** Times Books, 1993. © 1993 by Robert S. McElvaine. All rights reserved. Used by permission of Times Books, a division of Random House, Inc.

Meltzer, Milton. From **Violins & Shovels: The WPA Arts Projects.** Delacorte Press, 1976. © 1976 by Milton Meltzer. All rights reserved.

Montella, Frank. From **Memories of a CCC Boy,** in an interview with Kim Stewart. Cal State Fullerton and Utah State Historical Society Oral History Project, July 9, 1971.

Oettinger, Hank. From "Bonnie Laboring Boy," in **Hard Times: An Oral History of the Great Depression** by Studs Terkel. Pantheon Books, 1986. © 1970, 1986 by Studs Terkel. All rights reserved. Reproduced by permission.

Parran, Thomas. From "Shadow on the Land," in **Tuskegee's Truths: Rethinking the Tuskegee Syphilis Study.** Edited by Susan M. Reverby. University of North Carolina Press, 2000. © 2000 by The University of North Carolina Press. All rights reserved. Used by permission of the publisher.

Perkins, Frances. From **The Roosevelt I Knew.** The Viking Press, 1946. Copyright 1946 by Frances Perkins. Reproduced by permission.

Phillips, Cabell. From **From the Crash to the Blitz 1929–1939.** The Macmillan Company, 1969. © The New York Times Company 1969. All rights reserved. Reproduced by permission.

Plotke, David. From **Building A Democratic Political Order.** Cambridge University Press, 1996. © Cambridge University Press 1996. Reproduced by permission of the publisher and author.

Rauch, Basil. From **The History of the New Deal, 1933-1938.** Creative Age Press, Inc., 1944. Copyright 1944 by Basil Rauch. All rights reserved. Reproduced by permission.

Reid, Robert L. From "Introduction," in **Back Home Again: Indiana in the Farm Security Administration Photographs, 1935–1943.** Edited by Robert L. Reid. Indiana University Press, 1987. © 1987 by Robert L. Reid. All rights reserved. Reproduced by permission.

Roosevelt, Eleanor. From "Women in Politics," in **What I Hope to Leave Behind.** Edited by Allida M. Black. Carlson Publishing, Inc., 1995. Reproduced by permission.

Roosevelt, Franklin D. From "Hopkins Before 1941," in **Roosevelt and Hopkins: An Intimate History** by Robert E. Sherwood. Harper & Brothers Publishers, 1950. © 1948, 1950 by Robert E. Sherwood; copyright renewed © 1976, 1978 by Madeline H. Sherwood. All rights reserved. Reprinted by permission of Brandt & Hochman Literary Agents, Inc.

Rothstein, Arthur. From **Just Before the War** by Thomas H. Garver and Arthur Rothstein. October House Inc., 1968. Copyright 1968, Newport Harbor Art Museum, Balboa, California. Reproduced by permission.

Russo, Anthony. From "Prologue," in **Capone: The Man and the Era** by Laurence Bergreen. Simon & Schuster, 1994. © 1994 by Laurence Bergreen. All rights reserved. Reproduced by permission.

S., K. From **Recipes & Remembrances of the Great Depression** by Emily Thacker. Tresco Publishers, 1993. Copyright 1993 Tresco Publishers. All rights reserved. Reproduced by permission.

Schieber, Sylvester J. and John B. Brown. From **The Real Deal: The History and Future of Social Security.** Yale University Press, 1999. © 1999 by Yale University. All rights reserved.

Schlesinger, Jr., Arthur M. From **The Age of Roosevelt: The Coming of the New Deal.** Houghton Mifflin Company, 1988. © 1958, renewed 1986 by Arthur M. Schlesinger, Jr. All rights reserved. Reprinted by permission of Houghton Mifflin Company.

Steichen, Edward. From "Introduction," in **The Bitter Years: 1935–1941.** Edited by Edward Steichen. The Museum of Modern Art, 1962. © 1962, The Museum of Modern Art, New York.

Steinbeck, John. From **I Remember the Thirties.** Copyright 1960 by John Steinbeck.

Steinbeck, John. From **The Grapes of Wrath.** The Viking Press, 1939. Copyright, 1939, John Steinbeck. All rights reserved.

Stockard, George. From **Stories and Recipes of the Great Depression of the 1930's, Volume II.** Edited by Rita Van Amber. Van Amber Publishers, 1999. © Library of Congress. All rights reserved. Reproduced by permission of the author.

Stryker, R. E. From a letter in **Portrait of a Decade: Roy Stryker and the Development of Documentary Photography in the Thirties** by F. Jack Hurley. Louisiana State University Press, 1972. Copyright 1972 by Louisiana State University Press. All rights reserved.

Sueur, Meridel Le. From **Women on the Breadlines.** West End Press, 1984. © 1977, 1984 by West End Press. Reproduced by permission.

Sundquist, James. From **Dynamics of the Party System: Alignment and Realignment of Political Parties in the United States.** Brookings Institution, 1983.

Svobida, Lawrence. From **Farming the Dust Bowl: A First-Hand Account from Kansas.** University Press of Kansas, 1986. Copyright 1940 by The Caxton Printers, Ltd.; 1968 by Lawrence Svobida. All rights reserved. Reproduced by permission.

Swados, Harvey. From "Introduction," in **The American Writer and the Great Depression.** Edited by Harvey Swados. The Bobbs-Merrill Company, Inc., 1966. © 1966 by The Bobbs-Merrill Company, Inc.

Terkel, Studs. From "Concerning the New Deal," in **Hard Times: An Oral History of the Great Depression.** Pantheon Books, 1986. © 1970, 1986 by Studs Terkel. All rights reserved. Reproduced by permission.

Terkel, Studs. From "Three Strikes: Mike Widman," in **Hard Times: An Oral History of the Great Depression.** Pantheon Books, 1986. © 1970, 1986 by Studs Terkel. All rights reserved. Reproduced by permission.

Terrell, Harry. From "The Farmer is the Man," in **Hard Times: An Oral History of the Great Depression** by Studs Terkel. Pantheon Books, 1986. © 1970, 1986 by Studs Terkel. All rights reserved. Reproduced by permission.

Tugwell, Rexford Guy. From **The Bitter Years: 1935–1941.** Edited by Edward Steichen. The Museum of Modern Art, 1962. © 1962, The Museum of Modern Art, New York. Reproduced by permission.

Tully, Grace. From "Pearl Harbor News Reaches FDR," in **We Saw It Happen.** Simon and Schuster, 1938. Reproduced by permission.

Tyack, David, Robert Lowe, and Elisabeth Hansot. From "A Black School in East Texas," in **Public Schools in Hard Times: The Great Depression and Recent Years.** Harvard University Press, 1984. © 1984 by the President and Fellows of Harvard College. All rights reserved. Reproduced by permission.

Tyack, David, Robert Lowe, and Elisabeth Hansot. From **Public Schools in Hard Times: The Great Depression and Recent Years.** Harvard University Press, 1984. © 1984 by the President and Fellows of Harvard College. All rights reserved. Reproduced by permission.

Uys, Errol Lincoln. From **Riding the Rails: Teenagers on the Move During the Great Depression.** TV Books, 2000. © 1999, 2000 Errol Lincoln Uys. All rights reserved. Reproduced by permission of the author.

Van Amber, Rita. From **Stories and Recipes During the Great Depression of the 1930's.** Van Amber Publishers, 1999. © Library of Congress. All rights reserved. Reproduced by permission.

Wasserman, Dale. From "Troubles and Triumphs," in **Free, Adult, Uncensored: The Living History of the Federal Theatre Project.** Edited by John O'Connor and Lorraine Brown. New Republic Books, 1978. Reproduced by permission.

Watkins, T. H. From **The Hungry Years: A Narrative History of the Great Depression in America.** Henry Holt and Company, 1999. © 1999 by T. H. Watkins. All rights reserved. Reprinted by permission of Henry Holt and Company, LLC.

Weinberg, Sidney J. From "The Big Money," in **Hard Times: An Oral History of the Great Depression** by Studs Terkel. Pantheon Books, 1986. © 1970, 1986 by Studs Terkel. All rights reserved. Reproduced by permission.

Winslow, Susan. From **Brother, Can You Spare A Dime?: America from the Wall Street Crash to Pearl Harbor.** Paddington Press Ltd., 1976. © 1976 by Susan Winslow.

Wright, Richard. From "How 'Bigger' Was Born," in **Native Son.** Harper & Row, Publishers, 1940. Copyright 1940 by Richard Wright. Renewed in 1967 by Ellen Wright.

Wright, Richard. From **Uncle Tom's Children: Five Long Stories.** Harper & Brothers, 1938. Copyright 1936, 1937, 1938 by Richard Wright. All rights reserved.

Song lyrics appearing in *Historic Events for Students: The Great Depression,* were received from the following sources:

Guthrie, Woody. From "Talking Dust Bowl." © Copyright 1961 and 1963 Ludlow Music, Inc., New York, N. Y.

Warren, Harry and Al Dubin, lyrics from "We're In the Money." Music and lyrics by Harry Warren and Al Dubin. Copyright 1933, Remick Music, Inc. Reproduced by permission.

About the Series

Historic Events for Students (HES) is a new addition to the Gale Group's *for Students* line, presenting users with the complete picture of an important event in world history. With standardized rubrics throughout each entry, for which the *for Students* line is well-known, and a variety of complementary elements including illustrations, sidebars, and suggestions for further research, *HES* will examine all of the components that contributed to or sprung from a significant period of time, from ideologies and politics to contemporary opinions and popular culture.

A new one- to three-volume set of forty-five to sixty entries will appear each year. The topics are evaluated by an advisory board of teachers and librarians familiar with the information needed by students in today's classrooms. Essays contain consistent rubrics for easy reference as well as comparison across entries and volumes, and each volume contains a complete glossary, general bibliography, and subject index. Additionally, approximately one hundred images are included per volume, including photos, maps, and statistics to enhance the text and add visual depictions of the event.

The standardized headings found throughout *HES* let users choose to what depth they want to explore the subject matter. Take a quick glance at the topic via the Introduction, Chronology, and Issue Summary rubrics, or delve deeper and get a more inclusive view through the Contributing Forces, Perspectives, and Impact sections. A who's who for a particular issue can be found under the heading of Notable People, while excerpts of speeches, personal accounts, and news clippings can be located under Primary Sources. Ideas for further study can be found with Suggested Research Topics and the Bibliography, while numerous sidebars provide additional information on material associated with the issue being discussed.

Historic Events for Students is different from other history texts in that it doesn't just narrate the facts of an event from the past. It traces the social, cultural, political, religious, and ideological threads that combined to create an historic event. *HES* follows these threads to the end of the event and beyond it to discern how it shaped the history that followed it. The result is a comprehensive examination of the causes of and effects from a significant event in history and a greater understanding of how it influenced where we are today.

Introduction

Technologies and accepted behavioral norms comprising the human experience are constantly changing. Such change in society, however, does not occur at a consistent pace. Sometimes change may be slow and barely perceptible to the average person. At other times, extraordinary events spur change much more quickly. While such events most often involve times of war (the American Civil War, World War I, World War II, and the Vietnam War all resulted in fundamental changes to American society), other watershed events may be no less dramatic. The Great Depression was one such event.

Historical Overview—The Great Depression

Though signs of pending economic problems were surfacing in the United States throughout the 1920s, hardly anyone took notice as most people in the country enjoyed prosperity like never before. The dramatic stock market crash in October 1929, however, captured the attention of the American public. Many feared for the first time that the economic health of the United States might not be as good as it had seemed just a year or two previously. The period that followed, known as the Great Depression, may not have actually resulted from the stock market crash, but it is frequently linked to it in the public's mind.

The Great Depression was an extended period of severe economic hard times, first for the United States and then for many of the world's nations. Though the depression was rooted in earlier economic undercurrents, a cascade of economic events followed the stock market crash and exacerbated the problem. Many investors, including banks, lost their fortunes in the Wall Street crash as the value of stocks tumbled. This loss meant less money was available to invest in businesses, which led companies, now short on cash, to layoff workers. The rise in unemployment meant that the public had less money to buy consumer goods and pay back the bank loans it had accumulated in the liberal spending times of the 1920s. As a result, thousands of banks closed and more layoffs resulted from decreased purchases by consumers as inventories of goods mounted. By 1933 almost 25 percent of the U.S. workforce was unemployed, amounting to more than twelve million people. Those who kept their jobs saw their incomes decrease significantly.

The arrival of Franklin Delano Roosevelt to the White House as the thirty-second president of the United States in March 1933 significantly changed the relationship between Americans and their government. Through Congress, Roosevelt orchestrated numerous and diverse pieces of legislation designed to bring economic relief and recovery, and later reform, to the desperate nation. These laws and the resulting government programs are collectively known as the New Deal.

Though the New Deal would not lead to significant recovery, it did end the dramatic economic plunge Americans experienced through the early 1930s. It gave those most affected by the Great Depression food and shelter. For many more it reestablished hope for the future and faith in the U.S. economic system. Historically the federal government had largely been detached from the public's everyday life. The severity of the depression, however, made many Americans consider the possibility—and even to expect—that the government would take action to assure the wellbeing of the people it governed. Significant differences of opinion emerged over how far government should go in regulating business and guaranteeing the financial security of its citizens.

All of this took place at a time when American popular culture was gaining its own distinct character, unique from its predominant European roots. It also occurred in the midst of new mass production technologies in business, mass media, and mass consumerism. The United States would emerge as a profoundly different nation in 1940 than it had been in 1930.

Content

These volumes specifically address the actual event of the Great Depression rather than presenting a general treatment of the 1930s. They describe the events and issues surrounding the economic depression and the New Deal. The authors, editors, and advisors selected forty-five issues that take an inclusive look at the Great Depression as it affected such diverse elements of American society as economics, the arts, literature, mass media, ethnic and gender relations, the functioning of government, international relations, religion, politics, crime, public health, education, and everyday life.

The writers of these volumes, well-versed in the relevant historical issues, sought to provide a comprehensive treatment of each issue, yet in a concise, readily digestible format. They strove to provide an objective overview of each issue, helping the reader to experience and evaluate the diverse perspectives of often-controversial events. The reader is provided with sufficient background information to encourage the formation of his or her own opinions of the complex events and the contemporary reactions to them. In addition to in-depth text, this premier set of *Historic Events for Students* includes maps, statistics, photographs, sidebars, bibliographic sources, and suggestions for further research, designed to meet the curriculum needs of high school students, undergraduate college students, and their teachers.

How Each Entry is Organized

Each of the forty-five issue entries are divided into multiple headings for easy and complete reference:

- **Introduction:** briefly introduces the reader to the topic. Its connection to the Great Depression is established and some of the key concepts and events that will be addressed are presented.
- **Chronology:** a brief timeline is provided for each topic to place the various key events related to it into an easy-to-understand time-frame for the reader.
- **Issue Summary:** the primary source of information describing the topic, firmly set in the context of the Great Depression. The topic is thoroughly discussed, including governmental efforts made to resolve economic and social problems associated with it. The student will gain a keen sense of just how dynamic the topic was and the major consequences of the individual issues at the time. This summary is divided into subheadings that are unique to each issue.
- **Contributing Forces:** identifies the key social, economic, and political currents in U.S. history leading up to the topic. The section explores how the events and prevailing attitudes contributed to the particular issue and how they influenced the New Deal's response to the issue.
- **Perspectives:** prevailing and competing notions and opinions of the day are detailed and, where feasible, the varying viewpoints are distinguished at the local community level or among the general public; at the national level, including the country's political leaders; and internationally as the Great Depression became an increasingly global event. The discussion includes the perspectives of what should be done, if anything, by the federal government and what the implications were of government action or inaction.
- **Impact:** the long-term consequences of the issue and resulting government action are discussed. The New Deal's response to the Great Depression posed dramatic changes to American society. The events of the depression shaped the evolution of the social, economic, and political foundation of the nation after the 1930s and into the twenty-first century. This section highlights the lasting effects for that particular issue.
- **Notable People:** describes the lives and accomplishments of some of key individuals in the context of the specific issue. Each issue commonly has several key people associated with it, including people who advocated for or against government action and those who administered the New Deal programs.
- **Primary Sources:** provide first-hand accounts from the common citizen and notable people such as Franklin Roosevelt and Herbert Hoover. The Great Depression was a traumatic time. As a result emotions were openly displayed and opinions and

solutions hotly debated. There is no better way to experience the depression days than through the words of those caught in the turmoil.

- **Suggested Research Topics:** guide students to explore matters further. Many suggested topics ask the student to examine his or her own communities more closely and how New Deal programs might still influence their lives today.
- **Bibliography:** lists key sources used by the writer in researching the topic and also includes suggestions for further reading. The list of further readings is predominantly aimed at the reading level of the high school and undergraduate student and targets sources most likely found in public libraries and book stores.

Additionally, each entry is also accompanied by several sidebars presenting insights into various facets of the issue. The sidebars focus on different kinds of topics related to the particular issue, including descriptions of concepts, extensive biographies of the most important figures to play a role, or more thorough descriptions of particular agencies or other organizations involved in the issue.

Additional Features

In an attempt to create a comprehensive reference tool for the study of the Great Depression, this set also includes:

- A general chronology covers the Great Depression from its start to its finish to place the various issues and events into a historical context, including some key national and international events to underscore what the citizens and leaders of other countries were experiencing at the same time.
- A general bibliography consolidates the numerous and significant research on the Great Depression and offers an easy reference for users, with material divided into books, periodicals, novels, and websites.
- A glossary presents a number of terms and phrases introduced in the entries that may be unfamiliar to readers.
- A subject index provides easy reference to topics, people, and places.

Acknowledgments

A number of writers contributed to these volumes in addition to the lead authors, including Michael Vergamini, Dr. Richard Pettigrew, Dr. Doug Blandy, Dr. Stephen Dow Beckham, Linda Irvin, and Meghan O'Meara. Catherine Filip typed much of the manuscript. Much gratitude also goes to the advisors who guided the project throughout its course.

Comments on these volumes and suggestions for future sets are welcome. Please direct all correspondence to:

Editor, *Historic Events for Students*
Gale Group
27500 Drake Rd.
Farmington Hills, MI 48331-3535
(800) 877-4253

Chronology

1914 Industrialist Henry Ford introduces the moving assembly line to manufacture automobiles; the production technique will revolutionize U.S. industry over the next decade.

1914 World War I begins in Europe, placing a high demand of U.S. goods, though the United States does not itself enter the war for another three years; high wartime production levels will continue following the war, leading to a long term agricultural economic downturn.

1919 The peace treaty of Versailles ends World War I and leads to excessive economic demands on Germany.

1919 The General Motors automobile company introduces a consumer credit program that makes loans available to purchase cars; this program begins the popular installment plan for many other industries producing consumer goods.

1920 The Nineteenth Amendment to the U.S. Constitution is ratified, granting women the right to vote; women voters will become an important element of the Democratic Coalition 15 years later.

January 16, 1920 The Eighteenth Amendment, or the Prohibition Amendment, goes into effect nationwide, prohibiting the sale, transport, and consumption of alcoholic beverages in the United States.

1920s Continued expansion of farming production leads to soil exhaustion in some areas of the United States and expansion into marginal agricultural areas, setting the stage for future topsoil problems; record production causes continued decline in farm prices.

1922 Benito Mussolini takes over Italy, which becomes a fascist nation under his leadership.

1923 The U.S. stock market begins a six-year expansion as the value of stocks begins to climb.

1924 Congress passes the National Origins Act, reducing the number of immigrants allowed to enter the country to only 150,000 per year, and sets quotas favoring northwestern and southeastern Europeans.

October 6, 1927 The first talking motion picture is released, *The Jazz Singer,* starring Al Jolson.

November 7, 1928 Republican Herbert Hoover, an engineer with a reputation as a humanitarian, is elected to the U.S. presidency over Democrat Al Smith, the first Catholic to run for the U.S. presidency.

October 24, 1929 Known as "Black Thursday," the value of stocks plummets on Wall Street, costing many investors vast sums of money, and raises public concern over the health of the U.S. economy.

1930 As economic conditions in the United States continue to worsen following the stock market crash, Congress passes the Smoot-Hawley Tariff Act, which greatly raises taxes on foreign goods to boost sales of domestic goods. In application, however, the act instead causes foreign trade to greatly decline, decreasing the demand for U.S. goods.

1931 The U.S. economic crisis spreads to Europe as American investments decline and trade decreases; the United States pulls back from international affairs and looks increasingly inward.

May 1, 1931 The Empire State Building in New York City, the world's tallest building, is opened.

July 14, 1931 The German banking system fails as all banks in Germany close.

September 18, 1931 Japan begins a military expansion in the Pacific by invading Manchuria and seizing thc Manchurian railroad.

1932 With the farm economy in desperate condition, the Farmers' Holiday Association is formed in Iowa, which leads to farmer protests seeking government assistance.

January 22, 1932 To help an economy in crisis President Herbert Hoover creates the Reconstruction Finance Corporation, a federal agency designed to provide loans to struggling banks and businesses.

July 28 1932 Thousands of unemployed and financially strapped World War I veterans and their families, known as the Bonus Army, march on Washington, DC, seeking early payment of previously promised bonus pay. They are denied by Congress and routed violently by U.S. army troops.

October 24, 1932 Gangster Al Capone is sentenced to 11 years in prison for tax evasion.

November 8, 1932 Pledging a "New Deal" for Americans, Democratic candidate Franklin Delano Roosevelt is overwhelmingly elected president over the highly unpopular Hoover; Roosevelt will not be inaugurated until the following March.

February 1933 The U.S. banking crisis deepens as almost five thousand banks have closed and panic spreads among depositors; faith in the U.S. banking system hits an all-time low.

January 30, 1933 Adolf Hitler becomes Chancellor of Germany.

March 4, 1933 Roosevelt is inaugurated as president promising hope to American citizens, claiming the "only thing to fear is fear itself" and beginning a dramatic surge of legislation during his first one hundred days in office forming the New Deal.

March 6, 1933 President Roosevelt closes all U.S. banks, declaring a Banking Holiday, and Congress passes the Emergency Banking Act three days later in a successful effort to restore public confidence in the banking system; most banks reopen on March 13.

March 23, 1933 The legislature is dismissed in Germany and Hitler assumes dictatorial powers of the country.

March 31, 1933 The U.S. Congress passes the Civilian Conservation Corps Reforestation Act, creating the Civilian Conservation Corps (CCC) to provide jobs for young males.

May 12, 1933 Congress passes the Agricultural Adjustment Act and Emergency Farm Mortgage Act to bring economic relief to farmers, and the Federal Emergency Relief Act to provide relief for the needy.

May 17, 1933 The Tennessee Valley Authority (TVA) is created to establish a massive program of regional economic development for a broad region of the American Southeast.

June 16, 1933 Congress passes the Banking Act, reforming the U.S. banking system. The Federal Deposit Insurance Corporation (FDIC) is established to insure depositors' money; the National Industrial Recovery Act (NIRA) is created to regulate industry; and the Public Works Administration begins to provide funding for large public projects.

December 5, 1933 Prohibition ends in the United States after a nearly 14-year ban on the sale of all alcoholic beverages.

1934 Great dust storms sweep across the Plains of the United States; the hardest hit region of the southern Plains becomes known as the Dust Bowl. The drought persists for several years.

June 6, 1934 Congress passes the Securities Exchange Act to regulate the stock market and protect investors.

June 28, 1934 Congress passes the National Housing Act, creating the Federal Housing Administration to provide loans to home buyers and setting national standards for house construction; this marks the end of the First New Deal under the Roosevelt administration.

April 8, 1935 Kicking off the Second New Deal, Congress passes the Emergency Relief Appropriation Act, authorizing the creation of the Resettlement Administration and the Works Progress Administration.

May 11, 1935 Roosevelt creates the Rural Electrification Administration to provide electricity to rural areas through federal partnership with private farming cooperatives.

May 27, 1935 The U.S. Supreme Court issues several rulings against New Deal programs, including *Schechter Poultry Corporation v. United States,* striking down the National Industrial Recovery Act; the day becomes known as "Black Monday."

July 5, 1935 In reaction to the Schechter decision, Congress passes the National Labor Relations Act, recognizing the right of workers to organize in unions and conduct collective bargaining with employers.

August 2, 1935 Roosevelt establishes the Federal Art Project, Federal Music Project, Federal Theatre Project, and Federal Writers' Project to provide work relief for people involved in the arts.

August 14, 1935 Congress passes the Social Security Act, providing old age and unemployment benefits to American workers.

August 28, 1935 The Public Utility Holding Company Act is enacted by Congress, prohibiting the use of multiple layers of holding companies in the utility industry.

October 1935 Italy sends 35,000 troops and volunteers to Ethiopia, seeking to expand its rule into Africa.

November 9, 1935 In organizing unions for semi-skilled workers of mass production industries, John L. Lewis begins to break with the craft-oriented American Federation of Labor (AFL) and creates the Committee of Industrial Organizations (CIO), which later becomes known as the Congress of Industrial Organizations.

January 6, 1936 The Supreme Court rules the Agricultural Adjustment Act unconstitutional in *United States v. Butler.*

March 7, 1936 German troops retake the Rhineland region of Europe without conflict, beginning the German expansion through Europe.

August 1936 Athlete Jesse Owens, a black American, wins four gold medals at the Berlin Summer Olympics, conflicting with Adolf Hitler's white supremacy beliefs.

November 1936 Franklin Roosevelt wins reelection to the U.S. presidency by a landslide, winning a record 61 percent of the vote.

December 30, 1936 Seven General Motors plants in Flint, Michigan, are shut down by sit-down strikes; the company gives in to worker demands on February 11, 1937.

February 5, 1937 Roosevelt introduces a plan to reorganize the U.S. judiciary system. It becomes known as the "court packing" plan and attracts substantial opposition in Congress and the public.

June 22, 1937 Black American Joe Louis defeats Briton James Braddock to become the new world heavyweight boxing champion.

July 30, 1937 Japan invades China and begins a major offensive toward other countries in the Far East.

April 12, 1937 The Supreme Court begins making decisions supportive of New Deal programs by ruling in favor of the National Labor Relations Act in *National Labor Relations Board v. Jones & Laughlin Steel Corporation.*

May 1937 A steelworkers' strike at Republic Steel leads to a violent confrontation between striking workers and Chicago police, leaving ten people dead and 90 injured.

June 25, 1938 Marking the end of the Second New Deal, Congress passes the Fair Labor Standards Act, setting minimum wage and maximum hour regulations.

April 30, 1939 The New York World's Fair opens.

September 30, 1939 Germany invades Poland, starting World War II as France and Great Britain declare war on Germany.

May 1940 Germany invades Western Europe; France surrenders in June.

December 29, 1940 In a "fireside chat" over the radio, Franklin Roosevelt describes the United States as the "arsenal of democracy" to provide war supplies to those nations fighting German expansion. The country's war mobilization efforts help the economy and spur recovery from the Great Depression.

1941 A. Philip Randolph threatens to lead a march of black Americans on Washington, DC, protesting racial discrimination in the war industry; Roosevelt establishes the Fair Employment Practices Commission in response to the pressure.

December 7, 1941 Japan bombs U.S. military facilities in Pearl Harbor, Hawaii; the United States declares war on Japan and later Germany, entering World War II.

April 12, 1945 Franklin Roosevelt dies suddenly from a cerebral hemorrhage at 63 years of age.

April 30, 1945 With defeat imminent, Adolf Hitler commits suicide in Germany.

American Indians

1933-1941

Introduction

Since the colonial period in U.S. history, American Indians had continually lost lands to the expanding European settlements. By the 1830s major dislocations of Indian populations were occurring as much of the Indian population of the Southeast United States was forced to the "Indian Territory" of Oklahoma. A federal program to establish reservations for Indian peoples in their ancestral territories in the West grew through the mid-nineteenth century. This policy resulted in a dramatic decrease in the amount of land used by the American Indians. As the Indian land base eroded, so did their economic capabilities. Increasingly, federal policies sought to destroy tribes and promote the transformation of American Indians into English-speaking, Christian farmers.

Through another federal program, a land allotment program established in 1887, the federal government tried to break apart communal tribal land holdings and allot (assign a portion) the resulting small parcels of land to each native in an effort to make them landowning farmers. With on and off-reservation day schools and boarding schools, it tried to force this transition with each succeeding generation of native children. But many, both children and adults, did not have the training or interest in farming. Even if they did, much of the land set aside was too dry for agricultural use.

By the 1920s evidence abounded that American Indians were rapidly losing what lands they had left, were trapped in poverty, had substandard education,

Chronology:

1921: The proposed Bursum Bill in Congress causes pro-American Indian advocates to rally and fight this legislation which would have given ownership of Pueblo Indian lands to white ranchers.

June 2, 1924: The Indian Citizenship Act granting citizenship to all American Indians passes.

1928: An influential report requested by the U.S. Office of Indian Affairs titled *The Problem of Indian Administration,* also known as the Meriam Report, is published providing a blueprint for reform of government policies.

April 20, 1933: John Collier is named Commissioner of Indian Affairs.

April 16, 1934: Congress passes the Johnson-O'Malley Act providing federal funding for schools that have American Indian children enrolled.

June 18, 1934: Congress passes the Indian Reorganization Act (Wheeler-Howard Act) establishing the cornerstone of New Deal Indian policy.

1935: Congress creates the Indian Arts and Crafts Board to promote Indian cultural traditions.

1939: Senate Indian Affairs Committee recommends repeal of the Indian Reorganization Act but fails in its effort.

suffered from poor health, had limited life expectancy, and existed in overall desperate circumstances. With most Indians living on remote parcels of land, their conditions were depressed before the stock market crash in 1929 and subsequent impact of the Great Depression. Fact-finding reports such as the Brookings Institution's *The Problem of Indian Administration* (1928) had documented in detail their needs.

The prospects for change were strong when President Franklin D. Roosevelt (served 1933–1945) named Harold Ickes to serve as secretary of the interior. Ickes was a crusty, no-nonsense administrator who wanted the various bureaus in his department to operate efficiently and honestly. Ickes was a champion of civil liberties and comfortable with the perpetuation of tribes and traditional native cultures. He turned to John Collier, one of the sharpest critics of past federal policies, and named him to serve as U.S. commissioner of Indian affairs.

The 1930s marked a turning point in American Indian history. The New Deal brought to Washington, DC, new leaders and new ideas more sensitive to the multiculturalism of the United States. The New Deal consisted of a range of federal social and economic relief and recovery programs addressing a broad span of issues including work relief for the unemployed. Supporters of these programs, called New Dealers, were willing to advance programs and ideas that earlier administrations would not have considered. New Deal reform sought to improve the staffing and efficiency of federal government Indian programs. These new efforts became known as the Indian New Deal.

Collier's tenure as Indian commissioner from 1933 to 1945 was the longest of any in U.S. history. It was a period of major shifts in programs and actions toward tribes and individual American Indians. Although little immediate change in the Indian economic condition would occur, a foundation was built for later changes in the last three decades of the twentieth century.

Issue Summary

The Indian New Deal

During the Great Depression, the federal government sought to address a number of the accumulated problems in the administration of American Indian affairs. The New Dealers faced complex issues related to American Indians. Some of the new directions were crafted in Congress. A number were initiated in the U.S. Office of Indian Affairs (that would later be known as the Bureau of Indian Affairs—BIA), given congressional approval, and then were implemented by the Indian agency. The BIA is an agency in the Department of Interior responsible for ensuring the general welfare of American Indians. In general, the course of federal policy during the years of the Great Depression was to support the political and cultural existence of tribes (tribalism), slow down the efforts to force American Indians to adopt the dominant American culture's beliefs and ways of life (assimilation), improve delivery of social services, and support a multicultural nation.

These efforts essentially began on April 20, 1933, during the second month of the New Deal. On that date Secretary of Interior Harold Ickes appointed John Collier commissioner of Indian affairs. Collier, making a commitment that New Deal reforms would include American Indians too, aggressively sought to

Biography:

John Collier

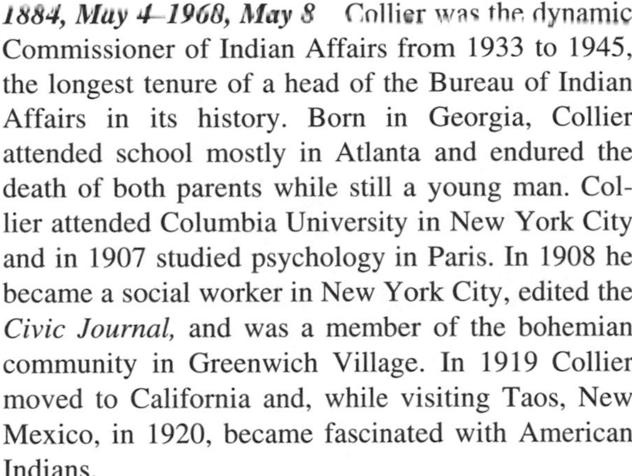

1884, May 4–1968, May 8 Collier was the dynamic Commissioner of Indian Affairs from 1933 to 1945, the longest tenure of a head of the Bureau of Indian Affairs in its history. Born in Georgia, Collier attended school mostly in Atlanta and endured the death of both parents while still a young man. Collier attended Columbia University in New York City and in 1907 studied psychology in Paris. In 1908 he became a social worker in New York City, edited the *Civic Journal,* and was a member of the bohemian community in Greenwich Village. In 1919 Collier moved to California and, while visiting Taos, New Mexico, in 1920, became fascinated with American Indians.

During the 1920s Collier served as the research agent for the Indian Welfare Committee of the General Federation of Women's Clubs. He then became executive secretary of the American Indian Defense Association. He mounted national opposition to the Bursum Bill, a bill that would have forced the Pueblo peoples of New Mexico to prove title to their lands. He also helped organize the All Pueblo Council, fought for tribal self-rule, and wrote a book titled *American Indian Life.* Collier defended American Indian rights and resources in a variety of publications. As a sharp critic of federal policy toward native peoples, he set the stage for the Brookings Institution's funding of a major study of the condition of American Indians. The study resulted in the publication of *The Problem of Indian Administration* (1928).

President Roosevelt named Collier head of the Bureau of Indian Affairs in 1933. Collier pressed for a number of major changes: an end to land allotment, extension of federal trust over individual and tribal lands, increasing the native land base, federal loans to tribes, encouragement of native arts and crafts, and preferential hiring of native people into the Office of Indian Affairs. Collier dreamed of an increasingly self-sufficient future for tribes through the Indian Reorganization Act. However, the law was significantly amended in Congress and lost many of the features Collier envisioned. He helped organize the Civilian Conservation Corps-Indian Division (CCC-ID) and promoted its work on reservation lands.

Collier's long run as head of the Office of Indian Affairs brought mixed results. Even though the IRA was not as Collier envisioned, he supported it and tried to implement it. However many tribes rejected the IRA. He was often at odds with the Senate Committee on Indian Affairs, especially when it was chaired by Burton K. Wheeler. Collier resigned as commissioner in 1945 and for the next six years taught at City College of New York. He died in Taos in 1968.

John Collier. *(Library of Congress.)*

---

rejuvenate Indian cultures and traditions. A key goal was to give tribes both legal and organizational capabilities to pursue economic development while maintaining their individual cultures.

Collier found a more receptive general public in 1933 for Indian policy reform than earlier existed. The widespread unemployment following the October 1929 stock market crash brought more sympathy in general for the poor. The seeming failure of individualism (to succeed on one's own initiative and skills) and capitalism (private ownership of a nation's means of production, distribution, and trade) made some more sympathetic toward the communal tradition of Indian culture.

Supporting Tribalism

For decades the federal government had sought the destruction of tribes. It had taken their lands, confined American Indians on reservations, mounted "civilization" programs to force cultural change, and divided up the lands of reservations into allotments. By the 1930s, however, it was clear that in spite of these many actions, tribes had not disappeared. Several of those serving in the New Deal wanted to support the existence of tribes but move them into the modern world.

The issues facing government planners, politicians, and tribes were numerous and complex, but several basic goals were adopted. For tribes to survive it was

Commissioner of Indian Affairs John Collier visits with Blackfoot Indians in Rapid City, South Dakota, on March 7, 1934. Collier was attending a conference which gave American Indians an opportunity to express their views on the Wheeler-Howard Bill. (Bettmann/CORBIS. Reproduced by permission.)

believed that tribes should adopt governing practices based on democratic principles. These would include majority rule constitutions, bylaws, elections, resolutions, and minutes of meetings. Tribes also needed to become economically self-sufficient by being permitted to charter corporations, borrow money, and develop their remaining lands and resources. Within this new strategy, traditional economies and cultural practices should also be supported. To accomplish this, they believed the federal government should encourage traditional arts, crafts, music, and language. The government should also refrain from further interference with American Indian religion. Several paths were followed in pursuing the goals of supporting tribalism.

Indian Reorganization

A sense of new direction swept through the Office of Indian Affairs with the appointment in 1933 of John Collier as commissioner. Collier saw tribes as playing a role in modern America. To achieve that dream, Collier began work immediately to change both the agency and the federal policy toward tribes. The highest priority was to open an avenue for the tribes to begin economic recovery in a way that formally recognized their unique legal status as somewhat independent nations existing within a nation—the United States.

Knowing that passage of legislation would be slow, Collier took a number of administrative actions to begin making progress towards his goals. First, to the consternation of missionaries, he established the principle of religious freedom throughout the agency school system and ended compulsory attendance at Christian services. Next, turning to the continuing loss of lands by Indians, in August 1933 he secured an order from Secretary of Interior Harold Ickes to stop further allotment of lands under the 1887 General Allotment Act until he could get Congress to pass a law negating the 1887 law. And lastly, regarding the economic problems of many Indian farmers, to help tribes financially he cancelled many debts that were charged against tribal funds. This was a major relief to Indian farmers who had used the loans to construct much needed irrigation systems for their fields.

To achieve long term reform Collier assembled a team in 1933 to draft reform legislation. What resulted was a fifty-page proposed bill titled the Indian Reorganization Act (IRA). The draft bill proposed several changes to increase economic benefits to American Indians.

The proposed legislation was composed of four basic parts, or titles. Title I would recognize the tribal right of self-government and seek economic development to foster tribal independence. Self-government included the rights to establish their own governments, tax tribal members and businesses, and have their own court system. Title II would establish Congressional support for Indian culture including arts, crafts, skills, and traditions. It would authorize Congress to fund Indian arts and crafts and provide funding for Indian education. Title III would end allotment of Indian lands, transfer allotments still in Indian ownership back to tribal communal control, restore lands depleted by erosion, and purchase lands for tribes that lacked a sufficient land base for economic self-sufficiency. Title IV would create a national Indian court system, a Court of Indian Affairs, to hear the cases involving the self-governing Indian communities formed under the IRA.

To gain support for his bill, Collier traveled throughout the West in March and April 1934, holding a series of meetings with tribes. A recently released report served to support Collier's push for reform. In 1934 the National Resources Board, established by the New Deal's 1933 National Industrial Recovery Act, found in one of its many resource planning studies that for 16 reservations 70 percent of the lands allotted to Indians and still owned by them were leased to non-Indians. Also 23 percent of the lands lay idle, unused for any particular economic purpose. Natives themselves used only 7 percent of the allotted lands.

Not all Indians, however, were supportive of the proposed reforms. Tribes who had successfully worked the allotments they had received in previous years were fearful of Collier's proposals to combine scattered allotments back into communal tribal lands. The Five Tribes of Oklahoma, consisting of the Cherokee, Chocktaw, Chickasaw, Creek, and Seminole, had such concerns. The Navajo opposed the proposed soil erosion control measures that would lead to reductions in livestock. Their herds of sheep and goats were important for prestige within the tribe and critical for actual physical survival at times. The sheep provided meat for food and wool for blankets. Other tribes opposed the representative form of governments proposed by Collier. The government form modeled after the United States was foreign to Indian traditions of hereditary tribal leaders and making decisions by consensus. In contrast, many in U.S. society considered this traditional Indian form of political authority communistic.

Even more of a challenge to Collier was convincing non-Indians of the reforms, particularly Congress. Eventually Congress found the proposed bill too radical. As a result they dropped most of Title II and all of Title IV. In addition the self-governing powers granted in Title I would be much more limited. The secretary of interior would retain close oversight over all tribal activities. Importantly the ending of the land allotment policy remained and was included in the final bill. However the Indians in Oklahoma who wanted to retain their individual ownership of allotments and lobbied against the bill were successful. As a result they were excluded from the final bill. Alaskan natives who, because of their remoteness, had a different history of relations with the U.S. government that did not include treaties and reservations were also excluded from the act. Congress had reduced the resulting act to only six pages from the original fifty pages.

A key provision of the IRA required approval by individual tribes of the act before they came under its general provisions. As it turned out, dozens of tribes elected not to participate. They either distrusted the provisions of the law or the intent of Congress. Some 250 tribes, bands, rancherias (small reservations in California), and pueblos held elections to decide whether to adopt IRA constitutional governments. Of those 174 tribes voted to accept IRA conditions while 78 voted against it. However, of the 174 who accepted it, only

Luther Standing Bear wrote books about Indian life and government policy during the Great Depression. (AP/Wide World Photos. Reproduced by permission.)

92 actually adopted IRA constitutions. Those who voted against IRA provisions or failed to adopt IRA constitutions could not receive federal funds to purchase land for economic development. To address Indians in Oklahoma and Alaskan natives in 1936, Congress passed the Alaska Reorganization Act and the Oklahoma Indian Welfare Act. These two acts provided some IRA benefits to tribes located in those areas. Some tribes rejecting the IRA, including one of the nation's largest tribes, the Navajo, still adopted bylaws similar to IRA constitutions to qualify for some benefits.

IRA constitutions adopted in compliance with the act recognized the authority of the secretary of interior to override any tribal actions if he so chose. To many tribes the IRA governments and constitutions would be an alien concept not integrating well with reservation life. Given close federal control and conflicts with traditional tribal leaders, they could exercise little power through them. In a sense the existence of IRA governments actually served in some cases to restrain development of independent tribal governments that may have been more effective in governing their communities.

As a result, the IRA accomplished some things and failed to do others. The IRA did stop any further allotment and extended federal trust (legal) responsibilities over both individual and tribal lands indefinitely. The IRA thus checked the continuing loss of American Indian lands through the allotment process. The IRA provided a major avenue for tribes to seek economic recovery, just as other New Deal programs financially helped the U.S. population in general. The IRA provided loan funds for tribal projects, assisted modestly in the efforts of some tribes to acquire new lands, and set the stage for a number of tribes to charter corporations and attempt business ventures. In California numerous landless tribes acquired mini-reservations (rancherias) by federal purchase of property. The rancherias attracted hundreds of native families who desperately needed a place to live. The IRA also encouraged dozens of previously disorganized tribes to adopt written constitutions, bylaws, election procedures, and forms of modern government.

The IRA contained disappointments as well. As amended by a Congress still interested in assimilation goals, the law did not provide for the court system envisioned by John Collier. By excluding the American Indians of Oklahoma and Alaska, the law missed dozens of tribal communities. Congress never adequately funded the IRA. Tribes could not really gain sufficient monies to effectively attain tribal economic recovery. Some tribes that developed constitutions under the IRA found that lawyers in the Department of the Interior had changed their constitutions, often weakening their self-governing authority.

In spite of these problems, as well as efforts in 1939 and 1943 to abolish the IRA by the Senate Indian Affairs Committee, the law remained in effect for those tribes that chose to organize and operate under it. Collier and his staff, in general, used the act to pursue their dream of increased tribal economic and political independence.

Despite its shortcomings the IRA brought the greatest change to U.S. Indian policy since the 1887 General Allotment Act. However the act contained far less change than Collier had sought. Collier had faced a hesitant Congress and opposition by a number of tribes. Still the IRA gave its name, "reorganization," to this era of U.S. Indian policy that lasted from 1933 to 1950. The law, in spite of the controversies surrounding it, pushed policy and programs in new directions driven by New Deal idealism of social and economic reform. The IRA became the centerpiece in what was labeled the Indian New Deal.

Johnson-O'Malley Act of 1934

Education problems were confronting the United States in general during the Great Depression. Just as school funding was severely dropping due to the economic crisis, the demand for better education was rising with the growth of major industries and the U.S. assuming a stronger role in global leadership. Indian education had always been a problem on reservations given their remoteness and lack of adequate funding. Indians who enrolled in public schools often faced racial discrimination and were discouraged from attending. By 1930 53 percent of Indian children were enrolled in public schools. The New Dealers decided to tackle the Indian education issue.

Given the financial conditions of the Great Depression, Congress concluded that for some parts of the country it was no longer feasible to operate separate health and educational facilities for American Indians living outside reservations. To do so was inefficient and uneconomical. In response Congress passed the Johnson-O'Malley Act (JOM) in 1934. The law was named for Hiram W. Johnson, chairman of the Senate Committee on Indian Affairs, and Thomas P. O'Malley, chairman of the House Committee on Indian Affairs. The goal of the act was to improve education, medical attention, agricultural assistance, relief of distress, and the social welfare of American Indians. Despite the range of social welfare issues addressed by JOM, most of its funding and programs were concerned with education. Though the legislation was largely designed to help Indians not living on reservations, Collier's Office of Indian Affairs applied it to reservation communities as well.

In hundreds of communities where American Indian children were enrolled in public schools, the federal government would pay public schools for expenses needed to educate Indian children in their districts. The law was amended in 1936 to make it easier for the states and federal government to cooperate to meet the act's objectives of educating Indian children. The amendment allowed federal contracts to go to parties other than the state. JOM proved successful in making it possible for many Indian children to switch from federal schools to better equipped and staffed public schools. With the availability of increased funds, public school districts welcomed Indian children to their schools.

More About...

Luther Standing Bear—A Native Spokesman

Luther Standing Bear (1868–1939) was born Ota K'te, a member of the Lakota people of the Sioux Nation. He grew up on the Pine Ridge Reservation in South Dakota and was one of the tribe's hereditary chiefs. As an outstanding student, he was taken from his family and tribe by the federal government and sent to Carlisle Indian School in Pennsylvania. He later wrote vividly in his autobiography, *Land of the Spotted Eagle* (1933) about this experience and his difficulties adjusting to existence in a government Indian school. He hated red flannel, shoes, and other things forced upon him.

Following completion of his education, Standing Bear found employment as a teacher, minister, and clerk. In 1898 Buffalo Bill Cody hired him to work in his Wild West Show. This employment led Standing Bear to California where he became an American Indian actor in numerous early Hollywood films. He became a member of the Actor's Guild of Hollywood and the Indian Actor's Association. In the 1920s and 1930s, Standing Bear fought to improve conditions for Indians on the reservations. He wrote several books about Indian life and government policy. He also was a member of the Oglala Council and the National League of Justice to the American Indian.

Standing Bear's other books included *My People, the Sioux* (1928), *Stories of the Sioux* (1934), and *My Indian Boyhood* (1988). He was a powerful, vivid writer.

Indian Arts and Crafts

Prior to the 1930s, the federal government had offered little encouragement or support to the artistic talents, music, or dance of American Indians. In fact most government educational programs were founded on the intent to destroy or alter native ways of life and assimilate American Indians into the surrounding majority culture. However the New Dealers of the Roosevelt administration were bringing to the nation a multiculturalism perspective built into the economic recovery programs. Having failed to get support for Indian arts and crafts through the IRA, John Collier pressed Congress further. Finally on August 27, 1935, Congress passed a law creating the Indian Arts and Crafts Board. This change was yet another program inspired largely by John Collier.

This law sought to encourage the production of traditional and contemporary arts and crafts by American Indians by expanding markets for their sale. To improve their marketability, standards for Indian crafts

Chief of the Yakima tribe greets presidential candidate Franklin D. Roosevelt before a speech to be given at the fairgrounds in Washington in 1932. (AP/Wide World Photos. Reproduced by permission.)

were adopted. The law provided for the trademarking of designs, opening of a sales art gallery in the Department of the Interior in Washington, DC, and the operation of American Indian art museums at Browning, Montana, Rapid City, South Dakota, and Anadarko, Oklahoma. The construction and operation of these museums and collections of artifacts helped to preserve and encourage native arts. Other projects included the operation of the Covelo Indian Market at the Golden Gate International Exposition (world's fair) in San Francisco in 1939 and 1940.

Part of the New Deal public works programs also focused on preserving Indian cultures. States, particularly New Mexico, designed such projects as part of their Works Progress Administration (WPA) program. Artists and musicians were hired to teach crafts and traditions almost lost. In addition as part of the fieldwork with tribes, Office of Indian Affairs employees worked to inventory, photograph, and document traditional arts and crafts in the 1930s. Special projects included an extensive photography project in 1941 and 1942 and Alfred W. Whiting's "Report on the Survey of Hopi Crafts" (1941–1942). These assessments of native arts permitted the Indian Arts and Crafts Board to address the misrepresentation of native arts, since often art and objects supposedly produced by American Indians were actually counterfeit.

Though some economic benefits for Indians were seen from these programs, it was almost negligible when compared to the desperate economic conditions of many tribal communities at this time. However, from this support a small group of Indian artisans was able to grow and influence students in future years.

Establishing Indian Law

Though the tribal court system did not survive in the congressionally-passed version of the IRA, Collier believed other avenues were open to increasing the protection of Indian rights. A part of the New Deal public works program (government funded jobs) compiled historical government records and placed them safely, at long last, into national archives, a place where official records and documents are kept. In a similar move, Secretary Ickes had the Department of Interior collect information on past Indian policies, relevant executive orders, acts of Congress, and court decisions.

Part of the New Deal for American Indians, therefore, was trying to sort out which laws and policies applied to them and if the laws or policies should be changed for the benefit of the tribes. Felix Cohen, a solicitor (lawyer) in the Bureau of Indian Affairs, and Nathan Margold, a solicitor for the secretary of interior, carried out much of this work. The materials ultimately filled volumes of three-ring binders. Cohen created a useful digest published as the *Handbook of Federal Indian Law* in 1941.

The Civilian Conservation Corps' Indian Division

On April 5, 1933, President Roosevelt signed an executive order creating the Civilian Conservation Corps (CCC), one of his personal favorites among the New Deal programs. The CCC employed young males between 18 and 24 years of age to perform conservation tasks. These included planting trees, fighting wildfires, building National Park facilities, constructing wildlife shelters, digging irrigation ditches for farmers, constructing trails, and numerous other activities. One of the most successful New Deal programs, the CCC lasted until 1943 and employed 2.5 million workers who lived in camps across the country.

Through the efforts of John Collier, the Office of Indian Affairs established the Civilian Conservation Corps-Indian Division (CCC-ID). This special branch of the CCC sponsored programs on reservations. Collier obtained $100 million from Congress for irrigation, soil erosion control, and road construction projects. Between 1933 and 1942, fifteen thousand American Indian young men served in CCC-ID.

CCC-ID served three major purposes. It provided training in useful skills, created a payroll for unemployed young men, and restored land affected by excessive soil erosion due to overgrazing. As required throughout the CCC program, those enlisted in this service personally kept about $5 per month for spending money and sent the other $20 in income home to their families.

Federally funded projects by CCC-ID designed to combat erosion included new systems for livestock grazing. Other projects on reservations included reforestation, spring and reservoir improvements, road and trail systems, fences, water systems, laying telephone lines, and construction of tribal facilities. In addition to restoration of lands still in tribal ownership, Collier also obtained one million acres of marginal farmlands through the New Deal's Resettlement Administration and Farm Security Administration to add to tribal base. Erosion control projects by the CCC-ID also were applied to these new lands as well. For new tribal facilities, the Office of Indian Affairs adopted a standard plan for tribal community buildings and clinics. CCC-ID constructed a number of these buildings to meet tribal needs on Indian lands across the country.

The CCC-ID program provided much needed employment on reservations. However little progress was actually made in making Indian farmers more economically competitive on the open market. Farmers still lacked capital to buy the necessary equipment.

New Deal programs such as the Works Progress Administration encouraged American Indians to preserve their Indian culture. This man uses his bow and arrow, made with WPA guidance, at the Tonawanda Indian Reservation near Akron, New York. (National Archives and Records Administration.)

End of the Indian New Deal

The various reform programs collectively known as the Indian New Deal were almost solely the result of efforts by Commissioner of Indian Affairs John Collier and Secretary of Interior Harold Ickes. President Roosevelt was largely uninformed about American Indian issues. The biggest successes came in stopping the loss of tribal lands through the 1934 IRA, which Collier had spent much of 1933 drafting, and passage of the Johnson-O'Malley Act providing funds to support Indian educational, social welfare, and medical needs. Also during his first year, Collier saw passage of the Pueblo Relief Act. This act increased monetary awards to the Pueblo Indians of New Mexico who had lost land and water through the Pueblo Land Act of 1924.

Collier, in his zeal for reform, pressed on with reforms dropped by Congress from the IRA bill before it was passed. This led to repeated battles between

Collier and Congress over budgets. Opposition over Indian New Deal programs also came from some Indians. Tribes in Oklahoma favored assimilation into white society and did not want to adopt the multiculturalism policies of Collier. Also, the Navajos of Arizona and New Mexico fought efforts by Collier to cut back the size of their sheep herds as part of the program to stop soil erosion. The sheep were vital to the Navajo way of life. After several years of battle between Collier and Congress to fund Indian New Deal programs, the budget demands of World War II (1939–1945) finally brought monetary support of the programs to an end.

Contributing Forces

U.S. Indian Policy

By 1870 military defeats and treaties had forced most surviving American Indians onto reservations set aside in remote areas of the West. U.S. society considered the American Indian a vanishing race. Almost every aspect of Indian life on a reservation was controlled or directly influenced by the U.S. Office of Indian Affairs. It had long been legally established that formal relationships with American Indian tribes were the responsibility of the federal government, not state or local governments. The agency regulated how tribal land and individual allotments owned by Indians could be used, and it provided healthcare and education for Indians. Indian agents had great power over Indians with little if any participation by Indians in their lives and property. Indians did not have the status of U.S. citizens but rather were members of "domestic dependent nations."

Public interest over Indian issues began growing late in the nineteenth century. Following the Civil War (1861–1865), frustrations grew over forcing social change to help the freed slaves in the South. Northern social reformers were meeting ongoing Southern resistance. As a result, by the late 1870s the attention of some social reformers shifted to the plight of American Indians. By the 1880s reformers decided it would be in the best interest of Indians if they were forced into mainstream American society. Their goal was to create an educated and economically self-sufficient Indian population. They believed the best way to do that would be to make them property-owning farmers. The desires of the reforms were much the same as land speculators and settlers who increasingly wanted access to lands and resources located within reservations. Through their combined efforts, Congress passed the General Allotment Act of 1887, also known as the Dawes Act. Through this legislation the United States adopted a policy of eliminating native traditions, Christianizing Indians, and making them into farmers and landowners to help with the assimilation process. The act launched a national program to divide up tribal lands into individual farms. Under this new policy the Office of Indian Affairs was charged with this division of the lands, education, and the training of farming skills as its main activities.

The General Allotment Act divided reservation lands into small parcels that would be assigned to individual tribal members. The federal government would hold the parcels for a period of 25 years, and then the ownership title would be transferred to the Indian allottee. The new individual owner would then begin paying taxes on it. Allotments at Makah Reservation, a heavily timbered property on the Olympic Peninsula in Washington, were ten acres. That was about all a man could clear in a lifetime of work with axe and saw. Many allotments in more open farming country were eighty acres. Grazing allotments in the dry, open rangelands were 160 acres or sometimes larger. However these parcels were often unsuitable for farming and Indians lacked agricultural tools.

With the increased need for agricultural products during World War I (1914–1918), the Office of Indian Affairs decided to speed up the process of giving full ownership of allotted lands to Indians so they could sell or lease the land for farming. To do this the agency introduced competency tests. Competency commissions would travel from reservation to reservation, supposedly to determine if individual Indians were capable of being productive landowners. The definition of competence was left somewhat vague at times. When an American Indian was deemed "competent," he or she (1) gained citizenship in the United States, (2) received a deed for the land, and (3) had to begin paying taxes on their new land. However, in the zeal to wrest lands away from Indians, the commission would often not even take the time to meet with the particular individual they were to assess but declared them competent nonetheless. The Indian would have little knowledge of this assessment. However, soon a non-Indian, often a land speculator, would approach the new Indian landowner to purchase their property for some amount usually well below market value. The Indian, having no means to pay taxes, had little choice but to get what money he could out of it. The General Allotment Act thus became an effective device for reducing the native land base and increasing local tax revenues.

A nightmare of mixed ownership of lands on reservations resulted from the allotment process. It created an even bigger nightmare of bookkeeping for

More About...

Bureau of Indian Affairs

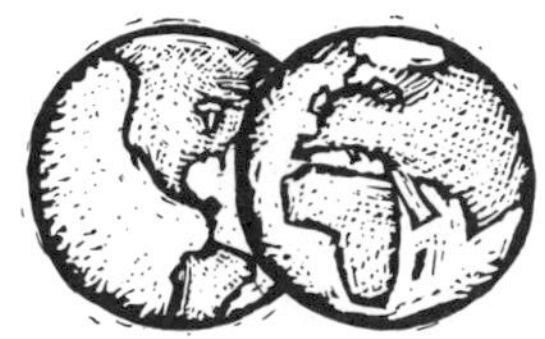

In 1786 the secretary of war was placed in charge of Indian affairs in the newly formed United States. Since contact with tribes was predominately through private and government trading houses, in 1806 a superintendent of trade was created to regulate trade with Indians. In 1834 Congress expanded the federal government's role in Indian matters with the creation of the Office of Indian Affairs in the war department. In 1849 oversight of Indian affairs passed from military to civilian control as the Office of Indian Affairs was transferred from the Department of War to the newly created Department of Interior. A commissioner of Indian Affairs headed the Indian agency and reported to the secretary of interior. Under the commissioner several superintendents administered over Indian agents who were assigned to particular tribes. The agents were responsible for distributing annual payments to tribes promised through treaties, regulating trade between Indians and non-Indians, supervising educational programs, and supporting missionary work. The agents operated fairly independently. Inefficiency and corruption came with the lack of oversight. From the 1850s into the 1870s a major focus of the agency was establishing a system of reservations to move Indians out of the way of westward-expanding U.S. settlement.

Following passage of the General Allotment Act in 1887, agents became increasingly responsible for making Indians into self-supporting farmers and abolishing Indian society. The agents had control over food distribution, farming tools, and military troops, thus holding a strong hand over Indian communities. Because education was such a strong part of the agency mission, by 1900 over half of the 4,260 employees of the Office of Indian Affairs were teachers or school employees. The agency grew from less than three thousand employees in 1890 to six thousand in 1918. By 1909 the agency was reorganized and superintendents and Indian agents were eliminated. In their place were schoolteachers to carry out U.S. policies of assimilation. Through the early 1920s, a major role of teachers was to discourage the speaking of native languages and following traditional customs such as dress and dancing. This repression of native culture lessened with release of the Meriam Report in 1928 which strongly criticized the agency's cultural assimilation policies. The report was filled with recommendations on improving the agency's education and healthcare programs. Under President Herbert Hoover (served 1929–1933) the agency began adopting some of the recommendations.

During the Great Depression, under the leadership of John Collier, the Office of Indian Affairs grew in size to twelve thousand employees in 1934. The budget also expanded briefly to $52 million from $23 million in 1933 at the worst of the Depression. However, the budget was trimmed back to around $12 million a year from 1935 to 1942 before being slashed to less than $1 million during the war years.

From 1909 to 1949 the agency's organization remained much the same with a Washington, DC, office and some eighty offices primarily located on reservations. By 1950 the Office of Indian Affairs became known as the Bureau of Indian Affairs (BIA), and the modern structure of the BIA came into being with a system of 12 regional offices administering ninety field offices. The responsibility of the agency included programs in health, education, welfare, law enforcement, forestry, job training, and irrigation. In 1955 healthcare was transferred out of BIA to the newly created Indian Health Service (IHS).

During the 1960s era, the Great Society programs of President Lyndon Johnson (served 1963–1969) provided assistance to Indians outside of the BIA programs. Assistance provided directly to tribes included housing and anti-poverty programs. It was during this period that the first Indian was appointed head of the BIA. President Johnson appointed Robert Bennett in 1966. Also the percentage of BIA Indian employees grew from 34 percent in 1934 to 78 percent by 1980. In 1977 under President Jimmy Carter (served 1977–1981), the position of the head of the BIA was elevated to assistant secretary of the Interior Department and the annual budget was $1 billion. Promoting tribal self-determination along with programs in education, economic development, and natural resource management remained the primary missions of the agency at the beginning of the twenty-first century.

tracing the heirs to allotments. The end result was that the allotment program dramatically increased the loss of lands held by tribes and individual American Indians. Also, fragmenting the reservation lands would strongly hinder wise and economic land use. The loss of lands occurred in two ways. First, unallotted reservation lands were sometimes identified as "excess" or unneeded and were sold to Euro-Americans. Secondly, lands transferred out of federal control to Indian ownership were usually lost, often within four years, because the new owners could not afford to pay taxes to the counties where they were located. This loss further reduced the native land base. When the act began in 1887, the tribes owned approximately 138 million acres. When the law was suspended in 1934, the total native land base had dropped to less than 48 million acres.

The allotment program promoted by the General Allotment Act was a major assault on tribalism. American Indian society is largely communal; in direct opposition to the concept of owning small individual farms.

A Further Decline in the Indian Condition

Under the policies of forced cultural assimilation prior to 1933, the physical and economic condition of American Indians further declined. Sanitation on remote reservations was very poor and employment was largely nonexistent. Infectious diseases such as tuberculosis and eye disease were much more common in Indian communities than in the general U.S. population. They also suffered high rates of infant mortality. Many Indians had to sell their land and live without any means of financial support. Despite the efforts of the federal government to make farmers out of Indians, the number of Indian farmers actually declined from 1900 to 1930 as did the amount of land farmed. Indian farmers were unable to compete in the growing agricultural industry which increasingly involved expensive mechanization. The demand for cash to buy machinery was more than they could raise.

When natural resources of value were discovered on Indian lands, usually the Indians would see little financial benefit. Private business and corrupt Indian agents would conspire to short change royalties owed to the Indian or tribal landowners. For example, oil discoveries on Indian lands, particularly in Oklahoma, in the early twentieth century commonly led to swindles. Much trickery occurred in taking lands away from Indian control.

In addition to economic and health issues, many Indian cultural traditions were lost during this period. During the 1910s the Office of Indian Affairs began an aggressive campaign to stop the practice of Indian ceremonies. The ceremonies such as the Hopi Snake Dance were labeled obscene, superstitious, and immoral by the federal agency. There was little appreciation of the ceremonies' religious value. Not only did the dances have religious worth, but they were becoming valuable from a tourism standpoint in the Southwest at Pueblos. However, termination of the Indian dances became a focal point of those promoting assimilation as they were considered unchristian traditions. The role of the Indian agent was to dissolve Indian culture as quickly as possible.

Other measures were also taken to assimilate Indians. During this time Indian children were taken from their families and sent to boarding schools away from their communities. There they were prohibited from speaking Indian language.

The legal status of Indians living in the United States was still largely unresolved as well. Several thousand American Indians served in World War I in the military forces of the United States, side by side with other Americans. However, almost one-third of Indians who entered military service were still not considered citizens of the United States. Native peoples remained in ambiguous legal status in the country where they were born and lived. Congress belatedly passed the Indian Citizenship Act of 1924 to correct this situation. Though Indians could still not vote in state elections, passage of this law raised national attention about American Indians.

The Pueblo Lands Issue

Another issue would also serve to raise public awareness of the Indian condition. A U.S. Supreme Court decision in 1913 suddenly called into question the land ownership of whites living in areas claimed by the Pueblo Indians in New Mexico. This issue gained national attention in 1922 when Senator Holm Bursum of New Mexico introduced the Bursum Bill.

The proposed legislation would have forced the Pueblo Indians to document ownership of their lands to defend them against their loss. This requirement was virtually impossible for Indians to comply with. The records of Pueblo lands dated far back through the territorial, Mexican, and Spanish administrations in the Rio Grand Valley. Many of the records simply did not exist. Others were often written in Spanish and kept in archives and libraries in Europe. They were well out of reach of the Pueblo members. In essence the bill would guarantee lands owned by Pueblos in New Mexico would be given to the white settlers who were considered illegal squatters by the Indian communities.

The proposed bill received much criticism in the press, and John Collier did much to increase public awareness of what he considered an unjust loss of land

The land and traditional way of life of American Indians was under enormous threat even before the height of the Great Depression. (Archive Photos, Inc. Reproduced by permission.)

by the Indians. The Bursum Bill caused hundreds of "friends of the American Indian" to rally and oppose its passage. Leaders in this effort included John Collier, author and activist for the preservation of Indian culture Mary Austin, and the American Federation of Women's Clubs. As a result of their efforts, Congress passed the Pueblo Lands Act in 1924 that was much more favorable to the concerns of the Pueblos than originally expressed in the Bursum Bill.

By the early 1920s the public began to recognize that the Office of Indian Affairs was doing a very poor job in managing tribally owned forests and mineral rights. John Collier, at the time a New York social worker, in particular began to speak out publicly against government policies of mismanagement and assimilation. He was hired by the American Federation of Women's Clubs to present his views. Collier contended American Indian traditions should be respected, not abolished.

Collier also founded the American Indian Defense Association, an activist Indian rights organization. Through the organization Collier pressed for Indian

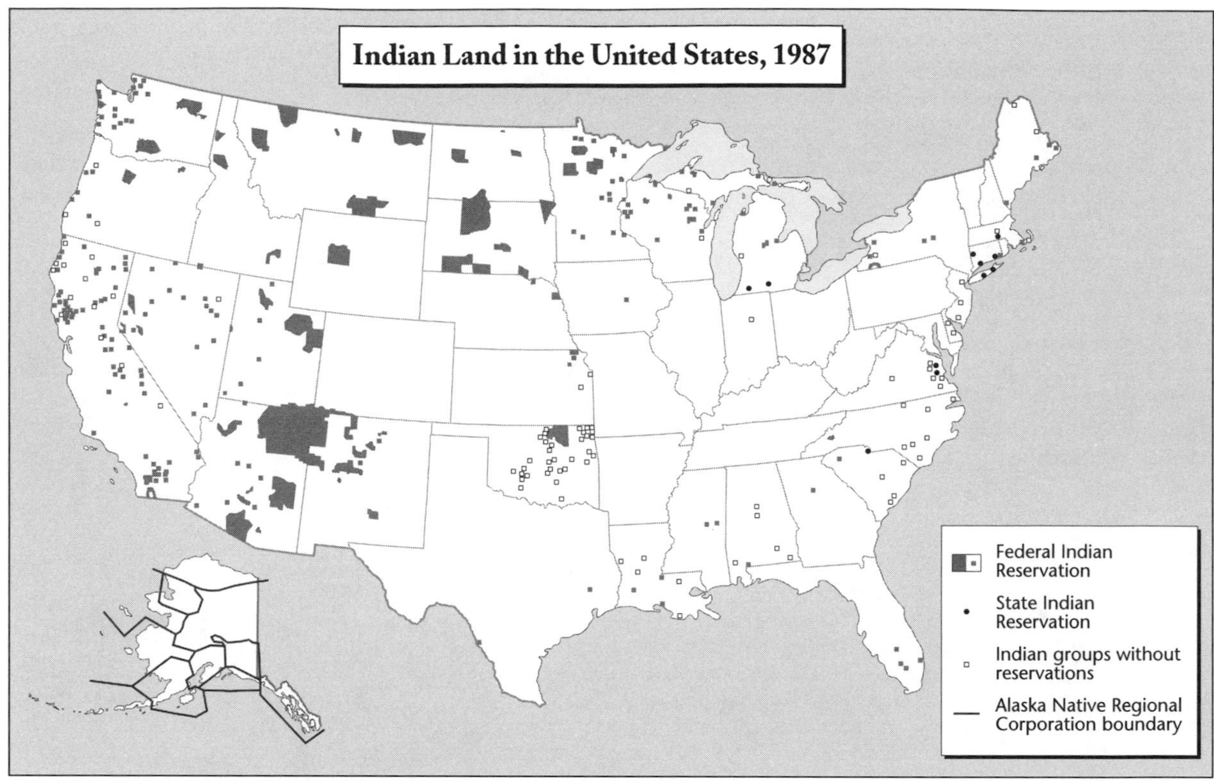

Map of Indian land in the United States as of 1987. (The Gale Group.)

reform to better protect the interests of Indians. Collier's campaign worked, and increasing public criticism of federal Indian policies led to the end of the suppression of Indian ceremonies and other traditions by 1925. Investigations of U.S. Indian policy also began to mount.

Indian Education through the 1920s

Since the late nineteenth century, the federal government had assumed the lead role in Indian education. Earlier, Congress had provided funds to religious missionaries to help "civilize" the native population. However, following the Civil War, it became apparent the government needed to assume a more active role. More Indians had become isolated on reservations, and many were not being reached by religious organizations. Indian children needed more preparation for assimilating into white society than they were receiving from scattered and inconsistent religious programs.

By 1880 the number of federally operated day schools and reservation boarding schools began growing. In 1879 an Indian school for teaching vocational trades opened in Carlisle, Pennsylvania. Girls were taught homemaking skills, while boys were taught blacksmithing, carpentry, and other industrial skills. Education consisted of four types of schools by 1900. These were on-reservation and off-reservation boarding schools, local day schools for Indians, and local public schools. In 1900 some 153 federal Indian schools of various types were in operation, including new boarding schools at Santa Fe and Phoenix.

Because of the lack of acceptance of Indian children in many public schools, the Office of Indian Affairs shifted in the 1920s to more exclusively Indian schools. The Office of Indian Affairs launched a campaign to organize the growing number of schools into an integrated system modeled after the public school system. A three-level system was established consisting of day schools for the beginning students, reservation boarding schools for intermediate instruction, and off-reservation vocational schools for the best students. Some schools also adopted an "outing" program in which pupils were hired out to local white families and businesses. This program gave students a chance to earn money and experience the non-Indian world. This system persisted into the 1930s.

Conservative white administrators and instructors dominated all schools through the early twentieth century. A key goal throughout the system was to destroy Indian culture in the pupils and prepare them for assimilation into white society. In the boarding schools, Indian youth were separated from family and friends, fed food strange to them, and forced to speak English. Punishment was often harsh. Through the 1910s a number of problems began adding up. Indian graduates were not finding many jobs in white society and returning to reservations with little job opportunity. School buildings were falling into disrepair. Overcrowding was causing major health problems. As always, parents did not like their children being removed from the home and the community, sometimes forcefully.

The Meriam Report

Charges of inefficiency and corruption within the Office of Indian Affairs led to various fact-finding studies in the 1920s. The leading critic was John Collier. In addition to corruption, he questioned whether education should stress manual labor skills, farming, and domestic labors set in an atmosphere of military discipline and English-only instruction.

The most substantial study came in 1926 and 1927, and was known as the Survey of Indian Affairs. The Commission of Indian Affairs requested the Institute for Government Research (IGR) to conduct the study. Lewis Meriam, who was on the IGR staff, led the study team. Another major figure of the team was Henry Roe Cloud, a Winnebago Indian educator who helped with tribal contacts. Funded by John D. Rockefeller, Jr., and promoted by the Brookings Institution of Washington, DC, the team engaged in fact finding and crafting of recommendations. The study focused on how social services provided to Indians compared to how similar services by the federal government provided for the general public.

The resulting 872-page report titled *The Problem of Indian Administration* (1928) identified the sorry state of affairs for American Indians. The investigators found widespread poverty, shockingly high disease rates, poor diets, short life expectancy, low levels of educational achievement, despair, and loss of resources. At that time of the Meriam Report 55 percent of American Indians had an annual income of less than $200 per year. Only 2 percent had incomes greater than $500 per year and the remainder had incomes in between.

The report, often called the Meriam Report after its team leader, tied many of the deplorable problems to the loss of lands through federal policies since the 1880s. It made a strong case for major changes in the administration of affairs relating to American Indians. Importantly, the report recommended that the federal government permit American Indians who chose to live by Indian cultural traditions to do so. The report also concluded that Indian schools largely lacked the resources needed to properly educate Indian children. This study became a blueprint for the New Dealers who wanted to change federal policy and programs in the 1930s.

Perspectives

The Public

The 1930s was a period of changing public perceptions of Indian peoples. Indians began finding some opportunities to represent their own interests in defining and implementing New Deal programs rather than having white supporters speaking solely for them.

Several major images of American Indians in the 1930s had been carried over from earlier times. These images dominated thought and debate over what should be done about the plight of the Indians. A prevailing image of Indians held by the reformers in the 1930s, who had moved away from assimilation to multiculturalism goals, was that of the good Indian or "noble savage." An image held by those who still promoted assimilation was one of the bad or degraded Indian. A third image common throughout the spectrum was that of Indians as relics of the past, an exotic dimension of human life found in the United States.

The noble savage perspective was a romantic notion of American Indians. The extension of the railroad into the American Southwest by the late nineteenth century opened up the world of the Indian Pueblo culture to white tourists and U.S. society in general. In addition more settlers poured into the Southwest, increasing interaction with the Pueblo communities. This increased exposure caused a romantic notion of native cultures to grow among many. John Collier, a social reformer from New York City, was one of those who visited the Pueblo area in 1920. He was immediately taken with this seemingly exotic culture. Collier became the leading promoter of reform in U.S. Indian policy.

This romantic viewpoint was also adapted by many Americans who had become disillusioned with the growing mass production and mass consumerism of American society and the increasingly crowded urban conditions. To them Indians seemed to have a superior spiritual life compared to whites. They lived a life of serenity in contrast to the increasing pace of the industrialized world. Puebloan artistic skills were similarly highly revered. Using this idealized perspective of

Indians from an Oklahoma tribe participate in the National American Legion convention in Louisiana. A key goal of the Roosevelt Administration was to support native American cultures. (AP/Wide World Photos. Reproduced by permission.)

Indian culture, reformers believed the native traditions should be preserved and honored for their values toward community and the land.

These same supporters who romanticized over Indian culture, however, still doubted Indian intellect. Just as promoters of assimilation spoke on behalf of Indian peoples that integration into mainstream society would be best for Indians, promoters of multiculturalism who opposed assimilation also believed they could best express what was best in preserving Indian culture. Neither side seemed interested in having Indians speak for themselves.

Another common public perspective was that of the "degraded" Indian. The degraded Indian, it was believed, was a result of his own natural laziness, dishonesty, and drunkenness. Stereotypes were portrayed in the local press with frequent mention of "fire water" and "wigwams"—making humor of the poverty that gripped Indian communities. The public used this portrayal to support the need to assimilate Indian peoples into white society so they would adopt more desirable social traits. Ironically, the racism rampant in America in the 1930s would frequently deny Indian peoples access to the economic opportunities in society.

Rampant among both reformers and those promoting assimilation was the perspective of Indian societies as relics of the past. To almost everyone Indians still seemed distant and unusual. References to Indian peoples and their communities in the media were usually in past tense. There was little public recognition that Indian peoples still existed and would continue to exist. Indian culture was considered a curiosity of the past, mostly surviving in books and museums. They were not considered a part of the present of the 1930s by many. Associated with this perspective was the lack of recognition of the significant differences between different tribal traditions.

The public began to experience a new, fourth image of American Indians during the Indian New Deal—the Indian citizen acting as an informed participant in New Deal developments. The New Deal gave Indians some opportunity to speak out in public on issues important to their tribes. Indians fluent in English were a surprise to many Americans. For some Indians the major provisions of the IRA proved controversial. Thousands of allottees viewed their land allotments as legally theirs. They did not want to turn over their lands to the tribes as the IRA directed. As a result, debate over the proposed IRA projected Indians as thoughtful political participants with differing points of view. This greatly differed from the single stereotypical images of Indians. Of course those Indians who expressed a viewpoint similar to local whites were considered thoughtful and responsible. If Indian views on proposed New Deal legislation were different from local white viewpoints, then the Indians were considered incompetent and to be representing communistic ideas of Indian tribal communal needs.

Clearly the Indians who represented their tribes in IRA governments and interactions with the New Dealers were living in two worlds. They were representing communities pushed aside and placed on remote reservations by U.S. expansionism of the nineteenth century. Yet they were striving to seek modern benefits offered by New Deal programs with a goal of future economic development. The conflict between the two worlds was evident to visitors at the 1933 Chicago World's Fair who viewed traditional Indian villages set in futuristic settings.

National Perspectives

For decades federal Indian policy was based on the destruction of tribes and the assimilation of American Indians. Thomas Jefferson (served 1801–1809), followed by other national leaders, had promoted these ideas since the birth of the nation. Even those who saw American Indians as equal in abilities and standing with Euro-Americans still advocated assimilation. They were unwilling to let the Indians retain their language, culture, religion, or tribal self-governance. The reservation system that grew during President Andrew Jackson's (served 1829–1837) administration in the early nineteenth century was driven by this agenda of destroying tribes and fostering assimilation.

By the first decades of the twentieth century it became clear that programs of assimilation did not end poverty or improve American Indian health. The native population continued to decline, just as it had since the arrival of Europeans in the Western Hemisphere four centuries earlier. In spite of the efforts of those enforcing assimilation policies to transform American Indians into English-speaking, Christian farmers, many Indians had not made the transition and clung to old ways of life.

The arrival of new leaders in Washington, DC, in the New Deal, including a number who had labored as social workers, raised the issue of supporting rather than destroying tribes and cultural identities of American Indians. The national perspective began changing.

Even as the New Dealers were introducing new national perspectives, the national press still projected the old perspectives. For example, the press covering news stories during the debate over the proposed IRA still used traditional terms to describe Indians—chiefs, braves, bucks, squaws, princesses, and papooses. All of these terms continued a national perspective of social inferiority of the Indian peoples. Similarly, during the drought of the Dust Bowl era of the 1930s, when winds were blowing massive clouds of dust from parched barren fields on the southern Great Plains, many stories covered the "rain dances" of the Plains Indians.

A great deal of misunderstanding of traditional Indian ceremonies, including the Snake Dance of the Hopis and the Sun Dance on the Plains, was relayed to the general public by these national news stories. As a result Indian religious activities were trivialized and placed in circus-like contexts. Other indications of the general perspective on Indian cultures also surfaced. Often in national news articles, whites were referred to by their last name whereas Indians were referred to by their first names. This portrayed Indians as childlike and undignified. This perspective supported proponents of assimilation who considered Indians naïve and vulnerable to the complexities of the modern world. They had to be taught the white man's ways for their own protection.

Adding to the national perspective of Indians was a biweekly magazine started by John Collier while promoting the Indian New Deal in the 1930s. Titled *Indians at Work,* the magazine presented favorable articles of Indians. The publication reflected Collier's own noble savage notions of American Indians. He portrayed Indians as wronged through actions by whites, such as having been robbed of their religions, traditions, and land through past government assimilation policies. Opponents of Collier countered that the social reform and experimentation was interrupting the progress of Indians in joining white society. Collier and the Indian New Deal, they claimed, were sending Indian peoples back to their primitive lifeways.

Perhaps the biggest aspect of Indian issues was that the debate was still largely between white reformers and white proponents of assimilation. Even John Collier operated largely in a paternalistic (acting as a parent to a child) manner, speaking for the Indian about what was best, in his opinion, for the Indian. Nonetheless Collier was promoting a multicultural viewpoint that Indian cultures and traditions should be respected and preserved. Though the lives of Indians were changing under the Indian New Deal, their public image, based on earlier stereotypes, was changing far less.

Some members of Congress still held to the view that multiculturalism was wrong for the United States. They believed assimilation, the key goal of the 1887 General Allotment Act, should continue to drive federal policy. They were not in favor of spending money to strengthen tribal authority or encourage the perpetuation of Indian arts, crafts, languages, religion, and culture. As a result, provisions of the IRA were never well funded.

Several other factors on the national level contributed to the shifts in federal Indian policy during the New Deal. Of significant importance among these events was the rise of an educated, able group of American Indian leaders. Sometimes called "Red Progressives," between 1900 and the mid-1920s these people pressed for reform of the Office of Indian Affairs, changes in Indian education, greater exercise of trust responsibility, and the extension of citizenship to all American Indians. Dr. Carlos Montezuma, a Yavapai physician and editor of *Wassaja,* was a sharp critic of the Office of Indian Affairs and called for its abolition. A traveling photographer had adopted Montezuma at a young age and moved him from the Southwest to Chicago. There he attended college and graduated from the Chicago Medical College of Northwestern University. Others, like Dr. Henry Roe Cloud, worked from within the Office of Indian Affairs to try to improve its delivery of services to native peoples. Cloud had attended government reservation schools as a youth. Through his own ambition, in 1910 he became the first American Indian to graduate from Yale University. He later received a doctorate in divinity from Emporia College in Kansas in 1932.

Impact

The Indian New Deal and Beyond

The New Deal dramatically changed the course of federal policy toward American Indians. Its impacts were many and highly significant. Perhaps most important economically was stopping the previous erosion of a land base. Except for some losses of land in the 1950s due to U.S. tribal termination policies, the land base preserved by the IRA remained intact through the remainder of the twentieth century and served as a foundation for future economic development projects.

Other important changes also occurred. Tribal governments regained a substantial footing for protecting tribal and individual rights and protecting natural resources owned by tribes. Indian New Deal legislation also extended federal benefits to tribal members for health and education services. The legislation encouraged tribes to adopt modern forms of government and set up a more formal process for tribal governments to interact with the federal government. It also provided loans to tribal governments for economic development.

The Indian New Deal had opened new opportunities in employment and job training to American Indians and established a foundation for future economic growth of tribal communities. For example, the Civilian Conservation Corps-Indian Division (CCC-ID) created jobs, started a flow of funds into reservations, and constructed important and needed infrastructure (roads, buildings, irrigation canals, etc.) on reservations.

For all these reasons, the Indian New Deal represented a major change in U.S. Indian policy. Tribes could now once again function as largely independent governments and gain a stronger hand in directing economic development. On the other hand, unemployment on reservations remained higher than national figures throughout the rest of the century, and most tribes were not able to fully achieve economic self-sufficiency.

The Indian New Deal reversed nationwide programs of forced cultural assimilation. Instead the federal government encouraged continued production of American Indian arts and crafts and stopped requiring attendance at Christian religious services in government schools. Under the Indian Arts and Crafts Board, tribal members could trademark their own art products and gain assistance in marketing their wares. Religious traditions were also saved and rejuvenated, and other aspects of cultural heritage were preserved.

The assembling of laws, court decisions, presidential executive orders, and other aspects of the legal history of tribes by Felix Cohen led to the publication of *Handbook of Federal Indian Law* (1941). Over the next sixty years, a major new branch of the U.S. legal system grew, known as Indian Law. Volumes by other legal scholars would follow in the next several decades addressing Indian legal rights.

Unfortunately, detrimental changes in U.S. Indian policy were soon to come. Many tribes suffered major political setbacks in the 1950s when Congress sought to abolish reservations and tribal governments. To do this Congress began terminating their federal recognition (trust status). This period became known as the Termination Period in U.S. Indian history. It was based once again on the ideas of assimilation that had fueled the Allotment period of 1887 to 1934. This action cut off federal social service benefits to terminated tribes, including healthcare and education support. Congress wanted to place tribes under state jurisdiction and responsibility. This effort continued until 1960 when opposition to this approach finally ended assimilation attempts.

Trust Responsibility

Trust responsibility refers to the federal government's legal obligation to act in the best economic interest of tribes. During the allotment period of 1887 to 1933, the federal government had trust responsibilities not only for the remaining tribal reservation lands, but also to protect the assets (timber, minerals, water, soil, and grazing resources) of individual allotments. The Office of Indian Affairs was to supervise the sale, lease, and administration of tribal lands and Indian allotments, and also receive, invest, and distribute the income from these lands to tribes and individuals. The Indian agency was to be a good steward of the assets of individuals and tribes.

Trust responsibility was defined early in U.S. history by the U.S. Supreme Court. In the 1831 case of *Cherokee Nation v. Georgia* the Court affirmed that the United States had a relationship to tribes much "as a guardian to a ward." As the stronger player in this relationship, the United States had a responsibility of trust to look out for its wards, in this case American Indians, and to protect them. This concept would appear later in councils with Indian tribes where the government negotiated treaties with tribes.

Despite this legal responsibility, for decades non-Indians, often working for the Office of Indian Affairs, plundered the assets of tribes and individual American Indians. Trespassers encroached onto reservations and allotments with livestock. They grazed the range and often destroyed the ground cover and caused erosion, while others stole timber from reservations. They cut the trees and hauled them off for their profit. When the Office of Indian Affairs set up a timber sale on Indian lands, at times they falsified the amount of timber or paid unfair prices for what they sold to lumber mills. Little oversight of the agency's actions existed.

Minerals on Indian lands, often having more value than forests, provoked even more plundering of the assets of American Indians. This problem was especially severe when oil discoveries promised to make the tribes in Oklahoma wealthy. Being shrewd crooks, often working with dishonest lawyers, bankers, and politicians, private individuals and federal officials created numerous ways to steal the wealth of natives. Often they insisted on being named guardians. Some American Indians, especially orphans, ended up with eight or ten guardians, each taking a fee for looking out for the "noncompetent" person. These events were scandals, only partially known but increasingly talked about in the 1910s and 1920s.

With the turmoil of the Depression in the 1930s and the advent of the Indian New Deal, Indian citizens could act as informed participants in New Deal developments. Several Indian speakers came into the public eye at this time to discuss issues important to their tribes. This included issues touched in the 1933 Indian Reorganization Act (IRA). The IRA granted new obligations to the traditional trust responsibilities, which had existed since the nineteenth century. With tribes now officially granted more rights in self-government and economic development—including taking advantage of their own natural resources and providing for cultural preservation—they could become more independent from the federal government's earlier domination of Indian affairs and preserve their way of life.

The IRA, however, was not without controversy amongst Indian tribes. Under Title III, the act transferred allotments of Indian land to communal tribal control. This troubled thousands of Indians, who considered the allotments as legally theirs and did not want to turn their land over to a communally controlled system. Vocal opposition to Title III in the 1930s gave Indians a higher profile publicly and with the government, and gained Indians status as thoughtful political participants.

More About...

Native American or American Indian?

Peoples whose cultures existed in North America prior to the arrival of the first Europeans are variously referred to as Native Americans and American Indians. Both terms are regularly used in U.S. laws addressing native issues and by the general public as well. Their use has varied through time, and neither are particularly appreciated by those to whom the labels are applied. The term "American Indian" was first used by the earliest European explorers in the sixteenth century. The word American comes from the first name of explorer Amerigo Vespucci, who landed on what is now the American mainland in the late 1490s. Indian refers to peoples of the Indian subcontinent who Christopher Columbus mistakenly thought he had contacted. As Europeans continued colonizing the New World, the term American Indian continued in use despite the wide variety of native groups that lived in North America and the fact it was not India that Columbus found. To the colonists all the native groups were primitive and uncivilized, thus a common name was collectively applied to all. The individual native groups had names for themselves in their own languages that commonly meant "the people" or "human beings."

By the mid-twentieth century the term Native American gained increasing use. Anyone born in North America of any ethnicity, however, could be considered a native American. By the 1980s American Indian became favored once again by native peoples. However, both terms are objectionable to natives because to them the terms reflect the racism of the dominant white society. American Indians prefer reference to their tribal affiliation when possible, such as Navajo or Oneida or Lakota. When referring to a group of people who are members of several tribes, then American Indian is preferred given the lack of any other commonly accepted term. However the use of Native American still continues as well.

It did not, however, stop the plunder of Indian resources. Just as before the Indian New Deal, resources continued to be diverted from reservations and allotments—to the detriment of the tribes. Among the most valuable of these resources in the American West were water and waterpower. Although reservations were mostly created to promote "civilization" through agriculture, non-Indians took the water that could have helped make farming possible. Power companies worked closely with Office of Indian Affairs officials to secure dam sites, often ignoring the tribal government. They would build hydropower facilities that flooded reservations.

After over a century of fraud, corruption, and just plain bad record keeping a major lawsuit was filed in 1996 on behalf of 300,000 Indians against the Secretary of Interior claiming that Indians had lost at least $10 billion through the years. Favorable rulings indicated the case would likely force major changes in how the federal government carried out its trust responsibilities.

Self-Determination Era

Another major period beneficial to American Indians began in 1970 when a program of tribal self-determination was announced in a speech by President Richard Nixon (served 1969–1974). The idea of political and economic self-determination emphasized again the independence of tribal governments. The Indian Self-Determination and Educational Assistance Act of 1974 built on the 1930s Indian New Deal policies. Through self-determination policies that included large amounts of grant monies, many tribes greatly increased their economic and political power. Tribes could gain more direct control over reservation social services such as reservation day schools and healthcare.

Thanks to the new policies, by the 1990s the Indian population was growing rapidly in size. Tribes were substantially influencing the economies of a number of localities in the United States. Industries exploiting the rich natural resources located on tribal lands, tourism, and commercial enterprises including gambling casinos began prospering in some areas. Organizations such as the National Congress of American Indians (NCAI) intensively lobbied both Congress and the White House for favorable consideration in any new U.S. domestic policies.

The Johnson-O'Malley Act of 1934, which had provided funds to support and care for American Indian students by granting federal dollars to state and local school districts, remained unchanged until it was amended by the 1974 Indian Self-Determination Act. The law greatly revised the Johnson-O'Malley Act by allowing the BIA to contract with Indians directly so they could provide for their own education needs. The JOM remained effective into the twenty-first century, playing a major role in supporting Indian education.

Its primary purpose was still to provide supplementary financial assistance to meet the specialized educational needs of American Indian children. JOM funds were in addition to other local, state, and federal monies.

In a precursor of later affirmative action (encouraging increased representation of minorities) hiring policies, the New Dealers also introduced new procedures in hiring that allowed members of tribes to gain employment in the Office of Indian Affairs. By the late twentieth century, the BIA had become not only predominately staffed by American Indians, but with an Indian as its head. Tribes had considerably more say in how BIA funds could be spent for Indian services.

Notable People

Felix Cohen (1905–1953). Cohen was the brilliant attorney who helped shape New Deal policy toward American Indians. Born in New York City, Cohen graduated from City College of New York, then earned a graduate degree in philosophy at Harvard in 1929 and a law degree from Columbia in 1931. When Franklin Roosevelt began his first term as president, Cohen left private law practice in New York to join Nathan Margold in the office of the solicitor in the Department of the Interior, in Washington, DC. Cohen's first assignment was to draft the Indian Reorganization Act (IRA).

Cohen, working closely with the Commissioner of Indian Affairs John Collier, charted a major change in federal policy toward American Indians in the IRA. Following passage of the IRA by Congress, Cohen and Collier toured the United States in 1934 to discuss the law's provisions. In the late 1930s, Cohen compiled the various treaties, laws, and court rulings relating to the affairs of native peoples. The materials eventually filled 46 volumes and were condensed into the landmark volume on Indian law *Handbook of Federal Indian Law* (1941).

Cohen also served as an attorney in a number of cases involving tribes. In 1947 he represented the All-Pueblo Council to force New Mexico and Arizona to provide public assistance to aged and indigent natives. In 1948 he left the Department of the Interior to engage in private practice, public service, and teaching. He continued to serve as general counsel for several tribes and published widely as a legal scholar.

Edgar Howard (1858–1951). Howard was the co-sponsor of the Indian Reorganization Act of 1934, sometimes known as the Wheeler-Howard Act. Born in Iowa, Howard attended Iowa College of Law but did not graduate. He was elected in 1923 to Congress and developed a reputation as a liberal Democrat. He introduced numerous bills permitting tribes to sue in the U.S. Court of Claims, tried to protect tribal and individual mineral resources on reservations and allotments, and by 1933 became chair of the House Committee on Indian Affairs. Howard lost his re-election campaign in 1934.

Darcy McNickle (1904–1977). McNickle was a member of the Flathead Tribe and an anthropologist who worked for the Bureau of Indian Affairs during the Depression. McNickle helped shape the creation of the National Congress of the American Indian (NCAI) in 1944. The NCAI became a major national organization representing tribal interests in the United States.

McNickle wrote several books including a novel, *The Surrounded, The Indian Tribes of the United States: Ethnic and Cultural Survival* (1962), *Indian Man: The Life of Oliver La Farge* (1971), and *Native American Tribalism: Indian Survivals and Renewals* (1973).

Nathan Ross Margold (1899–1947). Margold was an attorney and political activist who played an important role in shaping the reform of American Indian policies by the federal government during the New Deal. Born in Romania, Margold came to the United States in 1901, grew up in Brooklyn, and graduated from the City College of New York and Harvard Law School. He served as an assistant U.S. attorney in New York and in 1927 joined the faculty at Harvard Law School. His appointment at Harvard sparked an intense battle because he was Jewish. Margold return to New York in 1928 to enter private law practice.

In the early 1930s, Margold served as special counsel for the National Association for the Advancement of Colored People (NAACP). He helped develop the strategy for the future court proceedings that led to the integration of U.S. public schools in the 1950s. In 1933, as part of the Roosevelt administration, Margold became solicitor for the U.S. Department of the Interior. He played an important role in promoting tribal sovereignty and rights of American Indians during the New Deal. Margold also served as special assistant to the attorney general from 1933 to 1935. Roosevelt appointed him to the Municipal Court for the District of Columbia in 1942. He became a judge of the U.S. District Court for the District of Columbia in 1945. He died only two years later.

Lewis M. Meriam (1883–1972). Meriam, a statistician, headed the significant fact-finding commission studying the status of American Indians from

1926 to 1928. A graduate of both Harvard and the George Washington law schools, Meriam became a career federal employee in Washington, DC. He worked for the Office of the Census from 1905 to 1912, Children's Bureau from 1912 to 1915, and the Institute for Government Research from 1915 to 1920. In that year the institute became part of the Brookings Institution, with whom Meriam was associated until his retirement in 1951.

Funded by the Rockefeller Foundation through the Institute of Government Research, Meriam and a team undertook a national assessment of the condition of native peoples in the United States. Everywhere they found problems of poverty, poor health, short life expectancy, unemployment, low levels of educational achievement, loss of land, and failings in federal commitments to tribes. The team produced *The Problem of Indian Administration* (1928), popularly called the Meriam Report, which summarized its findings. Considered for Commissioner of Indian Affairs in 1933, Meriam withdrew and supported John Collier who was appointed.

Burton K. Wheeler (1851–1941). Wheeler was the co-sponsor of the Indian Reorganization Act of 1934, sometimes known as the Wheeler-Howard Act. Born in Massachusetts, Wheeler received his law degree from the University of Michigan. He was elected in 1923 to the Senate as a Democrat from Montana. Wheeler joined other liberals to work for reform as a member of the Senate Indian Affairs Committee. He sought to protect American Indian mineral and water resources. In 1934 he headed the Senate Committee on Indian Affairs and co-sponsored the Indian Reorganization Act, a bill he had not read. When Wheeler discovered the bill fostered tribal self-governance, a Court of Indian Affairs, and tribal land ownership, he turned against the draft bill and forced through a number of amendments. In 1937 he introduced a bill to repeal the Indian Reorganization Act, but it failed. Wheeler continued as a critic of New Deal policy toward American Indians until he lost his bid for reelection in 1946.

Primary Sources

The Plight of American Indians in the Early Twentieth Century

A 1928 report by Lewis Meriam for the Brookings Institute entitled *The Problem of Indian Administration* (1928, pp. 7–8) described the history of U.S.-Indian relations and the resulting sad state of the American Indian population. The report was highly influential in shaping New Deal Indian policies in the 1930s and beyond and noted the following:

> When the government adopted the policy of individual ownership of land on the reservations, the expectation was that the Indians would become farmers. Part of the plan was to instruct and aid them in agriculture, but this vital part was not pressed with vigor and intelligence. It almost seems as if the government assumed that some magic in individual ownership of property would in itself prove an educational civilizing factor, but unfortunately this policy has for the most part operated in the opposite direction. Individual ownership has in many instances permitted Indians to sell their allotments and to live for a time on the unearned income resulting from the sale. . . .
>
> Many Indians were not ready to make effective use of their individual allotments. Some of the allotments were of such a character that they could not be effectively used by anyone in small units. The solution was to permit the Indians through the government to lease their lands to the whites. In some instances government officers encouraged leasing, as the whites were anxious for the use of the land and it was far easier to administer property leased to whites than to educate and stimulate Indians to use their own property. The lease money, though generally small in amount, gave the Indians further unearned income to permit the continuance of a life of idleness.
>
> Surplus land remaining after allotments were made was often sold and the proceeds placed in a tribal fund. Natural resources, such as timber and oil, were sold and the money paid either into tribal funds or to individual Indians if the land had been allotted. From time to time per capita payments were made to individual Indians from tribal funds. These policies all added to the unearned income of the Indian and postponed the day when it would be necessary for him to go to work to support himself.

An outspoken critic of the Office of Indian Affairs, John Collier, was appointed the agency's head by President Roosevelt in 1933. Collier was instrumental in introducing sweeping new federal policies concerning American Indians. A key part of the programs was the Indian Reorganization Act of 1934, otherwise known as the Wheeler-Howard Act. Collier made the following observations regarding the act in his "Report of the Commissioner of Indian Affairs," published in the *Annual Report of the Secretary of the Interior* (1935, pp. 78–83).

> The repair work authorized by Congress . . . aims at both the economic and the spiritual rehabilitation of the Indian race. Congress and the President recognized that the cumulative loss of land brought about by the allotment system, a loss reaching 90,000,000 acres—two-thirds of the land heritage of the Indian race in 1887—had robbed the Indians in large part of the necessary basis for self-support. They clearly saw that this loss and the companion effort to break up all Indian tribal relations had condemned large numbers of Indians to become chronic

recipients of charity; that the system of leasing individualized holdings had created many thousands of petty landlords unfitted to support themselves when their rental income vanished; that a major proportion of the red race was, therefore, ruined economically and pauperized spiritually . . . .

Through 50 years of 'individualization,' coupled with an ever-increasing amount of arbitrary supervision over the affairs of individuals and tribes so long as these individuals and tribes had any assets left, the Indians have been robbed of initiative, their spirit has been broken, their health undermined, and their native pride ground into the dust. The efforts at economic rehabilitation cannot and will not be more than partially successful unless they are accompanied by a determined simultaneous effort to rebuild the shattered morale of a subjugated people that has been taught to believe in its racial inferiority.

The Wheeler-Howard Act provides the means of destroying this inferiority complex, through those features which authorize and legalize tribal organization and incorporation, which give these tribal organizations and corporations limited but real power, and authority over their own affairs, which broaden the educational opportunities for Indians, and which give Indians a better chance to enter the Indian Service.

Suggested Research Topics

- Why was John Collier a significant figure in helping change the course of federal policy toward American Indians in the 1930s? How might American Indians think of him?
- What was the promise of the Indian Reorganization Act (IRA) to tribes that adopted it? Where did the IRA fail to meet expectations? How did it influence U.S. Indian policy in the late twentieth century?
- How did the Indian Arts and Crafts Board seek to promote and protect American Indian artists? How much success in restoring cultural traditions did it have?

Bibliography

Sources

Brookings Institution. *The Problem of Indian Administration.* Baltimore, MD: The Johns Hopkins Press, 1928.

Cohen, Felix S. *Felix S. Cohen's Handbook of Federal Indian Law.* Albuquerque, NM: University of New Mexico Press, 1971.

Collier, John. "Report of the Commissioner of Indian Affairs," *Annual Report of the Secretary of the Interior, 1934.* Washington, DC: Government Printing Office, 1934, pp. 78–83.

Collier, John and Laura Thompson. "The Indian Education and Administration Research," *Sociometry* 9 (2/3) (May-August, 1946):141–142.

Kroeber, Alfred L. *Cultural and Natural Areas of Native North America.* Berkeley: University of California Publications in American Archaeology and Anthropology, Vol. 38, 1939.

Philp, Kenneth. *John Collier's Crusade for Indian Reform.* Tucson, AZ: University of Arizona Press, 1977.

Standing Bear, Luther. *Land of the Spotted Eagle.* Lincoln, NE: University of Nebraska Press, 1978.

Taylor, Graham D. *The New Deal and American Indian Tribalism: The Administration of the Indian Reorganization Act, 1934–45.* Lincoln, NE: University of Nebraska Press, 1980.

Washburn, Wilcomb E., ed. *Handbook of North American Indians: History of Indian-White Relations.* Vol. 4. Washington, DC: Smithsonian Institution Press, 1988.

Wilkinson, Charles F. *American Indians, Time, and the Law: Native Societies in a Modern Constitutional Democracy.* New Haven, CT: Yale University Press, 1987.

Further Reading

Bordewich, Fergus M. *Killing the White Man's Indian: Reinventing Native Americans at the End of the Twentieth Century.* New York City: Doubleday, 1996.

Champagne, Duane, ed. *Chronology of Native North American History: From Pre-Columbian Times to the Present.* Detroit, MI: Gale Research, Inc., 1994.

———.*Contemporary Native American Cultural Issues.* Walnut Creek, CA: Alta Mira Press, 1999.

Davis, Mary B. *Native America in the Twentieth Century: An Encyclopedia.* New York: Garland Publishing, Inc., 1994.

Deloria, Vine, Jr. *American Indian Policy in the Twentieth Century.* Norman, OK: University of Oklahoma Press, 1985.

Malinowski, Sharon, and Anna Sheets, eds. *The Gale Encyclopedia of Native American Tribes.* Detroit, MI: Gale Research, Inc., 1998.

National Congress of American Indians, [cited February 20, 2002] available from the World Wide Web at http://www.ncai.org.

Wilson, James. *The Earth Shall Weep: A History of Native America.* New York City: Atlantic Monthly Press, 1999.

See Also

Civilian Conservation Corps; Ethnic Relations

Arts Programs

1929-1943

Introduction

Imagine that you had spent your youth training for the theater only to discover that theaters were closing for lack of a paying audience, and that you had no opportunities to perform. Or consider yourself as a mid-career book illustrator discovering that your publisher, along with many others, was going out of business and you were now without employment or prospects, with a family to support. Or you might be an elderly painter who has an ongoing relationship with a patron. One day you receive notice that there will no longer be commissions coming your way because your patron can no longer afford to buy your work. Anticipating partial retirement based on this relationship, you are now faced with growing old and having to find employment.

As an actor, illustrator, or painter you are probably communicating your frustrations, fears, and anxieties to other artists finding themselves in a similar predicament. Angry that there seems to be no relief in sight from public or private sources, some of your colleagues, in desperation, are going on hunger strikes to bring public attention to their plight. Many are marching with thousands of others on city streets demanding some form of relief.

What you are imagining was very real to artists in the United States shortly after the onset of the Great Depression in 1929. It would be four very bleak and lean years before the government would recognize the artists' economic predicament and begin to initiate

Chronology:

1933: The Public Works of Art Project is initiated and continues to 1934.

1934: The Treasury Section of Fine Arts Section of Painting and Sculpture is initiated and continues to 1943.

1934: Diego Rivera's mural *Man at the Crossroads* is destroyed by orders of the administration of the Rockefeller Center.

1935: Federal One (consisting of the Federal Music Project, Federal Art Project, Federal Music Project, Federal Writers Project, and Federal Theater Project) is established as part of the Works Progress Administration.

1936: Federal Art Project artists are featured in the exhibit *New Horizons in American Art* at the Museum of Modern Art in New York City.

1938: The House Committee to Investigate Un-American Activities and the House Committee on Appropriations begin hearings on the Works Progress Administration (WPA), including Federal One.

1939: The American Art Today building at the New York World's Fair features art sponsored by the United State Government.

1939: The Federal Theater Project is closed by an act of Congress.

1942: National Art Week focus is on private rather than federal support for art.

1942: With the Labor Federal Security Appropriation Act, Congress terminates the Civilian Conservation Corps.

1943: An act of Congress terminates the WPA.

1974: The Research Center for the Federal Theatre Project established at George Mason University (on permanent loan from the Library of Congress).

1997: The National Archives and the Records Administration sponsor the landmark exhibit "A New Deal for the Arts." This exhibit includes representative works created by artists employed by the government between 1933 and 1943.

---

relief efforts. Even then relief would be intermittent and many musicians, actors, painters, dancers, and the like would disappear from the art world altogether. This cost to the creative life of the United States is incalculable. The relief that was received by artists was inconsistent and under constant threat of discontinuation. Despite these adverse circumstances, during this period artists would do some of the best work of their careers.

The story of art during the Great Depression is very much tied to federal relief efforts. During this period government support for the arts in America was at unprecedented levels never again equaled. Millions of children, youth, and adults in the United States were able to attend free or very inexpensive art classes, theater, symphony, opera, and other forms of art. Numerous publications documenting the cultural life of the nation were produced.

The purpose of this chapter will be to provide the details associated with these relief efforts, some of the people associated with them, and the ramifications for art and culture in the United States during and after the Depression. In doing so, questions like the following will be explored: What characterized the arts and art-making in the United States just prior to the Depression? In what ways did the federal government provide support to artists, and how did this influence art making and public access to the arts? What were some of the controversies surrounding federal relief efforts for artists? What are some examples of art and cultural development in the United States that were influenced by the Depression, but which did not receive public funding? Who were some of the key artists and arts administrators during the Depression? In what way is contemporary public support for the arts influenced by public support for the arts during the Depression?

Issue Summary

Art and Artists in the United States, 1929–1945

In the year prior to the stock market crash in 1929 there was a boom in the American art market corresponding to a boom in the American economy. However, it is important to recognize that this boom in no way indicates that American artists prior to the Great Depression enjoyed a comfortable and predictable living from their artistry. Many actors, stagehands, musicians and others associated with live theater, for example, were already out of work because of the mass popularity of motion pictures. Many American artists supplemented their incomes from art with other jobs. In addition, a report commissioned by President Herbert Hoover (served 1929–1933) in 1929 concluded that for most Americans there was not much interest in noncommercial forms of art.

As a consequence of American indifference and of art being a fragile source of income, artists were in dire straits shortly after the onset of the Depression. Records kept at the time show a drastic decline in the number of artists and art teachers in the 1930s. By mid-May 1932, 210 of the 253 theaters in the New York City region had closed.

To bring attention to their plight, artists began to organize hunger marches and outdoor sales of artwork. The first groups to respond were private charities that began to offer welfare payments to artists in New York City as part of aid packages for "white collar" workers. Another early relief effort was the Wicks Act of 1931, passed by the New York legislature. This act established the New York State Temporary Emergency Relief Administration. Harry L. Hopkins, as head of the New York agency, supervised the organization of relief work for unemployed artists. This administration employed one hundred artists. Hopkins became a close advisor to President Franklin D. Roosevelt (served 1933–1945). Roosevelt later appointed Hopkins as head of the Civil Works Administration and the Works Progress Administration, both of which would greatly impact the artists and arts of the Depression.

Federal Government Support for Artists and Art (1933–1945)

Four years after the stock market crash of 1929, and in the first year of President Roosevelt's administration, there was a federal response to the lack of jobs for the unemployed, including artists. During the first one hundred days of his administration, from March to June 1933, Roosevelt pushed through Congress an amazing amount of legislation designed to bring economic relief to those affected by the Great Depression. This period would mark the beginning of the New Deal. In November 1933 President Roosevelt signed Executive Order 6420-B, establishing the Civil Works Administration (CWA). The CWA initiated public work projects to employ workers from relief lists and from the ranks of the unemployed. They received minimum wages rather than relief payments. Because of the untiring efforts by advocates of the arts, "artist" was one of about one hundred professional job classifications receiving funding. The Public Works of Art Project (PWAP) was founded in December 1933 under a CWA grant. One million dollars was committed to PWAP. More than 3,600 artists participating in PWAP worked on the decoration of public buildings. Administrators of the program were inspired by Mexican muralist painters such as Diego Rivera, Jose Orozco, and David Alfaro Siqueiros, who were including social and political themes in their paintings in Mexico. As a consequence PWAP artists were expected to produce works that represented the American scene on public buildings as opposed to nonrepresentational or abstract murals. PWAP was the first federal art project sponsored by the federal government on a national scale.

Another program to assist artists existed under the U.S. Treasury Department, which was involved in providing relief to artists through the Section of Painting and Sculpture. Initiated in 1934, the Treasury Section of Fine Arts program ran until 1943. It concentrated on the acquisition (gathering) of paintings and sculpture for public buildings. Notable artists such as Thomas Hart Benton and Rockwell Kent advised Treasury Department officials on purchases. Officials believed that these efforts were in keeping with past state support of the arts.

The Treasury Relief Art Project was initiated in 1935 and ran until 1939. This project employed 440 artists from the unemployment register. Rather than an acquisition project, artists were employed to decorate post offices and other small public buildings.

Among the larger programs established to aid artists was Federal One. Established in 1935 Federal One was a part of the Works Progress Administration (WPA), the name for a group of agencies established by President Roosevelt to provide jobs for those who were able to work but unable to find employment on their own. Federal One specifically provided relief to visual artists, actors, musicians, composers, dancers, writers, and other people engaged in creating the arts. Its mission was to popularize the creation and appreciation of American art. Administrators hoped to produce art that would demonstrate the unique character of the United States and its citizens. Administrators tended to believe that this was best accomplished through art that documented everyday life through realistic depictions.

Federal One was also motivated by the Roosevelt administration's belief that art could serve in support

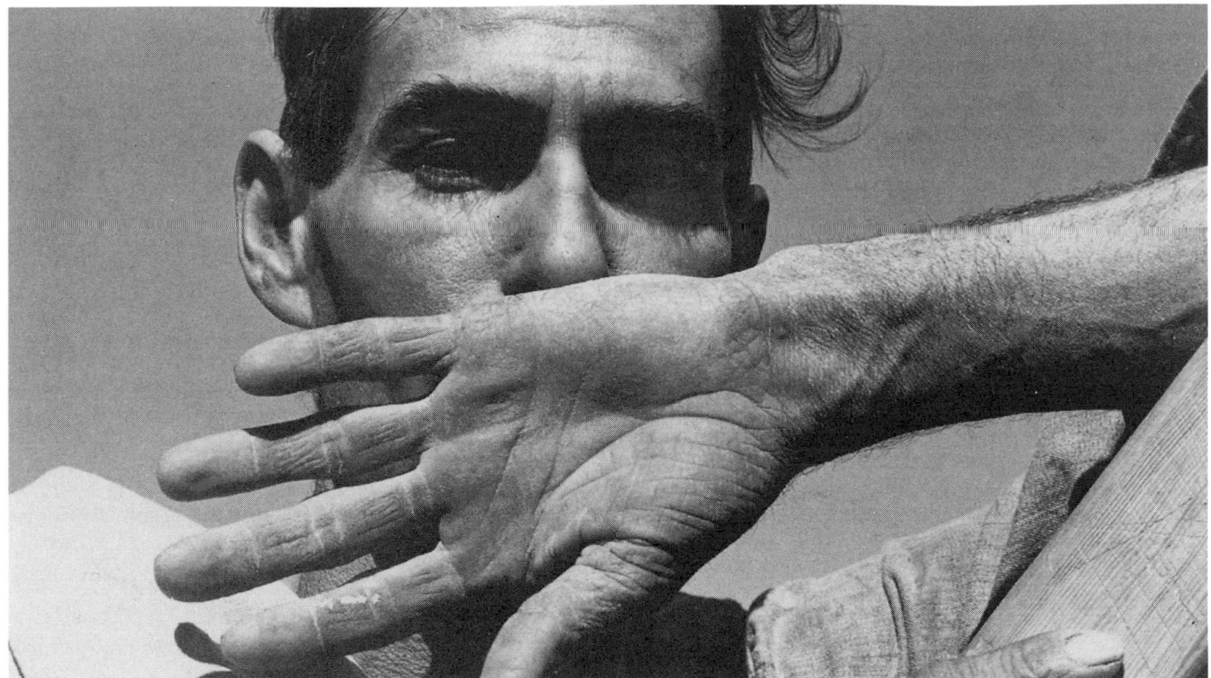

Photograph by Dorothea Lange titled "Migratory Cotton Picker, Eloy, Arizona." Lange became well known for her documentary photographs of victims of the Depression. *("Migratory Cotton Picker, Eloy, Arizona," 1940, gelatin-silver print, photograph by Dorothea Lange. The Museum of Modern Art, New York; gift of the photographer. Copy print ©1999 The Museum of Modern Art, New York. Reproduced by permission.)*

of President Roosevelt's public policies. Solidifying the nation's citizens in the face of economic hardship with art forms associated with the culture of the day was considered important to the everyday life of the nation. Significant to this vision was the belief that one could exercise his or her citizenship through making or appreciating art. In addition, the administration's populist orientation to art—the belief that art was intended to benefit the common people, not just the wealthy or educated—promoted artists as important workers making valuable contributions to national well-being.

Federal One consisted of five levels of administration overseeing five projects: the Federal Art Project, the Federal Music Project, the Federal Theater Project, the Federal Writers Project, and the Historical Records Survey. Holger Cahill was the national director working out of Washington, DC. Directly beneath him were field advisors who communicated with Cahill about Federal One operations. The nation was divided into 42 units, many based on state boundaries, all of which had appointed directors. Units were divided into districts with each having a supervisor. Local advisory committees advised district supervisors.

Federal One recognized four categories of artists. Those artists considered to be highly skilled and creative were identified as professional and technical workers able to supervise less skilled artists. Below this top category were skilled artists, intermediate grade artists, and the unskilled. Unskilled workers were employed as gallery attendants, messengers, and other support staff. There was recognition by some that artist labor differed from other types of labor. Artists resisted rigid schedules and fixed times. This was a contentious issue throughout the course of Federal One.

The WPA and Federal One were terminated by an act of Congress in 1943 for both political and economic reasons. Politically there were some that believed that the WPA, particularly Federal One, was a waste of resources. Others believed that private enterprise, and not the federal government, should provide what the WPA was set up to do. Some associated poverty with laziness and believed that those in need should not receive any type of public relief.

In the years before its termination, budgets were often cut and projects curtailed. Layoffs were common and encouraged Federal One workers to strike and demonstrate on behalf of the projects. This in turn enraged the opposition, which already believed that communists opposed to America's free market

A Federal Arts Project poster announces an exhibition of graphic arts. The Graphic Arts Division of FAP funded the creation of prints illustrating American Life. (The Library of Congress.)

economy had infiltrated the WPA. This opinion was fueled by the social and political content of the work by many Federal One artists that advocated for worker and human rights.

In the years prior to and during the Depression, the union movement and communism became inextricably linked in the United States. When some of the major labor organizations were beginning to form, such as the Committee for Industrial Organizations (later the Congress of Industrial Organizations, or CIO), the leaders of these labor organizations recognized that they needed to enlist the help of those with great leadership and organization abilities. In many cases, these leaders were communists and socialists, and their most common plan of action for unions to take was the strike. From that point on, the people of 1930s America associated the strike with communist beliefs and activities. Communism was seen as un-American and against the status quo, with such activities as striking upsetting the balance of power within a traditionally capitalist marketplace. Americans valued the free marketplace and saw communism as a threat to that tradition. Communism was also frequently the target of politicians who blamed the Great Depression on the "rise of communism" within the United States, which understandably led many Americans to develop an anti-communist attitude.

The United States economy was improving in the early 1940s in response to World War II (1938–1945) in Europe. This improved economy, coupled with the hostility held by some towards the WPA and Federal One, contributed to its demise.

Another large government program for artists was the Federal Art Project (FAP), which was divided into multiple divisions based either on media or around specific projects. One division was responsible for employing artists to create murals for public spaces such as hospitals and schools. The Painting Division employed artists to do easel paintings that illustrated aspects of American life. The Graphic Arts Division funded the creation of prints with much the same themes, as well as photographs that documented the WPA. Other artists were hired to produce sculpture, again primarily with American life themes. The Scenic Design Division produced models of historic buildings for architectural and educational purposes. Other divisions produced posters and stained glass. The Index of American Design employed artists to comprehensively document American folk art and antiques. Much of this documentation was exhibited in department stores around the United States. The Arts Service Division produced posters, handbills, and book illustrations. The Exhibitions Division was responsible for exhibiting the work of WPA artists.

The FAP also included an Art Teaching Division. Teachers worked in a variety of settings including hospitals, mental health facilities, settlement houses, and community arts centers educating the public about art. One hundred art centers were established in 22 states. A typical art center included an exhibition space and classrooms.

The mission of the community art centers was very much in keeping with the general mission of the WPA. Community art centers were viewed as a vehicle for bringing citizens' attention to art originating in the United States in contrast to contemporary or historical European artists. Community art centers also developed programs that would encourage connections between art and artists with the general public. This was part of an attempt to realize an authentic popular and mass art culture in contrast to the culture encouraged by the entertainment industries. The philosophical foundation of this approach to community arts was known as cultural democracy. WPA administrators believed that a culturally democratic orientation was in keeping with an American democracy in which people should have the right to contemporary cultural expression, as well as their cultural past. Such an orientation seemed very important to a country like the United States, with a citizenry claiming cultural roots from all parts of the world. Americans, a newly blended people, needed new cultural expressions in addition to ties to past ethnic artistry.

In 1997 the National Archives and Records Administration put together an exhibit of works created under the FAP. Exhibit curators discovered five themes that FAP artists addressed. These themes included rediscovering America, celebrating the people, work pays America, activist arts, and useful arts. Visitors to the exhibition saw an extensive collection of paintings, drawings, prints, sculptures, posters, and photographs that in combination tell a story of what life was like during the Depression and the significant ways in which artists contributed to national well-being at a time of social upheaval. Photographs documented artists at work, as well as the rural and urban landscape. Painting and sculpture provided glimpses into the domestic and work lives of Americans. Posters and handbills for theater productions were on display. Exhibited were examples from all visual art forms that communicated attitudes about the ways in which America should change in order to be more responsive to the working class and minority groups.

The Federal Music Project (FMP) provided relief and programs in ways similar to Federal Art Project. Directed by Nikolai Sokoloff, a former conductor of the Cleveland Symphony, the FMP employed musicians who participated in orchestras, chamber music groups, choral groups, opera, military bands, dance bands, and in theaters. At one point musicians were participating in five thousand performances before three million people a week. Performances took place in cooperation with local sponsors such as schools, colleges, or community groups. The FMP also coordinated music education programs in rural areas and urban neighborhoods. In 1939 it is estimated that 132,000 children, youth, and adults in 27 states received music education. Composers also benefited through FMP's Composers Forum Laboratory. The Forum sponsored performances of contemporary compositions. The FMP also included a project dedicated to documenting works by American composers. Works documented were performed. FMP employees also recorded American folk music.

Concentrating specifically on theater, the Federal Theater Project (FTP) was directed by Hallie Flanagan. Consisting of 31 state units and New York City, one thousand performances before one million people were given each month. Admission to productions was often free, meaning that for many this was their first exposure to live theater.

The ballet, "Guns and Castanets," was one of thousands of productions put on by the Federal Theater Project. (National Archives and Records Administration.)

The FTP stimulated theater in the United States. The project produced more than 1,200 plays introducing the work of one hundred new playwrights. The FTP also broadcast "Federal Theater of the Air" to an estimated 10 million radio listeners. To insure quality, the FTP published *The Federal Theatre Magazine,* containing reviews of FTP plays produced across the United States.

FTP-supported theater represented social issues; educational or informative works; new plays and musicals; plays never before presented in the United States, as well as standard classics; children's theater; and those works with significance to specific cultures, languages, or heritages. FTP additionally supported vaudeville, variety, circuses, marionette and puppet troupes, experimental theater, operas, and dance troupes.

Because the FTP was a relief effort, productions with large casts and extensive technical needs were favored in an attempt to put as many people as possible to work. Production budgets favored personnel costs and skimped on production materials. The FTP productions included many people who would later become significant in performing arts history. For example, noted actor and filmmaker Orson Welles directed *Macbeth* for the Negro People's Theater. Welles also directed Marc Blitzstein's *Cradle Will*

A crowd gathered outside of the New Lafayette Theater where Orson Welles' all-black production of "Macbeth" was staged for the Federal Theatre Project in 1936. (FDR Library.)

Rock. Within the history of American theater this musical is famous not only for its open support for American labor, but also for the circumstances of its premier. On the day "Cradle Will Rock" was scheduled to open, funding was canceled and the theater padlocked. The government's reaction was a result of the subject matter of the musical, which leaned toward left wing (socialist or communist) and unionist beliefs. Despite the injunction against them, actors and audience walked to a new theater. Because the actors and musicians union would not allow members to perform on the stage of the new theater, the actors and musicians performed from their seats in the audience, to great acclaim.

Operating without the fanfare of the FTP, the Federal Writers Project (FWP) was directed by Henry Alsberg until 1939. The FWP employed up to 6,686 writers working on projects in 48 states and the District of Columbia. By the conclusion of 1941 the FWP had produced 3.5 million copies of eight hundred titles.

The best-known books published by the FWP are associated with the American Guide Series. This series was planned to include illustrated guidebooks for every U.S. state and territory. Guides included maps, information on municipalities, natural features, and tourist attractions, as well as essays on history, folklore, politics, and local culture. Numerous city guides and local pamphlets were also published. Employees of the FWP completed studies of American natural and cultural history for children, youth, and adults. This included the compilation of archives of slave narratives and folklore.

The Historical Records Survey (HRS) was also a part of the FWP. The mission of the HRS was to inventory all county records in the United States in an effort to aid historians, government officials, and researchers. Field workers were employed to survey manuscripts and records associated with county offices, churches, women's organizations, vital statistics, federal archives, Civil Works Administration papers, and education.

Jesse Cornplanter makes a ceremonial mask at a community art center located at the Tonawanda reservation near Akron, New York. *(National Archives and Records Administration.)*

Agriculture Department—Resettlement Administration

The U.S. Agriculture Department, through its Resettlement Administration (RA), later the Farm Security Administration (FSA), was founded as a relief agency to provide such services as low-interest loans to farmers and reeducation for those from the cities who were being resettled on communal farms. One of the sections of the RA was the Historical Section, which was responsible for the compilation of historical information. In order to compile the historical information, the RA hired photographers to document life, primarily rural life, in the United States between 1932 and 1945. Under the direction of Roy Stryker, photographers produced 66,000 black and white photographic prints, 122,000 black and white negatives, and 650 color transparencies. Numerous documentary films were also produced as a result of the project. Notable contributors to this comprehensive project included Dorthea Lange, Walker Evans, Ben Shahn, and Marion Post Wolcott.

The RA also sought to document the folk music of the rural United States for eventual use by recreational leaders in new farming communities. Between 1936 and 1937, a section of the RA called the Special Skills Division was responsible for this task. Its workers traveled to the eastern and midwestern United States and recorded folk music in various languages, including Lithuanian, Swedish, Serbian, and Gaelic, as well as numerous songs from the Ozarks and Appalachians. Sidney Robertson, Margaret Valiant, and others, under the supervision of Charles Seeger, were responsible for the recording efforts. In total, 159 records were produced. The RA also distributed illustrated song sheets throughout rural communities based on these recordings.

Special Committee to Investigate Un-American Activities and Propaganda

There were other forces at work in American society during the Depression that were not compatible with those promoting the arts and culture within an unstable economy. Not everyone regarded the bringing together of artists as a cultural and political force as a positive development. Those same individuals and groups who were not sympathetic to organized labor also saw organized artists as a threat to American values. Organized labor was often paired in the minds of some with communism and social revolution, such as talk of overthrowing the United States government. This was true to such an extent that in 1938 members of the U.S. House of Representatives felt enough public support to create a committee to investigate threats to national security and potential subversion by United States citizens. The committee was named the Special

Committee to Investigate Un-American Activities and Propaganda in the United States. It later became the House Un-American Activities Committee (HUAC), famous for the investigation of Hollywood's film-making community. Known more commonly as the Dies Committee because Congressman Martin Dies of Texas chaired it, this committee began to immediately investigate Federal One for any subversive activities. The FTP was an early target. Dies pressed for government to ban the Communist Party, require all public employees to sign loyalty pledges, fire those who did not, and prohibit government interaction with labor unions. Dies believed communists controlled organized labor in general. Dies greatly disliked the New Dealers, including the head of the WPA Harry Hopkins, Secretary of Interior Harold Ickes, and Secretary of Labor Frances Perkins. Roosevelt personally opposed the idea of loyalty oaths. However, there was so much public fear of the spread of communism and fascism that the New Dealers of the Roosevelt administration were restrained in responding to the committee's charges. In addition, Congress' disdain for labor unions made organization by the actors and FTP workers unattractive as an effective response to save federal arts programs.

The Dies Committee had a profound effect on the arts in general, and the Federal Theater Project specifically. The FTP was shut down in 1939 in partial response to unsubstantiated claims of subversion. When the FTP ended on June 30, 1939, actors publicly expressed indignation through their performances. The endings to some plays were changed that night. In one case in New York City, stagehands knocked down the set in view of the audience at the conclusion of the performance. The FTP equipment that had accumulated over four years since 1935 were locked up in government warehouses. Many of the FTP actors and workers found jobs in commercial or community theaters. Eventually the social and cultural forces associated with this fear within the American public would contribute to the shuttering of the WPA and all of those projects associated with it.

Art Outside of Federal Relief Programs

Not all of the creative activity taking place during the Depression occurred as a result of federal relief. Budgets for the projects were not so large that all those in need could receive benefits. In addition, some artists were able to earn a living through association with patrons or teaching institutions. Examples of private projects from this period indicate the extent of creative activity and entrepreneurship that occurred beyond the involvement of the federal government. They demonstrate a connection with the American values, attitudes, and beliefs associated with the depressed economy and the federal response to it.

By 1932 commercial architects in the United States were being influenced by European Modernism or the International Style. The "towering" city cores that we associate with contemporary American urban areas are largely a result of this period. Both the Chrysler Building and the Empire State Building in New York City show the influence of this style. In this regard, American architects working in the International Style should be seen in contrast to those many other visual and performing artists of the period who were looking into America for themes that would help to unite the public during economic hardship. Two well-known architectural projects associated with the Depression years do exemplify an architectural response to the stress on the nation—Rockefeller Center and Broadacre City. One of these projects is commercial and the other domestic. One was fully realized, while the other exists primarily in the form of architectural models and writings.

Rockefeller Center is the largest private building project ever initiated in the United States. Located on three city blocks in midtown Manhattan, the Center includes fourteen original slab skyscrapers intended to house the then-new network broadcasting industry. Unique to the design was a community-oriented plan for multiuse facilities. Rockefeller Center integrates commercial business with restaurants and shops on multiple levels above and below the street. The center also includes gardens and an ice skating rink. It is its multiple use design and attention to outdoor space and community that speaks to its partnership with those other arts projects of the era that were created to bring people together.

Associated with Rockefeller Center is one of the most infamous examples of the conflict that can develop between artists and their patrons. The conflict also demonstrates the tensions that existed during the Depression between a troubled capitalist economy and socialist responses.

Diego Rivera was very well known internationally for the murals he created in Mexico celebrating his cultural heritage and communist ideals. In 1932 John D. Rockefeller commissioned Rivera to paint a mural for the lobby of the main building in Rockefeller Center. Proposed was a mural of workers and their encounters with industry, science, socialism, and capitalism. Rivera inserted into the mural an unapproved portrait of Vladimir Lenin, Russia's communist leader. Building managers ordered Rivera to remove the portrait because of its anti-capitalist intent.

Rivera refused. Demonstrations in support of Rivera began and there was an attempt to transfer the mural to the Museum of Modern Art. On February 10, 1934, however, Rockefeller Center workers destroyed the mural with axes.

In contrast to the controversy connected to the Rockefeller Center, Broadacre City was an unrealized ideal that had the support of President Roosevelt and others. Beginning in the early 1930s architect Frank Lloyd Wright began to promote a utopian response to what he saw as the urbanization of America. He referred to his idea as Broadacre City.

The Broadacre City plan was based on a view of urban living as inhospitable and uninhabitable. This view was shared by President Roosevelt and his advisor, Rexford Tugwell. Both thought of cities as rather hopeless. Roosevelt desired, if it were at all possible, to devise a way that would move everyone to the country or at least to suburban environments. Broadacre City was envisioned as located away from large metropolitan areas and containing values associated with democracy and community. The plan for Broadacre City took into consideration the automobile, communications systems, and power. Nature was revered within the plan, and the design was envisioned as cooperating with nature. Life in Broadacre City was to center on nature rather than the many technological distractions associated with cities. Integral to Broadacre City was the "Usonian" house. Usonia is an acronym that stands for "United States of North America" with the letter "i" included between the "n" and the "a" to make it a more pleasant sounding word. Adapted from Wright's prairie style homes, Usonian houses featured an attention to good design, nature, and spaciousness. Usonian houses were also designed to be affordable to middle-class families.

A model of Broadacre City was built and toured the United States. It was included in an exhibit at Rockefeller Center. Broadacre city was never built, and indeed Wright never intended it to be built. It was conceived as a model for suburban living and, in many ways, it succeeded in setting forth a blueprint for communities to come. Broadacre City featured architectural strategies such as underground power, highway overpasses, low-level lighting, and landscaping that are now taken for granted. Usonian homes were built, but never on the scale suggested by Broadacre City.

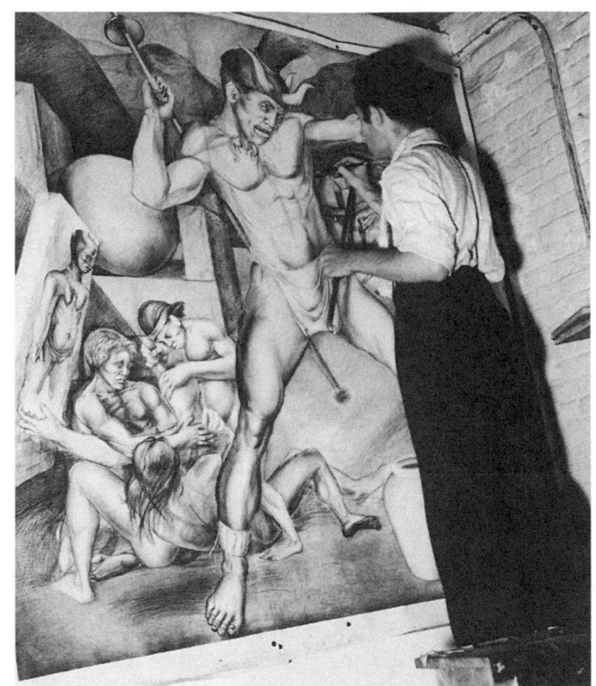

WPA artist Isidore Lipshitz works on his mural, "Primitive and Modern Medicine," under the direction of the Federal Art Project. (CORBIS. Reproduced by permission.)

Folk and Domestic Art

Some artists working during the Depression were not associated with any type of professional art world or related institutions, like museums and galleries. For example, Bill Traylor, a sharecropper and former slave in Lowndes County, Alabama, was forced into unemployed homelessness in Montgomery, Alabama, as a result of the falling price of cotton. To earn an income, Traylor established himself as a sidewalk storyteller, and by 1939 he was also known for his pencil and charcoal drawings. Traylor's drawings, displayed with clothespins on a clothesline, told stories of everyday life in his neighborhood in much the same way as photos by the Farm Security Administration photographers. Eventually Traylor was invited to join with other artists in Montgomery and exhibit his work in gallery settings.

Another example is Ben Hartman of Springfield, Ohio. In 1932, at the age of 48, Hartman lost his job at a local iron foundry. At that point he began what he referred to as his own WPA project. This project was to fill his backyard with a pond surrounded by small buildings covered with cement and stone. Hartman also created cement cast figures that peopled his landscape. Many of these figures were personages from history, radio, religion, and stories. Eventually Hartman's Rock Garden became know to tourists and became a destination point. Admission to the garden was a nickel or a dime. In exchange, Hartman would give guided tours of his creations.

Quilt-making enjoyed resurgence during the Depression years. This resurgence was probably associated with pubic interest in Americana, coupled with a need to conserve and reuse scarce materials. Making a quilt provided the opportunity to reuse materials for a utilitarian purpose while simultaneously providing a creative outlet and the chance to join with other quilt makers for a common purpose. Quilt making became so popular as a creative outlet that Sears, Roebuck and Company sponsored a quilt contest at the 1933 Chicago World's Fair.

Contributing Forces

Art and Artists in the United States, 1900–1929

At the beginning of the twentieth century, artists in the United States continued to be heavily influenced by art movements of the past. Collectors and the public were most comfortable with art inspired by classical styles borrowed from the Greeks and Romans, as well as with the conventions of the Italian Renaissance. This situation, however, was soon to change. Economic modernization, as well as scientific and technological developments rendered obsolete conventional ways of thinking and operating within the world. This change within American society had a profound impact on the arts as well.

In 1913 the Association of American Painters and Sculptors sponsored the International Exhibition of Modern Art in New York City at the 69th Infantry Regiment Armory. The purpose of this exhibit was to present the history of modern art from the nineteenth century through the work of contemporary European artists. The Armory show represented the United States' modernist rebellion against the academic art styles continuing from the nineteenth century. Despite a huge public protest against the art on display, collectors in the United States to a great extent began to favor artists, particularly European artists, working in such modern styles as Cubism and Futurism.

America's infatuation with modernism and modern art came to an abrupt end as a result of World War I (1914–1918). The United States entered a period of political and cultural isolationism as evidenced by the United States Senate's rejection of President Woodrow Wilson's (served 1913–1921) appeal for the United States to join the League of Nations. This was a period in which immigrants from Europe were suspected of harboring political and cultural points of view threatening to American democracy. It is not surprising that it was during this period that American collectors turned away from European artists towards American folk art, as well as toward artists and art representing American history and ways of living.

Art and Artists After 1929

The stock market crash of 1929 effectively ended an art market boom that begin in 1928. Suddenly, funding for any kind of art or artistic endeavor was gone. Artists scrambled to find money to feed their families as private support for the arts dried up.

The economic hardship experienced by artists that resulted after the stock market crash was made worse by the popularity of the movie industry. This was particularly true for actors and other professionals associated with theater. By the early 1930s theater productions were closing on a large scale due to poor audience attendance, thus putting large numbers of theater people out of work.

It was fortunate that as the social and economic standing of artists was plummeting, they were also being recognized within society as skilled professionals and laborers and therefore eligible for federal relief. It was also fortunate that American artists prior to the Depression had begun to concentrate on celebrating American life in their work. This allowed federal administrators to envision artists and artwork as being able to contribute to citizen solidarity in this period of economic instability.

Contributing also to the power of arts during the Depression was willingness on the part of artists to shift focus from the individual artist dependent on wealthy patrons to the power of worker groups and unions. Artists came together to assist one another and found encouragement and support to continue their artistic endeavors.

Perspectives

National Perspectives

Nationally, particularly among politicians, civil servants, and industrialists, Federal One was perceived as having mixed results. Some saw Federal One as plagued by conflicts between those believing in rigidly imposed hourly employment expectations and those who believed the creative process could not be bound by such standards of employment. Politicians, specifically Republicans and conservative Democrats opposed to the WPA, believed Federal One to be producing political propaganda for the political left. This generated a congressional backlash resulting in funding cuts and eventual termination.

On the other hand, some politicians, civic leaders, artists, and publicly minded citizens recognized Federal One as providing much needed work to artists, resulting in significant contributions to the creative life of the nation, as well as providing a training ground for new talent. For example, it is not insignificant that some believe that the most experimental theater that has ever taken place in the United States occurred under the auspices of the FTP. Others saw the WPA and Federal One as ultimately contributing to an organizational structure that helped the United States to organize efficiently once the war effort began.

Local Perspectives

On the local level responses to Federal One were more uniformly positive. Support of this opinion comes from the large numbers attending public performances and exhibits associated with Federal One projects, and participation in the programs and classes offered by the community arts centers. The success of Federal One on the local level is also evidenced by the fact that it has been credited for stimulating a second "Harlem Renaissance" in New York City. This second renaissance included such groups as the Negro Experimental Theatre, the Negro Art Center, and the Harlem Community Art Center among others. Federal One is credited with providing an environment in which black American artists could address socio-political issues relevant to civil rights initiatives. It is important to also recognize, however, that in some communities there was controversy around art forms produced by non-resident artists. Such controversy usually involved local residents believing that an outsider had in some way misrepresented them. Other controversies resulted from artists resisting local influence on the content of their artistry.

International Perspectives

It is important to consider the nationalism that infused the federal relief projects for the arts in an international context. Nationalism is when a nation places its needs significantly over the interests of other nations. Many nations around the world were experiencing nationalistic tendencies with different results. Both Germany and Italy, for example, were experiencing forms of nationalism that ultimately resulted in the Third Reich in Germany and Benito Mussolini's fascist government in Italy. In both Germany and Italy there was the recognition, like that in the United States, that the arts can be a very powerful tool in furthering a government's agenda. Like in the United States, artists in Germany and Italy participated in depicting the national scene. The results, however, were very different. Totalitarian policies in Germany and Italy were very controlling of what artists could and could not do. Artists that did not conform to such controls were likely to see their works destroyed. In the United States the executive branch of the federal government was much less controlling in this regard. Artists in the United States were more likely to feel such pressure in the private sector, as in the case of Diego Rivera and the administrators of the Rockefeller Center.

More About...

Harlem Renaissance

Contributing to the art and culture of the Depression period was the fact that the Depression was coinciding with an era in black American history characterized by the "New Negro." This was a term used by the black American community to take pride in race and culture. It encouraged black Americans to see themselves as talented artists, intellectuals, philosophers, and educators able to contribute to American society as a whole.

The epicenter for much of this creative energy was Harlem in New York City. Between 1914 and 1929, the population of Harlem grew from 14,000 to over 200,000 in response to increased job opportunities in the North and racial violence in the South. This period in Harlem was characterized by a celebration of black American culture in national publications, important art galleries, in film, and in music halls. The extraordinary efforts by black American artists contributed to a rise in race consciousness. Participants began to call this period a "Harlem Renaissance."

Impact

By the end of World War II (1939–1945) the realistic orientation of much of the art produced in the United States during the Depression was seen as quaint, socially claustrophobic, and not very personally expressive. Coupled with the influx and influence of European refugees, postwar America once again turned to European modernism and the abstraction associated with it. Coinciding with the post-World

War II "Cold War" of the 1950s and 1960s was the rise and dominance of abstract expressionism in art. Abstract expressionism is art that seeks to portray emotions, responses, and feelings rather than objects in their actual likeness. Many of the artists associated with this movement, like Jackson Pollack and Lee Krasner, had once been realistically oriented artists working for Federal One.

There is ample evidence that Federal One did encourage later career development and the facilitation of artist networks. For example, well-known and widely respected actors like Ernest Borgnine, Hume Cronyn, and Patricia Neal were all associated with the FTP. Writers such as Ralph Ellison, Richard Wright, Studs Terkel, John Cheever, and Zora Neale Hurston were associated with the FWP. There is reason to believe that the Federal Charter for a National Theater, signed by President Roosevelt in 1935, was sustained in part because of networks and experiences associated with the FTP. This charter was initiated by arts patrons from Philadelphia and New York who persuaded Congress to institute the American National Theater and Academy (ANTA). The purpose of ANTA was not to provide relief, but to provide historical and contemporary theater on a self-support basis. In the postwar period ANTA supported theater in colleges and universities, commissioned plays, and promoted experimental theater, television broadcasts of theater, and cultural exchanges.

Despite the rise and dominance of a modernist perspective in American arts following the Depression, Federal One and the socially relevant orientation of art during the Depression years continued to be an influence in the United States. For example, Baker Brownell, a Northwestern University scholar, began publishing on the role of art in community during the 1950s. He saw a close connection between the arts, economic development, and community planning. Associated with community theater and political activism in Wisconsin, Robert Gard wrote extensively during the 1950s and 1960s on the important relationship that exists between art and place in rural communities. He proposed that artists must connect with other civic associations to insure community health and vitality.

In 1965 President Lyndon Johnson (served 1963–1969) signed Public Law 89-209, which ultimately established the National Endowment for the Arts (NEA) and the National Endowment for the Humanities (NEH). Once again the federal government was subsidizing the arts in America. The purpose, however, was not to provide relief to artists, but to instead facilitate and encourage the creative life of the United States. The immediate outcome of this law was the proliferation of arts organizations to the present day.

Federal support for the arts remains controversial, particularly regarding grants made to individual artists or to institutions perceived as experimental or rebellious. Both endowments, however, are committed to making the arts accessible to citizens of the United States, while simultaneously protecting and preserving America's diverse arts and cultural heritage. Much of this work is accomplished by people who consider themselves to be "citizen artists" grateful to the artists who worked during the Depression in assisting the United States to survive intact a period of great financial instability and fragility.

Notable People

Marc Blitzstein (1905–1964). Blitzstein is credited with revolutionizing American theater both politically and stylistically. Under the auspices of the FTP, Blitzstein created a new theatrical form that was not fully musical theatre or opera. His work *The Cradle Will Rock* exemplifies a style combining popular music with social satire.

Hallie Flanagan (1889–1969). Hallie Flanagan organized and directed all aspects of the FTP, including play selection, the hiring of regional directors, and the budget. This work was consistent with her desire to establish a network of theaters across the United States that would meet the needs and reflect the lives of people. Flanagan was the first female winner of the Guggenheim Award, a fellowship awarded to professionals in various fields to further their development by allowing them to perform research in their area of expertise. Flanagan used her award to research European national theaters.

Harry L. Hopkins (1890–1946). Hopkins was the national director of the Civil Works Administration and the Works Progress Administration. He was a strong advocate for the incorporation of arts into the federal relief initiative.

William H. Johnson (1901–1970). Johnson joined the FAP as a painter and was assigned a teaching post at the Harlem Community Art Center. Johnson's first major solo exhibition was in 1941 at the Alma Reed Galleries in New York. The exhibition was reviewed by the two major art journals, *Art News* and *Art Digest,* as well as by all the large newspapers in New York. Johnson's paintings documented contemporary life in Harlem and illustrated urban dancing and fashion of the period, including the jitterbug and zoot suits. His paintings also provided glimpses into the pastimes of urban children and youth.

Bob Porterfield (?–1971). Porterfield was an out of work Shakespearean actor and promoter working as an elevator operator when he founded the Barter Theatre. Because of his background in promotions he was able to acquire publicity for this project. People could attend for the price of admission or the equivalent in produce. The Barter Theater was still in operation as of 2002.

Roy Stryker (1893–1975). Stryker directed the documentary photography project for the Farm Security Administration. Hundreds of thousands of images were produced by notable photographers. Their focus was on life in rural America during the time of the Depression. Stryker later directed documentary projects for the Standard Oil Company (1943–1950), the city of Pittsburgh (1950–1951), and Jones & Laughlin Steel (1952–1958).

Orson Welles (1915–1985). Orson Welles received national attention as a young director in the New York Federal Theatre Project. He received praise for his work on the *Swing Mikado* and *Faustus.* Later he became well known for his films, including *Citizen Kane.*

More About...

The Barter Theater

The Barter Theatre began in 1933, when Bob Porterfield had the idea to offer theater to people in exchange for the price of admission or the equivalent in produce. According to the Barter Theatre history (available from the World Wide Web at http://www.bartertheatre.com), the first theater ticket was traded for a pig. Porterfield proposed the idea to W.B. Gillesbie, the executive secretary of the Chamber of Commerce in Abingdon, Virginia. Though both Gillesbie and Porterfield recognized that offering theater in this way was out of the ordinary, they were committed to the idea. Porterfield received permission to bring twenty-two performers to Stonewall Jackson College for Women and make use of the Abingdon Opera House. The first show to be produced was *After Tomorrow.* The advertisement for the production read, "35 cents or the equivalent in produce." The house was full. Tickets were traded for all kinds of goods and services. Items included haircuts, corn, pigs, preserves, bacon, apples, cakes, and jellies.

Primary Sources

The Works Progress Administration—Federal One

In late July 1935, Hallie Flanagan accompanied Harry Hopkins, director of the WPA, on a train from Washington, DC, to Iowa City, Iowa. At a national theatre conference in Iowa City Hopkins was to announce Flanagan's appointment to head a nationwide federal effort to assist unemployed actors. While on their way to Iowa, Hopkins discussed with Flanagan the need for the administration, and particularly artists, to receive relief. According to Flanagan, Hopkins later developed these ideas into a public speech to the United States Conference of Mayors in Washington, DC, in November 1937. This passage is recounted in Hallie Flanagan's *Arena* (1940, p. 27).

> It costs money to put a man to work and that's why a lot of people prefer direct relief. These people (critics of the arts programs) say that if we make the working conditions decent and give people a reasonable minimum to live on, people will get to like their jobs. They suggest that we make relief as degrading and shameful as possible so that people will want to get 'off.' Well—I've been dealing with unemployed people for years in one way and another and they *do* want to get off—but they can't, apparently, get 'off' into private industry. Well—if they can't get off into private industry, where can they turn if they can't turn to their government? What's a government for? And these people can be useful to America; they can do jobs no one else can afford to do—these slums, for instance. No private concern can afford to make houses for poor people to live in, because any private concern has got to show a profit. Why, we've [the WPA] got enough work to do right here in America, work that needs to be done and that no private concern can afford to touch, to lay out a program for twenty years and to employ every unemployed person in this country to carry it out.

The Federal Theater Project

Milton Meltzer participated in the Federal Theatre Project. His book, *Violins and Shovels,* (1976) tells the story of his experience of the Great Depression and working with Federal One. In it, he explains, "Our family did not 'go broke' in the Depression. We started broke... Soon enough we found out that you didn't have to own stocks to feel the impact of the crash."

Many of those who participated in the Federal Theater Project went on to have successful careers in the entertainment business. For example playwright

Dale Wasserman would author "Man of La Mancha" and write the screenplay for the award winning motion picture "One Flew Over the Cuckoo's Nest." John O'Connor and Lorraine Brown quote Wasserman in their book *Free, Adult, Uncensored: The Living History of the Federal Theatre Project* (1978, p. 7).

> Federal Theatre was a wonderful, lucky thing because it kept alive possibilities in people who would never have made it otherwise, who would never have ended up in theatre at all. I myself might be one of them—I'm not absolutely sure. I was getting along barely; but living on about ten dollars a week while trying to practice one's art, you may not survive too long. So Federal Theatre gave me two excellent opportunities. One was to stay alive, which was rather nice, and the other was a chance to learn arts that I didn't know, that I was primitively ignorant about ... It was very important for me and it was ... a beautiful piece of luck when it happened.

Opposition to Federal Programs

Despite the creation of jobs brought about by government programs such as the Federal Theatre Project, federal projects in general that were initiated to counter the effects of the Depression were not without opposition. In 1938 the U.S. Congress House Committee on Un-American Activities, more commonly known as the Dies Committee, began to investigate the FTP as a threat to American democracy. Hallie Flanagan, the founder of the FTP, was adamant in her defense of the project and its contributions to democracy and to the United States. Even though by law political affiliations of participants in the WPA could not be collected, and that actors working in the theater were not permitted to join unions other than theater unions, the committee relentlessly pursued unfounded fears that theaters were becoming a hotbed of communism.

The Dies Committee filed a report with the U.S. House of Representatives on January 3, 1939, largely condemning use of federal funds to support theater productions through the FTP. The report, referenced in Flanagan's *Arena* (1940, p. 347) summed up,

> We are convinced that a rather large number of the employees on the Federal Theatre Project are either members of the Communist Party or are sympathetic with the Communist Party. It is also clear that certain employees felt under compulsion to join the Workers' Alliance in order to retain their jobs.

Suggested Research Topics

- To what extent were United States artists forced to leave the United States during the Depression to seek support abroad?
- Most of the literature documents the work of European-American and black American artists during the Depression. What contributions did members of other ethnic and racial groups make? For example American Indians, Mexican Americans, or Asian Americans?
- How were youth involved in the Federal Theater Project?

Bibliography

Sources

Adams, Don, and Arlene Goldbard. *New Deal Cultural Programs: Experiments in Cultural Democracy,* [cited April 4, 2001] available from the World Wide Web at http://www.wwcd.org/policy/US/newdeal.html.

African Americans in the Visual Arts, [cited April 25, 2001] available from the World Wide Web at http://www.liu.edu/cwis/cwp/library/aavaahp.htm.

Barter Theatre History, [cited February 26, 2001] available from the World Wide Web at http://www.bartertheatre.com.

Bjelajac, David. *American Art: A Cultural History.* New York: Harry N. Abrams, 2001.

Brown, Lorraine. *Federal Theatre: Melodrama, Social Protest and Genius,* [cited February 3, 2001] available from the World Wide Web at http://memory.loc.gov/ammem/fedtp/fthome.html.

Bustard, Bruce I. *A New Deal for the Arts.* Seattle: The University of Washington Press, 1997.

Buttitta, Tony and Barry Witham. *Uncle Sam Presents: A Memoir of the Federal Theatre 1935–1939.* Philadelphia: University of Philadelphia Press, 1982.

Harris, Jonathon. *Federal Art and National Culture: The Politics of Identity in New Deal America.* New York: Cambridge University Press, 1995.

McDonald, William F. *Federal Relief Administration and the Arts.* Columbus, Ohio: Ohio State University, 1969.

Spron, Paul. *Against Itself: The Federal Theater and Writers' Projects in the Midwest.* Detroit: Wayne State University Press, 1995.

Waldvogel, Merikay. *Soft Covers for Hard Times: Quiltmaking and the Great Depression.* Nashville: Rutledge Hill, 1990.

Whitman, Willson. *Bread and Circuses: A Study of Federal Theatre.* New York: Oxford University Press, 1937.

Further Reading

Education Teachers Resources. *Art and Life of William H. Johnson,* [cited April 25, 2001] available from the World Wide Web at http://nmaa-ryder.si.edu/education/guides/whj/whj-bio.html.

Federal Theatre Project Collection, [cited January 27, 2001] available from the World Wide Web at http://www.gmu.edu/library/specialcollections/theater.html.

Federal Theater Project Digitization Project, [cited January 29, 2001] available from the World Wide Web at http://memory.loc.gov/ammem/fedtp/ftwpa.html.

Flanagan, Hallie. *Arena.* New York: Duell, Sloan and Pearce, 1940.

Harlem 1900–1940, [cited April 25, 2001] available from the World Wide Web at http://www.si.umich.edu/CHICO/Harlem/text/introduction.html.

Langley, Stephen. *Theatre Management and Production in America.* New York: Drama Book Publishers, 1990.

Meltzer, Milton. *Violins and Shovels: The WPA Arts Projects.* New York: Delacorte Press, 1976.

New Deal for the Arts, [cited April 25, 2001] available from the World Wide Web at http://www.nara.gov/exhall/newdeal/newdeal.html.

O'Connor, John and Lorrain Brown. *Free, Adult, Uncensored: A Living History of the Federal Theatre Project.* Washington, DC: New Republic Books, 1978.

Waldvogel, Merikay. *Soft Covers for Hard Times: Quiltmaking and the Great Depression.* Nashville: Rutledge Hill.

See Also

New Deal (First, and Its Critics); New Deal (Second)

Banking

1929-1941

Introduction

America was in the depths of the Great Depression in early 1933. Bank "moratoria," or closures, rolled across the country beginning in 1930. Bank officials called moratoria "bank holidays," but there was no holiday spirit evident in the eyes of citizens standing before a bank entrance on whose door was a note announcing "closed by the Board of Directors until further notice." Panic, anger, and disbelief were the emotions experienced at the loss of one's entire savings. The American banking industry was in serious trouble and everyone knew it.

On Valentine's Day, 1933, the governor of Michigan proclaimed an eight-day "bank holiday" throughout the state, freezing 900,000 depositors' funds in the state's bank vaults. The closure was so unnerving, depositors throughout the country attempted to withdraw cash from their banks. "Holidays" spread to Indiana, Maryland, Arkansas, and Ohio. In the early morning hours of the day, as Franklin Delano Roosevelt was inaugurated the thirty-second president of the United States, the banks in Illinois and New York were closed. As dawn broke on March 4, 1933, the nation's banking system had no pulse.

Over the last two hundred years the United States banking system experienced a succession of crises. Each crisis weakened public confidence and prompted cries for reform. The bouts of bank failures reached a climactic point in 1933. Nearly 40 percent of America's banks had failed or had to merge. U.S. banks were

Chronology:

1920–1929: An average of 588 banks fail each year foreshadowing trouble.

October 28, 1929: The stock market crashes.

1930: The number of bank suspensions skyrockets to 1,300.

December 11, 1930: The Bank of United States in New York City closes.

1931–1932: More than 3,600 banks suspend operations.

January 22, 1932: The Reconstruction Finance Corporation (RFC) becomes law.

March 4, 1933: Franklin Delano Roosevelt is inaugurated as the thirty-second U.S. president.

March 5, 1933: President Roosevelt calls for Congress to meet in a special session on Thursday, March 9, 1933.

March 6, 1933: At 1:00 AM President Roosevelt orders a nationwide "bank holiday" from Monday, March 6, through Thursday, March 9.

March 9, 1933: Congress convenes and passes the Emergency Banking Act of 1933.

March 12, 1933: In his first fireside chat, President Roosevelt calmly and confidently speaks to the American public about the country's banking crisis.

March 13, 1933: Banks begin to reopen.

March 15, 1933: Banks controlling 90 percent of the country's banking resources have reopened.

June 16, 1933: President Roosevelt signs the Banking Act of 1933 (Glass-Steagall Act) into law.

August 23, 1935: President Roosevelt signs the Banking Act of 1935 into law.

reduced from 25,000 to 14,000 in the late 1920s. The prevalent thought of the day fostered by congressional hearings was that the failures were in large part due to unscrupulous bankers and banks investing in securities (stocks and bonds). The belief that banking failed due to stock speculation proved to be a misconception.

By 2000, with hindsight as an ally, the structure of the American banking system was recognized as the main weakness causing so many banks to close their doors. Although some large city banks did fail, 90 percent of the failed banks were small unit banks with few assets. Unit banks attempted to carry out an array of services operating out of only one location. Nationwide branch banking was prohibited. As the Depression wore on, more businesses failed, workers lost their jobs, and bank loans were not repaid. People withdrew their cash to live on, instead of saving it. Banks could not keep up with the demands for withdrawal of funds. Americans lost all confidence in the banking system and turned to Washington for answers.

By the time Franklin Delano Roosevelt was inaugurated, the banking system was paralyzed. Roosevelt took control and was able to stabilize the situation in eight amazing days between March 4, 1933, and the evening of March 12. Key actions of those days were the declaration of a nationwide "bank holiday" to allow breathing room for all, passage of the Emergency Banking Act, and President Roosevelt's first fireside chat, broadcast over radio to millions of anxious Americans. These actions restored public confidence in banks. On March 13, as banks began to reopen, deposits exceeded withdrawals and the American banking system was saved.

Building on the momentum of those first few days, Congress passed the Banking Act of 1933, commonly known as the Glass-Steagall Act, in June, and later the Banking Act of 1935.

The Emergency Banking Act had stopped the bleeding of American banks and restored confidence. The recovery and reform banking acts of 1933 and 1935 laid the foundation for far-reaching changes in the U.S. banking industry, including the establishment of the Federal Deposit Insurance Corporation (FDIC). In keeping with other New Deal legislation expanding the government into all walks of American life, the federal government became an increasingly important player in the oversight and regulation of the U.S. banking system.

Issue Summary

Bank failures during the 1920s were considered local failures. They did not tend to produce any general

The majority of banks that failed were small, rural banks. This closed bank is located in Haverhill, Iowa.
(The Library of Congress.)

loss of public confidence or produce banking panics of nationwide importance. In fact they went largely unnoticed by the American public, reveling in a seemingly strong capitalist business climate and a wildly escalating stock market. The 1920s failures were, however, symptomatic of the unhealthy state of the U.S. banking system.

The optimism of the 1920s came crashing down on October 28, 1929, when the stock market plummeted. The Great Depression began that Fall 1929. Growing numbers of businesses failed, employees lost their jobs, and farmers lost their farms. Many businesses and individuals, their incomes declining or disappearing completely, could not make payments on loans and mortgages (home loans). Further, the "collateral" that businesses and individuals had used to back up loans had lost much of its value. Collateral is something of value that a borrower agrees to hand over to the lender if the loan is not repaid. The deepening Depression also forced many depositors to withdraw their savings. Banks that were unable to collect on

Commercial Bank Suspensions, 1900-1936

Year	National Banks		State Banks	
1900 - 1909	118		375	
1920	7		136	
		Federal Reserve State Member Banks	Nonmember Banks	Total State Banks
1925	118	28	433	461
1929	64	17	547	564
1930	161	27	1,104	1,131
1931	409	107	1,697	1,804
1932	276	55	1,085	1,140
1933	1,101	174	2,616	2,790
1934	1	-	43	43
1935	4	-	30	30
1936	1	-	42	42

The toughest year for banks was 1933. Nearly 4,000 State and Federal banks closed their doors that year.

(The Gale Group.)

many loans had great difficulty meeting these withdrawal demands. Not surprisingly in such an unsteady financial climate, banks began to fail.

Bank Suspensions—1930

Banks began to close their doors in record numbers. In 1929, 651 banks suspended operations. In 1930 the figure skyrocketed to more than 1,300. Many banks forced out of business were small rural unit banks. Bank suspensions quickly spread over large geographic areas and into the cities.

In November and December 1930, after the stock market crash and the run on banks by a panicked public, banks experienced the sharpest increase in closures. In November a large Nashville, Tennessee, investment banking house, Caldwell and Company, collapsed due to poor performance on loans and investments. The collapse spread panic through Tennessee, Arkansas, Kentucky, and North Carolina, engulfing over 120 banks.

In December one of the most disastrous failures in American banking history occurred. The New York State Commissioner, on the morning of December 11, 1930, closed the Bank of United States in New York City. Although a private bank, the bank's name alone spawned fears that the whole United States banking system would fail. New York City's Bank of the United States had 57 branches throughout the city and some $220 million deposited in 440,000 accounts. More than three-fourths of the 440,000 depositors had accounts of less than $400. Many were Jewish immigrants, left unemployed in the wake of the stock market crash. Disillusioned and confused, depositors had no warning that inadequate supervision and mismanagement by those who owned and controlled the bank would lead to the loss of their savings. Citizens across the nation questioned the safety of their deposits. Two other large city banks closed their doors in December 1930. The Bankers' Trust of Philadelphia closed on December 22 and the Chelsea Bank and Trust of New York City closed on December 23.

The failures caused public confidence to sink to new lows. Strong banks struggled to solidify their positions. They made no effort to bail out the weaker banks. Depositors could not distinguish strong banks from weak banks and distrusted them all. Throughout the nation runs on banks accelerated, as did the private hoarding of gold and cash.

Nothing exhibited the public's lack of confidence in banks during the Depression more than bank runs. Runs began when depositors feared their bank was unsound. Rather than risk losing their savings, depositors rushed to withdraw their money. A mere rumor of trouble could start a run. Since banks do not keep enough cash on hand to cover all depositors, those first in line got their cash, but those last in line did not. Runs often ended with a bank's collapse.

Since few companies provided retirement pensions for workers in the 1920s and 1930s, many workers used banks to house their life savings. When banks failed many individuals were left with nothing.

Fearing that their savings would be lost, crowds form in front of New York's Bowery Savings Bank as they attempt to withdraw their money. The structure of the American banking system is recognized as the main weakness causing so many banks to fail. (UPI/Corbis-Bettmann. Reproduced by permission.)

Washington Gets Involved

During the boom of the 1920s bankers were thought of as thrifty, smart, hardheaded businessmen helping Americans reach their financial goals. By the early 1930s, Americans were suspicious and distrustful of these same men. Many felt that the unethical accumulation of wealth by some bankers was a root cause of the Great Depression. Hundreds of thousands of Americans now hoarded cash and gold. They preferred keeping it under mattresses and buried in cans in the back yard to depositing it in America's financial institutions. The money in circulation, called the money supply, shrank dramatically. No longer confident in bankers, the public turned to Washington for bank reform.

As early as 1929, President Herbert Hoover (served 1929–1933), in his annual message to Congress, called for Congress to consider revising the banking laws. He emphasized the lack of unity between national and state banks and the debates among bankers over branch banking. Hoover called for the formation of a joint committee of congressmen of both houses and other federal officials to investigate the entire banking system. Especially interested were two congressmen, Senator Carter Glass and Representative Henry B. Steagall. Senator Glass had served as a representative in the House of Representatives from 1902 until 1918. As chairman of the House Committee on Banking and Currency he "fathered" the Federal Reserve Bank Act of 1913. Between 1918 and 1920, Glass served as secretary of treasury under Woodrow Wilson. He resigned that position in 1920 to accept an appointment to the U.S. Senate, where he remained for 28 years. Among his many banking interests, Glass was particularly concerned with the banking system as it related to speculative investments in stocks. Speculative investing refers to buying stocks or bonds in hopes of making a large profit. This type of investing is considered very risky.

In 1930 Representative Steagall, elected to the House in 1914, became chairman of the House Committee on Banking and Currency, the same committee that Glass once chaired. Steagall's chief focus was federal deposit insurance, which was designed to safeguard the bank deposits of individuals. He had been a proponent of deposit insurance since the early 1920s, but had had no success enacting it.

Despite Hoover's request, no joint committee was established, but both the Senate and the House began banking studies in Spring 1930. In the Senate a subcommittee of the Banking and Currency Committee, with Senator Glass as chairman, began hearings. Steagall's House Banking and Currency Committee also initiated hearings to consider the entire banking situation. From the White House, President Hoover attempted to mobilize the banking community. In October 1930 he urged cooperation between bankers and federal officials to devise better policies to end the crisis.

As the state of banking deteriorated in 1931, federal bank authorities—the Federal Reserve Board and Treasury officials—demanded action from bankers and Congress. The Federal Reserve maintained a liberal lending policy and pleaded with banks to make loan money available to customers. But banks were determined to preserve what "liquidity" they had left. Liquidity, in banking terms, means being able to meet the cash needs of depositors wanting to withdraw funds. Banks faced the threat of depositors caught in the Depression continuing to withdraw funds for living expenses or joining in massive runs, eliminating the bank's liquidity. The value of collateral backing up existing loans continued to slide. Many businesses and individuals defaulted (did not keep up payments) on their loans. So banks defended their liquidity by keeping credit tight, refusing new loans, and halting investments.

Hearings continued in Congress in 1931, during which three major issues surfaced: (1) bank involvement with stock speculation; (2) federal deposit insurance; and (3) increased federal regulation of the banking industry.

Banks and Stock Speculation

Bank involvement with stock speculation surfaced as a concern in 1929, even before the stock market crash. As early as February 1929, the Federal Reserve Board warned banks against using Federal Reserve funds for loans to "affiliate" companies or individual brokers, who in turn used the money for speculating in the market. An affiliate is a firm closely tied to another firm; in this case, to a bank. Despite warnings, the loans continued. Most of the complex dealings between banks and their affiliates that purchased and sold stocks were legal under state laws. Banks could take advantage of the highly profitable "securities" business through these affiliates. The term securities refers to stocks and bonds.

Senator Glass, heading the Senate Banking and Currency Committee hearings, passionately believed that banks should not engage in securities speculation. He believed it was harmful to the Federal Reserve System since its funds were being used for risky speculation. He viewed stock market speculation by banks as irresponsible and contrary to the rules of good banking. He wanted "commercial" banking and "investment" banking separated. Commercial banks are those that accept deposits from customers and make personal, business, and industrial loans. Investment banking or securities banking activity consists of investing in stocks and bonds. Glass' hearings were directed at uncovering evidence of wrongdoing, in hopes of gathering support for separation of commercial and investment banking. He was successful. Soon many legislators became convinced that banking activities had to be completely separated from securities investment speculation. Likewise, as the hearings revealed cases of bank mismanagement of funds, the public became outraged. Although the mismanagement was carried out by only a few, the public's distrust of all bankers swelled. Bankers, on the other hand, thought the stock speculation issue was blown out of proportion. They argued that control over securities investment could be achieved through the banking industry's own self-regulation. They wanted no new laws that took management decisions away from them.

More About...

Federal Deposit Insurance Corporation

The most enduring and accepted agency to emerge from New Deal banking reform legislation was the Federal Deposit Insurance Corporation (FDIC). Originally proposed by Congressman Henry Steagall of Alabama, it became law on June 16, 1933, when President Franklin D. Roosevelt signed the Banking Act of 1933. Under provisions of the act, a Temporary Deposit Insurance Fund would begin operation on January 1, 1934. The permanent FDIC started up on July 1, 1935. Only banks certified as sound could join. Sound banks were well capitalized, and liabilities did not exceed assets. Originally, individual accounts up to a maximum of $2,500 were insured. That figure was later increased to $5,000.

The FDIC was an immediate and unparalleled success. It imposed a measure of unity on the U.S. dual banking system, returned depositor confidence, all but eliminated bank runs and failures, and protected the nation's money supply from wild fluctuations. By 1935 more than 14,400 banks had joined the FDIC, and bank failures dropped to 44 in 1934, and 34 in 1935.

By 2000 about 98 percent of all commercial banks were FDIC members. Individual accounts were insured up to $100,000. Each member bank pays a fee based on its average annual total deposits. The FDIC insurance fund is built up through these annual assessments. Should this fund ever prove insufficient to meet the needs of depositors, the FDIC is authorized to borrow up to $5 billion directly from the U.S. Treasury.

In 2000 FDIC operations were directed from Washington, DC, by a three-member board of governors. Regional FDIC offices existed throughout the United States. The FDIC also administered the Savings Association Insurance Fund (SAIF), which insures deposits of Savings and Loans up to $100,000.

Federal Deposit Insurance and Regulation

Deposit insurance was clearly the most controversial reform issue. Numerous bills were drafted and introduced into Congress to provide a measure of guarantee for deposits. Representative Steagall was the primary authority in Congress on deposit insurance. With the increasing crisis, public pressure for some form of deposit insurance gained popularity. Bankers strongly opposed deposit insurance. They felt that agreeing to deposit insurance was like agreeing to ensure everyone against all evils—impossible. Large banks, confident of their own ability to meet depositors' demands, believed the insurance plan would result in their having to cover losses to depositors of weak banks.

Throughout Senate hearings bankers almost unanimously fought against increased federal regulation. Bankers wanted no part in centralized power of the Federal Reserve Board. As the crisis deepened, however, the possibility of increased government control grew. Many viewed the basic problem to be the "hodgepodge" dual banking system of the United States and the many small unit banks. Lack of unity, plus self-interest for only local concerns, contributed to the national crisis. The banking community was unprepared to offer its own solutions for the declining situation, and it was inevitable that the federal government would step in.

By January 1932, when Hoover's voluntary schemes and Congress' investigations had led only to inaction, Hoover suggested an emergency step. He recommended establishment of the Reconstruction Finance Corporation (RFC). The RFC, headed by Jesse H. Jones, was endowed with up to $2 billion in working capital to make low interest loans to banks. Hoover expected the RFC loans to restore bankers' confidence to in turn make loans to business. Recovery would follow. On January 22, 1932, the RFC became law.

While Congress feverishly considered more substantial banking legislation, the RFC began operation. Bank suspensions fell to 68 in April 1932, as opposed to the high of 522 failures in October 1931. Nevertheless, currency hoarding continued by individuals and, disappointingly, banks did not ease credit by making loans.

Congress responded to the crisis by passing the Federal Home Loan Act of 1932. The act created the Federal Home Loan Bank Board (FHLBB) to oversee the operations of savings and loan banking institutions. Savings and loans made mortgage loans for home purchases. As more people could not make their loan payments, savings and loans failed—1,700 in the 1930s. The Federal Home Loan Bank Board did not have an immediate effect. Depositors lost all their money because deposit insurance did not exist. It would be two years before Congress passed the National Housing Act of 1934, creating the Federal

Banks insured by the Federal Deposit Insurance Corporation (FDIC) provided deposit insurance of up to $2,500 for each depositor account. (The Library of Congress.)

Savings and Loan Insurance Corporation (FSLIC) to insure each savings and loan account up to $5,000. The Housing Act also created the Federal Housing Administration (FHA) to protect mortgage lenders by insuring full repayment of mortgages if individuals could not make the payments.

The Election of 1932

Conditions were rapidly growing worse by the summer of 1932 despite Hoover's and Congress' efforts. Over 2,200 banks failed in 1931, and 1,400 more would fail in 1932. In November the nation turned its eyes to the task of electing a new president. Hoover's unpopularity virtually assured anyone running on the Democratic ticket a victory. The Democratic candidate was Franklin Delano Roosevelt. The Depression was the key issue of his campaign, with the banking situation near the top of the concerns list. The Democratic platform, which Roosevelt endorsed in its entirety, called for rigid supervision of national banks, a complete separation of commercial banks from investment banking, and a restructuring of the lending practice by the Federal Reserve Bank. Hoover's conservative views on banking were well known. By contrast Roosevelt's speeches sounded radical to bankers, but the public sensed hope in the words of the personable governor from New York. Roosevelt was elected the thirty-second president of the United States in November 1932. He would not be inaugurated until March 4, 1933. The four-month interim seemed to be an eternity to Americans hoping for relief from the new president. Hoover and his Republicans had no leadership capability left. Congress disagreed amongst itself. The shadows of disaster grew longer.

Bank Holidays

Since the early days of the Depression local bank "moratoria" had been used to help banks that were facing runs. A moratorium is a legal suspension of activity. This was normally done by declaration of a "bank holiday," a period in which a bank would be closed for business. In November 1932 the number of "holidays" increased, fueling growing alarm. Nevada declared a statewide holiday and, in the next two months, the West experienced an epidemic of bank failures. Early in 1933 Louisiana's governor declared a bank holiday. The real panic struck on St. Valentine's Day, February 14, 1933, when the governor of Michigan declared an eight-day bank holiday. Michigan's holiday tied up the funds of 900,000 depositors and froze $1.5 billion in bank deposits.

President Hoover, in a ten-page handwritten letter to President-elect Roosevelt, urged Roosevelt to

More About...

Bank Run Psychology

A major responsibility of a bank is to allow depositors to withdraw their funds whenever they desire. No bank, however, keeps enough cash readily available to satisfy its depositors if they all demanded their money at the same time. This situation—when many depositors want their money back at the same time—is known as a bank "run." Experience tells bankers that runs rarely occur. When people are confident they can withdraw funds at any time, they leave most of their funds in the bank until needed. Banks can therefore loan or invest a large percentage of funds deposited with them.

Why do banks' depositors suddenly line up outside of their bank and demand their money in cash? Two theories try to explain the panic phenomenon. In one, panics are seen as a kind of mass hysteria. They begin when depositors think other depositors are going to withdraw all their money. The bank works on a first-come-first-serve basis, so those first in line get their money. Those last do not. No study explains why depositors suddenly fear other depositors will withdraw, but in the 1930s a bank experiencing a run often collapsed.

In the second theory panics result from perceptions that the overall banking system is unsound. Depositors cannot distinguish the risk of one bank from another so they distrust all banks. This belief of unsoundness throughout an entire system sparks withdrawals of cash from banks within the system.

What put an end to the bank runs of the 1930s? The Federal Deposit Insurance Corporation (FDIC). The FDIC, established under the Banking Act of 1933, protected depositors from bank failures. If an insured bank fails, the FDIC pays the claim of each depositor up to $100,000. Often, with FDIC assistance, other banks have assumed all the deposits of failed banks. By 2000 virtually no depositor had incurred loses.

make an early statement reassuring the public that the banks were fundamentally sound. Roosevelt replied that the bank situation was so bad that no "mere statement" would help. Further, Roosevelt acknowledged that "very few financial institutions anywhere in the country are actually able to pay off their deposits in full, and the knowledge of this fact is widely held" (quoted in Helen Burns, *The American Banking Community and New Deal Banking Reforms, 1933–1935,* 1974). Roosevelt issued no statement. Meanwhile, "bank holidays" spread to Indiana on February 23, Maryland on February 25, Arkansas on February 27, and Ohio on February 28.

The banking pulse had all but stopped. Hoover refrained from acting independently, and Roosevelt felt he could not act cooperatively with Hoover. All committees, hearings, and investigations had failed. Neither bankers nor Congress had come up with a workable solution. Reform banking legislation lay buried in Senate and House committees.

By March 2, 1933, twenty-one states had declared moratoria. Around the clock conferences were held at the White House, Treasury Department, Federal Reserve, and banks throughout the country. Members of the new Roosevelt administration began work as soon as they arrived in Washington. Hoover administration members remained at their posts to help. It was hoped that at least closures of large banks in financial centers could be avoided.

On Friday, March 3, 1933, Roosevelt went to the White House for the traditional courtesy call on the outgoing president. Hoover and Roosevelt conferred about a nationwide bank holiday but by nightfall no statement had been made. At 3:00 AM, March 4, the governor of Illinois closed his state's banks. At 4:20 AM the governor of New York proclaimed a two-day holiday.

Eight Amazing Days

At dawn on Saturday, March 4, 1933, the nation's banks were paralyzed. At 1:08 PM Franklin Delano Roosevelt was inaugurated as president of the United States. In a strong, clear voice, President Roosevelt spoke to the anxious nation. In his inauguration speech he chided bankers, calling them "money changers" and saying they, "have fled from their high seats in the temple of our civilization." He announced that "there must be an end to speculation with other people's money, and there must be provision for an adequate sound currency." Roosevelt asked Congress for "broad executive power to wage a war against the emergency, as great as the power that would be given to me, if we were in fact invaded by a foreign foe" (quoted in Burns, pp. 40–41).

As soon as the inauguration ended, senators returned to the Senate chamber and immediately approved Roosevelt's cabinet appointments. A few hours later, in an unprecedented ceremony, the entire

A farmer and banker stand outside of the Farmers National Bank in Plain City, Ohio in 1938. Many farmers were unable to pay off loans, leading to failures of many rural banks. (The Library of Congress.)

Cabinet was sworn in. Meetings at the White House and the Federal Reserve continued non-stop for the rest of the day. Leading bankers, those "money changers," were told to come to Washington the next day, Sunday, March 5. President Roosevelt bowed out of the inaugural balls that evening.

William Woodin, the new treasury secretary; Raymond Moley, chief of Roosevelt's campaign "brain trust" and now an assistant secretary of state; Ogden L. Mills, outgoing treasury secretary; and Arthur Ballantine, outgoing treasury under-secretary, had been meeting since Thursday, March 2. They agreed that the only immediate way to halt the bank crisis was to declare a nationwide bank holiday to allow everyone some breathing room. When it became evident on March 5 that the hastily gathered bankers had no plan of their own to end the emergency situation, President Roosevelt made his decision. That evening Roosevelt issued his first proclamation, which summoned Congress to convene in an extraordinary session on Thursday, March 9. Treasury Secretary Woodin had agreed to have emergency banking legislation ready on March 9. Then at 1:00 AM Monday, March 6, believing the American banking system could not withstand the strain of another day, Roosevelt ordered a bank holiday to extend across the nation from Monday, March 6 through Thursday, March 9.

For the nation the holiday ushered in immense relief. At least for the moment the long economic descent was at a full stop. People rallied together in their predicament of not having access to their money. They wrote out IOU's, accepted scrip (printed IOUs), made jokes, and adjusted as cheerfully as they could to the bankless economy.

If banking was to be saved, however, it would be done in the halls of the U.S. Treasury, where tense discussions continued. Woodin, Mills, Ballantine, and George Harrison of the New York Federal Reserve Bank are largely credited with putting together the emergency bank bill. The provisions of the bill, for the most part, actually originated in the Hoover administration during 1931, 1932, and 1933. After an impassioned five days the bill was ready for passage. Congress convened at noon on Thursday, March 9. The president sent a strong message for immediate action. Representative Steagall read the provisions of the bill aloud to members of the House. Shortly afterward, House members shouted, "Vote! Vote!" The bill that most members had never even seen passed unanimously. Meanwhile, the Senate, growing impatient waiting for printed copies of the bill, substituted the House version, and passed the bill 73 to 7, just before 7:30 PM. An hour later the Emergency Banking Act of 1933 was at the White House for Roosevelt's final

More About...

A Moneyless Society

What would it be like to wake up and find out that the government had shut down all the banks, and the only cash available was what was in your wallet, or pockets, or "piggy" bank. Would out-of-control mobs roam the streets smashing store windows and taking all they could carry? Would families hide their jewelry and silver flatware? Would grocers hold off hungry crowds with shotguns?

Nothing like these scenarios played out on March 6, 1933, that historic Monday when all banks in America did close. No doubt some people rushed to the banks to see if they really were locked up, but for the most part people were relieved. President Roosevelt, at least for the moment, had stopped the bank runs. People actually laughed and joked about their common dilemma.

Experiences of comedy and practicality played out. Stranded salesmen hawked anything they had—the contents of their suitcases, even shoes, for a train fare home. Promoters of a Madison Square Garden boxing tournament accepted any usual item for admission. Employers postdated paychecks. Grocers, drugstores, gasoline stations, and hotels operated on credit. One of the most critical problems to develop was the inability to make change. If you needed bus fare but all you had was a $20 bill, bus drivers could not make change. Scrip, or paper IOUs, showed up in all forms in various communities. Bus tokens, foreign coins, and postage stamps all became part of the strange moneyless society.

Monday, March 13, when banks began reopening, came none too soon. In communities such as Detroit, where the bank holiday lasted four weeks, the humor in the situation began to wear off. Few wage earners could afford to miss many paydays. Just raising carfare for work or school had to be an ingenious endeavor. Relief applications poured in, and some began to go hungry, unable to cash their paychecks. The reopening of the banks helped stop this snowball effect, while Roosevelt's actions in declaring the bank "holiday" did help stabilize the banking industry.

---

signature. The entire process was completed in less than eight hours. Roosevelt then extended the bank holiday until Monday, March 13, to allow time to determine which banks could reopen.

Title I of the newly enacted Emergency Banking Act legalized Roosevelt's decision to declare a nationwide bank holiday. Title II dealt with the reorganization of the thousands of closed banks throughout the United States. It was based on the Bank Conservation Act, a bill that had not made it through Congress earlier in the year. Title III rejuvenated the RFC, authorizing it to purchase banks' preferred stock to provide them with long-term investment funds. The act also gave the president complete control of gold movements and made the hoarding of gold illegal. The act was passed out of necessity in a crisis atmosphere, but it was conservative legislation. It was a disappointment to those who had listened to the anti-bank rhetoric of Roosevelt's inaugural address and hoped for radical change. The bankers had feared radical changes. Despite the wording in his inaugural speech, Roosevelt's conservative handling of the banking crisis was simply in keeping with his own beliefs, which proved to be much more conservative than observers had originally thought.

On Friday, March 10, gold hoarders by the thousands lined up before regional Federal Reserve Banks. They were bringing back their treasure, which had suddenly become contraband. By Saturday night the Federal Reserve System had recovered $300 million in gold—enough to back up $750 million in new currency.

Meanwhile, under the powers granted by the Emergency Banking Act, examiners from the Treasury Department, the Federal Reserve System, and state banking systems undertook the task of determining which banks were sound enough to reopen beginning Monday, March 13. The biggest fear was that when the banks began to reopen, still-panicky depositors would withdraw their money and start the bleeding again. Largely to avert such a reaction, President Roosevelt broadcast the first of his radio fireside chats on Sunday evening, March 12. More than 60 million people heard his comforting voice as Roosevelt explained the actions of the past few days and what would happen on Monday. His message was that banks were once again safe for depositors' savings. On Monday morning, March 13, people again lined up in front of banks, but instead of withdrawing money they waited to deposit their money. In New York City alone, deposits exceeded withdrawals by $10 million. The bank runs were over. People had regained confidence in their political leadership and in the banking system. By March 15 banks controlling approximately 90 percent of the country's banking resources had resumed business. Throughout the country deposits exceeded withdrawals. Those banks found unsound remained closed, awaiting reorganization.

Two women use scrip money to purchase food. These paper coupons were used as temporary money following the closing of some banks. *(©Hulton-Deutsch Collection/Corbis. Reproduced by permission.)*

Pecora Hearings

While Roosevelt was busy restoring confidence in banks, Congress, in 1933 and 1934, investigated and punished old violations of the public trust. Senator Duncan U. Fletcher, chairman of the Senate Banking and Currency Committee, directed the "Pecora Investigations." Ferdinand Pecora, counsel (lawyer) to the committee, tirelessly led the investigations. The sensational hearings revealed the unethical and immoral side of bankers. Pecora found that Charles E. Mitchell, head of National City Bank and commanding a salary of $1.2 million, paid no income tax. He had also issued $256 million in Peruvian bonds he knew were worthless.

Pecora's investigation also revealed that the brokerage house of Lee, Higginson and Company had defrauded the public of $100 million. He found that former Secretary of the Treasury Andrew Mellon and banker J .P. Morgan also managed to not pay taxes, as had twenty of Morgan's partners. The reputation of bankers hit a new low. Public outrage over the fraud uncovered in the Pecora investigations led to demands for solid bank reform.

Banking Act of 1933 (Glass-Steagall Act)

By mid-March 1933 President Roosevelt focused on permanent banking legislation. For the next six weeks many conferences on banking were held in Washington, DC. Frequent White House visitors were Senator Glass, Senator Fletcher, and Representative Steagall. Separation of commercial and investment banking, the very controversial deposit insurance, branch banking, and increased Federal Reserve control all were major topics of discussion as the bill to create the Banking Act of 1933 developed. Originally President Roosevelt did not support the deposit insurance proposal, but he knew the power of public opinion. As a result of the strong public support, a deposit insurance plan was included in the new banking bill. Bankers remained bitterly opposed to the proposed insurance plan.

On May 10, 1933, Senator Glass introduced a completed bill to the Senate, and on May 17, Representative Steagall introduced a similar bill to the House. The full bill passed through Congress in mid-June. President Roosevelt signed the Banking Act of 1933 into law on June 16. Roosevelt congratulated Senator Glass at having fathered the first major banking measure since the Federal Reserve Act of 1913.

The Banking Act of 1933 included the following provisions: (1) commercial banking was separated from investment banking. Member banks had one year to divorce themselves from security affiliates; (2) a new agency within the Treasury Department, the Federal Deposit Insurance Corporation (FDIC), was created to provide deposit insurance up to $2,500 for each depositor account at all FDIC insured banks. All Federal Reserve member banks had to join the FDIC. State non-member banks could join if they became part of the Federal Reserve System by July 1, 1936; (3) national banks could establish branches on a statewide basis in states already allowing state banks to do so, but interstate branching was still not permitted; (4) the Federal Reserve was given more control over loans made to member banks; (5) Interest payments on checking accounts (demand deposits) were prohibited to eliminate competition among banks to pay higher and higher rates; and (6) officers of national banks had until July 1, 1935, to divest themselves of any loans granted to them by their own banks. Divest means to give up something of value, in this case, their loans.

The Banking Act of 1933, which was commonly called the Glass-Steagall Act, laid a foundation for far-reaching changes in the American banking industry. Its passage marked the completion of the remedial banking legislation of President Roosevelt's "first hundred days" in office. The bank reform act was not as conservative as bankers had hoped for, nor as progressive as liberals desired. It was an outgrowth of public demand, formed by government officials and congressmen. Bankers, having never agreed on a plan, did not play a major role. Glass-Steagall was devised as compromise legislation to get the wheels of banking turning again and to restore normalcy. Its elements began both recovery and reform of the banking industry.

Banking Act of 1935

President Roosevelt did not turn his attention to banking issues again until Fall 1934. At the time rumors abounded among bankers that a government-run central bank might be created to own and operate all banking activity in the country. Senator Glass forcefully asserted that he did not know a single responsible leader in Washington considering such a move. Throughout 1934 President Roosevelt, in public and in private, reaffirmed his support of the American banking system. Nevertheless, fear of further government control got bankers highly involved with the next banking bill, developed in late 1934 and 1935.

President Roosevelt had appointed Marriner Eccles as the new governor of the Federal Reserve Board in August 1934. Eccles' appointment paved the way for New Deal banking legislation in 1935. Several problems with Glass-Steagall concerned private bankers and government officials, including Eccles. Glass-Steagall required officers of national banks to divest themselves of all loans granted them by their bank by no later than July 1, 1935, though many officers wanted an extension. Additionally, the FDIC was set to begin formal operations on January 1, 1935. Most bankers considered the insurance rates to be charged by the FDIC as too high. In the administration camp, Eccles wanted a major restructuring of the Federal Reserve System. He wanted to centralize power with the Federal Reserve Board in Washington, DC, rather than in the twelve regional Federal Reserve Banks. Roosevelt agreed, knowing his relief proposals would require massive federal spending involving cooperation with the Federal Reserve Board.

President Roosevelt reasoned that the bankers wanted the loan time extension and lower FDIC rates enough to agree to centralizing of the Federal Reserve System. His assessment was correct, and a bill containing these elements moved through the House and Senate in the summer of 1935.

On August 23 President Roosevelt signed the Banking Act of 1935. Title I reduced the FDIC fees; Title II restructured the Federal Reserve System, centralizing power in the Federal Reserve Board located in Washington, DC; and Title III postponed the loan divestment. The Banking Act of 1935 authorized the FDIC to: (1) set standards for member banks; (2) examine those banks for compliance; (3) take action to prevent troubled banks from failing; and (4) pay depositors if insured banks failed.

The Banking Act of 1935 was a milestone in public policy, much like other New Deal legislation. That is, it was now the federal government, not individual bankers, that played the role of overseeing a more coordinated U.S. banking system. Responsibility for monetary management and credit control also rested with the federal government. Ever since 1935 the Federal Reserve Board has carried out its responsibility to stabilize overall economic activity while providing a flexible currency to meet the nation's money supply needs.

Contributing Forces

Unit Banks

Bank suspensions or failures were more numerous in the 1920s than in any decade between 1890 and 1920. Nationwide bank failures between 1892 and 1899 averaged ninety a year; between 1900 and 1909, 49 a year; and, between 1910 and 1919, 66 a year. Between 1921 and 1929 an average of more than six hundred banks failed every year. Explanation for the high failure rate of the 1920s lies in federal and state legislation adopted in the second half of the nineteenth century. The resulting structure or organization of U.S. banking allowed the development of thousands of independently owned state banks or "unit" banks. The unit bank is a full-service commercial bank operating out of only one office or location. In the first years of the twentieth century the number of small unit banks increased dramatically.

In 1900 there were approximately twelve thousand commercial banks—banks where services included deposits and personal and business loans. By 1920 the number had risen to thirty thousand. Continuing the trend, liberal banking laws of the "roaring" 1920s allowed commercial banks in some states to open with as little as $6,000 in start-up funds or

More About...

Types of Banks

Banks are business organizations that accept deposits from the public or other businesses, hold those deposits until demanded by the depositor (as with a check), make loans to individuals or businesses, and purchase securities (bonds and/or stocks). Banks earn money when the interest paid out to depositors is less than the interest income earned on loans and other investments. Every banking institution is chartered by either the federal or a state government and is subject to a variety of regulations. The term "bank" now also describes a variety of banking institutions. Savings and loan associations, savings banks, and credit unions are sometimes referred to as "thrifts," since one of their major purposes has traditionally been to encourage savings.

Different types of banks originated to serve different types of need. Commercial banks traditionally served the needs of business. Investment banks raised money for businesses. Savings banks and savings and loans originated to serve different requirements of low- and moderate-income individuals. Although traditionally different in purpose, banking institutions through time have increasingly provided more of the same services. Legislation through the last half of the twentieth century gradually broadened the scope of services at all institutions.

Commercial Banks. Commercial banks are the most important banks in terms of assets and range of services. They offer checking accounts, savings accounts, and retirement accounts. Traditionally, industrial and business loans dominated lending, hence the name "commercial" banks. Modern commercial banks meet the needs of individuals as well as businesses. Limited in their dealings in securities from 1933 until 1999, commercial banks began in 2000 to rapidly diversify into securities investments and insurance.

Savings and Loan Associations (S&Ls). S&Ls traditionally provided loans for housing-related purposes, including mortgages, home improvement, and construction. They chiefly relied on individual savings accounts for their funds. Modern S&Ls offer checking accounts, savings accounts, retirement accounts, consumer and business loans, and educational loans. In the 1980s and 1990s they have been allowed to diversify their lending.

Savings Banks. Savings banks originated in the early 1800s to encourage savings among the poor and working class by providing a safe haven for their deposits. Modern savings banks offer savings, checking, and retirement accounts and make personal and business loans.

Credit Unions. Credit unions' depositors are people with a common bond, such as teachers' credit unions or a certain university's credit union. They offer checking and savings accounts for their members, and loan funds, usually at interest rates lower than that of other institutions. Credit unions typically do not loan to businesses.

Investment Banks. Investment banks primarily raise money for businesses or for the government by buying and selling securities. To raise money or capital for a business, investment banks sell the company's stock, called shares, to investors, who become part owners of the business. Bonds issued by the government or by a business are borrowings from the investor. The investor who buys the bond becomes a creditor of the government or business. The government or business must eventually pay the money invested in the bond, plus interest, back to the investor.

Investment banks do not accept deposits or make loans. Between 1933 and approximately 1980, other banking institutions were prohibited from investment banking except to buy U.S. government bonds. Not until 1999 could other banks diversify widely into securities.

---

capital. Loans were freely made. Small rural banks made predominately agricultural loans to local farmers. Lack of enough capital, however, made the banks extremely susceptible to failure. A few bad loans could doom the tiny banks.

The late nineteenth century banking legislation ensured the predominance of the single office bank by all but banning any nationwide or statewide branching. In the early twentieth century, much discussion among bankers centered on branch banking. Branches

Commercial Banks in the United States, 1900-1936

Year	National Banks	Federal Reserve State Member Banks	Nonmember Banks	Total State Banks
			State Banks	
1900	3,731		8,696	
1905	5,664		12,488	
1910	7,138		17,376	
1915	7,597	17	19,776	19,793
1920	8,024	1,374	20,893	22,267
1925	8,066	1,472	18,904	20,376
1930	7,247	1,068	15,364	16,432
1931	6,800	982	13,872	14,854
1932	6,145	835	11,754	12,589
1933	4,897	709	8,601	9,310
1934	5,417	958	8,973	9,931
1935	5,425	985	9,078	10,053
1936	5,368	1,032	8,929	9,961

The number of commercial National banks, 4,897, hit its lowest point since 1900 in 1933. The total number of commercial State banks hit its lowest point since 1900 in 1933. (The Gale Group.)

are smaller arms of main banks and are located throughout a region. In 1900, 87 banks had established branches. In 1927 Congress passed the McFadden Act, allowing national banks to branch within the cities of their main offices. Still, by 1930 only 751 banks had branches. Like national banking, branching was concentrated primarily in large east coast cities. Nowhere had the growth of branch banking been uniform. Branch banking laws differed widely from state to state. Some permitted statewide branching of state banks; some permitted no branch banking. An advantage branch banking offered was a more diversified depositor base. If one branch was in trouble, another stable branch's gains could offset the troubled branches' loses.

Dual Banking and Federal Reserve Systems

The U.S. banking structure evolved through the nineteenth century as a dual banking system. Bank supervision was divided between federal and state government authorities. Under the dual system the federal government chartered national banks. The U.S. Treasury Department's Office of the Comptroller of the Currency provided supervision. State banks were chartered by the individual states. State authorities regulated them under varying state laws. This dual system offered no nationwide unity, but instead fostered a strong allegiance to local interests. Few individual banks comprehended U.S. banking from a national perspective.

In 1913 an avenue had opened for state-chartered banks to come under the federal umbrella. Passed that year, the Federal Reserve Act created twelve Federal Reserve Districts across the nation. A Federal Reserve Board was to oversee the entire system. The Federal Reserve System was charged with promoting economic stability. The act required all national banks to be members of the Federal Reserve System. A state bank, meeting minimum capital requirements, could also choose to become a Federal Reserve member.

The Federal Reserve Act was initially created to avoid the state-imposed prohibitions on interstate banking that made check clearance across state boundaries impossible. Each member bank had to maintain reserves deposited in its regional federal reserve bank. The reserve deposits allowed for a national check clearing arrangement. The other major advantage to joining the Federal Reserve System was a member could borrow, at discount rates, currency or loan-able funds from its regional federal reserve bank as needed. The disadvantage to joining the system was the reserve funds each member bank was required to deposit in its federal reserve bank did not draw any interest. The member bank's reserve funds essentially sat in the reserve bank earning the member bank no interest income instead of being deposited in another bank where the funds would draw interest. Thus it was more profitable for individual banks to not belong to the Federal Reserve System.

More About...

The Federal Reserve System

Under the Federal Reserve System the United States was divided into 12 Federal Reserve Districts, each with a Reserve Bank. The Reserve Banks carry out the day-to-day operation as the nation's central banking system. The Reserve Bank's services for depository banking institutions across the nation parallel the services those banks and thrift institutions provide to businesses and individuals. For example, banks and thrifts deposit money into their accounts, called reserve accounts, at their regional Reserve Bank. In turn the Reserve Bank makes loans to them. Reserve Banks also move coin and currency into and out of circulation, collect and process millions of checks each day, and supervise member banks for safety and soundness. Reserve banks provide the U.S. Treasury Department with its checking accounts and buys and sells government securities or bonds. A board of nine directors supervises each of the Reserve Banks.

Overseeing the entire system is the Board of Governors, commonly known as the Federal Reserve Board. The seven members of the Board of Governors are appointed for 14-year terms by the president and confirmed by the Senate. The appointments must fairly represent financial, agricultural, industrial, and commercial interests from around the country. The Federal Open Market Committee (FOMC) is the most important monetary policy-making body of the Federal Reserve System. The FOMC is composed of the seven members of the Board of Governors, plus five Reserve Bank presidents. The Reserve Bank presidents serve one year on a rotating basis, except for the president of the Federal Reserve Bank of New York, who serves on a continuing basis. United States monetary policy is set by the Board of Governors and the FOMC. Monetary policy is determined in three ways:

1. The Board of Governors sets reserve requirements. Member banks must keep a certain percentage of their deposits in a reserve account with their regional Reserve Bank. The Board may change the reserve percentage from time to time. For example, when the reserve requirement is 15 percent, a member bank must keep in its reserve account with the Reserve Bank $15 out of every $100 of its deposits. It then has $85 left from every $100 deposited to lend or invest. In this way the reserve requirement controls the amount of money available for lending. If banks are required to increase reserves there will be less money in circulation or money will be "tighter."
2. The boards of directors of the Federal Reserve Banks can change the rate of interest, or "discount rate," member banks are required to pay for loans from the Reserve Banks. Discount rate changes must be approved by the Board of Governors in Washington, DC. If an expansion of the supply of credit money is desired, the decision would be to lower the discount rate. A lower rate would cost member banks less when they borrow. Therefore they borrow more, making more money available for loans to customers. A low discount rate or a reduction in the rate makes clear that the Federal Reserve believes an increased supply of money would be in the public interest. On the other hand, a raise in the discount rate would discourage member banks from borrowing, making less money available for customer loans. A high rate or an increase in the rate indicates that the Federal Reserve believes there is too much money that would encourage inflation.
3. The Federal Reserve influences the money supply by buying or selling government securities (bonds). This process is called open market operations. The FOMC meets eight times a year to determine policy with respect to purchasing or selling government bonds. When the Federal Reserve Bank purchases government bonds, the money is deposited in a commercial bank. The bank's supply of money is increased so that more money is available for loans to businesses and individuals. When the Federal Reserve Bank sells government bonds, it receives money in payment for them from commercial banks. This results in less money to be loaned out to business and individuals.

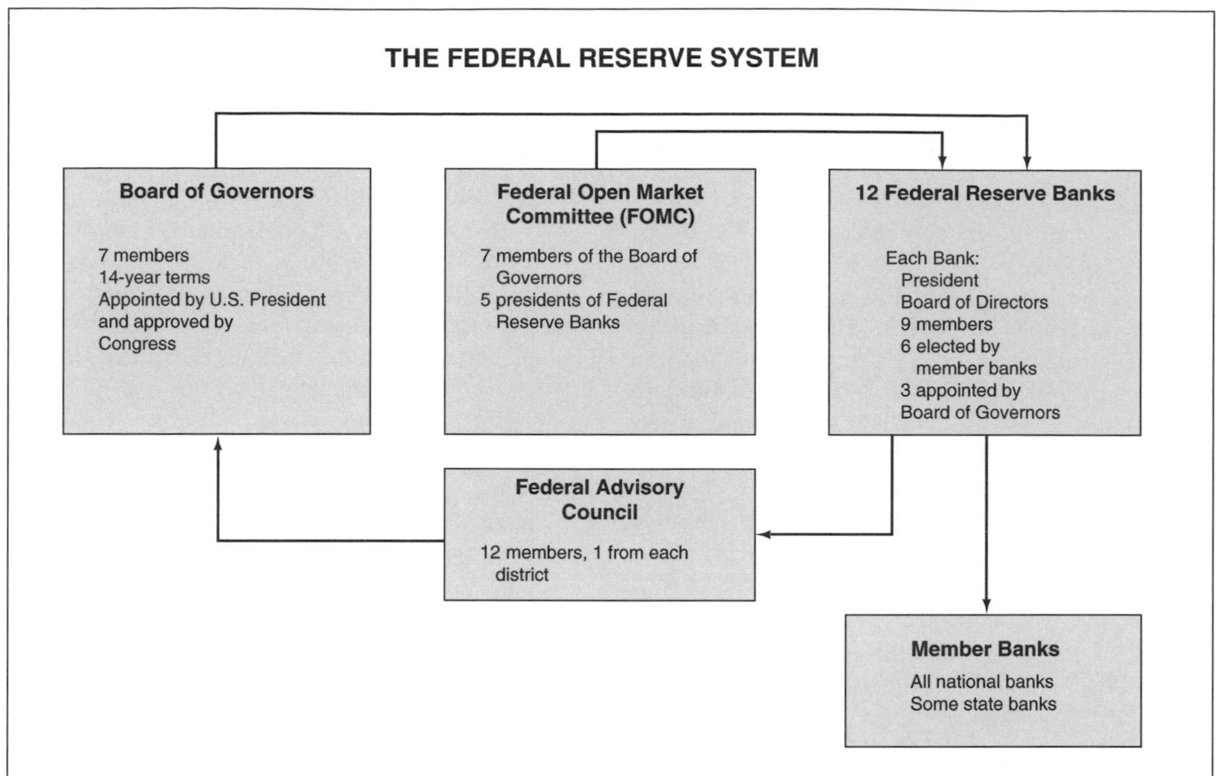

The Federal Reserve System was founded to provide the United States with a more stable financial system. *(The Gale Group.)*

Between 1900 and 1920, the number of state-chartered banks rose from over eight thousand to 22,267, but only 1,374 elected to become Federal Reserve members. Most did not join because they did not have enough capital, because they refused to deposit reserves in a non-interest bearing situation, and/or because they fiercely rejected federal supervision. By 1920 the 8,024 national banks had assets of $23.3 billion. The 1,374 state member banks of the Federal Reserve had assets of $10.4 billion. The 20,893 non-member state banks had assets totaling only $13.9 billion. The dual banking system continued to be a headache for federal regulators, who had no control over the large number of non-member banks. Many small, poorly regulated, and undercapitalized rural banks would fall prey to agricultural difficulties following World War I (1914–1918).

Agricultural Woes, Loan Speculation, and Reform

In the post World War I, period agriculture suffered from a decreased demand for its products. During the war Europeans, unable to grow enough food, bought American products. The high levels of American agricultural production continued after the war, but overseas demand halted, resulting in chronic U.S. over-production. Farm prices fell and farm income decreased. Through the 1920s farmers defaulted on loans and on mortgages. Deposits in local banks also drastically declined.

As a result bank failures in the 1920s were most prominent in the agricultural regions of the Midwest and Southeast. These rural areas did have the greatest increase in number of banks prior to 1920. A majority of bank failures between 1921 and 1929 were banks in communities of 2,500 or fewer inhabitants and with capital stock of $25,000 or less.

Unlike agriculture, businesses and industries had prospered in the 1920s. To many it seemed that the economic boom of the 1920s would go on forever. Banks competed aggressively with one another by offering higher rates to attract deposits. To cover the expense of high interest rates paid to customers, banks needed interest income. This income came from the interest banks charged on loans. Therefore they made loans easy to obtain. Banks readily extended credit for business ventures, real estate, and investments in stocks and bonds. Depositors who wished to invest in the stock market found credit easy to obtain. They could fund 90 percent of the price of purchasing the stock through bank loans or through stockbrokers who had obtained bank loans for stock purchase.

Prior to the stock market crash of 1929, member banks were able to use Federal Reserve System funds for many speculative (high risk) loans. The Federal Reserve had also followed the policy of "easy money," making more money available to member commercial banks to be loaned out. By the end of the decade individuals and businesses were unable to keep up with payments on loans. Banks in the 1930s would watch as many of these loans and investments became worthless.

As the 1920s drew to a close, the banking community was aware of the need for bank reform. A few bankers advocated either central banking or an extensive system of large, stable commercial banks with close government supervision. Many bankers supported branching, believing it would not only allow banks to grow but would better serve customers. They envisioned a stronger nationwide banking structure, as weak banks would be eliminated. On the other hand many bankers throughout the country were opposed to any expansion of branch banking. They feared a concentration of power in a very large bank with many branches, unfair competition, and a decline of the local bank that they believed best served each community. They feared it would end the dual banking system in America by concentrating the industry in large centralized banks. Likewise, many Americans were suspicious of powerful financial institutions, preferring only local control with a minimum of restraints on the opportunity to make money. America's bankers could come to no agreement, and no reform plan was ever put forth in the 1920s. Thus, in the economic turmoil of the 1930s, effective reform became a priority.

Perspectives

Presidents and Congressmen

President Herbert Hoover regarded the banking crisis as a crisis of confidence. He chose to combat the crisis with speeches repeatedly reminding the country that its banking and economic systems remained strong, and that the paralysis was produced by an unjustified lack of confidence. He believed conditions aided by voluntary cooperation between bankers, businessmen, workers, and consumers would correct themselves. Seeing himself as a leader and guide rather than as an activist, Hoover called conferences, suggested remedies, and worked for cooperative agreements. He realized reforms might be necessary, but he emphasized voluntary action from leaders of banking, industry, agriculture, and labor. Every slight economic upturn caused Hoover to announce the end of the Depression. But each message proved false, and Hoover's credibility plummeted.

Franklin D. Roosevelt knew Americans had lost confidence in the banking system, but he felt real problems were behind the lack of confidence. He felt a pressing need for banking reform, even as governor of New York (1928–1932). Roosevelt sensed little interest on the part of bankers, however, to make any meaningful changes. Likewise, during the first days of his presidency he found that bankers had little to offer in the way of suggestions or recommendations to solve the banking crisis.

Roosevelt believed banking should be strictly supervised, that banking ethics should always be maintained, and that depositors should be protected against bad banking practices. He did not, however, believe in government exclusively owning and operating banks. Nor did he believe in a concentration of all banking resources and control in one spot. Even while the Banking Act of 1933 was progressing through its final development, Roosevelt did not support deposit insurance. He wanted other plans substituted. Roosevelt, however, being a true politician, bent to the public will on the insurance issue.

Although bankers feared he wanted radical changes, President Roosevelt's banking policies were thoroughly conservative. His appointments in banking-related areas were conventional. For example, both U.S. Treasury Secretary William Woodin and Eugene Black, head of the Federal Reserve Board, were conservatives on money matters. The uniqueness of Roosevelt's policies lay in their swiftness and bold application.

Most congressmen were ready to follow the lead of the new president. Typically those on the far right felt the reform proposals were too liberal. The loudest cries, however, came from the left, or progressives. Having heard the president's inaugural address denouncing bankers as "money changers" fleeing from their "temples," they expected radical reform, but they vastly underestimated Roosevelt's true conservative nature on banking. They considered the Emergency Banking Bill, passed the evening of March 9, 1933, to be a conservative measure. The vote in the Senate was 73–7. The seven voting against the bill were not conservatives, but a small band of progressives.

Bankers

The banking community between 1930 and 1933 was fully aware of the need for reform. The division

President Franklin D. Roosevelt delivers his first fireside chat, in which he explained the measures he was taking to reform the banking system, on March 12, 1933. (AP/Wide World Photos. Reproduced by permission.)

of opinion on a course of action, however, reflected the numerous conflicts of interest and the enormous complexity of the situation. There were commercial banks, investment banks, savings and loan associations, and credit unions. There were large banks, small banks, national banks, state banks, sound banks, and unsound banks. There was contention between the national and state banks, urban versus rural banks, and east coast versus interior banks.

A few bankers advocated one central bank, owned and operated by the government, and opposed the regional operation of the Federal Reserve System with twelve districts nationwide. Yet most bankers were hesitant to advocate one central authority that would greatly increase the amount of federal control over banking. State bankers vehemently opposed federal control, an outgrowth of the long-time controversy over states' rights as opposed to federal power. Among bankers who did support bank reform there was a decided lack of unity on what action should be taken. Many believed that bad banks would always exist. Reform, most bankers believed, would have to come from rigid enforcement of existing laws and regulation.

As reform banking legislation moved through Congress, bankers voiced many objections. Out of harmony with the Roosevelt administration, in disfavor with the public, and in disagreement amongst themselves, bankers had little impact on the legislative process. The one subject they were united on was opposition to deposit insurance. Their attitude was that it would penalize the strong banks to the benefit of the weak banks, thereby further weakening the banking economy. Bankers believed deposit insurance was like trying to insure everyone against everything, and that simply was not the way the world worked, especially in the 1930s.

The Public

Bewildered and perplexed, the public saw the once proud and trusted banking community crumble, taking with it their life savings or that of friends or relatives. They had no way to distinguish a strong bank from a weak one and had lost confidence in them all. A single rumor could start a run. Keeping money in mattresses and buried in back yards became preferable to depositing funds in financial institutions.

As investigations progressed the public became outraged at the seemingly prevalent banking fraud. People were also discouraged at the banking industry's speculation in the stock market at the expense of depositors' funds.

More About...

Where Was the Federal Reserve?

As the unemployment rate edged to 25 percent, and numerous depositors lost money in the 1930s, bank after bank closed. Where was the Federal Reserve? The "Fed" was supposed to be the lender of last resort. That is, when a troubled bank could find no other bank to lend it money, it could turn to the Fed. The Fed would often lend the money a bank needed to get through its crisis. That is the way the system was intended to work. During the years of the Great Depression, however, the Fed did not do this. Many believe the economic woes of the Depression were made considerably worse because of the Federal Reserve's inaction. Looking back at the entire decade of the 1930s, economists suggest two reasons why the Fed did not act.

First, it appears Fed officials believed that failing banks were poorly managed and should be allowed to disappear. This was a common perception of the day in all areas of business. The problem with letting this happen in the banking industry was that one or two bank failures in an area could cause depositors to wonder if their own bank might also be in trouble. For every two banks that failed, perhaps fifty were in good shape, but the public could not tell which banks were in trouble and which were not.

Depositors would start withdrawing their money. Sometimes enough people did this to cause a "run" on the bank—a majority of depositors attempting to withdraw their money at the same time. Since banks loaned out money, no bank kept enough cash on hand to satisfy all customers at once. As a result those at the end of the line would not get their money. Even though the bank had been perfectly sound and well managed, depositor's fears caused their bank to fail. This scenario played out time and again across the country.

Second, economists suggest Fed officials were bowing to the wishes of big bank owners. The majority of failing banks were in small towns and rural areas. Big city banks did not like the competition of the many small banks. Big city bankers were happy to see small banks go out of business and pressured the Fed to do nothing to save the troubled banks.

However, the public had a new president with a confident smile, a calming voice, and a determination to take action. Within 35 hours of his inauguration, President Roosevelt brought the banking problem to a head, stopped runs, and centralized authority. The public would have followed him anywhere, cheering the entire way.

One issue the public and President Roosevelt were out of step on was deposit insurance. The public demanded it. Therefore, a reluctant Roosevelt yielded to them. It put confidence back in banking—a confidence Roosevelt realized must be restored. On this issue, the public had been correct.

Impact

An Enduring Federal Deposit Insurance Corporation (FDIC)

The FDIC, created by the 1933 Glass-Steagall Act, not only restored confidence in banks for Depression-weary depositors, it maintained high public confidence for the rest of the twentieth century. Depositors believed their money, insured by a large federal corporation, was safe. If their bank should fail, the FDIC would pay back their lost money. Therefore, most all Americas confidently deposited their money into banks. The FDIC directly reduced the rate of bank suspensions throughout the country. Between 1934 and 1940, approximately 450 suspensions occurred, down from almost four thousand alone in 1933. Only 112 total bank suspensions occurred between 1941 and 1960. A key benefit in belonging to the Federal Reserve System is that the FDIC automatically insures deposits in member banks. Of all the freshly created New Deal agencies none had more endurance and universal acceptance than the FDIC. Depositor confidence in individual banks is an important concern for the stability of the banking system. U.S. banks have not experienced economically significant or contagious runs since the FDIC's establishment. By the turn of the twenty-first century virtually no depositors had incurred loses.

Banking centered on maintaining financial stability between 1935 and 1970 by adhering to provisions set forth in the Banking Act of 1933 (Glass-Steagall

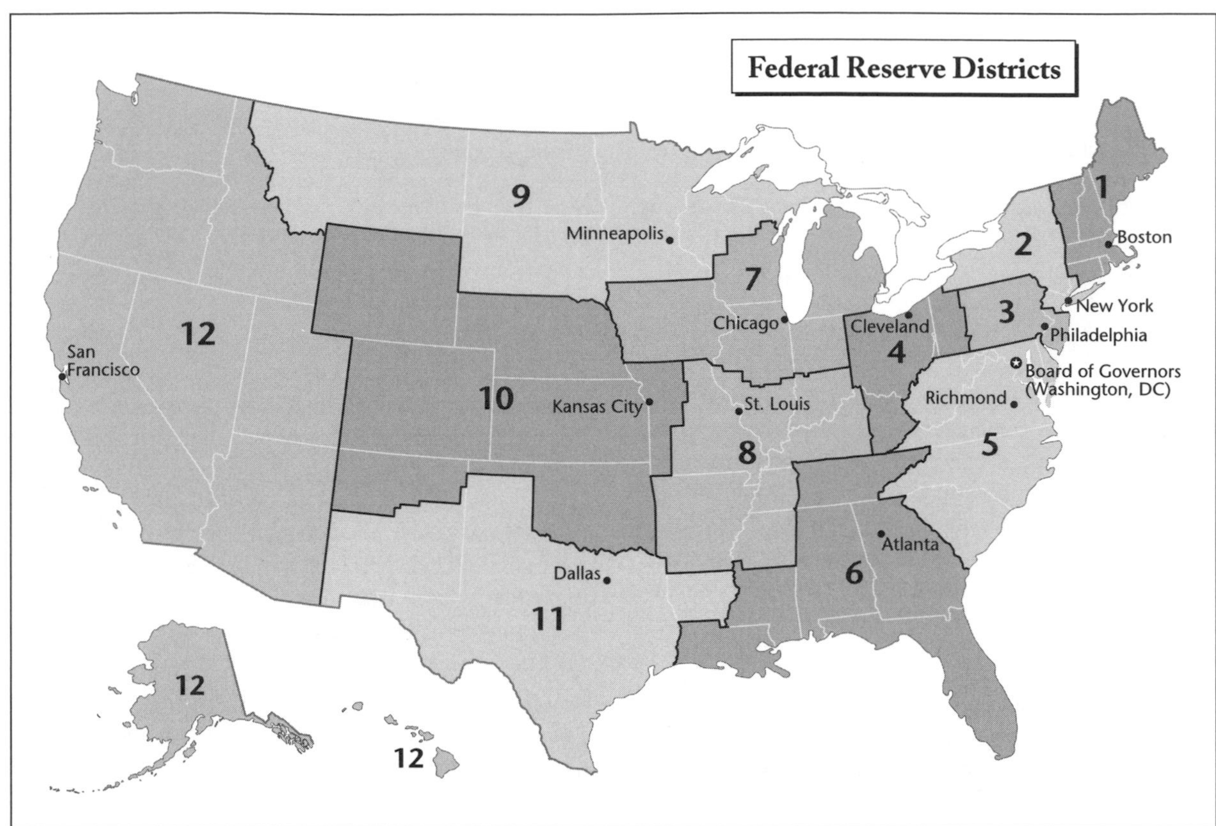

Map of the twelve Federal Reserve Districts, cities denoting the Federal Reserve Banks, and the Board of Governors in the United States. (The Gale Group.)

Act). In addition to the FDIC, the act prohibited interest payments on checking accounts and allowed the Federal Reserve to limit the interest paid on savings accounts. Both enabled banks to quit warring over higher rates to attract customers, saving them from paying interest rates they could not afford. Further, the Depression-spawned Glass-Steagall also separated commercial banks from stock brokerages. Although widely viewed as a major cause of bank failure in the 1930s, historians have since shown losses on securities played a very minor role in the failures. Only 7.2 percent, or 15 of the 207 national banks that actively dealt in securities, failed. This percentage is far smaller than the percentage of failed national banks that did not conduct both commercial and investment banking.

The failures, 90 percent of which were rural banks, were overwhelmingly caused because small unit banks that had too little capital concentrated loans in the depressed agriculture sector. Their loan portfolios had very little diversification. Nevertheless, commercial banking activities and securities investment remained divorced.

During the years after the end of World War II (1939–1945) through the 1960s, banks that had weathered the 1930s prospered in a stable atmosphere. Very few new banks were established. It was very difficult to obtain a charter since the perception persisted that too many banks existed in the early 1930s, partly leading to so many failures. Industrial loans dominated bank lending, although banks expanded consumer credit by offering credit cards as early as 1950. Mortgage lending also increased after 1963, when Congress passed legislation allowing national banks to offer terms similar to those offered by savings and loan associations. The few banks that did fail through this time period were small, and depositors lost no money thanks to the FDIC.

By 1971 the Glass-Steagall provisions separating commercial banks and investment firms, in addition to the interest rate caps imposed by the Federal Reserve in 1934, began to take a significant toll on banks. Investment and security firms established new types of funds directly competing with banks for depositors. Fewer regulations on the security firms gave them a distinct advantage. Security firms introduced the money market fund in 1971. This type of fund, in which anyone with the minimum amount required (usually one to two thousand dollars) could invest, paid a much higher interest rate than banks were allowed to pay. Many individuals and companies withdrew their deposits and put them in money market funds even though no insurance for the funds existed. An added benefit was that funds could easily be transferred from the money market accounts into mutual stocks funds.

To help banks keep their depositors, in 1980 Congress passed the Depository Institution's Deregulation and the Monetary Control Act (DIDMCA). At that time, the DIDMCA was the most important single piece of banking legislation since 1933 and the Glass-Steagall Act. Amending a small part of Glass-Steagall, it allowed banks to pay interest on checking accounts, called NOW accounts. The act also phased out interest rate caps, negating the 1934 regulation that had set maximum interest rates. The phase-out of interest rate caps was complete in 1987. The DIDMCA also raised the maximum FDIC coverage to $100,000 for each account deposited in FDIC-member banks. The act helped curtail the drain of deposits from banking accounts, but the inflation driven double-digit interest rates of the 1970s spelled trouble for the 1980s.

The 1980s Crisis

In the 1980s the banking and savings and loan industry (S&Ls) experienced the worst crisis of banking institutions since the Great Depression. Congress began to deregulate the S&L industry with the DIDMCA. The DIDMCA allowed S&Ls to pay higher interest rates to be competitive with money market funds. The DIDMCA also allowed S&Ls to offer adjustable rate mortgages (ARM). ARMs allowed the interest rates charged to home buyers on their mortgages to float with the market interest rates. S&Ls had been caught in a bind. During the 1970s inflation-driven interest rates had gone very high so S&Ls had to pay very high interest rates on depositors' accounts. But the long-term mortgages they held and received their income from were at much lower interest rates. Therefore the S&Ls were receiving considerably less income than they had to pay out. With ARMs interest, income could begin to match the rates S&Ls were having to pay out on depositors accounts.

The second major form of deregulation was the Garn-It, or German Depository Institutions Act of 1982. This act enabled S&Ls to diversify and invest in other types of loans besides home construction and purchase loans. They invested in many types of commercial loans, such as in office buildings, shopping centers, condominium projects, hotels, and resorts. S&Ls plunged into these often risky ventures. A third form of S&L deregulation was actually a change in accounting procedures which allowed S&Ls to appear to have more solid financial positions than they really did. The rapidly rising inflation rates of the 1970s and 1980s began to slow considerably by the mid-1980s. Real estate values turned downward, dropping below the value of the loans. Borrowers were not able to keep repaying the high debt payments and correspondingly high interest rates. A major example occurred in the energy-producing states such as Texas, Louisiana, and Oklahoma. Oil prices had jumped from $12 a barrel to $35 a barrel with predictions of $100 a barrel. Banks and S&Ls drastically increased their loans for oil production, but by 1986 oil prices collapsed back to near $12 a barrel, and repayment of loans was impossible. By the late 1980s, nine of the ten largest Texas banks failed, and the entire energy producing regions saw 500 banks and S&Ls fail.

Overall, the failures of the 1980s were largely due to deliberately high-risk loan strategies, poor and even foolish business judgments, excessive optimism, and sloppy accounting, all compounded by the declining values of real estate and oil and gas revenues. From 1980 to 1990, approximately 1,100 banks and S&Ls failed. Depositors did not lose their funds thanks to Depression-era legislation establishing depositors' insurance, FDIC, and FSLIC, established by the National Housing Act of 1934. However, the FSLIC was strained beyond repair and Congress took action.

Just as in the 1930s, the federal government intervened to solve problems and restore public confidence. Congress passed the Financial Institutions Reform, Recovery and Enforcement Act of 1989 (FIRREA). FIRREA created the Office of Thrift Supervision (OTS) under the U.S. Treasury Department. It took the place of the Federal Home Loan Bank Board (FHLBB) in oversight of S&Ls. FIRREA created the Resolution Thrift Corporation (RTC). RTC's sole purpose was to manage and dispose of the assets of S&Ls that failed between 1989 and 1992. FIRREA also eliminated the FSLIC, replacing it with the Savings Association Insurance Fund (SAIF), to be administered by the FDIC.

Secondly, Congress enacted the Federal Deposit Insurance Corporation Improvement Act of 1991. This act allowed earlier intervention by regulators into a troubled bank's affairs. They could intervene before a bank's capital fell too low. The Crime Control Act stiffened criminal penalties in 1990 for crimes related to financial institutions.

Glass-Steagall Repealed—1999

During the 1980s the Glass-Steagall Act, separating commercial banking from investment banking, came under repeated challenges. Bankers wanted to improve their competitive position by offering many more financial services. While bankers demanded repeal of the Glass-Steagall Act, the securities industry strongly opposed any changes. Congress was hesitant to give additional powers to banks.

Through the 1990s the economic thinking in the United States changed. A separation of commercial banking and investment banking seemed increasingly outdated in a global economy that favored diversification. Once designed to safeguard economic growth, Glass-Steagall now seemed to be an obstacle to it. Insurance companies had been similarly separated from both commercial banks and investment companies by another act passed in the 1950s. Banking, securities, and insurance industries all began to agree on the urgent need for reform so that they could merge operations. The competitive international world demanded large one-stop shopping financial institutions. Foreign financial institutions had been large integrated conglomerates for some time. In 1999, six decades after the passage of Glass-Steagall, President Bill Clinton (1992–2001) signed the Gramm-Leach-Bliley Financial Services Modernization Act. The act repealed the Glass-Steagall Act, which restricted the ability of banks and securities to intermingle. Gramm-Leach-Bliley enabled banks, security firms, and insurance companies to create financial conglomerates. Conglomerates engage in a wide variety of business activities. Financial conglomerates may offer such products as certificates of deposit, stocks, credit cards, insurance, mutual funds, mortgages, and auto loans.

By the late 1990s, a wave of mergers among financial institutions had taken place in anticipation of Glass-Steagall's repeal. Citicorp and Travelers Insurance merged in 1998. Its offspring, Citigroup, positioned itself to be the first real universal financial institution in the United States. At the beginning of the twenty-first century—in an America without Glass-Steagall—banks looked to go on-line and diversify their services further. Chase Manhattan, Fleet Financial, and Mellon Bank each have merged with on-line brokerages to put their services on the web.

Notable People

Eugene Robert Black (1872–1934). Eugene Robert Black practiced law in Georgia before becoming president of the Atlanta Trust Company in 1921. Appointed governor of the Federal Reserve Bank of Atlanta in 1927, Black frequently warned that the unhealthy state of the banking system in the 1920s would lead to a nationwide banking crisis. Widely respected in the conservative banking community, Black served as a link between the White House and the financial community. In May 1933 President Franklin D. Roosevelt appointed him head of the Federal Reserve Board. Black took a leading role in certifying banks to reopen after the "bank holiday." He also played an influential role in creating the Securities Act of 1933, the Banking Act of 1933, the Securities Exchange Act of 1934, and in extending the Reconstruction Finance Corporation. Eugene Robert Black died after a brief illness in December 1934.

Leo Thomas Crowley (1889–1972). Although hailing from a poor family, Leo Crowley had a keen sense for business and banking. By 1918 he was president of a paper supply company. In 1920 he became president of the State Bank of Wisconsin and director of First Wisconsin Bankshares Corporation. Crowley's finances took a downturn when his bank failed in 1932. He helped write Wisconsin's bank holiday proclamation in March 1933. Known as a conservative Democrat, Crowley supported Franklin D. Roosevelt in the 1932 presidential campaign. In February 1934 Roosevelt appointed him to head the new Federal Deposit Insurance Corporation, where he remained for twelve years. Crowley's expertise paved the way for many troubled banks to become part of the new insurance program.

Duncan Upshaw Fletcher (1859–1936). Fletcher was elected to the Senate in 1909. A moderate Democrat, he became chairman of the Senate Banking and Currency Committee in 1932. He was a faithful supporter of President Roosevelt and New Deal legislation. Fletcher directed the "Pecora investigations" of the banking community. The Securities Exchange Act of 1934 and the Banking Act of 1935 were both sponsored by Fletcher.

Marriner Stoddard Eccles (1890–1977). Born and educated in Utah, Marriner Stoddard Eccles as a young man managed his family's enterprises into a multimillion dollar empire. He successfully led the family banks through the banking panics of 1932 and 1933 with no failures. As the economy grew worse in that time period, he advocated increased consumer purchasing power and more private investment as a remedy. Eccles believed federal government spending could lead the way. President Roosevelt appointed Eccles chairman of the Federal Reserve Board in 1934. Eccles accepted on the condition that the board could be reorganized under the centralized control of the

Washington Federal Reserve Board. He also helped draft the Banking Act of 1935. Eccles served as chairman of the board until 1948 and remained a member until 1951.

Carter Glass (1858–1946). Carter Glass was born in Lynchburg, Virginia. His father was a newspaperman. As a young man, Glass became a reporter and writer for the Lynchburg Daily News, but soon entered politics. He served in the U.S. House of Representatives from 1902 until 1918, and chaired the House Committee on Banking and Currency, where he was the acknowledged "father" of the Federal Reserve Bank Act of 1913. Glass served as Woodrow Wilson's secretary of the treasury from 1918 to 1920 when he entered the Senate. He strongly advocated the separation of commercial banking and investment banking. He believed that speculative investment in stocks and bonds was not compatible with safe commercial banking practices. He helped author the Glass-Steagall Act (the Banking Act of 1933) that, among other things, separated commercial banking from investment banking. The act also created the Federal Deposit Insurance Corporation, a provision to which he was opposed. Glass was a popular states' rights conservative Democrat. Stubborn and independent-minded, he opposed most New Deal programs. Glass remained in the Senate until his death in 1946.

George Harrison (1887–1958). Harrison was appointed deputy governor in 1920, governor in 1928, and president in 1936 of the Federal Reserve Bank of New York. He was a major contributor to the Emergency Banking Act of 1933, the Banking Act of 1933, and the Banking Act of 1935.

Jesse Holman Jones (1874–1956). Jones, a "self-made man" from Texas, had business interests in real estate, construction, banking, newspaper publishing, and oil. In January 1932 President Herbert Hoover appointed Jones as one of the seven directors of the newly created Reconstruction Finance Corporation. President Franklin D. Roosevelt advanced Jones to chairman of the RFC in 1933, a position he held until 1945.

Ogden Mills (1884–1937). Mills served as secretary of the treasury under President Herbert Hoover. He unselfishly gave immeasurable assistance to the incoming Roosevelt Administration in early 1933, playing a central role in developing the Emergency Banking Act of 1933 during the nationwide bank holiday.

Raymond Moley (1886–1975). After President Roosevelt's election in 1932, Raymond Moley served as Roosevelt's close advisor, playing an influential role in creating the legislation of the "first hundred days." He was instrumental in the actions taken in the days surrounding Roosevelt's inauguration, which averted a banking disaster. Moley was one of President Roosevelt's advisors who called for a nationwide bank holiday.

Henry Morgenthau, Jr. (1891–1967). Morgenthau served as secretary of treasury under President Franklin D. Roosevelt for eleven years, from 1934 until 1945. He replaced the ailing Secretary of the Treasury William H. Woodin.

James Francis Thaddeus O'Connor (1885–1949). President Franklin D. Roosevelt appointed O'Connor comptroller of the currency. O'Connor served in this Treasury Department office until 1938. He presided over the examination and certification to reopen thousands of banks closed during the nationwide bank holiday in March 1933.

Ferdinand Pecora (1882–1971). Born in Nicosia, Sicily, Pecora's family immigrated to the United States in 1887. Pecora graduated from New York law school in 1906. In January 1933 Pecora was hired as legal counsel to the Senate Banking and Currency Committee for its investigation into banking and securities fraud. In that role, Pecora exposed tax and securities fraud and numerous unethical business practices by such banking giants as J.P. Morgan, Winthrop Aldrich of Chase National Bank, and many others. His investigations led directly to the Securities Exchange Act of 1934. Pecora served as one of the original members of the Securities and Exchange Commission.

Henry Bascom Steagall (1873–1943). Henry Steagall was elected to the U.S. House of Representatives in 1914 and remained in the House 28 years until his death. Steagall became chairman of the House Committee on Banking and Currency in 1930. He aided President Herbert Hoover in the creation of the Reconstruction Finance Corporation.

Steagall supported Franklin D. Roosevelt in his bid for the presidency and in March 1933 helped rush the Emergency Banking Act of 1933 through the House of Representatives. A few months later Steagall was influential in drafting the Banking Act of 1933, commonly known as the Glass-Steagall Act. This act included provisions for the Federal Deposit Insurance Corporation (FDIC), which provided deposit insurance to depositors. Long advocated by Steagall, the FDIC provided effective protection to depositors' funds and created lasting confidence in the banking system.

William Hartman Woodin (1868–1934). A lifelong Republican, Woodin became close friends with, and an associate of, Franklin D. Roosevelt during the time they spent together working on the Warm Springs Foundation in February 1933. President-elect Roosevelt appointed Woodin as secretary of treasury for his new administration. Woodin played a critical role in the weeks surrounding Roosevelt's inauguration, with the decision to call a nationwide banking holiday and the putting together of the Emergency Bank Act of 1933. A conservative in money matters, Woodin presided over the development of the Banking Act of 1933 (the Glass-Steagall Act). He resigned his post in January 1934 because of illness and died in May 1934.

Primary Sources

The First Fireside Chat—March 12, 1933

The following is part of President Roosevelt's historic first fireside chat (quoted in Samuel J. Rosenman, *The Public Papers and Addresses of Franklin D. Roosevelt,* 1938, vol. 2). His confident, calming voice over the radio waves explained the nationwide bank holiday and reassured Americans as the banks prepared to reopen the next morning.

> I want to tell you what has been done in the last few days, why it was done, and what the next steps are going to be... First of all, let me state the simple fact that when you deposit money in a bank the bank does not put the money into a safe deposit vault. It invests your money in many different forms of credit—bonds, commercial paper, mortgages and many other kinds of loans. In other words, the bank puts your money to work to keep the wheels turning around. A comparatively small part of the money is kept in currency—an amount which in normal times is wholly sufficient to cover the cash needs of the average citizen. In other words, the total amount of all the currency in the country is only a small fraction of the total deposits in all of the banks.
>
> What, then, happened during the last few days of February and the first few days of March? Because of undermined confidence on the part of the public, there was a general rush by a large portion of our population to turn bank deposits into currency... The reason for this was that on the spur of the moment it was, of course, impossible to sell perfectly sound assets of a bank and convert them into cash except at panic prices far below their real value....
>
> It was then that I issued the proclamation for the nationwide bank holiday ... The second step was the legislation ... passed by the Congress ... to extend the holiday and lift the ban of that holiday gradually. This law also gave authority to develop a program of rehabilitation of our banking facilities ... The new law allows the twelve Federal Reserve Banks to issue additional currency on good assets and thus the banks which reopen will be able to meet every legitimate call ....
>
> As a result, we start tomorrow, Monday, with the opening of banks in the twelve Federal Reserve Bank cities—those banks ... have already been found to be all right .... On ... succeeding days banks in smaller places all through the country will resume business, subject, of course, to the Government's physical ability ... to make common sense checkups ... It is possible that when the banks resume a very few people who have not recovered from their fear may again begin withdrawals. Let me make it clear that the banks will take care of all needs—and it is my belief that ... when the people find that they can get their money ... the phantom of fear will soon be laid. I can assure you that it is safer to keep your money in a reopened bank than under the mattress.
>
> There will be, of course, some banks unable to open without being reorganized. The new law allows the Government to assist in making these reorganizations quickly and effectively ... I do not promise you that every bank will be reopened or that individual losses will not be suffered, but there will be no losses that possibly could have been avoided; and there would have been more and greater losses had we continued to drift. I can even promise you salvation for some at least of the sorely pressed banks .... Confidence and courage are the essentials in carrying out our plan. You people must have faith; you must not be stampeded by rumors ... We have provided the machinery to restore our financial system; it is up to you to support and make it work. Together we cannot fail.

Monday, March 13, 1933

Will Rogers, lecturer, humorist, and social critic, commented on the success of President Roosevelt's first fireside chat that dealt with the banking crisis. His words are reproduced in Susan Winslow's *Brother, Can You Spare a Dime? America from the Wall Street Crash to Pearl Harbor: An Illustrated Documentary,* 1979).

> Mr. Roosevelt stepped to the microphone last night and knocked another home run. His message was not only a great comfort to the people, but it pointed a lesson to all radio announcers and public speakers what to do with a big vocabulary—leave it at home in the dictionary.
>
> Some people spend a lifetime juggling with words, with not an idea in a carload.
>
> Our President took such a dry subject as banking (and when I say 'dry,' I mean dry, for if it had been liquid, he wouldn't have to speak on it at all) and made everybody understand it, even the bankers.

At the Treasury Department

Raymond Moley, a close advisor to President Roosevelt and an assistant secretary of state, observed that the men who worked together to find solutions during the bank crisis of March 1933 had "forgotten to be Republicans or Democrats...we were just a bunch of men trying to save the banking system." The Emergency Banking Act of 1933 and the Banking Act of 1933 resulted. The preceding passage can be found in Helen Burns' book, *The American Banking Community and New Deal Banking Reforms, 1933–1935,* 1974.

Federal Deposit Insurance Corporation (FDIC)

The following statements are from a committee report at the 1934 annual meeting of the American Bankers Association (quoted in Helen Burns, *The American Banking Community and New Deal Banking Reforms, 1933–1935,* 1974). The FDIC was originally established with the Banking Act of 1933. Bankers opposed FDIC's creation. This report represents a dramatic swing in opinion of deposit insurance by the bankers.

> There is no question but that the law guaranteeing deposits has reestablished the confidence of many thousands of small depositors throughout the United States. This has given a certain stability to the banking situation that might not otherwise have existed under all the conditions that have prevailed.

Suggested Research Topics

- Imagine what it would be like if banks closed suddenly for one week. How would you live? Could you get to school or work? What likely alternate ways of paying for necessities would develop?
- The first two national banks were the First Bank of the United States and the Second Bank of the United States. What were their functions and did they survive? What role did the issue of states' rights play?
- Research the organization and function of the modern Federal Reserve System (FRS). Further study the two main committees that direct FRS policies, the Board of Governors and the Federal Open Market Committee.
- Alan Greenspan became chairman of the Federal Reserve Board in 1987 and was very prominent in keeping American economic policy stable at the end of the twentieth century. Explore his early life, including influences and interests, and his career as an adult.

Bibliography

Sources

Benston, George J. *The Separation of Commercial and Investment Banking: The Glass-Steagall Act Revisited and Reconsidered.* New York: Oxford University Press, 1990.

Burns, Helen M. *The American Banking Community and New Deal Banking Reforms, 1933–1935.* Westport, CN: Greenwood Press, 1974.

Glasner, David, ed. *Business Cycles and Depressions: An Encyclopedia.* New York: Garland Publishing, Inc., 1997.

Kennedy, Susan E. *The Banking Crisis of 1933.* Lexington: University Press of Kentucky, 1975.

Roosevelt, Franklin D. *The Public Papers and Addresses of Franklin D. Roosevelt.* New York: Random House, 1938.

White, Eugene N. *The Regulation and Reform of the American Banking System, 1900–1929.* Princeton, NJ: Princeton University Press, 1983.

White, Lawrence J. *The S&L Debacle: Public Policy Lessons for Bank and Thrift Regulation.* New York: Oxford University Press, 1991.

Wicker, Elmus. *The Banking Panics of the Great Depression.* New York: Cambridge University Press, 1996.

Winslow, Susan. *Brother, Can You Spare a Dime? America from the Wall Street Crash to pearl harbor: An Illustrated Documentary.* New York: Paddington Press, 1979.

Further Reading

American Bankers Association. [cited February 20, 2002] available from the World Wide Web at http://www.aba.com.

Bondi, Victor, ed. *American Decades: 1930–1939.* Detroit: Gale Research Inc., 1995.

Compton, Eric N. *Principles of Banking,* 4th ed. Washington, DC: American Bankers Association, 1991.

Federal Deposit Insurance Corporation. [cited February 20, 2002] available from the World Wide Web at http://www.fdic.gov.

Federal Reserve System. [cited February 20, 2002] available from the World Wide Web at http://federalreserve.gov.

Fitch, Thomas P. *Dictionary of Banking Terms.* New York: Barron's, 1990.

Horn, James D. *The Desperate Years: A Pictorial History of the Thirties.* New York: Bonanza Books, 1962.

Leuchtenburg, William E. *Franklin D. Roosevelt and the New Deal: 1932–1940.* New York: Harper & Row, 1963.

McElvaine, Robert S. *The Great Depression: America, 1929–1941.* New York: Times Books, 1993.

Phillips, Cabell. *From the Crash to the Blitz: 1929–1939.* Toronto: The Macmillan Company, 1969.

Schlesinger, Arthur M., Jr. *The Coming of the New Deal: The Age of Roosevelt.* Boston: Houghton Mifflin Company, 1988.

See Also

Causes of the Crash; Global Impact; Housing; New Deal (First, and Its Critics)

Black Americans

1929-1941

Introduction

"Let Jesus lead you and Roosevelt feed you" (quoted in Robert S. McElvaine. *The Great Depression: America, 1929–1941,* 1993). These words were spoken by a black minister to his congregation shortly before the 1936 presidential election.

Hard times were nothing new for black Americans. After all, Southern slavery had ended only a few generations earlier. Nonetheless, the Great Depression made things worse. Black workers were normally the first to lose jobs at a business or on a farm. Often they were denied public works employment supposedly available to all needy citizens. Individuals were even threatened at relief centers when applying for work. In deep frustration many blacks called President Franklin D. Roosevelt's programs a "raw deal" instead of a "new deal." Some charities refused to provide needy black persons food, particularly in the South. To make matters worse, violence rose against blacks during the 1930s, carried out by whites competing for the same jobs. As a result, black Americans suffered more than any other group during the Great Depression.

Racial discrimination was seen in federal housing, social security, and youth programs. Labor unions, including the American Federation of Labor (AFL), actively pursued discriminatory practices. These activities included exclusion of blacks from union membership, lobbying Congress to keep anti-discrimination clauses out of New Deal laws, and striking against companies that employed blacks in jobs desired by whites.

With First Lady Eleanor Roosevelt personally taking up the cause of racial equality, initial steps were directed toward racial harmony by the mid-1930s. The Roosevelt administration ended racial discrimination in some federal programs in 1935. In addition, significant amounts of relief were targeted for black Americans. Consequences of these changes appeared in the 1936 presidential election. The majority of black voters voted for Roosevelt, bringing to an end a 75-year period of black allegiance to Republican candidates. Shortly after the elections, a Black Cabinet, composed of black American government employees, was formed to advise the president. But the president's and Mrs. Roosevelt's support did not come without controversy and loss of political support for the New Deal programs, particularly among Southern Democrats. World War II (1939–1945) finally brought economic relief to black Americans. But significant advances in racial equality would not come until the civil rights movement pressed for changes in the 1950s and 1960s. The New Deal was a period of great economic suffering, small political gains, and lost social opportunities.

Chronology:

1929: The radio program *Amos 'n' Andy,* exploiting all stereotypes held by white America of blacks, becomes the most popular radio program in the nation, attracting 60 percent of the radio-listening public.

1933: The number of lynchings of blacks in the United States during the Great Depression peaks at twenty-eight.

1935: President Franklin Roosevelt issues an executive order prohibiting discrimination in new Works Progress Administration projects, one of the first anti-discrimination measures in U.S. history.

1936: Mary McLeod Bethune becomes head of the National Youth Administration's Division of Negro Affairs, the first black American to head a government agency.

1937: Roosevelt appoints NAACP attorney William Hastie as the first black federal judge in U.S. history.

1939: The denial of world famous American opera singer Marian Anderson the opportunity of performing in a private concert hall in Washington, DC because of her race leads to a major public backlash against racism in the nation.

1939: Roosevelt's Attorney General Frank Murphy establishes the Civil Rights Section in the federal Justice Department.

1941: Roosevelt signs an executive order prohibiting racial discrimination in the defense industry, the first such proclamation since Reconstruction in the 1870s.

Issue Summary

Tough Times Turn Harder

Racism in the 1920s invaded every aspect of life in the United States. Many people outwardly expressed such feelings in public with few reservations. Given this longstanding social atmosphere, black Americans naturally suffered greatly when the economy declined in 1929. Those employed were often the first to be laid off when company fortunes fell. The slogan "Last Hired, First Fired" became well known. By 1932 black Americans had a 50 percent unemployment rate compared to 25 percent in the U.S. population in general. With unemployment escalating, jobs previously considered "Negro occupations" suddenly became attractive to the larger population. These jobs included domestic help, elevator operators, street cleaners, garbage collectors, waiters, and bellhops. Blacks were considered fit for only low paying dirty jobs no one else wanted. In Atlanta the slogan "No Jobs for Niggers Until Every White Man Has a Job" became popular among whites. Those blacks able to keep their jobs sometimes had their wages cut in half. The Pulitzer Prize winning novel *To Kill a Mockingbird* by Harper Lee, written years later in 1960, was based on the racial prejudices of the 1930s. The story focuses on the courtroom trial of an unjustly accused black man. It examined the ignorance, prejudice, and hate that characterized that period. An award-winning movie was later adapted from the book.

Depression in the Rural South

In 1930 over two million males worked in agriculture. Of these over 835,000 black farmers and laborers faced particularly difficult times in the rural South. Less than 13 percent of black farmers owned their own land. The rest worked as sharecroppers and

A woman and her baby inside their slum apartment in Washington DC in 1937. Many black people were deprived of adequate food, shelter, clothing, education, and health care during the Great Depression. (The Library of Congress.)

tenant farmers on farms of large landowners. Approximately 40 percent of black workers in the nation in the 1930s were farm laborers, sharecroppers, and tenant farmers. Not only was a declining economy a threat to their employment, new machines, such as mechanical cotton pickers, displaced many farm workers. For those black sharecroppers still working, discrimination in pay was common. White sharecroppers received an average income of $417 a year compared to $295 for blacks. Not surprisingly with such low wages, living conditions were deplorable. Many black families lived in one- or two-bedroom shacks with no electricity, insulation from the winter cold, or running water. Relief through private organizations in the South was rarely available to needy blacks. Sharecropper families would often drift from one farm to another every three years or so in search of better living conditions.

Some sharecropper unions formed to seek better conditions. But these groups often met harsh resistance from the large white landowners and local law authorities. The Croppers' and Farm Workers' Union and the Share Croppers' Union were formed in 1931. Both met with violence. In Alabama just before Christmas in 1931 a force of vigilantes and authorities attacked an entire black population in Reeltown, Alabama, to break up union activities. Hundreds were injured and two killed. The incident did bring increased public sympathy to the plight of black sharecroppers.

As the economy struggled through the 1930s, jobs grew even scarcer. Competition between whites and blacks brought added hostility. The number of lynchings of blacks by white mobs increased from eight in 1932 to 28 in 1933, 15 in 1934, and 20 in 1935. Lynching is a form of mob violence in which a mob, operating in the name of justice but without holding a trial, executes a person suspected of committing some offense. Usually the victim is tortured and their body mutilated in some way. Hanging was a common form of lynching, though some victims were burned alive. Almost all occurred in the South. The number of lynchings finally dropped to two in 1939 as economic conditions improved for whites. However, blatant racism, the most dominant factor contributing to these murders, still propelled lynchings in the South for the next several decades.

Hard Times in the Urban North

The Great Migration of southern rural blacks to northern industrial centers seeking employment decreased some during the Great Depression as job opportunities declined. At least if they stayed on the farm they could grow some food in the garden, even if they were not making money. Still, 400,000 blacks made the journey north during the 1930s. At least two benefits of living in the North inspired their continued migration. One benefit was to escape the racial violence of the South. Secondly, blacks experienced less discrimination by relief organizations in the North.

For those already living in the North, the steadily growing black population only meant greater hardships. More and more people were competing for fewer and fewer jobs. Black Americans organized cooperative groups such as the Colored Merchants Association in New York City to help each other. "Jobs for Negroes" organizations appeared in several cities. These groups bought food and other goods for black residents in large volume so they could get lower prices. Boycotts were also organized against stores that served mostly black customers but employed few black workers.

Blacks faced yet another obstacle during the Great Depression. With husbands unemployed or taking pay cuts, the incomes of their wives became that much more critical. But with hard times for everyone, many white women began seeking jobs for the first time. They took jobs traditionally held by black women such as maids, housekeepers, and cooks.

With the increasing loss of jobs, blacks became disproportionately represented in breadlines at relief centers. Not all impacts were economic. As black unemployment rose, membership in clubs, churches, and other organizations declined. Black society was unraveling and many personal relationships were lost.

Little Relief From Hoover

As the Depression was hitting black American laborers hard, some new opportunities for other blacks were appearing. Black representation in the federal government workforce increased in President Herbert Hoover's (served 1929–1933) administration. Known as a humanitarian and a reformer, Hoover appointed more blacks to mid-level federal positions than his predecessors. He also began a program to fight the high illiteracy rate among blacks. Hoover argued for the equal opportunity of both black and white sharecroppers to own land. However, Hoover's economic policies did little to help most black Americans. In 1930 Hoover created the Reconstruction Finance Corporation (RFC) to turn the struggling economy around. But the RFC primarily gave loans to railroads, banks, and insurance companies with hope they would create new businesses and jobs. The effort to boost the economy did not trickle down to black workers as Hoover had envisioned.

Black American Population, 1900-1940

Year	Population	Percent of Total Population
1900	8,833,994	11.6%
1910	9,827,763	10.7
1920	10,183,131	9.6
1930	11,091,143	9.0
1940	12,665,513	10.3

The percentage of black Americans in the total population remained steady from 1900 to 1940. (The Gale Group.)

The 1932 Presidential Election

Hoover's policies did little to economically help black Americans. He even refused to be photographed with blacks. Still, 66 percent of blacks who voted cast their ballots for Hoover over Democratic candidate Franklin D. Roosevelt in the 1932 presidential election.

Roosevelt's campaign had offered little to blacks. Despite pressure from the National Association for the Advancement of Colored People (NAACP), the Democratic Party refused to adopt a position prohibiting racial discrimination. In fact a stark level of racism was openly displayed in the Democratic Party. For this reason it was in Franklin D. Roosevelt's best interest during his 1932 presidential bid to not express any anti-discrimination feelings. Being a northern Democrat, Roosevelt was careful not to say anything that would upset southern party leaders and lose their support. Roosevelt's campaign staff had no blacks. He even issued a public statement earlier in 1929 denying he had eaten lunch with blacks. Earlier yet he had quietly stood by as President Woodrow Wilson (served 1913–1921) instituted a racial segregation system in the Navy during World War I (1914–1918).

No Relief from the First New Deal

Despite the black vote overwhelmingly going to Hoover, Roosevelt readily won the presidency. Once in office President Roosevelt continued an effort to not disturb southern Democrats. Early New Deal programs did not address the plight of black America directly. Any efforts by him to improve race relations, Roosevelt believed, would significantly undercut support for his main economic recovery measures. Southern support in Congress would be lost. If the critical economic legislation did not pass, both white and black Americans would be hurt. Therefore, President Roosevelt resolutely refused to make civil rights and racial equality a priority for the New Deal.

The son of a sharecropper helps out on a North Carolina tobacco farm in 1939. Black sharecroppers, facing low wages and deplorable living conditions, usually moved from farm to farm in search of better living conditions. (The Library of Congress.)

With no New Deal legislation addressing racial discrimination, discriminatory practices were widespread in the new programs. For example, many of the National Recovery Administration's (NRA) programs establishing standard wage rates did less to help blacks than whites. Many black jobs were still in the South where regional wage rates were established lower than other regions of the country. In fact the program did not even cover many black occupations such as farm labor and domestic helpers. Consequently, the NRA programs in effect perpetuated racial pay discrimination. Even in situations where blacks might receive equal pay as whites, it often meant unemployed whites would replace the blacks. Or, businesses simply ignored the NRA guidelines and paid the white workers more than blacks for the same jobs. They argued that the lower standard of living of blacks meant they could live on less.

Similarly, Congress passed the Agricultural Adjustment Act in May of 1933 to provide economic relief to the nation's farmers. The act created the Agricultural Adjustment Administration (AAA) to pay farmers to not grow crops on parts of their farms. The goal was to decrease the production of crops so that market prices and the farmers' incomes would eventually go up. But this program essentially reduced the incomes of black farmers. For those blacks that owned land, routinely they held less land than white landowners. With less acreage available to qualify for payments, they received smaller government payments. Removing land from production was too great a hardship for many. Since they left no land unplanted, they received no government payments. The agricultural program meant that many black farmers could no longer afford to keep their own land.

Most black Americans did not own the land they farmed. This made them even more vulnerable to the AAA's crop production control measures. So they could qualify for the AAA benefit checks, often the white landowner would pull the acreage they had leased to tenants. They would frequently keep the benefits for themselves and not share it with the tenant farmers as required by the act. The number of sharecroppers declined from over 390,000 in 1930 to less than 300,000 in just a few years.

Black farmers had little means to correct the problems. To gain farmer support for the early New Deal programs, the programs relied on local administration. This effort to encourage grassroots support meant those traditionally in power—the white landowners and business leaders—would control how federal benefits were distributed. County committees set up to run the AAA programs banned black participation. As a result the AAA continued the poor condition of rural black Americans in the nation. In 1934 the average income of black cotton farmers was less than $200 a year.

The popular Tennessee Valley Authority (TVA) program, also created in 1933, initially offered hope to blacks in parts of the Southeast. But the program essentially barred blacks from skilled and management jobs. Blacks were even barred from the new federal model town of Norris, Tennessee. Norris, named after Senator George W. Norris of Nebraska who sponsored the TVA act, was built by TVA to house construction workers who were building the Norris Dam, the first major dam built by TVA. Given the local oversight of hiring workers and managing the projects, black Americans were excluded both from higher paying construction jobs and residence in the company town. As a result, blacks in the area continued to live in shacks with no electrical wiring. Consequently, the black tenant farmers in the region received little benefit from the cheap electricity generated by the new TVA hydroelectric dams.

Why Not Promote Civil Rights?

Despite the activism of the New Deal President Roosevelt consistently rejected appeals by the black community to correct some of the social injustices imbedded in American society. White supremacy still ruled American politics, and President Roosevelt rightly figured that anyone who promoted civil rights issues would quickly lose political support to accomplish much of anything.

In 1933 Franklin Roosevelt, while constructing his New Deal program, rejected pleas to include civil rights issues. Roosevelt commented (quoted in Robert S. McElvaine, *The Great Depression: America, 1929–1941,* p. 188),

> First things come first, and I can't alienate certain votes I need for measures that are more important at the moment by pushing any measures that would entail a fight. I've got to get legislation passed by Congress to save America.

To his advisor Walter White, Roosevelt argued (McElvaine, p. 189),

> The Southerners by reason of the seniority rule in Congress are chairmen or occupy strategic places on most of the Senate and House committees. If I come out for the anti-lynching bill now, they will block every bill I ask Congress to pass to keep America from collapsing. I just can't take that risk.

By 1937 and 1938, however, Roosevelt's support on the New Deal was waning. Despite his choice not to actively seek to improve the situation for blacks, he lost support from the conservative element of the Democratic Party, partly over racial equality issues.

Eleanor Roosevelt

One person was particularly responsible for changing the attitude of the federal government toward helping black Americans. That person was First Lady Eleanor Roosevelt. Eleanor had long held strong sympathies for the less fortunate in society. But she was especially struck by the uproar caused in 1933 by her simply having lunch with a black woman in Florida. Intent on making a difference in public attitudes toward racism, she took up the black cause for social justice and economic betterment. Her outspokenness on civil rights issues served to greatly raise public awareness of the problems. In a 1934 speech to a conference on black education, Eleanor Roosevelt stated that "the day of working together has come, and we must learn to work together, all of us, regardless of race or creed or color ... We go ahead together or we go down together." (quoted in Robert S. McElvaine. *The Great Depression: America, 1929–1941,* 1993).

The First Lady used many avenues to promote black issues. She held weekly press conferences with women reporters, she conducted lectures across the country, and she had her own radio program, and wrote her own syndicated newspaper column, "My Day." Also, while traveling widely, she became her husband's eyes and ears, particularly regarding issues concerning the underprivileged and racial minorities. While in Puerto Rico in early 1934, Eleanor made a point of being photographed where the public back home could see the dire living conditions in parts of the Caribbean.

Eleanor also used her unique access to policymakers as First Lady to strongly lobby for greater federal assistance to the black community and recognition of civil rights. As an example she addressed congressional committees, conferred with committee chairmen, and wrote letters to members of Congress demanding that childcare assistance be provided.

At a Glance

"Don't Buy Where You Can't Work"

Black Americans used many tactics during the Great Depression to try to expand jobs for blacks. One approach in the northern cities was the "Don't Buy Where You Can't Work" campaign. The strategy targeted those white merchants who primarily served a black community but refused to hire black employees or only hired them for low-paying positions. Blacks would boycott targeted stores. In New York City, the Reverend John H. Johnson formed Citizens League for Fair Play. They would establish picket lines outside the targeted store then take photographs of blacks that crossed the picket lines. The local black newspaper would publish them.

This strategy greatly discouraged potential shoppers from crossing picket lines and being revealed to their friends and neighbors. The amount of business was considerably reduced. When this tactic was applied to Blumstein's Department Store, the store finally relented after six weeks of boycotts and hired black clerks and professional staff. This campaign constituted the nation's first affirmative action hiring program, giving hiring preferences to minority groups previously excluded. The strategy brought economic gains to the black communities. In 1938 the New York Uptown Chamber of Commerce agreed to hire blacks in one-third of all executive, clerical, and sales jobs in retail businesses.

Unlike her husband, the president, Eleanor also publicly supported the passage of anti-lynching bills.

This role of social activism was unprecedented for a First Lady. Her action led to inclusion of black Americans into the political Democratic coalition, aligning the black vote with the party for the rest of the twentieth century. Speaking out against racial segregation in public places, Eleanor became the target of intense abuse from white racists.

Eleanor continued her crusade even after the Great Depression and New Deal years and Franklin's death in April 1945. The following December President Harry Truman (served 1945–1953) appointed Eleanor to be a member of the U.S. delegation to the United Nations (UN). As chairwoman of the Commission on Human Rights she was instrumental in drafting the historic UN Declaration of Human Rights.

Support from the Left and Labor

Communists, socialists, and major labor organizations joined the push for racial equality. The Communist Party eagerly took up the black cause in the United States. Aggressive public efforts by the party served to substantially increase public awareness of black issues. The Communists staged demonstrations and took legal actions. The party also worked on a day-to-day basis supporting activities aimed at combating hunger and unemployment. However, a proportionally small number of blacks ever actually joined the party.

The Socialist Party through the United Colored Socialists of America also took up black interests. They aggressively challenged racial discrimination in labor unions. The Socialist Party also lobbied for anti-lynching laws and equal voting rights. In the South they organized sharecroppers unions, including the Southern Tenant Farmers Union.

In 1935 the Committee for Industrial Organization formed within the American Federation of Labor (AFL). Under leadership of John L. Lewis the CIO represented mass production industries that employed many black American workers. The AFL focused more on skilled workers. Unlike the AFL the CIO recruited blacks to its membership. Lewis also headed the United Mine Workers of America, which recruited both whites and blacks. Other influential organizations became members of the CIO, including the United Automobile Workers (UAW). Black representatives attained leadership roles in these unions. Thanks to CIO efforts eventually the AFL opened its membership to blacks as well. By 1939 blacks were well accepted in labor unions. Through the 1930s the CIO was one of the most important supporters of civil rights.

Riot in Harlem

The only race riot to occur during the Great Depression erupted in New York's Harlem on March 19, 1935. On that day a rumor began quickly spreading that police had brutally beaten a black Puerto Rican youth suspected of stealing a knife from a store. Although in actuality the youth was released unharmed, violence erupted. Store windows were smashed and stores looted through the night. Three people were killed and one hundred injured. Considerable property damage resulted to about 250 shops. The incident alerted President Roosevelt to the increasing explosive nature of race relations in the North as well as the South.

The New Deal Reaches Out

By early 1935 President Roosevelt began to take more direct action in black issues. In May 1935 he issued Executive Order 7046 prohibiting discrimination in the newly created Works Progress Administration (WPA). Within a few short years after President Roosevelt's order between 15 and 20 percent of WPA workers, or about 230,000, were black. Their inclusion enabled many blacks to economically survive the Depression. Reflecting the low economic status of black Americans, the minimum wage of WPA—set at $12 a week—was twice the amount many had previously earned. The Civilian Conservation Corps (CCC) proved less responsive, largely due to its greater reliance on local implementation. Only about 250,000 black American men (7 percent) served in the CCC through the decade. Some areas would not select blacks for CCC work positions at all. In Georgia where 36 percent of the population was black, less than 2 percent of the CCC enrollment was black.

Sensitive to the criticism that his farm policies were harmful to the small farmer, Roosevelt created the Resettlement Administration (RA) in 1935. Roosevelt named Will Alexander, who had focused on black poverty issues throughout his career, to lead the agency. For the rural poor, the agency sought to end sharecropping, tenant farming, and migratory labor, and to promote land ownership. One of the RA's initial goals was to resettle 500,000 farm families onto their own productive lands. The program attracted considerable opposition from existing white landowners who relied on such cheap labor. As a result the agency fell short with only 4,441 families eventually relocated. The RA also sought to relocate the poor from urban slums into planned towns in the suburbs. This program met the strong resistance of real estate developers. Though the initial goal was the creation of 25 towns, only three were actually constructed and settled.

The New Democratic Coalition

The humanitarian interests of Eleanor Roosevelt and others, in addition to Franklin Roosevelt's increasing recognition of the growing importance of the black vote in national politics, led President Roosevelt to include blacks in the new Democratic coalition he was building. American attitudes toward race were changing, and blacks were becoming more politically organized. Even before Roosevelt began to take steps for inclusion, the black vote had begun swinging away from Republican candidates for the first time in the 75-odd years since the Civil War (1861–1865). In the 1934 midterm elections, Arthur Mitchell became the first black Democrat to win a seat in Congress, upsetting a black Republican incumbent in Chicago.

The 1936 presidential election marked a historic turnaround in party allegiance by black voters. Whereas Hoover won 66 percent of the black vote in 1932, Roosevelt won 76 percent of the black vote only four years later. Many blacks voted for the first time, encouraged by Roosevelt's actions. Just as President Roosevelt had earlier anticipated, however, in reaction to his increasing support of civil rights issues, the southern Democrat support of New Deal programs waned. Many feared that not only was Roosevelt introducing socialism to America but racial equality as well. Some charged Roosevelt with instituting a second Reconstruction period. The first Reconstruction was when the Federal government had tried to force social and economic change on the South following the Civil War. Actually the "second Reconstruction" would not happen until the 1960s, three decades later. But President Roosevelt was beginning to lay the foundation for increased activism.

New Hope

Following reelection, President Roosevelt began taking more assertive steps for racial equality. At the time when no blacks were in high enough positions in government to advise the president, Roosevelt appointed forty-five blacks to various federal positions. In 1936 Roosevelt informally assembled a group of black leaders who held mid-level government positions to advise him on black issues. Such a group had never before existed. They called themselves the Federal Council on Negro Affairs, but soon the press began calling the group the "Black Cabinet." The group would periodically visit the White House to meet with the president.

The Black Cabinet included: William H. Hastie, an attorney in the Interior Department; Robert C. Weaver, an economist in the Interior Department; Edgar Brown of Civilian Conservation Corps; Robert L. Vann, editor of the Pittsburgh Courier and special assistant in the Justice Department; Lawrence A. Oxley, a social worker in the Department of Labor; and, key organizer Mary McLeod Bethune, administrator in the National Youth Administration. This advisory group was one way in which President Roosevelt reached out to black Americans. As a result the Democratic Party gained the support of black Americans across the nation, but few tangible results came from the cabinet's activities.

Biography:

Mary McLeod Bethune

1875–1955, Bethune was a black woman born to a South Carolina sharecropper's family with seventeen children. She won scholarships to college and after graduating set up a school for black women in Daytona Beach, Florida. In 1923 the school merged with Cookman Institute in Jacksonville to become Bethune-Cookman College with Bethune president. She founded the National Council of Negro Women and gained respect nationally as vice president of the NAACP.

A respected educator, she became an advisor to President Calvin Coolidge in the 1920s. In 1927 she began a personal friendship with Eleanor Roosevelt and through the years greatly increased Roosevelt's understanding of black problems and issues. Bethune was instrumental in organizing President Franklin Roosevelt's "Black Cabinet."

She was appointed assistant to Aubrey Williams, director of the National Youth Administration (NYA), and became head of NYA's Division of Negro Affairs. She was the first black American to head a government agency. The NYA was considered a model of government assistance for blacks. Bethune reportedly helped some six thousand black Americans complete their educations.

Bethune also organized conferences in 1937 and 1939 on the impact of federal policies on black Americans. The conferences highlighted several key issues of black Americans at the time: (1) unemployment and lack of economic security for blacks; (2) a need for educational and recreational facilities; (3) poor health and housing situations; and (4) fear of mob violence.

Judge William H. Hastie is awarded the Spingarn Medal, an honor by the NAACP for outstanding achievement by a black American. Hastie was the first black American Federal judge to be appointed. (AP/Wide World Photos. Reproduced by permission.)

The president resisted the push for anti-lynching laws and prohibitions against the poll tax, two major civil rights goals of the 1930s. He feared losing critical support of the southern Democrats for his New Deal programs. Still the cabinet represented political access to the White House never before enjoyed by black Americans.

Despite the lack of significant promotion of civil rights by the Roosevelt administration, New Deal programs did begin increasing their assistance to blacks. The Public Works Administration (PWA) provided some public housing for black tenants. The PWA even constructed several racially integrated housing projects. In addition 31 percent of PWA wages went to black workers in 1936. In another historic move, one of the first racial hiring quota systems was introduced into government. Secretary of Interior Harold Ickes directed the hiring of black workers on PWA projects

Biography:
A. Philip Randolph

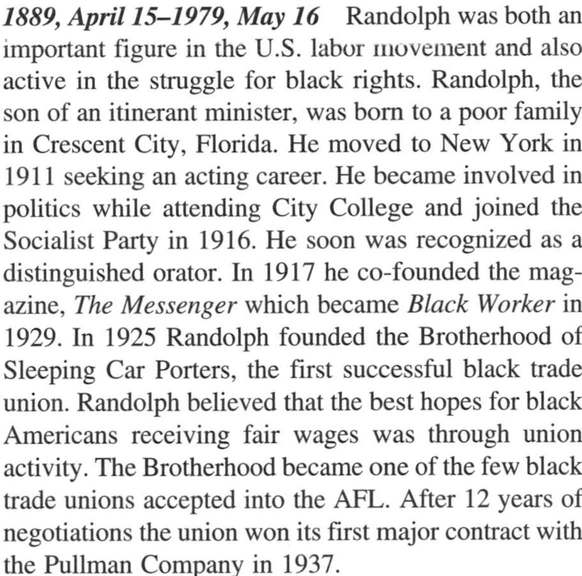

1889, April 15–1979, May 16 Randolph was both an important figure in the U.S. labor movement and also active in the struggle for black rights. Randolph, the son of an itinerant minister, was born to a poor family in Crescent City, Florida. He moved to New York in 1911 seeking an acting career. He became involved in politics while attending City College and joined the Socialist Party in 1916. He soon was recognized as a distinguished orator. In 1917 he co-founded the magazine, *The Messenger* which became *Black Worker* in 1929. In 1925 Randolph founded the Brotherhood of Sleeping Car Porters, the first successful black trade union. Randolph believed that the best hopes for black Americans receiving fair wages was through union activity. The Brotherhood became one of the few black trade unions accepted into the AFL. After 12 years of negotiations the union won its first major contract with the Pullman Company in 1937.

With government and industry mobilizing to prepare for World War II, Randolph became a leader in fighting for black job opportunities in both. A climax came in 1941 when Randolph threatened to lead a march on Washington, DC, on June 25 to demand better jobs for black Americans in the defense industry. President Roosevelt, not wanting to see such a demonstration at that time, signed an executive order barring discrimination in defense industries under contract with the federal government and within the federal government itself. The order also established the Fair Employment Practices Committee. Following the war Randolph led a crusade for ending racial segregation in the armed forces. He was once again successful with President Harry Truman signing another executive order on July 26, 1948, prohibiting racial segregation in the services.

When the AFL and CIO merged in 1955, Randolph became vice president and sat on the executive council of the combined organization. Becoming an elder statesman for the growing civil rights movement, Randolph helped organize with Dr. Martin Luther King the August 1963 march on Washington, DC. Two hundred thousand whites and blacks united seeking an end to social injustice. Randolph remained the president of the Sleeping Car Union until 1968.

---

in proportion to their presence in the local workforce. Other milestones occurred. In 1937 President Roosevelt appointed NAACP attorney William Hastie as the first black federal judge in American history. Two years later, in 1939, President Roosevelt's Attorney General Frank Murphy established the Justice Department's Civil Rights Section.

The Civilian Conservation Corps, created in 1933 to work on public projects, expanded the number of black workers from 6 percent in 1936 to 11 percent by 1939. Photography sessions of President Roosevelt with black leaders began to occur, and civil rights delegations visited the White House. Still, racial discrimination was widespread in New Deal programs. The rise of black ghettos was in part a result of New Deal public housing policies that did not go far enough to help blacks.

Activism Within the Black Community

Organization within the U.S. black community itself increased. In 1936 Ralph Bunche and John Davis formed the National Negro Congress (NNC). The organization brought together all existing black political groups to press for economic recovery. Representatives of nearly six hundred participating organizations elected A. Philip Randolph its first president.

In 1937 the Carnegie Corporation hired Swedish economist Gunnar Myrdal to study race relations in the United States. A number of scholars assisted in the study. In reporting his findings, Myrdal wrote the influential 1944 publication *An American Dilemma: The Negro Problem and Modern Democracy.* The problem, as Myrdal concluded, was not the natural capabilities of black Americans. The problem was white racism and policies promoting racial inequality.

Blacks and the Arts

Some WPA programs not only provided employment to black Americans, but promoted social justice as well. The Federal Theater Project introduced new ideas to America, including racial equality. Blacks were portrayed as highly capable, equal human beings. Sixteen black theater groups were established around

More About...

National Negro Congress

The U.S. Communist Party (CP) aggressively took up the issues of black America in the 1930s. The CP fought for legal rights and jobs for blacks in the courts and politics. Though many blacks were grateful for whatever source of support they could muster during these particularly difficult times, few actually joined the CP. One of the exceptional cases of formal interaction was through the National Negro Congress (NNC) formed in 1936. The NNC grew out of a 1935 conference organized by black leader Ralph T. Bunche and civil rights activist John P. Davis. Bunche was chairman of Harvard University's political science department. The conference, titled the "Status of the Negro in the New Deal," was held at Howard University in Washington, DC. The conference focused on the major issues of lynchings and violence against blacks. It also considered the lack of support coming from President Roosevelt and his New Deal programs. The president did not want to antagonize southern Democrats and lose their crucial political support for his economic measures. The NNC brought together a diverse range of people including Communist sympathizers, Socialists such as labor leader A. Philip Randolph, and liberals such as the leaders of the National Association for the Advancement of Colored People (NAACP).

The NNC's focus through the late 1930s was on opposition to lynching and the Scottsboro 9 case, in which nine black Alabama youths were unjustly accused of sexually assaulting two white girls. The NNC was also involved in labor and foreign issues. The organization sought to organize workers in mass production industries and join the CIO. The NNC also supported the Spanish republican government against local fascist forces and Ethiopia against invasion from fascist Italy. Pacts between Communist Russia and Nazi Germany caused a major split among members of the organization. It became further weakened with the entrance of the United States into World War II. Following the war the NNC was absorbed into the Civil Rights Congress in 1946, which fought for civil rights on a broader scale. Several former NNC members played crucial roles in the 1950s civil rights movement.

the country. Though casts remained racially segregated, the characters in the plays were not. A major milestone came when a black production of a Shakespearean classic, *Macbeth,* appeared in Harlem. Young Orson Welles directed the play. It was set in Haiti with Voodoo priestesses serving as the play's witch characters. The play proved a major success.

Other WPA programs also promoted black achievements. The Federal Music Project staged concerts involving works of black composers. The Federal Art Project employed hundreds of black artists. The WPA taught almost 250,000 blacks how to read and write.

The Federal Writers Project provided opportunities and early training for young black writers and scholars. Zora Neale Hurston wrote the novel *Their Eyes Were Watching God,* first published in 1937. The novel focuses on a proud, independent black woman's search for identity while experiencing three marriages and a search for her roots. Richard Wright, born on a Mississippi plantation, won a WPA writing prize in 1938 with *Uncle Tom's Children,* a collection of short stories of black life in the South. In 1940 he published *Native Son,* a story about blacks migrating to northern cities and the racism they faced. The book passed John Steinbeck's *Grapes of Wrath* on the best sellers list. Another black author, William Attaway, in 1941 published *Blood on the Forge,* a book about the lives and hardships of black workers.

Because the theater and writing projects promoted interracial understanding, they attracted strong resistance from white supremacists. The programs came under investigation of the U.S. House of Representatives' Un-American Activities Committee. The Committee charged the programs with conspiracy to subvert American ideas and beliefs.

A Start

Some gains for black Americans occurred under New Deal programs, more so in the late 1930s. They not only provided economic relief to many blacks, but also increased the overall quality of life. Life expectancy at birth of black Americans increased through the 1930s. For black women it increased from 49 to 55 years of age (compared to 63 to 67 for white women) and from 47 to 52 for black men (compared to 60 to 62 for white men). Black illiteracy dropped during the decade from over 16 percent to 11.5 percent by 1940.

Much was left to later generations to correct. With resurgence of political conservatism in 1938, President Roosevelt had little inclination to push the black cause further. As the economy began to improve in

1940 and 1941, black Americans were the last to get off of relief programs. Jobs opened sooner for whites.

The arrival of World War II opened up many new economic opportunities for white Americans, and eventually for blacks as well. Defense-related industries expanded, leading many more blacks to move from the rural South to northern cities. Yet in 1940 less than 2 percent of workers in the growing aircraft industry were black. One company even stated that blacks would only be considered for janitorial jobs. Such discrimination was promoted by craft unions such as the International Association of Machinists. Black women faced even greater discrimination. They were relegated to domestic service jobs. A. Philip Randolph of the Brotherhood Car Porters and head of the NNC threatened to lead a march on Washington, DC in 1941 to protest job discrimination. On June 25, 1941, President Roosevelt, wishing to forestall the march, issued an executive order prohibiting discrimination in defense industries and creating the President's Committee on Fair Employment Practices (FEPC). This order was the first proclamation of its kind since Reconstruction of the 1870s. The FEPC was given the responsibility to hold public hearings when complaints arose concerning business hiring practices and to propose new public policies. However, since FEPC had no enforcement powers and little budget or staff, neither business leaders nor even many government officials took it very seriously. Even Roosevelt provided little support for fear of angering southern Democrats. It soon faded away in 1943.

Though Roosevelt had addressed racial discrimination and segregation to various degrees in government agencies and government contractors, the armed forces remained a segregated world. The marines and coast guard barred blacks altogether. Activists were continually challenging the armed forces to open up more opportunities, but segregation would not end in the military until the late 1940s under order of President Harry Truman (served 1945–1953).

Contributing Forces

Black Americans had historically been among the nation's most underprivileged segments of society. During the early nineteenth century, black slaves were a key element of the U.S. economy providing cheap labor for the South's agricultural region. Freedom following the Civil War brought little relief, as white supremacy remained a key part of American daily life and segregation became the norm. Segregation means maintaining a separation of the races.

Though racial segregation had been addressed by the Roosevelt administration in government agencies and contractors during the Great Depression, it wasn't until the late 1940s that blacks and whites were allowed to work side-by-side in the armed forces. (National Archives and Records Administration.)

Jim Crow Laws

Following defeat of the South in the American Civil War the U.S. government attempted to force social and economic change in the South. This program was known as Reconstruction. These efforts met strong southern resistance. By 1877 reform programs had lost their momentum, and white southerners regained control of the region. Political leaders began promoting segregationist policies and reversing the few gains in racial equality achieved through Reconstruction policies.

State legislatures created a legal system, referred to as Jim Crow laws, separating the races in every aspect of daily life. This system particularly affected access to public facilities. Anyone even suspected of having black ancestry was subjected to these segregationist policies. The name Jim Crow came from a popular white minstrel show performer of the 1800s who played a black character. The name became a derogatory symbol for blacks.

Jim Crow laws survived legal challenges in the 1890s. The U.S. Supreme Court ruled in *Plessy v.*

Ferguson that racial segregation was legally acceptable to promote the public good. The Court's "separate but equal" doctrine resembled more "separate but unequal" treatment. It dominated segregationists' policies through the 1930s and beyond. Racism became the legacy of slavery.

Jim Crow laws required the separation of races in every facet of life, including transportation, schools, lodging, public parks, theaters, hospitals, neighborhoods, cemeteries, and restaurants. Business owners and public institutions could not allow black and white customers to intermingle. Inter-racial marriages were prohibited. Blacks had to live with inferior facilities, access, and service. The objective was to deprive blacks of key economic and social opportunities. They were also deprived of adequate food, shelter, clothing, education, and health care. The laws also limited black voting rights through various discriminatory voting requirements, including literacy tests and poll taxes. Whites controlled political power.

The National Association for the Advancement of Colored People (NAACP), created in 1909, took the lead in combating Jim Crow laws. The NAACP began legally challenging housing segregation during the 1910s. NAACP lawyers soon gained a major victory in a Louisville, Kentucky, case. In *Buchanan v. Warley* (1917), the U.S. Supreme Court ruled that government-supported segregated housing laws were unconstitutional. However, the NAACP suffered a major setback nine years later when challenging private contracts banning the sale of housing to blacks. In *Corrigan v. Buckley* (1926), the Court ruled private individuals had the right to discriminate in such sales. The *Corrigan* decision dominated legal views on racial segregation into the 1930s.

The Great Migration

Between 1910 and 1930 approximately one million southern blacks moved to northern cities. They were escaping racial discrimination, poverty, crop failures, and lynchings, as well as seeking employment in the new industrial centers. However, once in the North many found they lacked adequate skills and education. They ended up with jobs as laborers or servants or remained unemployed. Unsanitary conditions, run-down housing, poverty, crime, and despair characterized the growing black ghettos.

Racism in America

In the 1920s U.S. society was strongly and openly racist. The entertainment media often portrayed black Americans as stupid and laughable. With white actors speaking the parts of black characters, the radio program called *Amos 'n' Andy* began in 1928. It exploited all the stereotypes held by white America at that time. By 1929 it was the most popular radio program in the nation, attracting 60 percent of all radio listeners. "Darky" jokes were popular, and amusement parks had games called "Hit the Coon and Get a Cigar." Racism and discrimination clearly carried over into the job market. During the economic prosperity of the 1920s, black unemployment rates remained high.

Associated with racism and white supremacy were lynchings. Lynching had long been a violent tradition in the South. From 1889 to 1933, some 3,745 people, mostly black Americans, had been lynched. The most incidents occurred in 1892 with 255 lynchings. Rarely did local police authorities pursue those committing the murders, as it was predominately a white attack on blacks for some alleged crime against a white. Often the actual victim of the lynching was innocent. Lynchings in the South continued into the 1960s with murders of civil rights workers.

With a rash of lynchings and race riots from 1911 through 1916, the NAACP formed an Anti-lynching Committee. The committee began compiling data, investigating the specific cases of lynching, and organized business and political leaders. It also conducted a major fund raising campaign to provide a legal defense for those arrested in a race riot in East St. Louis, Illinois, in 1917. A "Silent Protest Parade" was also held in New York City in July 1917. The march attracted more prominent black Americans to the organization. In 1919 the NAACP published "Thirty Years of Lynching in the United States, 1889–1918." However, racial violence only escalated in 1919. The most violent incident occurred in Phillips County, Arkansas, when over two hundred people, mostly black Americans, were killed by a large group of armed whites. The whites were attacking blacks thought to be organizing to combat social injustice in the South. The NAACP lawyers defended many blacks that were arrested. The court proceedings led to a successful U.S. Supreme Court decision in 1923, *Moore v. Dempsey,* which overturned the previous conviction of a black. The decision provided a guarantee of legal protection from mob actions. Through the 1920s the NAACP focused on anti-lynching legislation.

The notion of equality before the law in the United States, though supposedly affirmed for black Americans by the Fourteenth Amendment to the U.S. Constitution following the Civil War, still had a long way to develop. The emphasis of courts was still on protection of property rights under the Constitution rather than individual rights. In addition to Jim Crow laws enforcing public segregation, other traditional dis-

Richard Wright won a WPA writer's award for his novel Uncle Tom's Cabin, *a collection of short stories about black life in the South.* *(AP/Wide World Photos. Reproduced by permission.)*

criminatory practices persisted. Black Americans had limited access to the U.S. judicial system. The system rarely protected blacks in the early twentieth century. For example, blacks were routinely denied the right to fair trial. One way this was done was by prohibiting blacks from testifying in a court of law against a white person. Obviously, mob actions against blacks, including lynchings, were a stark denial of a fair trial when accused of a crime. Black Americans were clearly not treated equally under the law.

Artistic Advances

Despite the rampant racism in America during the 1920s, a number of black performers became accepted in the entertainment world. Jazz had only recently grown out of black folk blues. Exotic nightclubs featuring black jazz musicians became very popular with white society, such as the Cotton Club in Harlem. Louis Armstrong and Duke Ellington would become the nation's leading jazz musicians.

Literary contributions also blossomed. Black writers produced numerous works and in a different style than earlier. Instead of imitating white works, the new works explored black life and culture in both the northern industrial cities and rural South. A striking example of this development in New York City has been called the Harlem Renaissance or the New Negro Movement. Notable among the movement's authors was Langston Hughes, James Weldon Johnson, Countee Cullen, Jean Toomer, Wallace Thurman, and Claude McKay. The onset of the Great Depression brought an end to the movement, as the writers scattered looking for employment. The musicians, however, grew into legendary figures.

Even with the predominance of racism, acceptance of cultural works by blacks was growing in mainstream American culture. This trend may have served to open the door to some black leaders gaining access by the late 1920s to positions of slightly greater authority.

Voting Patterns of Black Americans

Following the end of the American Civil War the nation adopted the Fifteenth Amendment to the U.S. Constitution, granting black Americans voting rights. However, the amendment was only a brief declaration that races should be treatment equally. The matter of actually establishing voter qualifications was still left strictly to the states. The prospect of a black vote was met with strong resistance throughout the South. Intimidation by such white supremacist organizations as the Ku Klux Klan became increasingly violent in an attempt to prevent blacks from voting. The Klan's hooded midnight riders terrorized blacks by burning crops, whipping, clubbing, and murdering victims. By 1900 all 11 former Confederate states made it virtually impossible for blacks to vote.

The southern states carefully worded their voting requirements to avoid obvious Fifteenth Amendment violations. As long as state voter eligibility requirements did not openly discriminate on the basis of "race, color, or previous condition of servitude," they were not considered unconstitutional. Though appearing to apply to all men equally, in actuality the requirements were directed against persons of color. States used a variety of measures to exclude the black vote: literacy tests, white-only primaries, poll taxes, and grandfather clauses. These techniques proved successful in excluding blacks from political participation until the mid-1960s. Consequently, whites completely dominated all levels of government in the Southern states through the 1930s and for the following few decades.

By the 1890s the popular voter eligibility requirements in the South were the grandfather clause and literacy tests. Grandfather clauses required all voters to show that their ancestors were eligible to vote in 1866. Blacks in 1890 had no ancestors who were eligible to vote in 1866 because the Fifteenth Amendment had not been passed yet to grant such rights to blacks. If a person could not show proof of 1866 voting ancestors, then they had to pass a literacy test. Nearly all black men in the South were disqualified from voting. As was often the case, most whites did not have to take literacy test, even though many could not read, because typically most white men had ancestors eligible to vote in 1866. Finally, in 1915 in *Guinn v. United States,* the U.S. Supreme Court unanimously ruled grandfather clauses unconstitutional.

With the ban on grandfather clauses, white-only primaries became the next barrier raised to block black voters. Under laws adopted by most Southern states, political parties could set their own rules for membership. The Democratic Party became organized as private clubs in each state and excluded all blacks. Only party members could vote for candidates in its primaries. Since the Democratic Party overwhelmingly dominated politics in the South, whoever won the Democratic primaries would readily win the general election. Any black votes cast in the general election were, therefore, usually meaningless. The Supreme Court unanimously ruled in *Grovey v. Townsend* (1935) that since the political parties had become private clubs and not part of state government, their actions were not restricted by the Constitution. White-only primaries would continue into the 1940s.

Another common barrier to black voters and to poor whites was the poll tax. The poll tax was simply a fee charged at the polling (voting) place. Since many black Americans could not afford to pay the tax, by the early twentieth century some states began to see poll taxes as a means to exclude blacks from the political process. The Court in *Breedlove v. Suttles* (1937) upheld the poll tax as constitutionally valid because it was applied to both black and white voters. The poll tax persisted until 1964 when the Twenty-fourth Amendment to the Constitution was ratified, abolishing the poll tax in federal elections.

Those black Americans who were able to exercise their right to vote, voted overwhelmingly Republican from the 1870s through the 1920s. They were voting for the party of Abraham Lincoln who had finally given black slaves their freedom. Given their recent emergence from slavery and extensive discrimination by whites, which maintained political control, the black population held little political power. Taking the black vote for granted through the years, the Republican Party actually offered little to black Americans. The Democratic Party, however, offered even less. A black had never been seated at a Democratic National Convention prior to the 1930s. In 1928, when the Democratic convention was held in Houston, Texas, several black alternates were seated behind chicken wire, separated from the white delegates. This lack of political power, in addition to low economic status, left black Americans particularly vulnerable to the impacts of the Depression.

Perspectives

Local Perspectives

Black Americans entered the Great Depression already economically deprived. As Clifford Burke later commented, "The Negro was born in depression. It didn't mean too much to him, The Great American Depression ... The best he could be is a janitor or a porter or shoeshine boy. It [the Great Depression] only became official when it hit the white man" (quoted in Studs Terkel's *Hard Times: An Oral History of the Great Depression,* 1986). The introduction of New Deal work relief programs in 1933 raised some hope for federal assistance. But because local governments dominated by white supremacists guided politics administered many New Deal programs, little help arrived.

"There will be no Negroes pushing wheelbarrows and boys driving trucks getting forty cents an hour when the good white men and white women, working on the fields alongside these roads can hardly earn forty cents a day." This comment by a Georgia official, recounted in Robert S. McElvaine's *The Great Depression: America, 1929–1941* (1993), describes a commonly held perspective on the local administration of New Deal benefits. The combination of longstanding racism and increased competition over jobs led to considerable hard feelings. This situation was especially strong in the South. In many areas black Americans were excluded from federally sponsored work programs. In fact, some relief programs such as those led by the AAA actually contributed to a further decline in the black condition. The AAA programs favored the large farmer who had enough land that he could cut back production on in order to qualify for government payments. These payments greatly supplemented farmers' incomes. The small farmers found it even more difficult to compete in the marketplace. In addition, sharecroppers were kicked off lands that were taken out of production. As a result, the programs ran many small black farmers and sharecroppers out of business.

With little relief coming from the New Deal, blacks soon lost confidence in the programs. For example, black newspapers characterized the National Recovery Act (NRA) as standing for "Negro Run Around" and "Negroes Rarely Allowed." Wage standards developed by the NRA setting wage rates did not meet the needs of black Americans. Most black occupations, such as farm workers and domestic help, were excluded from the program. Wage rates were also set according to region. Most blacks lived in the rural South where pay rates were low. Even if a black person did have a job favorably affected by the wage rates, they likely lost the job to unemployed whites. In many cases the NRA codes were ignored as employers paid lower wages to blacks than to whites. Some relief started coming in the mid-1930s as President Roosevelt became more sensitive to the criticisms of advocates for the needy. Still, hopes were largely unanswered, as it took World War II to bring relief on a larger scale.

Realizing little help was coming from the federal government, local efforts seeking better economic conditions rose in both the South and North. In the South sharecroppers and tenant farmers formed local organizations such as the Southern Tenant Farmers Union. The union started in Arkansas and spread to other states. Store boycotts in northern cities sprung up as part of the "Don't Buy Where You Can't Work" program. In Cleveland the Future Outlook League was formed, seeking to establish a fully economically self-sufficient black community within the larger city. In Harlem the Citizen's League for Fair Play promoted greater employment opportunity for blacks. All of these movements led to opening up some employment opportunities and encouraged a number of new black businesses.

National Perspectives

On a national level, black Americans, who composed only 10 percent of the population and had traditionally been economically downtrodden and politically voiceless, had a major mountain to climb for relief.

You kiss the niggers,
I'll kiss the Jews,
We'll stay in the White House
As long as we choose.

This poem (from McElvaine's *The Great Depression: America, 1929–1941,* 1993) was a popular fictional characterization of President Roosevelt speaking to Eleanor. It was a criticism of Eleanor's promotion of black equality. This prose represents well the racism that pervaded American society in the early 1930s. Not only did Eleanor become the target of such hate for promoting black issues nationally, but President Roosevelt did as well for reaching out to various ethnic and religious groups in building his new democratic coalition. Despite Roosevelt's stance, however, racism was also a part of the Democratic Party. Senator Ellison D. "Cotton Ed" Smith of South Carolina walked out of the 1936 Democratic National Convention when he learned that a black minister was to give the invocation to the convention.

Despite such public views, the Roosevelts were successful in bringing diverse groups together politically for the first time in American history. President Roosevelt won by a landslide in the 1936 presidential election. Seventy-five percent of black voters voted for Franklin Roosevelt.

Though successful in the November 1936 elections, Roosevelt's inclusion of black Americans into his new democratic coalition was more than many party traditionalists could stand. Though popular with the public, he lost the support of the southern Democrats in Congress for his programs. Just as he had feared in 1933 when he dodged civil rights issues for fear of losing key support for his economic recovery programs, his initiatives steadily lost the support of the more conservative congressmen through 1937 and 1938 with his inclusion of black Americans. As a result the New Deal era drew to a close.

International Perspectives

Racism was not unique to the United States in the 1930s. Preaching racial and religious hatred, Adolf Hitler gained political power in Germany in the late 1920s and became the leader of Germany in 1933.

Hitler claimed the Germans formed a "master race" that would rule the world. He considered blacks an inferior race. As a result, the Nazi Party in Germany most vigorously promoted the rise of racism in Europe through the 1930s. Black Americans were among the first Americans to condemn Hitler and Nazism. The Summer Olympics were held in the German capital of Berlin in 1936. When black American track star Jesse Owens won four gold medals, Hitler walked out of the stadium.

Black Americans were outraged when Italy invaded Ethiopia in 1935, one of the few independent black nations in the world at the time. Black Americans raised funds for medical supplies for Ethiopia and some even traveled to Ethiopia to help defend it.

U.S. Senator Theodore Bilbo of Mississippi once noted that race consciousness was growing in various countries around the world. He called racial values "the only hope for future civilization" and commended the Germans for the importance they placed on it. Bilbo so strongly supported racial values that, in 1938, he sought a $1 billion congressional appropriation to deport all black Americans to Africa. Such were the hurdles black Americans faced in their quest for economic relief and racial equality.

Impact

The historic civil rights movement of the 1950s resulted in major legal gains in the 1960s. It clearly owed part of its success to the gains made in the 1930s. Black Americans had been appointed to the highest public offices in U.S. history. A key group, the Black Cabinet, personally advised the president on a regular basis. First Lady Eleanor Roosevelt personally promoted black issues. Segregation was banned in federal office buildings. Many blacks received federal relief to cope with the Depression.

Yet despite these gains during the 1930s, black Americans were still dependent on whites in government to speak on their behalf. Some black leaders, such as Ralph Bunche, argued that the New Deal sustained an inferior attitude in blacks. The New Deal had not challenged existing patterns of black and white relations. For example, liberal whites assumed lead positions in seeking social change. Black leaders were kept in the background. Secretary of Interior Harold Ickes was one of those white leaders. He firmly believed that black Americans were part of the larger group of citizens the "New Democracy" was intended to aid through the welfare state. As a result, actions by blacks on their own behalf were stalled until the civil rights movement of the 1950s and 1960s. What the New Deal did offer was a rebirth of the ideal of racial equality in American public life. That notion had earlier died at the end of Reconstruction in the late 1870s.

Changes in American Politics and Law

The Depression era created lasting political associations in America. These included the link between liberalism and the quest for social justice, and the link between economic conservatism and racism. Perhaps most importantly, beginning in the 1930s the federal government became a key factor in civil rights issues. The Black Cabinet and President Roosevelt's appointees, including Ickes, Hopkins, Alexander, and Williams, brought the recognition of civil rights issues into the New Deal.

One of the lasting legacies of Roosevelt to the black cause was the appointment of eight Supreme Court justices during his lengthy tenure as president. Seven of these justices became advocates for civil rights. They set the stage for the Warren Court of the 1950s and 1960s that made landmark decisions directly affecting racial equality.

Social Progress Stalled

Despite important gains made in public attitudes and positions of blacks in government, some viewed the New Deal era as a setback in the struggle for civil rights. The growing momentum within the black community of the early twentieth century was sidetracked by the country's urgent pursuit of economic recovery programs. As a result, blacks would have to wait until after World War II to pursue racial justice. Changes in public attitude translated to little concrete change in New Deal programs. Black sharecroppers, unskilled laborers, and domestic helpers still had twice the unemployment rate as whites. Jim Crow laws and public segregation continued for twenty more years.

The onset of World War II forced President Roosevelt and the federal government to confront race issues more directly. The hiring quota system Secretary Ickes introduced in the WPA set a precedent for the wartime Fair Employment Practices Commission. It also served as a model for civil rights legislation and court decisions of the 1960s and 1970s. Job opportunities for blacks boomed through the war years, only to decline afterwards.

Despite the stalled momentum for sweeping social change, two lasting changes brought by the New Deal era were the increase in black expectations of racial equality and the decrease in open white hostility. White supremacy was far less tolerated in public.

Civil Rights Movement

The civil rights movement grew following World War II, building on the factors of increased public awareness of black issues, increased black expectations, and the role of the federal government. The movement became a "freedom struggle" by black Americans in the 1950s and 1960s. The goal was equality with white Americans. Equality meant freedom from discrimination in employment, education, and housing, the right to vote, and equal access to public facilities such as theaters, inns, and restaurants.

The 1954 U.S. Supreme Court landmark decision in *Brown v. Board of Education* had proved the spark for change. The ruling directly struck down segregation in public schools. But the historic ruling also closed the door on the "separate-but-equal" doctrine supporting Jim Crow laws.

Black activists sought to extend the *Brown* ruling and racial reform to other aspects of life. In 1955 Rosa Parks, a secretary for the NAACP, was arrested in Montgomery, Alabama for refusing to give her seat on a city bus to a white man as required by city law. This incident led to the rise of a young 27-year old preacher, Martin Luther King, Jr. King preached nonviolent, civil disobedience tactics. This strategy contrasted to both the Ku Klux Klan's violent terrorism and the NAACP's quiet legal approach.

King founded the Southern Christian Leadership Conference (SCLC) in 1957 to provide leadership to the movement. But white resistance to racial equality led to years of conflict. Highly publicized confrontations followed in 1957 at Little Rock, Arkansas, and in 1962 at the University of Mississippi.

The high point of the civil rights movement came on August 28, 1963 when 250,000 thousand persons marched on Washington, DC. They urged the federal government to support desegregation and protect black voting rights. King gave his famous "I Have a Dream" speech, preaching nonviolent action. Congress responded with passage of the sweeping Civil Rights Act of 1964, prohibiting discrimination in public places. This action came almost three decades after President Roosevelt had issued his limited order addressing discrimination in federal office buildings.

White violence, including assassination of a NAACP leader and murders of civil rights activists, followed. Mounted police using tear gas, dogs, and clubs attacked black protest marches in the South. Urban riots across the country in 1965 called attention to the plight of blacks. In reaction Congress added the Voting Rights Act in 1965 expanding voting rights of blacks.

King, who had received the Nobel Peace Prize in 1964 for his leadership role in the movement, was assassinated in Memphis, Tennessee in 1968. Race riots erupted in the following week in 125 cities, as black America's most effective leader was gone. Congress passed the Fair Housing Act, banning racial discrimination in most housing, six days after King's assassination. This bill corrected the housing discrimination that persisted from the New Deal's housing programs. However, with its leader gone and unity no longer evident, the civil rights movement's national thrust faded. The movement had altered the fundamental relationship between state and federal governments and compelled the federal courts to more effectively protect constitutional civil liberties. The federal role in civil rights issues begun in the 1930s was further expanded. Many others soon benefited from the movement's gains in social justice, including women, the disabled, and other victims of discrimination who had little voice in the 1930s.

Notable People

Will Alexander (1884–1956). A white Methodist minister in Tennessee, Alexander became increasingly concerned with rural black poverty. He left the ministry to become executive director of the Commission on Interracial Cooperation in 1919. He then became president of Dillard University in New Orleans in 1930. In 1935 Alexander was appointed assistant administrator of the New Deal's Resettlement Administration to give aid to poor farmers. When the agency became part of the new Farm Security Administration, Roosevelt appointed Alexander to lead the new agency. Alexander left the agency in 1940.

Marian Anderson (1897–1993). Anderson was a world famous black American contralto singer. In 1925, early in her career, she appeared with the New York Philharmonic orchestra. Anderson traveled throughout Europe in the early 1930s, earning great praise for her performances. She became recognized as one of the world's top opera singers. In 1935 she returned to the United States to perform at Carnegie Hall in New York City. In March of 1939, the Daughters of the American Revolution (DAR) refused to allow Anderson to give a concert in a private hall in Washington, DC. In reaction, Eleanor Roosevelt, along with others, resigned from the organization.

They had federal officials arrange for Anderson to give a free concert on the steps of the Lincoln Memorial on Easter Sunday instead. The denial of Anderson to perform at the private hall triggered a

Marian Anderson performs on the steps of the Lincoln Memorial in 1939. Although one of the world's top opera singers, she was denied access to a larger audience due to the racial discrimination and segregation of the times. (AP/Wide World Photos. Reproduced by permission.)

major reaction against racism in the nation. Tens of thousands of letters and telegrams were sent to DAR offices in protest. An estimated crowd of over 75,000 attended the outdoor event. According to a nationwide Gallup poll, Eleanor's resignation from DAR received a 67 percent approval from the public.

Given that a decade earlier blacks had been roped off across the road at the dedication of the memorial, the integrated concert crowd reflected a major change in public attitudes through the 1930s. In 1955 Anderson became the first black to perform at New York's Metropolitan Opera. In 1958 President Dwight D. Eisenhower (served 1953–1961) named her as a delegate to the United Nations General Assembly. President Lyndon B. Johnson (served 1963–1969) awarded Anderson the Presidential Medal of Freedom in 1963, and she received a Grammy music award for Lifetime Achievement in 1991.

William H. Hastie (1904–1976). Hastie earned a law degree from Harvard University and taught at Howard University in Washington, DC. He worked on many NAACP legal cases. Roosevelt appointed Hastie to a lawyer position in the Interior Department, and he became part of Roosevelt's "Black Cabinet." In 1937 Roosevelt appointed Hastie the first black federal judge in American history, as district court judge in the Virgin Islands. In 1939 he returned to Howard University as law school dean. During World War II he served as a civilian aide to the secretary of war. In 1946 President Harry Truman (served 1945–1953) appointed Hastie governor of the Virgin Islands, and in 1949 he was appointed judge on the U.S. Court of Appeals.

Harold Ickes (1874–1952). A social activist his entire career, Ickes served as secretary of interior to Roosevelt. He had earlier been president of the Chicago chapter of the NAACP. Ickes was Roosevelt's key advisor on black issues. Ickes, through his own initiative, took measures to end segregation in the Interior Department by hiring black lawyers, engineers, and architects. Ickes established the first minority quota hiring system. He demanded that all Public Works Administration contractors employ black workers in proportion to the number of blacks living in the local area of the particular project.

Joe Louis (1914–1981). Louis, a large black man born in Alabama and raised in Detroit, became a professional boxer in 1934. He won the heavyweight title in June 1937 by knocking out white boxer James J. Braddock. The rise of Louis as a champion prizefighter made him a folk hero among black Americans during a difficult period. His victories over whites, particularly German fighters, gave a great moral lift to black Americans in their quest to gain racial equality. Louis held the world heavyweight boxing championship longer than any other boxer. He retired from the ring in 1949 and later had an unsuccessful comeback attempt.

Eleanor Roosevelt (1884–1962). Eleanor married Franklin D. Roosevelt in 1905 and raised five children while her husband chased political ambitions. Following volunteer work during World War I, including Red Cross activities, Eleanor chose the course of social reformer and political activist and became active in the Democratic Party. She supported child labor laws, legislation to protect women, and social services to mothers and children. In the 1930s Eleanor took up the cause of black Americans, promoting anti-lynching laws and bringing NAACP leaders to the White House. She became very popular among the black population for promoting their issues at such a high level.

Robert C. Weaver (1907–1997). Roosevelt appointed Weaver in 1933 as an advisor on black economic problems and a member of Roosevelt's "Black Cabinet." He had earlier earned a Ph.D. in economics from Harvard. From 1937 to 1940, he served as special assistant for the U.S. Housing Authority. Weaver became the first black cabinet member in U.S. history in 1966 when President Lyndon B. Johnson named him secretary of housing and urban development. In 1969 he became president of Bernard M. Baruch College.

Walter White (1893–1956). After establishing the Atlanta chapter of the National Association for the Advancement of Colored People (NAACP), White became executive secretary of the organization from 1931 to 1955. During the 1930s White spent considerable effort seeking passage of an anti-lynching law, but without success. He also lobbied for voting rights, school desegregation, and many other civil rights issues. White kept ongoing communications with First Lady Eleanor Roosevelt. As a national spokesman for black issues, White was successful in raising public awareness of the plight of black Americans and laying the foundation for the civil rights movement of the 1950s and 1960s.

Primary Sources

Racial Discrimination During the New Deal

During the Great Depression, black Americans not only faced racial discrimination in employment, but in economic relief programs as well. They often received inferior food and goods, if any at all. Evelyn Finn of Louisiana reminisced a number of years later, after the end of the New Deal. Finn's memories are recounted in Studs Terkel's oral history volume on the Great Depression, *Hard Times: An Oral History of the Great Depression* (1986, p. 319).

> Negroes'd go in town and get their rations. But they couldn't eat it. Full of worms and weevils. They would tell me when they come into the store. They couldn't use half of what they got. But they went and got it. Otherwise, they wouldn't get anything. Because who dished it out would say: 'If you don't take it, there's no use to give it to you.' That's what they'd give the Negro.

A *Time* magazine story, "Jim Crow Concert Hall," recounted on March 6, 1939, how singer Marian Anderson was refused a date to perform at the private Constitution Hall in Washington, DC.

> One of the greatest concert singers of this generation is Marian Anderson, a Philadelphia-born Negro contralto. Since she skyrocketed to fame in Salzburg four years ago, the music-lovers and critics of the world's musical capitals have counted it a privilege to hear her sing. Last week it looked as though music-lovers in provincial Washington, DC might be denied this privilege. Reason: Washington's only large concert auditorium, Constitution Hall, is owned by the Daughters of the America Revolution, who are so proud they won't eat mush—much less let a Negro sing from their stage.
>
> Last January, when Contralto Anderson's manager tried to book Constitution Hall for a concert in April, D.A.R. officials said they were sorry but the hall was taken. When alternative dates were suggested, the D.A.R. frostily replied that *all* dates were taken. Sympathetic protests began to pour in from all sides: last week they reached peak proportions ... This week while the Daughters continued to preserve a thin-lipped silence, Daughter Eleanor Roosevelt announced in a syndicated Scripps-Howard column that she was resigning from the D.A.R. in protest.

Suggested Research Topics

- Imagine being a black American living in the early twentieth century in the United States. Describe the benefits you might expect from the New Deal programs.
- What were the lasting effects of the New Deal for black Americans and the dream of social justice?
- Conduct more research on people like William H. Hastie, Marian Anderson, and Mary McLeod Bethune to find more out about their lives during the Great Depression and beyond. What types of struggles were unique to them because of their race?

Bibliography

Sources

Greenberg, Cheryl Lynn. *"Or Does It Explode?": Harlem in the Great Depression.* New York: Oxford University Press, 1991.

"Jim Crow Concert Hall," *Time,* March 6, 1939.

Kelley, Robin D.G., and Earl Lewis. *To Make Our World Anew: A History of African Americans.* New York: Oxford University Press, 2000.

Kirby, John B. *Black Americans in the Roosevelt Era: Liberalism and Race.* Knoxville: University of Tennessee Press, 1980.

McElvaine, Robert S. *The Great Depression: America, 1929–1941.* New York: Times Books, 1993.

McMillen, Neil R. *Dark Journey: Black Mississippians in the Age of Jim Crow.* Urbana: University of Illinois Press, 1989.

Nordin, Dennis S. *The New Deal's Black Congressman: A Life of Arthur Wergs Mitchell.* Columbia: University of Missouri Press, 1997.

"Only Decent Manner," *Time,* March 20, 1939.

Sitkoff, Harvard. *A New Deal for Blacks: The Emergence of Civil Rights as a National Issue, the Depression Years.* New York: Oxford University Press, 1978.

Terkel, Studs. *Hard Times: An Oral History of the Great Depression.* New York: Pantheon Books, 1986.

Further Reading

Appiah, Kwame A., and Henry L. Gates, eds. *Africana: The Encyclopedia of the African and African American Experience.* New York: Basic Civitas Books, 1999.

Egerton, John. *Speak Now Against the Day: The Generation Before the Civil Rights Movement in the South.* New York: Alfred A. Knopf, 1994.

Hampton, Henry, and Steve Fayer. *Voices of Freedom: An Oral History of the Civil Rights Movement from the 1950s Through the 1980s.* New York: Bantam Books, 1990.

Mead, Christopher. *Champion: Joe Louis, Black Hero in White America.* New York: Penguin Books, 1986.

Oshinsky, David M. *Worse than Slavery: Parchman Farm and the Ordeal of Jim Crow Justice.* New York: Free Press, 1996.

Stewart, Jeffrey C. *1001 Things Everyone Should Know About African American History.* New York: Doubleday, 1997.

See Also

Effects of the Great Depression—LBJ's Great Society

Causes of the Crash

1919-1929

Introduction

The crash of the stock market in October 1929 was not so much the cause of the Great Depression as it was a confirmation that economic conditions in the United States had reached a crisis. The economic problems were long in the making, and a product of diverse factors that had worsened in the 1920s.

One of the key factors that influenced all the other factors in the 1920s was the lack of national economic planning or any other substantial form of active government oversight in the economy. The Republican administrations of Warren G. Harding (served 1921–1923), Calvin Coolidge (served 1923–1929), and Herbert Hoover (served 1929–1933) embraced a *laissez faire* philosophy. *Laissez faire* means being relatively free of government control or regulation. These presidents did not plan, nor did they attempt to regulate, banking, stocks, bonds, or other basic aspects of the economy. They also did not gather adequate statistics that, if analyzed, would have highlighted growing problems in stock market investing, agriculture, international finance, and buildup of inventories of consumer goods.

For much of the 1920s, the United States seemed prosperous. Many people were employed, and consumer goods—automobiles, appliances, furniture, and other commodities—flowed out of factories faster than ever. The satisfaction of America's workers was evidenced by the decline in membership and significance of labor unions. A number of Americans were

Chronology:

1776: British economist philosopher Adam Smith publishes *The Wealth of Nations* which greatly influenced economists and politicians through the twentieth century.

1792: The New York Stock Exchange is founded by a group of 24 men under a tree in New York City.

1914–1918: Widespread war leaves European economies in disarray, while the United States emerges as an industrial leader.

November 1920: Warren G. Harding is elected president, leading to 12 consecutive years of Republican control of the White House and strongly pro-business government policies.

October 24, 1929: The first day of panic strikes Wall Street when 12.8 million shares of stock are sold, many at significantly lower prices than their value only a few days earlier. This day became known as Black Thursday.

October 29, 1929: Wall Street has its only 16 million-share day, with 16,410,000 shares sold. The day became known as Black Tuesday.

March 5, 1933: The New York Stock Exchange closes until March 14 for a national bank holiday.

June 6, 1934: Congress passes the Securities Exchange Act to correct the problems leading to the October 1929 stock market crash.

gripped with speculative fever. They invested in unseen real estate, foreign currency, and even stocks in new companies that had yet to manufacture a good. This speculation at such a high level was clearly unhealthy. When the stock market began to plummet, some confronted it with disbelief. Others had already experienced depressed times.

Besides lack of government involvement and over-speculation in stocks and real estate, other possible causes of the Great Depression that have drawn attention include a widespread get-rich-quick mentality, overproduction and low prices for farm produce, a belief that national economies naturally decline in predictable patterns, and a large gap in wealth between the rich and common citizens. Each of these possible causes will be explored below. One fact stands out. The "big crash" was a clear warning sign of deep national economic troubles. These problems continued to worsen through 1932, and their effects stubbornly remained for another ten years.

Issue Summary

Whose Fault Was It?

Historians and economists have devoted much attention to the consequences of the Great Depression and its worldwide impact during the 1930s. For many years, however, little energy was devoted to finding the causes of the calamity that so seriously affected the lives of tens of millions of people. The most likely causes identified remain hotly debated into the twenty-first century. They include economic regulation by government, the occurrence of business cycles, the distribution of wealth, public attitudes about money, the unregulated stock market, a slumping agricultural economy, and the struggling international economy. The following factors have each been identified as possible causes.

Little Government Oversight of Business

Up through the nineteenth century a prevalent belief was that conducting business represented a basic form of property right that should be protected from any form of government regulation. Related to this belief, many rationalized that unrestricted economic systems would behave like a living organic system in nature. It would regulate itself to maintain a healthy condition. One form of self-regulation was propelled by the self-interest of business owners. British economist Adam Smith had earlier argued that the "invisible hand" of the marketplace would serve as a check and balance system in a nation's industrial economy. Smith contended that humans are driven both by personal passions to compete and succeed and a desire to self-regulate their actions, driven by the human ability to reason and sympathize. Because humans have this capacity to self-regulate, Smith concluded that economic markets should be free of government restraint. In Smith's economic model, the free market would be self-correcting and lead to a steady growth in national economics. Government involvement would only serve to inhibit this growth. Such was the birth of *laissez faire* government policy (business largely free of government regulation). This perspective was quite revolutionary in contrast to the centrally controlled economies of the feudal period in Europe in which craft guilds were the dominant organization for producing goods.

Smith's theories had been born during a time when small local craft industries dominated. By the late 1920s, about two-thirds of American industry was controlled by large, publicly owned corporations, many of them "holding companies." Holding companies hold the ownership of other corporations and may provide some general direction and management. Mergers of smaller companies formed other large corporations. By 1929 these companies controlled vast empires. Two hundred of the largest corporations owned half of U.S. businesses. The influence of small individual owners who closely watched the course of their companies' operations had diminished significantly. As the Great Depression began unfolding, some question arose whether Smith's "invisible hand" still played an effective role in balancing a modern industrial economy. Considerable control of industry was in the hands of only a few. While the administrations of Presidents Harding, Coolidge, and Hoover believed the rules of Adam Smith still applied, industrialists were no longer playing by those rules. Some alleged that such pervasive widespread corporate control proved detrimental to the continued health of the economy as a whole. They lacked vision to look ahead.

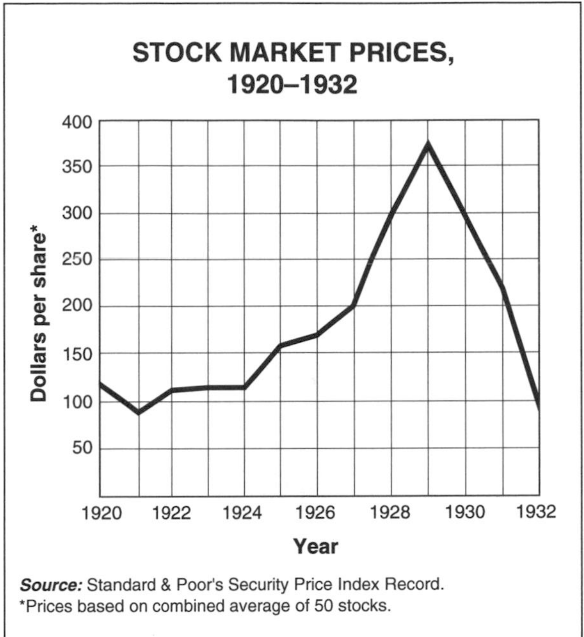

Stock market prices based on the combined average of fifty stocks, 1920–1932. (The Gale Group.)

For example, Samuel Insull of Chicago created a complex pyramid of public utility holding companies. Insull ended up controlling an eighth of the electrical power in the United States. His collection of companies was worth almost $3 billion. Insull's empire finally went bankrupt in 1932. He could no longer afford to pay interest on stocks and bonds back to investors because of declining income during the Great Depression. With large numbers of holding companies and corporate mergers dotting the U.S. industrial landscape of the 1920s, economist Adam Smith's model of business owners maintaining a competitive balance in markets no longer seemed to be the case. Owners had become increasingly detached from the social situation influenced by their companies.

Business Cycles

Somewhat related to the Adam Smith belief that a business economy will tend to satisfactorily regulate itself was the belief that business will tend to go through "natural" cycles of decline and expansion. Any governmental intervention in these cycles would tend to disrupt the system's natural operations and enhance any problems. The United States had previously experienced a number of economic panics, slumps, and depressions. These came in 1819, 1837, 1857, 1873, 1893, and 1914. Many people, including President Hoover, believed that the events of October 1929, which dramatically worsened by 1931, were merely part of a regular cycle of downturns that had historically beset the nation's free market economy.

National economies are known to fluctuate up and down over time. Levels of employment, industrial and agricultural production, and prices for commodities and produce vary almost continuously. Perceiving economic systems as some sort of "natural" system, many economists in the early twentieth century analyzed economic trends in terms of business cycles, where an almost predictable pattern could be identified and explained. These business cycles were thought to operate on different levels—daily, seasonally, annually, and longer periods of several years. Each long-term cycle was composed of an economic expansion period in which the economy was strong and increased, and an economic contraction period in which the economy would decline.

Many, including President Hoover, argued in the early part of the Depression that what was happening was only the "natural" performance of the economy as it went through its regular business cycle. If left alone, the system would once again improve before long. They argued that these cycles occurred every fifty years or so, with one cycle having occurred from 1792 to 1850 and a second from 1850 to 1896. They claimed that the Depression was simply the natural financial contraction following an economic expansion that lasted from 1896 into the 1920s.

Unemployed and broke as a result of the stock market crash, one-time millionaire Fred Bell sells apples at his stand on the street in San Francisco, California, on March 7, 1931. (AP/Wide World Photos. Reproduced by permission.)

Later in the twentieth century, economists increasingly accepted that such long-term patterns cannot be predicted as if some sort of "natural" cycle. Through the years it became recognized that many forces are at work to influence economic downturns. National economies are subject to such historic events as epidemics, earthquakes, floods, wars, and social strife, as well as climate changes and cultural customs. Therefore, long-term cycles may not always self-regulate, and economic declines may not be so "natural" and have an anticipated automatic improvement. Consequently, business cycles as a cause for the Depression ranks low compared to the other factors considered.

Wealth Distribution

In spite of the general prosperity in America in the 1920s, wealth was not shared equally. Many believe that a wealth distribution tilted so strongly to the rich getting richer was an important factor contributing to the nation's economic instability and ultimately the Great Depression. The unequal distribution of wealth meant workers in general were unable to enjoy higher wages and afford the very goods they were producing.

An unequal distribution of wealth has characterized much of human history. Many people have only a few material goods and a limited ability to change their situation. A few people possess much wealth. This concentration of assets—in land, possessions, or money—gives the wealthy incredible political and economic power. By the 1920s the maldistribution (greatly uneven distribution) of wealth in America was accelerating, and it posed dramatic consequences for the health of the nation's economy. What greatly affected the economy in the 1920s was that the few who were wealthy were growing richer at a rapidly increasing rate. The ability of the superrich to spend their money in ways that would stimulate the economy was quite limited compared to the years following World War II (1939–1945). This increasingly concentrated wealth contributed to one of the most serious problems of the 1920s.

In the years 1919 to 1929, workers increased their output by some 43 percent. In the six years between 1923 and 1929 alone, worker output increased by nearly 32 percent. Worker wages also increased during this period, but only by 8 percent. This rise was much less than the increase in product output. As a result, profits for corporations soared in that six-year period, increasing by 62 percent. Obviously most of these profits went to the rich, not to the workers. What was going wrong in America was that the workers were increasingly less and less able to purchase the manufactured goods they were producing. The country appeared prosperous, but in reality it was headed for a big fall. Unsold inventories of manufactured goods were steadily rising. Even though the wealthy spent money on luxury items, the longer-term problems for the economy were mounting and could not be counteracted by this spending.

The problems were offset for a time by fairly healthy investment by the wealthy in businesses. Many factories acquired new machinery with updated technology. Likewise, thousands of banks, feeling confident about the nation's economic health, hired architects and constructed substantial bank buildings. A sturdy structure with metal doors, marble lobby, brass grills at the tellers' cages, and wood-paneled offices for the officers made a positive public statement. In this way the money was being redistributed to workers through the wages they earned to make the new machinery and construct the bank buildings.

The government did little to address the growing uneven distribution of wealth. In fact, government policies aided the rich in becoming richer. Tax cuts for the wealthy in the 1920s helped them retain even more income. At the same time, when workers tried to organize and work through unions to gain health and wage benefits, the government was hostile to such activities. The government did not support a union's right to strike or enter into collective bargaining agreements to improve the position of workers.

The final undoing of the false prosperity of the 1920s came when workers—the great bulk of them not sharing in the rapid build-up of wealth—deluded themselves into believing that they too were participating in the economic boom. This occurred when people were allowed to borrow money to buy goods. They were also allowed to pay back their loans over longer periods of time. This type of consumption was promoted by new glitzy advertising, and it propelled the nation into a frenzy of personal borrowing and spending. Installment buying provided immediate gratification. For example, a person could buy a radio, a vacuum cleaner, a washing machine, or a car, gain possession of the item, and then pay for it over the following months or years. A problem with this method of consumption was that it obligated a person to pay—including interest—over a long period of time, and sometimes the item wore out before it was paid for. Another problem was that if a person lost employment and had no savings, the lender showed up to repossess the item. This situation, which frequently occurred, contributed to the ill health of the economy. Banks were also loaning out lots of money to people to buy stocks and investments in real estate property. Both were chancy speculations on future trends. These practices placed the banking system in a precarious situation.

Get Rich Quick

The new appeal of mass marketing combined with a booming economy and soaring stock market to create a get-rich-quick mentality that gripped many Americans in the 1920s. This mindset made many people reckless with their money—even those without a great deal to spend. Foolish spending and a change in thinking about savings contributed to instability in the economy. Many Americans in the 1920s grew to believe that it was possible to get rich without working. Others thought that fortune was just around the corner. It was during the 1920s that materialism rose to hew heights in U.S. society. Mass production and mass media were fueling a new mass consumption never witnessed before. Industrialization had transformed society, and it was reflected in the literature of the time. These attitudes fostered reckless investment and speculation. They also were a mirror to changing attitudes about the relationship between work and wealth.

At a Glance

An Anonymous Ditty from the Great Depression

A popular saying in 1929–1930 stated:

Mellon pulled the whistle,
Hoover rang the bell
Wall Street gave the signal
And the country went to hell.

The best-selling book in the United States in 1925 and 1926 was Bruce Barton's *The Man Nobody Knows: The Discovery of the Real Jesus.* An advertiser by trade, Barton looked at some of the New Testament and wrote a tale for modern American readers loosely based on the life of Jesus. He said that Jesus took a dozen men from the lower ranks of society and welded them into a business organization that changed the world. He used the biblical phrase "Knock and it shall be opened unto you" to try to persuade his readers that Jesus was the greatest salesman who ever lived. Hundreds of thousands of Americans believed him, or at least, they bought or borrowed his book. The popularity of Barton's crass use of Christianity confirmed the materialism of the 1920s.

Another example of the get-rich-quick mentality was found in the essay, "Everybody Ought to be Rich," written by John J. Raskob. Published in the *Ladies' Home Journal* in 1929, this article proposed the creation of a company whereby small investors might pool their money, invest in stocks, and become wealthy. In a sense Raskob anticipated the creation of mutual funds, an investment in which small investors put their assets into a common fund that purchased stocks. The title of Raskob's essay was indicative of the attitudes of the 1920s.

This fascination with wealth and material gain gripped the United States in other ways, such as grand architecture, booming real estate markets, and an increase in the public consumption of luxury goods. The construction of movie palaces—elegant buildings with design themes based on architecture from Spain, ancient Egypt, or China—drew millions of viewers to films which portrayed life in fictional but romantic ways. The tales of movies often celebrated riches and success, while the lives of the players in the films seemed exotic, adventuresome, and wonderful. In many ways Americans were lured further into materialism and financial irresponsibility by the media.

Americans consumed the flood of advertising and enticing images pouring at them. They heard commercials on the radio, flocked to movies telling fictional tales of alluring adventure and romance, read billboards along the roadside, or encountered handsome display ads in magazines and newspapers. They were advised to purchase deodorants to avoid body odor, cleanse their mouths with mouthwash to avoid bad breath, and scour their hair with special soaps to rid their scalps of dandruff. Millions could not resist. Like the glamorous movie stars, they wanted to look good, smell good, and have adventures. The consequences of this get-rich-quick mentality were seen in the wild rise and fall of real estate values in Florida and California.

Florida Real Estate Boom and Bust

For a time in the mid-1920s Florida was the nation's hottest real estate market. A few dollars down might hold a lot (a small parcel of land) until weeks or months later when it could be sold for fantastic profit. The lure in Florida was not only its splendidly appealing weather but also the clever promotion by real estate agents who fed the boom with brochures, signs, and promises. Thousands invested in lots in Coral Cables or other "instant" towns in Florida. Improved transportation and higher wages encouraged people from the North to make more and more trips to the South. Developers wanted to believe that Florida would become a holiday destination and that the entire peninsula would soon be populated with sun-worshipers. This promotion led to the belief that all land in Florida would be valuable, including beaches, bogs, swamps, and scrubland. Promoters in Florida subdivided land and sold it for a 10 percent down payment. Buyers were purchasing property that seemed to have little use, but their intent was not to develop it or to live on it. The reality was that land in Florida was increasing in value daily and could be sold at a profit in a short time. Florida real estate was in the grip of a speculative frenzy.

By 1925 real estate in Florida was so popular that some developers were selling twenty lots on a single acre of land. Lots promoted as being on the seashore were often 10 to 15 miles away from the water. Suburbs also became farther and farther away from towns. Sometimes the farmland or scrubland was equipped with eloquently named streets lined with sidewalks and street lamps. Taxes and assessments amounted to several times the current value of the property. The subdivision of Manhattan Estates claimed to be "not more than three-fourths of a mile from the prosperous and fast-growing city of Nettie." The truth, however, was that the town of Nettie did not even exist.

When some investors actually went to visit the lots they had purchased, they found them to be miles from the seashore or underwater in a swamp. Similar real estate promotions drew investors to Venice or Huntington Beach in southern California. The narrow lots lay blocks and blocks from the much-desired shoreline. The lots were often without nearby streets or utilities. Most proved to be worthless, costing buyers millions.

In 1926 two hurricanes tore through Florida. Hundreds were killed, roofs were torn off of houses, water was everywhere, and yachts were even tossed from the ocean into city streets. The storms caused a lull in the real estate boom in Florida. Property owners were in need of assistance. Peter King, an official of the Seaboard Air Line and a sincere believer in the future of Florida, tried to convince the nation that the "Sunshine State" was not too dramatically harmed. He claimed it was the same old Florida with its nice climate. Investors in the Florida market, however, were not so sure. Loans were not paid, and the land often returned to the original owner.

By 1927 the Florida boom was over. Many had lost their investments. People, however, remained optimistic that other opportunities to make a quick fortune would come along. The stock market was becoming an attractive place to invest, and the possibility of losing money there was not seen as much of a threat.

The Soaring Stock Market

In the late 1920s Americans invested their money in the stock market because it seemed safe and a sure way to make much more. Stocks are certificates of ownership in a company. A stock's value is often linked to the performance of the business or industry. Businesses needed to sell stock in order to raise money to expand their endeavors, and people were willing to purchase these offerings, believing that the business will do well, their stock value will increase, and money can be made. Only 2 percent of Americans were purchasing stock by the mid-1920s. Buying and selling stock shares was largely uncontrolled, as few government regulations existed. The growth in stock values had been so pervasive that many people who bought shares did not realize they could easily lose all of their money. Share prices during the 1920s went up because companies encouraged people to buy on credit. This was called "buying on margin" and enabled speculators to sell shares at a profit before paying what they owed. The result was that the money invested in the stock market was not actually there. For example a person buying on margin purchases a $100 stock for $10 of his own money and borrows the other $90 to complete the purchase. The investor does this in the belief the stock's value will go up. If it doubles you have $110 and pay the $90 back. If it goes down to $50 then the creditor will demand payment of the loan to save himself. During this period of get-rich-quick mentality, the stock market appeared to be a winning solution for many.

Investors were not protected from fraud or hype and often bought misleading stocks. Companies told the public that they were doing well, but the public had no means of confirming whether the companies' financial reports were reliable. It was difficult for investors to know exactly what they were buying. Some Americans began predicting that the stock market was going to crash, but during the 1920s few people really believed them, as the nation seemed so wealthy and powerful.

A great Bull Market gripped Wall Street in 1928 and 1929. Tales began to circulate—and were documented in the financial pages of the newspapers—that a few dollars invested in the right stock today might be worth hundreds of dollars within weeks. Many of the tales were true, even if the stock values were inflated (valued more than their actual worth). So the speculation began to grow. In early 1928 the Dow Jones industrial average was 191; in September 1929 it was 381. The Dow Jones & Company computes Dow Jones stock price averages. Begun in 1897, Dow Jones computes the averages from a set number of selected industrial stocks. The average serves as an indicator reflecting the general trend in prices of stocks and bonds in the United States. The rise from 191 to 381 indicated an overall doubling in the value of stocks during that brief time period. This indicates great profits in buying and selling stocks could be had. The federal government was also playing a part in the frenzied speculation as well. In 1927 the federal banks lowered their interest rates on loans to a low 3.5 percent. This action further enticed many more to speculate in stocks.

On September 3, 1929, the stock market reached an all-time high in the number of stocks being traded. Trading was occurring at a frantic rate as people were trying to get a share of the action. In the following weeks, however, prices of stocks gradually began to fall. Then, on October 24, more than ten million shares were sold, and prices fell dramatically as sellers tried to get out of the market. Trying to bolster stock market trading, that evening Charles E. Mitchell, chairman of the National City Bank, issued a statement saying that because of the large amount of shares sold, many were now underpriced and would be a good bargain for prospective investors. Alarm over the selling was widespread, however, and there were few buyers. On October 29 over 16 million shares were sold. In less than a month the value of stocks had declined by almost 50 percent; many were now worthless. This plunge of stock and bond values would continue until 1932.

At a Glance

- In 1929 some two hundred corporations owned almost half of American industry. These two hundred corporations, with $81 billion in assets, represented 49 percent of the corporate wealth of the country and 22 percent of the overall national wealth.
- In the 1920s more than 1,200 corporate mergers eliminated more than six thousand small companies.
- The Brookings Institution's report, *America's Capacity to Consume* (1934), reported: (1) the top 0.1 percent of American families in 1929 had a combined income equal to the bottom 42 percent in the country; (2) the 24,000 richest families had annual incomes in 1929 of over more than $100,000, and 513 families earned more than $1,000,000, while 71 percent of all American families (including single adults) had annual incomes under $2,500 and, (3) between 1920 and 1929, persons in the top 1 percent of income gained a 75 percent increase in income.
- By 1929 three of every five cars and 80 percent of all radios purchased in the United States were bought on an installment plan. The amount of money owed on installment plans in the United States increased from $1.38 billion in 1925 to $3 billion in 1929.
- In 1929 the average per capita income for all Americans was $750 per year, but for those persons engaged in agriculture it was just $273.

Crowds walk past the New York Stock Exchange Building on October 24, 1929. Approximately 12.8 million shares were sold on this day, many at significantly lower prices than their value only a few days earlier. (AP/Wide World Photos. Reproduced by permission.)

The stock market crash had a tremendous impact on the whole population, not just those who actually owned stock. When investors bought stock, businesses were able to expand production. However when stock prices began to drop, companies were unable to raise the money needed to run their businesses. Within a short time 100,000 American companies were forced to close, and consequently many workers became unemployed. During this era, no federal or state assistance for the unemployed existed. As a result, the purchasing power of Americans fell dramatically. This in turn led to even more unemployment.

Banks also failed. Pressed to meet "margins calls" to pay for stock purchases, investors withdrew their deposits. Like the public in general, however, many banks themselves had invested the customers' deposits they were holding into the stock market. Many banks lacked sufficient cash reserves to meet creditor withdrawals. As confidence in the U.S. banking system waned, depositors would sometimes spark a "run" on a bank, depleting all its cash on hand. In their panic, they often caused the bank's failure.

The mere rumor that a bank was in trouble could cause a run. Because no bank kept enough money on hand to meet all depositors demands at once, those first in line got their money, and those last in line did not. Usually the run caused the bank to face closure, as it immediately depleted all its on hand funds.

Speculators launched new companies and promoted sales of stock in what were sometimes called "Ponzi schemes." These were fraudulent investment plans where the initial investors fed off the cash of later investors. Usually in a Ponzi scheme the company had few assets and little potential to make money for people other than those who created it and got out of the investment in time. Eventually the schemes would collapse. This was a "buying on margin" scheme where investors bought stock using borrowed money for the prospect of getting rich. This posed a great financial risk, and a number of such investors lost everything.

When the federal government stepped in, it often did so too late. In the waning months of 1931, for example, the number of banks failing was increasing. Nearly 15 percent of the nation's banks went out of business between 1929 and 1931. With a banking crisis looming, the Hoover administration joined bankers and insurance company executives to raise $500 million for the National Credit Association (NCA). The organization was to assist banks beset by depositors wanting to withdraw funds. The NCA, however, took little action. By the end of 1931, it had loaned only 2 percent of its funds to troubled banks.

Agricultural Decline

Did a struggling agricultural economy of the 1920s also contribute to the Great Depression? Some thought so and found the seeds of trouble in the lowered prices for farm commodities following World War I (1914–1918). The prosperity of American agriculture, which employed fully one-quarter of workers in the United States in the 1920s, relied on market conditions overseas.

During World War I, the demand for agricultural products grew dramatically. Disruptions in production due to the war in Europe left millions of people hungry. Wheat, corn, dried fruit, meat, and other commodities produced in the United States found strong markets in Europe. For example, U.S. farmers produced less than 690,000 bushels of wheat prior to World War I, but were producing over 945,000 bushels by war's end. At the conclusion of the war, however, several changes were occurring. A number of European countries resumed production and filled the need of their citizens with locally produced commodities. Other nations, beset with economic problems, were unable to resume purchasing foodstuffs from the United States.

International competition was another reality by the 1920s. Argentina, South Africa, and other nations sold meat and cereal crops on the world market and competed strongly with American producers. Still, U.S. agricultural production remained relatively high. Farmers were still producing over 800,000 bushels of wheat a year in 1930. Farmers were growing more than they could sell.

As a result, U.S. crop surpluses grew as farmers kept up the World War I production pace, and prices fell. The downward spiral in the American agricultural economy continued through the 1920s and reached near crisis level in 1929. By then wealthy U.S. investors had cut off loans to other nations, further reducing their ability to purchase farm products from the United States. U.S. investors were busy investing at home in the stock market and American businesses. In addition, due to high tariffs, Americans were not buying foreign-made goods, so no money was flowing to Europe that they in turn needed to buy American food. As a result, the world market was oversupplied with food, foreign nations were less able to purchase U.S. produce, and the American farmers were caught in the middle. For many farmers the Great Depression started immediately after World War I and just got worse after 1929.

The Hoover administration attempted to help out. In 1929 the Agricultural Marketing Act created a Federal Farm Board. The board was designed to assist

STAGE BROADWAY SCREEN

VARIETY

PRICE 25¢.

VOL. XCVII. No. 3 NEW YORK, WEDNESDAY, OCTOBER 30, 1929 88 PAGES

WALL ST. LAYS AN EGG

Going Dumb Is Deadly to Hostess In Her Serious Dance Hall Profesh

DROP IN STOCKS ROPES SHOWMEN

Kidding Kissers in Talkers Burns Up Fans of Screen's Best Lovers

Hunk on Winchell

MERGERS HALTED

Talker Crashes Olympus

HOMELY WOMEN SCARCE; CAN'T EARN OVER $25

Demand for Vaude

FILTHY SHOW OF SHUBERTS GOOD FOR SCREEN

Pickpocketing Dying Out

Ads for Execs

Soft Drink Smuggling

Flirting Contest

Studio in Church

BROOKS COSTUMES

The October 30th edition of the "Broadway Variety" announces the stock market crash of 1929. (UPI/Corbis-Bettmann. Reproduced by permission.)

locally established farm cooperatives, private organizations through which farmers could work together in solving agricultural problems. Congress gave the board $500 million to support the cooperatives. Basically, these federal efforts were to try to establish stability in farm produce marketing. The assumption by Hoover and his advisers that the financial difficulties in agriculture were primarily marketing problems, however, proved mistaken. With the declining agricultural economy, farm foreclosures were leaving banks with a large amount of property they could not readily sell. Between 1926 and 1928, almost 1,600 banks failed and closed their doors.

Thus, the falling demand for U.S. agricultural products after World War I, overproduction by U.S. farmers, the drop in grain prices, and the government's belief that difficulties stemmed mainly from marketing problems collectively contributed to the deteriorating situation in American agriculture. With agriculture being a highly significant part of the nation's economy, this was one likely cause of the Great Depression. The factors were complex and not well understood at the time. Even decades later debate continued about which parts of the agricultural problems were the most important in contributing to the downward spiral of the economy into the early 1930s.

International Conditions

The condition of the international economy was another factor contributing to the onset of the Great Depression. The 1920s were a time of weakness and instability as once-strong European nations struggled to rebuild from the destruction of World War I. For example, Germany was once a powerful industrial and economic force. Following defeat in World War I, however, it was partially occupied by victorious forces and assessed stiff monetary penalties by other nations, including Great Britain. As a result, Germany suffered pronounced economic instability. Also, Great Britain, though victorious in war, had slipped as a stabilizing force in Europe by the 1920s, in part due to the economic drain of the war. Many looked to the United States to play a stabilizing role in helping construct a post-World War I economic order. The United States, however, turned inward, wanting to focus on its own affairs. Stung by the horrors of war, the nation largely shied away from the responsibility of greater international involvement. The turning inward and away from cooperation and interaction with other nations became known as isolationism.

The United States isolated itself, even though it came out of World War I as a creditor nation with a tremendous industrial capability. Creditor nation means the United States had loaned money to other nations to fight the war and to rebuild war-damaged infrastructures (roads, bridges, buildings, etc.). These nations now owed money back to the United States. U.S. private investors continued loaning money to European organizations, helping to stabilize the European economies while making money. By 1928, however, U.S. investors, who were commonly the wealthiest Americans, found that the U.S. stock market was more lucrative an investment than making interest off foreign loans.

Another key factor in international finance during this period was the matter of tariff protections. Tariffs are taxes placed on goods imported from foreign nations. Tariff protections mean that the taxes are raised sufficiently high to discourage people from buying foreign goods, purchasing goods made by U.S. manufacturers instead. The United States wanted to be the world's banker, food producer, and manufacturer while buying as few foreign goods as possible. Supporting this desire, President Hoover promoted U.S. exports to foreign countries while encouraging high tariffs (taxes) on imports. Raising tariffs, however, had another result. Because Americans bought fewer imported goods due to the high tariffs, so little money flowed to European countries they could not buy American exports, nor could they pay their war debts back to the United States. In addition, in retribution foreign nations would raise tariffs in their countries on U.S. goods. This would further discourage purchase of U.S. goods. Many believed these tariffs were bad policy, hurting other nations, and, in turn, hurting the Americans who supported them.

This self-centered national business perspective only served to limit markets for U.S. goods. If domestic markets should slump, which they did in late 1929, American businesses would be obliged to fall back on foreign markets to make up the sale in goods. In addition, the decline in foreign sales only further caused inventories of unsold American goods to grow and prices to decline further, creating company losses. In fact, after the Depression had begun to set in, the U.S. response was only to raise tariffs yet again with the 1930 Hawley-Smoot Act. Many believed this move only plunged the U.S. economy into deeper depression by even further limiting potential markets for U.S. goods.

End of the Road

The apparent prosperity of the 1920s was real but proved to be very limited in term. Clearly, many things were not well in the nation's economy. Danger signs, largely unread, appeared with the decline in purchasing power, rising unemployment, a stagnant real estate market, growing inventories of manufactured goods, and the lack of financial regulations. The national economy was no longer stable. Although many politicians and investors remained hopeful that prosperity was once again just around the corner, the stock market crash confirmed the harsh realities of the American economy. Taking a "wait and see" attitude, the Republican administrations of the 1920s contributed to these causes of the Great Depression. The nation lacked adequate safeguards to stop these cascading sequences of events. The federal government, with planning and action, might have intervened and stemmed some of the difficulties. But embracing Adam Smith's theories of government non-involvement in business, the government leaders chose not to act. The stock market's crash of 1929 was a confirmation to the nation that the prosperity of the 1920s was at an end, and marked the nation's slip into the Great Depression of the 1930s.

Contributing Forces

Stock Markets

A stock represents an ownership interest in a business. Stock certificates are documents that show evidence of that ownership. Stocks are also divided into smaller units of ownership called shares. Selling shares of stocks is one common way companies can

Stock Market Performance, 1929, 1932

Stock	High Day Sept. 2, 1929	Low Day Nov. 13, 1929	Final Low July 8, 1932
Allied Chemical	354	198	45 1/2
American & Foreign Power	160 1/8	51	2 1/2
American Telephone & Telegraph	302 1/2	207	72 1/8
Auburn Auto	497	130 1/4	44 7/8
General Electric	391	173	9 3/8
International Telephone & Telegraph	147 1/2	53 1/2	3 7/8
Montgomery Ward	134 1/2	49 7/8	4 3/8
Radio	98 1/2	28 3/4	3 5/8
U.S. Steel	257 5/8	151 1/2	21 1/2

Stock prices of these companies lost considerable value in just a few years. (The Gale Group.)

raise capital (money) for expanding and growing. Stock exchanges encourage people to put savings into corporate investments. The ownership interest a person specifically gains by buying stock of a particular company is usually spelled out in the company's charter or bylaws. The interests include certain rights, such as the right to receive dividends (periodic payments from the company's profits), to vote for company officers and on basic company changes, and to gain information on the performance and health of the company. Stocks are different from bonds. Companies sell bonds to rid themselves of debt. Bondholders are paid interest periodically on their invested money and then paid a certain sum of money when the bond's maturity date is reached.

Stocks are frequently sold through stock exchanges. Stock exchanges have a long history, dating back to the Middle Ages of Europe when early traders sold shares in agriculture and other interests. The French stock exchange began in the twelfth century when merchants would gather in front of a particular family's house to trade (buy and sell) stocks. The emergence of great world trading centers in the sixteenth and seventeenth centuries led to the need for banks and insurance companies. At times these institutions had funding shortages and needed to raise money by selling stock. As a result, stock exchanges grew in various countries, including Great Britain and Germany. By the nineteenth century, trading in stocks had become common in all industrialized nations.

The first stock exchange in the United States was established in Philadelphia, Pennsylvania in 1791. The following year 24 merchants and brokers, trading largely under a tree at 68 Wall Street, established a New York stock exchange. Government bonds and stocks of insurance companies and banks were the most commonly sold securities (stocks and bonds). In 1817 the New York brokers formally organized as the New York Stock and Exchange Board, and in 1863 it became the New York Stock Exchange. Other stock exchanges came along during the Civil War (1861–1865), including the American Stock Exchange. As commercial activity in the United States expanded through the nineteenth century, the stock exchanges expanded, providing capital for the rapid industrialization following the Civil War. With an economic downturn in 1837 that led to many investors losing their money, the exchange began demanding that companies disclose their financial condition to be able to sell stocks through the exchange. There were still no government requirements through the 1920s as business activity continued to increase.

The Rise of Corporations

Corporations are companies that have registered at a public office or court to gain official recognition under state law. By registering the corporation becomes a legal entity separate from its owners and managers. It can have a life beyond its original owners. Being considered a "person," corporations can sue and be sued, can purchase property, and make contracts with others. In this way investment through the stock market in corporate stock is encouraged, since stockholders owning a share of the company have limited liability for corporate actions. A stockholder would lose no more than what he had invested. Shares can easily be transferred from one investor to another, in essence changing ownership.

The process of incorporating businesses is relatively recent in history. Not until the mid-nineteenth century did corporations become the primary form of private company ownership. Until then corporations were more commonly semi-public enterprises, often

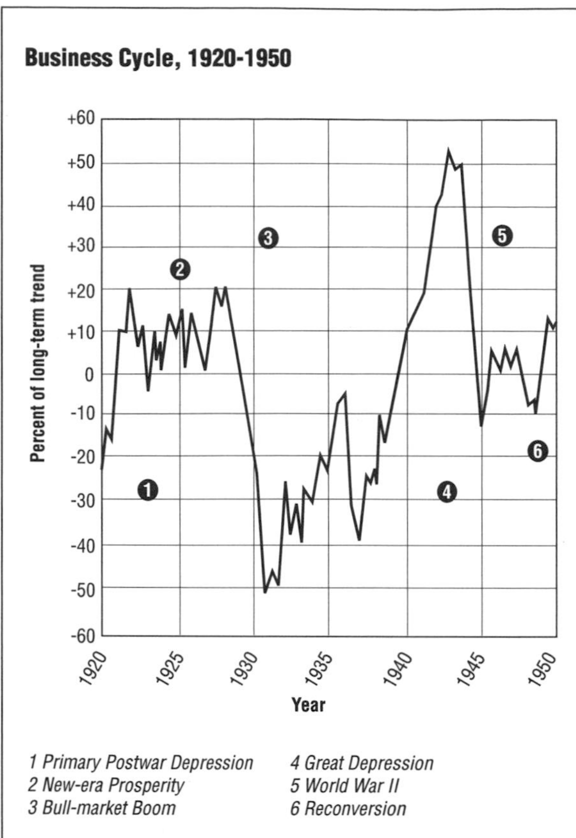

United States business activity, 1920–1950. (The Gale Group.)

involved in overseas exploration, trade, and settlement. This included the great trading companies in the seventeenth century, such as the East India Company and Hudson's Bay Company, who were granted trading monopolies for certain regions. These organizations operated as a part of the state, but for private profit guided by public charters. The charters established in detail how the enterprise would operate. The American colonies such as Virginia and Pennsylvania were first settled by such corporations as part of business ventures.

In the United States, corporate charters were initially for public service companies constructing bridges, roads, canals, and docks in addition to private banks and insurance companies. By 1811 New York passed a general incorporation law making it easier for private companies, such as manufacturers to become corporations. By the mid-nineteenth century all states had such laws. With the growth of industries requiring more capital than ever, states competed to attract businesses. One way to compete was to make the individual state laws for chartering corporations as routine as possible for the businesses. With freedom of interstate commerce (trade between states) guaranteed, businesses could shop among states for the best deal. One of the first to use these new incorporation laws were railroad companies who needed considerable capital. Steel and coal industries grew with the railroads. Following the Civil War, industries dramatically expanded from 1870 to 1910, and incorporating became much desired. Giant corporations developed, such as Standard Oil Company and United States Steel which became monopolies in their industries. Public concern over the growing powers of some of the giant corporations led to public support for government antitrust actions to preserve competition.

By the 1920s several hundred giant corporations dominated business in the United States. Their influence was immense—socially, politically, and economically. Strong individuals accumulated much wealth and power. They lobbied for *laissez faire* government policies that left them free to maximize their profit with minimal government oversight.

Agricultural Expansion

Several changes came in the agricultural industry by the 1920s, leading to financial problems. These issues involved overproduction following World War I, the need for greater capital for purchasing newly available farm machinery, a decreased demand for livestock, and the expansion of agricultural areas through government land reclamation projects. During World War I, Herbert Hoover, who served at that time as food administrator, encouraged vast increases in agricultural production. With agriculture in the United States booming in the 1910s and prices soaring, farmers used their new-found profits to purchase machinery to increase production. Steam plows, combines, seed drills, and commercial fertilizer helped them operate farms efficiently and with substantially larger yields. The shift from subsistence farming (where a family largely lived off what it produced) to commercial farming (where a family specialized in one or two crops and used mechanized machinery) had started after the Civil War. The process accelerated and, by the early twentieth century, had become the prevailing pattern in American farming.

The investments to engage in commercial farming were expensive. Many farmers went into debt, borrowing against their land to invest in new devices. Long term, this pattern contributed to a glut of products that had to compete on the world market. The process worked, however, when markets were good, especially during World War I. The United States had the opportunity to fill a production void left by Euro-

A New Yorker offers to sell his roadster after losing his money in the stock market crash. Few people anticipated the event that would usher in the Great Depression. (UPI/Corbis-Bettmann. Reproduced by permission.)

pean nations engaged in war. The predicament of farmers in debt became a major crisis when markets vanished or shrank. For instance, after World War I, when European states resumed their production of goods for the world market, international competition got stiffer again.

Like the crops, problems of over-supply also affected livestock raising. Tens of thousands of farmers in the 1910s raised horses and mules. For a time the demands of the military during World War I created a brisk market for these animals. Suddenly, in 1919, after the war was over the United States shifted from the use of draft animals to automobiles and trucks. An estimated 25 million acres of land that had been devoted to the livestock production of horses and mules suddenly had no immediate use. Much of it was converted to cropland, further adding to the over-supply problem. These farmers faced difficult times by 1920.

Another factor that would affect American agriculture in the 1920s was the creation of new agricultural lands. Congress passed the National Reclamation Act of 1902, creating the Reclamation Service. The agency, renamed the Bureau of Reclamation in 1923, mounted major projects to irrigate arid lands in the American West which affected 17 states.

The federal government constructed dams, ditches, siphons, canals, and head gates to distribute water to millions of acres on which farm families settled. These "reclaimed" lands began to produce potatoes, sugar beets, grain, alfalfa, and other commodities needed to compete on a national and international market.

Prohibition and the implementation of the Eighteenth Amendment in 1920 also was a financial setback for some farmers. Prohibition stopped the production of beer, wine, and grain-based liquors throughout the country. Owners of vineyards and hop farms were put out of business overnight or had to make dramatic changes in production. Grain producers who sold to distilleries also lost their markets. The nation's experiment with prohibition came at an economic cost to special sectors of the agricultural economy.

Perspectives

No National Planning

In the late nineteenth century, Herbert Spencer championed *laissez faire* policies in America. His teaching, lectures, and books proved highly popular, especially with the wealthy, whose positions and prosperity were justified by what Spencer said regarding letting the economy manage itself without outside forces such as the government regulating it. A consequence of the country embracing *laissez faire* was that in the early twentieth century the federal government did little economic planning. It adhered to a hands-off policy regarding the economy, believing things would work themselves out over time.

Another source of inaction was the political philosophy of President Calvin Coolidge. Coolidge, vice-president under Harding in the early 1920s, succeeded to the presidency upon Harding's death. Coolidge believed in a balanced budget and little action by the government. Thus, for nearly six years, as warning signs accumulated about the growing disease affecting the American economy, the Coolidge administration did nothing.

Herbert Hoover, who followed Coolidge as president, had gained an international reputation as an engineer and businessman, a relief administrator, and as secretary of commerce starting in 1921. Despite a more humanitarian perspective than Coolidge, neither he nor his administration were willing to engage in large-scale government economic planning. Hoover, elected president in 1928, stressed voluntary cooperation between business and government. Neither he nor his associates saw the government in an active, regulatory role.

The positions of the Coolidge, Harding, and Hoover administrations in the 1920s were strongly pro-business. The federal government cut taxes for the wealthy, discouraged the formation and actions of labor unions, and generally embraced a *laissez faire* attitude toward the economy. The federal government did little planning and avoided intervention in the business affairs of the country.

Public Demand For Goods

The desire to get a share of material possessions increased among Americans after 1900. Millions of immigrants had poured into the country since the Civil War. Many had found jobs and owned land. Advertising and promotion of material goods danced before their eyes, likely contributing to attitudes of get-rich-quick and spend now. Availability of easy money through loans allowed the public to buy the newly available goods, but placed many heavily in debt.

The 1920s in America were good times. Employment was increasing, and companies were continuing to produce at high levels. While wages were not going up, they remained stable. Although many lived in poverty, more and more people experienced a rising standard of living and more comfort than ever before. Businesses were doing well, and people were purchasing cars, real estate, carpet sweepers, radios, and wringer washing machines.

The nation became interested in the radio and the automobile. Companies such as Radio Corporation of America (RCA), Ford, and General Motors grew and prospered. Investors buying stock in American businesses considered the investments almost guaranteed moneymakers. The market did not look weak, and businesses gave financial reports, though sometimes false, to support those beliefs. With no government regulations to protect potential investors, companies could exaggerate claims of financial success and offer false promises of hot new products that might soon be expected on the market. Sometimes companies offering stock only existed on paper and completely falsified their company reports. The public investor had no way to know if what they were reading or hearing from the stockbrokers was true or not. With stocks of many real companies doing very well, how was an investor to know what was a bad investment?

International Perspectives

Foreign nations looked to the United States with envy during the boom years of the 1920s. The impact of World War I on Great Britain, Germany, and the United States set the stage for many of the economic problems of the later 1920s. While U.S. citizens enjoyed a rise in power and influence, the British saw a decline. Following its defeat, Germany found its economy in disarray, and the nation largely dropped from major influence. European perspectives of the United States began to further sour by the late 1920s. With the U.S. farm economy in decline, the United States put tariffs on foreign goods to try to persuade people to buy American goods. Although a seeming international truce in the use of tariffs by one nation on the goods of another had been reached in 1927, Congress passed the Hawley-Smoot Tariff Act in June 1930. This large increase in taxes on foreign goods forced American consumers to buy less from foreign countries. European countries lost much needed income as a result. Foreign countries retaliated by putting high tariffs on American goods, making American exports too expensive for their residents. Because of the tariff war, exports from all countries declined, as did public spending.

To make matters worse in international relations, with the U.S. stock market soaring by 1928, many wealthy U.S. financial leaders were taking their money out of European investments and putting it in Wall Street stocks. As American investment in Europe declined in 1928 and 1929, Europe's economy also declined. Several European nations thus suffered eco-

John Poole, president of the Federal American Bank, attempts to calm the nerves of thousands of depositors as they start a run on the bank in 1931. *((c) Hulton-Deutsch Collection/CORBIS. Reproduced by permission.)*

nomic instability. The worst situation, however, was in Germany, where runaway inflation ruined the value of the currency, the German mark. Eventually, at one stage in the spiraling economy, postage stamps cost millions of marks. The German mark was virtually worthless, and the nation's economy was on the verge of collapse. The unemployed and disenchanted in Germany responded positively to the patriotism and militarism of Adolf Hitler and the National Socialist (Nazi) Party, a development that would have large impact in the coming years.

The increase of tariffs and withdrawal of investments had clearly shown the United States was unwilling to assist the European nations in need. The Hawley-Smoot Act demonstrated once and for all that the United States preferred to focus internally on its own needs and not the growing international economic problems. Much of Europe was dismayed with the United States' isolating itself rather than assuming a stronger world leadership role. Many in the United States lacked the understanding of the impact of international inaction by the United States. The loss of

U.S. goods and money in Europe directly contributed to worsening economic and political problems of that region.

Impact

The Crash Arrives

The stock market crash of 1929 ended a decade of prosperity. The crash did not cause the Depression, but rather was evidence of the weakness of the economy. The economic success of the 1920s was unevenly distributed, with great wealth in the hands of only a portion of the country. There were not enough people with money to purchase all of the cars, refrigerators, clothing, and other products pouring out of the newly expanded American factories. Prosperity had been built on an unstable foundation that crumbled in 1929 with the stock market crash. America began to slip into the Great Depression.

Few people anticipated the stock market crash in the fall of 1929. Even fewer believed that it would cause the entire economy to go into a tailspin. By 1932 the average income had plunged to half of what it had been in 1929. At least one out of four Americans who had a successful job in 1929 was now out of work. As people began to lose their jobs and had no money on which to live, they also lost their homes. In 1930 over two hundred thousand evictions occurred in New York City alone. Despair was felt throughout the country as even the middle class watched in horror as savings and dreams disappeared.

Men were no longer the breadwinners, and they struggled to find food for their families. Some had to sell apples on street corners. Other hungry Americans took advantage of soup kitchens. These kitchens were organized by the Salvation Army and by churches to try to bring relief to the hungry and poor. The suicide rate during the Depression was high, and 1932 marked the most devastating year for those who had no hope. In 1932 more than twenty thousand Americans committed suicide; 16,453 of them were men. Women were also confronted with despair and depression in the 1930s. Often they were better able to cope with the problems of the era by fulfilling their expected social roles of keeping busy at home. Women would still cook, clean, and watch over their children while their husbands hopelessly searched for work and food day after day.

Not all women, of course, stayed at home. Though historically facing significant discrimination in the workplace prior to the 1930s, the number of married women in the labor force increased by 52 percent during the Great Depression. By 1940 over four million married women had jobs, representing about 15 percent of all married women in the nation. During the Depression they faced common accusations of taking jobs that could have gone to unemployed men. They were mostly able to hold jobs not normally sought by men at the time, such as in clerical positions, beauty salons, nursing, and dental hygiene. Even where they were able to keep jobs, women still commonly were paid less than men doing the same work.

The stock market crash of 1929 signaled the beginning of the most significant decline in the American economy in the nation's history. Even a decade later Americans suffered from the fallout of this event. The decline of stock values wiped out savings, destroyed public confidence, drove banks and businesses into bankruptcy, caused numerous suicides and mental breakdowns, and shattered delivery of public services.

The stock market crash became a benchmark for measuring future conditions in the stock market. For millions the events of 1929 remained a dark, bitter memory at the beginning of hard times and great suffering due to unemployment. The United States faced another major economic slump in the early 1980s. The jobless rate hit almost 11 percent by the end of 1982, the highest since the Great Depression. Approximately 12 million people were looking for jobs, the most since 1933. Bankruptcies also reached the highest level since 1932, including the closing of many banks and savings and loans. There were two million homeless living in cars and tent cities, reminiscent of the Hoovervilles of the Great Depression. Just as it had earlier, farming income also suffered, and conflicts arose in farming communities when banks tried repossessing farms and equipment from farmers who could no longer make payments on loans. The similarities to the Great Depression for many were very unsettling. Massive government spending by the federal government under President Ronald Reagan (served 1981–1989) on defense helped pull the economy out of the slump.

Remedies of the 1930s

The stock market crash unleashed events that proved exceedingly difficult to turn around. President Hoover tried but failed to respond successfully to its consequences. President Roosevelt's New Deal tried a variety of programs to bring about relief, recovery, and reform. First of all, in response to the thousands of banks that were closing all over the country, in March 1933 President Roosevelt declared a "bank holiday," closing banks to the public for a week. During

Hard economic times during the Depression meant that this hotel, located in Vincennes, Indiana and started in 1929, remained unfinished in 1938. (The Library of Congress.)

this time Roosevelt sent auditors to check the solvency (stability) of the individual banks. Those with sufficient assets to survive were permitted to reopen. Those virtually broke remained closed to restore long-term confidence in banks. This emergency measure proved highly successful in preserving the U.S. banking system at a moment of grave danger. The public once again began placing their money in banks with peace of mind. Next, Congress passed the Banking Act of 1933, commonly known as the Glass-Steagall Act. The act created the Federal Deposit Insurance Corporation (FDIC) to protect bank deposits, which were previously not guaranteed in the event of something like a bank run. The result was that the number of bank failures declined sharply and even temporarily came to a halt. With depositors assured that, even if their bank collapsed, the government would insure their deposits, confidence in the banking industry was stabilized, and people began to have more faith in putting their savings into banks.

More About...

The Securities and Exchange Commission

The Securities Exchange Act of 1934 established the Securities and Exchange Commission (SEC). Working with Congress and other federal agencies, the SEC's primary concern is with enforcing the securities laws and protecting investors who interact with these various organizations. The creation of the SEC ensured that the stock market would not be a free-for-all, but rather a more closely monitored and regulated industry than it was in the 1920s. Congress hoped to put faith back into the investor and to guarantee that the market would not experience a crash as severe as the one of 1929.

Because investors have no guarantees that securities (stock and bonds) cannot lose value, the SEC makes sure all investors have access to basic reliable information before making purchases of securities. The SEC requires almost all companies selling stocks publicly to provide financial reports to the public. The SEC also oversees the stock exchanges, brokers, dealers of stocks, and investment advisors. Companies must tell the truth about their business, their stocks, and what risks might be involved.

The SEC is composed of five commissioners, appointed by the U.S. president, who oversee the agency. In order to ensure that the Commission remains non-partisan, no more than three commissioners may belong to the same political party. The first chairman of the SEC, appointed by President Franklin Roosevelt, was Joseph P. Kennedy, father of President John F. Kennedy (served 1961–1963).

The SEC is composed of four divisions. The first is the Division of Corporation Finance. It provides administrative interpretations of the Securities Act of 1933, the Securities Exchange Act of 1934, and the Trust Indenture Act of 1939. This division also recommends regulations to implement these statutes. The second is the Division of Market Regulation, which establishes and maintains standards for fair, orderly, and efficient markets. It does this by regulating the major securities market participants such as brokerage firms. Third is the Division of Investment Management. This division oversees and regulates the investment management industry and administers the securities laws affecting investment companies and investment advisors. Finally, the fourth is the Division of Enforcement, which investigates possible violations of securities laws. With these four divisions, the SEC is able to monitor and regulate the market closely to protect investors from fraud and unstable conditions.

The SEC requires public companies to disclose meaningful information to the public so that investors can judge whether the company's securities are a good investment. Such information, which may be contained in what is known as a stock prospectus, should include all the factors surrounding the offering of the stock, the names of the company's officers and their salaries, names of others who hold 10 percent or more of stock already sold, a detailed description of the business, and the financial condition of the company. Some of this information would be included in company performance reports that are commonly available to the public.

The SEC oversees other key participants in the securities market, including stock exchanges, broker-dealers, investment advisors, mutual funds, and public utility holding companies.

In addition to the changes in banking, the federal government also faced stock market problems. Congress needed to reaffirm the public's faith in the stock market by providing some form of protection to private investors. Ferdinand Pecora, an assistant district attorney of New York, was hired by the Senate to conduct an investigation of stock market activities. A series of hearings took place to identify problems and solutions. The investigation lasted from 1932 into 1934. The resulting report identified numerous problems with stock market trading and led to a public demand for change. The Pecora investigation uncovered widespread fraud and corruption involving the sale of stocks. The fraud included major misrepresentation of what the companies and stocks represented, including the selling of stocks of fictitious companies. Potential returns on the investments were often exaggerated and high-pressure sales techniques were applied. Government regulation of the stock market was needed. On March 29, 1933, President Roosevelt sent a message to Congress demanding that stock brokers and others who sell stock be held accountable for their actions.

As a result, Congress passed the Securities Act of 1933 and the Securities Exchange Act of 1934. These laws were designed to help restore investor confidence in the market by providing more structure and government regulation. These laws were based on two ideas. First, companies offering stock on the market had to tell the public the truth about their businesses, the securities they sold, and the risks involved in investing. Second, people who sold and traded securities—brokers, dealers, and exchanges—were to put investors' interest first and treat them fairly and honestly. Violations of the laws could lead to criminal prosecution by the government and civil lawsuits by investors against the companies. In order to monitor the companies and individuals, Congress created the Securities and Exchange Commission (SEC) with the second act. This was the first time that the federal government had become directly involved in the stock market activities, and the confidence of the public in buying stocks was once again restored.

Notable People

Herbert Hoover (1874–1964). Hoover was born in West Branch, Iowa, in 1874. Orphaned at the age of nine, he lived with a variety of relatives in Iowa and spent his teenage years in Newberg and Salem, Oregon. Although his parents belonged to a "progressive" branch of the Quaker religion, his religious training was quite rigorous as his mother was an ordained Quaker minister. In 1895 Hoover graduated with a degree in geology from Stanford University and became a mining engineer. Hoover's career in mining was a success, and by 1895 he had become a millionaire. He supported the branch of progressivism that stressed cooperative economic organization, self-regulation by businesses, and voluntary activity through American society. These beliefs greatly influenced his response to the mounting economic problems that beset the country during his involvement in government. Hoover served as head of the Commission for the Relief in Belgium, as President Woodrow Wilson's U.S. food administrator (served 1917–1919), and as director general of the American Relief Administration in Europe. He became such a popular philanthropist that both the Republican and Democratic parties wanted him to be their presidential nominee in 1920. Hoover did not wish to run for president and instead served as secretary of commerce for Presidents Harding and Coolidge. In 1928 Hoover ran for the presidency and was elected under the Republican ticket.

Andrew William Mellon (1855–1937). Andrew Mellon was born in Pittsburgh, Pennsylvania. In 1886 Mellon, along with his brother Richard, took over his father's banking firm. As his experience in the banking industry grew, Mellon later established other banks. He also expanded his holdings in key American industries such as oil, locomotives, coal, hydroelectricity, bridge building, public utilities, steel, and insurance. Mellon played an important role in the founding of the Aluminum Co. of America. In 1921 Mellon resigned his position as president of the Mellon National Bank to become U.S. secretary of the treasury, serving until 1931. From 1931 to 1932, he served as ambassador to Great Britain.

In his position as treasury secretary Mellon favored high tariffs, reduction of the national debt, low personal and corporate taxes, low excise taxes, and government assistance to agriculture through the purchase and sale of commodities abroad. An active art collector, Mellon helped create the National Gallery of Art in Washington, DC, to which he donated 369 paintings and portraits, as well as monetary contributions.

John Jakob Raskob (1879–1950). Raskob, an American financier, was born in Lockport, New York, in 1879. An attorney, he moved to Ohio and became involved in industry. In 1902 he settled in Wilmington, Delaware, to run E. I. du Pont de Nemours and Company, a manufacturer of dynamite, gunpowder, and chemicals. Following World War I, Raskob invested in General Motors to help build the automotive company and its financial subsidiary, General Motors Acceptance Corporation.

A multimillionaire by the 1920s, by 1934 Raskob became an outspoken critic of President Roosevelt's New Deal. Raskob and other U.S. business leaders considered Roosevelt and his New Dealers an increasing threat to the U.S. capitalist system. Government was becoming too intrusive in private economic matters in their mind. Thoughts of New Dealers regulating the stock market and other economic reform proposals such as the Agricultural Adjustment Act, which attempted to control agricultural production, prompted Raskob to take action. Raskob's views were summed up in the article "Everybody Ought to be Rich," for *The Ladies Home Journal.* Though Raskob had earlier helped build the Democratic Party, his increasing dislike for Roosevelt led him, along with the Du Ponts, to found the American Liberty League in 1934. At that time the League became the leading voice from the right in opposition to the New Deal. They sought to shove the Democratic Party in a more conservative direction with less business regulation and lower taxes for the wealthy. It soon became apparent to much of

More About...

The Holding Company

The phenomenon of large corporate holding companies probably attracted relatively little awareness from the average American during the 1920s. Few realized the growing concentration of economic power in the country. Holding companies would operate in the following manner: A group of businessmen would form a company and sell its stocks on the lively stock market of the 1920s. With the money gained from the stock sales, they would then use the money to buy enough stocks from other existing companies to gain control of them. When the businessmen wanted to make even more money, they would create a second holding company and sell stocks. The immediate companies established by the businessmen were not actually producing any commodities, only the corporations they had purchased were producing goods or services. It was all a money game on paper, creating a complex web of companies designed to earn money for the businessmen. With the money gained from the sale of stock from the second holding company, the businessmen would buy all of the stock of the first holding company, which had no actual value beyond the businessmen's purpose of generating money to buy the stock of legitimate companies. This process could go on indefinitely as the businessmen would then establish a third and fourth holding company, each time making more money off of the stock investments and gaining increasing control over a growing number of corporations. Because of the complex relationships among holding companies, it was difficult to determine at any one time just how many existed.

Following the crash of the stock market, the public no longer had money to buy such stocks. In addition, the corporations bought by the businessmen running the holding companies were making less money as fewer goods were being sold. The holding companies were no longer bringing in money to pay the interest on investments that had been made earlier. Often, trying to pay interest to investors, they would have to take away earnings from the lower corporations. As a result, fewer goods were being produced, unemployment increased, and the nation's general economy further declined. Recognized as a contributor to the Great Depression, Congress eventually outlawed the giant holding companies.

---

the public that the League existed primarily to represent the self-interests of the rich who had founded it. Therefore its following was small and short lived.

Adam Smith (1723–1790). Smith is a major figure in the history of economic thinking and greatly influenced U.S. economic policies up through the 1920s. Smith was born in 1723 in a prosperous Scottish fishing village near Edinburgh to a well-to-do family. At age 14 he entered the university at Glasgow, at the time a major intellectual center. Graduating in three years, Smith then continued his education at Oxford. At the age of 27, in 1751 Smith became a professor at Glasgow. There Smith mixed with a wide circle of aristocrats, government leaders, world merchants, and intellectual figures, including the highly regarded philosopher David Hume. Hume became a longtime friend of Smith's. Possessing a keen interest in trade and business, Smith published his first work on the principles of human nature in 1759.

In 1763, while living in France, Smith was hired as a personal tutor for the family of British leader Charles Townshend. There Smith worked on the epic book *The Wealth of Nations* that was published in 1776. The book is recognized as the first great work on political economy and the rise of orderly societies. In it Smith explored the "laws" regulating the distribution of wealth in a society. The work represented the prevailing thoughts during the Enlightenment of Europe, an age in which major breakthroughs in science and philosophy were occurring. The inevitable progress of human societies was a prevalent theme. *The Wealth of Nations* greatly influenced the tendency toward *laissez faire* government policies of the various Republican administrations through the 1920s.

Primary Sources

The Stock Market Craze

John Hersch worked with a stock brokerage house in Chicago at the time of the stock market crash. He described in Studs Terkel's *Hard Times: An Oral His-*

tory of the Great Depression (1970, p. 75) the hectic stock market days of the late 1920s and the rampant investing going on.

> The Crash—it didn't happen in one day. There were a great many warnings. The country was crazy. Everybody was in the stock market, whether he could afford it or not. Shoeshine boys and waiters and capitalists .... A great many holding company pyramids were unsound, really fictitious values. Mr. Insull was a case in point. It was a mad dream of get-rich-quick.
>
> It wasn't only brokers involved in margin accounts. It was banks. They had a lot of stinking loans. The banks worked in as casual a way as the brokers did. And when they folded ....
>
> I had a friend in Cincinnati who was young and attractive. He had a wife and children and he was insured for $100,000. Life was over as far as he was concerned. He took a dive (jumped to his death), to collect on insurance policies. It's unthinkable now, when you know how many people have been able to come back.

October 24, 1929

Elliott V. Bell was a reporter for the *New York Times* when the stock market crashed in 1929. He recounts that day—with its sweeping highs and lows—in David Colbert's *Eyewitness to America* (1998, pp. 424–428).

> October 24, 1929, ... was the most terrifying and unreal day I have ever seen on the Street. ... The market opened steady with prices little changed from the previous day, ... then around eleven o'clock the deluge broke.
>
> It came with a speed and a ferocity that left men dazed. The bottom simply fell out of the market. ... Thousands of traders, little and big, had gone "overboard" in that incredible hour between eleven and twelve. Confidence in the financial and political leaders of the country, faith in the "soundness" of economic conditions had received a shattering blow. The panic was on.
>
> After the meeting [of bankers], Mr. Lamont walked across Broad Street to the Stock Exchange to meet with the governors of the Exchange. ... He said: "Gentlemen, there is no man nor group of men who can buy all the stocks that the American public can sell."....
>
> The streets were crammed with a mixed crowd—agonized little speculators, walking aimlessly outdoors because they feared to face the ticker and the margin clerk; sold-out traders, morbidly impelled to visit the scene of their ruin; inquisitive individuals and tourists, seeking by gazing at the exteriors of the Exchange and the big banks to get a closer view of the national catastrophe; runners, frantically pushing their way through the throng of idle and curious in their effort to make deliveries of the unprecedented volume of securities which was being traded on the floor of the Exchange....
>
> I remember dropping in to see a vice-president of one of the larger banks. He was walking back and forth in his office. "Well, Elliott," he said, "I thought I was a millionaire a few days ago. Now I find I'm looking through the wrong end of the telescope."

Suggested Research Topics

- Review newspapers for the days October 24–31, 1929, and assess the extent to which reporters grasped the seriousness of the crash of the stock market.
- Examine the actions of Andrew Mellon as secretary of the treasury in the 1920s and identify what steps he took to try to keep the United States prosperous.
- Investigate the real estate boom in Florida or southern California in the 1920s, and assess the lack of realism displayed by investors in buying properties in these states.

Bibliography

Sources

Bordo, Michael D., Claudia Goldin, and Eugene N. White, eds. *The Defining Moment: The Great Depression and the American Economy in the Twentieth Century.* Chicago: University of Chicago Press, 1998.

Glasner, David, ed. *Business Cycles and Depressions: An Encyclopedia.* New York: Garland Publishing, Inc., 1997.

Leuchtenberg, William E. *The Perils of Prosperity.* Chicago, IL: University of Chicago Press, 1993.

McElvaine, Robert S. *The Great Depression: America, 1929–1941.* New York: Times Books, 1993.

Myers, William Starr and Walter Newton, eds. *The Hoover Administration: A Documented Narrative.* New York: Charles Scribner's Sons, 1936.

Parrish, Michael E. *Anxious Decades: America in Prosperity and Depression, 1920–1941.* New York: W.W. Norton, 1992.

Further Reading

Allen, Frederick Lewis. *Only Yesterday: An Informal History of the 1920's.* New York: Harper & Brothers, 1931.

Barton, Bruce. *The Man Nobody Knows: A Discovery of the Real Jesus.* Indianapolis: Bobbs-Merrill Company, 1925.

Chandler, Lester V. *America's Greatest Depression, 1929–1941.* New York: Harper & Row, 1970.

Galbraith, John Kenneth. *The Great Crash, 1929.* Boston: Houghton Miffin Company, 1954.

Green, Harvey. *The Uncertainty of Everyday Life 1915–1945.* New York: Harper Collins, 1992.

Jacobson, Matthew. *The Money Lords: The Great Finance Capitalists, 1925–1950.* New York: Weybright & Talley, 1972.

Parrish, Michael. *Anxious Decades: America in Prosperity and Depression, 1920–1941.* New York: W. W. Norton, 1992.

Phillips, Cabell. *From the Crash to the Blitz, 1929–1939.* New York: MacMillan, 1969.

Terkel, Studs. *Hard Times: An Oral History of the Great Depression.* New York: Pantheon Books, 1986.

See Also

Banking; Employment; Farm Relief; Global Impacts; Interwar Era; Labor and Industry; New Deal (First, and Its Critics); Reconstruction Finance Corporation

Civilian Conservation Corps

1933-1941

Introduction

"It is my belief that what is being accomplished will conserve our natural resources, create future national wealth and prove of moral and spiritual value not only to those of you who are taking part, but to the rest of the country as well." These words of support for the Civilian Conservation Corps (CCC) program were spoken by one of its most ardent supporters, President Franklin D. Roosevelt (served 1933–1945), in a speech on July 8, 1933, while greeting CCC enrollees (quoted in Franklin D. Roosevelt's *The Public Papers and Addresses of Franklin D. Roosevelt,* 1938, p. 271).

The Civilian Conservation Corps (CCC), which lasted from 1933 to 1941, became one of the most notable programs launched by the federal government in response to the Great Depression. The purposes of this agency were to provide relief to millions of young men who needed jobs, to provide modest food and shelter to those in need, to offer instruction in basic work skills, and to build facilities and make improvements on public lands and Indian reservations.

By 1933 millions of young Americans were unemployed. The early onset of tough times in the mid-1920s kept a generation from working and securing experience that would enable them to become productive laborers. Compelled to remain with their parents and siblings, these young Americans were restless and frustrated. The CCC enrolled American males between the ages of 18 and 25, placed the CCC

Chronology:

1933: Emergency Conservation Work Act creates the Civilian Conservation Corps (CCC).

April 7, 1933: CCC inducts first enrollee 37 days after inauguration of President Franklin D. Roosevelt.

1933: President Roosevelt names Robert Fechner national director of the Emergency Conservation Work Act and head of the CCC.

1933–1948: CCC creates 725 cubic feet of records (Record Group 35), including 10,850 still images, motion pictures, architectural plans, and 691 cubic feet of written records in the National Archives.

1934: Clarence S. Marsh is named to head education programs in the CCC.

1935: More than 500,000 men enroll in over 2,600 CCC camps across the United States.

1935: CCC companies secure special assignment to assist the U.S. Grazing Service in implementing the Taylor Grazing Act of 1934 on public lands in the American West.

1937: CCC gains permanent status as a federal agency.

1940: John T. McEntee is named second director of the CCC.

1941: Congress begins investigations to determine whether or not the CCC remains vital to the nation's interests.

1941–1947: More than 150 CCC camps across the country begin to house conscientious objectors who declined military service.

1942: Congress withdraw funding of the CCC and its programs end.

1943–1948: CCC liquidates its operations and facilities, turning some over to other federal agencies and activities.

companies under U.S. Army control, relocated the men to work sites, established camps where they would live and work, and mounted projects which would benefit both them and the nation.

Critics charged that the CCC was a thinly veiled attempt to build up the nation's military forces. The 1930s were years of American neutrality and disinterest in military preparedness. The close relationship between the young laborers in the CCC and the military structure of the organization drew the attention of those committed to peace and disarmament.

The CCC sought to create a positive atmosphere wherein young men could learn job skills, engage in projects needed by the nation, earn a modest salary, and return a large portion of their earnings to their parents to help them cope with their basic needs. For many young men, the CCC was a ticket to adventure. Enlistment in the CCC offered a chance to travel to new parts of the country, especially to the federal lands of the American West. The CCC afforded a break from the grinding monotony of enduring a poverty-stricken existence at home.

CCC-ID, the Indian Division of the CCC, enlisted American Indian young men in projects to provide special assistance to tribal communities. These segregated units of the CCC worked on reservations to build needed improvements. Another special division of the CCC was assigned to helping the U.S. Grazing Service carry out the Taylor Grazing Act of 1934.

Though the CCC proved to be an expensive program through the years, the work of the CCC survives into contemporary times. As of the early twenty-first century, the public still used CCC-built campgrounds and walking trails popular for outdoor recreation, reservoirs to water cattle on the open range, various stone structures including National Park facilities, water towers, and pump houses for irrigation. They also had fought many forest fires and planted over two billion trees. At its height in 1935, the CCC employed over 500,000 young men placed in over 2,600 camps.

Issue Summary

Unemployed American Youth

The Civilian Conservation Corps (CCC) was created in 1933 by the Emergency Conservation Work Act to provide work for young men who were jobless because of the Great Depression. President Roosevelt sought to put these men, ages 18 to 25, to work on resource conservation projects across the United States and intended the CCC to help solve two of the country's most serious problems, unemployment and resource degradation. The projects provided for work in reforestation, road construction, prevention of soil erosion, park and flood control projects, and construction of facilities on federal lands and Indian reservations.

Distress during the Great Depression fell heavily on young Americans. Estimates by 1933 suggested that as many as 250,000 teenage hoboes, male and female, roamed America. Some were "street kids" and others were "boxcar kids," riding the rails to escape their problems. Some teenagers left their homes because they sought adventure. Many more ran away to escape poverty and the burden they caused their parents. Tens of thousands looked for work, but few found it.

Creation of a Peacetime Army

President Roosevelt wasted no time: he called the 73rd Congress into Emergency Session on March 9, 1933, to hear and authorize his program. He proposed to recruit unemployed young men, enroll them in a peacetime army, and send them into battle against destruction and erosion of the nation's natural resources. Senate Bill 5.598, introduced on March 27, 1933, went through both houses of Congress and was on the President's desk to be signed on March 31, 1933. Roosevelt promised that he would have 250,000 men in camps by the end of July 1933 and hoped to launch an historic mobilization of men, material, and transportation on a scale never before known in time of peace. Only 37 days had elapsed from Roosevelt's inauguration on March 4, 1933, to the induction of the first enrollee on April 7.

After the authorization of the CCC, the program faced an immediate problem. The majority of the unemployed youth was concentrated in the East, while most of the projects were in the West. The army was the only agency with the capability of solving the problem and became involved in the program from the beginning. Mobilizing the nation's transportation system, the army moved thousands of enrollees from induction centers to work camps. Officers of the army, coast guard, marine corps and navy worked together temporarily to command camps and companies. The presence of the army also created the necessary organization that was needed for the program to function in a systematic way. The CCC possessed a military organization with officers and enrollees. In the field most of the enrollees worked for the National Park Service, Soil Conservation Service, Grazing Service, or Forest Service. In camp they lived under army regulations. Although building designs were standardized, enrollees personalized the camps with their own landscaping, decorations and building improvements. The men lived by military schedules, ate in mess halls, and lived in tents or simple wood barracks. Many CCC facilities looked like army barracks housing troops in basic training.

More About...

"Striking a Chord: Loveless CCC"

The song "Striking a Chord: Loveless CCC" was popular among railroad "wanderers" in the 1930s. Although the CCC offered an opportunity for a young man to work and send money to his family, work and life were not easy (available from the World Wide Web at http://www.pbs.org/wgbh/amex/rails/sfeature/lovelessccc.html).

Why did I ever join the C.C.C.?
Oh, why did I join the C.C.C
Why did I join the C.C.C.?
This old hard labor's killing me.

They treat me like a dirty dog
I have to slave down in a log
And they feed me like a hog
Oh, why did I join the C.C.C.?

I haft to work most ever day
Five bucks a month is my pay
I'm just a wasting my life away
Oh, why did I join the C.C.C.?

The Lieut. sure is hard-boiled
His hands and clothes are never soiled
When I come in all day I've toiled
Oh, why did I join the C.C.C.?

These O.D. clothes sure is hot
They'll make you scratch a whole lot
They'll make you wish you'd never got
Into this old C.C.C.

There's an empty cot in the barrack tonight
There's a C.C.C.'s head hanging low
The axe and saw hang on the wall
Now he's gone where the C.C.C. boys go.

There's a place for every C.C.C.
Where the leader takes care of his own
How happy I'll be when I leave the C.C.C.
And there'll be no K.P. at home.

Criticisms from the Peace Advocates

Many critics of the CCC were concerned with the Department of War's involvement. They feared that the CCC was a means to put guns into the hands of young men and to prepare them for war. A growing concern was that CCC workers would have their shovels replaced with rifles. However, the focus of the CCC did not go astray, and the program remained true to its goals of resource conservation and solution to unemployment.

The military was not the only government agency to get involved in the CCC. The Department of Labor was responsible for the selection and enrollment of applicants. The Departments of Agriculture and Interior helped plan and organize work to be performed in every state. By working together and pooling resources, the federal government was able to create a national program that was efficient and successful.

Career army officers played a central role in shaping the layout and construction of CCC camps, establishing discipline, and laying down expectations for recruits. The CCC, however, did not require uniforms, drill young men in marching and weaponry, or require such protocols as salutes and deference to officers.

Civilian Control of the CCC

In April 1933 Roosevelt appointed Robert Fechner the national director of the Emergency Conservation Work Act. Although Roosevelt thought of the CCC as his special project and retained some decision-making power, Fechner grew in authority and proved an honest and capable administrator. In addition to Fechner's role, an advisory council had oversight of the program. The council consisted of representatives of the secretaries of war, labor, agriculture, and interior. Never before had there been an agency like the CCC in the United States.

The coordination between the several branches of government in peacetime was unique and proved highly successful in achieving its goals in regard to the CCC. Such cooperation seen in the CCC program was carried over to some other New Deal programs, including the Works Progress Administration (WPA) and the National Youth Administration (NYA). However, this era of such sweeping cooperation came to a close by the beginning of World War II (1939—1945). Political conservatives who disliked large government programs took stronger control of Congress by the start of the war. Big business, which largely disdained close coordination, took the lead on war efforts and gained support in curtailing New Deal government programs. Renewed efforts at social reforms in the 1960s were unable to achieve the degree of cooperation that the early New Deal years gained.

CCC Recruits

Requirements for joining the CCC were simple. Enrollees had to be aged 18 to 25, single, healthy, and unemployed. They signed up for six months of service, which could be renewed three times for a total enlistment of two years. They were expected to work at whatever job they were assigned. In return, the men received room, board, clothing and thirty dollars each month. The program required that $25 a month be sent home to the man's family to provide some financial relief. Cities and rural areas all across the nation felt the economic impact of the money that was sent home. The remaining $5 was for the men to spend and was often used to buy necessities at the camp canteen. Communities close to the work camps also benefited from many local purchases, and this sometimes staved off failure of small businesses.

Expansion of the CCC Mission

Although relief of unemployed youth was the original objective of the CCC, in early 1933 two important modifications became necessary. The first change extended enlistment coverage to 15,000 American Indians whose economic difficulties had largely been ignored. American Indians were able to work on projects that aided them in protecting their heritage as well as more typical conservation projects. For example, the Haida and Tlingit of Southeast Alaska restored and replicated totem poles in the Tongass National Forest, thus preserving their artistic and cultural traditions. Their projects included construction of plank slab ceremonial houses at Totem Bight near Ketchikan and at Chief Shake's Island in the middle of Wrangell Harbor—complete with replicas of totem poles—and handsome totem pole parks at Sitka and Saxman.

Before the CCC program was terminated, more than 15,000 American Indians were enrolled in CCC-ID (Indian Division) and were paid to help reclaim the land that had once been their exclusive domain. Other projects included construction on reservations of tribal halls, clinics, roads, reservoirs, fences, and telephone systems.

The second modification made to the CCC authorized the enrollment of about 25,000 older local men (called LEMs) who, because of their special skills or experience, trained unskilled enrollees. Communities near the work camps demanded that their own unemployed be eligible for hire and, because of the obvious need for this mentor program, their requests were satisfied. By working with local experts, enrollees were able to make a transition from city folk to expert handlers of axe and shovel. The LEMs trained the young men in skills such as masonry, carpentry, engine repair, blacksmithing, fire fighting, trail construction, and forestry.

A third unplanned modification was made in 1933 when President Roosevelt, through Executive Order 6129, authorized the immediate enrollment of about

President Franklin D. Roosevelt eats lunch with Civilian Conservation Corps members in 1933 at Camp Fechner, Virginia. (AP/Wide World Photos. Reproduced by permission.)

25,000 veterans of the Spanish American War (1898) and World War I (1914–1918), with no age or marital restrictions. These men were at first housed in separate camps and performed conservation duties suited to their age and physical condition. Many war veterans participated in the CCC and took advantage of the opportunity to rebuild lives disrupted by earlier service to the United States. These older men understood military discipline and the value of hard work to achieve specific objectives.

In addition the CCC drew a fairly wide response from black Americans. The program did not discriminate on the basis of race or creed. By 1940, 250,000 black American recruits had served in the CCC. The CCC developed 83 all-black camps in 12 southern states and 151 mixed-race camps elsewhere in the country.

Mission in Education

The Emergency Conservation Work Act did not mention education or training and, not until 1937, were CCC recruits formally introduced to such programs. However, in 1934, President Roosevelt appointed Clarence S. Marsh as the first director of education. The education aspect of the CCC was often criticized, and some suspected that, at the camp level, it might interfere with the work program. This did not happen, and only in the later years of the program was training authorized during normal working hours.

Eventually, the CCC education program taught more than 40,000 illiterates to read and write. Many young men received high school diplomas and were trained in a variety of trades that helped them when they finished the program. As the CCC program progressed and education courses became available, many of the work camps offered journalism. Most camps published their own newspapers, or the young men wrote regular columns for the local town papers. Some camps built small dark rooms where the recruits learned how to develop photographs. Sometimes they submitted these photos to the regional CCC monthly newspapers.

Highly important in education were the on-the-job skills imparted to the recruits. The young men learned how to operate horse-drawn and mechanically powered equipment. Each camp had a blacksmith shop where a number of recruits mastered engine repair and general equipment maintenance. The men also mastered the use of shovel, axe, and saw and, in many units, became adept builders of fences, roads, trails, bridges, and structures such as barracks, barns, guard stations, ranger stations, and lookouts. Skills in carpentry, stone masonry, wiring, and plumbing were central to the CCC projects.

Two laborers at work in Prince George's County, Maryland, in August 1935. CCC men lived by military schedules, ate in mess halls, and lived in tents or simple wood barracks. (The Library of Congress.)

High Point Years, 1935–1936

By 1935 the program was well under way. Gone were the early days of drafty tents, ill-fitting uniforms, and haphazard work operations. Enrollees proved to be hard working, well fed, and providing for their families while they improved millions of acres of federal, state, and local lands. The CCC received acknowledgment through reports in major newspapers, even those that opposed other phases of the New Deal. The director's office was flooded with letters and telegrams from people all over the country requesting new camps in their states. Eventually, there were camps in all states including Hawaii, Alaska, Puerto Rico, and the Virgin Islands. CCC workers were performing over one hundred different types of jobs.

The years 1935–1936 witnessed not only the peak in size and popularity of the CCC, but also the first major attempt to change the system, which had proved to be workable and successful since early 1933. Harry Hopkins was a new advisor to the program and established and coordinated ground rules for the selection of enrollees. His new procedures relied on federal relief rolls and did away with the more locally controlled quota systems used by local authorities. The quota systems had been based on recruiting from different racial groups in proportion to their presence in the local population. The system greatly limited the number of black American enrollees and other minorities who were highly represented on the relief rolls. Use of relief rolls would potentially increase the number of minorities enrolled. Recruiting from federal work relief rolls required a national federal coordination of the 48 states. This approach was opposed by political conservatives who resented the greater intrusion of the federal government into what they considered a responsibility of the states to provide for their citizens. The change produced confusion, and recruiting efforts were greatly affected. The CCC sought to employ 600,000 men, but by September 1935 there were only about 500,000 men located in 2,600 camps across the country. Fechner, the director of the program, struggled to meet the enrollment requirement. Then another change to the program was revealed to him. Roosevelt informed Fechner that there was to be a drastic reduction in the number of camps and enrollees in an effort to balance the federal budget in an election year. In order to get reelected, Roosevelt had to cut government spending, and this invited trouble for the CCC program.

President Roosevelt's proposed reduction in spending resulted in public outrage. The CCC was at the height of its popularity, and no one wanted camps to close, especially in their own state. Both Republicans and Democrats sought to reverse Roosevelt's policy on the proposed budget cut. Roosevelt wanted the budget reduction to begin in January 1936 and he proposed that by June approximately 300,000 men would be enrolled in 1,400 camps. Dissent to the proposal was so strong that Roosevelt and his advisors believed the public outcry to be a threat to their whole legislative program. Roosevelt retreated, and called off the proposed cut on the CCC, advising Fechner that all existing camps and personnel would remain.

Improvements on Federal Lands

The CCC developed many types of projects, including forest preservation, drainage improvements, park restoration, disaster relief, and grazing and wildlife protection. The CCC built fire towers, fought forest fires, and controlled soil erosion on millions of acres of land by planting trees. Man-made drainage systems helped reclaim 84.4 million acres of good agricultural land. Forty-six camps were assigned to the drainage program, most of them American Indian enrollees.

In 1937 members of the CCC were called upon to provide flood relief in the Ohio and Mississippi valleys. Other disasters that the CCC participated in were the floods of Vermont and New York in 1937 and the New England hurricane of 1938. Workers were also called upon during the blizzards of 1936–1937 in Utah where one million sheep were stranded and in danger of starvation. CCC crews braved snowdrifts and the bitter cold to save the flocks. Workers also sought to protect natural habitats of wildlife, were involved in stream improvements, restocked fish, and built dams for water conservation.

Many of the CCC projects, however, also harmed native animals. The CCC was directed to kill prairie dogs, coyotes, jackrabbits and other "varmints." This task was done by dispensing poison by hand. Enrollees also pulled weeds and dug out "invading" plants deemed harmful to livestock.

Several units of the CCC worked with the U.S. Grazing Service, established in 1935, to implement the Taylor Grazing Act (1934) on public lands. These companies worked in remote parts of the American West to build roads, corrals, drift fences, reservoirs, and to make spring improvements. They fought fires, dug out livestock and haystacks buried in snowdrifts, and stretched telephone lines. The projects mounted in conjunction with the U.S. Grazing Service were vital in assisting ranchers and farmers in maintaining their flocks and crops during the Great Depression.

At a Glance

Civilian Conservation Corps History Source

The National Association of Civilian Conservation Corps Alumni (NACCCA) maintain a headquarters at 16 Hancock Avenue, St. Louis, MO. 63125 (P.O. Box 16429, St. Louis, MO., 63125). Among its many activities is maintaining a national list of CCC camps, listed by state, and preserving the history of the CCC. Information is available on the World Wide Web at http://www.cccalumni.org.

A Civilian Conservation Corps Museum is located in Grayling, Michigan, in North Higgins Lake State Park. The facility includes a well-preserved barracks and tells the story of the CCC in Michigan. Information is available on the World Wide Web at http://www.sos.state.mi.us/history/museum/museccc/index.html.

Permanent Federal Agency Status

The Civilian Conservation Corps approached maturity in 1937 with thousands of enrollees passing through the system and returning home to boast about their experiences. Hundreds more demonstrated their satisfaction with the CCC by extending their enlistment. By this time life in the camps was fairly routine with work every day except Sunday.

In April 1937 Roosevelt sought to make the CCC a permanent agency. Even though the success of the corps was apparent, Congress never considered it to be more than a temporary relief organization with an uncertain future. Many saw the CCC as a solution to unemployment rather than a continuous agency working to protect the dissipation of the nation's resources. Congress refused to make the CCC permanent, but did extend its life for two more years.

Changes and Termination of Funding

Major changes that brought about the demise of the Conservation Civilian Corps began to occur in 1939 with changes in both the United States and Europe and within the structure of the CCC. England and France were being drawn into World War II (1939–1945), which directly affected the United States, causing jobs to become more plentiful. As a result, applications for the CCC declined. However, the most significant change to the CCC was Roosevelt's plan to reorganize the administrative functions of some federal agencies. The Federal Security Agency (FSA) was created to consolidate several offices, services, and boards under one director. The CCC lost its status as an independent agency, and was brought under control of the FSA. Fechner was furious, especially when he learned that the director of the FSA would have authority over him. In angry protest Fechner submitted his resignation but, probably at Roosevelt's request, later withdrew it.

A year of change for the CCC began in 1940 with Fechner's death from a heart attack. Fechner was replaced as director of the CCC by John T. McEntee. McEntee had an entirely different personality, especially lacking the patience and friendships that Fechner had possessed. Tension between the Department of the Interior and the director's office increased. Although the CCC was facing new problems, the program remained popular with the public. In response Congress appropriated $50 million in funding for the CCC to last through 1941, but Congress would never again be so generous. Other major problems were

CCC workers dig holes for a fence under construction in Greene County, Georgia in May 1941. (The Library of Congress.)

developing in Congress, especially in the area of defense and concern over the war in Europe.

By the middle of 1941, the CCC was in serious trouble. There was a lack of new applicants, enrollees left work camps for jobs, and public support was weakening. Many were beginning to question the necessity of the CCC when unemployment had almost disappeared. Many CCC workers were finding better jobs that paid more than the $30 a month rate. Most agreed that more work could be done, but ensuring the country's defense became a central concern. As the war progressed, the nation became focused on the war effort. The joint committee of Congress, authorized by the 1941–1942 appropriations bill, was in session to investigate all federal agencies to determine which ones, if any, were essential to the war effort. The CCC came under review in late 1941, and the committee determined that it was to be abolished by July 1, 1942. The CCC was never abolished but, instead, Congress refused to appropriate the CCC any additional funds. In 1942 many politicians were trying to pass legislation to fund the CCC, but their efforts failed. The agency's assets were liquidated, and the Civilian Conservation Corps dissolved.

With the entry of the United States into World War II in 1941, more than 120 CCC camps across the country began to receive young men who refused the draft and induction into the armed forces. The camps housed conscientious objectors, or "conchies." These men resumed many of the activities that the CCC had done, including fighting forest fires and replanting over burned areas. The Conscientious Objectors' Public Service Camps finally closed in 1947.

Contributing Forces

Several factors set the stage for the programs of the CCC and its general success between 1933 and 1942. This federal agency reached out through its employment of more than three million young men to become a major success of the New Deal.

Homeless American Youth

Thousands of young Americans left home to try to find jobs or to lessen the burden on their parents and siblings during the 1930s. An estimated 250,000 teenage hoboes roamed America. Between 1929 and 1939, the Interstate Commerce Commission logged the deaths of 26,647 trespassers on railroad property and noted another 27,171 who were injured.

A number of those involved in the New Deal were aware of the dangers to health and life of so many young people wandering across the land. With this in mind, the CCC was the first New Deal program aimed specifically at providing relief for homeless and unemployed young people. The CCC became a means to reduce the numbers who were "riding the rails" and living in poverty, hunger, and danger.

Needs in National Forests and Public Rangelands

Since its creation in 1906, the U.S. Forest Service had lacked personnel and appropriations to mount programs to develop a management infrastructure. The CCC became the innovative agency to provide the much-needed assistance so long awaited by the forest rangers. CCC crews opened thousands of miles of trails and roads by hand labor. They stretched telephone wires and erected lookouts atop lofty peaks where monitors watched for fires. They built guard stations, ranger stations, warehouse complexes, playgrounds, campgrounds, and day recreation sites in the national forests. When peace came in 1945 and America's economy improved, the recreation boom of the 1950s on federal lands was directly a result of CCC labors in the 1930s.

Passage of the Taylor Grazing Act in 1934 brought more than 150 million acres of public lands under the administration of the U.S. Grazing Service and, after 1946, under its successor, the Bureau of Land Management. Between 1935 and 1942, the numerous CCC companies in western states worked directly with the Grazing Service to construct improvements on the public range. These included drift fences, corrals, spring surrounds, and reservoirs. CCC men opened trails, eradicated poisonous weeds, sewed nutritious grasses, and poisoned "varmints" believed detrimental to the health of the range.

Needs of American Indians

American Indians suffered terribly in the years leading up to the Great Depression. All aspects of American Indian life were touched by poverty. In the early 1900s, infant mortality rates were twice the national average. American Indians were seven times more likely to die of tuberculosis than was the general population. Indian boarding schools were overcrowded and staffed with unqualified personnel that provided poor medical care and an unhealthy diet. Under these conditions Indian literacy rates remained low. The infrastructure of their reservations was crumbling or nonexistent.

The federal government mounted reforms to respond to some of these issues. The CCC-Indian Division was created to help American Indians build and rebuild their own facilities on their own lands. The CCC-ID employed more than 80,000 American Indians who built clinics, community buildings, roads, reservoirs, and telephone systems. The CCC-ID generated jobs, skills, and important long-term benefits for tribes.

Needs of Rural Residents

As the Great Depression deepened, older men also found themselves unemployed. Skilled laborers such as carpenters, farmers, lumbermen, miners, and others found themselves idle. Job scarcity in the rural areas of the United States devastated local economies.

The arrival of 150 or more green recruits at CCC camps convinced older, local resident men that they had important things to offer the CCC. The Local Experienced Men (LEM) recruits were those over age twenty-five who became the teachers at the CCC camps. These men knew blacksmithing, carpentry, equipment operation, fence and corral building techniques, cooking, and plumbing. Their involvement helped the CCC succeed and also provided jobs for unemployed men and some stimulus to local economies.

Adaptive Use of CCC Camps

When Congress withdrew funding of the CCC in 1942, the federal government converted dozens of camps into alternative facilities during World War II. More than 150 facilities became Public Service Camps that housed conscientious objectors, men who declined to fight but who were willing to work in alternative service during wartime. Nearly 50,000 war objectors became medics and served with the military; 13,000 elected not to have anything directly to do with the war effort and were placed under the National Service Board for Religious Objectors (NSBRO). This board operated 143 camps, and the federal government ran another eight. Most provided assistance to the Bureau of Reclamation, Forest Service, Soil Conservation Service, and the Farm Security Administration. The "conchies," as they were often called, fought fires, planted trees, helped to check erosion, and continued CCC programs.

In early 1942 President Roosevelt issued Executive Order 9066. This measure mandated the removal of persons of Japanese American descent, whether citizens of the United States or not, residing in the states of California, Oregon, and Washington, but not in Hawaii or Alaska (in the war zone). Over 100,000 people were relocated and held in internment camps for the duration of World War II. In a number of instances, these facilities included the recently abandoned CCC camps in Idaho, Nevada, and California.

A poster promoting the CCC. The agency employed millions of young men during the Great Depression. *(The Library of Congress.)*

Perspectives

Local Perspectives

The CCC was viewed with mixed feelings by local communities. A number of Americans were suspicious of the "city boys" who came in from far across the country to mount projects close to the homes, farms, and properties of those who had resided in an area for a long time. Some feared threats to local morality, but most realized that the CCC was a great infusion of talent and energy for projects much needed and long overdue.

Local communities soon became accustomed to hosting monthly dances, baseball and basketball games, and attending open houses at the CCC camps. Isolated residents found fellowship and friendship with the CCC men who lived nearby, and many CCC men decided to settle down and marry young women who lived near the camps where they had served.

The shipshape manner in which the CCC operated its camps, its sense of discipline, and the many projects and good deeds accomplished by the CCC won over almost all of the critics. When CCC men fought fires, cleared snowdrifts, helped farmers get hay to their snowbound livestock, or provided rescues of those swept up in disasters and accidents, the appreciation was widespread. Similarly, CCC work in construction of parks, playgrounds, flood control facilities, and soil conservation projects attracted local support and favorable attention.

In southeast Alaska the CCC-ID projects helped preserve rapidly decaying totem poles and, for a time, perpetuated traditional arts by enabling a younger generation to work with surviving master carvers. The CCC-ID projects in the Tongass National Forest today draw tens of thousands of tourists who visit the totem parks and native cultural centers and museums in the state.

National Perspectives

The CCC met a great human need. It took homeless men from the streets and boxcars and gave them bed, board, and modest income. The CCC also created a flow of income to the families of recruits. This was founded on the principle of each man sending home $25 per month for the support of his family.

The CCC met a great need for improvements on federal lands, especially on the public land of states west of the Mississippi River. The CCC built parks, playgrounds, roads, and much-needed buildings on Indian reservations and national forests. On the public domain, it helped implement the mandates of the Taylor Grazing Act.

Critics of the CCC who feared it was merely a guise to prepare America for war, found little evidence to support their suspicions. The role of the army in the CCC was largely structural. The army did not impose a military regimen or drill the recruits in anticipation of war. Instead, it brought stability and order to a rapidly mobilized peacetime force of young men whose assignment was to do "good works" all across the land.

Impact

The CCC left many legacies. Many small towns in America never before had improved parks, secure playgrounds, trails, and community buildings. The CCC developed remarkable buildings and roads in the national forests. Crews built guard stations, ranger stations, lookouts, trails, bridges, roads, and campgrounds. A two-mile river trail in the Grand Canyon, constructed by the CCC in the 1930s, took two years to complete. Many of the cabins in Yellowstone National Park were built or rebuilt by the CCC.

Much of the post-World War II recreation on public lands was a direct consequence of the facilities constructed by the CCC. Similarly, the U.S. Forest Service, when it increased staffing and began to shift from merely caring for the land to preparation of timber sales, made use of the warehouses, office compounds, and other facilities built in the 1930s by the CCC.

The CCC also enlivened many rural communities. A CCC camp brought a new spirit to many areas. The young men played basketball and baseball against local teams. They came to dances, and many met and married local women and settled in the areas where they had come to work. Many of the recruits had never before been away from home. The CCC enabled them to see new parts of the country and to pick up important vocational skills many would use in jobs for the remainder of their lives.

The closing of CCC operations in 1942 and the abandonment of its facilities led to other uses of the camps. More than 150 Public Service Camps housing conscientious objectors who declined to fight in World War II were established in former CCC camps. These men continued many of the programs started by the CCC, especially fighting fires and reforestation. Some CCC camps were also converted into relocation centers for Japanese Americans subjected to Executive Order 9066.

Aside from the many roads, bridges, lookout towers, and other physical reminders of the CCC, the program became a model for later youth programs. In 1964, as part of President Lyndon Johnson's (served 1963–1969) Great Society programs, Congress passed the Economic Opportunity Act. The act created the Job Corps to provide educational and vocational training to 16- to 24-year-old young men and women. The program was directly patterned after the CCC and prepared youth to enter the job market. As with CCC alumni, graduates of the Job Corps have frequently pointed back to the Job Corps experience as life changing.

At a Glance

Achievements of the Civilian Conservation Corps

Between 1933 and 1940 the CCC had accomplished the following:

- Enrolled 2.6 million men
- 2.2 million aged 18 to 25
- 185,000 veterans
- 50,000 American Indians
- 20,000 residents of U.S. territories
- Planted 1.85 billion trees
- Constructed 106,800 miles of roads and trails
- Laid 73,590 miles of telephone lines
- Constructed 42,780 bridges
- Erected 49,500 buildings
- Laid 4.89 million check dams in gullies
- Built 17.1 million rods of fences
- Thinned 3.4 million acres of forests
- Impounded 5,575 ponds with diversion dams
- Made 18,000 spring and well improvements
- Expended 9.3 billion man days fighting fires

Additionally, before the CCC was terminated, more than 80,000 American Indians were involved in its programs. By 1942 the CCC's accomplishments included 3,470 fire towers erected, 97,000 miles of fire road built, and more than 3 billion trees planted. In Michigan alone, between 1933 and 1942, the CCC planted 484 million trees, spent 140,000 days fighting forest fires and constructed 7,000 miles of truck trails, 504 bridges and 222 buildings.

Notable People

Robert Fechner (1876–1940). Appointed by Roosevelt to be the national director of the Emergency Conservation Work Act, Fechner, along with an advisory council, oversaw the CCC program. Fechner was born in Tennessee but largely educated in Georgia. For many years he worked as a railroad machinist and traveled widely throughout the South, Mexico, and Panama. He then became a labor organization specialist and dispute arbitrator. In 1901 he was a national leader in the campaign for a nine-hour workday, and in 1915 he helped lead the efforts for the eight-hour movement. Fechner worked hard to garner cooperation of the Departments of Agriculture, Interior, War, and Labor and headed the CCC from 1933 until his death on January 1, 1940.

Harry Hopkins (1890–1946). Born in Sioux City, Iowa, Hopkins attended Grinnell College, where he was instilled with social ideals and Progressive political values of honest government, public service, and aid to the "deserving" poor. After graduating Hopkins

CCC laborers riding through the Lassen Volcanic National Park in Forest, California in 1933. The CCC improved millions of acres of federal, state, and local lands. (USDA-Forest Service/Corbis-Bettmann. Reproduced by permission.)

became a social worker in New York City. Supported by Dr. John A. Kingsbury of New York's Association for Improving the Conditions of the Poor, Hopkins rapidly rose as an administrator. In 1923 Hopkins became president of the American Association of Social Workers and the following year director of the New York Tuberculosis Association. The unemployment crisis of the Great Depression changed Hopkins's career, and in 1931 he became director of Governor Franklin D. Roosevelt's Temporary Emergency Relief Administration, which provided jobs for New York's unemployed. After Roosevelt became president, Hopkins was appointed head of the Federal Emergency Relief Administration (FERA). Hopkins influence also persuaded Roosevelt to create the Civil Works Administration (CWA) to provide work relief for all able-bodied unemployed workers. When the CWA ended in 1934, Hopkins then became head of the Works Progress Administration (WPA), which was to provide the largest amount of relief labor for the projects. Hopkins had health problems throughout his life, but shortly before he died he received the nation's highest civilian honor, the Distinguished Service Medal.

James Joseph McEntee (1884–1957). A labor arbitrator and government administrator, McEntee was born in New Jersey. He attended parochial schools and became an apprentice machinist, working his way up until he became an officer of the International Association of Machinists. During World War I, President Woodrow Wilson (served 1913–1921) named him to the New York Arbitration Board. During the 1920s, he helped settle newspaper strikes and worked in railroad contract agreements. At the request of Robert Fechner, a longtime friend and colleague, McEntee was named in 1933 as assistant director of the CCC. He succeeded Fechner in 1940 and continued to direct the CCC until it was abolished in 1942. McEntee tried to strengthen the central administration of the CCC, a position opposed by Secretary of Interior Harold Ickes. McEntee returned to the Machinists' Association and his work with organized labor following the termination of the CCC.

Franklin Delano Roosevelt (1882–1945). Born on his family's estate in Duchess County, New York, Franklin Delano Roosevelt was the son of James Roosevelt, a wealthy gentleman, and Sara Delano. Roosevelt was the thirty-second president of the United States. As a young boy, he had Swiss tutors who supervised him at home and on the family's annual travels through Europe. In 1900 Roosevelt entered Harvard College where he became president of the student newspaper. In 1905 he married his distant cousin, Eleanor Roosevelt, who was President Theodore Roosevelt's niece. He attended Columbia Law School and passed the bar, though he never completed the requirements for his degree.

Roosevelt began his involvement in politics in 1910 when he was elected the Democratic senator of the state senate of New York. After Woodrow Wilson was elected president, Roosevelt was appointed assistant secretary of the navy and thus began his career in Washington politics. In 1920 Roosevelt secured the Democratic Party's nomination for vice-president but lost to the Republican Party.

In August 1921 Roosevelt developed polio, and within days he lost the use of both his legs. Months later, doctors told him he would never walk again. He disguised his paralysis for public purposes by wearing heavy leg braces and supporting himself with a cane. So effective was Roosevelt's deception, and the cooperation of the press in preserving it, that few Americans knew during his lifetime that he was largely confined to a wheelchair.

Roosevelt was elected governor of New York in 1928 and again in 1930. Under the Democratic ticket, Roosevelt was elected president in 1932 as the country began to fall into the Great Depression. He was well known during his presidency for his "fireside chats" over national radio. He was the first leader whose voice was part of the country's everyday life, and people were glued to their radios to hear of government proposals and plans. Roosevelt also created the New Deal, a plan to turn around the depressed economic situation in the United States.

Primary Sources

Life in the CCC

Frank "Bo" Montella was born in Brooklyn, New York, in 1921. At the age of 17 he joined the CCC and was assigned to San Juan County, Utah. Montella was interviewed by the California State-Fullerton/ Utah State Historical Society on July 9, 1971 about his days in the CCC (available from the World Wide Web at http://www.sanjuan.k12.ut.us/sjsample/CCC/CCCHOME/Montella.htm).

> Being First Sergeant in the camp, my responsibility was to keep the camp in tip-top shape with good living conditions in which the fellows cooperated well. If they didn't then we would assign them extra duties... We also learned how to survey. James Albertano, as a boy, was a dropout, but he just took a notion that he wanted to be a surveyor. Old Chap Blake, our camp engineer, would take anybody in there and try to teach them to survey. Albertano wasn't a high school graduate but he got together with Old Chap Blake and learned surveying. And do you know what he turned out to be? He turned out to be one of the vice-presidents of James White Engineering in Denver. He took correspondence courses and he studied a little more. But that's what I say, every one of the boys that I know personally from the CCC's progressed. I think it was a great organization. To tell you the truth, if they had it today, I'd go in it today. That's the truth.

Another veteran of the CCC was Norman A. Myers. Myers enrolled in CCC Company 754 and came to western Oregon in the Umpqua National Forest, near Tiller, Oregon, in the summer of 1933. He wrote letters home twice a week in 1933 and 1934 describing his experiences with CCC. The letters were later published by the Forest Service in *Norman A. Myers Letters to Home: Life in C.C.C. Camps, Douglas County, Oregon* (1983, pp. v, 11, 15, 83).

> A total of 100 men in Dodge County [Nebraska] applied for enrollment in the CCC and this Selection Committee found exactly 100 met all requirements for the Corps. The principal consideration used in this selection was need. Only single men between the ages of 18 and 25 who had dependents were eligible... The physical examinations were given under the direction of Major Philpot of the U.S. Army. Due to the early arrival of most men, the physicals were started during the mid-morning hours. Only three of the 162 men could not be enrolled... I had my first taste of real work today [June 19, 1933]. It is not going to be hard when I get used to it. We start to get our tools at 8 in the morning and check them in at 11:45. We get our tools at 1 p.m. and have our tools in by 4. This seems to be short hours. The men are under the forest ranger bosses while out of camp... The first part of the week [June, 1933] we worked in an awful steep canyon burning brush. My legs sure got tired. Then we moved up the canyon about half a mile to a level valley to clear timber for a road to Summit, a lookout station. Passed it going to work today and can see at least 50 miles from there. It is 2,000 feet higher than the camp and only 4 miles away. There are no fires now. A little too damp. Soon will move into new tents with floors in. Helped unload three loads of lumber at off times this week. Thursday they started to dynamite stumps. Tried to get on but didn't. I guess I look to sloppy. You have to do whatever they give you anyway. Thurs. afternoon we all got a lesson in chopping by a forest ranger... We were issued swell boots (leather) Saturday morning [January 21, 1934] and I am going to take good care of mine so I can have them when I get home. I have a pair of good loggers [boots] I bought for $3.00 so I will have a lot of shoes. I ordered a gray army locker for $3.50 so it will take most of the month's paycheck. I still have $4.00 left from my last check so I have plenty. I am going to save a little every month so I have some when I go back. They took our measurements yesterday and they said it was for army dress uniforms. This is just a rumor though.

Suggested Research Topics

- What was the role of the CCC in development of city parks, state parks, and recreation facilities on federal lands? Assess the criticisms that the CCC was a paramilitary organization designed to get the United States involved in World War II.
- How do autobiographical reminiscences by recruits confirm that service in the CCC changed their lives? Be able to discuss the organization of the CCC and the benefits it accorded to those enrolled in it.
- Identify the impact of the Civilian Conservation Corps on U.S. public lands, national forests, state and city parks, and Indian reservations. Why was the work of the CCC of critical importance to the administration and management of national forests?
- How did Public Service Camps housing conscientious objectors during World War II continue the labors of the CCC?

Bibliography

Sources

Breaman, John, Robert H. Bremner, and David Brody, eds. *The New Deal: The State and Local Levels,* Vol. 2. Columbus, OH: Ohio State University Press, 1975.

Davis, Kingsley. *Youth in the Depression.* Chicago: University of Chicago Press, 1935.

Guthrie, John D. *Saga of the C.C.C.* Washington, DC: American Forestry Association, 1942.

Harper, Charles Price. *The Administration of the Civilian Conservation Corp.* Clarksburg, WV: Clarksburg Publishing Co., 1939.

"Loveless C.C.C." Copied literatim from the text in Herman Beeman's ballad book. Song written by Beeman's bunk-mate in Brokenair [sic] CCC Camp, Oklahoma,1937. From *Voices from the Dustbowl: The Charles L. Todd and Robert Sonkin Migrant Worker Collection, 1940–1941,* Library of Congress.

McEntee, James J. *Now They Are Men: The Story of the CCC.* Washington, DC: National Home Library Foundation, 1940.

Merrill, Perry H. *Roosevelt's Forest Army: A History of the Civilian Conservation Corps, 1933–1942.* Montpelier, VT: Perry H. Merrill, 1981.

Montella, Frank, "Memories of a CCC Boy: Frank Montella Interview," interview by Kim Stewart, July 9, 1971, Cal State Fullerton and Utah State Historical Society Oral History Project.

Myers, Norman A. *Letters to Home: Life in C.C.C. Camps of Douglas County, Oregon, 1933–1934.* Edited by Gerald W. Williams. USDA-Forest Service, Umpqua National Forest, Roseburg, OR, 1983.

Roosevelt, Franklin D. *The Public Papers and Addresses of Franklin D. Roosevelt.* New York: Random House, 1938.

Salmond, John A. *The Civilian Conservation Corps, 1933–1942: A New Deal Case Study.* Durham, NC: Duke University Press, 1967.

Further Reading

Brown, Nelson C. *The Civilian Conservation Corps Program in the United States.* Washington, DC: Government Printing Office, 1934.

Cohen, Stan. *The Tree Army: A Pictorial History of the Civilian Conservation Corps, 1933–42.* Missoula, MT: Pictorial Histories Publishing Company, 1980.

Cole, Olen Jr. *The African American Experience in the Civilian Conservation Corps.* Gainesville, FL: University Press of Florida, 1999.

Drake, Darwood. *Looking Back.* Chicago: Adams Press, 1989.

Hayden, Ernst A. *The United States Civilian Conservation Corps of the 1930s.* Callahan, CA: Ernst A. Hayden, 1985.

Howell, Glenn. *CCC Boys Remember: A Pictorial History of the CCC.* Medford, OR: Klocker Printery, 1976.

Hoyt, Ray. *We Can Take It: A Short History of the CCC.* New York: American Book Company, 1935.

Lacy, Leslie Alexander. *The Soil Soldiers: The Civilian Conservation Corps in the Great Depression.* Radnor, PA: Chilton Book Company, 1976.

Melzer, Richard. *Coming of Age in the Great Depression: The Civilian Conservation Corps in New Mexico.* Las Cruces, NM: Yucca Tree Press, 2000.

Ryan, J.C. *The CCC and Me.* Duluth, MN: J. C. Ryan, 1987.

Schultz, Michael John. *In the Shadow of the Trees.* Thomaton, ME: Dan River Press, 1997.

Wecter, Dixon. *The Age of the Great Depression, 1929–1941.* New York: Macmillan, 1948.

See Also

Black Americans; New Deal (First, and Its Critics)

Crime

1920-1940

Introduction

In America, just as in many countries, outlaw heroes and larger-than-life lawmen historically have appeared and been looked to by the public in response to certain situations. These situations may include unjust or unpopular government regulation, concentration of wealth in the hands of a few, or widespread poverty. All of these situations existed in the United States during the early years of the Great Depression, 1929–1933. Preceding and through the early Depression years the government banned alcohol in what became known as the Prohibition years, 1920–1933. This policy was highly unpopular with the public. At the same time, a very small percentage of Americans controlled a high percentage of wealth in the country. As a result, due to the extreme economic depression, many middle class citizens experienced poverty for the first time in their lives. To the workers and needy the early years of the Depression brought desperation and conflict. Crowd violence in the form of food riots and unemployment protests of the early years of the Depression gave way to labor strikes and violent clashes with troops and law authorities in the later 1930s. At the beginning of the Depression the U.S. government had appeared ineffective at solving many problems affecting the average citizen.

In the midst of the Great Depression, faced with economic hardship and desperation, the American public needed heroes. Thirsty Americans especially needed someone to outsmart the government's ban on alcoholic beverages. Quick to respond to the call

Chronology:

1920: Prohibition begins as the Eighteenth Amendment and the Volstead Act make the sale and consumption of alcohol illegal.

1920–1933: Bootleggers, by supplying illegal alcohol to the public, become wealthy and public cult heroes as the Great Depression sets in and respect for the government declines.

1931: Gangster movies *Little Caesar* and *Public Enemy* premier in Hollywood glorifying the financial success of gangsters during a time of economic depression.

1931: In New York City, Lucky Luciano and Meyer Lansky murder old line Mafia heads and form the new American Mafia.

October 24, 1931: Al Capone, the nation's most notorious gangster, receives an eleven-year prison sentence for income tax evasion.

1933–1934: Midwestern outlaws rob and murder in America's heartland gaining notoriety from a public whose confidence in the U.S. banking system and the government is shaken by the Great Depression.

December 5, 1933: Prohibition ends with the repeal of the Eighteenth Amendment as the New Deal begins, restoring public faith in government and the U.S. economy.

1934: Congress passes and President Roosevelt signs Attorney General Homer S. Cumming's anti-crime package.

1933–1935: J. Edgar Hoover's Special Agents capture or kill all of the famous Midwest outlaws.

1935: The Hollywood gangster movie *G-Men* opens in cinemas reinforcing the growing public respect for federal government.

1936–1940: J. Edgar Hoover shifts the FBI's focus to fascists and communists.

throughout the 1920s, ethnic gangs in the ghettos, which were once groups that were loosely associated through criminal activity, organized and had been delivering the "goods," specifically bootlegged liquor. As a result, by the late 1920s, these criminals, now operating in well-structured groups generally referred to as organized crime, were established and wealthy. Powerful members of organized crime units, or gangsters, such as Al Capone of Chicago became public figures of mythical proportion. In addition, by 1933, outlaws in the Midwest began racing through the heartland robbing banks. To some citizens who had lost all their savings in bank closures, these outlaws were often seen as contemporary Robin Hoods. On the other hand to those who lost their money in bank robberies, it was another cruel feature of the Great Depression.

The presidential inauguration of Franklin Delano Roosevelt in March 1933 saw the advent of the New Deal—Roosevelt's plan for relief, reform, and recovery. Government suddenly seemed responsive to the common man. These new government programs designed to raise employment and restart the economy rekindled a spark of hope in Americans that their economic woes would come to an end. Due to this renewed faith in their government and new hope for the future, Americans began to view crime more negatively and as something that must end.

Thus, the expanding role of the federal government in people's daily lives during the Great Depression was not only in economic programs regarding business and finance, but in law enforcement as well. Congress passed expanded anti-crime legislation and the Federal Bureau of Investigation (FBI) grew into America's finely tuned investigative arm under the leadership of J. Edgar Hoover.

Such violent events as gangster wars, outlaw raids, food riots, unemployment protests, and labor confrontations that played out on the streets of America proved to be one of the hallmarks of the Great Depression.

Issue Summary

The Great Depression and Crime

The onset of the Great Depression in the years of 1929 to 1933 brought some continuity but also major changes as well as public exposure to crime. Organized crime that rose with the beginning of Prohibition and gained much media and public attention through the 1920s continued through Prohibition's end in 1933. Bootlegging, which proved extremely profitable for gangsters, involved the smuggling of liquor across borders and delivering it to establishments known as speakeasies that illegally sold liquor, or to private customers. Usually the corruption of local law authorities aided the success of such criminal operations that often were reliable systems of supply for their customers. A new crime wave catching public attention, however, was street crowd violence. This social response to the new economic crisis became increasingly pronounced during President Herbert Hoover's (served 1929–1933) tenure in the White House. Hoover showed little sympathy for those who had fallen on hard times, and his efforts at recovery proved ineffective. As a result many of those affected, as the unemployment rate climbed from three percent in 1929 to 25 percent in 1933, felt a growing sense of hopelessness and despair. The U.S. economic system based on free market capitalism was being seriously called into question for the first time and financial leaders were viewed with rising disdain. Mass demonstrations were occurring and many feared a loss of government control leading to anarchy, or lawlessness, was not far away.

The mob violence of the early years of the Great Depression decreased as President Roosevelt, through his personal charm and new programs, reestablished public confidence in the United States. The quick resolution of a national banking crisis in March 1933 in which many banks had been going out of business and the quick adoption of radically new economic programs through his first one hundred days of office began to renew hope. Though violent incidences out of frustration over the lingering Great Depression continued, the focus of public crime shifted to labor strikes that only rarely involved battles between labor activists and the police.

Many factors led to major changes in public reaction to crime. The federal government's inability to first control organized crime through the 1920s and then solve the economic problems of the Depression in the early 1930s fed the public's lack of confidence in government and in the future of the nation. In a way the more notorious criminals were seen as a sort of hero reflecting the traditional U.S. model of individualism and economic success. The combination in the early 1930s of the rise of street mob violence, the seeming threat of anarchy, President Roosevelt's effectiveness in at least stopping the decline of the economy, and the increasing size of the federal government to cope with social and economic problems, however, led the public to disdain crime again. The majority of Americans sought a restoration of law and order to accompany the slowly recovering economy.

More About...

Bootlegging

Bootlegging is a term originated by early Native American traders. Since it was either illegal or severely frowned upon for a Native American to have a bottle of liquor, they carried their bottle in their boot. Hence early on a bootlegger was a person who illegally transported liquor.

Bootleggers made huge profits during Prohibition, from January 1920 until December 1933, when the Eighteenth Amendment was repealed. Best estimates put American consumption of bootleg liquor at more than 100 million gallons annually during this time. Most of the liquor came into the country over land through Canada and Mexico or by boat. The wealth accumulated by gangs distributing and selling liquor allowed organized crime to expand and prosper.

Bootlegging did not disappear, however, with the repeal of Prohibition. A person making batches of "mountain dew," also known as "moonshine" or "white lightening," could sell the product at lower prices than legal liquor because the seller did not pay any alcohol taxes. Bootleg liquor, however, often had serious consequences for the buyer.

Some producers mistakenly used methyl alcohol (rubbing alcohol) in production of bootleg liquor. One batch made in Atlanta, Georgia, in 1951, killed 42 of its consumers. Producers were also known to add lye to whiskey to give it a sting or to mix in ether or fuel oil. Taking a drink of bootleg liquor wasn't always a safe bet, but in the time of Prohibition, many were willing to take that chance.

Crowd Violence

Following the crash of the stock market in October 1929 the national economy began a steady downward spiral. Unemployment was increasing, banks were failing, companies were filing for bankruptcy, and homes and farms were foreclosed on and repossessed by banks. President Hoover's personal aloofness portrayed an uncaring administration as he ineffectively emphasized voluntary efforts by industry to curb layoffs and private charities to provide relief. A sense of public helplessness led to hopelessness and then anger and despair by those most affected by the downturn. A number of important events followed that further dramatized this trend.

March 6, 1930, was declared an International Unemployment Day by the U.S. Communist Party, which was trying to take advantage of the growing public unrest to further its political agenda and increase its membership. Protest marches were held throughout the nation demanding government action to assist the unemployed. In the previous month several thousand had marched in Chicago, Cleveland, Los Angeles, New York, and Philadelphia and clashed with police setting the tone for further demonstrations. One of the more violent events on March 6 occurred in New York City when 35,000 people, both workers and the unemployed, gathered to hear Communist Party leaders, including William Z. Foster, speak at Union Square. At least three hundred police lined around the event that began peacefully until the crowd heard they were denied a permit by the city to march to city hall and about two thousand began marching anyway in defiance. Their intention had simply been to demand action by the city in providing more job relief. On their way to city hall, however, they were met with police both on foot and on horses armed with nightsticks. On that same day in Washington, DC, police used teargas to disperse a similar rally in front of the White House.

Other forms of crowd disturbances were occurring at this time. Food riots broke out in 1930 and 1931 in a number of U.S. communities. Some notable disturbances occurred in Minneapolis and St. Paul, Minnesota; Van Dyke, Michigan; San Francisco; and Oklahoma City. In Minneapolis a crowd of women broke windows of a grocery store and surged in to raid the store shelves. Another Minneapolis grocery store raid in February 1931 led to the arrest of seven raiders. Throughout the spring and summer of 1931 hunger and unemployment marches with related violence occurred in cities across the country.

One of the most notable events occurred in 1932 when up to 20,000 veterans of World War I (1914–1918) and their families, many out of work, arrived in Washington, DC, from across the country. Calling themselves the Bonus Expeditionary Force, or more simply the Bonus Army, they came to support a proposed bill in Congress that would pay a bonus to war veterans for their services. Congress had approved the bonus in 1924 to be paid in the form of a life insurance policy in 1945. The new bill proposed to pay each veteran $500 cash immediately instead of deferring the payments. President Hoover initially received the Bonus Army peacefully providing food and supplies. When the new bill was defeated on June 17 in the Senate President Hoover requested that the crowd disband and return home to avoid further violence. About two thousand remained, however, to protest the defeat of the bill. Violent confrontations with the police led to four being killed. By July 28 Hoover decided to remove the remaining Bonus Army members and one thousand U.S. soldiers along with tanks and machine guns under the command of General Douglas MacArthur and Major Dwight D. Eisenhower were sent to clear the veterans. The military charged aggressively through the area against men, women, and children, with bayonets drawn and tear gas bombs exploding. Shantytown structures that had been erected through the previous months caught fire. Two veterans were shot and wounded and more than 60 injured. One of the most devastating events of the day occurred when a baby died from tear gas exposure. The public was outraged by the government's harsh actions.

Violence was in no way limited to cities and industrial workers. Since World War I farmers had been producing too much food. As a result they were getting very low prices for their crops. Many could not make ends meet or afford to make their farm mortgage payments to the banks. Banks were foreclosing on those who could not make their payments, taking possession, and then selling the farms at auctions to recover what money they could. Seeing no help coming from Hoover, in 1933 farmers in the Midwest began taking matters into their own hands. They began organizing to push for mortgage relief legislation and a guarantee that at least their farming production costs would be covered. Some went beyond lobbying to forcefully stopping eviction sales and intimidating judges, bankers, and insurance agents. In Dennison, Iowa, a crowd of farmers attacked collection agents and sheriff's deputies attempting to foreclose on a farm. Such violence in early 1933 was growing so much that the governor of Iowa placed six counties under martial law, which meant suspending local civil laws and placing military forces—in this instance armed National Guard troops—in control to maintain peace. Some warned President-elect Franklin Roosevelt that economic strife was so widespread and severe that a violent revolution was brewing in the Midwest farm region. Farm relief became a top priority of Roosevelt's first New Deal programs.

Labor Strife

As part of the New Deal, Congress passed laws favorable to labor. The laws recognized the right of workers to organize and collectively bargain, or negotiate working conditions as a group with company leadership. Passage of these acts, however, fell far short in solving U.S. labor issues. Many companies were slow to recognize unions or to sit down at the

The Memorial Day Massacre, as it came to be known, took place outside the Republic Steel plant in Chicago on May 30, 1937. Ten strikers were killed by police after the demonstration turned violent. (AP/Wide World Photos. Reproduced by permission.)

bargaining table. In many cases labor leaders had to resort to more aggressive tactics to force union recognition. Throughout much of 1934 the level of violence between labor activists, local authorities, and company security guards rose to levels the nation had not seen for several decades. The Communist Party aided many of the strikes and protests. Others, however, occurred without any political or organized labor involvement.

One such strike occurred at several factories in Toledo, Ohio, where automobile parts were manufactured. In early February 1934 a labor strike in Toledo appeared quickly settled and resulted in improved pay and an agreement to further discuss further union recognition. One factory, however, pulled out of the deal. In reaction factory workers joined by some unemployed workers established picket lines around the plant. The company obtained an injunction, which

At a Glance

What's a Gangster to Do?

With the end of Prohibition in 1933 gangsters had to find new business ventures in Depression America. Many went back to old standbys of gambling and prostitution, while innovators found new lucrative rackets of loan-sharking, labor racketeering, and drug trafficking.

After gambling, loan-sharking was the major source of steady income for organized crime. Gamblers and high-risk credit individuals who could not obtain a loan from a legitimate bank often became customers to loan sharks. Typically, loan sharks charged "six for five." For every five dollars borrowed, six must be paid back each week. That amounts to a 1,004 percent loan rate per year! One investigation in New York found the organized crime syndicate netting 3,000 percent. In contrast, a less expensive loan shark was loaning money to customers for a rate of only 585 percent.

Labor racketeering became another popular venture for gangsters. Members of criminal groups worked their way into positions of authority in labor unions. Once inside the unions they used pension and health funds to invest in high-risk ventures or to loan themselves money that they never paid back.

Drug trafficking was a natural extension of bootlegging, supplying the demand of an illegal substance desired by the public such as opium, heroin, marijuana, cocaine, or amphetamines. By 2000 drug trafficking and laundering money of the proceeds were organized crime's biggest businesses.

---

is a court order prohibiting a certain action, against the pickets. The injunction limited how many could picket at any one time and where. The injunction, however, was largely ignored as more picketers joined, eventually growing to ten thousand protesters. To enforce the court order police moved in with tear gas, fire hoses, and guns. They were joined after several hours of battle by seven hundred National Guard troops. During the confrontation the National Guard opened fire killing two strikers and wounding 15 others. A truce was finally called and a negotiated settlement reached after two weeks of discussions, resulting in workers receiving a 22 percent raise as well as union recognition.

The West Coast witnessed such violent outbreaks as well. The International Longshoreman's Association in San Francisco, California, went on strike on May 9, 1934, and consisted of a labor walkout and the forming of picket lines. The workers demanded formal recognition of their union and improved working conditions. Companies that were responsible for loading and unloading ships held out, not giving in to workers' demands. By July 5 the companies decided to begin operations again by crossing the picket lines with trucks to haul goods under police escort. Violence erupted with protesters and police using clubs, stones, tear gas, and eventually guns. Two strikers were killed and many injured as the National Guard arrived to restore order. In reaction to the violence the strike spread to other unions who joined in. Within a few days, however, the strike was ended. The longshoremen eventually won most of their demands through later negotiation.

Violence continued through the mid-1930s as many companies resisted union activity at their places of business. On January 11, 1937, a sit-down strike at a General Motors automobile plant in Flint, Michigan, led to a clash between strikers and the police involving rocks, bottles, tear gas, and pistols. The violence in Flint was unlike any seen in any other sit-down strike, however, it was only as a result of company guards and police trying to prevent food delivery to the strikers inside. Strikers overcame the guards and took over the gate, and with police intervention a riot ensued. A 1937 strike at a Republic steel mill in South Chicago led to a Memorial Day battle between picketers and police, leaving ten strikers dead, 30 wounded and another 28 picketers injured

Finally workers at the Goodyear Tire Factory in Akron, Ohio, tried a more peaceful strategy—a sit-down strike. The workers shutoff their machines and refused to leave until the company recognize their union. The success of the strike led to other workers around the country adopting this more peaceful approach. Approximately 170 sit down strikes occurred in U.S. factories through 1937. By the early 1940s the industrial mobilization for World War II (1939–1945) and the resulting full employment eventually led to a major decrease in violent labor actions.

End of the Gangster Period

In March 1930 gangster Al Capone returned after nine months in jail to a far different place than the rowdy and vigorous Chicago he had left. The stock market crash of 1929, which occurred during his stint in jail, had provoked a collapse of the nation's economy, causing the previous sense of security and confidence to evaporate. Every day more Americans lost their jobs and found it increasingly difficult to put food on the table.

For favorable publicity and a personal desire to help, Capone opened a soup kitchen at 935 South State Street in Chicago. Three times a day his kitchen fed the hungry, and on Thanksgiving Day alone, five thousand men, women, and children were fed. Capone often wondered why the government was wasting its time trying to prosecute him when such pressing social problems like feeding the hungry existed.

Capone also exhibited generosity on a private level. Friends report he helped the elderly people of Chicago earn a few dollars and stay off welfare. One of his tactics was to ask if he could rent the person's garage or basement, saying he might need the space. Capone never actually used the space, but he would pay rent each month. By the end of 1930 Al Capone had never been more popular. His life was taking on mythical proportions as a real life Robin Hood, an outlaw who gives generously to the poor and needy. He seemed to have genuine regard for the underprivileged as much as he had little regard for public agencies and seemingly inept law enforcement.

In an effort to feed the hungry, and gain a little positive publicity in the process, Al Capone opened this soup kitchen in Chicago in 1931. *(National Archives and Records Administration.)*

Despite the new public acceptance of Capone, the federal government did not change its opinion of him. It continued to consider him a criminal who needed to be brought to justice. The Internal Revenue Service (IRS) pursued a determined and exhaustive investigation into Capone's tax records. Likewise Eliot Ness and a fearless group of men he recruited, dubbed the "untouchables" because they could not be bribed by criminals to look the other way, wreaked havoc on Capone's breweries as they uncovered Prohibition violations. Eventually, tax evasion charges led to Capone's conviction. On October 24, 1931, Capone was shocked when the court handed down an 11-year prison sentence. He would eventually be released due to ill health in 1939 and die in 1947. Less than two years after Capone's conviction Prohibition would be officially ended and the era of gangsters who bootlegged alcoholic beverages would draw to a close.

Crime in the Movies

As the Great Depression worsened in the early 1930s, economic paralysis took hold of the country. A shop closed in one neighborhood, a factory in another, and a bank in yet another. Disillusionment with American institutions, including the government, big business, and the legal system, ran high. Uncertain and frustrated Americans became a receptive audience to the entertainment and escape of Hollywood movies. As unemployment numbers moved steadily upward to 15 then 25 percent of the population, weekly movie attendance continued to average sixty to seventy million. Although they could barely afford to be there, Americans continued to find respite from the worries of real life by attending movies.

The movies often provided an outlet for feelings of frustration, loss, struggle, and hope. Viewing the travails and triumphs of characters on the big screen allowed audiences to forget their own worries for at least the duration of a movie. One genre of movies that became very popular during the Depression was the gangster movie, which began to depict the gangsters' new standing in national society. Hollywood presented crime as a highly successful and organized business, and often depicted criminals as essentially likeable despite their unlawful activity. *Little Caesar* (Warner Brothers, 1930) was the first great gangster "talkie," a movie with sound. Caesar Enrico Bandello, "Rico," played by Edward G. Robinson, followed all the idealized stereotype of an American's climb from the bottom rungs of society upward to success. Rico was a thinly disguised, fictional version of Al Capone. He robbed and murdered, but at the same time was

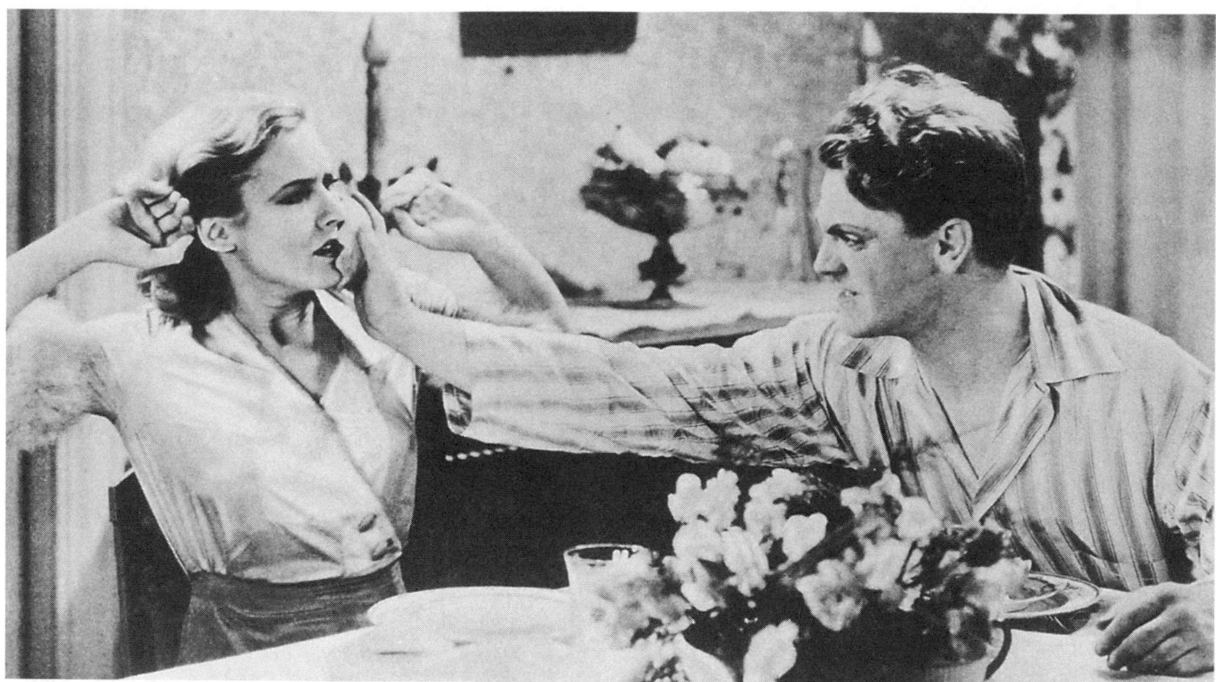

A 1931 movie still from the film The Public Enemy *starring James Cagney. The movie contained unintentionally glorifying scenes of bootlegging and emphasized the high life style of gangsters during the depths of the Depression.* *(Warner Bros./Archive Photos. Reproduced by permission.)*

kind and generous. Ultimately and morally, since his success was outside the law, his story ended in death.

With the box office success of *Little Caesar,* some fifty gangster films appeared in 1931. Civic groups and parent-teacher associations denounced the glorification of the gangster and the disrespect shown to law enforcement authorities. Despite the clamor, a great many people, young and old, packed the movie houses. Actor James Cagney drew more audiences when he appeared on the screen as Tommy Powers in *Public Enemy* (Warner Bros., 1931). Cagney's character was irresistibly appealing to moviegoers. Tommy Powers was industrious, classy, a wise guy, and a ladies' man, who never wavered from the system of values held by fellow thieves. Only when his criminal conduct pushed too far outside the law did he become doomed to die. Cagney's character was not seen as vicious or troubled, rather he was considered to be a man who had directed his rage against injustice.

The heyday of American gangster movies was 1930–1931, however, by 1932 the anti-gangster crusade began to gain momentum and fewer gangster movies were made. Historians look back to the gangster films and speculate as to why so many Americans spent so many hours inside the theaters. It seems that during even the most wrenching years of the Depression crime and the criminal were closely tied to success. Crime figures in the movies were shown as rugged individualists who on their own initiative raised themselves from poverty to a life of financial wealth. Success starved Americans could triumph through the fictional stories in films. Americans, however, often held conflicting attitudes towards individual success. Those attitudes included admiring approval and, at the same time, a jealous disapproval. Therefore, the success of gangster films may have represented to some a self-centered, greedy rise to the top much like the rise of very wealthy Americans whom many blamed for their economic woes. A gangster character's ultimate failure then also represented social justice to this group of moviegoers. Still another group of moviegoers may have simply identified with the fictional characters as men who worked hard but failed, just as the moviegoer who had worked and failed due to the economic collapse that resulted from the Depression.

Birth of the American Mafia

The poor economic conditions actually helped stabilize organized crime. Many Italians and Jews living in the ghettos had been ready to rise out of the

More About...

The Juvenile Delinquent

By the late 1930s Americans had become acutely aware that the Depression years had taken a toll on families. As a result troubled homes were producing troubled kids. Between the film releases of *Public Enemy* (1931) and *Dead End* (1937), Hollywood, in step with the latest social thought, found a way to show how a child's environment could lead to juvenile delinquency. Gangster movies of the early 1930s had presented crime as an oftentimes glamorous lifestyle and did not explore its causes, but that would later change along with public attitudes about crime and criminals.

By 1937 Hollywood had changed its emphasis dramatically. *Dead End* explored the lives of five very believable teenage boys from the East River slums of New York. Their parents, unemployed, drank and argued and their home surroundings were filthy. The "friends" fought amongst themselves, swam in the polluted East River, and mimicked the toughest hoods of the day. The gangster myth buried, *Dead End* linked hoodlums and crime with upbringing in squalid conditions.

James Cagney, the gangster in *Public Enemy* and the lawman in *G-Men*, gave another brilliant performance in the 1938 film *Angels with Dirty Faces,* playing the character of Rocky. To the dead-end kids of *Angels,* Rocky was a hoodlum hero who had grown up in their neighborhood. Father Jerry, a friend of Rocky's since childhood, came to him on death row and asked Rocky to destroy his own popular hero image by dying like a coward, resisting his death sentence like a man afraid. As Rocky and Father Jerry walk the last few steps together, finally, Rocky complied by being dragged screaming and sobbing to the electric chair. The dead end kids were told he died "like a yellow rat" (Clarens, *Crime Movies: An Illustrated History.* p. 155). Father Jerry then urged the boys, despite the lifestyles from which they came, to find a better way.

---

ghetto, just as the Irish had earlier, but the battered national economy froze them in place. Most young people living in ghettos remained trapped there, with crime being one of their few hopes for making a decent living. With a steady supply of new recruits, organized crime grew and became more sophisticated.

Alongside the rise of the gangster movies in 1930 and 1931 came the very real gangster war, specifically the Castellammarese War in New York City. By September 10, 1931, Lucky Luciano and his allies, including Jewish boss Meyer Lansky, had risen to the top of the crime world. Together, Luciano and his allies succeeded in murdering old line "bosses," a term used by organized crime to describe a leader, and in so doing, formed the new American Mafia, a secret criminal organization composed primarily of people of Italian and Sicilian ancestry.

Five New York crime families emerged in the aftermath of the crime war. They formed a new alliance, or syndicate, sometimes referred to as the Luciano-Lansky plan. The new Mafia had no tolerance for the old Italian Mafia's ideas. The old Mafia believed in a certain "honor" which demanded ethnic purity, allowed warring against other Italians, and concentrated on settling old vendettas rather than making money. The new Mafia organized the various ethnic groups into an efficient, cooperative underworld syndicate whose sole goal was making money. They only killed those who stood in the way of profits. Luciano also reinstated the "Commission" as a leadership body for the crime organization. Ironically this "Americanization" of the Mafia took place at approximately the same time that Al Capone was seeing his career end in a tax evasion trial. The new syndicate had become so wealthy during the last years of Prohibition that it was able to withstand the effects of the Depression, at least for awhile.

By 1932 it was clear through increasing opposition and the government's inability to enforce alcohol restrictions that Prohibition would soon end. It finally did with passage of the Twenty-first Amendment on December 5, 1933, making the sale and consumption of alcohol legal again. The bootleg gangs of Prohibition, which had become organized crime syndicates, managed to stay together and returned to their earlier businesses of gambling and prostitution. More importantly, the new Mafia also moved ahead into new ventures of labor racketeering, which uses the power of labor unions to control business and industry, loan sharking, and drug trafficking.

The criminal exploits of John Dillinger fascinated the public during the early years of the Great Depression. (AP/Wide World Photos. Reproduced by permission.)

The Outlaws

The continued economic downturn of the Great Depression led to yet another crime phenomenon that caught the country's interest. A new breed of criminal arrived—the Midwest outlaw. These rural bandits appeared on the scene and briefly operated in the Midwest and South in 1933 and 1934. Traveling in fast-moving cars, toting Tommy guns and sawed off shotguns, they struck at isolated banks and filling stations. They would shoot up buildings and people before roaring away with their stolen money, and they preyed on inept and corrupt local police.

Descended from American frontier outlaws of the nineteenth century, these bandits—John Dillinger, George "Baby Face" Nelson, Charles "Pretty Boy" Floyd, George "Machine Gun" Kelly, Bonnie Parker and Clyde Barrow, and "Ma" Barker and her sons—stole only a fraction of the money that Al Capone and other East Coast gangsters made. Gangsters considered these bandits small time thrill seekers. The Depression weary public, just as it had done with the fictionalized silver screen gangsters, tended to romanticize the outlaws as daring and resourceful Robin Hoods.

By 1933 many Americans in the heartland had lost jobs and seen their farms foreclosed by the banking establishment. Nearly helpless against these economic forces, people welcomed stories of banks being held up by outlaws boldly taking what they wanted at gunpoint, who easily escaped with the goods. When "Pretty Boy" Floyd, waving a machine gun, rushed into a bank, he often took, in addition to cash, mortgage notes on local families' homes and farms, which he promptly destroyed. It was actions like these that provided a measure of public support for the outlaws. While not condoning the brutality employed by the outlaws, Americans felt that government in general—and public officials in particular—were ineffective in dealing with the problems of the day, be they economic or criminal. The outlaws and their ability to evade the police further reinforced this belief.

Among the outlaws, John Dillinger emerged as one of the most infamous as he projected an appealing bravado, leaping over barriers to grab moneybags from hapless bank tellers. Newspapers reported his every move as he roamed and robbed from state to state. Although Dillinger had killed ten men, his ability to break out of jail and elude police fascinated the public. He was finally gunned down in July 1934 as he left a movie house where he had watched Clark Gable in "Manhattan Melodrama," a New York gangster film.

The New Deal Responds to Crime

Although gangsters and outlaws captivated America's imagination, their brutal activities coupled with the horror of a high profile kidnapping case leading to the murder of the infant son of popular aviator Charles Lindbergh, increasingly caused the public to believe a moral as well as economic crisis was at hand. By 1933, as Franklin Delano Roosevelt (served 1933–1945) assumed the presidency, Americans began to look to the federal government not only for economic relief and jobs, but also for a solution to the crime problem.

Local enforcement agencies, riddled with corruption and hampered by restrictive laws, had been unable to cope with the growing lawlessness. Now every new bank robbery and kidnapping was proof to many Americans that criminals were at war with society.

Just as President Roosevelt took over the reigns of federal government in Washington, DC, MGM Studios released a film, *Gabriel Over the White House,* that illustrated the shift in public attitude towards crime and criminals. In *Gabriel* a U.S. president is able to put a quick end to crime by allowing speedy trials and firing squads. Clearly the movie industry and many in the public were no longer enamored with crime and violence. Although such a radical course was outside the boundaries of a democratic society and therefore beyond President Roosevelt's consideration, the movie illustrated that some people were reaching a desperate willingness to abandon democratic principles in favor of immediate action.

While not acting with the flourish and flash of a Hollywood movie, Roosevelt did take action to bring crime under control. He selected Homer Stillé Cummings as his Attorney General in charge of the Department of Justice, which included the Bureau of Investigation. In 1933 and 1934 Cummings served as Roosevelt's chief architect for the New Deal's war on crime. As with the economic recovery programs, the goal was to instill public confidence in government and U.S. society.

In early 1933, despite his efficient organization of the Bureau of Investigation, neither its leader, J. Edgar Hoover, nor his bureau was well-known outside of government circles. Hoover's top-notch corps of Special Agents was severely limited under the law to carrying out basic tasks such as trailing prostitutes or violators of antiquated laws such as the Migratory Birds' Act, which placed restrictions on the hunting of migratory birds. Special Agents could neither make arrests nor carry guns. The Federal Bureau of Investigation as Americans knew it at the end of the twentieth century did not yet exist.

An Anti-Crime Plan

On June 17, 1933, a major incident known as the Kansas City Massacre startled the country and solidified the growing anti-crime sentiment. Unarmed police officers and Special Agents were escorting Frank Nash, a bank robber and prison escapee, back to confinement. Three men with machine guns ambushed the party and opened fire, killing four officers, including one of the Special Agents. The incident enraged the nation. Cummings translated that anger into a plan of action in the form of a federal anti-crime package sent to Congress in 1934 that was approved in May of the same year. Any theft of $5,000 or more that was carried across state lines, as well as robberies of national banks, illegal use of telephone and telegraph wires, and attacks on federal officers, were all made federal offenses. Practically any other type of crime in which the criminal crossed a state line to avoid prosecution became open for pursuit by federal agents. Additionally, it was at this time that Congress granted Hoover's Special Agents the authority to carry guns and make arrests.

FBI Director J. Edgar Hoover extends his hand to FBI Agent Melvin Purvis. Purvis and his men were responsible for trapping and killing the notorious John Dillinger. (©Bettmann/Corbis. Reproduced by permission.)

From his experience in the first hundred days of the New Deal, Cummings knew success for the war on crime depended on restoring the public's confidence in law enforcement. President Roosevelt, during the first hundred days of his administration beginning in March 1933 was able to restore public confidence in government by almost overnight solving the desperate banking crisis in America and initiating a number of innovative economic recovery programs collectively known as the New Deal. These programs addressed a wide range of the U.S. economic system including farms and industry. To similarly restore public confidence in law enforcement, Cummings decided that he would commit the federal government to pursuing criminals whose convictions promised the greatest

President Franklin D. Roosevelt, signing a crime bill in 1934. Behind him, from left to right are: Attorney General Homer Cummings, FBI Director J. Edgar Hoover, Senator Henry F. Ashurst, and Assistant Attorney General Joseph B. Keenan. (AP/Wide World Photos. Reproduced by permission.)

publicity payoff. Cummings targeted celebrity criminals who had become symbols of the crime problem. By taking down these figures, Cummings intended to improve the public's perception of law enforcement and confidence in government.

Immediately agents from the Bureau of Investigation swept down on the infamous Midwest outlaws. Agent Melvin Purvis, chief of the bureau's Chicago office, and his men gunned down John Dillinger, then officially labeled Public Enemy No. 1, in July 1934; Charles "Pretty Boy" Floyd in October 1934; "Baby Face" Nelson in November 1934, and "Ma" Barker and her son Freddie in 1935. Special Agents, along with local law officers in Louisiana and Texas, hunted down Bonnie Parker and Clyde Barrow, who had been on a nationwide crime spree that began in 1932. They were wanted for robbery, kidnapping, and murder. Thirteen people had fallen to the Barrow gang's guns, and several of the victims were police officers. One of the largest manhunts of the time was launched, involving the FBI and several state and local law enforcement agencies. A local posse, including Texas Rangers, finally gunned them down on May 23, 1934.

Although Attorney General Cummings was the nation's unchallenged symbol of law enforcement by the end of 1934, America in the fifth year of Depression still looked for larger-than-life myths and action heroes. One year later J. Edgar Hoover displaced Cummings as the public's new top law enforcement figure. This was largely due to the release of Warner Brothers' sensational 1935 hit *G-Men.* Hollywood breathed new life and credibility into the law by trading the old gangster myth for a new one of tough policemen. James Cagney, who had portrayed Public Enemy No. 1 in 1932, was the heroic lawman in *G-Men.* Just as the New Deal ushered in a new cooperation among individuals and levels of government to redeem the economy and assist society, Hollywood's "G-men" helped redeem American law enforcement in public opinion. It was in 1935, when opinion of law enforcement was making a comeback, that the name of the Bureau was changed to the Federal Bureau of Investigation (FBI).

Organized Crime Continues Through the Depression

While J. Edgar Hoover's law enforcement organization destroyed the Midwest outlaws quickly and efficiently, the national organized crime syndicates encountered few difficulties from the FBI. Though it kept a low profile, organized crime continued to grow throughout the remainder of the 1930s. Despite the success against outlaws, Hoover chose not to battle organized crime. Perhaps he was reluctant to risk making a poor showing against the powerful underworld that would jeopardize the FBI's rise in public respect. Instead he preferred easier targets that would garner plenty of publicity for himself and the agency.

Through the remainder of the 1930s Hoover remained a publicity hound. In 1936, after FBI agents and the New York City police located bank robber and kidnapper Harry Brunnette, Hoover personally led the charge on the apartment. The newspaper headline read "25 G-Men led by Hoover capture bandit in West 102nd St."

In 1936 President Roosevelt ordered J. Edgar Hoover to compile information on any fascist and communist activities in the United States. The duty would be the FBI's main focus through the remainder of the New Deal and Great Depression. Fascism, a system of government characterized by dictatorship, militarism, and racism, had taken hold in Benito Mussolini's Italy and Adolph Hitler's Germany. Fascism and Josef Stalin's brand of communism in the Soviet Union were seen as threats to America's democratic principles. As some European countries succumbed to these politically radical ideologies, the American Depression continued. Fears that these radical political ideas would take hold in America's weakened economic situation abounded. European Fascists did have their supporters in the United States and the American Communist Party saw an opportunity to advance its cause through the labor unrest of the time. Hoover vigorously pursued domestic surveillance efforts such as wire-tapping. He also kept lists of the names of "questionable" individuals. With the outbreak of World War II in 1939, the FBI's responsibilities concerning national security drastically escalated and the war on crime was temporarily put on hold.

Contributing Forces

Early Outlaws

The social and economic roots of crime in America are embedded in part in the stories of the Western outlaw. America's nineteenth century saga, set in the rugged, often violent frontier, revolves around famous outlaw gangs—the James brothers, the Daltons, and Billy the Kid. According to legend the James gang robbed banks and railroads but never bothered farmers. Billy the Kid stole from middle class and rich people and gave it to the poor. Like the bandits of the nineteenth century, gangsters of the 1920s and 1930s also became legends. Early Hollywood silent movies included Westerns pitting outlaws against lawmen. The gangster's world, however, was not set in the western landscape but in America's cities.

Immigrants

Individuals associated with highly organized street gangs of French and Italian cities and with violent political activists from Ireland were among those who immigrated to America from Europe in the late nineteenth century. These individuals oftentimes brought with them to their new country the gang associations of their old home. In 1878, the Italian government began an anti-Mafia campaign. Many of the blood loyal members of the Mafia, or *mafiosi* of Sicily left for North African ports and for the United States. A majority of those coming to America settled in cities, among them New York, Chicago, Baltimore, Boston, Detroit, Cleveland, and New Orleans. This influx laid the foundation for the brutal criminal society of the 1920s and 1930s.

In the 1890s and early 1900s ethnic groups struggled to survive in U.S. cities. They violently clashed with each other and with the law to gain economic, political, and social power within their communities. The earlier immigrants had largely come from northern and western Europe and they were not receptive to this new wave of immigrants that by the 1890s was coming primarily from Eastern and Southern Europe. Social and cultural differences proved to be too pronounced. The numerous gangs that evolved had colorful names, such as the Dead Rabbits, Blood Tubs, Bowery Boys, Whyos, and many more. Although the older Mafia was reestablished in New York City by the 1890s, it had little money and its gang activities remained localized.

Police forces swelled in response to a public outcry for control of the increasing street violence. Frequent arrests were made as the gangs faced increasing police pressure to curtail their activities. Shortly before the start of World War I one of the few major street gangs of this period still surviving under the increased police pressure was the 1,500-member Italian Five Points Gang in New York City. In 1915, a sixteen-year old named Alphonse Capone joined the Five Points Gang.

As World War I began, gangs crumbled with their members heading off to war. A few years later, however, the new and significant opportunity for the future of crime and criminals in America presented itself—Prohibition.

Labor Strife

The United States has the bloodiest labor history of any industrialized nation. The earliest deaths related to labor strikes occurred in 1850 when police killed two New York tailors while dispersing a crowd of strikers. A severe economic depression in 1873 triggered a number of violent strikes through the following years. In 1877 the first national railroad worker strike led to over one hundred deaths. As the strike spread, coal miners, farmers, and others joined railroad workers in attempting to stop rail traffic. State and federal troops were called in to forcefully end the strike.

Between 1875 and 1910 state troops were called on almost five hundred occasions of labor unrest. On May 1, 1886, workers across the United States went on strike demanding eight-hour workdays. In Chicago police attacked the strikers killing two. Three days later the workers gathered again to protest the police action. As a confrontation with police developed once again, someone threw a bomb in the crowd of police killing eight policemen. Four were eventually convicted in trial and hanged for the bombing. Violent confrontations continued six years later in 1892, when eight thousand state troops were sent to a steel mill in Homestead, Pennsylvania, after armed strikers turned back an attack by company security guards. The U.S. army was used in 1894 at a Pullman railroad strike and several mining strikes in the Rocky Mountain region.

One of the more famous incidents in the early twentieth century occurred in 1913. Known as the Ludlow Massacre, National Guardsmen attacked a tent city holding striking Colorado miners, killing 11 children and two women. Other bloody strikes occurred in the Northeast during the time just prior to World War I. By the 1920s as the economy was booming the number of strikes and related violence greatly decreased.

Prohibition

The United States government in 1920 introduced the prohibition of the manufacture and sale of liquor and with it a measure to restrict liquor consumption. This ban, not respected by many in the public, would prove to be the nation's single most disastrous social experiment of the entire twentieth century.

Congress passed the Eighteenth Amendment to the U.S. Constitution in 1918. The individual states had ratified the amendment by January 1919. On January 17, 1920, Prohibition officially became law. The Eighteenth Amendment prohibited "manufacture, sale, or transportation of intoxicating liquors...for beverage purposes." Congress passed the Volstead Act to enforce the amendment. The Volstead Act defined "intoxicating liquors" as any beverage containing more than one-half of one percent alcohol. Beer contained between three and seven percent and wine 12 to 15 percent. Thus, all alcoholic beverages fell under the ban.

Veterans returning home from the World War I were angered and amazed at the new law. Those Americans who planned to continue drinking stocked up on supplies. Those who planned to give it up treated January 16, 1920, like New Year's Eve, with their resolutions to stop drinking slated to begin the next morning. Saloonkeepers mainly moved their bottles of liquor under the counters and continued to serve customers. After about one year under Prohibition, people who had at first determined to follow the law became impatient with its restrictions and increasingly unwilling to follow it. Saloons continued to go underground with their liquor sales and many began to operate as "speakeasies." Speakeasies were usually disguised as more commonplace businesses such as barbershops or ice cream parlors. Patrons would "speak easy" to a doorman and tell him who sent them or give him a password to gain entrance. According to various estimates, New York's 16,000 saloons grew to between 32,000 and 100,000 "speaks." Furthermore, unlike saloons, women were welcomed at the speakeasies. Speakeasies dealt in large stocks of beer, wine, and liquor—all illegal. Supplying thousands of speakeasies required a great deal of organization and led to the development of organized crime.

The Irish had dominated criminal street gangs throughout the 1880s and 1890s. By Prohibition the Irish had largely vacated the worst ghettos, leaving the cities' criminal breeding grounds to Italians and Jews. With young men returning from the war gangs regrouped and began a new industry—bootlegging. Bootlegging involved illegally getting liquor into the hands of the thirsty public. Due to the outrageously inflated prices of alcohol, crime would pay and pay handsomely.

Al Capone was in jail when the stock market crashed in October 1929. He returned to a far different place than the vigorous Chicago he had left. (Archive Photos, Inc. Reproduced by permission.)

Organized Crime

Organized crime has been a term applied by law enforcement and the public to various kinds of criminal activity through history. By the 1860s certain kinds of gambling operations began to be increasingly coordinated in some city neighborhoods. These gambling operations became widely popular as forms of illegal lotteries would be accessible through barbershops, bars, newspaper stands, and other locations. By the 1880s horseracing became a national sport and the focus of organized illegal betting operations.

Public lawlessness and a crime spree in the 1920s was an outcome of Prohibition its supporters had never anticipated. In cities around the country criminal gangs who before 1920 limited their activities to thievery, gambling, and murders transformed into organized groups of bootleggers intent on supplying America with illegal alcohol. Gangsters became millionaires. Bribery and corruption of law enforcement officers became widespread. Newspapers profiled gangsters' lives and activities on the same pages with the Hollywood stars. The most prominent among them was Alphonse Capone whose brief career at the top as a crime boss, from 1925 to 1927, brought him lasting notoriety at legendary proportions. At the same time the overall prosperity of the 1920s led to a decrease in labor strikes and violence.

Only half a year before the stock market crash of 1929, as people still thought only in terms of money and success, Capone's life captivated Americans, who marveled at his wealth and power. He had reached across ethnic boundaries to form racketeering ties with Jews, Italians, Poles, and blacks. His empire, built on prostitution, gambling, and above all, bootlegging, reached from New York to Chicago. Capone maintained his base in Chicago, clearly the geographic center of the underworld; a winter retreat at Palm Island, Florida; and a summer hangout in Lansing, Michigan.

Capone's organization dominated the City of Chicago through intimidation not only in business but also in politics. The mayor feared him and the police were oftentimes corrupt and turned a blind eye to Capone's illegal doings. Newspapers estimated his income at more than $100 million a year. Capone, thanks to the much flaunted laws of Prohibition, was the grandest success story Chicago had seen in the "roaring 20s."

Although Capone seemed invincible his popularity in Chicago caught the attention of federal government forces. Only a few days after taking office in March 1929, President Herbert Hoover (1929–1933) pressured the U.S. Treasury Department to spearhead a campaign to bring down Capone. Elmer Irey of the Internal Revenue Service (IRS) Special Intelligence Unit was to obtain evidence of tax evasion by Capone. In case tax evasion charges were insufficient, evidence of Prohibition violations were also collected. In charge of amassing proof of Prohibition violations was a daring young Prohibition Agent, Eliot Ness. All would work together with U.S. District Attorney George E.Q. Johnson who was in charge of Capone's prosecution.

Compared to the power Capone wielded, the federal agents seemed an insignificant presence. Capone was seen as economically successful and effective at what he did, which happened to be operating a crime syndicate. Overlooking the persistence of the federal agents, however, proved Capone's undoing. After attending an Atlantic City, New Jersey, crime organizational meeting in May 1929, Capone and his bodyguard went to a movie in Philadelphia. When the movie was over the two were arrested for carrying concealed deadly weapons. They were sentenced to jail for one year. Released on March 17, 1930—three months early—for good behavior, Capone returned to his home in Chicago. Though his popularity remained high with the public, his power was declining. The competition between different gangs for the bootlegging action continued.

A Tolerant Public

Under the restrictions of Prohibition, alcohol became a symbol of independence and sophistication. People wanted to drink and were not willing to let the Eighteenth Amendment and Volstead Act stop them. Many Americans came to feel that the Prohibition law was misguided or even wrong and, therefore, should be ignored.

Prohibition made the suppliers of alcohol—gangsters—not only well paid but also well liked. Those who didn't support Prohibition thought of bootleggers as Robin Hoods, supplying what they needed in opposition to government policy. Escapades of the bootleggers offered exciting entertainment in the newspapers and clubs. Gangs' violent behavior seemed far removed from the lives of most citizens and so caused little alarm outside of law enforcement.

Prohibition saw the rise of many crime legends. The public was aware of certain individuals who carried out their crimes with flair and style. Dwarfing them all in the public imagination was Al Capone. Capone was daring and ruthless and had systemically murdered all gang leaders who tried to rival his power. Al Capone's yearly income topped $100 million (the equivalent to $3 billion in 2000 dollars) in liquor sales alone. Capone commented that all he ever did was supply goods to meet a demand—a very popular demand. Wealthy criminals bought off politicians and police in great numbers. If bribery failed to work, the bootleggers resorted to violence to get their way.

Organized Crime

Near the end of the 1920s gangs were becoming so organized that they held a national convention on December 5, 1928, in Cleveland, Ohio. Some historians date the beginning of modern nationally organized crime to this meeting. Twenty-three mafiosi, all Sicilian, gathered from cities such as Chicago, New York, Detroit, St. Louis, Tampa, and Philadelphia. Being a non-Sicilian, Capone could not participate, but he was represented. Many of those at the meeting would eventually head Mafia crime families. The purpose of the meeting was to discuss mutual interests and problems. Capone and other leaders realized their profits depended on organization and cooperation between criminal groups. So the suggestion for a national syndicate, which is an association of individuals or groups which agree together to carry out certain activities, to coordinate criminal activity nationwide was proposed. The mutually suspicious gang and Mafia leaders rejected the plan, but the meeting did lead to cooperative projects such as an execution service later called Murder, Inc., and to a national betting service that provided major income to the gangs and the Mafia after the repeal of Prohibition.

Despite the organization and cooperation of the Cleveland meeting, another bloody, rival gang-related act would take place on February 14, 1929. The St. Valentine's Day Massacre played out in a garage on the north side of Chicago. Dressed as police officers, four men brutally gunned down seven members of the Bugs Moran gang, the last rival gang of Capone's in Chicago. Although never proven, a shocked nation widely believed the murders could only be the work of Capone.

In May 1929 another underworld "convention" was held in Atlantic City, New Jersey. Crime leaders from around the country divided the United States into territories. They also established a nine-member national "Commission" for consultation and conflict resolution. The roots of an organized crime syndicate were in place. Organized crime had positioned itself in a powerful way only months before the onset of the Great Depression.

Public Trust in Law Enforcement

Where were law agencies during the 1920s as gangs were advancing into organized crime syndicates? Throughout Prohibition organized crime in cities essentially had many legal authorities, including police, judges, and lawyers, on its payroll. For example, a difficult law officer could be easily murdered. The political and governmental power structure of many cities and several states came largely under mob control.

On a national level the Federal Bureau of Investigation was still developing its powers as an arm of law enforcement. When Attorney General Harlan Fiske Stone selected Hoover to head the Bureau of Investigation in 1924 Hoover inherited a Bureau rampant with scandal and corruption. At that time the Bureau employed 441 Special Agents. Hoover immediately fired the agents he considered to be unqualified and set about improving the organization. To make the Bureau respectable Hoover assembled an elite group of men who were white, between the ages of 25 and 35, and college graduates. For his new agents he demanded rigid conformity with his rules and a strict moral code. In 1928 Hoover personally established a training school for new agents.

Hoover, a stickler for order and efficiency, devoted much of his energies and skills to making the Bureau a textbook example of a perfectly organized and well-controlled bureaucracy. Within two months he had directed the Bureau to take over control of fingerprint collections nationwide. By 1926 law enforcement agencies nationwide were contributing fingerprint cards to the Bureau of Investigation.

Hoover made these advances at the Bureau against a backdrop of bootlegging, gangsters, and a public distrustful of law agencies. Although it had evolved into a finely tuned government agency, the Bureau's agents had not yet seen any action against the nation's lawless heroes. In fact Special Agents were initially not authorized to carry guns. The actual direction Hoover's men would take to restore the country's laws and morals would not be apparent until the 1930s.

Perspectives

The Public View on Gangsters and Outlaws

Perspectives of Americans on gangsters and outlaws changed dramatically between the early years of the Depression and the middle to late years of the 1930s. In the Prohibition years of the 1920s and early 1930s, Americans viewed bootleggers as champions. Bootleggers found ways to beat the unpopular anti-alcohol law and brought liquor to thousands of speakeasies, where the public happily consumed the illegal beverages. As the bootleggers organized their efforts and became wealthy, Hollywood began to romanticize them in the early 1930s gangster movies. In 1930 and 1931, as the Depression deepened, Americans flocked to the movie houses. The fictionalized gangsters of the films caught audiences' imagination. They were just as enthralled with the imaginary tales of gangsters based on Al Capone as they were captivated by Capone's real life. Americans related to the individual success of these characters and kept up hope that they too would succeed once again.

By the time the Midwest outlaws such as John Dillinger appeared in 1933, Americans tended to ignore the brutality of such criminals and instead turn them into folk heroes. The outlaws regularly outsmarted local police, whom Americans had for many years viewed as incapable of reining in crime.

During the same period, however, civic groups, churches, and parent associations became increasingly alarmed at what they perceived to be the growing presence of violence and its affects on society. They feared a moral decay was developing and became more outspoken against the glamorization of crime and criminals. Their anti-gangster crusade and calls for film censorship began to have an effect in the early to mid 1930s, and fewer gangster movies were made.

When Franklin D. Roosevelt assumed the presidency in 1933, he called for a New Deal of relief programs to assist people struggling with the Depression. A more hopeful America became caught up in a new spirit of cooperation and, with a rebirth of positive feelings towards the government, public opinion turned away from lawbreaking criminals. The gangsters and outlaws were increasingly looked upon as symbols of an undesirable moral decay. By 1935, the Special Agents of the Bureau of Investigation, under Hoover's leadership, had eliminated the most famous outlaws. Hollywood, getting into the spirit of supporting government, produced *G-Men,* which helped revive public opinion of the law in the eyes of many Americans. Just as federal programs were helping citizens to survive the Depression, federal lawmen were becoming the new heroes of the public.

The Public and J. Edgar Hoover

J. Edgar Hoover became the number one figure of law enforcement in American popular culture. He enjoyed the media attention and sought out all the publicity he could. Hoover began to speak to groups about criminals, calling them "mad dogs with guns in their hands" and "public rats." By 1936 Hoover's FBI, prompted by growing concerns over fascism and communism in Europe and rumblings of the same at home, began to keep lists of "questionable" persons, those who might turn into enemies of democracy. Hoover was able to accomplish this information gathering under the guise of investigating activities and people with connections to communism and fascism in the United States. Roosevelt had first charged Hoover with collecting and providing information to the government on fascist and communist groups in the country. Hoover took liberties with this "permission" and interpreted Roosevelt's request by beginning domestic surveillance on anyone he deemed suspicious.

Though many Americans during the early years of the Great Depression sympathized with gangsters and outlaws, by 1933 most ordinary Americans shared Hoover's beliefs about law and order. Just as the public had once admired Al Capone's flouting of the unpopular Prohibition law and his assistance of Chicago's poor when the government was not providing help, Hoover was now admired by that same public, who looked to him for direction and security against the organized gangs that remained in the wake of Prohibition. Some became concerned, however, that Hoover was crossing a line between law enforcement and forcing the law. They feared that Hoover was disregarding civil liberties in his zeal for justice. A few congressmen, along with members of the American Civil Liberties Union and some citizens, shared these apprehensions. As World War II (1939–1945) approached, however, fear of fascists and communists in the country increased, and Hoover's tactics appeared justified.

Impact

The legacy of crime resulting from the Great Depression has three fronts: (1) crowd street violence spurred by economic desperation and labor's effort to achieve union recognition by employers; (2) continued existence and expansion of organized crime; and, (3) the continued existence and expansion of federal law enforcement, most notably the Federal Bureau of Investigation (FBI).

Street Violence

Violence resulting from food riots, farmer protests, and unemployment marches largely subsided as the New Deal gained momentum in 1933 and 1934. Labor violence became less pronounced with the industrial mobilization for World War II. New forms of violent protest came in the 1950s as part of the civil rights movement in which black Americans sought to end racial discrimination and segregation (keeping races apart in public places). The push for recognition of civil rights for racial minorities during the 1930s had been largely suppressed by the New Deal. Roosevelt had sought to maintain the loyal support of white Southern Democrats so as to get his economic recovery programs through Congress. Following World War II the patience of black Americans had further eroded over unjust racial segregation laws. Civil disobedience strategies inspired by Dr. Martin Luther King drew attacks from local police forces just as labor strikers had in the 1930s. The National Guard and U.S. troops were used to restore peace. These forms of confrontation gave way to race riots in the mid and late 1960s. Major clashes in inner cities across the United States left behind considerable property damage and racial tensions.

Anti-war protests beginning in 1966 against U.S. involvement in Vietnam also led to numerous incidents of street violence. Two notable incidents were the riot between protesters and police outside the Democratic National Convention in Chicago in 1968 and the shooting of protesters by National Guard troops on the campus of Kent State University in 1969. As food riots and unemployment unrest were largely quelled by New Deal policies, civil rights confrontations resulted in the passage of major legislation in the mid-1960s, and anti-war protests contributed to the withdrawal of U.S. forces from Southeast Asia.

Organized Crime

Organized crime involving the rise of the American Mafia, largely unchallenged during the Great Depression, continued through the century. The FBI focused first on gangsters and outlaws and then political extremists. Local authorities dealt with street crowd violence and labor strife. However the face of organized crime changed in America between the 1930s and 2000. The Irish and Jewish gangs of the early twentieth century virtually disappeared. New criminal gangs of black Americans, Asians, Jamaicans, and Latin Americans, all dealing in drugs, besieged the traditional American Mafia.

The focus of the federal government after World War II continued to be the activities of Italian Americans. Congressional investigations in the 1950s and 1960s identified what it believed was a secret society of the Mafia that operated throughout the United States overseeing illegal activities. Twenty-four separate organizations composing the Mafia operated in twenty cities involved in gambling, drug trafficking, and loan sharking. The highly popular 1972 movie, *The Godfather* popularized the notion of a tightly- knit Mafia underworld.

A tool to assist law enforcement in curtailing crime, called the Organized Crime Control Act, was passed by Congress in 1970. Central to this act is the Racketeer Influenced and Corrupt Organizations Act (RICO). Notably, "Rico" is also the name of the gangster in the popular 1930 film *Little Caesar.* As part of the Organized Crime Control Act, RICO is actually a

Biography:

Alphonse "Al" Capone

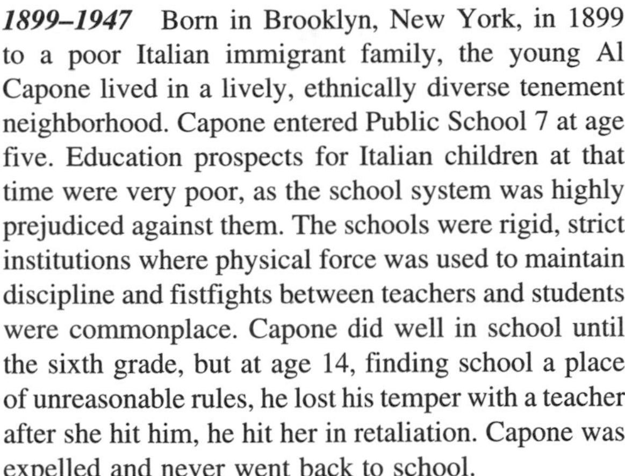

1899–1947 Born in Brooklyn, New York, in 1899 to a poor Italian immigrant family, the young Al Capone lived in a lively, ethnically diverse tenement neighborhood. Capone entered Public School 7 at age five. Education prospects for Italian children at that time were very poor, as the school system was highly prejudiced against them. The schools were rigid, strict institutions where physical force was used to maintain discipline and fistfights between teachers and students were commonplace. Capone did well in school until the sixth grade, but at age 14, finding school a place of unreasonable rules, he lost his temper with a teacher after she hit him, he hit her in retaliation. Capone was expelled and never went back to school.

Young people in Capone's neighborhood ran in gangs—Italian gangs, Jewish gangs, and Irish gangs—which were not violent but merely boys who hung out together. Few slum schools had playgrounds or recreation activities so the formation of gangs substituted for this lack. Capone belonged to the South Brooklyn Rippers, Forty Thieves Juniors, and the Five Point Juniors, while at the same time he worked dutifully for years to help support his family. There was no indication he would go to a life of crime until his friend Johnny Torrio, from the neighborhood, who would later become a gangland leader, got 18-year-old Al Capone a bartending and bouncer job at the Harvard Inn. It was there, in a fight, that the left side of Capone's face was scared. From this injury Capone permanently acquired the nickname of "Scarface."

Capone's father died suddenly of a heart attack in 1920, when Capone was 19. Historians believe this lack of parental authority marked the beginning of Capone's criminal life. Torrio had moved to Chicago and called Capone to join him. Torrio became an influential lieutenant in Chicago's Colosimo mob, which engaged in the Prohibition-spawned rackets of brewing and distributing beer. Torrio and Capone took full advantage of the "business opportunities," and Torrio soon gained full control of the gang.

In 1925 Torrio was seriously wounded in an assassination attempt and while he retired to Brooklyn, Capone took charge of the Colosimo gang. Capone had a fearless reputation, which grew as he eliminated rival gang after rival gang. By 1927 Capone had a bootleg monopoly across Chicago and Cook County. Capone pocketed well over $100 million a year from beer and liquor sales, gambling, dog tracks, dancehalls, and prostitution. Through bribery he kept law enforcement and politicians both in check.

Although he was in Florida at the time of the St. Valentine's Day Massacre on February 14, 1929, Capone was very likely behind the event. Several associates of the rival gang headed by "Bugs" Moran were murdered. Although Capone did not realize it at the time, the massacre and the publicity stemming from it, much of which glamorized Capone to the public, caught the attention of federal government law enforcers.

In 1928 26-year old Ness, a Prohibition federal agent, was put in charge of gathering information on Al Capone's illegal activities. Assembling an incorruptible and fearless squad of nine agents, Ness and his men wreaked havoc on Capone's bootlegging activities. They raided and destroyed equipment in his breweries and distribution centers. Ness' men were nicknamed the "untouchables," and were later immortalized in the popular 1950s television series "The Untouchables," as well as in a 1987 Kevin Costner movie of the same name.

In 1931 a federal jury convicted Capone of income tax evasion and the judge sentenced him to eleven years in prison. Released from Alcatraz after eight years, Capone, now suffering from complications of syphilis, retired to his Palm Island, Florida, home where he died in 1947.

---

group of laws that define and set punishment for racketeering. Racketeering is very broadly defined and includes many categories of activities common to organized crime such as extortion, money laundering, bootlegging, and kidnapping. By 1975 the National Conference on Organized Crime estimated that what was considered organized crime cost the American economy over $50 billion a year. During the 1980s and 1990s many bosses and members of organized crime were convicted and sent to prison under RICO.

By 2000 organized crime became more associated with the "war on drugs," a massive law enforcement effort to stop international drug trafficking. What was now considered organized crime was associated with no particular ethnic group but with drug cartels. Its definition included not only organized groups but any collection of individuals engaging in continuing criminal activities, including street gangs.

Organized crime was difficult to eliminate because it is actually comprised of complex and loosely coordinated activities by diverse groups. It was made up of a variety of enterprises that are not necessarily centrally controlled by any particular group or organization and alliances may constantly shift. In addition organized crime had gone global. According to Louis J. Freeh, a former director of the FBI, worldwide alliances in 2001 were being forged in every criminal field, from trafficking in drugs and money laundering, to counterfeiting, to the illicit sale of nuclear materials. The challenge of containing or eradicating organized crime remained a problem, just as it was during the Great Depression.

Further Growth of the FBI

During the Great Depression the FBI gained greatly in public respect. Federal law enforcement grew along with other parts of the federal government dealing with economic recovery. Following World War II in 1945, the FBI began undergoing further change. Both its size and jurisdiction (range of authority) greatly expanded. The FBI began conducting background security investigations for the White House and other government agencies. Headed by Senator Estes Kefauver of Tennessee, a committee of congressmen traveled the country in the early 1950s investigating all levels of corruption, including the organized crime syndicate. Organized crime, however, did not receive full attention of the FBI until 1972 following J. Edgar Hoover's death. At the time of his death Hoover had been with the Bureau for almost 55 years, 48 of those years serving as its director. He believed to the end that he and his Special Agents had been the guardians of the country's moral values.

In 2000 the FBI, adhering to its motto of Fidelity, Bravery, and Integrity, served as the U.S. Department of Justice's principle investigative arm. Compared to its lack of federal jurisdiction in 1930, the Bureau in 2000 had investigative jurisdiction over violations in more than 200 categories of federal crimes. The FBI also investigated violations under the Civil Rights Act of 1964. It also continued its background investigations for the Executive Branch and government agencies. As of 2001 the FBI had five top priority areas: domestic terrorism; national foreign intelligence; organized crime/drug cases; violent crimes; and white-collar crimes.

Notable People

James Cagney (1904–1986). Among the films actor James "Jimmy" Cagney starred in are *Public Enemy* (1931), *G-Men* (1935), and *Angels with Dirty Faces* (1938), which reflected Depression America's social thinking. First he was the gangster hero, next the lawman hero, and lastly a hoodlum produced by a harsh Depression-era childhood. All of the films were well received by audiences.

Homer Stillé Cummings (1870–1956). Cummings served as attorney general under President Franklin D. Roosevelt from 1933 to 1939 and was Roosevelt's chief architect for the federal government's war on crime. It was his anti-crime package, passed by Congress in 1934, that allowed major expansion of federal law enforcement jurisdiction which resulted in the dramatic expansion of FBI power.

During the first few years of the New Deal from 1933 to 1935 Cummings was the undisputed head of American law enforcement. In fact the American public was more interested in Cummings than in J. Edgar Hoover until Hollywood premiered *G-Men* in 1935, which popularized federal agents.

John Herbert Dillinger (1903–1934). Dillinger was born in Indianapolis, Indiana, and raised by an older sister after his mother died when he was three years of age. After dropping out of school he joined the navy but got in trouble and was given a dishonorable discharge. Soon he was arrested for armed robbery and sent to a state prison.

After being released in May 1933, however, he went on a crime spree in Indiana and Ohio robbing banks. For the next 14 months Dillinger would become one of the Midwest outlaws that gained great public notoriety during the darkest period of the Great Depression. Arrested in September 1933 he broke out of jail the following month. Dillinger was extremely daring, even raiding two police stations to obtain guns and bulletproof vests.

After numerous bank robberies and other crimes, Chicago law authorities assigned 40 men to his case in December 1933. After holding up a bank and killing a guard in East Chicago, Indiana, Dillinger was once again arrested, this time in a Tucson, Arizona hotel. Again Dillinger escaped with a handmade toy gun, taking hostages and leaving in a sheriff's car. Crossing state lines in a stolen car, he became the target of J. Edgar Hoover and the FBI. Dillinger continued a crime spree from Minnesota to South Dakota, shooting his way out of two FBI traps in Minnesota and Wisconsin.

By May 1934 substantial rewards were issued for his capture and, to elude authorities, Dillinger had plastic surgery to permanently disguise himself. After robbing a bank in South Bend, Indiana, and killing a police officer during the robbery, Dillinger returned to Chicago. On July 23, 1934, a girlfriend of Dillinger's tipped off the FBI of his whereabouts. While leaving a movie theater Dillinger was gunned down by a force of FBI agents and local police led by FBI Agent Melvin Purvis.

J. Edgar Hoover (1895–1972). Hoover was born in 1895 into a primarily white, Protestant, middle class neighborhood in Washington DC known as Seward Square, located just three blocks from the U.S. Capitol building. His family had been government civil service workers for years. Hoover was closest to his mother, Anne, who was his moral guide and disciplinarian and whom he lived with until her death in 1938.

Hoover was a competitive student and desired to enter politics. He had a stuttering problem that he overcame by acquiring the habit of talking very fast. "Speed" became his nickname. As the United States entered World War I in 1917, Hoover went to work at the Department of Justice as a clerk, where he was recognized as extremely efficient and politically conservative.

In 1919 the Red Scare, or Communist scare, swept America as people got caught up in the fear of Communist supporters inside the United States. Communism was a new political belief system, recently initiated in Russia after a violent overthrow. Attorney General A. Mitchell Palmer placed Hoover in charge of investigating radical groups. Hoover planned raids, later called the "Palmer raids," in three cities, which led to mass arrests and deportations of suspected Communists.

In 1924 after the war, Attorney General Harlan Fiske Stone appointed Hoover as head of the Department of Justice's Bureau of Investigation (later renamed the Federal Bureau of Investigation). Hoover had long coveted the position and set about improving the Bureau's power and capabilities during the bootlegging Prohibition era of the 1920s. He immediately fired all Special Agents he considered unworthy and built an elite corps of young, white, college-educated men. Hoover demanded total conformity and a strict moral code, which resulted in the entire Bureau being reorganized with engineer-like efficiency and the beginnings of a crime laboratory.

In 1933 and 1934 Attorney General Homer S. Cummings decided Hoover's men would investigate, pursue, and arrest or gun down the infamous Midwest outlaws, who were in the midst of a bank robbery spree throughout the Midwest. Hoover's Special Agents, popularly referred to as "G-Men," helped restore the American public's faith in law enforcement.

By 1936, with the next world war looming, President Franklin D. Roosevelt instructed Hoover to keep him informed on fascist and communist activities within the United States. This became Hoover's main focus as he increased domestic surveillance and developed his list of "questionable" individuals.

To the generations coming of age in the 1960s and 1970s Hoover's tactics of widespread surveillance and wiretapping and his maintenance of detailed files on numerous innocent citizens seemed a threat to every American's personal freedom. As a result he lost popularity. He remained, however, in office until his death in 1972, after almost 55 years with the Bureau, serving 48 as the director of the FBI.

Meyer Lansky (1902–1983). Meyer Lansky, born Meyer Suchowljansky in Grodno, Poland, came to the U.S. in 1911 when he was ten years old. After a brief stint at a tool and die factory, Lansky linked up with Bugsy Siegel and with him began a minor criminal enterprise—the Bugs and Meyer mob—at the age of 16. He gradually expanded his exploits into gambling and bootlegging. Lansky, operating his criminal gang out of New York City, was known as the Jewish Godfather of the Mafia. He helped "Lucky" Luciano develop organized crime in the 1930s and was thought of as the "brains" of the two. He was very influential in his advice and guidance to many other Mafia leaders. After an attempt to avoid U.S. law enforcement by moving to Israel in 1970, he was successfully returned to the U.S. Lansky was put on trial three times for everything from tax evasion to contempt of court for failure to appear before a grand jury. The contempt charge was the only charge for which he was actually convicted. The other two charges were dropped, and the contempt conviction was overturned. Lansky passed away at home in January of 1983.

Charles "Lucky" Luciano (1897–1962). Luciano, based in New York City, was regarded as the most important Italian American gangster in the history of organized crime. Between 1930 and 1931, in New York City, Luciano cleaned the Italian underworld of old line leaders and established the American Mafia. Along with Meyer Lansky he invigorated "the Commission," the Mafia ruling body. U.S. attorney

Thomas E. Dewey sent Luciano to prison in 1936. Luciano aided the World War II effort while in prison by instructing his gangsters to protect the U.S. eastern seaboard waterfront. He also had his Old World Mafia contacts help the Allies during the invasion of Sicily. Dewey had Luciano's sentence suspended in 1946 and deported him to Italy.

Primary Sources

Hoover Defends Attack on Bonus Army

In the spring of 1932 thousands of unemployed World War I veterans and their families began gathering in Washington, DC, in hastily built shantytowns. Known as the Bonus Army, their goal was to lobby Congress into providing bonus pay to them immediately rather than waiting until 1945 as Congress had originally scheduled their bonus pay for serving in the war. At first President Herbert Hoover had provided some food and supplies while waiting for Congress to act on a proposed bill that would have met their demands. When the bill was defeated, however, Hoover asked the veterans to leave and go home. Most did, but two thousand stayed to continue their protest. After violent clashes with local police, Hoover sent in the U.S. army to remove those Bonus Army members remaining. After a bloody confrontation leading to their removal Hoover held a news conference on July 29, 1932, to justify the heavy-handed approach of the U.S. Army that led to many injured and the death of a child from tear gas exposure. At the news conference with reporters the president made the following comments. (quoted in Herbert Hoover. *Public Papers of the Presidents of the United States: Herbert Hoover, 1932–1933.* Washington, DC: United States Government Printing Office, 1977, pp. 347–348).

> A challenge to the authority of the United States Government has been met, swiftly and firmly.
>
> After months of patient indulgence, the Government met overt lawlessness as it always must be met if the cherished processes of self-government are to be preserved. We cannot tolerate the abuse of constitutional rights by those who would destroy all government, no matter who they may be. Government cannot be coerced by mob rule.
>
> The Department of Justice is pressing its investigation into the violence which forced the call for Army detachments, and it is my sincere hope that those agitators who inspired yesterday's attack upon the Federal authority may be brought speedily to trial in the civil courts. There can be no safe harbor in the Untied States of America for violence.
>
> Order and civil tranquility are the first requisites in the great task of economic reconstruction to which our whole people now are devoting their heroic and noble energies. This national effort must not be retarded in even the slightest degree by organized lawlessness in the country. The first obligation of my office is to uphold and defend the Constitution and the authority of the law.

Al Capone

Anthony Russo, who became a surrogate son to Capone, speaks about Capone's humanity during the Depression (as quoted in Laurence Bergreen, *Capone: The Man and the Era,* pp. 15–16).

> Anyone ever needed any help who went to him, they got it. He helped those old people in Chicago, those old Italians during the Depression. If it hadn't been for him, half of them would have been on welfare, or worse, but he always had ways of helping them earn a dollar. He never let anyone think he was just giving them something. He'd say, `I'll rent your garage. I may need it.' Or, `I'll rent your basement. I may need it.' Never using it, but he would pay them anyway. In those days back in Chicago he'd pay 'em $75 a month; it was a lot of money back in 1930. He was just that way. During the Depression he even ran soup kitchens in Chicago. He fed many and many a bum. I don't know what he gained by being kind to those kind of people because they couldn't do anything for him; he was doing it for them. But that's the kind of individual he was. He just liked people.

Suggested Research Topics

- Research what it takes to become an FBI Special Agent in the early twenty-first century. What are the requirements for employment and what kind of lifestyle is demanded of the candidate? Find out what subjects are taught at the training school located in Quantico, Virginia.
- What type of environment did Bonnie Parker and Clyde Barrow grow up in? Might their lives have turned out differently if they had come of age in a more prosperous time, or do you think a life of crime was inevitable?
- Counterfeiting is big business for organized crime in the twenty-first century. Describe up to seven ways counterfeited money can be recognized.

Bibliography

Sources

Bergman, Andrew. *We're in the Money: Depression America and Its Films.* New York: New York University Press, 1971.

Bergreen, Laurence. *Capone: The Man and the Era.* New York: Simon & Schuster, 1994.

Clarens, Carlos. *Crime Movies: An Illustrated History.* New York: W.W. Norton & Company, 1980.

Fox, Stephen. *Blood and Power: Organized Crime in Twentieth-Century America.* New York: William Morrow and Company, Inc., 1989.

Hoover, Herbert. *Public Papers of the Presidents of the United States: Herbert Hoover, 1932–1933.* Washington, DC: United States Government Printing Office, 1977.

Kobler, John. *Capone: The Life and World of Al Capone.* New York: G.P. Putnam's Sons, 1971.

McCarty, John. *Hollywood Gangland: The Movies' Love Affair with the Mob.* New York: St. Martin's Press, 1991.

McElvaine, Robert S. *The Great Depression: America, 1929–1941.* New York: Times Books, 1993.

McWilliams, Peter. *Ain't Nobody's Business If You Do: The Absurdity of Consensual Crimes in a Free Society.* Los Angeles: Prelude Press, 1993.

Milner, E. R. *The Lives and Times of Bonnie and Clyde.* Southern Illinois University Press, 1996.

Powers, Richard Gid. *G-Men: Hoover's FBI in American Popular Culture.* Carbondale: Southern Illinois University Press, 1983.

———. *Secrecy and Power: The Life of J. Edgar Hoover.* New York: The Free Press, 1987.

Raine, Linnea P., and Frank J. Cilluffo, eds. *Global Organized Crime: The New Empire of Evil.* Washington, DC: Center for Strategic and International Studies, 1994.

Rosow, Eugene. *Born to Lose: The Gangster Film in America.* New York: Oxford University Press, 1978.

Ruth, David E. *Inventing the Public Enemy: The Gangster in American Culture, 1918–1934.* Chicago: The University of Chicago Press, 1996.

Volkman, Ernest. *Gangbusters: The Destruction of America's Last Mafia Dynasty.* Boston: Fabor and Fabor, 1998.

Further Readinng

Baxter, John. *Gangster Film.* New York: A.S. Barnes & Co., 1970.

Bondi, Victor, ed. *American Decades: 1930–1939.* Detroit: Gale Research In., 1995.

"Crime Library Website." [cited February 19, 2001] available from the World Wide Web at http://www.crimelibrary.com

"Federal Bureau of Investigation." [cited on February 19, 2001] available from the World Wide Web at http://www.fbi.gov

Hall, Angus. *Crimes and Punishment, Volume 2.* New York: Marshall Cavendish, 1986.

Kelly, Robert J. *Encyclopedia of Organized Crime in the United States: From Capone's Chicago to the New Urban Underworld.* Westport, CN: Greenwood Press, 2000.

Kennedy, Ludovic. *The Airman and the Carpenter: The Lindbergh Kidnapping and the Framing of Richard Hauptmann.* New York: Viking, 1985.

Nash, Jay R. *Bloodletters and Badmen: A Narrative Encyclopedia of American Criminals From the Pilgrims to the Present.* New York: M. Evans and Company, Inc., 1973.

Sifakis, Carl. *The Encyclopedia of American Crime.* New York: Facts on File, Inc., 1982.

———. *The Mafia Encyclopedia.* 2nd Ed. New York: Checkmark Books, 1999.

Toland, John. *The Dillinger Days.* New York: Da Capo Press, 1995.

Democratic Coalition

1933-1941

Introduction

"The immediate future of the Progressive movement is at stake. If you should fail of reelection, the Progressive movement as we have understood it, the aim of which has been to bring about a reasonable economic and social reconstruction of the country in the interest of the average man without a violent swing to the left, will, in my judgment, have gone down into a tragic grave." Anticipating the 1936 presidential elections although they were a year away, Secretary of Interior Harold Ickes wrote these words in a letter dated September 7, 1935, to President Franklin D. Roosevelt (served 1933–1945). They were recounted by David Plotke in *Building A Democratic Political Order* (1996, p. 80). At the time Ickes wrote the letter, the nation was experiencing a long period of economic strife, the rise of radical political movements, and numerous social protests

The Great Depression of the 1930s proved to be a major political crossroads for the Democratic Party, much as the Civil War (1861–1865) was an important event for the Republican Party. A disastrous series of national elections for the Democrats through the 1920s had left the southern states and a few northern city political machines as the only reliable supporters of Democratic candidates. Through the political skills of President Franklin D. Roosevelt, however, a diverse voting bloc came together. Included in this bloc were organized labor, poor and lower class workers, northern city political organizations, political liberals, intellectuals, farmers, racial and ethnic minority groups,

southerners, and social reformers. Through New Deal reforms, by 1936 the Democrats had become the protector of jobs for the workers, bank accounts for depositors, stock purchases for investors, and financial security for the aged and infirm. These programs, supported by this voting bloc, constituted what would become known as the Democratic Coalition. Though never formally organized into the political party, this Coalition would sustain the Democratic Party through much of the next three decades.

The impact of the Coalition's common interest in political candidates proved remarkable. It was during the 1936 national election that this radical political realignment in the United States took shape and by 1940 it was well established. The average presence of Democrats in the Senate between 1916 and 1930 was 44 percent. Between 1932 and 1940 it rose to 67 percent. It was primarily among business groups and the professional elites that the Democrats could not establish a bond. Business support remained limited and unenthusiastic despite Roosevelt's successful efforts in quickly resolving the March 1933 banking crisis and, as some claimed, saving capitalism.

Roosevelt and the Coalition also brought profound changes to Democratic ideals. The early nineteenth-century Democratic Party goals of a balanced federal budget and limited government greatly changed. Although Roosevelt personally favored a balanced budget, he realized the only way to fund New Deal programs was with large deficit spending. Government size and power grew to new levels.

Chronology:

November 1932: U.S. voters elect then-governor of New York Franklin D. Roosevelt, to the presidency, unseating President Herbert Hoover.

March 31, 1933: President Roosevelt signs the Civilian Conservation Corps Act to provide jobs for America's youth.

May 12, 1933: President Roosevelt signs the Agricultural Adjustment Act providing relief to farmers.

June 16, 1933: President Roosevelt signs the National Industrial Recovery Act recognizing the right of labor to organize unions.

June 26, 1935: Roosevelt establishes the National Youth Administration which becomes a major form of assistance to black American youth.

July 5, 1935: Congress passes the National Labor Relations Act to reaffirm the right of workers to organize and to protect workers from intimidation from employers.

August 14, 1935: Congress passes the Social Security Act which benefits the aged and infirm.

August 28, 1935: Congress passes the Public Utilities Holding Company Act to appeal to consumers.

August 30, 1935: Congress passes the Wealth Tax Act to shift the tax burden away from the lower class.

November 1936: President Franklin Roosevelt achieves reelection in a landslide victory thanks to the newly emerging Democratic Coalition of special interest groups.

June 25, 1938: Congress passes the Fair Labor Standards Act, the last New Deal piece of legislation.

November 1940: President Roosevelt is reelected to a third term as the Democratic Coalition becomes more firmly established.

Issue Summary

The Republican Fall

Just when it looked as though the Republican Party was going to continue to ride an endless wave of economic prosperity that had been accompanied by a series of 1920s presidential elections, the economy suddenly took a major downward turn. The stock market crash of October 1929 was followed by three years of severe economic decline. Banks closed, homes and farms were lost to foreclosure, businesses went bankrupt, farm produce prices continued to fall, and factories cut back production and laid off workers. By 1931, 1,300 banks had failed. The Republicans and President Herbert Hoover (served 1929–1933), who appealed to private charity groups to assist the needy, were overwhelmed by the severity of the situation. Meanwhile, New York governor Franklin Roosevelt was aggressively establishing relief programs in that state, as well as promoting pension plans for the aged.

By the summer of 1932, 12 million people were unemployed, and the Great Depression had a firm grip on the nation. The nation's problems were so dramatic that many began questioning the basic economic system of the United States. Many blamed big business for the Depression and scoffed at the Republican pro-big business ideas of increased mass production and a

Herbert Hoover, right, and Charles Curtis, left, 1928 Republican candidates for president and vice president, respectively. Hoover lost his 1932 bid for re-election to Democrat Franklin Delano Roosevelt. (AP/Wide World Photos. Reproduced by permission.)

laissez faire economy. *Laissez faire* economy means minimal government regulation over business. The new mass-production industries and the dramatic downturn of the economy created a working class more prone to question the authoritarian behavior of employers, meaning that an employer made decisions and set policy without any responsibility to their employees. Labor unrest in the population increased from 1929 to 1933 as conflicts exploded between employers and workers. This discontent, however, was neither organized nor politically focused. Having enjoyed the fruits of prosperity during the 1920s, many workers felt it unnecessary to join a union. Popular protests involved consumers, tenants, laborers, and the unemployed. Unrest was prevalent in the rural areas as well. Efforts to organize agricultural workers increased.

Republicans lost voters by the thousands with their harsh treatment of the Bonus Army in 1932. The Bonus Army was a large gathering of World War I (1914–1918) veterans in Washington, DC. They were seeking early payments of promised bonus checks for their military service. Such indifference shown toward the growing hardships of U.S. citizens by the Hoover administration was leading to greater social disorder in the nation.

President Herbert Hoover's unwillingness to take strong direct action to relieve the people's misery opened the door for the Democratic Party in the presidential elections of November 1932. The Democratic National Convention of August 1932 nominated Franklin D. Roosevelt as their candidate for president. An organist pounded out "Happy Days Are Here Again!" as the delegates paraded around the convention floor. It would become the Democratic theme song at all later party conventions. Roosevelt handily won the primary and the national election. The national election victory was not yet the work of a Democratic Coalition. Instead, the voting was more anti-Republican than pro-Democrat. The Republicans had simply failed to keep their promise of continuing economic prosperity and to show sufficient compassion for the victims of the economic depression. Roosevelt's victory was actually neither well funded nor well coordinated by the Democratic Party.

The New Dealers Arrive

Roosevelt and the New Dealers came from the urban progressive wing of the party. Progressivism called for using the powers of government to solve social and economic problems. Progressives believed the government should take a more aggressive role in relieving people's hardships and overseeing business activities. Roosevelt's first one hundred days of office, beginning on March 4, 1933, were filled with an incredible amount of social and economic legislation. The legislation that became collectively known as the New Deal included bank reform, regulation of the stock market, farm bills, public works programs, and low-interest loans for homeowners. These new pathways quickly labeled Roosevelt's administration as the most daring in U.S. history. In their flurry of activity New Dealers sought to make everyone satisfied, and for the first six months they were fairly successful. Even most businessmen, who had historically supported Republican candidates, refrained from criticizing the Democratic president.

By 1934 the Democratic Party was becoming better organized. James Farley, manager of Roosevelt's successful 1932 campaign, had been named head of the national party organization. Historically in U.S. politics, when a party gains greatly in a presidential election year it will lose seats in Congress the following midterm election. With the Democratic Party under Farley's guidance, however, the 1934 elections proved dramatically different. The public gave Roosevelt and the Democrats a strong vote of confidence. This victory came as much from Roosevelt's impressive efforts at helping the average citizen through his New Deal economic relief programs than any increased structural organization of the voters over the previously two years. The Democratic majority in Congress held to 319 seats in the House to 103 for the Republicans and 69 out of 96 seats in the Senate.

Actual success in leading the nation to an economic recovery did not come as quickly as many New Dealers had hoped. Importantly, however, the First New Deal measures of 1933 and 1934 halted the dramatic economic decline. Unemployment rates began a steady decline from 25 percent in 1933 to 14 percent in 1937. But momentum in New Deal policies was distinctly waning by late 1934. Roosevelt decided to take a different course to reinvigorate economic recovery efforts. He began looking in 1935 at building a stronger role of government in U.S economic affairs.

What became known as the Second New Deal began in early 1935 and carried strongly through to 1936. The Wagner Act, which supported labor activities, and the Social Security Act, which provided financial security for the aged and infirm, would set new standards. It was during this second push that Roosevelt began to solidify a broad-based constituency that would become known as the Democratic Coalition.

More About...

Origins of the Republican Party

The Republican Party was born in 1853 and 1854, through two organizational meetings held in New Hampshire and Wisconsin, and its first convention in Jackson, Michigan. People forming the party shared a common antislavery viewpoint that other political parties would not embrace. They were especially opposed to the Kansas-Nebraska Act of 1854. The act opened the door to slavery in the two newly established U.S. territories. Success at the polls came quickly for the Republicans as their first presidential nominee, John C. Fremont, carried 11 states in the 1856 presidential elections. The Republicans were almost instantly the key challenger to the Democratic Party in the North. Their next candidate, Abraham Lincoln, won 18 northern states in the 1860 presidential elections, enough to win the election against a Democratic Party that was in turmoil.

With Lincoln's victory, a chain reaction of secession by Southern states from the United States resulted. Since the Democratic Party had its stronghold in the South, the Republicans were soon left to run the federal government with little political opposition. Following the Civil War the Republicans established a long period of political domination, winning 14 out of 18 presidential elections between 1860 and 1932. The party traditionally promoted high protective tariffs, limited government, low taxes, and a *laissez faire* outlook for big business. In addition to big business, farmers who largely opposed both government and the powerful new industrialists of the North formed part of its key supporters. The party would remain one of the two primary political parties of the United States into the twenty-first century, promoting much the same values as it had since the beginning of the twentieth century.

The president shifted focus from trying to please everyone to focusing more on the common worker. Having passed major reform legislation the previous year, President Roosevelt had great confidence heading into the 1936 presidential campaign.

President Franklin D. Roosevelt delivers his inauguration address after taking the oath of office for his second term in 1937. In his speech, he promised to continue to push his New Deal legislation. (Bettmann/CORBIS. Reproduced by permission.)

Republicans a Minority Party

Franklin Roosevelt's victory in 1933 began a prolonged period in which the Republican Party became a minority party. The progressive wing of the Republican Party largely supported New Deal programs of the Democrats, which created further problems for Republicans.

In the years following his 1932 election defeat, Hoover and Republican Party chairman Henry Fletcher continued to speak out in opposition to Roosevelt's New Deal. But as the economy steadily improved into 1936, their arguments were attracting fewer followers.

Election of 1936

With the 1936 election approaching, the Democratic Party was still not particularly well organized. The condition of the party was actually not of keen interest to Roosevelt. Few in Roosevelt's first administration had strong ties with the Democratic Party. They were mostly independent progressive liberals. Though many voted Democrat they were not among the party leaders. They came from professional and administrative backgrounds and not from the party organization. Roosevelt's popular support was more a combination of small formal organizations such as the city political machines and masses of voters not associated with any formal political organization but affected in major ways by New Deal legislation. These included laborers, farmers, youth, black Americans, immigrants, and intellectuals. Each faction, in a sense, represented a separate social movement. They were becoming what would be called the Democratic Coalition.

Some popular movements promoting social reform did not join the Democratic Coalition. These included Upton Sinclair's "End Poverty in California" (EPIC) campaign, Huey Long's "Share Our Wealth" movement out of Louisiana, and Francis Townsend's Townsend Clubs. These independent movements reached their peak in membership in 1935. By 1936 the popularity of these more radical movements was declining. The public was hopeful about Roosevelt and his New Deal policies. Many followers of the declining movements would ultimately settle into the Democratic Coalition.

The Democratic Party platform for 1936 contained much more of a social and economic reform orientation than in 1932. Roosevelt integrated themes of progressivism, or modern reform, democracy, or social equality, and populism, or favor toward the common person. This combination attracted a large array of people. He hammered at what he called selfish elites such as big business, accusing them of blocking the nation's progress. When reaching out to this broad base, Roosevelt rarely mentioned the Democratic Party in his major speeches. He attempted to reach the poor, the first- or second-generation immigrants, and the working class. Many of those individuals had never voted or supported a political party in the United States before. In addition he rarely mentioned the Republican Party. Rather, he attacked Alfred Landon, his Republican opponent, and others by personal name only. In this way he appealed to the Progressives who had previously supported Republican candidates.

While Landon and the Republicans criticized Roosevelt's deficit spending and "runaway bureaucracy," they were hard pressed to criticize many of the more popular New Deal accomplishments. Still, the Republicans charged that unemployment was a continuing problem, Roosevelt had not balanced the federal budget, and the National Industrial Recovery Act (NIRA) and other New Deal measures threatened free enterprise. Roosevelt countered that free enterprise had actually been saved by his New Deal measures, and the public was feeling more secure that the economy would not worsen any further. Roosevelt and the New Dealers tried to appeal to various special interest groups. For example, as the New Deal was entering its fourth year in the summer of 1936, farmers were receiving far more attention than they had from all other previous presidents. The New Deal provided farm price supports, loans, technical assistance, and electricity. Until the 1930s farmers still read by kerosene lamps and used wood stoves for heat and cooking.

To the southerners and northern big-city political machines who had supported the Democrats in the past, Roosevelt successfully added Catholics, Jews, black Americans, immigrants, the unemployed, intellectuals, radical and moderate labor, farmers, and liberals. Catholics believed his New Deal policies were in perfect step with the Catholic idea of social justice. Jews turned strongly to Roosevelt because of his social policies and his belief in the worth of the individual and would overwhelmingly vote Democratic for decades. Black Americans saw hope with First Lady Eleanor Roosevelt's public opposition to racial discrimination. Farmers and laborers saw great attention paid to their problems by the First New Deal measures. The unemployed were helped by the public works programs. And the immigrants, intellectuals, and liberals were simply in tune with progressive politics. All were impacted positively by New Deal policies. Votes came from previously Republican supporters, people who had not voted before, and youth who could vote for the first time in 1936. The Democrats gained between six and seven million voters from these sources. Some estimated that between 60 and 75 percent of Roosevelt's support actually came from new voters.

Vice President John Nance Garner prepares to call the Senate to order. Garner served as vice president under FDR for two terms. (AP/Wide World Photos. Reproduced by permission.)

With this newly emerging Democratic Coalition, Roosevelt dealt Republican presidential candidate Landon a crushing defeat in November 1936. Landon won only Maine and Vermont in the electoral college. It was the worst defeat in presidential elections in U.S. history. In electoral votes Roosevelt won 523 to 8. The charismatic Roosevelt also carried other Democratic candidates on his shoulders. In the resulting 75th Congress, the Democrats outnumbered Republicans 331 to 89 in the House and 76 to 16 in the Senate. It was an increase of 12 seats in the House and 7 seats in the Senate. The Democratic Party, considered nothing more than a doomed minority party in 1928, had made a stunning turnaround in just eight years.

The 1936 election represented a revolution in national politics, with the diverse groups of the Democratic Coalition expending considerable influence. The New Deal had supported vigorous government

More About...

Black Americans Switch

Even with Roosevelt handily winning the 1932 presidential election, 66 percent of the black vote still went to Hoover. This represented a long-term voting pattern of black Americans since the days of President Abraham Lincoln (served 1861–1865) and the 1870s Reconstruction period. Reconstruction was a federal government program under Republican Party influence formed to create social and economic change in the South. But the increasing interest of President Roosevelt's wife, Eleanor, and the president's growing awareness of the importance of the black vote in national politics inspired a major change in blacks' political allegiance. During this time blacks were becoming more politically organized, and public attitudes toward race were changing outside the South. The 1934 midterm elections had indicated that blacks were beginning to turn away from the Republican Party after 75 years of strong support.

Although Roosevelt did not support civil rights issues because he did not want to lose the southern Democrats' support, some New Deal programs provided assistance to blacks. Secretary of Interior Harold Ickes directed the hiring of black workers on Public Works Administration (PWA) projects in proportion to their presence in the local workforce. The PWA also provided some public housing for black tenants, even constructing some racially integrated housing projects. In addition, 31 percent of PWA wages went to black workers in 1936.

As a result of various factors—Eleanor's active involvement, New Deal general benefits, and the Republicans' striking lack of concern for black issues—the 1936 presidential election saw a historic turnaround. An astounding 76 percent of the black vote went to Roosevelt. Many blacks voted for the first time, encouraged by Roosevelt's actions.

Following the 1936 reelection, President Roosevelt appointed 45 blacks to various federal positions. A number of those appointees formed the "black cabinet" of advisors to the president, including National Association for the Advancement of Colored People (NAACP) attorney William Hastie, who was appointed as the first black federal judge in American history.

Roosevelt worked to cement the black vote in the late 1930s in other ways as well. The Civilian Conservation Corps, created in 1933 for young adults to work on public projects, expanded the number of black workers from six percent in 1936 to 11 percent by 1939. Photography sessions of President Roosevelt with black leaders began to occur, and civil rights delegations visited the White House. Still, racial discrimination was widespread in New Deal programs, and it would not be until the 1960's Great Society programs of President Johnson that the black support for the Democratic Party would be further strengthened.

---

spending and the expansion of federal authority, equal opportunity, social reform, and economic security. The lower end of the social scale surged to the voting booths. They developed a deep loyalty to Roosevelt and the Democrats. Many segments of U.S. society were obviously in need of and ready for an expanded government.

Midterm Elections of 1938

The road was not always smooth in these first years of the Coalition. The midterm election of 1938 showed how the loose-knit coalition of interest groups, though destined to be long lasting, could also be vulnerable. A series of events in 1937 greatly undercut Roosevelt's popularity. In an effort to gain support for his New Deal reforms, Roosevelt pursued a highly unpopular proposal to add seats to the U.S. Supreme Court in early 1937. That was followed by a major economic downturn, leading to increased unemployment and decreasing farm produce prices. In addition, fighting between two labor unions, the American Federation of Labor (AFL) and the Congress of Industrial Organizations (CIO), following the CIO's split from the AFL the previous year, further heightened labor unrest. The New Deal appeared to be in disarray. To make matters even worse, Roosevelt decided to personally campaign against certain conservative Democratic congressmen running for reelection. The president had become weary of conservative Democrats joining with northern Republicans to block New

President Franklin D. Roosevelt seated with his wife, Eleanor and his mother, Sara, before a radio broadcast of one of his "Fireside Chats" in 1936. (Archive Photos. Reproduced by permission.)

Deal legislation. Known as the "purge of 1938," Roosevelt's political involvement in local elections was very unpopular with the public.

As a result, the Republican Party made a mild comeback in the 1938 midterm elections. The southern Democrats, alarmed by deficit spending, social security, and labor reform, supported conservative Democratic and Republican candidates. The public and Congress lost much enthusiasm for Roosevelt's programs.

This dissatisfaction was reflected in the midterm elections of 1938 in which many conservative Democrats and Republicans won seats. Republicans gained 75 seats in the House and 7 in the Senate. The number of Democratic-held seats in the House declined from 331 to 261 and the number of Senate seats from 76 to 69. The Republicans also gained 13 governorships. After eight long years, the Republicans were on the road back. During this time southern Democrats feared the New Deal would increasingly attack racial segregation traditions of the South. This would only add to the New Deal's existing pro-labor policies that greatly bothered the South as well.

The Republican association with southern Democrats continued to gain strength through the next few years. Though they were able to bring New Deal initiatives to a practical halt, they still could not defeat Roosevelt in 1940. Germany's defeat of France and aggressive actions by Japan in the Far East alarmed the public. As a result, they chose Roosevelt's increasingly internationalist perspective over the Republican isolationism. In addition, increased defense spending by Roosevelt in 1940 created thousands of new jobs and greatly improved the national economy. The combination of southern Democrats and northern Republicans had successfully blocked New Deal initiatives following 1938 until foreign affairs took over from domestic issues.

The progressive liberals who orchestrated the New Deal believed that given the size and complexity of U.S. society, interest groups were a key way of gaining political strength. A big drawback was that reliance on such a network of interest groups would likely not sustain a long-term existence because of inherent competing interests between the groups. For example, there was considerable tension between the southern Democrats and the pro-black movement. This tension came to the forefront with the southern Democrat support of the Dixiecrats in 1948, the Republicans in the 1950s and early 1960s, George Wallace in 1964, and Richard M. Nixon (served 1969–1974) in 1968. More and more through the 1960s southern Democrats were leaving the

Democratic Coalition. Laborers, farmers, city dwellers, youth, blacks, consumers, and others had their own needs. For this reason the leadership of the administration had to be flexible and pragmatic, or realistic. The New Dealers had to make sure no one group dominated over the others. The Democratic Coalition was also not open to formal organization. Many of the groups were populist oriented and suspicious of large organized groups. This network was counter to the Republican's rigidity and exclusiveness. This political force, though primarily supporting Democratic candidates, was never formally integrated into the Democratic Party.

Contributing Forces

Birth of a Strong Party

The beginnings of the Democratic Party can be traced as far back as 1792. It was then that a group of influential citizens began organizing to support Thomas Jefferson (served 1801–1809) for the presidency. They opposed the Federalists Party, led by Alexander Hamilton and John Adams (served 1797–1801), who promoted a strong central government. Supporters of the new party feared a strong national authority would threaten individual liberties. They supported Jefferson's vision of a peaceful agrarian, or farm-based, nation in contrast to Hamilton's ideal of a complex industrialized nation. Though it was built on the principles of representing the common man, the party's earlier leaders were actually all aristocrats. Besides Jefferson, they included future presidents James Madison (served 1809–1817), James Monroe (served 1817–1825), and John Quincy Adams (served 1825–1829). Jefferson, Madison, and their followers began calling themselves Republicans to show their loyalty to the country. So the Democratic Party actually started out being called the Republican Party. The modern form of the Democratic Party began to emerge following the War of 1812 as the party of Jefferson broke into factions. One faction became the Democratic-Republican Party led by future president Martin Van Buren (served 1837–1841). Their main focus remained fighting the Federalist's efforts to create a strong centralized government. The southern plantation owners, farmers everywhere, and immigrants in the cities were the core of support of Democratic-Republicans. They also drew from groups considered outside the society's mainstream—ethnic and religious minority groups. Many of these groups feared powerful governments and were unaccustomed to the unbridled capitalist system for which little government involvement existed. It was the common citizen versus the nation's ruling elite.

The Democratic-Republican Party successfully promoted the candidacy of Andrew Jackson (served 1829–1837) for president in 1828. Jackson was the first actual populist, or "man of the people," to represent the party and was called the first westerner since he was from Tennessee which was considered the western frontier at that time. Serving as the party's leader, Jackson was the national symbol against greed and unfairness. During Jackson's presidency in the 1830s the party switched its name from Democratic-Republicans to simply Democrats. The Democrats controlled the White House, Congress, and state offices from the mid-1830s to the Civil War. Democrats Van Buren, James K. Polk (served 1845–1849), Franklin Pierce (served 1853–1857), and James Buchanan (served 1857–1861) followed Jackson to the White House. Democrats only lost the presidential elections of 1840 and 1848 during that lengthy period.

The Party's Demise

By the 1840s the issue of slavery began to cause major strains within the Democratic Party. Particularly divisive was the issue of slavery spreading to the western territories. The party essentially split in two. Jefferson Davis of the southern Democrats promoted the protection of slavery in all new territories. The northern Democrats, led by Stephen A. Douglas, believed settlers within each territory should resolve the slavery issue. Douglas and his followers were able to successfully seek passage of the Nebraska-Kansas Act of 1854. The act gave residents of those two new territories the right to decide the slavery issue within their respective territories. Rather than once and for all putting the slavery issue in western territories to rest, however, it only served to further inflame the debate.

Fighting within the party came to a head in 1860 when the northern Democrats nominated Douglas for president and the southern Democrats nominated John Breckinridge. The Democratic split brought immediate and long-term political implications. A newly formed antislavery political party calling themselves the Republican Party nominated Abraham Lincoln their presidential candidate for the 1860 elections. With the Democrats split, Lincoln was able to win the majority of electoral college votes.

Through the next forty years, the Democrats held the White House for only eight years—two terms by Grover Cleveland (served 1885–1889, 1893–1897) toward the end of the nineteenth century. Following the Civil War the Republican Party aggressively pressed for social change in the South during the Reconstruction period of the 1870s. In reaction southerners throughout the region continued to support the Democratic Party, forming what became known as the Solid South. They would continue to support the Democratic Party through much of the twentieth century, forming a major traditional element of the Democratic Coalition.

Strongly supported by the industrial North, the Republican Party became aligned with big business. The party favored policies promoting a free market system with little government involvement. The Democrats remained more agrarian oriented. Democratic constituents largely opposed big business and high tariffs, or taxes, on imported goods.

In the 1890s another major issue would once again split the Democrats. The split was over the free-silver issue. Due to a sharp economic depression in the 1870s, a Free Silver Movement grew. The movement promoted unlimited coinage of silver. This would mean that the U.S. government would coin any silver brought in to the U.S. Mint. Supporters, including farmers and silver mine operators, wanted silver for currency as Congress had earlier eliminated it in 1873 in favor of using gold only to support the U.S. monetary system. Farmers believed they would get better prices for their crops with this proposed policy of unlimited silver coinage. In response to this pressure, Congress reintroduced the silver dollar in 1878. The movement for free silver subsided. An economic downturn beginning in 1887, however, brought the issue back to the forefront. Farmers once again demanded unlimited coinage of silver. Such an introduction of more money into circulation would cause the value of the dollar to decline and therefore the prices of crops to increase. Congress once again responded with the Sherman Silver Purchase Act of 1890. The act greatly increased the rate at which the government was purchasing silver from the public. Continuing economic troubles led Congress to have a change of heart about the increasing reliance on silver, and it repealed the act in 1893. Farmers of the South and West were irate and condemned the action as the coinage of silver had kept their crop prices up. With farmers a key element of the Democratic Party, the silver issue entered party politics. William Jennings Bryan won the 1896 Democratic presidential nomination, strongly supporting free silver against the advice of President Grover Cleveland. Bryan sought to bring back to the Democratic Party the western populism of Andrew Jackson's days. As Cleveland had warned, Bryan lost the election badly to William McKinley (served 1897–1901), and the Republicans dominated again. The Republicans passed the Gold Standard Act in 1900, once again making gold the sole standard for currency as it had been prior to 1878 and ending the free silver controversy. The United States would no longer rely on two rare metals, silver and gold, to support the value of its coins and paper money.

The New Freedom

It would take a split in the Republican Party—much as the Democratic Party had earlier split over slavery and free silver—to open the door for the Democrats' return to the White House. By the late 1890s the party became split between progressives and conservatives. Theodore Roosevelt (served 1901–1909), leader of the progressive wing of the party, gained control when President William McKinley was assassinated in 1901. Among the initiatives Roosevelt promoted was increased antitrust action. Roosevelt served for two terms before giving way to fellow Republican William Howard Taft (served 1909–1913). Dissatisfied with the conservative policies of Taft, Roosevelt took many Republicans with him in forming the Progressive Party in 1912 to challenge Taft's reelection. In the 1912 presidential elections Taft ran for reelection on the Republican ticket, and Roosevelt represented a third party called the Progressive Party. This split in the Republican vote opened the door for Democrat Woodrow Wilson.

Democratic candidate Woodrow Wilson promoted progressive reformism. He called it the New Freedom. Progressive reformism called for using the powers of government to solve the growing social and economic problems. The idea was counter to the prevailing ideas of limited government, especially in social and economic issues. The public had grown weary of the vast fortunes made by big business leaders such as John Rockefeller, J.P. Morgan, and Andrew Carnegie. Several big corporations controlled a good deal of the nation's wealth. Wilson focused on using government to support individualism against the large corporate forces that manipulate the system. Seeking economic reforms, the public elected Woodrow Wilson (served 1913–1921) president. The Republican vote was split between Taft and Roosevelt.

Back in a leadership position the Democrats called for a progressive income tax (higher tax rates for those who make more money), pro-labor legislation, direct election of senators, an inheritance tax, voting rights for women, and reduction of tariffs, as well as other reforms. The progressive philosophy of the New Freedom, with its expanded role for government, created a foundation for Roosevelt's later New Deal programs.

Though facing stiff opposition for his programs, Wilson was able to obtain legislation regulating industry and banking. Also, a constitutional amendment

Alfred E. Smith was a popular figure within the Democratic Party. He served as governor of New York for four terms (1919–1920, 1923–1928) and faced Herbert Hoover in the 1928 presidential election. (UPI/Corbis-Bettmann. Reproduced by permission.)

permitting income taxes passed. The Clayton Antitrust Act provided greater authority for antitrust action, and the Federal Trade Commission was created to oversee business activity. Corporate giants such as Standard Oil Company of New Jersey were put on notice that their activities would be under much greater government scrutiny. The Child Labor Act prohibited goods made by children from interstate commerce. The Federal Reserve System, created by the Federal Reserve Act of 1918, set up a central banking authority in the United States. The system makes loans to commercial banks and prints the nation's paper currency.

Wilson was also the first president to speak before a major labor union, the American Federation of Labor (AFL) convention. Though women still had no vote, a women's bureau was established by the Democrats to encourage their participation in political developments. Congress would finally pass the women's voting rights constitutional amendment in June 1919.

Elements of the future Democratic Coalition were coming together, but it would take Roosevelt's more aggressive New Deal programs to complete the process of organizing the diverse support. Wilson, however, was unable to bring the black vote to the Democrats. Like Roosevelt in later years, Wilson did not want to lose the support of southern Democrats. Therefore he did not touch on civil rights issues. Black leaders such as Booker T. Washington were highly disappointed in Wilson and the Democratic Party. Wilson did reach out to the Jewish community by nominating Louis Brandeis to the U.S. Supreme Court in early 1916. Brandeis became the first Jew to serve on the Court.

Wilson also favored an internationalist perspective, looking for cooperative relations in contrast to the Republicans' strong bent toward nationalism, which means a strong devotion to one's own country above other countries. This appealed to the politically liberal internationalists who formed another, later, element of the Democratic Coalition. It was Wilson's internationalist perspective that led to the formulation of the League of Nations following World War I. President Wilson worked hard to sell his idea of the League of Nations to stabilize world politics following the war. He believed the international body was essential to prevent future wars. The strong opposition against it within his own country, however, stunned Wilson. The unexpected harsh opposition to Wilson's internationalist position was one factor leading to the return of the Republicans to the White House.

Return of the Republicans

By 1920 the postwar economy was booming. Due to this unparalleled prosperity, the public concern over corporate greed and control had declined. The public call for government regulation over business that the Democrats had promoted died down. People also wanted little U.S. involvement in foreign affairs after the horrible experience of World War I. The Republicans, with their pro-big business philosophy, regained the White House and rode the strong wave of economic prosperity throughout the following decade.

As the fall 1920 presidential elections approached, the Democrats began involving women more in the party. They wanted to be remembered for spearheading the drive to pass the Nineteenth Amendment to the U.S. Constitution, granting women voting rights. The amendment was passed by Congress in June 1919 and ratified by the states in August 1920. This support would add another voting bloc to the future Democratic Coalition.

The Republicans won the presidential elections of 1920, 1924, and 1928 with Warren Harding (served 1921–1923), Calvin Coolidge (served 1923–1929), and Herbert Hoover(served 1929–1933). Harding won a landslide victory over Governor James Cox of Ohio, bringing the Republicans back into power once again.

Cox had carried only some of the southern states. The electoral vote was 404 to 127. The Republicans also made great gains in both houses of Congress as well. The defeat left the Democrats in disarray for over a decade. The Republican administration brought back a strong pro-big business perspective and a *laissez faire* approach to government.

Despite scandals and corruption in the Harding administration, the Republicans maintained a strong following. They simply sat back and let the booming economy go its own way. The Wall Street boom and urban economic prosperity dominated public opinion. During this decade the Democrats were split between the southern and agrarian forces and the steadily rising urban immigrant element who favored the more socially progressive perspective of the Democratic Party. Because of this internal turmoil, the Democratic Party had to settle for a compromise nominee for the presidential election of 1924, John W. Davis. Once again it led to a landslide for the Republicans. It was the worst defeat in history for the Democrats.

Although the Democratic Party struggled nationally through the 1920s, some local Democratic organizations were able to successfully move forward, including party machines in Chicago and New York. A strong combination of Irish Americans and immigrants helped maintain these strongholds. Following the 1924 disastrous defeat of the Democratic presidential candidate, the New York Democratic organization began taking charge to rebuild a national organization. They sought a break from the Ku Klux Klan (KKK), a racially motivated hate group whose members claimed to be Democrats. They also pushed for the end of Prohibition, a highly unpopular law in the form of a constitutional amendment that banned alcoholic beverages. Many Americans blatantly ignored Prohibition.

In 1928 the Republicans turned to Herbert Hoover, a safe choice, while the Democrats selected flamboyant New York governor Alfred Smith, a Catholic. Though still continuing the Democratic losing streak, Smith fared much better. He carried the 12 largest cities and attracted the most votes of any previous losing candidate in U.S. history. With the loss, however, many in the party came to the conclusion that the Republicans would continue to benefit from seemingly endless prosperity, and the Democrats would become a permanent minority party. The party had lost most northern governorships except one, Franklin Roosevelt's victory in New York. Roosevelt showed he was a tough campaigner who could connect with the common person despite his aristocratic New England background.

Following the stock market crash of October 1929, public attitudes began changing once again. Massive unemployment, continued problems with the farm economy, and loss of savings by U.S. citizens brought President Herbert Hoover and the Republicans into great public disfavor. The mood of the American public had significantly shifted by 1932 from what it had been prior to the October 1929 stock market crash. The people were ready for a change, but they knew more about what they did not want than about what they needed. What was clearly needed was new leadership to help chart a new course for the nation. This could not be crafted overnight; it would take months if not years. It would delicately combine the desires of many different social groups—workers, framers, homeowners, racial and ethnic minorities, religious groups, and political progressives—together to support a common long-term goal.

Perspectives

A Mass Political Movement

Prior to the 1930s political involvement had been out of reach to many in the nation. Through their *laissez faire* policies, Republican administrations during the 1920s had encouraged the growth of large corporations that increasingly controlled the economy and society. These corporations were in turn controlled by a small group of business elites. The social base for the Republican Party was strongly linked to the Anglo-American segment of society and Protestant religious association. Adding to this white, Protestant domination, state laws and cultural traditions in the South hindered most black Americans from voting. Companies used various means, including violence, to limit labor union development and keep power away from lower-class workers, many of whom were recent immigrants. Lower and middle class urban workers and ethnic groups could find no place in the dominant political parties. The economic crisis of the early 1930s and the arrival of the New Deal brought this form of social and political domination to an end.

The rise of the Democratic Coalition in the mid-1930s represented a major change in American politics. Social groups that were politically marginal in previous decades saw considerably more opportunities to become involved. The Democratic Coalition involved the rise of mass political forces largely operating outside the traditional political organizations, including both the Republican and Democratic parties. New movements and interest groups formed and sought political strength to bring about social and economic

More About...

Elections of 1940 and 1944

As the 1940 Democratic nominating convention approached, President Franklin Roosevelt did not express a strong desire to run for a third term. Secretary of State Cordell Hull appeared to be the front runner for the nomination. But Roosevelt and other party leaders did not feel Hull was sufficiently supportive of New Deal policies. With world war looming, Roosevelt decided to run for an unprecedented third consecutive term and received the party's nomination. The public was greatly alarmed by Germany's defeat of France, and a sense of emergency was rising concerning foreign issues. The Republicans nominated Wendell Willkie, a Wall Street lawyer who represented the unpopular utility industry. Willkie actually supported some New Deal accomplishments and took an internationalist position not too different from Roosevelt's. Given the lack of a dramatic difference between Willkie and Roosevelt on a number of issues, the nation chose to stay with whom they knew best. In addition Roosevelt had boosted defense spending, creating thousands of jobs and turning the economy around once again. Roosevelt defeated Republican Wendell Willkie handily with a 449 to 82 electoral vote tally. Roosevelt drew almost 55 percent of the popular vote and carried every region of the country except the Midwest. The Democratic Coalition held together with southern Democrats and labor joined by ethnic populations. The 1940 election had further solidified the Democratic Coalition.

Four years later, with the nation in the midst of World War II, President Roosevelt chose to run yet again for a fourth term. He easily defeated Thomas Dewey 432 to 99 in electoral votes. Only three months after his fourth inauguration, however, Roosevelt died. He had been suffering a decline in health for some time, but due to the war crisis the public had not been well informed. Vice-president Harry Truman assumed the presidency for the next seven years. In reaction to Roosevelt winning a third and fourth term as president the Twenty-Second Amendment to the U.S. Constitution was adopted in 1951, limiting U.S. presidents to two consecutive terms.

reform. Greater economic security was a major goal. Some groups immediately became highly active, such as labor. Others would become even more active later, such as black Americans did when the civil rights movement finally gained increased Democratic Party support in the late 1940s.

To confound some Democratic Party leaders, these diverse groups of the Democratic Coalition were not actually linked strongly to the party, although the party greatly benefited. Even Roosevelt was more committed to his New Deal than he was to maintaining and nurturing the Democratic Party. President Roosevelt was a shrewd political compromiser in orchestrating the diverse Coalition. He was continually willing to compromise on some issues to gain overall support for his national policies. Although most New Dealers serving Roosevelt were Democrats, they were not associated with the Democratic Party organization. Rather they came from other sources, such as universities and businesses. This even included the president's top advisors.

The New Deal combined a renewed democratic spirit with the earlier progressive political trend, creating a major change in society. Through the Coalition a much broader range of people and groups were engaged in politics and the coordination of economic developments. The crucial years of the Democratic Coalition emergence were 1935 to 1937. It was an unprecedented mobilization of the general population responding favorably to the New Deal's major policy changes.

The Democratic Party Organization

Although by the mid-1930s the Democratic Party was a long-standing major political party, it had little structure. It was actually more of a hodgepodge of informally linked small organizations. The national party leadership had become disorganized and weakened from the election failures of the 1920s. By 1936 the main support for Democratic candidates, including Roosevelt, came from masses of unorganized voters—the poor in the cities and countryside, farmers, youth, black Americans, ethnic minorities, labor, and the college educated. As a result, support for the Democratic Party greatly expanded but the party itself changing very little. It was the Roosevelt administration and the various motives of the Democratic Coalition, not the Democratic Party, which led to political changes in the 1930s.

The party leadership saw diverse parts of the population come together with a common political interest, at least in candidates for public office. They would, however, be supporting the same candidates for very different reasons. Of these diverse groups, only labor became a formally organized political force in a traditional sense.

Other factors also kept the Democratic Party from more definitively absorbing the Democratic Coalition. The Democratic Party political machines, which were long-lasting local political organizations with formalized leadership, mostly existed in the East and Midwest and persisted through the 1930s. They served to select local candidates and energize Democratic voters in their areas. The traditional party leaders who led big-city political machines felt more threatened by, rather than enamored of, the growing Coalition. They believed that if they opened the party leadership door to these new political interest groups, they would lose their own leadership and power, and the Democratic Party would become too democratic. Besides, the traditional Democratic power base and leadership were more politically conservative than the New Deal and many of its followers.

Ironically the Coalition would eventually weaken local party organizations by not working within the established party structure. Major policy developments through the 1930s continued to ride on Roosevelt's charm and charisma, not on the growth and strengthening of the Democratic Party. Another factor also inhibited improvement of the party structure. The Democratic supporters had become so numerous that party workers did not feel the need to spend much effort organizing. During the 1936 election, fewer than twenty people were on the national party staff. The new political power was coming more from popular movements than the Democratic Party itself.

In some places new grassroots political organizations with deep political attachments to the Democratic Party appeared, many through networks of farmers in rural areas. But they were clearly separate from the traditional party machines and party leadership.

Laborers Organize

These new grassroots groups also developed where labor had become strong and well organized. America's labor, long suppressed from organizing, began to emerge in association with the progressive liberals of the New Deal. The result was a major new labor movement. Substantial barriers had blocked America's labor force prior to the Great Depression. Anti-union sentiments of the public and the Republican administrations through the 1920s were followed by the onset of the Great Depression, which cost many laborers their jobs. The support of laborers for Roosevelt began to grow when the federal government responded to dramatic strikes in 1934 by trying to seek a settlement with management. Previously the government would often send police or troops to control labor activists.

This show of support by New Dealers for the rights of laborers to seek better working conditions led the public to take the labor movement more seriously. As a result union activism began spreading to a broader spectrum of the poor and working class. With major Democratic victories in the midterm elections of 1934, laborers were encouraged to press harder for labor law reform.

Such reform was reflected in the National Labor Relations Act (NLRA) of 1935 recognizing the rights of laborers to organize. Popular support of the New Deal shown by the 1936 presidential election results illustrated further that employers would have to deal more seriously with laborers and their unions. Some even credited labor for carrying Ohio, Illinois, Pennsylvania, and Indiana for Roosevelt. Unions had worked hard recruiting voters to support the New Deal. They conducted education programs for workers and the public in general. They viewed the 1936 election as vital for the future of organized labor. In contrast, business became increasingly hostile to Roosevelt. Whereas bankers and stockbrokers contributed 24 percent of donations to Roosevelt's campaign in 1932, they only provided 4 percent in 1936.

The perspective of the Roosevelt administration regarding labor issues was further demonstrated in late 1936 and early 1937 when Roosevelt and Michigan governor Frank Murphy refused to use force to break up sit-down strikes in Flint, Michigan. This government reaction, still very uncharacteristic of government responses to strikes in those days, brought considerable public complaints to the White House. The refusal to act was interpreted as further support for labor's right to organize and for employees taking questionable legal actions when management refuses to bargain. Then in 1937 the U.S. Supreme Court ruled in *NLRB v. Jones & Laughlin Steel Corp.* that workers have a right to organize and select their leaders free of employer intimidation. The support received from Roosevelt, the favorable Court ruling upholding the NLRA, and labor's successes in organizing for the 1936 election gave laborers a major new level of public respect.

Lack of International Pressure

As the Democratic Coalition first began emerging, the international picture was grim. By the mid-1930s the Great Depression had spread globally. Political turmoil in Europe was increasing as aggressive fascist movements gained strength. In Russia a violent communist government had become well

More About...

The Influence of Labor

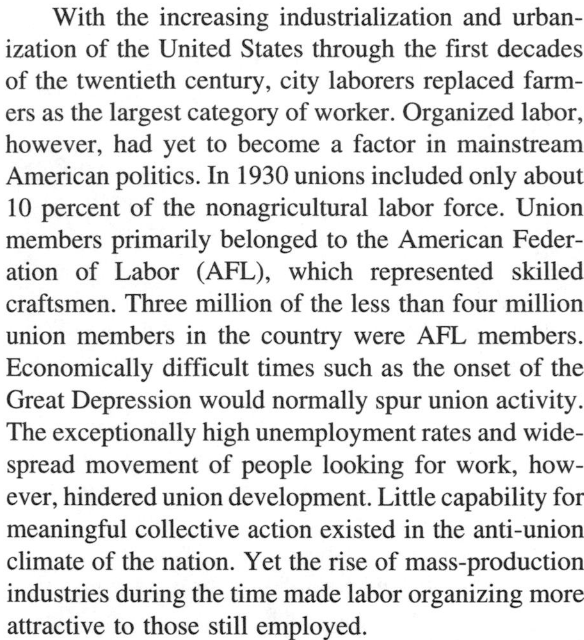

With the increasing industrialization and urbanization of the United States through the first decades of the twentieth century, city laborers replaced farmers as the largest category of worker. Organized labor, however, had yet to become a factor in mainstream American politics. In 1930 unions included only about 10 percent of the nonagricultural labor force. Union members primarily belonged to the American Federation of Labor (AFL), which represented skilled craftsmen. Three million of the less than four million union members in the country were AFL members. Economically difficult times such as the onset of the Great Depression would normally spur union activity. The exceptionally high unemployment rates and widespread movement of people looking for work, however, hindered union development. Little capability for meaningful collective action existed in the anti-union climate of the nation. Yet the rise of mass-production industries during the time made labor organizing more attractive to those still employed.

In the early 1930s the AFL often supported local Democratic Party organizations. Their influence was modest, however, and labor played no central role in President Roosevelt's first election in 1932. The major turning point was passage of the National Industrial Recovery Act (NIRA) in 1933 during Roosevelt's first months in office. NIRA was the first federal law to recognize workers' rights to organize and negotiate with employers over working conditions. Still, by 1935 only 13 percent of the nonagricultural labor force were union members, and by 1936 well-established unions were still few. But the labor movement was beginning to be taken much more seriously. Passage of the National Labor Relations Act (NLRA) in July 1935 again gave much stronger legal support for unions. Better known as the Wagner Act, it protected unions from unfair employer practices, promoted union recognition, and supported collective bargaining. Still, fierce resistance by employers made union organizing very difficult. The urban working class and poor carried little political strength other than through their individual votes. Improvement in economic conditions in 1935 and 1936 allowed workers to be able to organize. The principal aims were improving wages and working conditions, and unionization. People who supported unionization in the 1930s were considered radical.

Despite these slowly developing gains, labor knew they had a friend in the White House unlike any before. In the fall of 1936 the skilled crafts unions of the American Federation of Labor (AFL) and the newly emerging Congress of Industrial Organizations (CIO), representing unskilled and semiskilled industrial workers, rallied to President Roosevelt's support. Though still in its early growth stage, organized labor made a significant contribution to the Democratic Coalition and Roosevelt's reelection.

The 1936 reelection victory of Roosevelt meant a lot to unions as well as to Roosevelt. The unions were taken more seriously and resistance from employers was somewhat lessened. As a result unions would see their membership double from four million in 1936 to eight million in 1938. During the 1936 campaign labor had entered politics in a new and powerful way and would become a long-term part of the Democratic Coalition. By 1937 the more favorable climate for labor activity spurred many more strikes as unions fought for recognition from employers.

Labor became the most powerful component of the emerging Democratic political bloc, the Democratic Coalition. It reflected a significant mobilization of working-class citizens. Despite labor's role supporting the New Deal, few labor representatives were actually recruited to play key roles in the New Deal or the Democratic Party. Labor, therefore, lacked direct power in the national party but was a significant supporter in the voting booth. Labor's main political power was through local party organizations in urban industrial areas. Rather than working through the party, labor had more direct access to the administration itself to an extent not seen before.

---

established. Because of the disorder abroad few international pressures were being placed on the United States by other nations that were too preoccupied with their own problems. The time was ripe in the United States for political experimentation. President Roosevelt and the New Dealers knew they had a unique opportunity to try something new while not being distracted by international events.

Additionally, the controversy between Republican isolationism (opposing political or economic alliances with other nations) and Democratic internationalism (a policy of cooperation with other nations) was not forced to the forefront. Therefore Roosevelt did not have to take a strong foreign stance that could have caused the Republicans to become better organized in opposition. Foreign relations clearly became secondary to domestic developments. Roosevelt had personally believed that U.S. economic security could be improved with greater international involvement. He kept that unpopular viewpoint largely to himself, however, so as not to upset his fragile political coalition of support. He waited until the European situation had so deteriorated by the later 1930s that isolationism was no longer a feasible option for the U.S. government.

Impact

Transition to the Fair Deal

With Roosevelt naming Republicans Henry Stimson secretary of war and Frank Knox secretary of the navy, the Republican Party continued to be stymied in making political gains through the war years. A number of New Deal programs persisted beyond World War II (1939–1945). Much of the general public remained largely satisfied into the 1960s with the benefits they were receiving from social security and other programs. Many southern whites remained loyal Democrats. The lower- and working-class Americans in all regions still supported government welfare programs and maintained a strong support for Democratic Party candidates following World War II.

President Harry Truman (served 1945–1953) sought to promote many New Deal ideas and keep the Coalition together. Truman identified full employment legislation, civil rights, and slum clearance as the key party issues for the late 1940s. With the transformation of American culture to an urban society through the first half of the century, jobs became a top social and economic issue following World War II. In response, the Employment Act of 1946 became a hallmark of Democratic postwar policy. The act stated that it was the government's responsibility to maintain full employment. It also established the Council of Economic Advisors to assess employment issues. Truman's viewpoints regarding racial discrimination brought nothing but wrath from the southern Democrats. Many began searching for other political alternatives, including independent parties or even the Republican Party. Concerns by the southerners were rising in general over what they considered an erosion of traditional American values. They often blamed northern Democrats for bringing unwanted change.

In addition, a wave of labor strikes in the auto and steel industries increased public sentiment against unions. In response, a conservative Congress passed a series of antilabor bills, including the Taft-Hartley Act of 1947. That act, passed over Truman's veto, prohibited some forms of union activity and expanded the rights of management.

Public support of Truman and the Democrats was weakening, and the Democratic Coalition was beginning to fracture. Truman's support of labor and blacks was drawing increased criticism, especially from southerners. In fact, the midterm elections of 1946 led to a Republican-controlled Congress. As a result, Truman's social initiatives were being blocked in congressional committees. Despite his critics, during the 1948 Democratic convention, Truman insisted that a civil rights bill be supported that would guarantee voting rights for black Americans. This position led the southern Democrats to bolt from the party and nominate their own candidates on a Dixiecrat ticket. They were even able to keep Truman off the ballots in four southern states. Truman sought to keep the Coalition alive by rallying the black and labor vote. He became the first U.S. president to campaign in Harlem.

Truman's campaign faced another obstacle as well. Henry Wallace, Roosevelt's former secretary of agriculture in the New Deal and vice-president during the early part of World War II, formed the ultraliberal Progressive Party to run for president. The Progressive Party posed a political threat to Truman by attracting votes of Democratic Coalition members away from the Democratic Party ticket. The Democrats were badly fragmented among Progressives, southerners, and the mainstream party.

Given the disarray of the Democratic Party, predictions were that Truman had no chance of victory against Republican candidate Thomas Dewey. In a startling upset, however, Truman pulled off the victory, winning the electoral vote 303 to 189. The strength of the New Deal's Democratic Coalition had once again prevailed. The election victory was seen as confirmation of the continuing overall support for New Deal social policies. The withdrawal of the Dixiecrats from the party during the election campaigns and the eventual withdrawal of southern Democrats as well, however, gave indications of things to come for the Coalition.

Fresh from victory, Truman pushed a legislative agenda he called the Fair Deal. The Fair Deal promoted expansion of medical insurance, repeal of the

Taft-Hartley Act, an increase in minimum wage, and increased social security payments. As he received limited support from Congress, Truman was only able to win a minimum wage increase and a housing bill.

A Republican Interlude

With postwar prosperity continuing into the 1950s, the American middle class, including professional workers, expanded. Many of these middle-class workers were changing political party allegiance from Democrats to the more pro-business Republicans, weakening the influence of the Democratic Coalition. In addition, the southern support of the Democratic Party was further weakening due to growing fears over forced racial integration. Sweeping Supreme Court civil rights decisions and more forceful federal government actions to combat white supremacy in the South alarmed southern whites. The Republican Party embraced lower taxes for the rich, a strong anti-Communist stance, and resistance to racial desegregation. Adding to its support from the business community were the growing middle-class suburbanites and southerners dissatisfied with the antisegregation positions of Truman and the Democrats. Governor Adlai Stevenson of Illinois, running on the Democratic ticket, lost badly to war hero and Republican Dwight D. Eisenhower (served 1953–1961) in the 1952 presidential election. Eisenhower won in the electoral votes 442 to 89.

The Democrats would quickly rebound in 1954 to gain control of both the House and Senate by narrow margins. Again Stevenson won the Democratic nomination for president in 1956 only to lose to Eisenhower. The Democrats, however, retained the control of the House and Senate. Rising unemployment in the late 1950s led to substantial gains in the House and Senate for the Democrats in the 1958 midterm elections. So for much of the 1950s the Democrats retained control of Congress but had lost the White House to a moderate Republican.

The Democrats Return

In preparation for the 1960 presidential elections, major changes began occurring in U.S. politics. Two substantial defeats of Democratic old guard leader Adlai Stevenson led to a decline in the influence of party machines. They gave way to new organizations greatly influenced by young party volunteers new to the political scene. Their impact was immediate as youthful senator John F. Kennedy won the party's nomination in a close battle. Thanks to the reemergence of the Democratic Coalition, he then defeated Eisenhower's vice-president, Richard M. Nixon, running as the Republican presidential candidate. Up to that time, the 1960 election was the closest popular vote in a presidential election. With 68 million votes cast, Kennedy (served 1961–1963) won by less than 119,000. In electoral votes Kennedy won 300 to 223. With continued Democratic control of Congress, Kennedy attempted to inject Washington with an energy not seen since Roosevelt's first term. Though his popularity with the public soared, he could not maneuver his bills through a Congress in which conservatives ruled from both parties. While Kennedy was successful in establishing the Peace Corps, for example, his civil rights bill went nowhere.

With an eye toward the 1964 elections Kennedy strove to once again strengthen the Democratic Coalition. He wanted to rebuild support from the South that had gradually been lost since 1948. As part of this effort, he decided to journey to Texas in November 1963. His assassination in Dallas thrust vice-president Lyndon Johnson, into the presidency. Johnson (served 1963–1969) had been an administrator of New Deal programs in Texas in the early 1930s and a strong supporter of Roosevelt in Congress in the later 1930s.

Capitalizing on new support following Kennedy's death, Johnson pressed for a massive social agenda as part of his Great Society program. Democratic supporters, including both registered Democrats in the party as well as those composing the Democratic Coalition who were not affiliated with the party, sought a renewal of New Deal social activism within the healthy economy. The civil rights struggle of the 1950s and early 1960s had led to the rebirth of this liberal idealism. Because the Great Society was to be built in a period of prosperity rather than during the Depression years of the New Deal, President Johnson believed the Great Society could reach beyond what the New Deal was able to achieve.

Key parts of the Great Society were Johnson's war on poverty and civil rights legislation. Johnson had considerable success during 1964 and 1965 in passing many bills and establishing a number of programs. Legislative accomplishments included the landmark 1964 Civil Rights Act, the 1965 Voting Rights Act, housing laws, a funding bill for education, and the establishment of Medicare. Despite Johnson's sweeping victory in the 1964 presidential elections over Republican candidate Barry Goldwater, a large number of southern white voters, still angry over civil rights legislation, swung toward the Republican candidate, highlighting a continued weakness in the Coalition. Nonetheless, the Democrats established winning margins of 295 seats to 140 in the House and 68 to 32 seats in the Senate.

Just as Roosevelt could not capitalize on his 1936 landslide election victory due to his unpopular efforts at reorganizing the U.S. Supreme Court, Johnson was also soon sidetracked. The ever-expanding Vietnam War (1964–1975) began attracting more and more of Johnson's and Congress's attention. The Great Society agenda was losing momentum by 1967. Race riots in the nation's cities, escalating crime rates, and massive antiwar protests brought the Great Society to a premature end.

End of the Democratic Coalition

Frustrated and exhausted by the turn of events, Johnson stunned the nation by deciding not to run for reelection in 1968. The assassinations of Martin Luther King, Jr. and Robert F. Kennedy in early 1968 also greatly set back Democratic hopes of renewing efforts to press social issues. In fact, the tumultuous events of 1967 and 1968 would spell the end of the long domination of U.S. politics by the Democratic Party that had begun in 1932. For 28 out of 36 years, the Democrats held the White House, and even during the eight years they did not, they still controlled Congress for much of that time.

By 1968 the fragmentation of the Democratic Party over the Vietnam War opened the door for Republican control of the White House for most of the next 24 years, from 1969 to 1993. With a national crisis fueled by violent race relations, antiwar protests, rising crime rates, and increasing taxes to support social programs, many felt that the New Deal's promise of continuing long-term economic growth and improving the standard of living from generation to generation no longer existed.

With the Democratic Party in turmoil and split over the Vietnam War, the Republicans, behind Richard Nixon, swept into office in 1968. The Democrats had chosen Hubert Humphrey from Minnesota, a New Dealer and vice-president under Johnson, as its presidential candidate. The Democratic Coalition, however, could not be revived. Labor had been ignored by the Great Society programs, black Americans were disheartened by the slow pace of integration, youth and liberals were staunchly opposed to the Vietnam War—which many called "Johnson's War"—and the southerners were dissatisfied with the Democratic liberal social agenda.

The Republicans maintained a firm hold on the White House for the next 25 years with the exception of the four years between 1977 and 1981. The Democratic Coalition forged by Roosevelt three decades earlier was indeed over. The disastrous 1972 elections involving Democratic candidate George McGovern marked the first time in U.S. history that the Democrats would lose the entire South. With the Democratic Party supporting civil rights, the antiwar movement, and women's rights, southern Democrats who supported Republican Barry Goldwater in 1964 went with independent presidential candidate Alabama governor George Wallace in 1968, or Republican Richard Nixon in 1972. McGovern won only one state in 1972, Massachusetts. Nixon captured 521 electoral votes to McGovern's 17.

Between the continuing Vietnam War and the political scandal of Watergate, President Nixon ran into his own problems. Forced to resign the presidency in 1974, Nixon was replaced by his vice-president Gerald Ford (served 1974–1977). Capitalizing on the Republican's controversies, Governor Jimmy Carter of Georgia led the Democrats briefly back to the White House in 1977, but the old Democratic Coalition did not play a prominent role. Carter (served 1977–1981) received little support from unions and the northern city political machines. Rather than promoting New Deal/Great Society types of programs as Roosevelt, Truman, Kennedy, and Johnson did before him, Carter preached limited government. In a very narrow victory Carter defeated President Ford with 297 electoral votes to 240. Carter, with his southern roots, did return the South temporarily to the Democratic fold. Carter pushed for banking and airline deregulation, but his support of issues important to blue-collar workers was much less enthusiastic than his Democratic predecessors.

It was during this period of the 1970s that the political voice of the lower class and poor began weakening further. Political campaigns became increasingly expensive, leading to the rise in influence of political action committees (PACs). PACs are organizations formed by corporations, unions, and other groups whose purpose is to raise and distribute campaign funds to political candidates. These organized groups gained great power after 1971, replacing the more grassroots neighborhood and local political organizations that had been key elements of the Democratic Coalition. The American working class, a major component of the Democratic Coalition, was also losing its influence. By 1970 the growth of labor unions had come to a halt. From 1970 to 1986, even as the overall number of workers increased, the percentage of those who were labor union members dramatically dropped from 28 percent to 17 percent. By 2001 less than 14 percent of American workers belonged to unions, the lowest number in six decades. The traditional highly unionized manufacturing industries were being replaced by technology and service industries that offered low-wage, part-time jobs not represented

James A. Farley played a key role in Franklin D. Roosevelt's presidential campaigns in 1932 and 1936. (The Library of Congress)

by unions. Many manufacturing industries were relocating to foreign nations that offered cheaper labor and few unions. Unions had been the last formal link that had endured since the New Deal between working-class voters of the Democratic Coalition and the Democratic Party. Black Americans, ethnic minorities, and women replaced labor and the working class as the keys to Democratic support. The old coalition was being replaced by a much different one.

Since Carter was unable to build much popular support during his term in the White House, in 1980 the Republicans swept back in behind Governor Ronald Reagan of California. Under Reagan (served 1981–1989), the Republicans once again promoted a strong pro-business environment and cuts in social programs that provided benefits to the poor. They introduced "supply-side" economics, as well as lower taxes and higher military spending. Supply-side economics meant that businesses were given breaks to stimulate production and economic growth. When companies prospered, they believed that prosperity would "trickle down" to the workers. An economic boom did follow later in the 1980s but was accompanied by skyrocketing federal budget deficits. Riding the wave of a popular tax revolt and growing lower- and middle-class resentment of government and black Americans, Republicans also controlled the Senate from 1981 to 1987, wielding power they had not enjoyed since the 1920s. Reagan, leader of the conservative wing of the Republican Party, represented the ultimate end to New Deal politics of social reform. Despite Reagan's popularity, the Democrats regained control of Congress in 1984. Democrat leadership remained in disarray through the 1980s, however, offering Senator Walter Mondale as a presidential candidate in 1984 and Governor Michael Dukakis of Massachusetts in 1988, both of whom were soundly defeated.

In 1992 an economic downturn with rising unemployment, coupled with the third-party candidacy of Ross Perot from Texas, opened the door for Governor Bill Clinton of Arkansas to lead the Democrats back to the White House. Clinton (served 1993–2001) won 370 electoral votes to 168 against Republican president George Bush (served 1989–1993). The popular vote was much closer, with Perot winning 19 percent of the vote. The Democrats once again controlled both the White House and Congress after the 1992 elections. This Democratic resurgence did not signal a return of traditional principles supported by the old Democratic Coalition. Bill Clinton brought a more conservative, business-oriented administration. Still campaigning against New Deal-era social reforms such as welfare and government regulation, however, the Republicans took control of both houses of Congress in the midterm elections of 1994. The Republicans held full control of Congress for the first time in forty years. Despite the strong Republican showing in 1994, with the assistance of a strong economy, Clinton easily defeated Republican presidential challenger Senator Robert Dole in 1996, despite major personal controversies. The Republicans would once again regain the White House in the 2000 presidential election with an exceptionally narrow victory by George W. Bush (served 2001–) over Vice-President Al Gore.

Through the twentieth century, from Woodrow Wilson to Lyndon Johnson, the Democratic Party worked for the common citizen and the underdog in society, remaining a staunch supporter of civil rights. Taking a more centrist philosophy, Clinton veered from this tradition. As it had during the New Deal and Great Society, however, the Democratic Party remained the main voice for the poor and homeless, though they were the least likely groups to actually vote. Still the political trend was for the Midwest farmer, black Americans, Jews, women, factory workers, and conservationists to vote predominately for Democratic candidates. Business leaders, young professionals, and opponents of abortion and gun control sided with the Republican candidates as the nation headed into the twenty-first century.

Notable People

James A. Farley (1888–1976). Farley was born to a brick manufacturer in Grassy Point, New York, in 1888. From his early youth, he demonstrated a knack for political involvement. After earning a bookkeeper degree, he found employment with Universal Gypsum Company. While working for Universal Gypsum, Farley ran for town clerk in Stony Point, New York, in 1912. He was the first Democrat to win a Stony Point election since 1894. Over the next few years, he established a strong connection with leaders of the New York Democratic Party and became a supporter of Al Smith for governor. Farley's own political career continued to build as he became chairman of the Rockland County Democratic Committee in 1919 and was elected to the New York State Assembly in 1922. Meanwhile, his business career was also growing. In 1926 Farley left Universal Gypsum to form his own building material company. It soon merged with five other companies to form the General Building Supply Corporation with Farley as president. In 1928 Farley became secretary of the New York State Democratic Committee and helped manage Franklin Roosevelt's successful campaign for governor. By 1930 Farley had become chairman of the party's state committee as Roosevelt won reelection to the governor's post.

Following his successes in New York , which had become a place of political leadership for the party, Farley accompanied Roosevelt onto the national political stage. Along with Louis Howe, Farley laid the groundwork for Roosevelt's successful presidential bid in 1932. As a reward for his party work Roosevelt appointed Farley to the U.S. postmaster general position in 1933. He also became chairman of the Democratic Party National Committee that year. As a New Dealer Farley diligently kept records of how each member of Congress voted on New Deal measures and rewarded them accordingly through the president. In 1936 Farley skillfully directed Roosevelt's reelection and played a key role in forging the new Democratic Coalition. Although Farley continued as postmaster general and chairman of the Democratic Party National Committee for four more years, his relationship with the president cooled. In 1940 he disagreed with Roosevelt over the decision to seek a third term and resigned his two posts. Following his resignation Farley became chairman of the board for Coca-Cola Export Corporation where he remained until 1973.

Louis M. Howe (1871–1936). Howe was born in Indianapolis, Indiana, but grew up in the resort town of Saratoga Springs, New York, where his father owned a weekly newspaper. Following his father into journalism, Howe landed a job as a correspondent's assistant for the *New York Herald* in the state's capital, Albany, in 1906. In 1911 he was introduced to the young state senator Franklin D. Roosevelt. The following year, while Roosevelt was fighting typhoid fever, he hired Howe to lead his reelection campaign. After experiencing rousing success Howe became an assistant to Roosevelt in the future president's various appointments and elected positions through the 1910s and 1920s. In early 1932 Howe was joined by James Farley to develop much of Roosevelt's campaign strategy to win the Democratic presidential nomination and the successful campaign for the White House later that year. Howe advised Roosevelt through the crucial first three years of the New Deal and plotted the strategy for reelection in 1936. Howe played a key role in forging the Democratic Coalition. Having suffered failing health through the first four years in the White House, Howe died in April 1936. Much credit went to Howe for the Democratic Party's rise to its level of prominence in the 1930s.

Alfred Landon (1887–1987). Landon was the Republican candidate to oppose President Franklin Roosevelt in the 1936 presidential elections, a time in which the Democratic Coalition first made its presence felt. He grew up in Marietta, Ohio, before moving with his family at age 17 to Independence, Kansas. Landon gained his law degree from the University of Kansas but soon became a successful independent oil driller. Landon was politically a Progressive (believing in modernizing reform of the nation) and managed the 1928 campaign of Clyde Reed for governor of Kansas. Landon became state chairman of the Republican Party and assumed a moderate political position that would be more acceptable to the conservative wing. In 1932 Landon was nominated for governor of Kansas by the party and won a close election. As governor during the Great Depression, Landon gained respect for actions taken to protect farmers from losing their farms and avoid bank closures. Landon implemented New Deal programs in Kansas, including actively participating in industrial recovery actions for the oil industry. As a result, he was the only Republican governor that was reelected in the 1934 midterm elections.

Landon's popularity continued to climb as he gained the Republican nomination for the presidential race of 1936. Landon, disillusioned over the new policies' lack of success in his state, strongly attacked the

New Deal, claiming it failed to achieve its goals of recovery and full employment. But his criticism was not well received, and he fell—the newly rising Democratic Coalition's first victim.

Frank Murphy (1890–1949). Murphy was born in Harbor Beach, Michigan, and graduated from the University of Michigan with a law degree in 1914. He served in Europe during World War I as a captain with the American Expeditionary Force. Following the war he held several positions including assistant U.S. attorney and judge in Detroit. He became part of the city political machine in the Democratic Party and was elected mayor of Detroit in 1930. At that time approximately 500,000 people were unemployed. Murphy established a $14 million work relief program to ease the hardships. Murphy was reelected mayor in 1932 but resigned when President Franklin Roosevelt appointed him governor-general for the Philippines in 1933. He returned to Michigan in 1936 to win the governorship. Murphy quickly established what was called the "Little New Deal" for the state. The state legislature passed workmen's compensation, old age assistance, and greater funding support for education.

Murphy, along with Roosevelt, gained notoriety in early 1937 when he refused to send state troops to break up "sit-down strikes" in the automobile industry. This action helped solidify labor unions as a key part of the Democratic Coalition. It was, however, an unusual move to side with the strikers, and his general popularity declined for doing so. Murphy lost his reelection bid in 1938. In 1939 Murphy joined President Roosevelt's cabinet as attorney general. The following year Roosevelt appointed Murphy to the U.S. Supreme Court where he became a key defender of civil liberties and the rights of labor unions to demonstrate and strike. Murphy served on the Court for nine years.

Primary Sources

President Franklin Roosevelt spoke the following words in a speech during the presidential election campaign in Detroit, Michigan, on October 15, 1936. He was reviewing his record of helping the diverse groups of America during his first term of office. Roosevelt was particularly emphasizing his assistance to labor, as he was speaking in the heart of the automobile manufacturing region (Roosevelt, 1938, pp. 495–499):

> I am standing at the spot in front of the City Hall to which during the four terrible years, from 1929 to 1933, thousands of unemployed men and women of Detroit came to present problems of human existence to a great Mayor, Frank Murphy ...
>
> Relief and work relief through the use of Federal funds saved American humanity, and as the months went by it saved also the solvency of cities and States in every part of the Nation.
>
> After we had stopped the immediate crisis, our next step was to restore the purchasing power of the people themselves. I need not recite you the many steps we took. You are as familiar with them as I am. In great part you are glad today, I am sure, that we took these steps.
>
> The problem involved building up purchasing power of every kind. In restoring it there is one element often overlooked by those who dwell in great industrial cities—the building up of the prices which farmers obtain for their farm products ...
>
> In all other fields of production prices and values also rose. Miners went back to work. Eastern factories opened their closed doors.
>
> The dollars that we spent in relief, in work relief, in CCC camps, in drought relief, in cattle and hog buying and processing, each of those dollars went to work. They were spent in the shops of the city and in the stores of the small towns and villages. They were spent again by wholesalers who bought from manufacturers and processors. They were spent again in wages to those who worked in the purchases from those who produced the raw materials back in the mines and on the farms. And once again they were spent in the stores of the cities and the shops of the small towns and villages. You know how many of these dollars have finally come to the City of Detroit in the purchase of automobiles ...
>
> It is my belief that the people of Detroit, like the people of the rest of the country, are going to ask on November 3rd that the present type of Government continue rather than the type of Government which in its heart still believes in the policy of *laissez faire* and the kind of individualism which up to only three and a half years ago, frankly, put dollars above human rights.

Suggested Research Topics

- What was the role of American women in the Democratic Coalition? Could there have been more significant efforts by the New Dealers to focus on gender inequalities without endangering the Coalition?
- How well did the diverse groups composing the Coalition blend together? How could a coalition of interest groups keep from disintegrating due to conflicts?
- President Franklin Roosevelt's charm and charisma were major factors in building and maintaining the Democratic Coalition. What were the pros and cons in passing the Twenty-Second Amendment limiting presidents to two consecutive terms? What if that restriction had already existed? With Roosevelt

unable to run, would Cordell Hull have been able to further cement the Coalition?

Bibliography

Sources

Andersen, Kristi. *The Creation of a Democratic Majority, 1928–36.* Chicago: University of Chicago Press, 1979.

Burner, David. *The Politics of Provincialism: The Democratic Party in Transition, 1918–32.* Cambridge, MA: Harvard University Press, 1986.

Craig, Douglas B. *After Wilson: The Struggle for the Democratic party, 1920–34.* Chapel Hill: University of North Carolina Press, 1992.

Dark, Taylor E. *The Unions and the Democrats: An Enduring Alliance.* New York: Cornell University Press, 2001.

Goldman, Ralph M. *Search for Consensus: The Story of the Democratic Party.* Philadelphia: Temple University Press, 1979.

Parmet, Herbert S., and Marie B. Hecht. *Never Again: A President Runs for a Third Term.* New York: Macmillan, 1968.

Plotke, David. *Building a Democratic Political Order: Reshaping American Liberalism in the 1930s and 1940s.* New York: Cambridge University Press, 1996.

Roosevelt, Franklin D. *The Public Papers and Addresses of Franklin D. Roosevelt. Vol. 5, 1936.* New York: Random House, 1938.

Rutland, Robert A. *The Democrats: From Jefferson to Clinton.* Columbia: University of Missouri Press, 1995.

Ware, Alan. *The Breakdown of the Democratic Party Organization, 1940–80.* New York: Oxford University Press, 1990.

Wood, Clyde P. *The Nemesis of Reform: The Republican Party During the New Deal.* New York: Columbia University Press, 1994.

Further Reading

Democratic National Committee, [cited November 2, 2001] available from the World Wide Web at http://www.dnc.org.

Fish, Bruce, and Becky D. Fish. *The History of the Democratic Party.* Philadelphia: Chelsea House Publishers, 2000.

Lutz, Norma Jean. *The History of the Republican Party.* Philadelphia: Chelsea House Publishers, 2000.

Radosh, Ronald. *Divided They Fell: The Demise of the Democratic Party: 1964–96.* New York: Simon & Schuster, 1996.

Republican National Committee, [cited November 2, 2001] available from the World Wide Web at http://www.rnc.org.

See Also

Black Americans; Effects of the Great Depression—LBJ's Great Society; Employment; Ethnic Relations; Housing; New Deal (Second); Social Security; Women in Public Life; Works Progress Administration

Dust Bowl

1931-1939

Introduction

"Three little words achingly familiar on a Western farmer's tongue, rule life in the dust bowl of the continent—'if it rains.'" In this simple statement, Associated Press reporter Robert Geiger introduced the term "Dust Bowl" to the nation on April 15, 1935, upon reporting on the great dust storm of the previous day. Use of the term quickly spread across the nation.

Between 1932 and 1939, a series of disastrous dust storms struck the southern Great Plains of the United States. Particularly hard hit were western Kansas, eastern Colorado, northeastern New Mexico, and the Oklahoma and Texas panhandles. Though dust storms also occurred elsewhere on the Plains, the effects were far less severe. Soils of this region had always been prone to dust storms in the past, but during the drought of the 1930s they became far more vulnerable. Farmers had removed millions of acres of the natural grass sod to plant wheat during the previous twenty years. When the wheat failed to grow as the decade-long drought arrived in 1931, the soils were left exposed to the strong winds that annually sweep across the region. Millions of tons of blinding black dirt would sweep across the Plains, turning plowed fields into sand dunes. The social and economic impacts on farming communities were particularly severe given the drought's occurrence during the Great Depression.

The extended drought became the worst in U.S. history. Over 75 percent of the nation was affected, including 27 states that were severely impacted. With dire estimates concerning the loss of valuable topsoil in the United States, public concern began to increase over the future of American agriculture. In 1935 Congress passed the Soil Conservation Act, which squarely placed the federal government in the role of promoting farmland conservation for the first time. Programs were devised to teach farmers new farming practices that would make soils less vulnerable to water and wind erosion. Local conservation districts were created to instill the soil conservation ethic in various rural communities. These national programs, though at first resisted by local farmers as foreign ideas, soon made a major difference in conserving and rehabilitating valuable crop production land. The farmland conservation programs remained a critical part of American agriculture into the twenty-first century.

In the end, a wide range of New Deal programs were created that proved useful in tackling Dust Bowl problems. They included the Federal Emergency Relief Administration, the Federal Surplus Relief Corporation, the Civilian Conservation Corps, the Works Progress Administration, and the Drought Relief Service. These programs helped many of the Dust Bowl residents survive long enough for the rains to return and for the renewed demand for wheat brought on by World War II (1939–1945).

Chronology:

1914–1929: Farmers plow up millions of acres of natural grasslands on the Plains.

1931: The drought begins during the summer and will continue throughout the decade.

1932: The weather bureau reports 14 dust storms.

1933: The frequency of dust storms increases, with 38 recorded.

September 19, 1933: The Soil Erosion Service (SES) is created in the Department of Interior.

April 2, 1935: A dust storm from the Plains blows into Washington, DC, as H.H. Bennett, director of the SES, is testifying before a congressional committee about the need for a national soil conservation program.

April 14, 1935: The great black blizzard hits, causing dramatic destruction to farmlands.

April 27, 1935: The Soil Conservation Service is created in the Department of Agriculture, assuming the role of the SES in addition to expanded responsibilities.

March 3, 1937: Arkansas becomes the first state to enact the Standard State Conservation Districts Law.

1939: Drought comes to an end as rains return in the fall.

Issue Summary

The Unforeseen Arrives

As the United States entered the 1930s, Great Plains farmers were among the most prosperous in the nation, while farmers in other regions struggled. The 1931 growing season brought a record-breaking wheat crop and the future prospects seemed unlimited. A drought that had begun in the eastern United States the previous year, however, began moving west to the Great Plains. Many did not consider it significant at that time.

One of the first effects of the drought was the prevention of winter wheat crops from achieving sufficient growth in the fall of 1931 to protect the soil from windstorms. As a result, dust storms began by late January 1932 on the southern Plains. Storms swept across the Texas panhandle with sixty miles per hour winds and thick dust clouds that reached ten thousand feet into the air. From that point onward the storms steadily worsened. Fourteen storms were recorded in 1932, then 38 in 1933. The storms blew away valuable topsoil and covered farms in drifts of dust as if it were snow. With expectations that drought would soon end, farmers kept plowing and sowing wheat. Not only were dust storms of this type never seen before, but record high temperatures occurred as well. In 1934 in Vinita, Oklahoma, the temperature topped 100 degrees for 35 straight days only to reach 117 degrees on the 36th day.

By late 1934 the Dust Bowl area extended over 97 million acres in eastern Colorado, western Kansas, eastern New Mexico, and the panhandles of Oklahoma and Texas. The size of the area most severely affected each year would vary in location and size within the Dust Bowl. The period with the largest area affected at one time was between 1935 and 1936 when 50 million acres were affected.

A dust storm, on the verge of engulfing two houses during the Great Depression. These storms blew away topsoil and covered farms in drifts of dust. *(The Library of Congress.)*

The Character of Dust Storms

The nature of the storms would vary with the seasons. During the summer months, winds would come from the southwest. But the worst storms came during the winter months as strong winds blew from the north. The storms, particularly the winter ones with boiling dust clouds thousands of feet into the sky, carried millions of tons of dirt. They brought brief periods of total darkness during the daylight hours and left behind longer periods of half-light.

The dense clouds of blowing dust would force residents to seek shelter. Businesses and schools would close. Like snow, dust would pile in drifts against buildings and fences. Often drifts reached up to the windowsills, and people would have to shovel their way out of the front door following a dust storm. People got dust in their eyes, mouth, and noses. Everyone could feel the grit in their teeth and in their food.

Various measures were taken to protect against the storms. In some areas schoolchildren were required to wear gauze masks. Farmers and other residents would hang wet sheets in the windows and doorways to catch the dust. They would stuff window frames with gummed tape and rags, often in futility. Housecleaning after a storm could involve removing buckets full of dirt. People would wear handkerchiefs over their faces and put Vaseline in their nostrils.

Women found it difficult to prepare meals. They would knead bread in dresser drawers covered with a cloth with two holes cut in it for them to place their hands through. Baking in the oven was preferred over stovetops because of the protection from dust. Meals were immediately eaten when prepared before dust could cover them. Water and milk would be placed in tightly sealed Mason jars, which were normally used to preserve fruits and vegetables.

The worst dust storm came on Sunday, April 14, 1935, in the southern Plains, catching many unaware. Dust storms had been blowing for weeks. One toward the end of March destroyed five million acres of wheat crops. But the sun broke out that morning, and people ventured about going to church and other activities. Suddenly a fast moving black cloud appeared on the horizon. As it struck, residents outside fled for cover. This one proved the last and most severe for that year. One Kansas farmer was later found dead by suffocation in his car, having become lost in the storm. The event became known as "Black Sunday."

As if drought, heat, and dust storms were not enough, another natural disaster occurred in 1935. Like a plague, thousands of jackrabbits swept out of the parched hills, stripping what little vegetation was available, including farmers' struggling crops. Although the exact reason for this bizarre occurrence is unknown, many speculate that the rabbits were driven out of the hills because of the dust storm's effect on their food supply. Farmers banded together to conduct rabbit drives in an effort to exterminate them. Forming long lines, farmers swept across areas driving the rabbits into hastily built pens where they were clubbed to death.

The toll on the region was mounting by the end of 1935. Experts presented dramatic statistics at a meeting in Pueblo, Colorado, in December 1935. Soil scientists estimated that 850 million tons of topsoil was lost to winds on the southern Plains during 1935. Over 4.3 million acres were affected. Dire forecasts warned yet more acres of topsoil would be affected that following spring.

The dust storms continued to be severe through 1936 and 1937 and then lessened in 1938 and 1939. Relief arrived finally with the rains. The first rains arrived in the fall of 1939, followed by more continuous rainfall through the 1940s. Support of the major war effort increased the demand for wheat once again. The area had largely recovered by the early 1940s, supporting golden fields of wheat.

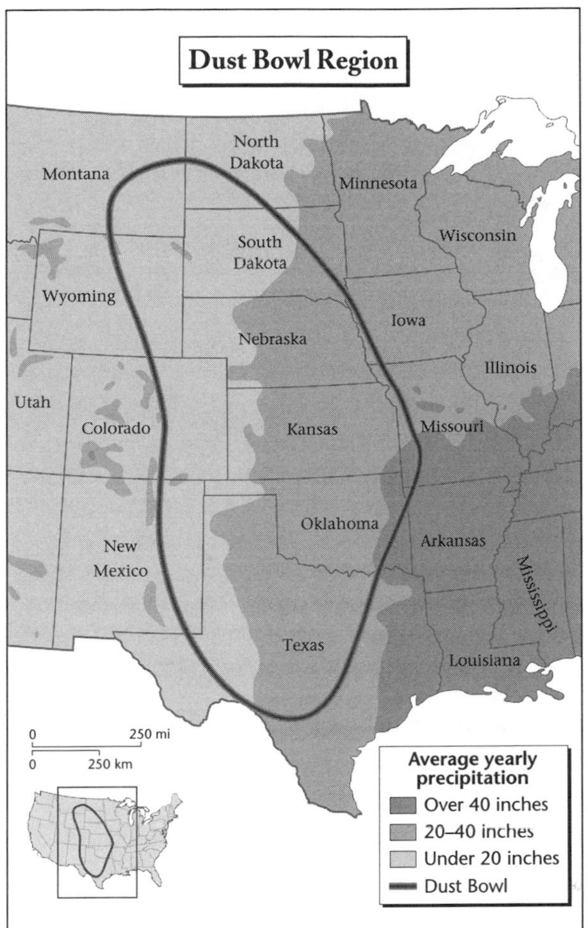

Map of the Dust Bowl region indicating average yearly precipitation. (The Gale Group.)

A Rural Society Unravels

The social and economic toll of the storms was dramatic. Though only a few deaths were directly attributed to the dust storms, many suffered from "dust pneumonia." Children were particularly susceptible to the health problems. People would spit up clods of dirt, sometimes the width of a pencil and three to four inches long. People tried various home remedies to clear the dusty phlegm from their throats and lungs. Inhalation of dust particles increased the number of deaths from pneumonia and other illnesses.

The dust storms were especially hard on farm animals. Animals died in the fields with their stomachs

Two young girls pump water during a dust storm. Children were particularly susceptible to health problems caused by dust storms. (AP/ Wide World Photos. Reproduced by permission.)

coated inside with two inches of dirt. For range cattle the dust combined with tears, cementing their eyes closed. Blindness, thirst, and exhaustion would then take their toll. Chickens smothered in hen houses. Horses and mules could be better protected with masking over the eyes and feedbags over their muzzles.

Having lost their crops and livestock, thousands of families left the region by the mid-1930s. Many had lost their farms to bank foreclosure. A foreclosure is when a homeowner does not keep up with their loan payments, and the bank takes the house and sells it to repay the house loan. Often they packed up the car with their belongings and simply drove away. Of those leaving about 200,000 headed west to the agricultural fields of California. Those that left hoping for greener pastures in California still struggled. If they were able to find work, they were not treated well and wages were extremely low. They also had no permanent home and conditions in work camps were unsanitary at the very least. This migration out of the Dust Bowl during the 1930s became the largest migration in U.S. history. Approximately 2.5 million people had left the region by 1940.

Economic impacts were extensive. The Depression had already taken its toll on the region with lowered crop prices. The dust storms devastated the region even further. Crop failures led to stagnation of towns. Eventually about one-fourth of the residents left the region looking for new opportunities elsewhere. The formerly tight-knit rural communities broke apart socially, and many were left dependent on federal relief programs. Banks and businesses failed, and schools were boarded up. Life was no longer the same for either those leaving or those staying.

Relief Through The New Deal

Having hit a postwar slump in the 1920s, the agricultural industry continued to suffer nationwide economic problems into 1933 when President Franklin D. Roosevelt (served 1933–1945) took office. As a result, much of the earliest New Deal activity addressed farm issues. Some of these benefited Plains farmers as they did farmers in other regions. The Agricultural Adjustment Administration (AAA) paid farmers to reduce production. For Dust Bowl farmers, their AAA payments came primarily for reducing wheat and hog reduction. By the time the program took effect, however, the drought was having its own effect in reducing crops. Therefore few could actually benefit from the aid.

Other types of aid also became available. The Emergency Farm Mortgage Act, passed in May 1933,

More About...

"The Plow That Broke the Plains"

In 1935 the Resettlement Administration hired journalist and film critic Pare Lorentz to produce a film on the Dust Bowl. Lorentz was nationally known for his articles appearing in *Fortune* and *Harper's.* He was an ardent supporter of New Deal policies. The intent of the agency was to create a Hollywood-quality commercial film to educate the public about the fragility of the land and the need to reform farming practices.

Lorentz wrote, directed, and edited the film entitled *The Plow That Broke the Plain.* Shot on location in various areas of the Great Plains, he captured the realities of the poverty, drought, and dust storms. The musical score and narration balanced beautifully with the visual documentation.

Despite the small budget and hardships in production, the thirty-minute film received great reviews from film critics and an enthusiastic public response. Some reviewers, however, labeled it a propaganda film for New Deal policies. Major film studios, fearful of controversial subjects and focused on Shirley Temple movies and screwball comedies, refused to distribute the film. As a result, the short-subject film debuted in May 1936 at the Rialto Theater in New York City and was shown in a limited number of independent neighborhood theaters. The film received a strong endorsement from President Franklin Roosevelt.

With the popularity of *The Plow,* Lorentz next produced *The River.* This film focused on the need for flood control in the Mississippi River Valley, as well as soil erosion from agricultural practices. During its filming major flooding of the Ohio River occurred in January 1937, providing graphic footage of the issues. The film was shown internationally and won first prize at the Venice Film Festival. Success of *The Plow* and *The River* led President Roosevelt to form the United States Film Service to produce more films to educate the public about social issues and to promote support for New Deal relief and planning agencies.

---

provided $200 million in federal funds to refinance mortgages of farmers facing foreclosure. In addition the Farm Credit Act, passed that same month, created a network of local banks and credit associations to provide low interest loans to farmers. In June 1934 Congress passed the Frazier-Lemke Farm Bankruptcy Act, sponsored by Representative William Lemke and Senator Lynn Frazier, both of North Dakota, that limited the ability of banks to repossess the farms of those financially struggling. The act passed despite President Roosevelt's opposition.

Unfortunately in 1935 the act was found to be unconstitutional. In its place, that same year, the Farm Mortgage Moratorium Act was introduced into the Senate by Frazier and into the House of Representatives by Lemke. The Supreme Court upheld the Farm Mortgage Moratorium Act as constitutional in 1937.

By spring of 1934, after two full years of drought and windstorms, livestock feed in the region was largely depleted. Predictions indicated conditions were not expected to improve any time soon. On May 18, 1934, the AAA created the Emergency Cattle Purchase Program to purchase and destroy thousands of starving cattle. The Drought Relief Service (DRS) was established to coordinate relief activities. The DRS designated certain counties as emergency areas. The first cattle purchases came in June 1934. The DRS would purchase the cattle for $14 to $20 a head, often above market value. Those unfit for human consumption were destroyed. Over half of those purchased fell into this category.

Those cattle still having some food value were given to the Federal Surplus Relief Corporation for distribution to needy families. Though the program saved many from bankruptcy, farmers found the extensive cattle slaughter one of the toughest actions to suffer through. It was difficult for farmers to give up herds they had managed for years, and the prospect of having to establish a new herd after the drought ended was daunting. Not having the responsibility of feeding cattle when they barely could feed their families, however, was a welcome relief for most farmers helped by the program.

With dust storms lasting for weeks on the Plains during the early part of 1935, President Roosevelt and Congress took action. President Roosevelt signed the Emergency Relief Appropriation Act on April 8. The act not only led to creation of the Works Progress Administration (WPA), a major New Deal works program, but also provided $525 million for drought relief.

On April 30, 1935, President Roosevelt signed an executive order creating the Resettlement Administration (RA), to administer the financial aid for Dust Bowl farmers. Rexford G. Tugwell, a professor of economics and close presidential advisor, was appointed as the director of the RA. The program was for those who had exhausted all other means of getting credit. RA loans were made available to purchase such necessities as food, clothing, feed, and fertilizer. The agency would design a farm management program for each farmer who received the aid. The goal was for the farmers benefiting from the aid to become self-sufficient once the drought had ended, and they were once again able to raise and harvest crops to support their families and properly manage their farms.

The RA, however, was not strictly limited to resettlement efforts and financial and educational support of farmers. Another significant area of the RA was the Historical Section, headed by Roy Stryker. The purpose of the Historical Section was to document relief efforts of the RA as well as the conditions under which struggling farmers and their families lived—especially those in the Dust Bowl and those who had fled the area and headed for California. Several talented and famous photographers were employed by the Historical Section.

Dorothea Lange was famous for her photograph of a weathered and worn mother seven with two of her children burying their faces in her shoulders and an infant in her lap. It was titled *Migrant Mother.* The woman was representative of the struggle and poverty of those who had left the Dust Bowl in search of something better. Thousands of photographs like Dorothea Lange's were taken to document the plight of the American farmer. The pictures were distributed to newspapers all over the United States for publication to accompany news stories. The photographs were instrumental in publicizing and making real the problems in the Dust Bowl and the West.

The RA was in operation until 1937 when it was integrated into the Department of Agriculture and renamed the Farm Security Administration (FSA). Rexford Tugwell left, but Stryker stayed on as head of the Historical Section, which continued to function in its same capacity until 1942 when it was transferred to the Office of War Information.

When the U.S. Supreme Court ruled the Agricultural Adjustment Act unconstitutional in early 1936, Congress quickly passed the Soil Conservation and Domestic Allotment Act to insure continued aid to farmers. The Agricultural Adjustment Administration (AAA) remained in operation following the Court ruling. But now its emphasis shifted from paying farmers to limit production to paying farmers for planting soil-conserving crops such as grasses, legumes, and feed crops. The shift particularly benefited Dust Bowl farmers, and nearly all participated. AAA payments became the major source of farm income by 1937.

One of President Roosevelt's personal favorites among the New Deal programs was the Civilian Conservation Corps (CCC). The CCC employed youths between 18 and 24 to perform conservation tasks, including tree planting, stocking fish, constructing wildlife shelters, digging irrigation ditches, and numerous other activities. By September 1935 more than five hundred thousand CCC workers lived in camps across the West.

With conditions worsening in the Dust Bowl region, Roosevelt sought to apply the CCC programs to the region. A grand scheme was devised, called the Prairie States Forestry Project. Roosevelt sought to plant 220 million trees across the Great Plains from northern Texas to Canada in a one hundred mile-wide zone. The trees, including green ash and red cedar, would serve to break the winds and greatly reduce wind erosion. They would be planted along fence lines separating properties and along roadways.

Estimated to cost $75 million over a 12-year period, the program saw only limited success. Critics claimed the effort was largely futile since no related effort was established to control the amount of plowing and planting going on.

Rise of Conservation

In addition to their social and economic effects, the storms were an environmental disaster. Valuable topsoil was literally blown away from vast areas, leaving only a bare hard ground. At the beginning of the Dust Bowl era, little scientific knowledge was available on preventing wind erosion.

Farming techniques to prevent water erosion from seasonal rains, such as contour plowing, strip plowing, and terracing, had little effect on wind erosion. Contour plowing means tilling a slope back and forth at the same elevation rather than tilling up and down a hill. Strip plowing leaves untilled strips of land between the tilled and planted strips. Terracing involves changing a sloped hillside into a stepped series of flat planting areas. Some local efforts at soil conservation developed, including the invention of the chisel plow, by Fred Hoeme of Hooker, Oklahoma, which has narrow curved bottoms that break up soil without bringing it up to the surface and subjecting it to erosion. Federal efforts, however, would prove much more effective through time.

Media Depictions

A number of media resources are available on the Dust Bowl, bringing the experience vividly to life. These include:

Places in the Heart. This 1984 movie relays a fictional account of a widow struggling to care for her children in a small Texas town during the Great Depression. When her husband is killed in an accident, Edna Spalding must provide for her two children. Mose, an out-of-work black man, comes along with a plan to help Edna and himself. Together, they plant cotton on her land, hoping its crop will provide them with money and allow Edna to pay her mortgage. The two must rely on each other, as little help is to be found. A tornado and the Ku Klux Klan, who disapprove of Mose, are just a few of the obstacles to stand in their way. The movie stars Sally Field, Danny Glover, and John Malkovich.

Voices From the Dust Bowl: The Charles L. Todd and Robert Sonkin Migrant Worker Collection, 1940–41. An on-line presentation by the American Folklife Center, Library of Congress, of interviews documenting everyday life of Dust Bowl refugees. The recordings were made at Farm Security Administration migrant work camps in central California in 1940 and 1941. The collection includes traditional ballads, camp meetings, conversations, storytelling, and personal experiences. Available from the World Wide Web at http://memory.loc.gov/ammem/afctshtml.html.

Surviving the Dust Bowl. The Public Broadcasting System produced this 1999 program as part of their "The American Experience" series. The program includes both a video and website complete with narrative, images, and teacher's guide. Information available from the World Wide Web at http://www.pbs.org/wgbh/amex/dustbowl.htm.

Out of the Dust. A book and an audio cassette of first-person, free-verse poems that read as a novel telling the story of a 15-year-old girl who helps her family struggle through the Dust Bowl years on an Oklahoma farm. Written by Karen Hesse. Listening Library published the cassette in 1998, and Scholastic Paperbacks published the book in 1999. Both are winners of various awards.

Federal efforts toward soil conservation began at the first of the decade. To combat erosion, in 1930 Congress authorized the Department of Agriculture to establish a series of soil erosion experiment stations and to set up demonstration projects. In September 1933 the Soil Erosion Service (SES) was created, located in the Department of Interior, to operate the stations and promote farmer cooperation.

The SES soil scientists and other specialists worked with farmers to demonstrate the new farming practices. The demonstration areas became showplaces to encourage others to adopt the new techniques. In 1934 SES's research at the wind erosion station in Dalhart, Texas, found that not burning or having livestock graze the remaining stubble of wheat after harvest made a major difference in wind erosion. This crop residue held the soil in place. In addition, trees were planted in rows to provide windbreaks. The SES also provided farmers with equipment, seeds, seedlings, and advice on how to plan their planting and harvesting to reduce soil erosion.

Less than two weeks after the epic Black Sunday dust storm, Roosevelt signed the Soil Conservation Act on April 27, 1935. Congress declared soil erosion "a national menace." The act shifted the Soil Erosion Service from the U.S. Department of Interior to the U.S. Department of Agriculture and renamed it the Soil Conservation Service (SCS). The SCS assumed much broader responsibilities than its predecessor did. With Hugh H. Bennett named as director, the SCS launched an extensive conservation program. Since preaching was not enough to change old ways, the

Many farmers were forced to abandon their land due to dust storms. The plowed fields of this Oklahoma farm have been replaced by sand dunes. (Corbis-Bettmann. Reproduced by permission.)

SCS also offered a program to pay farmers to practice these new soil conservation techniques. Farmers were paid about one dollar an acre for the areas to which they applied the new farming techniques.

When soil conservation demonstration projects began in 1934 under the Soil Erosion Service, only 10,454 acres were involved. With conversion of the SES to the Soil Conservation Service, and the addition of WPA and CCC labor, the acreage increased to 600,000 acres by the end of 1936 using contour plowing, strip cropping, and terracing.

Besides providing loans to farmers, the Resettlement Administration also focused on removing Dust Bowl farmers from farmland that was prone to erosion and relocating them onto less vulnerable acreages. The lands that were acquired from the displaced farmers were re-seeded into grass to prevent further wind erosion.

With farmers still slow to adopt the new farming practices being introduced by "Washington outsiders," it was recognized that voluntary acceptance, not national enforcement, would be most effective. On February 27, 1937, President Roosevelt introduced a new program encouraging states to individually pass conservation district laws. Under the laws farmers would establish their own local conservation districts. The Department of Agriculture would assist regions through these local organizations.

In March Arkansas became the first state to pass the Standard State Solid Conservation Districts Law. The first actual district to be organized was in North Carolina in August. Use of the districts allowed expansion of the conservation program beyond demonstration areas. The SCS programs promoting new farming techniques through local districts began seeing positive affects. By 1938 it was estimated that 65 percent less soil was eroding despite continuing drought and windstorms. A highly successful grassroots system of farmers was established that would persist beyond the Dust Bowl years.

Contributing Forces

The Great Plains of the United States is a broad, mostly flat, treeless expanse of dry grasslands covering parts of ten states and stretching from the Canadian border south to the Rio Grande in Texas. U.S. military expeditions that journeyed through the region in the early nineteenth century called the area the Great American Desert and declared it "almost wholly unfit for cultivation." The extensive natural grasslands tra-

Due to a serious drought, this family is forced to leave their family farm in Pittsburg County, Oklahoma, in 1935. More than 350,000 "Okies" headed west in search of work. (Liaison Agency. Reproduced by permission.)

ditionally supported mostly stock raising until wheat farming began expanding toward the end of the nineteenth century. The sod roots of the natural grasslands had anchored the soil and retained water from rains and snow.

Droughts and dust storms were no strangers to the Great Plains, particularly the more southern region. Dry spells were known to occur at regular intervals. Such events were noted from the time the region was first settled, including a severe drought in the early 1860s. More favorable weather in the 1870s led to increased agricultural settlement.

The thick sod was initially resistant to the traditional plows, but the introduction of steel plows proved highly effective in breaking the sod for planting. Drought returned in the late 1870s, slowing the farming movement. The worst dust storm recorded for the nineteenth century occurred on March 26, 1880, and affected an area from Las Cruces, New Mexico, to Iowa, to eastern Missouri. Several states and private organizations provided some relief to the struggling farmers during these periods of drought, primarily by providing them with seed and food.

Good weather returned again in the 1880s. In periods of above-average precipitation, lush grasslands with rich-looking dark soil lured many farmers to the Great Plains.

Even private railroad companies and state governments were actively recruiting farmers to the region. They were trying to stimulate business and tax revenue. Some states, such as Kansas, mounted advertising campaigns. In Kansas homestead entries rapidly escalated from 3,547 in 1884, to 9,954 in 1885, and 20,688 in 1886. Drought came again from 1887 to 1897, however, causing population declines in some areas of the Plains.

Despite drought years and short-term setbacks in the 1890s, the southern Plains actually filled with farms between 1886 and 1910 as wheat farming and cattle raising generally prospered. Drought struck again between 1910 and 1913. Some farmers lost 70 percent of their cattle herds during that period. The occurrence of several severe dust storms between 1912 and 1914 raised the issue of wind erosion and what to do about it.

One outcome of the periodic droughts was that farmers learned what crops were more resistant to drought than others. "Turkey Red" wheat, brought by Russian-German immigrants in the early 1870s, proved one of the hardiest. More and more farmers turned to this strain of wheat.

The return of rain in 1914, the push by the federal government to grow more wheat for the war effort, and the resulting high prices overshadowed concerns of future droughts and winds. In addition new improvements in farm mechanization enabled farmers to tend to far greater acreages of crops. By 1924 another 17 million acres of prairie land had been converted into wheat fields. A drought between 1917 and 1921 did little to slow development. An additional 15 million acres were converted between 1924 and 1929. In the southern Plains wheat acreage increased 200 percent between 1925 and 1931. Weather stayed highly favorable for most of the span between 1914 and 1931.

During this period farmers in the region would leave little crop residue on the ground following each harvest. They would let livestock graze the freshly harvested fields, cleaning off any remaining vegetative material. During these boom years the farmers enjoyed great harvests, unsuspecting of what lay ahead. During planting season plowing and breaking sod often went on 24 hours a day in shifts, stopping only for servicing the tractor every six hours or so. Cultivation of the same fields continued year after year, pulverizing the soil into a fine dust.

The prosperity led to absentee ownership and "suitcase" farming, in which little care was given to protecting the land. "Suitcase farmers" were people who resided elsewhere, such as east coast businessmen, who would come out, plant seed, and then return home until harvest season. Years of over-cultivation and generally poor land management extending from the late nineteenth century through the 1920s led to severely abused land that was unfit and unprepared to deal with severe drought conditions.

Perspectives

Residents of the Dust Bowl referred to the period as the "dirty thirties." They greatly disliked the term "Dust Bowl," believing it only served to further decrease property values and discourage business prospects in the region. But the label stuck from Geiger's first use of it in April 1935. Even Soil Conservation Service maps soon used the term in marking the area most affected by the drought and storms.

Dust Bowl Refugees

One-fourth of the population of the southern Plains left during the Dust Bowl years, including 200,000 to California. More than 86,000 arrived in California from the drought states between June 1935 and September 1936 alone. California residents and authorities did not warmly receive the refugees. Foreseeing this coming trend, in early 1935 the city of Los Angeles formed the Committee on Indigent Alien Transients. Scorn was directed at transients who had no visible means of financial support and whose legal residence was other than California.

The migration had actually begun in the 1920s while the agricultural industry was experiencing economic woes and increased mechanization of farms was displacing farm laborers. But the Great Depression and Dust Bowl conditions caused a dramatic increase in the flow of immigrants. Most arrived between 1935 and 1937, primarily by automobile, following U.S. Highway 66 across the Southwest.

To turn away "undesirables," the Los Angeles police chief even sent 125 policemen to the state borders with Arizona and Oregon. The press labeled the contingent the "bum brigade," as they stopped every vehicle entering California for two months, asking for proof of money or employment. The American Civil Liberties Union filed a lawsuit against the city, object-

More About...

"Dust Bowl Ballads"

In May 1940 RCA Victor released an album by folksinger Woody Guthrie entitled *Dust Bowl Ballads.* Guthrie was born in Okemah, Oklahoma, on July 14, 1912. Living in the panhandle of Texas, he began to take up song writing seriously by the mid-1930s. One of the first original songs he wrote was inspired by Black Sunday, the great dust storm of April 14, 1935. The dust storm also inspired Guthrie to leave the panhandle and begin traveling and singing in bars. His journeys carried him to California where he witnessed the border blockades set up to keep unemployed "Okies"—like himself—out.

Following his viewing of the newly released movie *The Grapes of Wrath,* Guthrie wrote a song about the lead character, "Tom Joad." This song, together with 12 other songs, including "Dusty Old Dust (So Long, It's Been Good to Know You)," "Dust Pneumonia Blues," "Dust Can't Kill Me," "Dust Bowl Refugee," and "Do Re Mi" were released on the album. Guthrie wrote in the liner notes, "They are 'Okie" songs, 'Dust Bowl' songs, 'Migratious' songs, about my folks and my relatives, about a jillion of 'em, that got hit by the drought, the dust, the wind, the banker, and the landlord, and the police, all at the same time."

Though the album was not a big seller, it clearly became part of the Dust Bowl saga. The following lyrics are from Guthrie's song, "Talking Dust Bowl," which he wrote while riding the rails in 1936 and 1937.

Back in 1927, I had a little farm, and I called that heaven.
Prices up, and the rain come down;
I hauled my crops all into town, got the money ...
Bought clothes and groceries ... fed the kids
And raised a big family

But the rain quit and the wind got high
Black old dust storm filled the sky;
I traded my farm for a Ford machine,
Poured it full of this gas-i-line
And started-rockin' and a-rollin'
Deserts and mountains-to California ...

Got to California so dad gum broke,
So dad gum hungry I thought I'd choke;
I bummed up a spud or two,
Wife fixed up some tater stew.
We poured the kids full of it ...
Looked like a tribe of ther-mometers a runnin' around.

---

ing to the practice. An assessment by the California attorney general that the practice was unconstitutional brought it to a close.

John Steinbeck, Woody Guthrie, and others wrote articles, books, and songs about the migrant experience on the road to California. In 1936 Steinbeck wrote a series of articles titled "The Harvest Gypsies" for the *San Francisco News.* He followed that with the epic novel *The Grapes of Wrath* (1939). Guthrie produced a 1940 album titled *Dust Bowl Ballads.* The Dust Bowl refugees were called the derogatory term "Okies" regardless of whether they were from Oklahoma or some other region. "Arkies" was also used, though less commonly.

Though Okie migration has been commonly attributed to people escaping from the Dust Bowl of the southern Plains, many also came from sharecropping and cotton farms of the Southeast. The Okies not only replaced Mexicans in the California fields as a cheap labor source, but they also replaced them as the key target of prejudice as well.

Their poverty also brought other major social problems. They lived in unhealthy conditions on the outskirts of towns and placed heavy burdens on local hospitals, schools, and social services. The plight of the Okies became the subject of John Steinbeck's novel *The Grapes of Wrath* (1939). The Resettlement Administration built several camps for migrants to improve sanitation and protect the migrants from local hostile groups.

Depictions of the "Okie" life in California led to congressional hearings by the Select Committee to Investigate the Migration of Destitute Citizens. Hearings were held across the country. The committee issued a report in 1941 titled *Interstate Migration* that fixed firmly in the mind of America the image of Dust Bowl refugees.

Local Perspectives—The Last Man's Club

Following the catastrophic dust storm of April 14, 1935, many Plains' residents began moving out of the region. In response to the worsening conditions on the

Abandoned buildings line this street in Caddo, Oklahoma in June, 1938. The exodus of farmers due to drought and dust storms left many small towns deserted. (The Library of Congress.)

Plains, the Resettlement Administration was created in the spring of 1935. One agency administrator recommended that the federal government purchase over two million acres of farmland in Colorado, Kansas, New Mexico, Oklahoma, and Texas and permanently move hundreds of farm families to other locations. President Roosevelt opposed the proposal, claiming it should be the decision of the farmers whether to remain and fight through the situation or to move elsewhere.

Hearing of the proposal, rumors began circulating across the Plains that the federal government would soon be forcing many to leave the area. Despite the hardships endured, many in the area were determined to stay put and outlast the drought to save their homes and farms. John L. McCarty, the young editor of the Dalhart, Texas, newspaper, led a charge to resist any such efforts if they should appear.

McCarty also lashed out at those who blamed the situation primarily on the farmers for not farming properly, rather than on natural factors such as drought and wind. McCarty published a pledge in his newspaper vowing to be the last man on the Plains and daring others to join him. In response people from all walks of life—bankers, farmers, doctors, and teachers—came to the newspaper office to sign the pledge to stay. The Last Man's Club came to symbolize the determination of many to join together and fight against the Dust Bowl hardships. Soon, however, many farmers begrudgingly accepted the new soil conservation farming practices promoted by the Soil Conservation Service.

Government Response to Refugee Problem

Some 40 percent of the Dust Bowl refugees who became migrant workers ended up picking grapes and cotton in the San Joaquin Valley. They replaced the 120,000 Mexican workers who were repatriated (sent) to Mexico during the Great Depression. Many migrants earned between 75 cents and $1.25 a day and lived in tarpaper shacks lacking plumbing. The resulting pollution from wastes led to outbreaks of disease, including typhoid, malaria, smallpox, and tuberculosis.

President Roosevelt sought to assist the migrants who were living in such makeshift camps along the rural roads and who were subject to attacks by groups of vigilantes. The New Deal's Farm Security Administration built 13 camps, each housing for temporary periods three hundred families in tents on wooden platforms. Families were expected to work to pay for their room and board.

Major Writings

The Grapes of Wrath

In 1939 John Steinbeck published a work that would become an integral part of the American literary canon. *The Grapes of Wrath* tells the story of a family from the Oklahoma Dust Bowl, following them on their journey to California in search for work as migrant farm laborers in order to survive. Tom Joad, the eldest Joad son, and protagonist, arrives home from jail only to find that his family had been evicted from their Dust Bowl-ravaged farm. The family decides, as many Dust Bowl families during the depression did, that California, with its orchards and fields, is the place for them to find work and salvation from their poverty.

Steinbeck was born and raised in Salinas, California, not far from many migrant farms. Steinbeck was horrified and angered by the living conditions and poor treatment of the migrant farm workers. He was compelled by what he saw to write about the situation. He wrote a series of articles titled *The Harvest Gypsies* for the *San Francisco News.* His work journals, kept during the time that he was researching and writing *The Harvest Gypsies,* focus on the desire to write a book that could accurately portray the migrant workers in California and inspire readers to action to solve the problems of the migrant laborer. It was this series that inspired Steinbeck to create a fictional account of a migrant family.

Steinbeck's novel, though a work of fiction, was strongly grounded in reality. Steinbeck tirelessly researched the topic of migrant families, making four trips to migrant farms. Steinbeck interviewed the migrant workers closely observing their speech and mannerisms, so that he could accurately represent them within the framework of *The Grapes of Wrath.*

Although it opened many readers' eyes to the problems that assailed the Dust Bowl refugees, the novel was seen as controversial when it was released. It supported organization of migrant workers and collectivism to solve the problems of poverty and unemployment. These topics were considered "un-American" and "communist" by some who associated labor movements and "sharing the wealth" with left-wing political movements such as communism. Steinbeck, however, made a concerted effort not to appear communist, so as not to offend farmers. It was burned in Salinas, Steinbeck's hometown, and it was banned in towns all over the country.

Regardless of the disdain that people had for the ills that the novel revealed and the solutions proposed, namely the mistreatment of desperate and impoverish migrant families, the book did exceptionally well. In 1940 it received the Pulitzer Prize and was made into a film starring Henry Fonda and directed by John Ford. When Steinbeck received the Nobel Prize in 1962, it was largely due to *The Grapes of Wrath*. To date, *The Grapes of Wrath* has sold over 14 million copies, and has been translated into virtually every language on earth. Steinbeck's work has set the tone for many works about the Dust Bowl—from books to films—that have been created since.

Impact

A New Outlook

Events of the Dust Bowl contributed to an official change in policy by the federal government toward conservation of natural resources. Perhaps best exemplified by the Soil Conservation Act of 1935, for the first time Congress was asserting that conservation of farmlands was in part a responsibility of the federal government. For sixty years the Soil Conservation Service (SCS) played a major role, beginning with its demonstration projects in the 1930s using WPA and CCC labor, then by shifting to work with local conservation districts.

By October 1980 over 2.8 million acres of former cropland had been converted back to grassland. Also, the use of drought-resistant crops greatly decreased wind erosion. As a result, not only was the environment stabilized, but the cycles of human migration in and out of the drought-prone area had ended. Farms were much more able to withstand the periodic episodes of drought.

Drought in Armour Station, Missouri caused this lake bed to dry up. Damaging farming techniques was one of the causes of soil and water erosion during the Great Depression. (UPI/Corbis-Bettmann. Reproduced by permission.)

Similarly, Congress looked at the deterioration of public lands in the West through the effects of drought and overgrazing. Historically, the federal government had the policy of passing titles of public lands into private ownership when someone wanted them. Local ranchers could graze lands still owned by the United States.

The uncontrolled grazing led to overgrazing, however, and by 1934 it was evident federal measures were needed to conserve natural resources on the remaining federal lands. Thus, Congress passed the Taylor Grazing Act in 1934. The purpose of the act was to attempt to reverse the effects of decades of overuse, but little could be done. The Taylor Grazing Act helped stop further deterioration but failed to reverse the damage. Under the act Roosevelt was allowed to take 140 million acres of federally owned land and disallow public use of these lands for grazing, which contributed to erosion and degradation of the topsoil. The act also established the U.S. Grazing Service to administer a system of grazing districts. A permit system controlled the number of cattle ranchers could graze in particular areas. District, state, and national advisory boards composed of ranchers would make policy recommendations to the Service. The Grazing Service became part of the newly formed Bureau of Land Management in 1946.

The "Filthy Fifties"

With favorable weather present once again, and the heavy demand for wheat during World War II, another five million acres of the Plains was converted to crops between 1941 and 1950. Dust storms, however, would revisit the Great Plains once more beginning in June 1950. The Department of Agriculture created the Great Plains Committee early in 1950 to study the problem and make recommendations. The biggest dust storm during the "filthy fifties" arrived on February 19, 1954. Some claimed the storm was worse than those of the 1930s. Because economic times were generally good, panic and migration out of the area did not occur as before.

The area affected by dust storms in the 1950s was actually larger than in the 1930s and included the entire Dust Bowl area. A total of $70 million in government funds was spent between 1954 and 1956 on drought emergency conservation measures. The Great Plains Committee developed recommendations for converting croplands back to prairie grass and discouraging further plowing of new areas. The Great Plains Agricultural Council took the committee's recommendations and developed a long-range plan to reduce the need for periodic emergency measures on the Plains. Seeking to establish agricultural stability,

President Dwight Eisenhower (served 1953–1961) sent the proposal to Congress to establish the Great Plains Conservation Program in January 1956. As in the 1930s, conservation districts guided this program. It was signed into law in August 1956. Success of these programs seemed apparent when a drought in the 1970s proved far less damaging to the region.

Conservation Districts

The formation of conservation districts, which began in 1937 to guide introduction of soil conservation practices, was one of the few grassroots approaches implemented by a New Deal program. It also proved to be one of the most successful. By 2001 nearly three thousand conservation districts existed, one in almost every county in the nation.

Besides addressing soil conservation, the districts also assisted farmers in water, forest, wildlife, and other natural resource issues. The districts go by various titles including "soil and water conservation districts," "natural resource districts," "resource conservation districts," and others. The main goal is to develop local solutions to natural resource problems affecting over 778 million acres of private land across the nation. Over fifteen thousand volunteers serve in elected and appointed positions on district governing boards.

In 1946 the National Association of Conservation Districts (NACD) was formed to represent the districts on the national level. The NACD develops national conservation policies and lobbies state and national lawmakers. The NACD also promotes sharing of ideas among the districts.

Notable People

Hugh H. Bennett (1881–1960). Known as the "father of soil conservation," Bennett was named director of the newly established Soil Erosion Service (SES) in 1933 and later the Soil Conservation Service in 1935. Bennett had worked for the Department of Agriculture since the early 1900s. He combated the commonly accepted notion by the federal government and the public that soil was an indestructible resource that could not be exhausted.

In 1928 he co-authored an agency bulletin entitled *Soil Erosion: A National Menace.* Bennett also published numerous articles on soil conservation in popular and scientific journals. The mission of the SES was to reform farming methods so as to stop the erosion caused by dust storms. Bennett promoted the position that the farmers' agricultural practices were more to blame for soil erosion than the natural forces. This unpopular position was initially not well received by farmers and others.

In a rather odd twist of fate, just as Bennett was testifying before a congressional committee in Washington, DC, on April 2, 1935, a major dust storm blew into the city from the Plains. Bennett dramatically threw back the committee room's curtains to reveal a dust-filled, blackened sky. It was the first time that a dust cloud had made it that far east. It had dropped 12 million pounds of dust in Chicago on its way.

This was the first occasion for millions of citizens in the East to experience a dust storm. Due to Bennett's efforts Congress declared soil and water conservation an urgent national priority. The legislature passed the Soil Conservation Act of 1935, designed to improve farming techniques. Bennett led the charge in returning a large part of the Great Plains to natural grasslands.

Lynn Frazier (1874–1947). Lynn Frazier was born near Medford, Minnesota in 1874. He moved to the Dakota Territory, which would become North Dakota, with his family in 1881. He graduated from the University of North Dakota in 1901 and pursued agriculture as a career. In 1917 he was elected Governor of North Dakota and served until 1921. He was elected to the United States Senate in 1922 and served from 1923 to 1941. While in the Senate he introduced two bills, both of which passed, to assist farmers struggling due to the Depression and the effects of the Dust Bowl. Both bills were introduced with William Lemke, a North Dakota congressman. The first bill, which became the Frazier-Lemke Bankruptcy Act, was declared unconstitutional. The Farm Mortgage Moratorium Act, meant to help the same people as the Frazier-Lemke Act, was passed and upheld by the Supreme Court. Frazier was the sole author of the Farm Mortgage Moratorium Act. Frazier left the Senate in 1941 and returned to agriculture. He died in 1947 in Maryland.

William Lemke (1878–1950). William Lemke was born in Albany, Minnesota to a farmer and his wife. Lemke graduated from the University of North Dakota in 1902 and Yale University in 1905. Lemke studied law at both the University of North Dakota and Georgetown, and was admitted to the bar in 1905. He began practicing in Fargo, North Dakota. In 1921 and 1922 he served as attorney general of North Dakota. He was elected to the House of Representatives in 1932 and served until 1941.

Known as the "Prairie Rebel" for his staunch support for agrarian relief despite opposition, Lemke cosponsored a bill with North Dakota Senator Lynn

Frazier to provide relief for farmers by protecting farms from being foreclosed on during difficult times. The Frazier-Lemke Bankruptcy Act was passed, but President Franklin Delano Roosevelt was opposed to the act. It was later found unconstitutional, but Lemke assisted Frazier in the introduction of a bill to take the place of the Frazier-Lemke Act. The Farm Mortgage Moratorium Act was passed in 1935 and upheld as constitutional in 1937. Lemke was disillusioned by Roosevelt's opposition to the Frazier-Lemke Bankruptcy Act and ran against him in the 1936 presidential election as the Union party candidate. He lost and continued to serve in the House until 1941 when he returned to his law practice. He was again elected to Congress in 1943 and served until his death in Fargo, North Dakota, in 1950.

Primary Sources

No Place To Go

Dust Bowl refugees arriving in California were not welcomed with open arms. The following account, from a *Collier's* magazine article by Walter Davenport entitled "California, Here We Come" (August 10, 1935), describes an exchange at the California border between a California border official and a Dust Bowl refugee:

> They straggled in across the Yuma bridge down in the southeast corner of the state looking much like war-zone refugees. There were a number of disconcerted Californians there, official and otherwise, engaged in the wholly futile business of shooing them off ...
>
> But far more active at deploring was a young man with downy, blond mustache. We took turns guessing what he represented. He was dressed in nicely fitting khaki, long trousers, (and) a stiff-brim campaign hat ... Very erect and primly severe, [a man] addressed the slumped driver of a rolling wreck that screamed from every hinge, bearing and coupling. 'California's relief rolls are overcrowded now. No use to come farther,' he cried.
>
> The half-collapsed driver ignored him—merely turned his head to be sure his numerous family was still with him. They were so tightly wedged in, that escape was impossible. 'There really is nothing for you here,' the neat trooperish young man went on. 'Nothing, really nothing.'
>
> And the forlorn man on the moaning car looked at him, dull, emotionless, incredibly weary, and said: 'So? Well, you ought to see what they got where I come from.' And he drove right on, fearful perhaps, that once stopped his car would never start again.

The Skeptic

Many farmers resented government actions to restore the lands, just as many initially resisted efforts to apply soil conservation farming techniques. Ann Marie Low, born in 1912, made the following entry in her diary on August 1, 1934. She reflects on her family's history of trying to make a living on the Plains in southeastern North Dakota. She later published her writings in *Dust Bowl Diary* (1984):

> The country is overrun with surveyors these days. The Missouri River Diversion Project has three automobiles full of them running around. Others are here about this game refuge idea, and some on a shelterbelt project. The Missouri D.P. people are going to turn this area into a huge lake. The game refuge people are going to let it revert to the wild. The shelterbelt people intend to put in a lot of trees to keep the wind from doing damage to the farms the other two outfits intend to eliminate ...
>
> GEE-EE-WHIZ! Each group is going contrary to the next. We seem to have a bunch of bureaucratic idiots running around at taxpayers' expense determined to ruin this area somehow.
>
> Our bountiful and interfering government sometimes creates awful messes. When this region was opened to homesteaders, the government and railroads encouraged people to come in here for an almost free 160 aces. The broken lives and broken hearts that caused was criminal. People back East had no idea a 160-acre tract here does not make a viable farm.
>
> Grandpa realized that. He started out with 480 acres and planned to get more. The drouth [sic] of the 1880's cost him his preemption and tree claim. The fire forced him to mortgage the remaining 160 acres. It was a man-killing struggle, but his family managed to hang on until the prosperous times after 1900.
>
> Then during the war the government cried out for all the wheat it could get. People came in there, bought small farms on mortgages, and planted wheat on land which should never have been plowed. After the war, prices dropped drastically. These people have never been able to pay their mortgages. The government has never done a thing to protect them against terrible gouging of the wheat and cattle markets and of the railroads.
>
> Now another prolonged drouth has struck at a time the whole country is suffering a severe depression. Men like Dad and the Holmes brothers, who have been here a long time, who have plenty of land and no mortgages, have a chance to hang on until better times come again. Better times will come.

The Approaching Cloud

Lawrence Svobida was a Kansas wheat farmer during the 1930s. He saw firsthand the storms and the resulting destruction around him. His observations and thoughts were published in his memoirs, *Farming the Dust Bowl* (1986). The following vividly describes the approach of a dust storm:

> ... At other times a cloud is seen to be approaching from a distance of many miles. Already it has the banked appearance of a cumulus cloud, but it is black instead of

white and it hangs low, seeming to hug the earth. Instead of being slow to change its form, it appears to be rolling on itself from the crest downward. As it sweeps onward, the landscape is progressively blotted out. Birds fly in terror before the storm, and only those that are strong off wing may escape. The smaller birds fly until they are exhausted, then fall to the ground, to share the fate of the thousands of jack rabbits which perish from suffocation.

Suggested Research Topics

- Identify the Dust Bowl region on maps and research information on the weather patterns, water sources, soils, natural vegetation, and terrain of the region.
- If you were member of a farm family in the Dust Bowl during the 1930s, what would you choose to do? What would you be leaving if you chose to go to California or some other region?
- Write a first-hand account of a person caught in a major dust storm and its effects on his or her farm and daily life. Discuss the health problems, effects on livestock, and impacts on the crops.
- What relief programs were available to Dust Bowl residents, and what did they have to offer? How effective were the programs? What would have happened to the residents if the programs had not been available?

Bibliography

Sources

Bonnifield, Paul. *The Dust Bowl: Men, Dirt, and Depression.* Albuquerque: University of New Mexico Press, 1979.

Gregory, James N. *American Exodus: The Dust Bowl Migration and Okie Culture in California.* New York: Oxford University Press, 1989.

Hurt, R. Douglas. *The Dust Bowl: An Agricultural and Social History.* Chicago: Nelson-Hall, 1981.

Riney-Kehrbeg, Pamela. *Rooted in Dust: Surviving Drought and Depression in Southwestern Kansas.* Lawrence: University Press of Kansas, 1994.

Shindo, Charles J. *Dust Bowl Migrants in the American Imagination.* Lawrence: University Press of Kansas, 1997.

Worster, Donald. *Dust Bowl: The Southern Plains in the 1930s.* New York: Oxford University Press, 1979.

Further Reading

Booth, David. *The Dust Bowl.* Kids Can Press, 1997. (for youth)

Brink, Wellington. *Big Hugh: The Father of Soil Conservation.* New York: MacMillan, 1951.

Davidson, James A. *Patches on My Britches: Memories of Growing Up in the Dust Bowl.* 1st Books Library, 1998.

Dyck, Mary K. *Waiting on the Bounty: The Dust Bowl Diary of Mary Knackstedt Dyck.* Iowa City: University of Iowa Press, 1999.

Jennings, Walta S., and Nancy J. Shaver, eds. *Poke Greens for Breakfast?: True Stories of Rural Arkansas, Oklahoma Dust Bowl Days, and South Dakota Sheep Wagon Tales.* Writers Club Press, 1999.

Long, Philip S. *Dreams, Dust and Depression.* Calgary: Cypress Publishing, Inc., 1972.

Low, Ann Marie. *Dust Bowl Diary.* Lincoln: University of Nebraska Press, 1984.

Meltzer, Milton. *Driven From the Land: The Story of the Dust Bowl.* New York: Benchmark Books, 2000.

National Association of Conservation Districts (NACD), [cited October 12, 2001] available from the World Wide Web at http://www.nacdnet.org.

National Resources Conservation Service (NRCS), [cited October 12, 2001] available from the World Wide Web at http://www.nrcs.gov.

Rutland, Richard A. *A Boyhood in the Dust Bowl, 1926–34.* Niwot, CO: University Press of Colorado, 1997.

Stanley, Jerry. *Children of the Dust Bowl: The True Story of the School at Weedpatch.* New York: Crown Publishing, 1992.

Stein, Walter J. *California and the Dust Bowl Migration.* Westport, CN: Greenwood Press, 1973.

Steinbeck, John. *Their Blood Is Strong.* San Francisco: The Simon J. Lubin Society, 1938.

Svobida, Lawrence. *Farming in the Dust Bowl: A First-Hand Account From Kansas.* Lawrence: University Press of Kansas, 1986.

See Also

Farm Relief

Education

1929-1941

Introduction

Although the Depression began in the fall of 1929, its ominous cloud did not overshadow schools until the fall of 1932 when many citizens facing unemployment or reduced incomes could no longer pay their property taxes. Retrenchment became the buzzword for budget cutbacks, resulting in reductions in the hours schools operated, increased class sizes, and decreases in teachers' salaries. Poor school districts in rural areas closed their doors. Black students—facing racism, poverty, and neglect—were severely impacted. Adding to school funding problems was the trend for youth to stay in school longer since employment was tough to find during the Great Depression. As a result, more youth were seeking an education.

The Depression greatly transformed teachers' working conditions. Educators observed the deterioration of school programs they had spent years building. Teachers had to try to teach undernourished children whose families had been devastated by unemployment and could no longer afford to eat well. Teachers fought back against retrenchment. Membership in organized teachers' unions rose significantly. Educators radicalized and called for teachers to take charge of creating an entirely new social order, redistributing the wealth for a fairer America. Experimental schools such as folk schools and labor colleges trained students for the new order by teaching courses in labor organizing, political reform, civil rights, and reform in housing and healthcare. Conservative groups such as the American Legion perceived civil rights and organizing activities

Chronology:

1931–1932: Depression spawns cuts in educational budgets, affecting teacher salaries and programs offered.

February 18, 1932: George S. Counts, professor from Columbia University, launches the social-reconstructionist reform movement in education with a speech to a teachers' convention in Baltimore, Maryland.

1932: Highlander Folk School of Monteagle, Tennessee, opens, offering an alternative form of education.

1933: Membership in teachers' unions such as the American Federation of Teachers (AFT) increases rapidly in reaction to budget and staff cuts due to the Depression.

1933: The Eight-Year Study, under the direction of the Progressive Education Association, begins. Its goal is to determine if progressive education prepares students for college as well as a traditional education.

March 1, 1933: John Dewey speaks before a school supervisors' convention in Minneapolis, Minnesota, where he accuses the U.S. Chamber of Commerce of being an enemy of public education because of its proposed radical cuts in education programs.

April 17, 1933: Marking one of the first New Deal economic relief programs of President Franklin Roosevelt's administration, the first Civilian Conservation Corps (CCC) camps open. Those CCC camps will conduct various education programs for underprivileged youth throughout the Depression.

April 24, 1933: Demanding back pay, five thousand Chicago schoolteachers march on city hall.

April 1, 1934: Approximately 20,000 schools, mostly rural, are closed due to funding problems.

June 26, 1935: The New Deal establishes the National Youth Administration (NYA) as a division of the Works Progress Administration (WPA).

1936: The U.S. Supreme Court in *Murray v. Maryland* orders the University of Maryland Law School to admit a black American student or create a segregated law school for him alone.

1938: The WPA, created three years earlier, claims to have taught over one million people to read and write.

1941: The Eight-Year Study ends. Evaluators proclaim progressive education a success.

for unions as communistic. Alarmed by the new rhetoric, they feared communism was creeping into all levels of public schooling.

The economic upheaval of the 1930s actually spurred some lasting positive changes. The portion of school budgets from state funds increased. School systems became more efficient by combining small schools and standardizing curriculum and school facilities. Teachers demanded and won higher standards for the teaching profession. Although often at odds with traditional public school philosophy—that only regular teachers in regular schools could teach—New Dealers, those who supported President Franklin D. Roosevelt's (served 1933–1945) reform and relief plan called the New Deal, reached out to the most needy students by teaching them in settings other than traditional schools. They helped those in school stay in school and demonstrated that students previously not experiencing success in school only needed to be given a chance in alternative settings with effective instruction.

The most dismal years for schools were between 1932 and 1936. By 1939 educators observed that Americans' desire to maintain and improve public education was very deep rooted. They clamored for more education, not less. The overall upward trends for U.S. education that started in the 1920s had begun again. The deflection downward for state and local educational support during the Depression had been only a temporary setback.

Issue Summary

The Great Depression became a time of crisis in public education in the United States. Because of the

At a Glance

Schoolchildren Learn a Savings Lesson

With the support of the National Education Association, the Savings Bank Division of the American Bakers Association promoted savings or thrift campaigns for America's schoolchildren. Beginning in 1920 schoolchildren had been learning about finance and the personal discipline of saving. By 1930, with accounts totaling more than $29 million, almost 4.5 million children in 14,000 schools participated in the program. The schoolchildren soon became casualties, just as their parents were, of the Great Depression. As banks began closing with the worst years between 1930 and 1933, children lost their entire savings. Teachers, disillusioned at the lessons children learned, sometimes made up the losses from their own meager salaries. Nothing, however, could compensate for the loss of confidence in banks and the dismay at losing savings at such a young age.

lack of employment opportunities, more youth were likely to stay in school longer. School attendance, however, would actually decline through the 1930s due to budget crises of local school districts. The rise of unemployment and cuts in pay meant less tax revenue for schools. In addition, many business leaders in the communities pressed, often successfully, for reducing state and local taxes. These reductions led to further cuts in school budgets. This trend came at a time when increased sophistication in industry demanded a better-educated workforce. Fearing that the growing number of idle youth, out of school and with no job prospects, would turn to radical political movements as was happening in Europe at the time, the New Deal social and economic programs under President Franklin Roosevelt's leadership would attempt to remedy this situation. The Works Progress Administration (WPA), Civilian Conservation Corps (CCC), and National Youth Administration (NYA) would address student needs by offering classes, often vocational in nature, to teach needed skills for future employment. Though the programs served numerous youth, it was still a small percentage of those out of school.

A Shift in Educational Support

The 1920s were marked by an economic boom following World War I (1914–1918). Many students, teachers, and school districts throughout the decade enjoyed steady funding support. More students than ever before were attending schools. Many teachers were hired to meet the demand, and average annual pay increased from $871 in 1920 to $1,420 in 1930. While some school districts were left behind, many experienced unprecedented levels of funding and support. Many educators, like most Americans, were unprepared for the harsh times that laid ahead.

In October 1929 the U.S. stock market crashed, and the value of stocks plummeted. By 1932, on average, stocks were worth only one-fifth of their value before the crash. Profits of corporations went into a tailspin, falling from $8.6 billion to minus $2.7 billion. Income from the agricultural industry decreased by one-half, manufacturing by approximately two-thirds, and construction by four-fifths. Americans' combined personal income decreased from $85.9 billion to $47.0 billion as estimated unemployment rose to 25 percent of the workforce. These losses occurred because of many reasons. Besides lack of government regulation of business and overspeculation in stocks and real estate, other possible causes that have drawn attention include: (1) a widespread "get-rich-quick" mentality; (2) overproduction and low prices of farm produce; (3) belief that national economies naturally decline in predictable patterns; and (4) a large gap in wealth between the rich and common citizens.

While businesses and individual Americans struggled to readjust to the most serious economic depression in recent history, the effect on schools was delayed. From the day of the collapse in 1929 through much of 1931, the devastating economic downswing was not seriously felt in most school districts. Through the first two years of the Depression, most local superintendents viewed the economic trouble as a temporary storm they could weather. Even President Herbert Hoover (served 1929–1933) declared it a temporary state of affairs that would soon run its course. He would take little action regarding schools. Because budgets were planned a year in advance, they typically reflected the same optimism of the 1920s. The U.S. Office of Education found that schools actually had budgeted slightly more for 1931–1932 than for 1930–1931. Most school districts operated independently of the government and could levy property taxes to meet their needs up to a point. A majority of citizens found a way to pay those taxes in 1930 and 1931. Furthermore, the decline in overall prices meant those tax dollars bought more. Superintendents' pay

Rural schools were often plagued by squalid classrooms, inadequate books and equipment, and non-attendance by students during the Depression. (Corbis-Bettmann. Reproduced by permission.)

increased in 1931–1932 from $4,000 to $4,200 a year, and teachers' salaries held steady. School enrollments continued to grow.

By 1932 the handwriting was on the wall. The shock came with unmistakable force in late 1932. Many property owners could no longer continue paying property taxes. Property taxes, which in large part funded public schools, had skyrocketed during the prosperous 1920s. Many citizens missed payments due to cuts in salary or job loss. In addition, taxes that were collected and meant for health and sanitation projects, highway construction, conservation, and education were now being devoted to providing relief to those in need.

Tax leagues forced reevaluations of real estate downward and demanded cuts in taxes and in public spending. Superintendents turned to their traditional business allies for help, but businessmen needed tax cuts to lower expenses. Schools needed tax dollars to survive, but businesses needed tax breaks so they could cover their costs. Businessmen's groups such as the U.S. Chamber of Commerce and the National Committee for Economy in Government complained of the high taxes for education and claimed America could no longer afford universal public education. They wanted school budgets cut and a limited number of basic subjects taught. The Chamber of Commerce called for shortening the school day, increasing class size, shortening the school year, reducing teachers' salaries, charging high school students fees, charging for textbooks, and discontinuing kindergartens and night classes. The word that came into common use to describe cutbacks was retrenchment. Some even called for school closure. They demanded that loans made to schools by businessmen for expansion in the 1920s be repaid. The focus of education began to shift back to earlier perspectives in history. These views were that education was primarily meant for the brightest youth. This shift would support reductions in funds needed for education.

During late 1932 the Depression deepened. The public became more and more critical of the industrial and commercial leaders who spearheaded campaigns to cut taxes and school services. There was a growing conviction that wealthy, wicked men in high places were at fault for the Depression. Educators attacked their former business allies as traitors who were helping to destroy schools. Nevertheless, retrenchment began in earnest.

Retrenchment

Retrenchment affected school districts throughout the country, especially in more rural areas. Many rural schools were already underfunded during the 1920s. During the Depression these schools found it necessary to sometimes cut teachers' salaries, stop purchasing supplies, or to simply close their doors when money ran out. By 1930 over three million children between seven and 17 years of age were out of school. For example, in the South, Georgia closed the doors to over 1,300 schools, affecting over 170,000 children; in Alabama in 1932 and 1933 most children had no school to attend as five out of six schools were closed; and Arkansas's school year was shortened to less than sixty days. In West Virginia one thousand schools were closed. In Iowa, where schools depended almost solely on property taxes, a salary of only $40 a month for all teachers was established. By April 1934 many districts had greatly shortened the school year. An estimated 20,000 schools across the nation that had taught over 10 million students had either severely shortened their school years or closed completely. Some 2,600 had closed completely. There were 25,000 fewer teachers nationwide in 1934 than four years earlier. The states most affected by retrenchment were in the South and Great Plains, but parts of Michigan, Ohio, and Montana were greatly affected also. Racial minorities were particularly hard hit. In the mostly rural South, 95 percent of black Americans of high school age were no longer in school. Attendance in rural schools in general was down 60 percent.

For the most part, before retrenchment, large city schools were better funded than rural schools. School terms in cities were generally longer than in rural schools, teachers' salaries were much higher, and more classes were held and were therefore more easily combined when funds dropped and some teachers had to be dismissed. Thus, a 30 percent drop in funding was considerably more detrimental in Arkansas than it was in New York. Retrenchment effects, however, varied from city to city and even within the same urban areas. For example, in the early 1930s, Detroit city schools saw their revenues drop over a two year period by almost 30 percent from almost $18 million to less than $13 million. But schools in affluent Detroit suburbs like Grosse Pointe were barely affected. School districts in cities such as Chicago, burdened with heavy debts from building programs and civic governmental corruption, suffered greatly. And some cities had placed the limited city revenue into unemployment relief, rather than into their schools. For example, Baltimore spent only half as much money on public schools as did Boston, although Baltimore had a much larger population. Los Angeles schools, however, suffered less than the large east coast cities' schools.

Educators, who had little taste for cutting budgets, searched for ways to reduce expenses. This was especially difficult at the high school level, where the number of students enrolled actually grew during the Depression, despite the overall decline in total number of students in lower grades due to the cutbacks. In the early twentieth century, it was not uncommon for teenagers to quit school early to join the work force, but as employment became increasingly hard to find, the number of students staying in school until the twelfth grade increased. From 1929 to 1934, the number of high school students grew from about 3.9 million to more than 5.6 million. To worsen matters, class sizes were also further increased as a way in which to save money. From 1930 to 1934 the average class size in high schools grew from 20.6 pupils to 24.9. National figures, however, mask considerable differences between districts. Some cities expanded class size to over forty students. Besides increasing class sizes, another cost-cutting measure was the emergence of "social promotion," or passing children from grade to grade rather than holding them back until certain

More About...

What Is Progressive Education?

The 1930s, due to financial pressure from the Great Depression and lack of federal support under the New Deal programs, were a period of considerable debate and creativity in education. Progressive education became a key idea under debate. But just what progressive education represented was often hard to describe and varied from one educator to the next. One perception of what progressive education consisted of, as contrasted with traditional education, was offered by Helen Hay Heyl in an article title "The Two Extremes" published in the November 7, 1932, issue of *Journal of Education* (p. 602; reprinted in Tyack, et al. *Public Schools in Hard Times: The Great Depression and Recent Years,* 1984, p. 151). The accompanying table illustrates how some educators saw the two methods of education in the 1930s.

Traditional vs. Progressive Schooling
A Comparison from the 1930s

Traditional School	Progressive School
Child is sent to school and is kept until four o'clock, after which he is released home.	Child goes to school and cannot get there early enough, he lingers in shops, laboratories, yards, and libraries until dusk or urgent parents drag him homeward.
This is a school for listening.	This is a school for working.
Children are pigeonholed in long rows of desks.	Children are seated in groups at tables with comfortable chairs.
Children sit quietly studying their lessons.	Children sit working at projects, asking questions as needs arise. They "learn by doing" under wise teacher-guidance.
Movement means marching in rows at a teacher-directed and controlled signal.	Movement means purposeful activity, with consideration for the rights of others, and leads to self-direction and self-control.
Child learns unquestioning obedience to authority.	Child learns obedience through participation.
Keynotes: memorize, recite, pay attention.	Keynote: Experiences leading to growth.
Child's mind is submitted to the grindstone of an educational discipline which dwarfs his capacity to think for himself.	Child is taught to think, to develop tolerant understanding, to question critically, to evaluate.
Aim: Mental discipline, which it is believed will produce good citizens.	Aim: Growth and tolerant understanding, which it is believed will produce good citizens and the improvement of the social order.

Comparison of Traditional and Progressive schooling from the 1930s. (The Gale Group.)

academic standards had been met. Also, the falling birth rate and subsequent decline in elementary school enrollment allowed districts to save money by closing smaller elementary schools. In normal times closure of such schools would have caused parental protest, but these were not normal times. As long as there was room in a larger school, smaller facilities shut the doors with little public objection. In retrospect, historians argue that such measures—larger classes, social promotion, and school consolidation—actually made instruction more efficient.

The worst period psychologically was the budget planning in 1932 for the school year 1932–1933. Fear of what catastrophes lay ahead caused budget-cutting hysteria for many districts. Some educators feared the depressed conditions might be permanent. Most hard-pressed urban districts cut teachers' salaries. From 1929–1930 to 1933–1934, the average teacher salary dropped from $1,420 to $1,227, a decrease of 13.6 percent. Depending on the district, however, pay cuts of 25 to 50 percent were not uncommon. By 1934 almost 300,000 rural teachers earned less than $650 a year, the minimum wage of factory workers under the National Recovery Administration (NRA). Approximately 85,000 earned less than $450 per year, which today is equivalent to only about $5,800 per year. Typical of American workers in general, the prospect of losing their jobs was a constant worry for teachers. Between 1930 and 1934, large numbers of superintendents and principals did lose their jobs. In worst-case scenarios, school boards filled superintendent and teaching positions by selecting from the lowest bidding applicant. In one North Dakota system, teaching jobs went to teachers bidding as low as $30 a month. Teachers were obviously shaken and demoralized by the plunge of their income.

Another sacrifice educators had to contend with was the elimination of classes and programs of a practical nature that had been instituted during the 1920s under the banner of "progressive education." These

Children in a North Dakota school learn to read and write. Reduced funding during the Great Depression meant that many schools had to eliminate classes such as home economics and the arts to concentrate on core classes like English and math. (The Library of Congress.)

programs were sometimes called "fads and frills." They included health services, physical education, night schools, adult education, summer schools, kindergartens, the arts, vocational classes, and home economics. These new programs were reduced or eliminated in many school systems as they cost more to teach than traditional core subjects such as English, social studies, and math. Some educators, however, argued that these were the programs precisely needed for the 1930s, as more students from poor families remained in school. They argued that the "new student clientele" required a corresponding adjustment in curriculum. Some schools did choose to cut college preparatory courses such as Latin and advanced algebra. After reaching a high of $90.22 in the 1929–1930 school year, the national per pupil expenditure declined to $83.22 per pupil in 1931–1932. The decline became a collapse after 1932, when the average dropped to $73.96 for 1932–1933, and only $66.53 in 1933–1934.

Black schools and students were perhaps the most negatively affected by retrenchment. Indeed, one educational study committee commissioned by President Herbert Hoover at the beginning of the 1930s described black students as "by far the most heavily disadvantaged group of children in the entire field of education" (Tyack, *Public Schools in Hard Times: The Great Depression and Recent Years.* 1984, p. 32). With the ever-worsening economic conditions in the early 1930s, many rural blacks moved into the cities. City school boards responded by establishing industrial high school programs to keep unemployed black teens out of trouble. Industrial high schools taught practical skills such as car repair, bricklaying, carpentry, cooking, and sewing. Yet the training black youth received generally provided no advantage, as the Depression caused the elimination of jobs in industry. Blue-collar and service industry jobs traditionally held by blacks were given to whites first. When black Americans asked that industrial schools teach traditional subjects so their students could move on to college, southern school boards answered by discontinuing the building of industrial schools altogether.

The Depression affected rural black areas more because their school budgets were already minimal. The average black family income, already very low, decreased dramatically. All that blacks could contribute to maintain their schools was labor. White school boards were more reluctant than ever to fund black schools. Books, supplies, and transportation were virtually nonexistent. Teachers' salaries could not be maintained, and some black schools could not pay for heat or electricity. A sense of desperation plagued black educators, who appealed to white philanthropists for help, often without success. Philanthropists are wealthy individuals who contribute money to charitable causes.

Despite the many obstacles, some positive changes occurred for black students. Donations by northern white philanthropists allowed black colleges to maintain and expand. Most importantly, a major change occurred in northern cities when budget cutbacks resulted in desegregation of some school systems. In 1932 the Educational Equality League of Philadelphia was formed to promote desegregation and the hiring of black teachers. A key argument most relevant to the times of the Great Depression was that the combining of black and white schools would be more economical. Some progress was seen in the Philadelphia area as one suburb integrated its public schools in 1934. By May 1935 the Philadelphia Board of Public Education had a black member. Spurred by the need to trim expenses, it was during this time that segregated education in the United States was first challenged. Although still much less than the percentage of whites, the percentage of blacks attending high school nationwide more than doubled between 1930 and 1940, and the number of graduates tripled.

Educators Respond to Retrenchment

The most frightening aspect of the Depression for educators was the uncertainty of how long retrenchment would continue. Educators felt abandoned by former business allies who in the 1920s supported schools with loans, donations, and advocated higher taxes. Local school boards were composed almost entirely of wealthy business leaders, but they now were chief proponents of cutting taxes, the lifeblood of schools. The optimism of the 1920s for universal schooling—schooling of all children—had faded. In response educators began to organize into unions. They viewed education as entrenched in a state of emergency and thus moved forth into concerted action.

As labor rights struggles were forged in the industrial sector in the 1930s, so were they also in the field of education. Like workers in industry, teachers struggled for higher wages and more control in their workplace. School boards composed of wealthy businessmen and administrators opposed them, saying schools must be run like businesses, and teachers were merely employees whose every action should be controlled. Teachers considered themselves professionals with some leeway in making decisions. Most hesitated to join unions, fearing this would indicate they were laborers and not professionals. The two leading educational organizations fighting for teachers were the American Federation of Teachers (AFT), founded in 1916, and the National Education Association (NEA), begun in 1857.

Unions Membership in teachers' unions such as the AFT dramatically increased. To its public school locals, the AFT added 33 college locals. Teachers pressed for higher pay, greater job opportunities, retirement pensions, and enforcement of higher teaching standards. Through time they became more outspoken and politically active. Other AFT members argued for changes in the U.S. tax structure. They argued that while underpaid teachers paid their taxes, many of the wealthy were not. Even those teachers who had lost their jobs had formed their own union, the Unemployed Teachers' Association.

More About...

American Federation of Teachers and the National Education Association

The story of teacher unionism is a history of both the American Federation of Teachers (AFT) and the National Education Association (NEA). Founded in 1916, today the AFT is a union affiliated with the American Federation of Labor and Congress of Industrial Organizations (AFL-CIO). Members not only include teachers but counselors, school custodians, school bus drivers, and college and university faculties.

The AFT's major goals are promoting overall professionalism in teaching, assuring fair wages, improving working conditions, increasing job security, better school construction standards, and teacher participation in forming school policies and programs. Objectives are accomplished through discussions between teacher representatives, administrators, and collective bargaining. The AFT has approximately 2,200 local unions.

The NEA is a professional educational organization with over two million members, predominately teachers. The NEA has chapters in all states and Puerto Rico, and represents U.S. citizens teaching abroad. The NEA holds annual meetings to establish policies where state and local associations send delegates to the Representative Assembly.

The NEA's major objectives deal with bettering public education, classroom conditions, and assuring fair salaries and benefits for school employees. The NEA achieves its goals through legislative and judicial efforts and collective bargaining. The NEA also publishes a number of periodicals, including a monthly newspaper, the *NEA Today.* The NEA also aids university students studying to become classroom teachers.

The AFT and NEA originally organized in two distinct ways. The AFT organized on the basis of local unions. Its influence was within local communities, but it had little presence on the state or federal scene. The strongest local groups were in Chicago and New York. It did not move its headquarters to Washington, DC, until the 1950s. The NEA, on the other hand, was a visible presence in Washington by the 1930s. The NEA focused on state associations, and only in the late 1960s did it strengthen local chapters.

The NEA spent much of the 1920s working to raise teachers' salaries as part of a program to better standards in general. It spent much of the 1930s trying to preserve its principle of educational standards in the face of severe school funding difficulties. During the 1930s financial strain, the NEA found itself in turmoil and out of favor with President Roosevelt, who referred to its leaders in Washington as the "school crowd." President Roosevelt preferred relief programs to reach the most needy over increased federal aid to education.

The AFT attracted the younger, more militant, teachers during the 1930s and was politically active at local levels. Chicago was AFT headquarters. The most radical group was AFT Local #5 in New York City, which was heavily communist influenced. Local #5 organized the Harlem Committee for Better Schools. With the approach of World War II, the communist delegates became too much for the noncommunist delegates. Most AFT unions abandoned their broader social reform goals and settled into focusing on higher teacher wages, strong pensions, and smaller classes during and after the war.

By 1933 the NEA, an organization that had loudly celebrated the business community as generous allies, now condemned that broad spectrum of businessmen seeking school funding reductions as exploiters and sinister agents reaching into communities to destroy schools. This was in response to many businessmen demanding budget cuts, loan repayments, and tax cuts. Although the rhetoric was strong, in reality, most educators were deeply distressed by the suffering of fellow teachers and students and angered by school cuts, but few had turned into true radicals. Most desired to realign and again cooperate with the business community in their respective towns.

Conflicts between businessmen and educators were present nationwide. For example, throughout the 1920s the Chicago schools had been badly managed and suffered at the hands of crooked politicians and wealthy property holders who dodged paying property taxes. In 1929 the wealthy organized and pressed for decreases in school spending, including suspending

Many teachers demonstrated during the Depression as a result of cutbacks that increased class sizes and reduced resources. These members of the New York City Teacher's Union local marched on the State Capitol to demonstrate for improvements in education. (Bettmann/CORBIS. Reproduced by permission.)

the wages of teachers while increasing teacher workloads. By 1932 the city owed teachers $20 million, or $1,400 apiece. Teachers were paid in scrip, paper IOUs, that banks would not accept. Funding was diverted away from school maintenance to repay debts to businessmen. Teachers neared the breaking point as they depleted their savings, cashed in insurance policies, cut back on necessities such as food, and sold their homes.

Some teachers turned militant, leading protests against local governments. In Chicago in April 1933, 14,000 teachers, with the support of several thousand students and parents, marched on city hall. When the demonstration fell on deaf ears, several thousand then vandalized banks not honoring teachers' scrip. To punish the teachers, the Chicago school board, dominated by business leaders, fired 1,400 teachers following the end of the school year and dramatically cut back the number of schools. School programs were slashed and the size of classes increased.

Efforts in other areas to protect schools from cutbacks fared better than in Chicago. In Detroit Mayor Frank Murphy and school superintendent Frank Cody successfully resisted budget cuts. Teachers and trade unions, whose members included many parents of Detroit students, organized to elect a school board that would combat efforts by members of the business community to trim school budgets. In the south the Florida League for Better Schools denounced businessmen's groups and succeeded in passing a gasoline tax to benefit schools and guarantee teachers' salaries. In California the California Teachers' Association (CTA) defeated proposed budget cuts and closure of kindergartens. California teachers even saw an increase in pay.

In 1932 the NEA established the Joint Commission of the Emergency in Education to combat efforts of the U.S. Chamber of Commerce. The Chamber had proposed sweeping educational cuts—such deep cuts that many educators labeled the businessmen as "wreckers." Educators and the general public believed the wealthy business community was continuing the irresponsible actions that had landed the nation in the economic disaster of the Depression. Many businessmen, angered and alarmed by teachers' rhetoric, began to charge that educators were communistic and filling students' heads with radical ideas. The battle gained momentum through the Depression years. To strengthen their defense, teachers began embracing different concepts, including social reconstructionism. This further antagonized the conservative business groups.

The Social Reconstructionism Philosophy

In the early 1930s, many influential educational leaders felt pushed by the Depression to urgently seek reform. They sought to move from the progressive education philosophy of the 1920s to a new, more radical philosophy. This philosophy was known as social reconstructionism. Social reconstructionism challenged teachers to take an active role in reform of the social order. To the reconstructionist the Depression seemed to have proven that greedy capitalism was cruel and inhuman. Most social reconstructionists believed that through schools, American life could be changed for the better. Many believed the time of capitalism was over—that community cooperation and collectivism, or shared ownership of goods, should be the new order. Some radical reconstructionists encouraged teachers to join in socialist or communist labor organizing. Others stressed teaching the construction of a new social order.

The philosophy of social reconstruction formed at Columbia University Teachers' College as professors there pondered the relationship between education and social change. This small band of progressive educators included among others George Counts, William H. Kilpatrick, Harold Rugg, John L. Childs, and R. Bruce Raup. Well-known educator John Dewey closely linked himself to the group. This group became the most influential leaders of educational philosophy during the early- and mid-1930s. The Depression convinced them that collectivism was necessary and the old social order was doomed. The reconstructionists, or "frontier thinkers," as they called themselves, believed that they should inspire educators with a sense of direction as to where society should be moving. They hoped by a peaceful evolution to clarify American's needs and assure that abundance was properly redistributed. They wanted progressive teachers to turn classrooms into a forum for political education. In February 1932 Professor Counts gave a talk to the Progressive Education Association (PEA), challenging its members with reconstructionist ideas. His address so moved the audience that rather than applauding, they sat in awed silence. Two days later he took the ideas to the NEA. To teachers the message of social reconstruction—that they could actually build a new social order—was compelling. It was also reassuring, since a new order seemed to be desperately needed. It called for centralized governmental economic planning, a national education system, a professional and organized American teaching force, and sought to break the power local businessmen held over education.

Not all progressive educators subscribed to the social reconstructionist philosophy. Many believed the Depression required administrators and teachers to focus on increased efficiency. They criticized reconstructionists as "romantics," believing any challenge to the business community was doomed to failure. Nevertheless, Professor Counts and other social reconstructionists held the attention of some educators for a time. In the end the majority of educators were not nearly as influenced by the "frontier thinkers" as they were by cutbacks in their own school systems. The talk of new social orders and collectivism made little practical sense to them. A superintendent from Minnesota said the social reconstructionist should "be put in the rear seats and muzzled." Social reconstructionist thinking caused a conservative backlash toward the new philosophy. Conservatives regarded the philosophy as left-leaning or communistic. Lumping all educators together, groups such as the American Legion and the Daughters of the American Revolution (DAR) attacked schools as pools of communist propaganda. They attempted to have school boards restrict curricula of public schools and demand teachers sign loyalty oaths.

Loyalty Oaths First adopted by state legislatures in the 1920s, state laws required teachers to take loyalty oaths in which they swore to not teach ideas "subversive" to mainstream American ideas. The consequence of breaking thc oath was dismissal, and no one could afford to lose his or her job during the Depression. By 1936, 21 states made teachers take loyalty oaths. Fourteen of those states had begun loyalty oath administration since the beginning of the Depression.

Also, in 1935 the U.S. Congress attached a last minute rider to an appropriations bill for the District of Columbia. Known as the "red rider," it required teachers to sign a statement that said they would not teach any communistic ideas. It also asked: "Do you believe in God? Do you believe in any of the doctrines of communism? Do you approve of Dr. George S. Counts' writings? Have you been to Russia?" (Tyack, p. 64). The red rider violated the constitutional right to free political expression. It also violated the principles of academic freedom whereby teachers are free to teach without being forced to adhere to certain political or "ideological agendas." Congress repealed the rider in 1937.

Great Depression financial pressures, in addition to existing politically conservative attitudes trying to maintain stability as they perceived it, led to many other attacks on academic freedom. William Randolph Hearst, publisher of a national chain of newspapers, filled his papers with warnings of the "red," or communist, menace in schools. He and his reporters practiced "red-baiting," portraying individuals as communists or communist sympathizers regardless of whether they were or were not involved with the Communist Party.

Educational Experiments

Despite harsh economic times and criticism from conservatives, the 1930s produced a number of experiments in education, especially at the college level. Most experiments were in search of a new progressive educational approach or a new social order reflective of the reconstructionist philosophies. Although some would succumb to the financial strain of the Depression, they pioneered new curriculum and administrative procedures that more mainstream universities would adopt in the coming decades. Such experimentation took place in higher level learning institutions that included folk schools, labor colleges, the New School for Social Research, and various other small schools with alternative approaches.

Folk Schools Folk schools, which originated in Denmark, stressed interpersonal relations, and students and teachers lived together and worked together to sustain the operation of the schools. Free of the usual memorization and recitation school work common in other schools, folk schools instead offered courses in political and social reform, labor organizing, and folk music as a type of oral history. One of the better known folk schools in the United States was the Highlander Folk School in Monteagle, Tennessee. Others were located in North Carolina, Pennsylvania, and Missouri.

Labor Colleges Labor colleges existed in the United States as early as 1903 with the opening of the Work People's College, a Finnish immigrant college in Duluth, Minnesota. The Brookwood Labor College of Katonals, New York, founded in 1921, and Commonwealth College of Mena, Arkansas, founded in 1925, derived from socialist labor movements. Like folk schools, students and teachers donated labor to maintain services at the schools. Innovative curricula included labor history and economics, labor organization, instruction for adult industrial workers and farmers, class consciousness, and activist theater with socialist themes. At Commonwealth such traditional college social activities as fraternities, sororities, and varsity sports were prohibited. Nationally known liberal personalities such as social worker Jane Addams, scientist Albert Einstein, educators George S. Counts and John Dewey, and author Sinclair Lewis defended thc colleges against attacks by conservative groups.

Brookwood and Commonwealth finally succumbed to the financial and conservative political pressures of the Depression in the late 1930s. Nevertheless, their graduates made important contributions to the labor movement as labor organizers and leaders. Work People's College suspended classes in 1941, as its Finnish students assimilated into American society.

Other Progressive Institutions Other educational institutions known for their variety of experimental philosophies were Bennington College, Rollins College, Black Mountain, Reed College, and Swarthmore College. Bennington College in Bennington, Vermont, opened in 1923 to study quality higher education for women. Classes provided creative, progressive instruction to women. Rollins College in Winter Park, Florida, offered students a wide range of instructional freedom of choice. Black Mountain College near Black Mountain, North Carolina, was founded in 1933

More About...
The Eight-Year Study

Beginning in the 1920s educators planned and carried out studies of new curriculum to determine its overall effectiveness for students. These studies greatly expanded in the 1930s, often taking the form of surveys. These studies frequently had mixed results. The interpretation of results generally depended on the viewpoint of the group examining the educator's conclusions.

The most important curricula survey of the 1930s was the famous Eight-Year Study, undertaken by the Progressive Education Association's Commission on the Relation of School and College. The survey, which ran from 1933 to 1941, evaluated the collegiate success of students who graduated from selected progressive high schools across the nation compared to their peers who graduated from more conservative or traditional high schools. Traditional high schools employed the decades-old methods of memorization and college-preparation classes in classical studies of Latin and Greek. They were geared toward the most elite social classes and most gifted students. The new progressive approach included more hands-on, student-orientated, discussion-filled classes rather than memorization. Latin and Greek were generally not part of the curriculum. The study sought to determine if students who had received progressive education were better at thinking creatively in problem solving than students receiving traditional education emphasizing memorization. If progressives could demonstrate their students indeed outperformed traditional students, the case would have been made for progressive education over traditional education.

The study was overseen by leading progressive educators and well endowed by the Carnegie Foundation and the General Education Board of the Rockefeller Foundation. Thirty-six hundred students from 27 secondary schools took part in the study. The students from selected progressive high schools were tracked throughout their college years. The three hundred colleges that took part in the study dropped entrance exams, which included translating Latin, since progressive students had not taken such courses.

Though those conducting the study proclaimed in 1941 that progressive education was distinctly superior in teaching school children how to think critically, others claimed that the students' personal backgrounds, such as growing up in affluent communities with better school facilities, could have contributed significantly to the higher performance. Those students from progressive high schools had just as successful college careers as those from traditional high schools.

Of course, overall interpretations differed by group. For example, conservatives said colleges had lowered standards for progressive students, making them appear to do better than they actually did. Nonetheless, the Eight-Year Study became a model for similar later surveys in California and Michigan.

---

by a group of dissident professors from Rollins. Like folk schools, Black Mountain focused on interpersonal relations between teachers and students as a community. Black Mountain gained a reputation for its progressive art program. Swarthmore College near Philadelphia, Pennsylvania, gained respect for its honors program and was imitated by other universities in the 1940s. Reed College in Portland, Oregon, was already established before the 1930s as an institution with excellent academic credentials. Reed refused to field competitive athletic teams, banned fraternities and sororities, was highly selective of students upon whom it imposed difficult examinations, and encouraged strong participation of faculty in the university administration. Black Mountain closed in 1956, but at the beginning of the twenty-first century, Bennington, Swarthmore, and Reed continue to flourish.

School Funding

The state funding of schools was one of the most important changes in public education during the 1930s. Education is not mentioned in the U.S. Constitution, but the Tenth Amendment gives states any powers not specifically reserved for the federal government. Hence control of education lies with the states. Legally, the state governments had monetary and regulatory responsibilities over public education, but they had long given these responsibilities to the county and city governments. Schools traditionally had been almost entirely funded through local property taxes. Citizens pay property taxes based on the value of land and structures they own. For years the rich districts had better schools because their higher property values brought in more tax money.

Hard pressed during the Depression as property values plummeted, educators turned to the state legislatures for funding. Since teachers had become more organized as a professional group during the early 1930s, they were able to lobby successfully for increased state support of schools. They found allies in the real estate business since more state funding to schools would decrease their reliance on property taxes of local governments. Property would then be easier to sell. In some states a minimum funding level was set, affecting all school districts. They were assured that their funding would not fall below that level. Localities were also given freedom to spend the funds they had largely as they saw fit. Between 1930 and 1940, the proportion of school budgets supported by the state nearly doubled to 30 percent of all funding. In 1930 only seven states had financially supported local schools to that extent. That figure increased to 18 states by 1934.

The New Deal and Education

In the depths of the Depression, in late 1932, Franklin Delano Roosevelt was elected President of the United States. Many educators eagerly awaited his inauguration in March 1933. The rhetoric of Roosevelt seemed to express their deepest hopes. They hoped Roosevelt and his New Deal would carry schools and teachers to recovery. The New Deal was a collection of economic and social programs created by Congress and the president to assist those suffering from the effects of the Great Depression. In this educators were disappointed. Their hope turned to disillusionment, then to anger as the New Deal created its own educational alternatives alongside public schools. For the most part, the New Deal failed to deliver federal assistance to schools. The Roosevelt Administration chose to leave public schools out from under the New Deal umbrella, and as a result, professional educators and New Dealers become adversaries rather than allies. One key factor contributing to this situation was that many educators wished to emphasize education for the brightest students, not the general population. They considered blacks and other minority groups incapable of learning beyond the basics. New Dealers had an entirely different outlook. New Dealers, supporting universal education, believed the most needy and the illiterate deserved a chance for an education. They began developing programs to help students that had left schools as well as those still enrolled in the traditional schools.

A large number of professional educators held to the notion that education could only take place in school classrooms with a credentialed teacher guiding instruction. With this view educational leaders attempted to protect their jobs during the Depression times. Much to the professional educators' dismay, New Dealers would soon readily hire nonprofessionals to teach in the alternative New Deal programs. Tensions rose between New Dealers and teachers' groups.

Roosevelt Although Roosevelt's reputation among conservatives was that of a spendthrift, he actually worried about the federal debt a great deal and attempted to control spending. He did not push for any federal public school funding. He was concerned that federal aid to schools would drastically increase the debt. Compared to other sectors of the economy, he viewed schools as in pretty good financial shape and teachers as relatively well paid. As governor of New York before taking over the presidency, Roosevelt believed in state and local control of schools, and there was no evidence he had changed his conservative position. President Roosevelt, along with his wife, Eleanor, simply saw too many other pressing needs to pursue federal school funding. In addition, Roosevelt never felt like a kindred spirit with educators. He referred to them as "the school crowd." In fact, he and John Studebaker, the commissioner of education, had a very tense relationship. Roosevelt consistently excluded Studebaker when formulating policy. If he needed advice on education matters, he turned to university presidents, professors at the New School, individuals on his staff with social work experience, and to his wife and her friends.

Politics also played a role in keeping education at a distance. President Roosevelt was a politician of the highest order. A political coalition of labor and urban liberals had formed to support the New Deal social and economic relief programs. Roosevelt feared that providing federal funds to public schools would create friction between the largely Catholic labor movement and urban liberals over federal funding for parochial schools. Parochial schools are private schools, most commonly run by the Roman Catholic Church, and are independent of state control. Southerners were another group whose support was vital to New Dealers. Providing federal funds to southern school districts would raise local fears that the federal government would force an end to racial segregation in public schools. Thus, any activist federal education policy might disrupt the New Deal support base.

Roosevelt's political impulse said to leave education alone, but his humanitarian nature called to him to help the needy. Rather than ask Congress for relief money to aid all school systems throughout the nation, Roosevelt created alternative education agencies to help the most needy. Those agencies included the Tennessee Valley Authority (TVA), the Works Progress Administration (WPA), the Civilian Conservation Corps (CCC), and the National Youth Administration (NYA). Roosevelt saw this approach as having a number of advantages. It delivered funds and services directly to people who needed the training for jobs and cost far less than general federal funding for the entire nation's school systems. Roosevelt could have control over the budgets, programs, and recipients of these specific programs headed by his appointees and could cut back the funding as economic conditions eased. Roosevelt believed the Democratic Party could reap political points from Americans to a much greater extent than it could from costly general federal funding.

The Roosevelt administration, though refusing to fund public schools directly, nevertheless answered and lent support in crisis situations. The New Deal's Federal Emergency Relief Administration (FERA) provided financial assistance to over four thousand rural schools by paying teachers' salaries. FERA paid out $44 million that helped some 150,000 students. With the New Deal relief programs in place for states through FERA and other programs, the New Dealers could threaten to withhold much-needed funding for other relief programs if states cut back school funding. This threat proved effective in maintaining state support for education. The Reconstruction Finance Corporation (RFC) helped schools pay off their debts by issuing loans. Roosevelt and the New Dealers found other ways to help schools. Through various public works programs between 1933 and 1939, such as the Public Works Administration (PWA) and the WPA, the New Deal was behind 70 percent of all school construction projects. In addition to the construction of new schools, federal relief workers also painted and upgraded thousands of other schools.

Educational Agencies of the New Deal

Other New Deal programs besides the PWA and WPA provided support for schools in some form. These included the Tennessee Valley Authority, the Civilian Conservation Corps, and the National Youth Administration. These agencies developed new methods to prepare people to ultimately find work producing goods and services.

The Tennessee Valley Authority had many goals—building dams, generating electricity, promoting flood control and soil conservation, supporting local industries, and creating waterways for commerce. It also had an education section in its Social and Economic Division. One part of its educational program was aimed at the entire nation. Films and visual exhibits illustrated the TVA's activities and helped to restore confidence to Americans. The other educational program was adult education for workers on the dams. They worked only five and a half hours a day, five days a week, as a way of spreading work around. The adult education was designed to produce foremen and skilled workers, previously in short supply in the Tennessee Valley. Workers could request what kind of classes they wanted. Offerings included carpentry, electrical work, auto mechanics, engineering assistance, scientific agriculture, literacy classes, economic studies, rural rehabilitation, and community organization. Classes were sex-segregated, and women learned about new home appliances and studied child care. Progressive educator Harold Rugg, far from disapproving of New Deal educators' efforts, regarded the TVA as "the finest 'social' laboratory in our country" (Tyack, p. 116).

Besides establishing work relief programs that constructed public buildings, including schools, the WPA also had the Emergency Education Program. Aimed toward younger children, the program offered nursery schools for children of poor families and classes in parenting for their parents. Between October 1933 and June 1934, almost three thousand such schools opened. By 1938 over 200,000 children had benefited from health services, supervised recreation, and social development activities such as music, storytelling, and drama. Ninety to 95 percent of its teachers came from relief rolls and were receiving financial assistance or other kinds of aid.

The WPA's largest educational program was its adult education. By February 1934 over 40,000 instructors taught over 1,500,000 individuals in an amazing variety of subjects from general academic courses to occupational classes. Approximately one-sixth of its teachers and students were black. Possibly one million people had learned to read and write through the program by 1938. It also directly contributed to public schools in the poorest sections of the country, providing health services, constructing furniture and teaching aids, and providing supplementary teachers who taught remedial reading and math. One of the most popular education-related programs of the WPA—which became a model for similar programs later in the century—was the provision of over one billion free hot lunches to needy students.

The CCC was created to provide jobs involving forestry work and environmental improvement for young, unmarried men between the ages of 18 to 25. The educational component evolved almost as an after-

Educational programs of the CCC focused mainly on vocational training such as auto repair. These skills could then be used for employment outside of the federal work program. (The Library of Congress.)

thought as to how to fill the men's free hours in the camps. From 1933 to 1942, the CCC had nearly 2.5 million enrollees assigned to almost 2,500 camps located across the nation. The CCC youth came predominantly from families on relief, and the average enrollee had finished only eight or nine school grades. Most wanted no more of traditional educational fare. Therefore, the educational program at CCC camps was flexible, voluntary, and offered a large choice of studies. Many CCC corpsmen took remedial classes to learn basics such as reading and writing, while others took traditional academic classes. Much instruction was directly related to the work of the camp, such as typing, surveying, drafting, construction, use of heavy machinery, driving trucks, and auto repair. This provided vocational skills for later employment outside federal work relief programs. Many camps had libraries, classrooms, and facilities for showing films. Though a large number of youth gained classroom skills, it was still small on a national scale. Over eight thousand received high school diplomas. Impressively, 96 enrollees received college degrees. Clarence S. Marsh, the Educational Director of the CCC, likened the program to "a great American folk school" (Tyack, p. 121).

Like the CCC, the National Youth Administration was a work relief project aimed at young people. While discipline of work in a military style was stressed in the CCC, the NYA focused on alternative teaching approaches. Aubrey Williams, director of the NYA, was a social worker and lay minister who believed in administering government programs to help bring about social justice. As did the CCC, the NYA dealt with impoverished individuals. Almost all participants were from families on some form of relief, and few had higher than an eighth-grade education.

Committed to giving youth a chance at life, the NYA even provided some high school and college students with cash through a work-study program to help with living expenses. The cash was intended to help the students stay in school. The simple ability to buy a pair of shoes enabled many to remain in school. To qualify for cash, the students had to take work-study jobs. Through these jobs they learned yet more skills. The NYA also provided training to youths no longer in school. Such training included work at fish hatcheries, road construction, building community centers, and being teacher's and nurse's aides. The NYA also established resident centers to teach various everyday skills such as machine and automobile repair, farming, welding, painting, and sewing, in addition to reading and writing. Approximately 300,000 black American youth were reached through the Division of Negro Affairs.

A survey in 1940 of 62,000 NYA students in 666 colleges showed that they academically outperformed their fellow students. Both the CCC and the NYA educational programs came at relatively low expense.

The New Deal education programs proved that groups of underprivileged youth who traditional educational systems might have written off as uneducable could learn. Their successes rebuked traditional educators' and conservatives' beliefs. New Dealers had consistently emphasized that the needy youth, when given access to appropriate education could compete with their wealthier peers. Many professional educators and conservatives, still angry about Roosevelt's snubs, joined together to fight the New Deal programs. Through World War II (1939–1945), the last of the New Deal programs related to education had been phased out. Nevertheless, models for education of the most poverty stricken had been established. The programs would serve as a blueprint for 1960s social programs begun under president Lyndon B. Johnson (served 1963–1969), who had served as one of the NYA's state directors in Texas.

Inequalities in Educational Support Continue

By the end of the 1930s, two themes in American education arose. First, education was a deep-rooted institution in U.S. society to which Americans remained committed even in hard times. Secondly, significant inequality existed between the country's school districts.

Despite economic challenges and conflicting educational philosophies, compromise and continuity persisted. The public's desire for education and its confidence in schools remained strong. Public education became woven into the life of not only the privileged but also the needy. People blamed the Depression on wealthy businessmen, not on the schools. They saw the schools as the solution that would unlock doors of opportunity for their children. Even in the depth of the Depression, rather than say education was unnecessary or not making a difference in people's lives, the public wanted more educational opportunities. By the 1930s elementary education through eighth grade had become the norm except in deprived areas serving black children in the South. The suggestion of closure of school systems because of monetary difficulties provoked outrage. The public knew children remained children just so long and could not wait for their education. Growth in high school enrollment kept school systems expanding even when funds were short. The public continued to have a great deal of faith in the professionalism of its teachers. The standards of training and certification for both teachers and administrators increased throughout the 1930s.

Inequalities in education between districts became clear during the 1930s. Using local property taxes as a means to fund schools served middle- and high-income districts reasonably well throughout the 1930s, particularly after the most dismal years between 1932 and 1935. Those school districts in poor localities, however, collected fewer property tax dollars because their property had less value. While many affluent districts barely felt affected by the Depression, poor districts were severely impacted. This inequality of funding continues to be wrestled with in the twenty-first century.

Contributing Forces

The U.S. Constitution does not provide for federal funding of public schools. In fact, in the eighteenth century no public general education existed. Such matters as education and health would be left to the states. It was not until the economic crisis of the Great Depression that the federal government, through New Deal programs, would enter the school scene.

Boom Years for Most

The 1920s were boom years for most schools in the United States. Increasingly more students attended school. The student population in grades kindergarten to 12 increased from 23.5 million in 1920 to 28.6 million in 1930. Enrollment at colleges and universities almost doubled in that time period rising from 598,000 to over 1.1 million. Teachers were hired to meet the demand and their salaries increased steadily. New schools were constructed, and a new concept, the junior high school, appeared, creating a separate middle school for generally the sixth, seventh, and eighth grades. New programs such as vocational education quickly expanded.

Schools operated with a business-oriented philosophy that served them well in the 1920s. Local school boards were mostly comprised of businessmen and the professional elite in the cities and in the more prosperous smaller districts. As a result, schools operated with corporate precision. The administrators were expected to manage districts on the basis of specialized professional knowledge, while not bowing to political factions and achieving the greatest results at the minimum costs. Businessmen cooperated with school administrators to improve education in the 1920s. They donated funds, initiated bond drives and advocated raising taxes. They generously loaned money for building new schools, then profited as the building contractors and suppliers of school needs.

Although constitutionally states were responsible for their systems of schooling, in reality responsibility was left to local districts, keeping schools close to the people in the communities. Schools were funded almost entirely from local property taxes.

Optimistic boom times generally prevailed in American public education during the 1920s. Since the American school system was not a single system, however, but consisted of over 145,000 local branches or districts, inequalities existed. While many districts were affluent, some contended with shocking scarcity of resources. Certain parts of the educational system in the agricultural, coal-mining, and textiles sectors were already in the throes of depression well before the stock market crash of 1929. A resulting problem for public schooling was inequality of school finance, especially in these rural and depressed districts. For example, the agricultural industry had struggled since World War I, leaving schools in farming communities with the lowest paid and most poorly trained teachers, the worst buildings, inadequate books and equipment, and highest rate of nonattendance. Between 1929 and 1930, there were approximately six thousand high schools with fewer than fifty students each, some with fewer than ten students. The majority of these schools were rural. Small high schools often offered narrow and restricted programs of study. The main problem of many rural youth, however, was not small high schools but no high schools. Elementary school districts covered all areas, but high school districts were spotty. Elementary districts in such areas could send their graduates to the nearest high school by paying tuition for them and if housing was available. As early as 1918, educators had developed a case for federal aid to needy districts. Little came of the campaign except a few visionary states began providing districts with "foundation grants," which was a flat sum of money per pupil per year. Areas where school funding was already a problem would be hardest hit by the Great Depression.

Schooling for Black Americans

America was racially segregated in the early twentieth century, which meant black and white students attended separate schools. In the 1920s as in all previous decades, most black Americans lived in poverty in communities with low-quality school facilities and low salaries for teachers. School boards, composed mainly of whites, blocked better funding for black schools. The average expenditure per pupil per year for black students was roughly 15 to 20 percent that for white students. Even though 25 percent of all students in the United States were black, only 12 percent of all education monies went to their education. School boards, especially in the southern states, refused to fund black education because most whites believed blacks were incapable of advanced learning. This widespread belief was accepted without question throughout the 1920s. Hence the barriers of poverty and racism combined to hold black education at woefully inadequate levels.

Denied funding by the white school boards, black communities during the 1910s and 1920s pooled their limited resources into programs of self-help. Former slaves donated their meager savings. Blacks banded together to farm land communally and donate profits to finance local schools. Those who did not have any money donated labor. People who lived in shacks built tiny schoolhouses. At least half of these schools had no desks, only rickety benches and a wood burning stove. By 1932, 3,464 schools had been erected in 880 southern counties. They were locally run with no government funds.

Despite the effort put forth for building schools, the southern black communities remained undereducated. Still only 25 percent of all black students could be served, and virtually all of the schools were elementary schools. Nearly half of all black students were in the first two grades, compared with 28 percent of whites. The mere handful of operating black high schools in the South were located in cities. By 1932, 230 southern counties still had no high school for black students. Nearly one-half of black Americans had never gone beyond the fifth grade. By 1930, while black students comprised approximately 10 percent of the general population, only 3 percent of high school students were black.

Spurred by a belief that black students were incapable of higher learning, northern white philanthropists funded a program to build industrial high schools for blacks in southern cities. The schools almost never taught traditional subjects such as literature, history, or math. Instead, they taught carpentry, bricklaying, auto mechanics, sewing, cooking, and laundry work. Industrial education aimed to prepare black Americans for "stable," but low-paying positions in the industrial workplace. The Depression would soon eliminate even those jobs.

Progressive Education

In the 1890s the chief challenge for America was dealing with problems brought on by urbanization, industrialization, and immigration. Many education reformers believed schools would have to help solve society's problems by teaching about real-life subjects.

The legality of segregated schools began to be challenged during the Great Depression, but it wasn't until 1954 that the U.S. Supreme Court ruled that separate schools for black and white students were not equal.

(The Bettmann Archive. Reproduced by permission.)

Throughout the 1800s specific subjects were taught by rote memorization. Lessons dictated by teachers were written down in notebooks, and students then learned by heart what they had written. Latin and Greek studies were emphasized in high schools with the belief they taught mental discipline. Students' desks were bolted to the floor. Students could not move or talk without permission.

Progressive education appeared around the turn of the century and sought to turn classrooms into places of active student participation. Subjects that related to everyday life were introduced. John Dewey, a well-known spokesman for progressive education and one of the most prominent figures in all of American educational history, established an educational laboratory at the University of Chicago. In the laboratory children learned "by doing." Curriculum was "child centered" and stressed individual talents. For example, children would build a small log cabin while studying about early homesteading in the U.S. West. The applied-learning tasks of the curriculum were forerunners of vocational education. Projects and creative arts allowed for individual expressions.

In the 1920s progressive education philosophies translated into elementary schools with science laboratories, art studios, gyms for physical education, kitchens, and gardens. High schools incorporated vocational education, home economics, physical education, health services, art classes, summer schools, night schools, and adult education. Highly conservative groups increasingly criticized progressive education programs as being expensive frills, liberal, and outright communistic, believing they trained workers for a cooperative society rather than the competitive capitalist society.

Loyalty Oaths

Conservative Americans feared communists would make inroads into American schools and subvert the minds of children. Frequently, conservative groups such as the American Legion and Daughters of the American Revolution (DAR), alarmed at the new progressive curriculum, charged it was tainted with communistic ideas. In 1928 the DAR accused the National Education Association (NEA), the professional organization of teachers, of being "sympathetic with communist ideals" (Bondi, *American Decades: 1930–39,* p. 156) and put out a pamphlet denouncing the organization.

The most popular means of assuring educators would not teach such "subversive" ideas or doctrines was the loyalty oath adopted by some states in the 1920s. The oath required teachers to swear allegiance to American ideas and to not teach subversive ideologies such as communism. The consequence of not taking the oath was dismissal. The prospect of dismissal would become highly intimidating during the Depression.

Perspectives

Business Community and Educators

Following a decade in which businessmen played a strong role in running school districts, the economic strife of the 1930s led to major change. By 1932 economically strapped businessmen changed direction. Instead of lobbying for higher taxes as they had before they became hostile to using tax money for funding schools, they now wanted to lower their own taxes because of the economic hard times. They also demanded that the loans to school districts be paid back.

The interaction between businessmen and educators also dramatically changed. Business organizations, such as the U.S. Chamber of Commerce, called for sweeping cuts in school programs and in funding. Educators were frightened over how far the retrenchment would be taken and felt betrayed by their former allies in the business community. The National Education Association (NEA) fought back against these new proposals. This was quite a reversal by an organization that celebrated its business association in the 1920s. Businessmen, angered by the educators fighting back, attacked harder themselves, especially in the years between 1932 and 1935. They accused educators of being communistic and spreading radical ideas among their students. Cooperation between the business and educational communities was not restored until the second half of the 1930s when economic conditions overall improved.

Militant Teachers

Teachers who had long desired greater control and advocated professionalization of their endeavors became more militant in the 1930s. They saw the day-to-day miserable situations that children were living under. Many school children were suffering from malnutrition. Teachers helped individually when they could on their limited incomes. They paid for school lunches for hungry kids or collected clothing for those students in need. Detroit teachers contributed $30,000 to a general relief fund.

Teachers joined unions by the thousands. Membership quadrupled in the American Federation of Teachers (AFT), which fought for the reclamation of lost pay, unemployment insurance, the planning of relief projects, and a decrease in retrenchment of public schools. Older teachers seeking retirement benefits and job stability were less militant than younger teachers. Communist teachers, the most militant, alienated the more moderate teachers. Most teachers were deeply moved by the suffering they saw and angered by school cuts, but few actually became radicals. The militancy of the teachers' organizations and unions subsided in the 1940s, although they continued to lobby for higher salaries, better benefits, and lower class size throughout the twentieth century.

Educational Progressives Versus Educational Conservatives

Progressives, organized and becoming a force by 1919, were interested in creating a better society through child center education. Teaching by rote memorization was out of favor. Progressives believed that allowing a child to be creative would better prepare him or her to solve problems and meet challenges as an adult. In progressive education the teacher was conceived as a friendly guide. Progressive ideas translated in the 1920s into hands-on learning in science laboratories, art studios, gymnasiums, projects of all varieties, and vocational classes such as electric shops and mechanical repair shops.

Social reconstructionists, considered more radical than progressives, called for indoctrination of students toward establishing a new social order. Social reconstructionists were deeply disturbed over the capitalist profit motives that they believed had led to the misery of the Great Depression. George Counts challenged his fellow educators in 1932 to take up the banner of social reconstructionism. They believed the educator could identify the prevailing social ills and deliberately use the schools to correct them. Many progressives actually opposed social reconstructionists, calling the reconstructionists "romantics" that would not be successful in taking the United States to a new social order. Although many bewildered educators were listening, these ideas made them nervous as conservative school boards controlled their jobs.

Educational conservatives had long been opposed to progressives and were even more opposed to social reconstructionism. They insisted classical curriculum such as Latin in high schools and colleges developed mental discipline and the ability to conquer difficult subjects. They had no use for spending time and money educating the general public. Educational

Students learn about insects at a school in Georgia in 1941. This type of Progressive educational approach is based on hands-on learning. (The Library of Congress.)

conservatives viewed school as another stage for competition where the most gifted win.

By the end of the decade, social reconstructionism faded. Its goal seemed unrealistic to educators and dangerous to many conservatives. The threat of war shifted the focus of educators. The ideas of progressivism endured and were put into practice when vocational education became an outright necessity to prepare individuals for jobs in the defense industries. Most likely the only lasting legacy of the more radical social reconstructionism was that it supplied conservatives with ammunition to claim that schools were a base of communistic subversion—a criticism that would be wildly pursued in the post World War II hysteria over communism.

The Politically Conservative

The rise of social reconstructionism during the Great Depression years led conservatives to believe communists were infiltrating into American life through the schools. Even progressive education was frequently the target of conservatives seeking to label it as communistic. Conservative groups such as the American Legion and the Daughters of the American Revolution (DAR) attacked schools as harbors of communist thought and propaganda. They attempted to force school boards to restrict the curriculum and demanded teachers sign loyalty oaths swearing they would not teach ideas or doctrines that went against mainstream thought.

William Randolph Hearst, a powerful newspaper publisher of the 1930s, frequently charged that the schools were full of communist subversives. Through his newspapers he often targeted teachers who he quoted out of context. The subject of hidden teacher plots proved a boon in selling more newspapers.

New Dealers Versus Educators

President Roosevelt and his New Dealers kept their distance from educational reforms. Roosevelt believed in state and local control of schools. Politically he did not want to upset the coalitions of urban liberals and largely Catholic labor by pursuing federal school funding for public schools and not for Catholic schools. Also he did not want to alienate southerners who believed federal school funding would lead to demands for segregation. Overall, an activist federal educational policy could disrupt the fragile coalitions of all these New Deal supporters. Rather than concentrating on federal funding, both Roosevelt and his wife, Eleanor, believed the New Deal education programs must reach the most needy, those already falling outside the traditional educational process. New Dealers talked of education for the masses and teaching skills to the poorest and least-educated Americans.

On the other hand, many conservative professional educators had long considered these same people, which the New Deal agencies taught, as incapable of education beyond a certain level. They believed the focus of education should be toward the gifted and rigidly held to the notion that education took place only in the classroom with credentialed teachers. Educators were also annoyed that monies flowed to the new agencies but not to established school systems. Even though it seemed as though New Dealers and professional educators would be kindred spirits in the cause of educational reform, they instead remained in opposite camps through the Depression.

Common Americans

The average American's faith in the value of education remained steadfast. By 1930 eight years of education had become the norm in all but the poorest regions. In the frightening times of the Depression, most people wanted schools to teach familiar subjects and themes. Families considered education necessary for new opportunities for their children and looked on in dismay when schools closed. They wanted more education, not less. The reformist issue of social reconstruction was an academic matter that did not reach into American homes.

Impact

Trends in Education

As the 1930s came to a close, the decade of scarcity altered the development of American public schools in the years to come. The Depression did not reflect trends in education that began in the 1920s. The percentage of children and teenagers aged five to seventeen attending school increased from 83.2 percent in 1920 to 94.2 percent in 1940. During World War II, the numbers dropped a bit because youth left school to work or go into the armed services. After the war, however, the rise resumed and reached 92.3 percent by 1950. The percentage of 17-year-olds who graduated increased steadily from 16.3 percent in 1920 to 57.4 percent in 1950, with the only downward dip occurring during the war. By 1998 over 80 percent graduated. Overall expenditures per student rose rapidly through the 1920s, decreased slightly during the harshest early Depression years, and rose steadily through the rest of the twentieth century.

The cost-saving closure of tiny rural schools and the consolidation of districts so that resources could be shared positively made public education more efficient. Between the school years of 1929–1930 and 1970–1971, the number of elementary schools declined from 238,306 to 65,800. The number of one-room schools went from 149,282 to 1,815. This allowed more efficient use of teachers, facilities, supplies, and transportation.

Following the federal government involvement in education through the New Deal programs of the CCC, NYA, WPA, and other agencies through the 1930s into the early 1940s, the federal government played a small role in education through the 1950s into the 1960s. National concerns over the quality of education in public schools arose again by the mid-1960s. President Lyndon Johnson's Great Society social programs addressed inner-city decay and the near collapse of school systems as white Americans moved out to the growing suburbs, reducing the tax revenues of the cities themselves.

An office of education was created in the U.S. Department of Interior in the mid-1950s. It grew later into its own Department of Health, Education, and Welfare. Congress established an actual Department of Education by 1980 that serves as a research center and database for educational activities in the nation, oversees financial aid for college students, and makes sure federal laws passed concerning civil rights and students with disabilities are followed. These last two areas were where federal funding in education was primarily focused by the end of the twentieth century. If local school districts do not follow laws in these areas, then the federal government may withdraw the small, but vital, amounts of funds provided. As it was before the Great Depression, general funding for public schools constitutionally rests with the individual states.

Black Students

Ironically, the Depression in some ways improved the situation of black education. Some northern schools began to abolish segregated education as a cost-saving measure in the 1930s. The National Association for the Advancement of Colored People (NAACP) won a series of Supreme Court challenges to segregation in the 1930s and 1940s. Yet the South resisted desegregation. In 1954 the NAACP mounted another legal challenge to segregation and won in *Brown v. Board of Education* which declared that any form of separate education is always unequal. Although it was a struggle, schools across the south desegregated.

More About...

Comparing Businessmen and Teachers Income

During the early years of the Great Depression, teachers were angered at businessmen's efforts to cut taxes, which schools needed for survival. The reason for the teachers' militancy against the business community lies partly in the annual incomes of the very wealthy compared to teachers and to the many families struggling with the economic collapse (partly adapted from Bondi, *American Decades: 1930–39,* 1995, p. 146; originally published in 1934 in the educational journal *Social Frontier*):

William Randolph Hearst, Newspapers—$500,000
B.D. Miller, Dime stores—$337,479
Charles M. Schwab, steel—$250,000
George Hill, tobacco—$187,126
R.B. Bohn, aluminum—$140,80
Arthur C. Dorrance, Soups—$112,500
College instructor—$1,500
Public school teacher—$1,200
Family on relief—almost $0

The newly built industrial high schools at least added to the number of black high schools available in southern cities. Many of these were used for decades. After desegregation the industrial high schools were open to all who wanted a vocational education. Often they were called technical high schools or "polytechs," meaning studies in multiple technical fields.

Progressive Education

Reform spawned by the progressive education movement began appearing in schools in the 1920s. The child centered, "learn by doing" approaches included science laboratories, vocational classes including shops and home economics, physical education, and art projects. After a temporary setback in the first half of the 1930s due to perceptions that these classes were unnecessary expensive "frills," progressive education expanded from primary grades to high schools. The education provided in New Deal agencies also incorporated many aspects of progressive education. The movement grew in the 1940s and resulted in the 1950s "life adjustment movement" with classes such as home economics, family life, health, and various vocational shops.

The launching of the Soviet Union's satellite, Sputnik I, in 1957 caused concern in the United States that American students were not keeping up with the Russians in educational pursuits. As a result, more traditional classes were returned to for a time. The pendulum, however, swung back to progressive in the 1970s. Throughout the remainder of the twentieth century, educators tried to balance child-centered, individual-development progressive ideas with required skills.

Educators who had demanded the building of a new social order abandoned their broad social reform goals. Instead, teacher unions concentrated on higher wages, pensions, high standards for credentialing teachers, and smaller classes. Teacher militancy over the issues often led to strikes. As a result, between 1960 and 1970 teacher's salaries increased by over 70 percent.

The experimental colleges that established new curricula and administrative methods continued to do so. For example, the Highlander Folk School that trained individuals for nonviolent protest in the 1930s continued to pioneer. In the 1940s and 1950s, it established "citizenship schools" to lead voter registration drives for black American voters. They continued to train leaders for roles in the civil rights campaigns of the 1950s and 1960s.

New Deal Educational Programs

New Deal agencies that had extensive educational programs—TVA, CCC, WPA and NYA—left a legacy that continues into the twenty-first century. The TVA's vast array of vocational classes such as carpentry, electrical courses, auto mechanics, agriculture science, community studies, and child care are prevalent in specialized public high schools and community colleges. Vocational classes prepare students for employment. Vocational education also includes business training, health care, industrial training, and computer applications and repair. Highly technical training classes in addition to basic reading and writing are also available in the armed services, much as they were in the CCC.

The WPA focused on adult education and preschool children. Millions participate in adult education today. Colleges and universities offer extension courses to adults so they may continue their formal education, learn a new skill, or develop a hobby. Most adult education classes are held at night to allow working people to attend. Likewise, high schools in many districts turn into adult education centers in the evenings, providing everything from remedial classes to special interest classes.

The WPA's Emergency Education Program for young children and their parents served as a model for the Head Start Program begun in the 1960s. Head Start provides child development programs for children from birth to age five, pregnant women, and their families. Its goal is to increase the school readiness of children from low-income families. Head Start continues to play a vital role in the lives of underprivileged families. Similarly, the WPA free hot lunch program for needy children was a forerunner of the later federally funded school lunch programs.

The NYA allocated its funds to help high school students stay in school according to the number of youth on relief in the district. Likewise, with Title I of the Elementary and Secondary Education Act of 1965, funds were allocated according to the number of children from poor families. Title I continues to assist underprivileged children by providing intensive help with the basic skills of reading, writing, and math.

Notable People

Charles Austin Beard (1874–1948). In the 1930s Charles Austin Beard was counted with John Dewey and George Counts as one of the foremost examples of U.S. teachers as political and social reformers. Beard grew up on a prosperous Indiana farm and graduated from DePauw University in 1898. During his undergraduate years, Beard spent a summer in Chicago and observed internationally noted social reformer Jane Addams' work at the Hull House. The Hull House, established by Addams in 1889, was a private organization that provided many social services to its local area within Chicago. Prominent among the services were educational courses of various levels and topics. Beard also traveled in Europe between 1898 and 1902 and in England observed socialists of the time who were attempting to build a Labour Party. Returning to the United States, he received his Ph.D. from Columbia University in 1904 and remained there until 1917. Although supportive of America's entry into World War I, he also believed antiwar protesters had the right to speak. When three Columbia instructors were fired for opposing the drafting of young men into the army, Beard resigned. He became a national symbol of academic freedom. With John Dewey, Thorstein Veblen, and James Harvey Robinson, in 1919 Beard founded the New School of Social Research. In the 1920s and 1930s, his fame and involvement in educational issues increased.

During the early twentieth century Beard authored numerous scholarly books on the U.S. government system. He also wrote well-received textbooks such as *The Rise of American Civilization* (1927)—a standard in high school and college classes. In 1932 Beard's *A Charter for the Social Sciences in the Schools* had an enormous influence on the way social studies was taught.

Mary McLeod Bethune (1875–1955). During the 1930s Mary McLeod Bethune was the most influential black American woman in the United States and the most influential black administrator in the New Deal. She possessed the ability to reassure whites, and at the same time, push for greater civil and social equality for blacks.

Bethune was born on a farm near Mayesville, South Carolina. She was one of seventeen children of parents who were freed from slavery after the Civil War (1861–1865). Her family recognized her superior intellectual abilities early in her life, and she was sent to mission school where she excelled. In 1894 she graduated from Scotia Seminary, a Presbyterian school for black girls in Concord, North Carolina.

In 1929 she founded and managed Bethune-Cookman College and kept it together through the Depression. By 1943 it was a fully accredited four-year institution and a leading southern teacher training college. In 1935 Bethune created the National Council of Negro Women (NCNW). She participated in many national organizations such as the National Association of Teachers in Colored Schools.

Bethune became a close friend and associate of Eleanor Roosevelt. In 1935 Bethune was appointed to the National Advisory Committee of the National Youth Administration (NYA). By 1939 she was Director of Negro Affairs for the NYA. She is credited with helping over 150,000 black Americans attend high school and 60,000 attend college.

Horace Mann Bond (1904–1972). Horace Mann Bond, an extraordinary black American scholar, labored with intelligence and diplomacy to improve education for black Americans. He despised segregation and quietly worked to abolish it, yet at the same time realized he must strive to improve education for black students within the confines of segregation. Born into a family that produced a number of scholars and civil rights leaders, Bond graduated from Lincoln University, a black college in southeastern Pennsylvania, in 1923. He received his Ph.D. in sociology from the University of Chicago in 1936.

Bond attacked a key issue of segregation—that intelligence testing proved the intellectual inferiority of black students. During the 1930s many asserted the decline of black schools was due to black indifference. Bond's studies clearly showed that poor financing by white-dominated school boards kept black schools substandard. Bond demonstrated exceptional black students were the products of well-financed and well-administered black schools, and poor educational performance was tied to political and economic exploitation of the black schools rather than any genetic characteristics.

Bond, despite his radical scholarly revelations, managed to survive as a black educator in the 1930s by tempering his articles. He advocated financing black schools on an equal basis instead of calling for an end to segregation. By 1939 Bond was a highly respected and influential black educator. In 1945 he became the first black president of Lincoln University. In 1957 Bond assumed the position as dean of the School of Education at Atlanta University, remaining there until his retirement in 1971. He tirelessly worked for improvement in black education and in the civil rights movements of the 1950s and 1960s.

George S. Counts (1889–1974). Born in Baldwin, Kansas, as a youth George S. Counts dreamed of being a trapper on the frontier. Instead he enrolled at the local Baker University. He had no early intentions of becoming a teacher, but after his marriage he began teaching high school science and math and within a year was a teaching principal. In 1913 Counts received a scholarship to study sociology at the University of Chicago. Counts shifted his focus to education shortly after arriving at Chicago. Chicago's School of Education was strongly influenced by the progressive teachings of John Dewey. Counts studied under some of the most distinguished educators and sociologists of the day. All of his teachers focused on education's role in the social and economic fabric of the country. Counts received a doctorate from Chicago in 1916 with a major in education and a sociology minor.

Counts held positions at a series of educational institutions over the next few years. During 1924 Counts co-authored "The Principles of Education," an overview of the philosophy of education favoring the progressive child-centered approach of John Dewey. In 1927 Counts moved to Teachers College, Columbia University of New York City. There he became one of several influential leaders on the cutting edge of educational reform.

Counts gained broad perspectives on education by studying approaches in other countries, including the Philippines and Russia. In Russia he studied the country's planned economic system and its organized school system. By the early 1930s, Counts was a well-known educator throughout the United States. At the onset of the Depression, many educators were still teaching students the merits of competitive capitalism even as it appeared to claim more victims every day. Counts believed teachers should lead society in building a new economical, political, and moral order that would solve problems and make social improvements.

Counts wrote "Dare the School Build a New Social Order?," a pamphlet that consisted of three papers he read to national educational meetings in February 1932. He demanded that educators become economic reformers and political activists involved with labor unions, farmers, and minority groups. This new educational philosophy was known as social reconstructionism.

Conservatives denounced Count's philosophy as communist. Counts was a reformer but not a communist. When elected president of the American Federation of Teachers (AFT), he began a purge to rid the union of communist influence, expelling communist-led locals, including New York Local #5. When a mandatory retirement policy forced his retirement in 1955 from Columbia, he continued to lecture across the country. He went to Southern Illinois University at Carbondale in 1961, remaining there for a decade. Counts continued as an activist his entire life.

John Dewey (1859–1952). John Dewey was perhaps the most influential American philosopher and educator during the first half of the twentieth century. The son of a Vermont grocer, Dewey attended public school in Burlington and graduated from the University of Vermont in 1879. He received his Ph.D. in philosophy from Johns Hopkins University in 1884 and served as an instructor in philosophy and psychology at the University of Michigan for most of the next ten years. Dewey's interest in education began at Michigan. His observations and studies convinced him that most schools taught only traditional classical classes. They failed to respond to a changing democratic social order or to recent findings in child psychology revealing how children learn best. Dewey began to search for a new modern approach for education.

In 1894 Dewey left Michigan to join the faculty of the University of Chicago where his research and writings in education would bring him national fame. Dewey's works, *My Pedagogic Creed* (1897), *The School and Society* (1899), and *The Child and the Curriculum* (1902) became the underlying basis of the philosophy of education he originated. The basic concepts of his philosophy proposed that education needed to be student-centered rather than subject-centered and that education through activities such as workshops, laboratories, and occupational programs would serve students and society better than the formal learning of traditional subjects. The "progressive" educational movement of the 1920s and 1930s embraced these ideas. Dewey established the University of Chicago's Laboratory Schools in which his educational theories and approaches could be tested.

In 1904 Dewey accepted the post of professor of philosophy at Columbia University in New York City. He would actively teach there for 25 years, attracting worldwide attention. His output of publications was tremendous. He also devoted time and energy to organizations and the formation of experimental schools.

During the 1930s and 1940s Dewey became the target of conservatives complaining that American schools were not training students adequately in the liberal arts, math and science. Critics also charged Dewey's progressive ideas caused a lack of discipline in schools.

Robert Fechner (1876–1939). Robert Fechner, born in Chattanooga, Tennessee, became a machinist's apprentice for the Georgia Central Railroads at age 16. Four years later he began traveling through Mexico and Central and South America as a machinist in the mining industry. Returning to Georgia in the late 1890s Fechner became involved in labor union activities, serving as an executive officer of the International Association of Machinists from 1913 to 1933.

President Roosevelt was impressed with Fechner's skill in negotiating labor disputes. Deciding he needed a labor leader to head the Civilian Conservation Corps (CCC), Roosevelt appointed Fechner as its director. Fechner insisted that the CCC was chiefly a work relief and conservation agency. He contended that education should not be a main priority. Under mounting pressure, Fechner relented and agreed to an educational plan with voluntary classes that did not conflict with working hours. Fechner was a conservative, fearful of radicalism, and was content to allow the CCC to operate under the racially segregated system of the army and the South. Perhaps in spite of Fechner, the CCC educational program became very popular and well attended by corpsmen. With the outbreak of war in Europe, Congressmen and military officers advocated turning the CCC into a military training program—a move Fechner opposed.

Glenn Frank (1887–1940). H. Glenn Frank served as the president of the University of Wisconsin from 1925 to 1936 when progressive governor Philip F. LaFollette fired him for being too conservative. Frank was an educational reformer during the 1930s, but he proposed more modest change during a period of radical ideas and reform approaches. He stayed in the center and became an outspoken critic of the New Deal, calling it a dictatorial government. Many Republicans hoped he would run for president in 1936, but he declined. He did help draft the 1940 Republican National Committee platform. He also ran for the U.S. Senate in 1940. While campaigning Frank was killed in an automobile accident.

Catherine Brieger Stern (1894–1973). Born in Breslaw, Germany, to Jewish parents, Catherine Brieger Stern earned a Ph.D. in physics and math from the University of Breslaw in 1918. Stern developed an avid interest in preschool education as she raised her own children. She developed new materials for teaching reading and math and opened Breslaw's first Montessori kindergarten. After publishing works in the educational fields of kindergarten and elementary education, Stern became too innovative for German Nazis. She immigrated to New York in 1938. Stern continued to develop challenging approaches to math and reading rather than to demand memorization. She authored influential textbooks, including *Children Discover Arithmetic: An Introduction to Structural Arithmetic* (1949). Stern's teaching methods continued to be widely used throughout the twentieth century.

Loyd S. Tireman (1896–1959). In spite of prejudice-driven opposition, Loyd S. Tireman established some of the first bilingual education programs in the United States. Tireman received his Ph.D. from the University of Iowa in 1927 and took a position with the University of New Mexico that same year. His interests revolved around the poor performance of Spanish-speaking children in public schools. In 1930 Tireman secured funding to open an experimental school, the San José Demonstration and Experimental School in Bernadillo County, New Mexico. San José became a model for teaching Hispanic students. Many educators of the 1930s believed minority students were incapable of learning to the extent white students could. Tireman's experimental school showed that the minority students could learn if given the proper curricula.

In 1938 Tireman founded the Nambé Community School. As in San José he abandoned curricula designed for white students and created curricula especially for Hispanic children. Nambé also taught adults scientific farming techniques with the help of several New Deal agencies.

Aubrey Willis Williams (1890–1965). Born into a poverty stricken family in Alabama, Aubrey Willis Williams left school at age seven to go to work. One of his earliest memories was the discriminatory treatment of the town's black residents. Williams absorbed the teachings of his religious mother and two Birmingham ministers, learning that Christian responsibility required caring for the physical as well as spiritual needs of the poor. Williams developed an attitude of outrage toward society's treatment of the very poor.

Not surprisingly, as an adult Williams entered the field of social work. In 1932 and 1933 he worked for the Reconstruction Finance Corporation (RFC), centralizing relief efforts in Texas and Mississippi. Williams' efforts caught the attention of Harry L. Hopkins who headed up the Federal Emergency Relief Administration (FERA). Hopkins appointed Williams his deputy within the FERA and the Civil Works Administration. The two shared views on relief issues and enjoyed a smooth working relationship throughout the New Deal years. In 1935 Williams became deputy director of the Works Progress Administration and executive director of the National Youth Administration (NYA). He held the post at NYA until just before it ceased operation in 1943.

Like Hopkins, Williams sought to bring about social justice and racial equality. He believed the government, with its vast resources, was the instrument to bring those at the lowest economic levels of society upward. A blunt man, he stated that educators should stop talking about the "glories" of free education which in reality did not exist for millions of children and young adults. Williams, as well as Hopkins and President Roosevelt, was not enthusiastic about an Office of Education plan to train youth in traditional school-based guidance centers. All three realized the youth unemployment problem involved up to one-third of the youth ages 16 to 24. Many had no money for shoes or lived in regions where schools were not even passably adequate. More school-based education was not a reality for these young people. So Williams, as director of NYA, developed work-study programs for poor high school and college students still in school. High school NYA students received an average $5.41 a month and college students $11.54 to $12.90. This was not much, but it was enough to keep students in school. For the youth already out of school and out of work, Williams' NYA developed paid work and training centers through local agencies. Williams sought to make his programs free of racial bias and to aid women as well as men. These objectives differed widely from the CCC, which largely operated under a segregated military system.

Williams remained in favor with President Roosevelt throughout the New Deal era, and they shared a mutual respect for each other. Williams spent the last twenty years of his life speaking out against racial discrimination in the South and against the witch hunt for Communists in the 1950s, the period of McCarthyism.

Primary Sources

"He must attend some kind of school."

The following excerpt is from a 1935 pamphlet by Kingsley Davis, entitled "Youth in the Depression," funded by the American Council on Education. First Davis describes how few students in the early 1930s made it through high school. He then relates in practical terms what the Depression was doing to youth and how it affected their schooling and job possibilities (quoted in Davis, *Youth in the Depression,* pp. 8–12):

> Every young man and young woman wants to get somewhere in the world. Except for a few who are too lazy or too discouraged, they are ambitious to become somebody. There are various ways of doing this, but most positions that are worthwhile nowadays require training. Before a boy can get a good job, he must learn something. He must attend some kind of school.
>
> Our schools act in much the same way as the sieves ... We may think of all the schools together, in all their branches, as a great sieve, or a series of sieves, by which young people are trained and sorted out for suitable positions in the business, industrial, and professional life of the nation. Many occupations, in fact, are closed to men who have not had a college training.
>
> Of course, schools are just one of the many kinds of training and grading places in which the younger generation proves its merits and qualifies for a place in social and business life ... But the schools show pretty well how the process works. Their selective action is shown partly by the number of boys and girls who drop out along the way. Out of 100 children who start in the first grade, about 50 enter high school; of the 50 who enter high school, only 10 ever graduate; of the 10, only about 3 enter college, and still fewer graduate from college.
>
> Don't make the mistake of thinking that only the "dumbbells" drop out. Many good students drop out because of ill health or poverty. Intelligent boys and girls often dislike school work. Sometimes they leave school to take a job, or so that they can get married sooner.
>
> Still, in the schools the sifting process is as work. It sorts out every year those who are ready for various kinds of employment ...
>
> But sometimes the machinery of our youth-sifting and youth-training system gets clogged. It clogs in a great crisis—a revolution, a famine, or some other disaster. It clogged badly in the Great Depression.
>
> What happens to the sifting process in a business depression?
>
> In the first place, millions of people are thrown out of work. Many who have proved their ability to do good work lose their jobs. Young people looking forward to a business position find nothing open to them. Even if they pass all the tests and examinations in the world, they will not get the places they seem to deserve.

In the second place, the public schools get so little money that they lose teachers and equipment. Parents, also suffering reduced incomes, are not able to send their children to school.

Finally, to make matters worse, business firms can't promote their men. Skilled trades can't take on new apprentices. Thus the industrial system enlists no new recruits.

So, you see, the whole machinery of sifting, or selection, breaks down. Boys and girls all over the country find nothing but a blank wall in front of them. With their parents suffering, their own futures clouded, the ordinary roads to success closed, they blindly seek a way out. In such conditions youth movements spring up. If the older people do nothing to help the young, they may take matters in their own hands and do things, often strange things, for themselves. Crimes committed by young people increase; revolution is not improbable. Anything may happen in a country where the normal selective processes become clogged.

Black Schools

Many schools in affluent white communities survived the worst years of the Depression sustaining very little negative impact. Most black schools, however, entered the 1930s underfunded. The extreme economic conditions of the Depression all but eliminated their budgets. The harsh realities of rural black education are graphically illustrated in the words of black American scholar Dopey A. Wilkerson in his book *Special Problems of Negro Education,* published in 1939 (reprinted in Bondi, *American Decades: 1930–39,* 1995, p. 151, originally from Tyack, 1984):

> The building was a crude box shack built by the Negroes out of old slabs and scrap lumber. Windows and doors were badly broken. The floor was in such condition that one had to walk carefully to keep from going through cracks and weak boards. Daylight was easily visible through walls, floors, and roof. The building was used for both church and school. Its only equipment consisted of a few rough hewn seats, an old stove brought from a junk pile, a crude homemade pulpit, a very small table, and a large water barrel ... Fifty-two children were enrolled. All these crowded into a single small room with benches for but half that number. The teacher and pupils had tacked newspapers on the walls to keep the wind out. Rain poured through the roof, and school was dismissed when it rained. No supplies, except a broom, were furnished the school by the district during the year.

Conditions in city schools were hardly better for black students. In this passage, a teacher describes an average Harlem school (quoted in Tyack, 1984, pp. 184–185):

> A typical Harlem school is like a prison, and a badly run one at that. Even the most diligent scrubbing cannot really clean a building built in the (18)70s or (18)80s ... The children...tuck their ... legs under benches too small for them in rooms unadorned, bleak and dingy. Teachers, trying to cope with classes whose numbers average slightly more than even those in other overcrowded sections, with children who have eye defects and toothaches and empty stomachs, suffer from frayed nerves and give way to harsh-voiced impatience ... Some bring with them indifference, some prejudice. Discriminatory practices are supposedly dealt with by the authorities; yet one teacher who snapped, "How dare you talk like that to a white woman?" was still teaching in the same school weeks after the incident.

Suggested Research Topics

- Evaluate the public education available to black American students between 1900 and 1939. Narrow the study to a specific geographic area or compare and contrast urban versus rural schools.
- Imagine, before you are allowed to teach, you must swear a loyalty oath that forbids you to teach certain ideas. Discuss the pros and cons of such a test. Are there any basic American principles that appear to be violated by such a test?
- Explore reasons why high school attendance increased during the 1930s Depression decade.
- Research public school funding at the beginning of the twenty-first century. How have state governments attempted to deal with inequity of funding between districts? Explore property tax funding versus funding from general state revenues.
- Study in depth the life of an influential Depression era educator of your choice. Suggestions are: Mary McLeod Bethune, Tom Dewey, Catherine Brieger Stern, Horace Mann Bond.

Bibliography

Sources

Anderson, James D. *The Education of Blacks in the South, 1860–1935.* Chapel Hill: The University of North Carolina Press, 1988.

Bondi, Victor, ed. *American Decades: 1930–39.* Detroit: Gale Research Inc., 1995.

Clark, Burton R. *The Distinctive College: Antioch, Reed & Swarthmore.* Chicago: Aldine Publishing Company, 1970.

Davis, Kingsley. *Youth in the Depression.* Chicago: The University of Chicago Press, 1935.

Dennis, Lawrence J. *George S. Counts and Charles A. Beard: Collaborators for Change.* Albany, NY: State University of New York Press, 1989.

Krug, Edward A. *The Shaping of the American High School: Vol. 2, 1920–41.* Madison, WI: The University of Wisconsin Press, 1972.

Murphy, Marjorie. *Blackboard Unions: The AFT and the NEA, 1900–80.* Ithaca, NY: Cornell University Press, 1990.

Tyack, David, Robert Lowe, and Elisabeth Hansot. *Public Schools in Hard Times: The Great Depression and Recent Years.* Cambridge, MA: Harvard University Press, 1984.

Wallace, James W. *Liberal Journalism and American Education, 1914–41.* New Brunswick, NJ: Rutgers University Press, 1991.

Further Reading

Altenbaugh, Richard J. *Education for Struggle: The American Labor Colleges of the 1920s and 1930s.* Philadelphia, PA: Temple University Press, 1990.

American Federation of Teaching, available from the World Wide Web at http://www.aft.org.

Davis, Maxine. *The Lost Generation: A Portrait of American Youth Today.* New York: The Macmillan Company, 1936.

Dennis, Lawrence J., and William E. Eaton, eds. *George S. Counts: Educator for a New Age.* Carbondale: Southern Illinois University Press, 1980.

Iversen, Robert W. *The Communists & the Schools.* New York: Harcourt, Brace and Company, 1959.

Kornbluh, Joyce L. *A New Deal for Workers' Education: The Workers' Service Program, 1933–1942.* Urbana: University of Illinois Press, 1987.

McCluskey, Audrey T., and Elaine M. Smith, eds. *Mary McLeod Bethune: Building a Better World.* Bloomington: Indiana University Press, 1999.

National Education Association, available from the World Wide Web at http://www.nea.org.

Nore, Ellen. *Charles A. Beard: An Intellectual Biography.* Carbondale: Southern Illinois University Press, 1983.

Urban, Wayne J. *Black Scholar: Horace Mann Bond, 1904–72.* Athens: University of Georgia Press, 1992.

U.S. Department of Education, available from the World Wide Web at http://www.ed.gov.

Wrigley, Julia. *Class Politics and Public Schools: Chicago, 1900–50.* New Brunswick, NJ: Rutgers University Press, 1982.

See Also

Black Americans; Civilian Conservation Corps; New Deal (First, and Its Critics); Riding the Rails; Tennessee Valley Authority; Works Progress Administration

Effects of the Great Depression —LBJ's Great Society

1963-1968

Introduction

"[W]e have the opportunity to move not only toward the rich society and the powerful society, but upward to the Great Society. The Great Society rests on abundance and liberty for all. It demands an end to poverty and injustice, to which we are totally committed in our time." President Lyndon B. Johnson (served 1963–1969) spoke these words at a college commencement ceremony on May 22, 1964, introducing the goals of his Great Society programs to the nation (quoted in Johnson, *Public Papers of the Presidents of the United States: Lyndon B. Johnson,* 1965, 1963–64, Book I, p. 704). The program would lead to landmark changes in civil rights laws and social welfare programs.

In the mid-1960s on the heels of President John F. Kennedy's (served 1961–1963) assassination, President Lyndon B. Johnson launched a massive legislative program of social reform. The nation's shock over Kennedy's death combined with an escalating civil rights movement and a growing public awareness of the poverty within the nation's own borders to provide a unique occasion for major social reform activity. In addition the nation was in a period of sustained economic growth. Money was available to fund reform programs, unlike during the economic hard times of the Great Depression. President Johnson realized he had to act quickly, anticipating the support of Congress and the public might not last long. The challenge Johnson perceived was how best to apply the nation's wealth to improve the quality of American life.

Chronology:

November 22, 1963: President John F. Kennedy is assassinated, creating a new mood in Congress and the public for major social reform.

November 27, 1963: President Lyndon Johnson, in an address to the joint session of Congress, urges the legislature to take action on Kennedy's legislative agenda, particularly a tax cut and civil rights bill.

May 22, 1964: President Lyndon B. Johnson announces plans at a University of Michigan commencement to attack poverty and social injustice as part of a Great Society program.

July 2, 1964: President Johnson signs the landmark Civil Rights Act prohibiting racial discrimination in public places.

March 6, 1965: President Johnson orders the first ground troops to Southeast Asia to defend South Vietnam from communist takeover.

April 1965: Congress passes the Elementary and Secondary Education Act, providing $1 billion in aid to improve public education.

April 1965: Following dramatic confrontations between the Alabama state police and protest marchers led by the Reverend Martin Luther King, President Johnson signs the landmark Voting Rights Act which banned certain requirements imposed on voters by states.

January 30, 1968: With over 500,000 U.S. troops in Vietnam, North Vietnamese forces launch a major offensive against South Vietnamese cities, leading to increased public opposition to the war and a drop in support of President Johnson and his programs.

March 31, 1968: President Johnson stuns the nation in a nationally televised address by stating that he would neither seek nor accept the Democratic party's renomination for the presidency.

By July 1964 several pieces of key legislation had passed, including the sweeping Civil Rights Act. Following his landslide presidential reelection victory in November 1964, President Johnson further expanded on his vision of a "Great Society." He declared "war on poverty" in a State of Union address on January 4, 1965. Johnson called for many actions, including federal support for education, expanding Social Security to the aged for medical care, and increasing voting rights protection. Through the next two years, the overwhelmingly Democratic Congress passed almost all of the proposed measures.

The Great Society was clearly created in the New Deal tradition. The uncommon nature of the first two years of Johnson's presidency reflected President Franklin D. Roosevelt's (served 1933–1945) first years. As in the 1930s, a special mix of factors came together, propelling social change much faster than the normal pace. As had Roosevelt, President Johnson played a central role in taking advantage of this opportunity. Congress responded to Johnson's lead much as it did to Roosevelt's during the first one hundred days of his presidency. A sweeping package of legislation passed, touching just about every aspect of American life and offering something for everyone.

Later, in *Lyndon Johnson and the American Dream* (1976, p. 226), author Doris Kearns Goodwin would summarize the vast diversity of what the Great Society programs had to offer:

> Medicare for the old, educational assistance for the young, tax rebates for business, a higher minimum wage for labor, subsidies for farmers, vocational training for the unskilled, food for the hungry, housing for the homeless, poverty grants for the poor, clean highways for commuters, legal protection for the blacks, improved schooling for the Indians, rehabilitation for the lame, higher benefits for the unemployed, reduced quotas (a set number of people from a specific nation or region) for the immigrants, auto safety for drivers, pensions for the retired, fair labeling for consumers, conservation for the hikers and the campers, and more and more and more.

Other major events, however, came along to prevent President Johnson from seeing many of his reforms fully take shape. Adding to the civil rights movement came the peace movement in response to the escalating Vietnam War, environmentalism, and women's liberation. Race riots swept across the nation. In reaction to these events, a white middle-class backlash erupted, destroying that fragile political environment in which Johnson was operating. Despite the major gains made in some specific programs, the Great

Society became considered by many as a lost opportunity to substantially improve the standard of living for all Americans.

Issue Summary

The Democratic Coalition, forged by President Franklin Roosevelt in the mid-1930s, remained a sufficiently strong political force to help President Lyndon Johnson shepherd social reform through Congress. The Coalition was a loose combination of diverse segments of U.S. society supporting New Deal politics and Democratic Party candidates for their own various reasons. New Deal politics meant having a strong federal government role in U.S. society through funding of public programs and oversight of various social and economic activities.

Unlike the New Deal, Great Society programs came at a time of economic affluence in the United States. From 1960 to 1965, corporate profits rose 67 percent, and take home pay of workers rose 21 percent. Very little inflation existed, and unemployment was at a low 3.9 percent in January 1966. Many believed the rapid economic growth was permanent. Great Society proponents wanted to tap into this affluence to fund the much-needed social programs to help those left behind in this economic surge.

Though President John F. Kennedy had plans to introduce social reforms as part of his New Frontier proposals, his administration was substantially sidetracked by foreign crises. In addition, conservatives of both political parties who dominated Congress largely blocked his domestic programs. Kennedy did gain approval of two programs, the Peace Corps and the Alliance for Progress. Both programs involved providing assistance to foreign nations. One, the Peace Corps, provided technical assistance through skilled volunteers, while the Alliance offered assistance through loans and other means.

In 1963 Kennedy submitted a civil rights bill to Congress designed to protect the rights of minorities seeking legal, economic, and social equality. Civil rights refer to the personal liberties promised in the Thirteenth and Fourteenth Amendments to the U.S. Constitution and in other laws. However the bill stalled.

President Kennedy's assassination in Dallas, Texas, on November 22, 1963, suddenly changed the politics of Washington, DC, at least for a period of time. The newly sworn president, Lyndon B. Johnson, was an exceptionally shrewd politician, and he fully understood that a unique opportunity to take action had arrived and might not last very long. Johnson seized the situation to break the congressional logjam. On November 27, 1963, five days after President Kennedy's assassination, Johnson addressed a joint session of Congress. While seeking to calm the nation and mark the transition to his presidency, Johnson strongly urged Congress to pass Kennedy's legislative agenda stalled in congressional committees. Johnson particularly focused on Kennedy's tax cut and civil rights measures. As Johnson stated, "No memorial oration or eulogy could more eloquently honor President Kennedy's memory than the earliest possible passage of the civil rights bill" (Johnson, 1965, 1963–64, Book I, p. 9).

Tax Cuts and Civil Rights

Congress responded quickly to Johnson's plea of November 27. The Tax Reduction Act was passed in February 1964, cutting corporate and individual taxes by over $11 billion. As intended, the tax cut further stimulated the nation's ongoing economic growth. Business investment and consumer spending both increased, leading to higher corporate profits as well as increased government tax revenues. The federal budget deficit would decrease from $6 billion in 1964 to $4 billion in 1966.

Also in February 1964, the U.S. House of Representatives passed an even stronger civil rights bill than what Kennedy had previously submitted. The bill, however, did not pass the Senate until June due to an 83-day filibuster by southerners opposed to the act. The debate was one of the longest in Senate history. On July 2, 1964, President Johnson signed the landmark Civil Rights Act into law. The act prohibited racial discrimination in places that commonly serve the general public (such as hotels, restaurants, and theaters) and prohibited racial and sexual discrimination in employment and unions. The act also gave the U.S. Justice Department authority to sue local school boards to end discriminatory practices. The Supreme Court upheld the act's constitutionality in the *Heart of Atlanta Motel v. United States* decision later that same year. The Civil Rights Act of 1964 marked the beginning of Johnson's Great Society program. It was the most important piece of legislation during the civil rights era of the 1950s and 1960s.

Later, President Johnson would declare it was not enough to legally prohibit racial discrimination; the social custom of racial segregation had to be changed as well, particularly in the South. Segregation is the practice of keeping races apart in public. Johnson introduced affirmative action, a program designed to

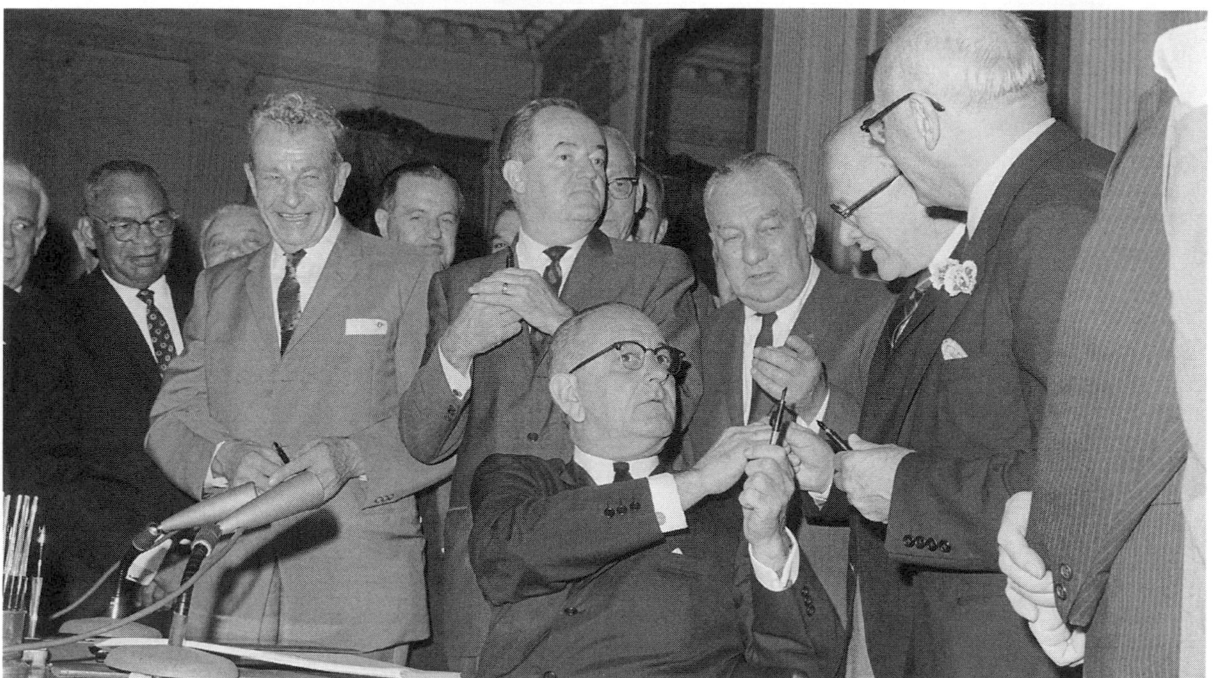

President Lyndon Johnson holds several of the pens used to sign the Civil Rights Act on July 2, 1964. The law prohibited racial discrimination in public places and was a cornerstone of Johnson's Great Society. *(Bettmann/Corbis. Reproduced by permission.)*

offer black Americans opportunities in areas where discrimination had a long history and still persisted. Affirmative action means that black Americans and other racial minorities might legally receive favored treatment in such business practices as hiring, school admissions, and job advancements. Many schools and businesses began adopting affirmative action programs of hiring and advancement. This program quickly proved effective and helped spur growth of a black middle class and largely black suburbs.

The New Deal did not tackle civil rights issues, such as racial segregation or discrimination, because Roosevelt did not want to lose the support of Southern democrats for his New Deal legislation. President Roosevelt had approached civil rights issues only as the industrial mobilization for World War II (1939–1945) was beginning, and as they pertained to hiring in the home front war-related industries. The military itself remained racially segregated.

War on Poverty

With the tax cut and civil rights bills successfully passed, Johnson turned to his more ambitious goals, including a declaration of war on poverty. Johnson firmly believed that bold government action could change the lives of millions who had no hope of attaining the American Dream, even during this time of prosperity.

Johnson had begun his congressional career in 1937 as a strong supporter of President Roosevelt and his New Deal policies. New Deal programs largely focused on public works programs. These programs used public funds to pay salaries for workers. They provided the unemployed immediate job relief as well as valuable job training. A major focus was on youth. In fact, Johnson had previously administered a New Deal youth program in Texas. Johnson borrowed directly from Roosevelt's New Deal strategies in formulating his own social reform program. Like Roosevelt in the 1930s, to spur social reform Johnson sought to centralize governmental powers more tightly under presidential control. Following the New Deal's blueprint, Johnson also looked at changing the responsibilities and authority of existing agencies to better achieve his reform goals.

Much like Roosevelt's Brain Trust that included his key advisers in 1932, President Johnson established special task force groups in 1964 to develop public policy options. Like Roosevelt's Brain Trust, the 17 task groups consisted mostly of scholars and experts. The groups worked in secrecy under the leadership of presidential aides Joseph Califano and Bill Moyers. Key issues of the mid-1960s included civil rights, poverty, urban decay, medical care for the aged, increasing pollution of the air and water, and inadequate public support for education and the arts. The key overall goals of the experts were to provide basic economic security and an improved quality of life to the public and to bring the poor into the ever-growing economy.

The experts identified a number of major behavioral problems in U.S. society they believed perpetuated poverty. To have any success in eradicating poverty, they believed these problems would have to be corrected. The problems included the rising number of broken households, escalating crime rates, high percentage of school dropouts, poor work habits, and increasing numbers of teen pregnancies. By mid-1964 the task groups had created a comprehensive legislative agenda to tackle these problems.

Unlike the public outcry for government action in the early 1930s, little grassroots support initially existed for President Johnson's antipoverty agenda. Consequently, the resulting legislative agenda developed by the task groups represented to many an elitist approach orchestrated by national leaders in power. The agenda lacked input from those who would be most affected by the programs, such as the poor and elderly. Like the New Deal, the proposed solutions would greatly expand government into a new bureaucracy unfamiliar to many. Soon programs would try a more community-based action approach to improve effectiveness.

Owing in large part to President Johnson's ability, with the Coalition's support, to guide legislation through Congress, the programs soon began to take shape. The main war on poverty measure, posing a strong resemblance to New Deal programs, was the Economic Opportunity Act (EOA) passed in August 1964. Johnson's war on poverty started with $1 billion dollars in federal funds in 1964 and an additional $2 billion through the next two years. The act created youth programs, small business loans, job training, and other antipoverty measures. Among the programs established was the Job Corps, modeled after the Civilian Conservation Corps (CCC). The program would teach young men new skills. Work training and work-study programs included the Volunteers in Service to America (VISTA). VISTA was basically a domestic peace corps through which middle-class youth were sent out to help poor neighborhoods. The act also created Project Head Start, an educational program for underprivileged preschoolers.

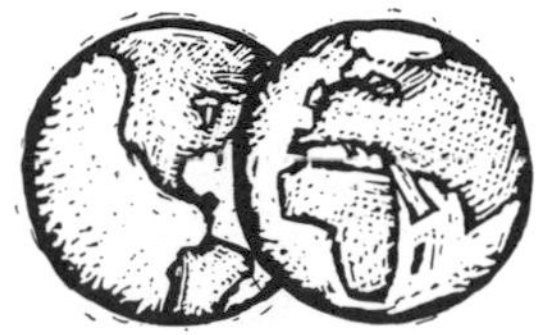

More About...

Civil Rights Act of 1964

The landmark act was designed to end discrimination based on race, color, religion, or national origin. The act is divided into separate sections called titles. Title I removed certain voter registration requirements. Title II prohibited racial segregation or discrimination in public places, such as hotels, restaurants, and theaters. Title III required desegregation of public facilities with the exception of public schools and colleges. Title IV required desegregation of public schools and colleges. Title V expanded the responsibilities of the Civil Rights Commission, and Title VI assured that federal assistance programs could not discriminate in the way they provide benefits. Title VII prohibited racial and sexual discrimination in schools, unions, and businesses involved in interstate commerce or contracting with the federal government. The title also created the Equal Employment Opportunity Commission (EEOC) to enforce provisions of the act.

The EOA established the Office of Economic Opportunity (OEO), charged with running the various antipoverty programs. Though located in the Office of President, the OEO introduced the idea of "community action." Through this approach communities had a greater role in determining how the programs were carried out. For example, the poor would be able to participate in establishing public works programs.

Johnson Gains a Mandate

Barry Goldwater of Arizona, one of the eight senators who had voted against the 1964 Civil Rights Act, was nominated as the Republican Party presidential candidate to oppose President Johnson in the November presidential elections. Goldwater provided a strong contrast to Johnson. Goldwater asserted that government had no business promoting social and economic change in such areas as racial discrimination and economic opportunity. He campaigned to make Social Security voluntary and to abolish the Tennessee Valley Authority. The election went in a landslide to Johnson. Johnson gained 61 percent of the popular vote, the most since President Franklin Roosevelt in 1936.

Young Congressman Lyndon B. Johnson shakes the hand of President Franklin D. Roosevelt. Johnson's Great Society programs were created in the tradition of Roosevelt's New Deal. *(©Hulton-Deutsch Collection/Corbis. Reproduced by permission.)*

Johnson received 90 percent of the electoral vote. Goldwater did gain impressive victories in the southern states, however, indicating a growing weakness in the Democratic Coalition. Nevertheless, for the time being Johnson was free to pursue his Great Society goals.

The first piece of Great Society legislation passed by the 89th Congress was the Appalachian Regional Development Act of 1965, designed to raise living standards in 12 states located in the Appalachian region of the eastern United States. The act provided financial aid for highways, health centers, and resource development. Unlike the later focus of Great Society programs on black inner city ghettos, this bill addressed poverty in white rural America.

Voting Rights

In the early 1960s, very few black Americans could vote in the South. They were commonly denied the right to vote by having to pass literacy tests, pay poll taxes, or being faced with physical threats. As with civil rights, voting rights issues were not addressed by the New Dealers in the 1930s. In 1964 the Twenty-Fourth Amendment to the U.S. Constitution was ratified, abolishing the poll tax in federal elections, but other impediments remained.

Public protests and voter registration drives designed to overcome these restrictions met with intense opposition from whites and local authorities. On March 7, 1965, Dr. Martin Luther King launched an all-out drive for black voter registration by leading a protest march from Selma to Montgomery, Alabama. In response Governor George C. Wallace sent the state police to intervene. The nation watched the resulting news films with alarm, as police brutally whipped unarmed marchers with clubs. President Johnson ordered U.S. troops to Alabama to end the violence.

Johnson also had the Justice Department draft a voting rights bill that he would present in a speech to a joint session of Congress on prime time television. The speech was epic and established Johnson as the nation's moral leader. Five months later Congress passed the Voting Rights Act. Designed to ensure voting rights for black Americans, the act outlawed state laws that imposed certain voting restrictions, such as literacy tests. The act specifically stated that a person's right to vote could not be denied on the basis of race, color, or membership in a language minority group. The act also gave federal officials authority to oversee, and in some cases supervise, voter registration.

The Voting Rights Act was very effective in bringing the voting right to thousands of southern blacks. The act had other effects as well. Persons running for public office had to tone down their white supremacy perspectives. White supremacy refers to the belief that white people have a natural superiority over blacks and must keep blacks socially and economically suppressed. Also, a significant increase in elected black officials resulted in areas previously controlled by whites.

The 1965 act actually targeted only seven southern states—Alabama, Georgia, Louisiana, Mississippi, North Carolina, South Carolina, and Virginia. In 1982 the act was extended to all states. Importantly, the act ended the long-held legal tradition allowing states to handle all matters related to voting and elections.

Education and the Arts

A former educator himself, President Johnson believed education was the key to ending poverty. Johnson expressed desires to be remembered in history as "the education president." The New Deal education programs had primarily focused on vocational training and programs for preschool children. Job training came through various New Deal programs, including the Tennessee Valley Authority (TVA), the Civilian Conservation Corps (CCC), the Works Progress Administration (WPA), and the National Youth Administration (NYA). Johnson had administered NYA programs in Texas. However the New Deal had not brought federal assistance to public schools.

A key Great Society program was designed to provide significant federal aid to public education. The Elementary and Secondary Education Act of 1965 offered funding assistance to public school districts. Johnson signed the act on April 11, 1965, at the one-room schoolhouse near Stonewall, Texas, where he had begun his education. His first teacher, Mrs. Kathryn Deadrich Loney, sat at his side, and former classmates attended as well. Among other things, the federal aid helped schools purchase textbooks and library materials. Funds were divided among the states based on the number of impoverished children in each state. This act was the first major federal aid package for education in U.S. history.

Other education bills followed as Congress also passed the Higher Education Act of 1965. The act provided federally funded scholarships and low-interest loans to needy college students. Later in 1967 Congress passed the Public Broadcasting Act creating the Corporation for Public Broadcasting and providing financial aid for educational television and radio.

In addition to education, President Johnson also sought other ways to elevate the quality of life and provide balance to the major technological advancements of the post-World War II period. While may New Deal programs, mainly in the WPA, focused on the arts, Johnson also sought to greatly increase public support for the arts. Whereas the New Deal assisted the arts through public works programs, Johnson would offer grants to applicants. Congress passed the National Foundation on the Arts and the Humanities Act in 1965. The act established various funding programs, including the National Endowment for the Arts (NEA). The NEA provides financial assistance to painters, actors, musicians, and others involved in the arts. Most of the grants go to institutions such as museums, theaters, and symphony orchestras. Some go to individual artists.

Housing

Adequate housing was a key concern of Johnson's antipoverty program. The New Deal first brought the federal government into housing issues through various programs. For example, the House Act of 1937 was the first federal housing legislation

Biography:

Lyndon Baines Johnson

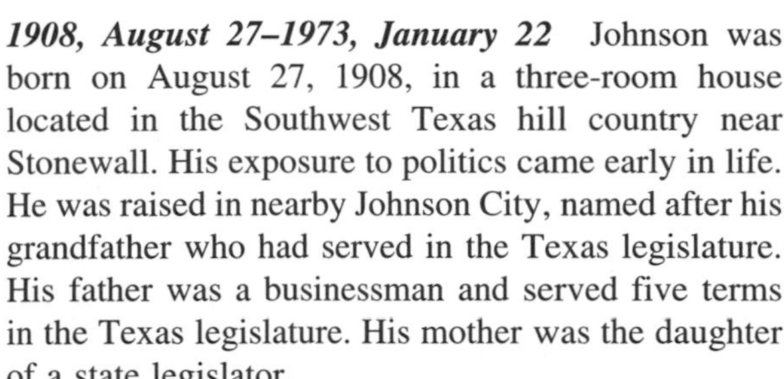

1908, August 27–1973, January 22 Johnson was born on August 27, 1908, in a three-room house located in the Southwest Texas hill country near Stonewall. His exposure to politics came early in life. He was raised in nearby Johnson City, named after his grandfather who had served in the Texas legislature. His father was a businessman and served five terms in the Texas legislature. His mother was the daughter of a state legislator.

Johnson attended Southwest Texas State Teachers College in San Marcos, Texas, in the late 1920s. While pursuing his teaching degree, he took a year off from college to earn money teaching at a predominantly Mexican American school in Cotulla, Texas. The extreme poverty there made a lasting impression on Johnson. As a result he maintained a closeness to the Mexican American community throughout his political career.

New Deal politics dominated Johnson's early formative years in Texas. In 1935 President Franklin Roosevelt appointed Johnson to be director of the Texas division of the National Youth Administration (NYA). For the next two years he helped put twelve thousand youth to work in public service jobs and helped another eighteen thousand go to college. He made a special effort to see that NYA programs reached black youth in the state.

Johnson ran successfully for a seat in the U.S. House of Representatives in 1938 as a supporter of Roosevelt's New Deal policies. Roosevelt quickly formed a strong interest in Johnson and helped him obtain key committee assignments and gain important water and electrification projects for his voting district in Texas. His 12-year stint as congressman was interrupted in 1941 when he became the first member of Congress to serve in active duty in World War II. Johnson won a Silver Star in combat.

In 1948 Johnson ran for a seat in the U.S. Senate and won a bitterly fought campaign marked by voter fraud on both sides. He was in the Senate for 12 years, becoming the youngest majority leader in the Senate's history in 1955 at age 46. During his tour as senator, Johnson exhibited talent in negotiating and bringing diverse political groups together in support of legislation. He was often ruthless, but his efforts actually pulled the Democratic Party together into a more effective organization. People referred to his maneuvering abilities in persuading senators to support his bills as "the Johnson treatment."

After losing a bid to become the presidential candidate for the Democratic Party in 1960, he stunned many by accepting John F. Kennedy's offer to be his vice-presidential running mate. Serving as vice-president from 1961 to 1963, Johnson was chairman of several important committees, including the Peace Corps Advisory Council and the President's Committee on Equal Employment Opportunity. Suddenly, Johnson's governing responsibilities dramatically changed. At 2:39 PM on November 22, 1963, following Kennedy's assassination, Lyndon Johnson was sworn in as president in Dallas, Texas, aboard the presidential plane.

The next year Johnson ran his own campaign for presidency and won handily over Republican Barry Goldwater, with an electoral college victory of 486 to 52. This margin was second only to Franklin Roosevelt's in the twentieth century at that time. With a strong Democratic majority in both houses of Congress, Johnson moved swiftly on his Great Society legislative agenda.

By 1968 the country had become torn with racial strife and antiwar protests. Military victory in Vietnam did not result from the escalation of U.S. involvement, despite such predictions from military leaders. Having lost significant public support for his programs. Johnson shocked the nation by choosing not to run again for president in 1968. Upon leaving the presidency in January 1969, Johnson retired to his ranch near Johnson City, Texas. He suffered a fatal heart attack on January 22, 1973. During his time in the White House, Lyndon Johnson had done more to expand the power and reach of the federal government than any other president since Franklin Roosevelt.

---

in U.S. history to recognize housing as a social need and use public funds to build housing for the poor. Most New Deal housing programs earlier in the 1930s had focused more on white, middle-class housing issues such as being able to make house payments during the Depression.

The Housing and Urban Development Act of 1965, following in the same spirit as the 1937 act, made available money for low-income housing in the form of rent supplements for the poor. Also in 1965 the Department of Housing and Urban Development (HUD) was formed to administer the federal housing programs. Creation of a full department raised the importance of the issue to a cabinet-level position, a position from which the president could be advised directly. The following year Congress passed the Demonstration Cities and Metropolitan Area Redevelopment Act. The act established a program to select "model cities" to rebuild slum areas, provide mass transit, and make other improvements.

Later, during Johnson's last full year as president, Congress passed the Civil Rights Act of 1968. The act was designed to end racial discrimination in the rental and sale of houses and apartments. Congress also provided over $5 million in federal funds to help the poor buy houses and rent apartments. Money was provided to build 240,000 low-rent public housing units and also to help moderate-income families afford better private housing.

Immigration

Not only did black Americans benefit from Great Society programs, but those wishing to immigrate to the United States did as well. The Immigration Act of 1924 and National Origins Act of 1929 had established strict limits on immigration of people based on what nation they were coming from. The restrictions were particularly tight for nations other than those in Western Europe.

Johnson's Great Society program greatly changed these immigration policies. The Immigration Act of 1965 replaced the national origins system of the 1920s and instituted less complicated restrictions based on the two global hemispheres of East and West. Significantly the act opened the door to non-European immigration. Major increases in Asian Americans resulted through the next thirty years.

Environmentalism

President Roosevelt had expressed a great deal of concern over environmental issues through his New Deal programs. In the 1930s environmentalism was commonly considered more as conservation of natural resources. The New Deal's Social Conservation Service taught farmers how to conserve soils. The Civilian Conservation Corps employed youth to replant forests, fight wildfires, and make range improvements to protect public grazing lands in the West. The 1960s brought a new perspective on environmentalism.

A public groundswell grew following publication of Rachel Carson's *Silent Spring* in 1962 to clean up and protect the nation's rivers. In 1965 Congress passed the Water Quality Act requiring states to clean up their rivers. In signing the bill, President Johnson declared "Today we begin to be masters of our environment." The act also gave the federal government authority to search out the worst polluters. Johnson proclaimed, "There is no excuse—and we should call a spade a spade—for chemical companies and oil refineries using major rivers as pipelines for toxic wastes. There is no excuse for communities to use other people's rivers as a dump for their raw sewage" (Johnson, 1966, 1965, Book I, pp. 1034–1035). Also passed in 1965 was the Wilderness Preservation Act which set aside over nine million acres of national forest lands for management as wilderness.

Air quality also became a target. Congress passed the Clean Air Act Amendment in 1965 directing the federal government to establish emission standards for new vehicles. In 1967 Congress went further by passing the Air Quality Act. The act set overall air pollution guidelines and increased the federal government's power to enforce air quality standards. Through the Great Society the environmental movement in the United States was born.

Consumer Protection

One of the last New Deal measures passed by Congress in the 1930s was the Food, Drug, and Cosmetic Act of 1938. The act greatly expanded consumer protection by giving broad powers to the Food and Drug Administration (FDA). The FDA could establish standards for the quality of food and drug products.

Increasing consumer protection concerns gave rise to several acts in 1966 and creation of a new major federal department. In a major breakthrough for consumers, Congress, building on the Federal Drug Act of the New Deal, passed the Truth in Packaging Act. The act set standards for the labeling of consumer products.

Congress also passed the National Traffic Motor Vehicle Act setting federal safety standards for automobiles and tires, and the Highway Safety Act requiring states to establish highway safety programs. Vehicles were now required to have headrests, padded dashboards, seat belts for all passengers, and other safety features. Additionally, Congress passed an act that President Johnson signed on October 15, 1966, creating the new cabinet-level executive department to oversee the various transportation programs affecting air, railroads, and highways.

Among other issues, opposition to the Vietnam War (1964–1975) eventually lead to the fracturing of President Lyndon B. Johnson's Great Society. (AP/Wide World Photos. Reproduced by permission.)

Adding to the earlier consumer protection bills and expanding FDA responsibilities, Congress passed the Wholesome Meat Act in 1967 and the Wholesome Poultry Products Act of 1968. A 1960 congressional investigation had earlier revealed that 25 percent of all commercially prepared meat products were not subject to inspection because they were not involved in interstate commerce. In response, Congress passed the meat act, which extended inspection requirements under the Federal Meat Inspection Act of 1906 to apply uniformly to all meat products shipped within the United States and to foreign countries. The 1967 act allowed states to operate their own inspection programs with substantial funding support by the federal government. The 1968 Poultry Act was modeled after the Wholesome Meat Act.

Ralph Nader, who formed a group of lawyers known as "Nader's Raiders," influenced other consumer protection laws. These included the Child Protection Act of 1966 banning dangerous toys, and the Flammable Fabrics Act of 1967 that included changes in children's clothing.

Great Society's Achievements

By the time the 89th Congress adjourned in October 1966, President Johnson had promoted two hundred pieces of legislation. Congress passed 181 of them. These bills addressed just about every social issue possible. Johnson saw this legislative package as building on the New Deal and perhaps even completing it. Like the New Deal, the Great Society posed a major change in the U.S. by further interjecting government into the everyday lives of citizens. The United States had joined the other industrial welfare states of Western Europe and Scandinavia in the public services provided its citizens.

The list of accomplishments by President Johnson and Congress was very impressive. Created were HUD, the Department of Transportation, the National Endowment for the Humanities and the Arts, the Corporation for Public Broadcasting, air and water standards, a Model Cities program for urban redevelopment, Upward Bound to assist needy high school students going into college, legal services for the poor, the food stamps program, and Project Head Start. Food stamps had first been introduced in 1939 but dropped during World War II. With a partial revival in 1961, Congress passed the Food Stamp Act in 1964 making the program a permanent fixture in assistance to the needy.

Opposition to the Great Society Grows

Public and political support for new Great Society initiatives soon came to an end in the late 1960s. The increasingly radical and violent civil rights movement,

More About...

The Welfare State

Welfare state is a governmental concept in which the state assumes a key role in protecting and promoting the economic and social well-being of its citizens. Welfare goals commonly include equality of opportunity, a fair and equitable distribution of wealth among citizens, and a responsibility of government to provide its residents with the minimal needs for a decent life.

A key feature of the welfare state is social insurance. The need for social insurance rose in industrialized states when the elderly or disabled found themselves unable to provide for themselves. Social insurance is designed to protect citizens from economic risks in life. Germany enacted the earliest social welfare laws in the 1880s. Through time, as other nations joined in establishing welfare programs, more types of risks were addressed. Important factors to be considered in establishing welfare programs are the types of risks to be covered, criteria for eligibility, levels of benefits, how the programs are administered, and how to finance the program. Debate over welfare state programs often focuses on balancing the desire to meet peoples' needs while still providing sufficient incentive to perform productive work.

In the United States, social insurance comes in the form of old age, survivors, health, and disability insurance. Mandatory contributions by workers and employers fund such programs. Other social programs focus on education, housing, and health services. Western European nations provide a much broader range of social services than the United States, particularly regarding healthcare coverage. The Netherlands, for example, offers social services affecting a person's life from birth to death. Antipoverty programs can also be part of a welfare state. The New Deal programs of President Franklin Roosevelt in the 1930s were based on welfare state concepts. President Lyndon Johnson's Great Society greatly expanded on these concepts.

---

together with a raging controversy over the Vietnam War (1964–1975) led to a fracturing of the coalition's diverse elements as it finally gave out in the 1960s.

Even while the Great Society's legislative agenda was still forming in 1964, signs of future political problems were appearing. During the 1964 presidential primaries, Alabama Democratic governor George Wallace attracted between 30 percent and 45 percent of the vote in strongly blue-collar areas of the North and Midwest. This strong showing revealed a basic weakness in the Democratic Coalition. In addition, a southern white backlash was growing against federal efforts spurred by Democratic Party leader Johnson to end long held segregationist attitudes and policies of the South. While embracing white supremacy views, however, Wallace still promoted a New Deal-like economic liberalism. For example Wallace promoted increases in Social Security, expansion of health care insurance, labors' right to collective bargaining, and better housing.

As the 1960s progressed, both the Vietnam War and liberal radicalism grew. Conflict within the Democratic Party between liberal factions and the socially conservative Wallace supporters escalated. During 1965 and 1966, the Great Society programs became increasingly intertwined with black American issues. Whites felt threatened by affirmative action policies and charged "reverse discrimination" by the government, schools, and employers. Many claimed the Great Society policies gave special privileges to blacks and exempted them from job and educational competition that whites must endure. It was long forgotten how black Americans lost jobs to unemployed whites in the Great Depression.

Whites also did not see the government programs teaching the values of self-reliance and the Protestant work ethic. As a result, the white backlash against Great Society ideals was even more apparent in the congressional elections of 1966.

Economic issues joined race as the basis for opposition to Great Society programs. Opposition came from the increasingly financially squeezed middle class. Spiraling taxes to pay for the Great Society's welfare programs drained monies from the working and middle classes.

Meanwhile, as the white backlash to Great Society programs grew, black Americans became increasingly frustrated over issues of poverty, joblessness, and inequality. The quality of life for those living in the inner-city slums was not showing any immediate

Support for the nonviolent approach to civil rights protest waned as activists were continually met with violence by police. Many activists turned to the "black power" movement for an answer. (AP/Wide World Photos. Reproduced by permission.)

improvement due to the government's actions. As throughout the twentieth century, inner-city residents still suffered from malnourishment, unemployment, decaying school buildings, and lack of sufficient medical care. It was becoming obvious that the needs of the black community exceeded what the government could provide.

Rise of Black Power

Tiring of Martin Luther King's nonviolent tactics, the black movement took on an increasingly violent nature. Groups such as the Student Nonviolent Coordinating Committee (SNCC), which previously supported King's nonviolent approach to the fight for civil rights, grew increasingly frustrated with the violence being perpetrated against civil rights activists. Stokely Carmichael, chairman of the SNCC from 1966 to 1968, was instrumental in shifting the focus from King's style of nonviolent civil rights activism to the more aggressive "black power" movement. Black nationalism spread through the northern ghettos. Rather than seeking integration into white society, the new black leaders called for separate self-sufficiency of black communities.

In Los Angeles the Watts riot in August 1965 presented a major turning point in the white perception of the black movement. The steadily increasing public support black issues had received through the early 1960s which led to the establishment of Great Society programs dramatically declined following the riot. Whites began increasingly viewing black ghettos as places lacking civility. The ghettos were seen as harboring drug addiction, high street crime, sexual irresponsibility and illegitimate births, and increased percentages of female-led households. In the next few years, the Watts riot was followed by riots in Cleveland, Ohio (1966), Newark, New Jersey (1967), Detroit, Michigan (1967), and Washington, DC (1968).

Various prominent black organizations began to appear. The Black Panther Party was founded in 1966, promoting revolution to combat violent police activities. Stokely Carmichael and others who distrusted white leaders behind the Great Society programs led the Student Nonviolent Coordinating Committee (SNCC). They called for "black power" by encouraging blacks to gain economic and political control of their communities. Fearing an approaching "race war," President Johnson established the National Advisory Commission on Civil Disorders to study the situation. The panel concluded that U.S. society was indeed close to breaking in two.

Great Society Becomes a Threat

By the late 1960s, racial integration was viewed with alarm by white communities. White residents feared inner-city crime would be transported out of the ghettos to the suburbs. The Republican Party seized on the increasing fears of white America by adopting a strong "law and order" theme. As a result, in 1966 conservative Hollywood actor Ronald Reagan, a Democrat turned Republican, swept into victory for governor of California, defeating the previously popular incumbent Democratic governor Pat Brown.

Given these growing stresses in the general population, the Democratic Party showed greater signs of unraveling. Middle-income Democrats felt threatened and forgotten by the Democratic Party. Liberal Democrats were considered their adversaries. Liberalism, they believed, posed a threat to their communities, their sense of fairness, their livelihoods, their children and safety, and their basic values.

The Presidential Election of 1968

With race riots and antiwar protests filling the streets and casualties mounting in Vietnam, public support for President Johnson and his programs was

National Guardsmen try to restore order during a riot in Detroit, Michigan in 1967. Race riots erupted in a handful of American cities as many black Americans felt their needs were not being met by Johnson's Great Society. (©Bettman/Corbis. Reproduced by permission.)

plummeting. Johnson, in a national address in May 1968, stunned the country by announcing he would not run for reelection. His announcement was soon followed by the assassination of presidential candidate Robert Kennedy in June in Los Angeles.

Based on his success in the 1964 presidential primaries, George Wallace decided to leave the Democratic Party and form the American Independent Party, running for independently for president. The race riots following Martin Luther King's assassination in April 1968 made George Wallace's presidential candidacy platform focusing on law and order even more attractive to a frightened white population.

Amid the turmoil within the party, a classic New Deal Democrat, Hubert Humphrey, who had been Johnson's vice-president, received the party's nomination. The Democratic Party convention in Chicago was held under siege as police rioted with antiwar demonstrators in the streets around the convention. During the convention changes within the party were beginning to take shape, with women, blacks, and youth gaining greater influence, and the influence of whites, labor unions, and traditional big city party leaders declining. The old Roosevelt Coalition was disappearing.

The November elections marked the end of the Great Society social reform period. Taking advantage of Democratic turmoil, the Republicans, seeking to broaden their popular appeal, offered a conservatism tailored to the middle class. They particularly aimed at the South and Midwest. It was in the 1968 elections that this new conservative movement came to the forefront. Wallace ran strongly in racially divided cities such as Cleveland, Ohio, and Gary, Indiana. Almost 10 million Democratic voters voted for Wallace. The white segment of the Democratic Party had become split as the working and lower-middle classes shifted toward Republican conservatism.

Humphrey won only 30 percent of the vote in the South. Wallace and Nixon split the rest. Johnson's political demise, Robert Kennedy's death, and Humphrey's election defeat essentially spelled the end for Democratic control of the White House for much of the 1970s and 1980s.

From 1968 through 1988, the Democrats won only one presidential election. In 1976 Jimmy Carter, who opposed New Deal type of programs and ran against a Republican Party severely wounded by the Watergate scandal, was elected. Traditional Democratic constituencies that were part of the Democratic

Coalition, including southerners, ethnic Catholics of the North and Midwest, blue-collar workers, and union members, became part of the new Republican conservatism. A politically conservative middle America had emerged, and dreams of further progress on Great Society programs had dwindled. Later, author James Sundquist summed up the factors leading to the backlash aimed at Great Society programs and New Deal politics in *Dynamics of the Party System: Alignment and Realignment of Political Parties in the United States.* (1983, p. 383):

> In the public's perception, al these things merged. Ghetto riots, campus riots, strcct crime, anti-Vietnam marches, poor people's marches, drugs, pornography, welfarism, rising taxes, all had a common thread: the breakdown of family and social discipline, of order, of concepts of duty, of respect for law, of public and private morality.

Contributing Forces

Birth of New Deal Politics

The New Deal programs and policies born in the 1930s marked a major change in American society. Government dramatically expanded into various realms of everyday life. Social reform programs primarily sought to help the working poor through economically tough times. The New Deal did not attempt to change society in a fundamental way, such as redistributing wealth. Also, no programs were specifically aimed at black Americans or any other minority groups. The New Deal's goals were short- and medium-term economic recovery and long-term reform, with social insurance a key part of the long-term focus. The New Deal, however different in specific goals from Johnson's Great Society, helped establish the precedent of using the government for the improvement and benefit of society that was necessary in the creation and implementation of many of the agencies and programs proposed in the Great Society.

The Warren Court

The substantial social activism coming from the legislative and executive branches of federal government in the 1960s was fueled in part by the judicial activism displayed by the U.S. Supreme Court beginning in the mid-1950s. Through new interpretations of the U.S. Constitution, including equal protection of the law, freedom of expression, rights of the accused, and representation in government, the Court, led by Chief Justice Earl Warren, had a profound effect on U.S. society.

Beginning with the landmark 1954 U.S. Supreme Court decision in *Brown v. Board of Education* ruling that school segregation was unconstitutional, numerous other critical Supreme Court decisions followed through the 1960s. Not only were existing rights strengthened, but a new right of privacy was established.

Key decisions also affected criminal justice procedures, such as prohibiting the use of illegally obtained evidence in trials and the creation of what became known as the Miranda rights protecting the accused from self-incrimination. The Warren Court, so-called after its chief justice, strove for social justice and the protection of individual rights from governmental powers. The Warren Court decisions first fueled and then supported Great Society measures. Together the Warren Court and the Great Society brought major social change and greatly increased public awareness of social problems in the nation.

The Persistent Democratic Coalition

A major political outgrowth of the New Deal in the mid-1930s was the creation of the Democratic Coalition. The Coalition was a fragile political union of liberals, members of the working class, southerners, and black Americans. President Roosevelt's decision not to press for prohibitions against segregation kept the southern support behind his New Deal policies, and black Americans needed the New Deal programs.

Following World War II into the 1960s, a number of New Deal programs remained largely intact. The general public remained fairly satisfied with the benefits they were receiving. Despite the continued white supremacy thrust of the South, southern whites still largely remained loyal Democrats, as they had been since the Civil War (1861–1865). Concerns by southerners over "creeping socialism" and subversion of traditional American values by northern Democrats persisted, but at a low level. Lower- and working-class Americans still supported government welfare measures and maintained an allegiance to the Democratic Party.

Many in the nation interpreted the victory of Harry Truman in the 1948 presidential elections as confirmation of the continuing overall support for New Deal social policies. This conclusion, however, was contradicted by some indications of the Democratic Coalition weakening, such as the withdrawal of southern Democrats—who became known as Dixiecrats and who were led by Strom Thurmond—from the party over civil rights issues in the 1948 election.

Other indications of a weakening Coalition arose. During the 1950s a growing segment of upper-middle-class business and professional workers began joining the Republican ranks. In addition, sweeping Supreme

Court civil rights decisions from the Warren Court, and more aggressive efforts by the federal government to combat white supremacy in the South energized a broader-scale resistance movement among southern whites. Nevertheless, the Democratic Coalition made it through the 1950s largely intact, as the Democratic Party candidate, John F. Kennedy (served 1961–1963), was able to narrowly defeat Republican candidate Richard Nixon (served 1969–1974) in 1960.

Perspectives

Supporters and Critics of the Great Society

Despite the unusually rapid pace of major bills introduced and passed by Congress between 1964 and 1967, social change in the 1960s was progressing even more quickly. These changes in U.S. society came faster than government reform efforts could keep up. This made government, despite all of the activity, seem unresponsive. Political radicalism and cynicism consequently grew even before the Great Society programs had fully begun to take effect. Given this response, Johnson increasingly steered the Great Society programs more to appeal to the middle class. As in the 1930s, radicals on the Left demanded more basic change in the nation's political, social, and economic institutions. Groups such as the Students for a Democratic Society (SDS) and SNCC sought to redistribute wealth as well as political power. They believed the Great Society was only addressing the symptoms of the social problems, not going after the causes.

Many of those in the middle, the centrists, believed that government had the capability to solve the complex social problems. President Johnson, for instance, believed that basic institutions of the United States were sound, they just needed some technical adjustments. Once the corrections were made, more people would have greater economic opportunities.

Critics to the Right called Johnson's Great Society programs, such as Economic Opportunity, "warmed-over" New Deal policies. In contrast to demands for more government, conservatives promoted free-market strategies. They opposed government intrusion into "natural" business processes. They argued that Great Society programs actually hindered opportunity, not enhanced it, by inhibiting the nation's economic growth through greater regulation and taxes.

One reason for the lack of substantial grassroots support for social reform in the 1960s was that the public was split over whether poverty was the fault of the individual or if the individual was a victim of society. For those who thought the individual was at a fault, they believed it was up to that person to help him or herself by improving his or her own life. In the 1930s protests and riots were limited because many individuals believed they were at fault for their problems.

Stemming from ideas planted in the minds of many Americans in the 1930s, others considered poverty to be a social problem, not an economic one. The New Dealers of President Roosevelt's administration believed the economic crisis of the Great Depression was not a result of the shortcomings of individual workers, but rather a result of a national economic system driven by the greed of major business leaders. For example, as profits had greatly increased in the 1920s before the crash of the stock market, wages of workers had increased much less. In addition, unemployment of the 1930s was a result at least partly of corruption in the trading of stocks on Wall Street. Therefore, they believed national economic problems

Major Writings

Influential Books of the Period

A number of books were published in the early 1960s that greatly increased public awareness of social problems within the United States and influenced Great Society programs. One influential book, published in 1960 titled *Delinquency and Opportunity* by Richard Cloward and Lloyd Ohlin, stressed that social forces created teen delinquency. Therefore, the problem of delinquency could be tackled through carefully designed social reform.

A 1962 book titled *The Other America* by Michael Harrington described the appalling poverty within the nation's borders. Another 1962 book, Rachel Carson's *Silent Spring,* substantially raised environmental concerns by focusing on the effects of pesticides on the environment. A young lawyer, Ralph Nader, wrote *Unsafe at Any Speed* (1965) which was very critical of the U.S. automobile industry regarding safety issues. All of these and many others greatly influenced public opinion as well as the direction of Great Society programs.

were a result of the social environment that shaped an individual's life from youth. Social reformers in the 1960s believed that if a person could acquire the necessary education and skills, then poverty would end. Though conservatives staunchly believed that only economic growth could cure the poverty and other social problems, poverty persisted during the years of substantial economic growth.

Additionally, though most poor Americans were white, almost all black were poor. Consequently, many saw poverty more as a racial issue. The Council of Economic Advisors in 1964 reported that 20 percent of Americans were poor. Of those, 78 percent were white, and 50 percent were elderly. Forty percent lived on family farms. Still, Great Society programs tended to focus on the urban black population.

Some claimed the Great Society a success because it produced substantial gains in civil rights, reduced the poverty level of many Americans, helped underprivileged children get a head start in school, and increased public awareness of pressing social issues. Critics claimed it led to creation of big government, interfered in the free enterprise system, and further trapped people in a cycle of poverty. Big government brought with it numerous regulations, increased waste and fraud, and a quickly rising annual federal budget.

A Vulnerable Coalition

In the 1930s some critics of Roosevelt saw him as a political opportunist who shaped his New Deal policies based on how it would benefit him politically rather than on what the public most needed. Similarly, some saw President Johnson's Great Society programs as a political strategy to keep the Democratic Coalition together.

The 1964 presidential election demonstrated that the Coalition was vulnerable, as a large number of southern white voters swung toward the Republicans. Although Johnson defeated his Republican opponent Barry Goldwater handily, Goldwater received many southern Democratic votes, highlighting a future weakness in the Coalition. Nonetheless, nationally Johnson's election was the largest percentage of victory ever in a presidential election, as he won 61.3 percent of the popular vote and all but six states: Arizona (Goldwater's home state), Alabama, Louisiana, Mississippi, Georgia, and South Carolina. In addition to winning the White House in a landslide, the Democrats also gained a strong hold on both houses of Congress. In the Senate, Democrats ruled 68 to 32 seats, and in the House 295 to 140.

During the political campaign, conservatives had called for economic growth policies of cutting both taxes and government spending, of reducing the power of labor, and making local governments responsible for aid to the needy. The 1964 election results clearly rejected these ideas, however, and created a liberal majority in Congress for the first time since the New Deal era of the early 1930s.

Democratic supporters sought a renewal of New Deal social activism within the postwar economic boom. The civil rights struggle of the 1950s and early 1960s had led to the rebirth of this liberal idealism. Because the Great Society was to be built in a period of prosperity rather than depression, like the New Deal, President Johnson believed the Great Society could reach beyond what the New Deal was able to achieve. With the commanding majority, the Democrats were able to alter House rules, making it easier to pass bills.

America Under Siege

As the Great Society programs were taking shape, the nation was increasingly experiencing both physical rebellion and intellectual protests. While nurturing the Great Society programs, Johnson sought to keep them distinct from all the other issues swirling around the nation. This was particularly true of the growing Vietnam War and its associated rising tide of anti-Americanism. Other demands for reform came from the counterculture and women's movement. Beginning in the mid-1960s, American traditional values were increasingly being challenged from many directions.

President Johnson's Great Society was caught in a collision between his own social reform activism coming out of Washington, DC, and the rapidly emerging grassroots activism across the nation. In addition, the Civil Rights Act not only was a landmark in outlawing fundamental discriminating practices in society, but it also spawned an increased white backlash against governmental integration policies. Candidates for public office opposing racial integration became more vocal, and racial violence grew.

Impact

New Deal and Great Society

The Great Society program was the most important expansion of the federal government since the New Deal. The numerous social and economic initiatives came largely between 1964 and 1967, greatly expanding federally funded social programs. Like the New Deal, the Great Society was amazingly vibrant during the early years of its existence. Also like the

More About...

The Vietnam War

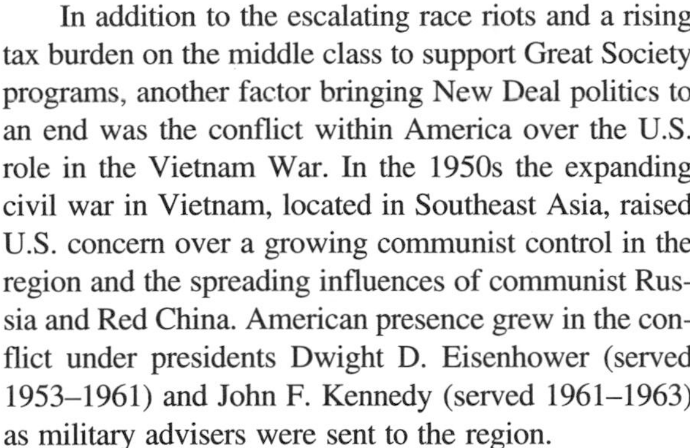

In addition to the escalating race riots and a rising tax burden on the middle class to support Great Society programs, another factor bringing New Deal politics to an end was the conflict within America over the U.S. role in the Vietnam War. In the 1950s the expanding civil war in Vietnam, located in Southeast Asia, raised U.S. concern over a growing communist control in the region and the spreading influences of communist Russia and Red China. American presence grew in the conflict under presidents Dwight D. Eisenhower (served 1953–1961) and John F. Kennedy (served 1961–1963) as military advisers were sent to the region.

In August 1964 the United States accused North Vietnam of attacking American warships in the Gulf of Tonkin. President Lyndon Johnson ordered bombing raids on North Vietnamese navy installations in retaliation. Two days later Congress passed the Gulf of Tonkin Resolution, giving Johnson broad authority to commit U.S. forces to Vietnam. Despite making campaign pledges in 1964 not to broaden American involvement in Vietnam, Johnson steadily increased the number of troops. In February 1965 he ordered massive bombing raids on North Vietnam to disrupt supply corridors leading from North Vietnam to the Viet Cong troops fighting in the South. By the end of 1965, 180,000 U.S. military personnel were in Vietnam, and this number steadily grew to 550,000 in 1968. American casualties grew also to five hundred a week by the end of 1967.

During this period public support of President Johnson fell dramatically. The war also took considerable sums of money away from Johnson's Great Society programs. Costs of the war rose to $25 billion in 1967 alone. Also, Johnson and his advisors had to divert their time and energies away from Great Society legislation to Vietnam.

Antiwar demonstrations that began primarily among college students in 1965 spread to other segments of the population by 1967. By 1968 key prominent political leaders were calling for an end to the war. With Johnson's popularity dropping to new lows in 1967, he faced antiwar demonstrations everywhere he went.

In late January 1968, the Viet Cong launched the Tet Offensive that temporarily pushed the war to Saigon, the South Vietnamese capital. The offensive, though not militarily successful, further damaged Johnson's credibility with the American public. On March 31, 1968, Johnson shocked the nation in a nationally televised address. He stated that he would not seek to run for the presidency in 1968, that he was ordering major reductions in the bombing of North Vietnam, and that he was initiating peace talks with North Vietnam.

In late October, just a week before the presidential election between his vice-president, Hubert Humphrey, and Republican candidate Richard Nixon, Johnson announced that the bombing of North Vietnam would stop altogether. Humphrey still very narrowly lost the election to Republican candidate Richard Nixon (served 1969–1974). The war and peace talks continued for the next several years. By the time the last U.S. troops withdrew from Vietnam in 1975, the Vietnam War had become the longest war in which the United States had ever been involved.

New Deal it interjected government into the world's private business more than ever before and extended social insurance programs, particularly medical care for the elderly.

The Great Society programs differed from New Deal programs in some basic ways, however. Great Society programs went well beyond social insurance—which was a key focus of the New Deal—to include racial segregation issues and voting rights, as well as a broader range of poverty issues. Whereas the New Deal focused on social classes, particularly the poor, the Great Society increasingly through the 1960s focused more on race and the plight of black Americans.

The Great Society's war on poverty increasingly targeted jobs, income, and housing for blacks. Many believe the most important achievement of the Great Society was President Johnson's translation of the civil rights movement into federal law. The Great Society offered the most important legal protections for civil rights since the Civil War. The Civil Rights Act of 1964 outlawed discrimination in education, employment, and public accommodations. The Voting Rights

Act politically changed the South. For the first time since the post-Civil War days of Reconstruction in the 1870s, black Americans could register to vote. President Johnson also appointed the first black American Supreme Court justice, Thurgood Marshall.

With this focus on racial issues, the Great Society programs served to further associate the Democratic Party with black America and at the same time turn away middle-class whites. This trend was a clear departure from the New Deal alliances, especially among the New Deal's Democratic Coalition. As a result, Democratic Party supporters became poorer and less likely to be white. For the next two decades, from 1968 to 1988, the only Democratic candidate to receive more than 40 percent of the white vote was Jimmy Carter. In 1984, 74 percent of white Protestant male voters voted for Republican incumbent Ronald Reagan over Democratic candidate Walter Mondale.

Also, unlike the New Deal labor relations and industrial production patterns, remained largely unaltered. In fact, the labor movement, so encouraged by Roosevelt's New Deal, was largely ignored by Great Society reforms much as the black American population was largely ignored during the New Deal. President Roosevelt had feared losing white southern support for his economic programs.

With all these differences between the New Deal and Great Society, one fundamental aspect was the same. Neither attempted to alter existing economic and political power structures. White intellectuals held political control over both programs.

Department of Transportation

Since its beginnings, the federal government had wrestled with what its role should be in promoting the nation's transportation systems. Through time, transportation responsibilities had steadily been added, but these responsibilities were scattered among various agencies. In June 1965 the head of the Federal Aviation Agency proposed a new cabinet-level department, an idea that had been considered for almost a century without action being taken.

Interested in improving public safety and establishing a coordinated transportation system, Johnson adopted the idea and pushed Congress for approval. As part of the Great Society programs, Congress established the U.S. Department of Transportation on October 15, 1966. The act represented a sweeping reorganization of the federal government. Many agencies that regulated various aspects of transportation were transferred to the new department, and its head serves on the presidential cabinet.

The Department of Transportation's primary function is to ensure safe, efficient, and economical transportation on the land and sea and in the air. The 12 major divisions of the department include the Federal Aviation Administration (FAA), the Federal Highway Administration, the Federal Railroad Administration, the National Highway Traffic Safety Administration, the U.S. Coast Guard, and various research programs.

Through these agencies the department oversees the air traffic control and air navigation systems; certifies pilots, aircraft, and interstate motor carriers; establishes safety standards for railroads; provides federal aid to construct airports, highways, and bridges, and to support Amtrak passenger rail service; supports vehicle and traffic safety programs; oversees the U.S. merchant marine; subsidizes mass transportation programs; and funds research programs related to transportation issues.

Healthcare and Other Achievements

The Great Society program, though having lost momentum by 1968, still offered some signs of success. The number of poor dropped from 25 percent of the U.S. population in 1962 to 11 percent in 1973. The Education Act provided the first substantial public funds for education. Healthcare became provided for the aged through Social Security benefits.

Programs with lasting social value included the resurrected food stamps program and Head Start. Medicare and Medicaid grew to be a major part of the federal budget and covered millions of people. Prior to passage of the Medical Care Act of 1965 only half of the elderly in the United States had health insurance. Introduced as Great Society programs, Medicare and Medicaid provide healthcare benefits to the aged and poor, respectively. Both programs went into effect in 1966. Medicare legislation, originally submitted by President Harry Truman (served 1945–1953), became the topic of congressional debate for almost two decades. Passed in 1965 as amendments to the New Deal's Social Security Act, the two programs represented a first step toward creating a system of national health insurance. This was the first major change in Social Security since it was first established as part of the New Deal in 1935.

Medicare benefits are available to everyone over 65 years of age regardless of financial need. Payments to hospitals and doctors are coordinated with the existing private insurance system in the United States. Medicare is composed of two related health insurance plans—a hospital insurance plan and a supplementary medical insurance plan. The hospital plan is funded through Social Security payroll taxes. Medicare pays costs for inpatient hospital care, nursing home care, and some home health care services. The plan meets most of the hospital expenses up to ninety days for each illness.

Most people covered by Medicare also enroll in the supplementary plan. Supported by general tax revenues and enrollees' monthly payments, the supplementary plan boosts payment amounts for medical services covered under the main insurance plan. The rapidly rising costs of Medicare through the 1970s became alarming. In response Congress set standards beginning in 1983 for charges of specific medical procedures in an effort to control the drain on public funds. Key problems affecting the program were that people were living longer, health care was becoming more expensive, and the percentage of elderly in society was increasing. By the 1990s Medicare costs were increasing 10 percent each year despite efforts to control expense. The primary success of Medicare was that by the end of the twentieth century most elderly citizens had health insurance.

Medicaid is designed to help low-income people under 65 years of age. It also helps the poor over 65 years of age by supplementing Medicare. States are required to offer the program to all persons on public assistance. States are left to determine who is actually eligible for coverage. The federal and state governments jointly fund Medicaid costs with the federal government providing 50 percent to 80 percent of expenses. As with Medicare, the costs of Medicaid rose quickly. By 1972 Congress began limiting the amount of expenses the government will pay. As a result, by the early 1980s increasing numbers of doctors refused to treat Medicaid patients because of the low rates of government reimbursements.

Other achievements under the Great Society had the federal government assuming new responsibilities over the environment, education, and the arts. The Great Society passed legislation amending the Clean Air Act of 1963 three times, establishing emissions standards for automobiles and stationary sources such as factories, increasing local air pollution control programs, and creating Air Quality Control Regions (AQCRs) to monitor air. By the 1980s America's air and water was cleaner than earlier in the century. During the first thirty years of the National Endowment for the Arts, the number of art organizations in the United States dramatically increased. The number of symphonies doubled, and the number of dance companies and theaters increased significantly.

The End of New Deal Politics

Because of the monetary drain posed by the escalating Vietnam War and the related decreasing public support for President Johnson, the push on the war on poverty and other Great Society programs ended prematurely, and many goals were not reached. Many of the social and economic problems fought by the Great Society programs in the 1960s, such as widespread poverty and city decay, persisted.. This ineffectiveness created disillusionment among Great Society supporters and inspired a conservative backlash. Conservatives would later argue that the New Deal and Great Society proved that government could not effectively solve social problems.

The 1972 presidential election between Republican Richard Nixon and Democrat George McGovern marked an end to Democratic liberal politics as a national force. With the Democratic Party supporting the antiwar movement, civil rights, gay rights, and women's rights, the Democratic voters who strayed to George Wallace in 1968 turned to Nixon in 1972. The new Republicanism relied on lower- and middle-class resentment of government and blacks.

A major political shift was evident for the next two decades, demonstrated by President Ronald Reagan's and President George Bush's administrations. The Republican Party used an anti-New Deal/Great Society argument to their advantage in the 1994 mid-term congressional elections. The Republicans swept into Congress blaming the Great Society and New Deal policies for many of the social problems plaguing the nation, involving poverty, welfare, education, growth of government regulation, public housing, and higher taxes

Declining Voice of the Poor

With the demise of the Democratic Coalition, the economic interests of the lower half of the wage earners were represented less and less in national politics through the 1970s and 1980s. As the middle class was increasingly pressed to pay for the new social programs, a tax revolt developed, lending further support to the growing Republican-led conservatism. The New Deal promise of continuing economic growth and improving the standard of life for each generation was no longer believed by many.

The Republicans adopted the push for major tax cuts. This strategy gained the Republican Party power not seen since the 1920s. Carrying this message forward in 1980 was Republican presidential candidate Ronald Reagan, who bridged the gap between the working class and the Republican elite, which was composed of top corporate supporters. As tax cuts took hold, government programs providing benefits to the poor greatly declined as did the political voice of the lower middle class.

This decline in the voice of the poor and lower classes was further aided by the growth of political action committees (PACs). PACs are organized interest groups that can provide political candidates considerable sums of money. As special interest lobbyists gained significant power, the working class lost influence. Lobbyists and PACs replaced the traditional neighborhood-based clubs and organizations as driving forces of political decisions. Other new changes in national politics included growth of political think tanks, media relations firms, expensive television commercials, and scientific polling strategies. All these factors led a shift to expensive technology and increased the importance of fund raising.

The increased importance of money was to the advantage of the Republican Party, which was becoming favored by corporate America due to its general stance of noninterference by the government in private business and industry. Wealthy business owners and corporations were more supportive of the probusiness platform of the Republicans. The Democrats lost some ground in this new political climate. The Democratic Party was known more as the party of the people, representing the interests of the average American and placing the protection of the interests of private citizens above those of corporate America. The affluent gained a greater influence on politics and an elite, independent group of public and private specialists determined political strategies and government policy. Corporate interests became more of a concern than those of common citizens.

By the late 1980s, most personal income gains were occurring in the top 5 percent of the population. In addition, with a greater emphasis placed on national defense budgets under Reagan, the portion of U.S. monies going to education, social services, health, housing, and other such domestic programs declined from over 25 percent of the national budget in 1980 to near 18 percent in 1987. These economic trends dramatized the post-New Deal period of American politics.

Declining Voice of Labor

By 1970 the growth of labor unions had come to a halt. From 1970 to 1980, the percentage of nonagricultural workers who were members of labor unions fell from almost 28 percent to 23 percent even as the size of the workforce increased. Through the 1980s, under Ronald Reagan's presidency, the decline accelerated, with the percentage dropping to 17.5 percent by 1986. During this time the manufacturing, mining, and construction industries gave way to the technology and service industries. These new industries were less susceptible to unionization and came to be characterized by low-wage part-time jobs.

Corporations became more boldly aggressive towards labor unions. They threatened to relocate manufacturing facilities to other countries that had cheaper labor standards or to the less unionized parts of the American South and Southwest. This decline of organized labor further weakened the traditional Democratic Party support. Unions were one of the last institutional links between working-class voters and the Democratic Party that had lasted since the Roosevelt days. Black Americans, ethnic minorities, and women replaced labor and the working class as the keys to Democratic support.

Notable People

Lady Bird Johnson (1912–). Given her political activity while First Lady, Lady Bird was often compared to Eleanor Roosevelt during her years in the White House. Lady Bird and Eleanor were quite different personalities, however. Eleanor liked to promote issues—even those not endorsed by her husband. Lady Bird was more focused on promoting issues important to her husband, President Lyndon Johnson. She vigorously campaigned on behalf of her husband's bid for the presidency in 1964 and was credited for gaining key votes from Texas. While in the White House, she concentrated on Head Start, the program designed to help preschool children from impoverished backgrounds. She left a lasting mark by raising national awareness of environmental protection issues through her "beautification" initiatives. For example, in an effort to improve the appearance of the nation's highways she successfully promoted passage of the Highway Beautification Bill in October 1965 despite strong opposition from billboard advertisers. Such active participation in the legislative process was rare for a First Lady. In 1969 she retired with Lyndon Johnson to their Texas ranch where she continued her environmental interests through the National Wildflower Research Center, which was renamed the Lady Bird Johnson Wildlife Center. She remains one of the more highly regarded First Ladies in U.S. history.

Reverend Martin Luther King, Jr. (1929–1968). Dr. Martin Luther King greatly influenced the course of the Great Society programs by dramatically leading a crusade to end racial segregation and protect voting rights of minorities A gifted student, King entered college at age 15 at Morehouse College in Atlanta and eventually earned a Ph.D. in theology from Boston University. While assistant pastor at the

Dexter Avenue Baptist Church in Montgomery, Alabama, King at the age of 26 in December 1955 became the chosen leader in an effort to end segregation on the city's public buses.

After successfully achieving integration on the Montgomery bus system, King broadened the civil rights movement by establishing the Southern Christian Leadership Conference (SCLC). King began operating throughout the South and the nation espousing, nonviolent resistance to what were considered socially unjust laws and practices.

King was a very skillful speaker and inspiring personality. His influence was at its height from 1960 to 1965, as he led nonviolent protest marches and demonstrations. In the spring of 1963, in an effort to end racial segregation at Birmingham lunch counters, he was jailed along with many others, including hundreds of school children. The Birmingham police had also turned dogs and fire hoses on the black demonstrators, drawing much national attention.

To further dramatize the plight of black Americans, King and other civil rights leaders organized the historic March on Washington on August 28, 1963. Two hundred thousand blacks and whites peacefully gathered on the Mall in Washington, DC, to hear King give his famous "I have a dream" speech. King demanded equal justice for all. The event strongly affected national opinion and led eventually to passage of the Civil Rights Act in July 1964, the first major act of President Lyndon Johnson's Great Society program. In December 1964 King received the internationally prestigious Nobel Prize for Peace.

Though still highly influential, a protest march in Selma, Alabama, in March 1965 promoting protection of voting rights avoided confrontation with Alabama state troopers by turning back. In reaction the growing number of black radicals withdrew their support for King and his nonviolent ways. Nevertheless, within days of the march President Johnson submitted a sweeping voting rights bill to Congress that was passed as the Voting Rights Act of 1965 five months later.

As violent racial confrontations began growing across the nation, King attempted to launch a campaign in Chicago against segregation in housing. This effort, however, did not successfully develop. Despite losing momentum King pressed on, attempting to form a coalition of both blacks and whites to fight poverty and unemployment. With plans under way for a Poor People's March to Washington in the spring of 1968, a sniper assassinated King at the age of 39. Though King's influence helped bring about an end to segregation laws in the South, racial problems of the northern cities and elsewhere proved too complex to solve in such a brief span of time.

Dr. Martin Luther King greatly influenced the programs of the Great Society by leading a crusade to end racial segregation and protect voting rights of minorities. (AP/ Wide World Photos. Reproduced by permission.)

George C. Wallace (1919–1998). Wallace, son of an Alabama farmer, worked his way through the University of Alabama Law School, graduating in 1942. Following service in World War II, Wallace served in various public offices, including state's assistant attorney, two terms as an Alabama legisla-

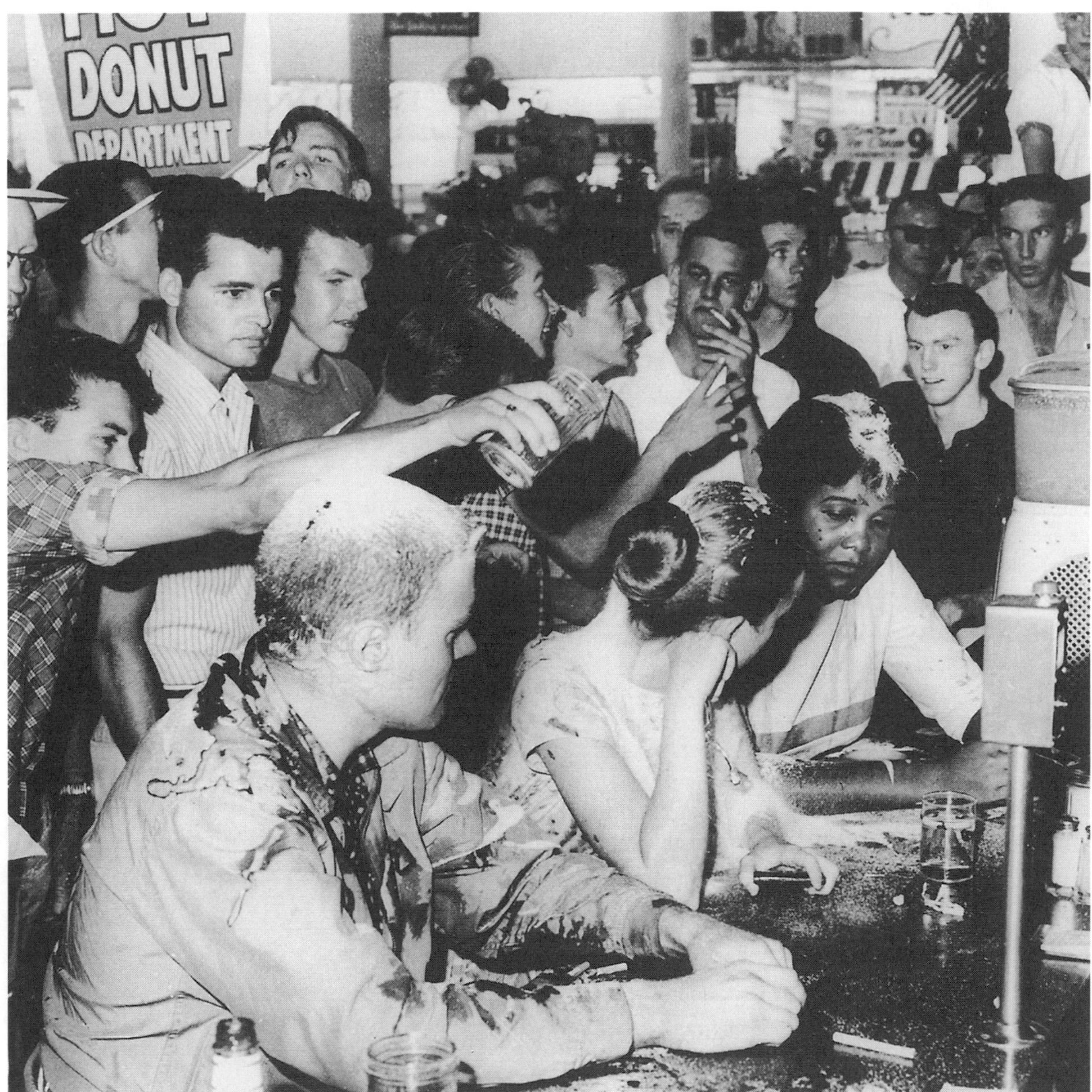

A mob harasses three segregation demonstrators during a lunch counter sit-in. Unlike the New Deal, President Lyndon Johnson's Great Society sought to directly tackle civil rights issues like race segregation and discrimination. (AP/Wide World Photos. Reproduced by permission.)

tor, and as a judge. After losing a race for the governorship to a segregationist, Wallace shifted from a moderate position on race relations to being an opponent of racial integration.

As a segregationist Wallace won the race for governor in 1962. In June 1963 Wallace gained national notoriety by blocking the enrollment of black students at the University of Alabama. He relented when the federalized Alabama National Guard came to enforce the enrollment. Similar confrontations occurred at other locations in the state.

In 1968 Wallace ran a tough campaign for the presidency as a third party candidate of the American Independent Party. He drew strongly from white southerners and blue-collar workers, normally Democratic supporters under the New Deal coalition. Wallace won 13 percent of the national vote and five southern states. With the Democratic vote split between Hubert Humphrey and Wallace, Republican candidate Richard M. Nixon won the election.

While campaigning for the presidency again in 1972, Wallace was shot and left paralyzed. Two years later, in 1974, he was reelected governor. By the 1980s Wallace renounced his segregationist viewpoints and sought reconciliation with black leaders. In 1982 he won the governor's race again, gaining substantial backing from black voters. Suffering increasing ill health, Wallace retired from politics in 1987.

Though unsuccessful in his bids for the presidency, Wallace greatly influenced American politics in general by pulling together the southern vote. This political development contributed to the ultimate demise of New Deal politics in particular.

Earl Warren (1891–1974). Warren was born in Los Angeles, California, the son of a railroad worker and immigrant from Norway. He earned a law degree from the University of California at Berkeley and served for a half century in public office. His positions included district attorney of Alameda County, California (1925–1939), California attorney general (1939–1943), and California governor for three terms from 1943 to 1953.

Thanks to his having helped Dwight Eisenhower win the 1952 presidential election, President Eisenhower rewarded Warren with a nomination for chief justice of the U.S. Supreme Court in 1953. The resulting Warren Court lasted until 1969 and introduced sweeping changes in U.S. constitutional law. The Warren Court was most noted for expansion of individual liberties, gaining equal representation of voters in elections, and protection of the rights of those accused of crimes.

On November 29, 1963, President Lyndon Johnson appointed Warren chairman of the commission created to investigate the assassination of President John F. Kennedy and the murder of Kennedy's suspected assassin, Lee Harvey Oswald. The Warren Commission Report was completed in September 1964 and later published. Earl Warren died on July 9, 1974, in Washington, DC. Warren is regarded as one of the great Supreme Court chief justices in U.S. history.

Primary Sources

Whereas President Franklin Roosevelt orchestrated the New Deal legislation with an air of optimism and charm, President Lyndon Johnson had a much more aggressive style. Stewart Alsop reported one such occasion in the *Saturday Evening Post,* December 14, 1963, entitled "The New President."

> The Majority Leader [Johnson] was, it seemed, in a relaxed, friendly reminiscent mood. But by gradual stages this mood gave way to something rather like a human hurricane. Johnson was, striding about his office, talking without pause, occasionally leaning over, his nose almost touching the reporter's, to shake the reporter's shoulder or grab his knee ... Appeals were made, to the Almighty, to the shades of the departed great, to the reporter's finer instincts and better nature, while the reporter, unable to get a word in edgewise, sat collapsed upon a leather sofa, eyes glazed, mouth half open.

The Beginnings of the Great Society

Lyndon Johnson was busily forming his legislative agenda for the Great Society programs in early 1964. He described visions for America in his Great Society speech of May 22, 1964, which is reproduced in Johnson's *Public Papers of the Presidents of the United States: Lyndon B. Johnson,* (1965, 1963–1964, Book I, p. 704):

> The Great Society is a place where every child can find knowledge to enrich his mind and to enlarge his talents. It is a place where leisure is a welcome chance to build and reflect, not a feared cause of boredom and restlessness. It is a place where the city of man serves not only the needs of the body and the demands of commerce but the desire for beauty and the hunger for community. It is a place where man can renew contact with nature. It is a place which honors creation for its own sake and for what it adds to the understanding of the race. It is a place where men are more concerned with the quality of their goals than the quantity of their goods.

A Plea For Voting Rights

The year 1965 was a tumultuous one in U.S. history. Confrontations were escalating between blacks and whites over the basic principles of freedom. In Selma, Alabama, Martin Luther King, Jr. led two attempts to march to Montgomery, Alabama, to protest the discrimination against blacks trying to register to vote in Selma. The first day, March 7, 1965, known as "Bloody Sunday," was marked with violence as state troopers beat and then arrested many of the marchers. King terminated the second march on Tuesday, March 9, and traveled that night to Washington, DC to prevail upon Johnson to step in on behalf of the protestors and the voting rights movement. Rising to the occasion, Johnson gave the following speech to a joint session of Congress and the country on national television. It proved a momentous speech which led to passage of the Voting Rights Act, and is reproduced in *Public Papers of the Presidents of the United States: Lyndon B. Johnson* (Book I, pp. 281–287):

> I speak tonight for the dignity of man and the destiny of democracy.

I urge every member of both parties, Americans of all religions and of all colors, from every section of this country, to join me in that cause.

At times history and fate meet at a single time in a single place to shape a turning point in man's unending search for freedom. So it was a Lexington and Concord. So it was a century ago at Appomattox. So it was last week in Selma, Alabama ...

There is no constitutional issue here. The command of the Constitution is plain. There is no moral issue. It is wrong—deadly wrong—to deny any of your fellow Americans the right to vote in this country. There is no issue of States rights or national rights. There is only the struggle for human rights. ...

This time, on this issue, there must be no delay, no hesitation, and no compromise with our purpose ...

What happened in Selma is part of a far larger movement which reaches into every section and state of America. It is the effort of American Negroes to secure for themselves the full blessings of American life. Their cause must be our cause too. Because it is not just Negroes, but really it is all of us who must overcome the crippling legacy of bigotry and injustice ...

I do not want to be the President who built empires, or sought grandeur, or extended dominion. I want to be the President who educated young children to the wonders of their world. I want to be the President who helped to feed the hungry and to prepare them to be taxpayers instead of taxeaters.

I want to be the President who helped the poor to find their own way and who protected the right of every citizen to vote in every election ...

God will not favor everything we do. It is rather our duty to divine His will. But I cannot help believing that He truly understands and that He really favors the undertaking that we begin tonight.

Suggested Research Topics

- Discuss the pros and cons of government involvement in the nation's social problems. Are such problems too ingrained in society to make them vulnerable to improvement by government? Was more radical action by Congress and President Johnson needed?
- Discuss the Economic Opportunity Act programs. Who were the programs intended to benefit? Why did these people need assistance? What economic programs at the beginning of the twenty-first century help needy people?
- Debate the effectiveness of Great Society programs. Did these programs encourage dependency of people on government benefits? Or did they give the people a needed boost to help themselves?
- Research the most pressing problems of your neighborhood or community. Propose a social program that would address these problems.

Bibliography

Sources

Bornet, Vaughn D. *The Presidency of Lyndon B. Johnson.* Lawrence: University Press of Kansas, 1983.

Carter, Dan T. *The Politics of Rage: George Wallace, the Origins of the New Conservatism, and the Transformation of American Politics.* New York: Simon & Schuster, 1995.

Dallek, Robert. *Lone Star Rising: Lyndon Johnson and His Times, 1908–1960.* New York: Oxford University Press, 1991.

Fraser, Steve, and Gary Gerstle, eds. *The Rise and Fall of the New Deal Order, 1930–1980.* Princeton, NJ: Princeton University Press, 1989.

Johnson, Lyndon B. *Public Papers of the Presidents of the United States: Lyndon B. Johnson.* Washington, DC: U.S. Government Printing Office, 1965–1966.

Kearns, Doris. *Lyndon Johnson and the American Dream.* New York: Harper & Row, 1976.

Patterson, James T. *America's Struggle Against Poverty, 1900–1980.* Cambridge, MA: Harvard University Press, 1986.

Schulman, Bruce J. *Lyndon Johnson and American Liberalism: A Belief Biography with Documents.* Boston: St. Martin's Press, 1995.

Further Reading

Andrew, John A. *Lyndon Johnson and the Great Society.* Chicago: I.R. Dee, 1998.

Califano, Joseph A. *The Triumph and Tragedy of Lyndon Johnson: The White House Years.* New York: Simon & Schuster, 1991.

Conkin, Paul K. *Big Daddy from the Perdernales: Lyndon Baines Johnson.* Boston: Twayne Publishers, 1986.

Frady, Marshall. *Wallace.* New York: Random House, 1996.

Johnson, Lyndon B. *The Vantage Point: Perspectives of the Presidency, 1963–1969.* New York: Holt, Rinehart, and Winston, 1971.

Unger, Irwin, and Debi Unger. *LBJ: A Life.* New York: Wiley, 1999.

U.S. Department of Transportation, [cited February 20, 2002] available from the World Wide Web at http://www.dot.gov.

See Also

Black Americans; Civilian Conservation Corps; Democratic Coalition; Education; Food; Housing; New Deal (First, and Its Critics); Social Security

Employment

1929-1941

Introduction

In the months following the stock market crash of 1929, the Great Depression swept across the industrialized world like a plague, out of nowhere and taking many down with it. Its most obvious characteristic was unemployment on a scale never before experienced. The other symptoms of the Depression were: massive decline of the value of money, the dramatic shrinking of demand for products, the continued slump in agriculture, the sudden collapse of the banking system, and the eventual decline in industrial production. These were all very baffling events to people trying to understand how the Depression occurred and what to do about it. But the greatest tragedy was the enormous unemployment and the resulting poverty that soon followed.

The level of unemployment was so great that it was difficult, if not impossible, to estimate, no reliable statistics being available. For the month of March 1933, when the Depression was near its worst, Robert Nathan, an economist in the Commerce Department, estimated that 15,071,000 people were unemployed. The American Federation of Labor, the nation's oldest national labor union, estimated that the number was higher at 15,586,000. In actuality both of these estimates were probably low. In 1936 the Bureau of Labor statistics determined that 1933 was the worst year and March of that year the worst month for joblessness in the history of the United States. It was estimated that 29.2 percent, close to a third of the labor force, was out of work. Nearly one out of five children was malnourished and

Chronology:

March 5, 1933: President Franklin Roosevelt upon taking office issues Proclamation No. 2038 convening Congress into Emergency Session.

March 31, 1933: Congress passes the Civilian Conservation Corps Reforestation Act.

April 5, 1933: President Roosevelt signs Executive Order No. 6101 creating the Civilian Conservation Corps.

May 12, 1933: Congress passes the Federal Emergency Relief Act.

July 8, 1933: Executive Order No. 6198 names Harold L. Ickes Federal Emergency Administrator of Public Works.

November 9, 1933: Executive Order No. 6420B establishes the Civil Works Administration.

February 15, 1934: Roosevelt orders the dismantling of the Civil Works Administration.

May 6, 1935: Executive Order No. 7034 establishes the Works Progress Administration.

June 26, 1935: Executive Order No. 7086 establishes the National Youth Administration.

families in the rural South and Midwest were quickly abandoning their farms. In several mountain communities in Appalachia, it was reported that entire families were reduced to eating dandelions and blackberries for their basic diet.

The great paradox of the Depression during the early 1930s was that the 1920s had been a decade of unprecedented prosperity. How had this reversal come about? There were many theories cast about but in 1933 nobody really knew for certain what had caused the economic downturn. The only thing people desperately came to believe was that something had to be done to put an end to it. This sentiment drove President Franklin Delano Roosevelt's (served 1933–1945) administration to experiment until solutions that worked were found, even if progress was measured only step-by-step and even if the approach to fighting the Depression required new ways of thinking. This was especially important for Americans to hear. When Roosevelt said in his first inaugural address that "The only thing we have to fear is fear itself," people understood it to mean that the worst enemy was inaction "—nameless, unreasoning, unjustified terror which paralyzes needed efforts to convert retreat into advance." The new President called for "action and action now" and above all else, this meant finding bold new ways to put people back to work.

Issue Summary

Unemployment Arrives

With the collapse of the stock market in October 1929, panic about the stock market's economic soundness led to immediate concern about the nation's economic health, and the resulting effect on income and employment. While only a small number of Americans were directly affected by the crash at first, it was an event of momentous significance in the minds of most people old enough to understand what had happened. Symbolically it appeared to herald the dramatic end of the commercial optimism that characterized the "roaring twenties" and for a long time thereafter the end of prosperity for the vast majority of Americans. The collapse of the stock market was also a point of reference for those who lived through this traumatic time. There was life before the Great Crash and then there was what followed. Even for those Americans who did not have money invested in the stock market, the event was a profound emotional turning point. But it also became a material turning point as well. In the wake of the crash the worst fears of Wall Street, which had tried to play down the crash in the hope of revitalizing confidence, were realized. Unemployment rapidly followed. Within five months unemployment more than doubled from 1.5 million in October 1929 to at least 3.2 million in March 1930.

President Herbert Hoover (served 1929–1933) insisted the unemployment was only a temporary situation that would right itself soon and confidently predicted on March 7, 1930, that the worst effects of the crash on unemployment would pass within 60 days. Hoover firmly believed that charities and private organizations could provide sufficient relief during the so-called temporary downturn. Yet employment only declined further. Early in the next year it had become obvious to anyone who witnessed the literal hundreds of people standing in bread lines and soup kitchens that the country was experiencing something much more than a mere setback. By the following winter it was generally recognized that the country was in the midst of a very deep depression.

The cold winter of 1932–1933 was particularly difficult in the large cities of the Northeast and Midwest. By this time, not only was much of the labor force unemployed, thousands were now homeless and had to endure the frozen temperatures as best they could on the street, many not surviving. In Chicago judges started refusing to evict families who could not make their monthly mortgage payments and the state legislature decided that banks could not repossess property. In a case that went all the way to the Supreme Court, the Justices held that the state of Illinois could allow judges to do this because it was a national emergency.

Some unemployed workers in large cities began forming loosely organized neighborhood councils that would negotiate food relief from state agencies and work to prevent cuts in relief. Members of these councils blocked sheriffs and police carrying eviction notices from entering into apartments, returned the furniture of evicted families back into their apartments, and packed courts to pressure judges to stop evictions. Some councils attempted to set up a barter system with local farmers so that work, such as the transportation of produce to markets, could be paid directly with food. Many unemployed councils eventually merged with the nationally organized Socialist Worker's Alliance. Although the councils never attracted more than a minority of the jobless, they did teach the skills necessary to organize as a political weapon. Many of those who later organized trade unions came directly out of the unemployed councils.

Despite the growing effort of the unemployed to organize, the relief systems already in place were woefully inadequate. By 1932 with unemployment rates exceeding 25 percent and business failures and home foreclosures increasing, communities of the homeless and unemployed formed. Tens of thousands of Americans were living in makeshift shacks of cardboard and scrap metal in empty lots, city parks and garbage dumps. Most of these communities consisted of hundreds of families living in conditions of squalor. In New York City, hundreds of people lived along the Hudson River between 72nd St. and 110th St. In Seattle a complex of shacks made from scrap wood and sheet metal arose in empty parking lots and train yards. In California groups of migrant farmers banded together as they lived out of their parked cars. The largest of these communities was in St. Louis where more than a thousand people lived in ramshackle housing. All of these large communities of the homeless were soon commonly referred to as "Hoovervilles," implying that President Hoover and the Republicans had been responsible for the economic downturn. The word itself came to represent the poverty and suffering wrought by the Great Depression.

Unemployment, 1933-1945

Year	Unemployed, in millions
1933	13 million
1934	11.4
1935	10.6
1936	9
1937	7.8
1938	10.3
1939	9.5
1940	8
1941	5.5
1942	2.6
1943	1
1944	.8
1945	1

The war effort ushered in declines in unemployment in the 1940s. (The Gale Group.)

Federal Emergency Relief Administration (FERA)

Recognizing that private and local relief efforts had been overwhelmed by the sheer magnitude of the Depression, the federal government launched an ambitious program to grant money directly to states for unemployment relief. In July 1932, during the last months of the Hoover administration, congressional democrats had authorized an already existing agency, the Reconstruction Finance Corporation (RFC), to loan $300 million at three percent interest to states and counties specifically for relief payment to the unemployed.

By the time Roosevelt took office, the $300 million had already been exhausted. It seemed to have made only a dent in helping the more than 15 million people out of work. Prominent progressive Senators and leading social workers throughout the country joined with the new administration in pushing Congress to approve a new national relief system. As a result Congress passed the Federal Emergency Relief Act on May 12, 1933, creating the Federal Emergency Relief Administration (FERA).Unlike the RFC that guaranteed and financed low interest loans, the FERA was authorized to spend $500 million in direct grants that were not to be repaid.

Cash payments were given directly to city and state work relief projects. This was an enormous change in the relationship of the federal government to the states. In fact the Hoover administration was

Federal Deficit, 1933-1945

Year	Federal Deficit, in billions
1933	$2 billion
1934	3
1935	1.8
1936	3
1937	2
1938	0
1939	2
1940	2
1941	5
1942	18
1943	54
1944	46
1945	45

The federal deficit grew as spending increased for the war effort. (The Gale Group.)

unwilling even to consider giving money directly to the states. Hoover argued in a campaign speech in Madison Square Garden on October 31, 1932, that such a program would give too much central power to the federal government and undermine American individualism and voluntary cooperation. He even suggested that the proposed New Deal was "un-American" and based on the "same philosophy of government that poisoned all of Europe" (from William S. Myers, ed. *The State Papers and Other Public Writings of Herbert Hoover,* 1934, Vol. II, pp. 498–413). Such arguments were frequently tossed about during the presidential campaign of 1932. Even when Congress was debating whether to pass the Emergency Relief Act, conservative members of the Senate argued that it would be the end of the Republic for it would heavily centralize government power in the federal government.

In fact the model for the FERA was not based on any system practiced in Europe, but instead on an experiment that had already been underway in New York. As governor, Franklin D. Roosevelt had been a believer in local responsibility for relief. Each city and town should take care of their own. In the face of mass joblessness afflicting his state, however, he changed his position. Governor Roosevelt called the state legislature in Albany into special session on August 28, 1931 (reprinted in Franklin Roosevelt. *Public Papers and Addresses of Franklin D. Roosevelt,* p. 788.) He told them,

> One of the duties of the State is that of caring for those of its citizens who find themselves the victims of such adverse circumstances as makes them unable to obtain even the necessities for mere existence with the aid of others...To these unfortunate citizens aid must be extended by Government, not as a matter of charity, but as a matter of social duty.

The New York legislature responded positively and Roosevelt created the Temporary Emergency Relief Administration. Prior to the New Deal, this effort became the nation's largest relief program. The administrator whom the governor appointed to run the program was a social worker by the name of Harry Hopkins. Once Roosevelt became president, he appointed Hopkins, who had now been running the relief programs in New York for over a year, to be the director of the newly created FERA. A fascinating personality, Hopkins not only had experience, but also tremendous ability. With little doubt Hopkins became one of the greatest administrators ever to serve the United States.

Harry Hopkins could be both compassionate and tough. He had an exceptional capacity to understand the politics of unemployment relief and strip complex problems to their essential elements. He enjoyed nothing more than learning the intricate details of how a bureaucracy worked, whether it was a relief agency or a state government, quickly grasping the problem and then cutting through the red tape. It was jokingly said that he could smell corruption from a mile away. British Prime Minister Winston Churchill once told Hopkins that he wanted to put him in the British House of Lords and entitle him "Lord Root of the Matter." But the truth is Hopkins was painstaking in keeping track of FERA funds allocated to different state agencies; when a discrepancy was found, he investigated immediately.

FERA was divided into four divisions. The Works Division tackled federal work projects such as building hospitals, roads, and bridges, and helped states that had already begun such projects. There was a division that handled relations with the states and a division that did research, collected information, and handled the finances. Lastly the Division of Rural Rehabilitation helped desperate farm families move to better land so they could rebuild their farms on more fertile soil. One of the strengths of FERA was the competence of the administrators who ran it. Hopkins appointed people of great ability and he commanded enormous loyalty from his staff. FERA administrators working under Hopkins constantly analyzed their own policies as to their effectiveness. When program deficiencies were found, they were often quickly restructured. When a new relief problem was discovered, such as the previously unimagined levels of poverty among sharecroppers in the Arkansas delta, administrators sought ways to tackle the problem with speed

Many unemployed people tried to earn a living by selling their wares as was seen in New York City on November 30, 1930. (AP/Wide World Photos. Reproduced by permission.)

and flexibility. Ideas for programs came from every possible source, for example, one day a tramp walked in off the street to sell the idea of hiring cartographers (mapmakers) to survey sunken ships in and around the coast. An assistant director liked the idea and a new project was born. It turned out that the tramp was a highly competent ship designer who had not received a commission since 1929.

The primary job of FERA was giving matching grants to states. For every $3.00 that a state was able to set aside for relief, FERA would "match" that amount with $1.00. This matching system offered two important advantages. First it encouraged states to establish and operate relief agencies rather than take the federal money and spend it on short-term projects. States had to make considerable investments both in terms of money and personnel. Therefore they would be especially careful in monitoring relief agencies to make sure they were operating free of graft or corruption. The second advantage was that the matching

Unemployment Rates of Women in Select Cities, January 1931

City	Percent of White Women	Percent of Black Women
Chicago, Illinois	20%	58%
Cleveland, Ohio	18	55
Detroit, Michigan	19	75
Houston, Texas	14	46
Pittsburgh, Pennsylvania	17	51
St. Louis, Missouri	16	48

Black women were much more likely to be unemployed during the Great Depression than white women. (The Gale Group.)

grant system encouraged both states and the federal government to raise more money overall. State officials knew that for every $3.00 they raised, it would be worth $4.00 once the amount was matched. Congress knew that for every $1.00 it was allocating, the states would throw in another $3.00. In theory it was an effective way to get both the states and the federal government to spend money on relief. But there was also the practical concern of simply having too little time to create an enormous federal bureaucracy to administer FERA grants across the country. It seemed it was much faster to use existing state agencies, at least initially.

Unfortunately Hopkins encountered a great deal of resistance from state legislatures who did not want to spend money on relief. Sometimes legislatures were not in session or were hampered by constitutional restrictions. States like Virginia and North Carolina refused to jeopardize their balanced budgets to spend money on relief. Some states even showed outright hostility, often reflecting traditional attitudes toward the poor. Georgia did not furnish its relief administrators with office space. Idaho's Governor C. Ben Ross prided himself on his ability to keep state spending at a minimum while still reaping the benefits of federal grants. In Oregon complete opposition existed to the very idea of relief itself. Oregon Governor Charles H. Martin, elected in 1934, believed that no able-bodied person should receive relief. He privately confided that the needy aged and feeble-minded should be chloroformed. The only threat Hopkins had at his disposal was to cut off funds to the uncooperative states, but both FERA administrators and local politicians knew that those who would really suffer would be the poor.

Tremendous variations also existed in the competence of relief administration at the local level. In places like New York, relief administrators could capitalize on the experience of social workers that had worked at the state government's Temporary Emergency Relief Agency, as well as the many private organizations that did charitable work. But in many Southern states it was another story. South Carolina and Mississippi had inadequately supervised and untrained personnel and poor salaries. The absence of social workers in Mississippi required that county relief directors would have to come in from out of state, which local politicians had no desire to tolerate. In addition there was often male opposition to female social workers in the more traditional areas of the South.

A significant drawback of the relief system to individuals was that relief recipients were given food coupons rather than money to purchase food. Often recipients felt the stigma of being treated as "charity cases." Some states even required that recipients of relief demonstrate their need through a "means test," a series of questions involving a person's residential, employment, and financial history that determined whether or not they were needy enough to warrant aid. Answering these types of personal, private questions to prove how poor one was could be very humiliating. In the South racial discrimination was near universal. Black Americans found it particularly difficult to get on the relief rolls and when they did get on they received less money than whites. Southern cities usually paid whites twice as much and in some rural "black-belt" counties, black American relief payments were as little as 30 percent of the payments in other areas. Hopkins fumed at the injustice but found he could do very little until the federal government had more direct control of relief.

Sometimes battles with local politicians became quite heated. In Ohio, Governor Martin L. Davy rewarded his numerous supporters with jobs in the Ohio Emergency Relief Administration. As it turned out, many of these supporters demanded kickback payments and were skimming money off the top of contracts with local businesses. Hopkins ordered a thorough investigation and uncovered conclusive evidence of corruption. He quickly ordered that relief operations in Ohio be "federalized," no longer under state control but rather direct control of FERA. When Hopkins threw out Governor Davy's men, the Governor retaliated by threatening to have him jailed when he visited Cleveland. But Hopkins was not deterred and came to Cleveland anyway and Davy backed down. He was not about to carry out this threat against the most trusted advisor of the President of the United States.

Both Roosevelt and Hopkins concluded that the FERA needed to move into work-relief, rather than direct relief. Work-relief, Hopkins believed, would provide proper jobs for the unemployed and reassure hostile conservatives in Congress that FERA relief payments were not subsidizing idleness. From a personal standpoint, Hopkins had been appalled at the unkind treatment the unemployed were receiving in many relief agencies. In addition it had become clear that any new relief plan could not depend on the unpredictable responses of state and local agencies. What was needed, Hopkins had concluded, was a relief organization that operated directly as a federal program. The timing at which this conclusion, that the federal government needed to commit itself to administering work-relief, could not have been more appropriate, because a potentially alarming crisis was looming on the horizon.

Civil Works Administration (CWA)

At first FERA planners had assumed that recovery measures would work quickly. Relief appropriations were made only two months at a time under the assumption that it would only be a matter of months before federal emergency relief would no longer be needed. But by October 1933 it became apparent that recovery was not taking place as quickly as originally hoped. Meanwhile FERA was rapidly running out of funds while millions were still unemployed. This was of tremendous concern, because winter was approaching. The memory of hardship experienced the previous winter left a vivid impression on the American psyche and the prospect of another such catastrophe was extremely frightening. Hopkins and his staff moved quickly to persuade Roosevelt to secure another $400 million for a work relief program. On November 9, 1933, Roosevelt signed an executive order creating the Civil Works Administration and appointed Hopkins to be its director. The Civil Works Administration (CWA) was launched with unprecedented speed, literally overnight the majority of state relief administrators became federal employees of the CWA. By mid-January, only two months later, the CWA employed 4,200,000 workers who received minimum wages for projects being developed all over the country.

The CWA was entirely a federal program. Its staff dispensed checks from the federal government and hired workers directly from the ranks of the unemployed. To Hopkins' immense satisfaction, there were no longer relief rolls or means tests. The program undertook nearly 180,000 projects, which were collectively referred to as public works. Five hundred thousand miles of secondary roads were built, forty thousand schoolhouses were either built or improved, thousands of playgrounds were constructed, nearly five hundred new airports were built, and hundreds of community swimming pools, parks, and waterways were established.

Although more than 90 percent of the projects involved construction and repair of public buildings, the CWA also hired scholars, artists, engineers, and teachers. Hopkins sought to utilize the skill and talent of more than manual labor. "We are not," Hopkins asserted, "going to permit CWA funds to be used for garbage collection or for cleaning of streets or for snow removal" (Schwartz, Bonnie F. *The Civil Works Administration, 1933–1934: The Business of Emergency Employment,* 1984, p. 45). In the Southwest CWA engineers helped farmers find methods to combat the drought that worsened agricultural conditions in the "dust bowl." Archeologists were hired to study and excavate prehistoric mounds of American Indian cultures, three thousand artists were hired to paint murals on public buildings, and forty thousand teachers were hired to teach adult illiterates. Surveys were made of harbors and historic sites, musicians organized two symphony orchestras in New York and Buffalo under the auspices of the CWA, and opera singers were sent on a tour of communities in the Ozark Mountains, most of whose audiences had never heard a recording, let alone a live performance, of classical music.

As an administrative feat, the organization of the CWA was nothing short of remarkable. Indeed nothing comparable in terms of mobilization of resources and personnel had ever been attempted in so short a time. Even the army was impressed by the magnitude of the operation and assigned a Corps of Engineers officer to determine exactly how the CWA had accomplished so much in so little time. The report of Lieutenant Colonel John C.H. Lee gave much credit to the ability of Hopkins and the able assistants he assembled and inspired. They worked tirelessly under him, he noted, and they mobilized as if reacting to a war emergency.

For the federal government to employ such a large workforce was an enormous managerial task that often required technical expertise, which was lacking among state agencies and local relief efforts. Therefore, engineers and business executives were brought in to supervise and plan projects. Contracts for supplies were made directly between the CWA and the supplier, much to the chagrin of many local politicians. As a result the CWA was markedly free of corruption.

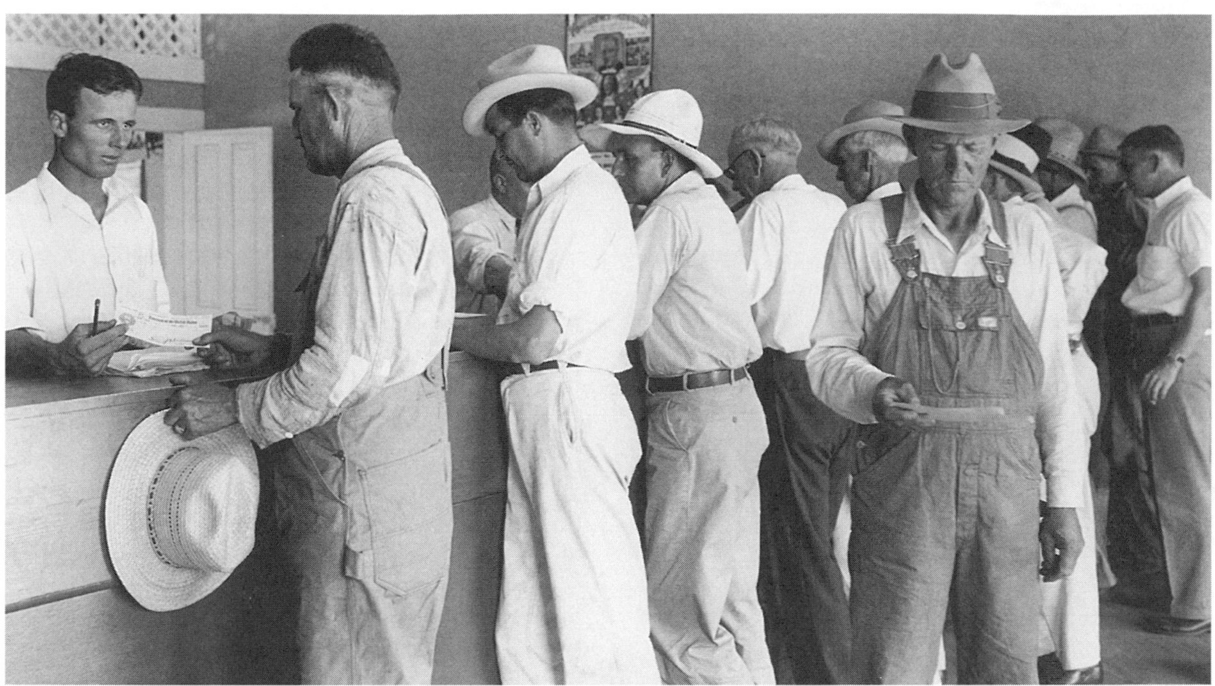

Farmers wait in line to receive benefit checks in Kaufman County, Texas, in 1934. Federal relief programs handed out millions of dollars to unemployed workers during the Great Depression. (Corbis Corporation. Reproduced by permission.)

In addition the generous wage rates were unique among the New Deal relief programs. CWA workers received wages that were related to the type of work they performed and were not necessarily based on need. Whereas the FERA made average weekly relief payments of $4.25 a week, the CWA paid an average weekly wage of $15.04 per person, comparable to wages paid in private industry.

Political Worries Over High Wage Rate Inevitably the high wage rate created some political anxieties. First there was concern about the budget. It became clear to Hopkins that the initial $400 million allotment would be exhausted by February if more funds were not forthcoming. When Hopkins approached Roosevelt for more money in early January, he was told that no more funds were available. Roosevelt would have had to siphon money from funds allocated to other agencies. Fortunately Congress stepped in and earmarked expenditures for the CWA, enough to keep the program running. However Hopkins was forced to lower wages and rotate workers in order to stretch out what little resources he had remaining. Administrators in the CWA were forced to the realization that the amount of funding necessary to keep the CWA in operation for anything more than a short-term relief period was never fully contemplated by either Congress or the administration.

The other significant political problem created by the wage rates of the CWA was that in some regions of the country the hourly rates were higher than local wages. The social impact of this fact should not be underestimated. Hopkins had no reliable statistics with which to compare wages in different parts of the country. Administrators in the FERA were a little suspicious since most of the complaints came from Southern farmers and industrialists. So Hopkins sent Lorena Hickok, his special field representative, to investigate. What she discovered, upon comparing hourly wages paid to textile workers in the Carolinas, was that CWA wages were higher. Poor sharecroppers now had an alternative source of income. As a result many were able to escape the financial domination of local landlords. Hickok became quite cynical at what she observed and attributed most of the opposition to the CWA to the "nervous landlord who realizes he may have to make better terms with his tenants and pay his day laborers more" (from Badger, Anthony J. *The New Deal. New York: Noonday Press,* 1989, p. 200; see also, *One Third of a Nation: Lorena Hickock Reports on the Great Depression.* University of Illinois Press: Urbana, 1981).

Where the CWA most strongly challenged the Southern social order, however, was in its payment of equal wages to black Americans, which tended to deplete the region's great resource of cheap labor. Hickok reported that white truck farmers in South Carolina complained that the CWA was creating dissatisfaction among black Americans because the CWA paid so much more than prevailing wages to black farm workers in the South. White farmers were anxious to have the CWA removed.

Hickok also voiced concern over what she perceived to be a view among the CWA workers that the program would be permanent. Roosevelt was himself fearful that the CWA would become a "habit" that the administration could not afford. The $200 million being spent each month on the CWA was a substantial increase above the $60 million that had been spent monthly on the FERA and Roosevelt feared a potentially endless drain on the federal treasury. Believing also that the need for general relief would diminish as the economy recovered, Roosevelt ordered the CWA terminated by the end of March 1934. The popularity of the CWA had also grown in Congress as the various successes of the program and its achievements in member's districts became apparent. Despite certain political shortcomings, there was little doubt that the CWA was a great domestic achievement. The model it put forward to combat the Depression, that of a massive federal relief effort, paved the way for what many New Dealers hoped would become a permanent and even larger program, the Works Progress Administration (WPA).

Public Works Administration (PWA)

The Public Works Administration (PWA) was responsible for the New Deal's early construction program. The popularity of a public works spending program had been around at least since the early twenties. At the time several economists called for creation of a reserve fund for public works, including Otto T. Mallery who published *The Long Range Planning of Public Works* in 1921. Likewise a number of construction trade groups were joined by social work organizations in advocating public works during the 1920s. With the economic collapse, several members of Congress, most notably Senator Robert Wagner of New York, Senator Robert La Follette of Wisconsin, and Edward Costigan of New Mexico, turned to the idea of public works as a relief measure. The idea had already gained earlier support and several plans existed. In fact the means for financing construction loans was already in place, with the Reconstruction Finance Corporation (RFC), created by the Hoover administration. In 1932 Congress gave $2 billion to the RFC to make loans for public works projects. It was hoped the funds would support projects that would produce work relief. Against the desire of many in Congress however, Hoover was hesitant to go forward very quickly on the appropriation. Much of the RFC's time was spent in drafting feasibility studies.

By the time Roosevelt was inaugurated, the demand for public works was quite vocal, although there were competing views on the underlying goals of a federal public works program. Some envisioned a massive works program that would stimulate the economy by "pump-priming." Pump-priming referred to the theory that if enough people received wages once again, that they would begin buying goods and services and the economy would eventually come back into balance. In the early 1930s, however, theorists often underestimated just how much "pump-priming" would be needed. Although disagreement existed as to how much of an expenditure of federal funds would be needed, it was clear to advocates of this plan, that a "pump-priming" stimulation of private purchasing power would require rapid expenditure. Thus huge projects that would take years would not sufficiently stimulate the economy to tackle unemployment in the short term. On the other side of the debate, some viewed public works as a means of providing short-term relief to the unemployed on less grandiose projects. And though perhaps an oversimplification, these competing views on public works can essentially be understood as coming down to large, long-term projects that employed fewer workers versus smaller, short-term projects that employed many. What eventually emerged was something in between. It was not entirely a federal program since the vast majority of projects were performed under contract with private construction firms. Nor was it entirely a relief program since contractors were allowed to hire the majority of their workers without regard for whether they were on relief or not.

The PWA was actually established under the National Industrial Recovery Act when it was passed on June 16, 1933. Roosevelt then turned over the administration of the program to Harold L. Ickes, the Secretary of the Interior. Ickes decentralized the PWA into state and local committees, partly to reward loyal Democrats. Ultimately $3.3 billion dollars was allocated to the program. Secretary Ickes then compromised with fiscal conservatives and adopted the RFC loan model. The PWA required that two-thirds of the cost of projects be secured by loans. The remaining

Jobs were so scarce as a result of the Depression that thousands would apply for a limited number of positions. This is part of a line of over 5,000 men who applied for 100 open porter jobs in New York City in 1938. Police were called in to keep order. (AP/Wide World Photos. Reproduced by permission.)

third would be funded by federal grants, which seemed like a practical compromise. However largely due to the loan security requirements, as well as the complex nature of the projects undertaken, the PWA was slow. Each loan had to be fully secured and fit into models of RFC contract requirements. This sometimes took months. The projects, such as dams, tunnels and canals, though impressive, were often quite elaborate engineering proposals and required a great deal of planning before construction could begin. As a result the PWA was somewhat disappointing in relieving unemployment. Many became disillusioned with its potential by the mid-1930s, including Roosevelt who became disenchanted with the slowness of the PWA. He soon began diverting PWA funds to agencies that could work faster, such as $400 million to start the CWA.

Another major problem was that too few workers were employed for the program to have much of a national effect on unemployment relief. At its peak in July 1934 only about 634,000 people were employed. Several months later in February 1935 that number fell to 282,000 reflecting the cyclical stops and starts of the construction industry. This was hardly conducive to "priming the pump" of the national economy. By the mid-1930s, Congress began allocating fewer funds to the PWA and instead shifted the burden of relief to the newly created Works Progress Administration after 1935. In fact the Emergency Relief Appropriation Act of 1935 only allocated $313 million to the PWA, hardly enough to undertake any new projects. In many ways Congress was financially tying the hands of the PWA until finally another $1.6 billion was appropriated in 1938. Even this was grudgingly given in part so the PWA could finish the projects it had begun. Eventually in 1939 Ickes turned the PWA over to the Federal Works Agency. That agency had been created as part of a consolidation of New Deal agencies in the Reorganization Act of 1939 and Congress ultimately abolished it in 1949.

Although the PWA failed to bring recovery in the short term, it would be a mischaracterization to call it a failure. In fact its long-term economic effects may have been the most significant of any New Deal public works programs. The projects themselves were of high quality and lasting. The Grand Coulee and Bonneville Dams on the Columbia, the Queens Midtown Tunnel, the All American Canal, the Imperial Irrigation District in Southern California, the Denver and Los Angeles water supply systems, the Triborough Bridge in New York City, the Lincoln Tunnel under the Hudson River, and the Overseas Highway from Miami to Key West were all PWA projects, to name a few. The PWA built 1,527 sewage systems, 2,419 waterworks, and 762 hospitals. In addition it constructed hundreds of bridges, viaducts, airports, and state and county public buildings. Through all these projects the PWA did stimulate some recovery in the construction industry and gradually over time, other investments were made around the projects themselves. For example reclamation projects gradually led to the formation of new farms in project areas; new highways attracted roadside enterprises; sewage systems, waterworks, and cheap electricity allowed for industrial expansion; and, so on. These long-term effects have never been fully studied but economist John Kenneth Galbraith has speculated that they were integral to the economic growth of America following World War II (1939–1945). When Roosevelt decided to move the PWA into the Federal Works Agency, and consequently take it away from Ickes, the Secretary of the Interior was upset. But in a letter to Roosevelt on June 26, 1939, he closed by writing, "instead of complaining, I ought to be thanking you for allowing me to be Public Works Administrator during the last six years...I have loved this job."

Works Progress Administration (WPA)

By authority of the Emergency Relief Appropriation Act, passed on April 8, 1935, President Roosevelt created the Works Progress Administration (WPA) by executive order a month later on May 6, which reflected a change in the approach to federal relief. Roosevelt wanted the federal government to "quit the business of relief." He wanted to create jobs, not government handouts. This was also what the vast majority of the unemployed wanted as well. Rather than being a withdrawal of the commitment of the federal government to relief efforts, work relief represented a progressive commitment to a larger-scale and longer-term relief program. In fact the WPA was intended to replace what were essentially viewed as emergency programs, the FERA and CWA, with a program that would be permanent. In the view of the administration, this could only be accomplished by turning relief programs back to the states.

In theory the role of the WPA would be to undertake public works, much as the CWA had done, but on a larger and more permanent scale. Like the CWA the WPA would also be involved in all manner of projects ranging from the employment of artists to creating public murals to the building of community centers. But the underlying objective of the agency was to employ workers on building projects of large-scale public works. This was not a new idea but rather the culmination of a series of experiments the most important of which was the earlier PWA.

The Emergency Relief Appropriation Act provided $1.4 billion to the program. Many of the leaders of the FERA, which officially ended at the end of 1935, were assigned to operate the WPA, including Harry Hopkins who became its director. From 1935 to 1943 the WPA spent over $11 billion building or improving public facilities, at its peak it employed 3.3 million workers. The projects included 2,500 hospitals, almost six thousand school buildings, one thousand airports or landing strips, thousands of public and utility parks, and hundreds of thousands of miles of streets, country roads, and sidewalks. Almost 40,000 people were employed in the Federal Writers, Music, Art, and Theater Projects. The WPA provided employment for almost one-third of the jobless with an average monthly income of $50.

Despite its accomplishments, some problems arose with the WPA. Due to the fact that the program was administered through individual states, minorities and women were frequently discriminated against. Also the businessmen complained of government competition in projects and organized labor complained about the lowered wage standards for construction. Finally Congress renamed it the Works Projects Administration and placed it in the Federal Works Agency in 1939 along with the PWA. Hopkins had resigned the previous year in 1938. As private industry gained strength again with the demands of World War II the WPA finally faded out by 1943. The WPA left a long lasting legacy, however, with its improvements made in public facilities throughout the nation.

Jobs For Young People

One limitation of the early New Deal efforts in combating unemployment was that programs, like the PWA and the CWA, tended to employ people who already had job skills of some kind, whether musicians, artists, mechanics, or teachers. Roosevelt had personally been concerned about what would happen to young people in the Depression who had no job training or not yet developed employable skills. Imagine coming out of high school and knowing that not only were their no jobs, but that there might not be jobs available indefinitely for unskilled workers. The prospects for young people were grim. Many New Dealers, including First Lady Eleanor Roosevelt, were afraid that young people would become alienated from American society and find outlets in political movements or organizations that were counterproductive to economic recovery and to American ideals. By the mid-1930s, this was an especially alarming concern to those who had observed how easily young people were being mobilized to partisan political ends in Hitler's Germany. One of these people was National Recovery Act administrator Edward A. Filene who after a brief trip to Germany, quickly concluded that the United States ignored its unemployed youth at its own peril.

President Roosevelt in fact had been concerned about young people from the very early days of the New Deal. The Civilian Conservation Corps, or the CCC, was a New Deal program specifically designed to target two problems in one: unemployment among youth and emergency conservation work. Soon after taking office Roosevelt presented Congress with an ambitious plan to help alleviate the severe unemployment problem among young men between the ages of 18 and 25. Roosevelt asked Congress for funding on March 21, 1933. Within 10 days he was given the authority to establish a conservation program under the Civilian Conservation Corps Reforestation Relief Act of March 31, 1933.

The program was the conception of the president himself. It was expected to provide jobs doing conservation work of various kinds for young men who came from families already on relief. By July 1933 over 239,000 young men were organized into work "companies" and assigned to a camp. The program was very expensive for the federal government but as a result of the projects completed, the country more than got its money's worth. CCC workers restored historic sites, built national park facilities, fought forest fires, enlarged reservoirs, and, most impressive of all, undertook an immense reforestation effort. The young men who worked on these projects were often referred to as "Roosevelt's tree army" because eventually they planted approximately two billion trees. This was an especially important conservation enterprise in fighting the dustbowl in the American southwest and Great Plains. Together with the "Shelterbelt Project," begun in 1936, the reforestation efforts of the CCC helped reverse the topsoil erosion due to misunderstood farming practices that had been destroying good farmland for decades.

Within a short period of time, the restrictions on age were lifted and eventually World War I (1914–1918) veterans could join the CCC. A separate division was also created under the Bureau of Indian Affairs that employed nearly 15,000 Native Americans on reservations across the country. Unlike other New Deal agencies, however, the CCC remained segregated when it came to black American enrollment. This was partly the result of little effort made to desegregate the corps by Robert Fechner, who served as the director of the CCC during its nine-year existence. There also was local opposition to enrolling black Americans. Surprisingly however, the CCC had been the first federal program that sought to eliminate racial discrimination. Representative Oscar DePriest of Illinois, the only black member of Congress, had inserted an amendment in the law stating that "no discrimination shall be made on account of race, color or creed." Southern states, particularly Georgia, simply ignored the provision, but the Labor Department, and particularly the U.S. Employment Service, kept pushing to get black Americans admitted to the CCC. Some 200,000 black Americans ultimately served in the CCC with 84 of the 152 "black" camps located in the South. Black American workers in these camps were paid the same amount as non-blacks and given equal rations of food, clothing and shelter. This represented a rise in the standard of living compared to that of most black Americans living in the South during the

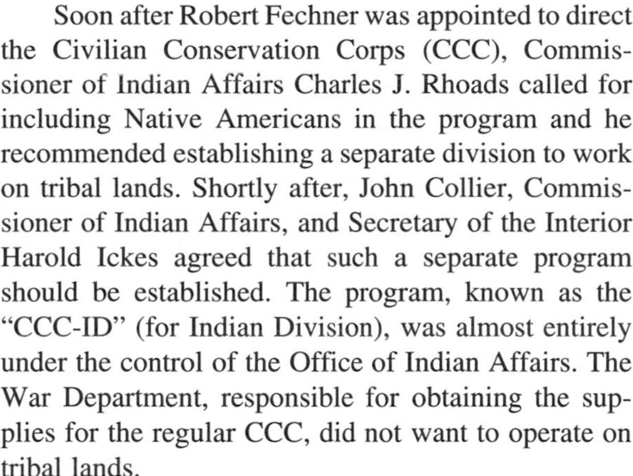

More About...

Indian Division of the Civilian Conservation Corps

Soon after Robert Fechner was appointed to direct the Civilian Conservation Corps (CCC), Commissioner of Indian Affairs Charles J. Rhoads called for including Native Americans in the program and he recommended establishing a separate division to work on tribal lands. Shortly after, John Collier, Commissioner of Indian Affairs, and Secretary of the Interior Harold Ickes agreed that such a separate program should be established. The program, known as the "CCC-ID" (for Indian Division), was almost entirely under the control of the Office of Indian Affairs. The War Department, responsible for obtaining the supplies for the regular CCC, did not want to operate on tribal lands.

Rather than undertake only conservation jobs, Collier stressed the importance of local participation by tribal leaders in developing the scope of projects. Six district offices administered the CCC-ID throughout the United States. In addition to the regular boarding camps of the CCC, there were also work camps and family camps as well.

The most severe conservation problem on tribal lands was soil erosion. In the 1920s and 1930s, Indians on reservation lands received only 20 percent of their income from farming or ranching, yet Indians held over 50 million acres of land. Unfortunately, most of this land was too dry to support grazing or agriculture. Therefore, a major goal of the CCC-ID was to increase the value of this land. Crews worked on irrigation projects, built dams and roads, planted trees, undertook soil erosion control measures, and even built housing and schools.

The impact on most reservations, which were the most poverty-stricken communities in the United States, was enormous. Agricultural yields at the end of the 1930s increased dramatically. Diet and healthcare improved and people from many tribes were brought together in the camps where they could meet and exchange ideas and friendship. For many reservations, it was the first time that full employment opportunities were available. Unfortunately it was also the last time that many tribes would experience that level of income until the 1970s or later.

1930s. Fechner had continuously received pressure to integrate the camps from various circles within the New Deal, especially from the Department of Labor. Eventually 71 camps were integrated by 1937. At its peak in 1935 the CCC had over 500,000 men working in 2,500 camps across the country. Each worker was paid $30 a month with anywhere from $23 to $25 to be sent home to their families. Workers were initially enrolled for a period of nine months to give as many young men as possible an equal opportunity. In little time, greater flexibility was established to allow the opportunity to re-enroll.

The selection standards of the CCC, however, did not allow young men to be enrolled who were already employed or were already in school or college. It turned out that nearly a third of the enrollees had not completed grade school or were illiterate. As a result the CCC encouraged educational programs and some 40,000 men learned to read and write while working in the Corps. Teachers from state schools and colleges were recruited by the Department of Education to help develop training programs in the camps. By 1940 every camp had an average of 18 instructors permanently assigned to it. Camps were eventually fitted with libraries and classrooms where both vocational skills in manufacturing and agriculture, and academic subjects were taught. During the history of the CCC over 25,000 young men received eighth grade diplomas, 5000 received their high school diplomas, and 270 were even awarded college degrees while serving in the Corps. By June 1941 over three million had served in the CCC for periods of up to two years. Their families received relief payments of around $25 a month and, perhaps more important, young men acquired job skills that would help them in the future. Eventually the coming of war spelled the end for the CCC. By early 1942 young men were enrolling or being drafted into the armed forces and federal funds were redirected to the war effort. Finally in June 1942 Congress simply appropriated enough operating funds to close the camps. Despite this unceremonious end, the CCC had undoubtedly been an exceptionally popular program. Its success continues to be recalled as an example of one of the New Deal's finest achievements.

National Youth Administration (NYA)

The CCC and the FERA employed or gave relief to hundreds of thousands of youths, yet millions more were still not affected by New Deal relief efforts. On January 26, 1935, President Roosevelt signed an executive order establishing the National Youth Administration (NYA) under the WPA. The NYA was designed specifically to meet the problems of young people and had two objectives. The first was to keep young people in school by providing them with part-time work so that they did not have to drop out. The second was to provide resources to local schools and colleges so that they would be able to train and educate young people. The NYA provided funds and set standards while school systems administered the programs at the local level. Later in the decade Student Work Councils were formed giving both the students and the community more control over the program. Each state received an allocation based on its student population, existing educational facilities, and number of families on relief. Colleges and universities received funds on the basis of the number of regularly enrolled day students. The NYA merely prescribed that the work should be "useful and practical." The institutions themselves made the project assignments that ranged from academic tasks to manual labor. In the high schools job emphasis was on construction, machine and auto shop, landscaping, health and sanitation as well as organizing recreation activities. In college, students worked in libraries, labs, and assisted professors in research. Between 1936 and 1943, a total of 2,134,000 students worked on NYA projects with more than two-thirds in high school. Pay levels for students were set by national criteria. College and graduate students received from $10 to $30 per month. The rate for high school students was no less than $3 and no more than $6 per month. Local schools fixed the number of hours for work but could not exceed four hours on school days.

The other major activity of the NYA was the out-of-school work program. This was essentially supervised work on local, public, educational, and health related agency projects. Young people were employed doing all manner of construction and repair, woodworking, hospital care and educational assistance and tutoring. In rural areas farm projects were organized at centers where young people lived together and produced food for people on relief. In urban areas special programs were developed to assist the handicapped and, in the case of New York, programs were developed to assist refugees, mainly Jews from Nazi Germany. Like the CCC the NYA had an impressive record of accomplishment, with over 1,500 miles of road paved, six thousand public buildings erected, a little over 1,400 schools and libraries constructed, and 2,000 bridges built by NYA workers. Most of these laborers in the out-of-school program received training in arc welding, machine tool work, and other industrial skills. To assist rural communities, "resident training centers" were established where young people could live for a period of time and receive training. Each of these centers also had a "Citizenship Instructor" who taught civics and other skills necessary to take an active role in their communities and local government.

By far the most impressive accomplishment of the NYA, from an administrative standpoint, was its cost. Because the agency could use state and local facilities and equipment, the cost to the federal government was substantially lower than the CCC. The cost of keeping a young person in high school, for example, was one-thirtieth the cost of keeping a young person in a CCC camp. The NYA was perhaps the only agency that numerically benefited women more than men. Women constituted a slight majority at the high school level and only a slim minority at the college level. In addition black Americans were enrolled in the program based on a non-discrimination policy and a division of Negro Affairs was established under the direction of the black American educator Mary McLeod Bethune, which targeted assistance to traditional black schools and colleges. By the time the war was underway armed forces' enlistments had drained most of the young men from the program, leaving it primarily benefiting young women. Congress felt compelled to reduce non-essential, war-related expenditures and the NYA was finally terminated in 1943. Interestingly it was two future presidents, Congressman Lyndon B. Johnson and Senator Harry S. Truman, who tried hardest to save the program.

The benefits of the NYA to the country did not end abruptly in 1943. Toward the late 1930s, when it appeared to NYA director Aubrey Williams that war was imminent, training programs focused on industrial war production were developed. The "resident centers" essentially became industrial training schools and once the war came, they were ideal locations for war plants. In the last year of the NYA, 1943, over 30,000 youths graduated from these centers and all were placed immediately in war industry jobs.

Contributing Forces

Early Beliefs About Unemployment

Throughout nineteenth century America, the conventional image of the unemployed worker was that of a lazy and worthless man whose own character flaws were to blame for his condition. The individual who had no job or became temporarily unemployed was quickly associated with those who suffered from afflictions such as intemperance or other vices. Whatever local relief was available in the almshouses was often just enough to maintain subsistence. Assistance was usually donations of food or clothing but rarely money. By the 1830s charitable groups that helped the poor emphasized more on reforming the individual. They would teach discipline and personal regeneration rather than provide actual material aid. Despite a severe economic downturn in 1819 and a more severe depression in the early 1840s, there was no sense that economic conditions and sudden downturns in the business cycle could cause displacement of large numbers of workers. In part this was because before the Civil War America was still largely an agricultural nation and a common perception existed that work could always be found on the land or in the building trades. Only a few observers began to look with misgiving at the plight of the unemployed in urban slums.

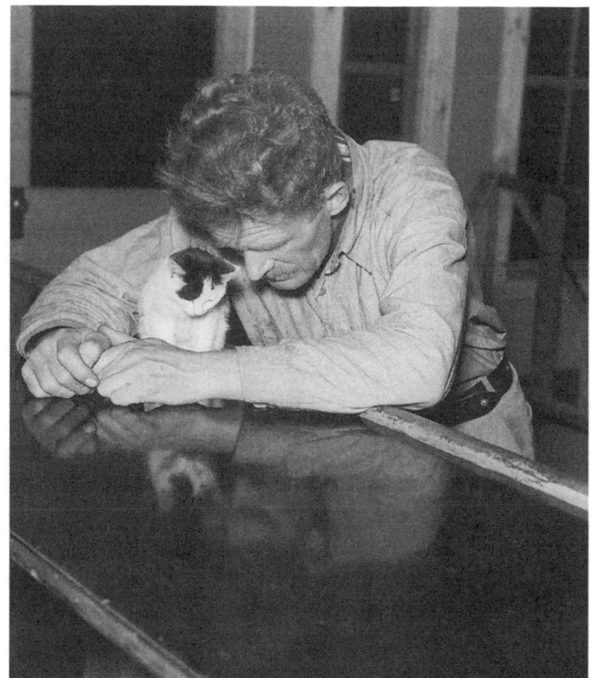

The image of the unemployed changed during the Great Depression. They were no longer seen as people with character flaws or failures but as unwilling casualties of a modern industrial economy. (The Library of Congress.)

The unprecedented industrial expansion following the Civil War made more and more workers dependent on the growing industrial economy. Yet when a massive depression hit the United States in 1873 putting thousands out of work, calls for public relief were quickly derided as socialist. Political machines in some of the largest cities, notably Boss Tweed's Tammany Hall in New York, assisted the needy unemployed. The machines, however, were so associated with corruption that reformers sought to abolish municipal relief altogether. People tended to distinguish between the "worthy poor," such as the aged, the infirm, and orphans, and the "indolent," those who would not work even if provided aid. Unemployed workers were more commonly associated with the "indolent," and it was widely believed that private philanthropy was sufficient to separate and assist the worthy poor from the unworthy poor. It was not until an extremely severe depression in 1893 that a perception arose that some of the "worthy poor" were affected by economic downturn for which they were not individually responsible. The 1893 depression was the first time public work relief was attempted in the United States. Work projects, however, were purposefully small, involved physical labor, and generally useless. Careful to avoid competition with the private market, workers were also underpaid.

Perceptions Toward Unemployment Change

Severity of the 1893 depression, the reform spirit of the early twentieth century progressive movement, and studies undertaken by sociologists and other experts gradually contributed to a shift in outlook. Economists, engineers, and "scientific managers" began to recognize that periodic fluctuations in the economy would periodically force people out of work. This, they acknowledged, was not caused by individual frailty, but by the result of disturbances in the industrial economic system. Given this intellectual framework, social workers and social engineers in the early years of the twentieth century also began to look differently at the individuals who suffered from these economic dysfunctions—the unemployed.

Social caseworkers became schooled in these new theories of sociology and obtained professional degrees from the University of Chicago and the New York School of Social Work. Their first challenge came during the recession of 1914–1915. Through the efforts of these early social workers, settlement houses and private charities in larger cities coordinated their efforts to devise small-scale work projects, such as street cleaning or clearing of empty lots. Usually these were organized for married men with dependents. They were paid wages in kind or in grocery orders. If they refused to work, however, they were usually taken off relief altogether. In this respect relief efforts resembled those of the nineteenth century. Significant new development did occur however. Caseworkers began to track and study the psychological dynamics of individual families and compile statistics. For the first time joblessness during the 1914–1915 recession was viewed as the result of disorders in the industrial system, problems which engineers and economists could solve. For the first time also the idea was advanced that the unemployed could be put to work on carefully designed projects, not as a relief measure, but as a way to increase the overall efficiency and productivity of the economy. That such technical expertise could be assembled to undertake such an endeavor was soon confirmed by the engineer's contribution to war mobilization during the World War I.

As Secretary of Commerce during the Harding Administration, Herbert Hoover initiated a meeting of trade association leaders, business academics, and "socially responsible engineers" to compile data and study the problem of economic displacement of workers. The committee, known as the Conference on Unemployment, would meet four more times and develop statistical methods for monitoring business fluctuations in the economy. The Committee's suggested that a federal agency was needed to create a permanent database and coordinate public works during periods of economic depression. Worthless, or "made work," was officially abandoned as a policy since it never absorbed more than a fraction of the unemployed. Instead, large construction projects that would in time pay for themselves were favored.

The Great Depression Arrives

It became clear when the Depression hit in 1929 that such an incredibly large extent of need of the unemployed was never fully anticipated by the experts on the Conference of Unemployment. First the Depression was far bigger than previous economic downturns and millions were unemployed. It was not clear whether this depression, unlike the Panic of 1873, the depression in the early 1890s, and the severe recession of 1914–1915, was due to a fluctuation in the business cycle or some indefinable industrial collapse of a different order. Second the Council's experts envisioned projects that would employ skilled workers in the construction trades. They never anticipated the massive unemployment in nearly every sector of the economy, affecting all economic classes, wrought by the Great Depression. The Depression was too extensive to be cured simply by more building. In fact construction had peaked in 1928 and city and county governments could not accelerate further building. Moreover the collapse of the bond market on Wall Street left financiers unwilling to issue bonds for civic improvements, therefore any that were planned quickly collapsed. Finally only local relief organizations existed to cope with the emergency and they were overwhelmed. Municipal intervention seemed inadequate, despite some heroic efforts, and states soon clamored for federal relief.

Early attempts by states and cities to fight the Depression did yield some valuable experience, however. Relief efforts were diverse and by far the most comprehensive was New York's Temporary Emergency Relief Administration organized by then Governor Roosevelt. Cities, however, also developed new approaches to deal with the crisis. For example, Philadelphia organized a committee of Unemployment Relief that brought together business leaders and social workers, organizing a wide range of programs funded by both private and municipal funds. A general relief system was established, low interest loans created, work relief programs organized, a homeless shelter for men built, and school breakfasts given to children. The program was ambitious, broadly conceived, well coordinated in the community and soundly managed, soon, however, private donations evaporated and by the winter of 1930–1931, municipal funds dried up as well. The Committee, led by Horatio Gates Lloyd, a long time proponent of local relief, was forced to recognize the futility of continuing without direct federal assistance.

Detroit had nearly the opposite approach. Staggering under the virtual absence of public charity organizations, no attempt was made, nor was it possible, to organize a concerted community response. Instead the city offered direct aid to the unemployed. After Mayor Frank Murphy was elected in 1930 on a platform of public relief, he quickly reorganized the welfare department, set up emergency relief lists, and created a Homeless Men's Bureau. City government expanded to meet the crisis almost as quickly as the expansion rapidly depleted the city's funds. After the winter of 1930–1931 Murphy realized the situation was hopeless and called for federal assistance, the first plea of many to follow. All eyes turned to Washington.

Perspectives

National Perspectives

The New Deal relief programs drew many criticisms. During the 1930s much faultfinding and negative attitudes were aimed toward recipients of aid. There was tremendous concern that the New Deal was merely subsidizing the idle with the dole. This, it was

Despite the accomplishments of federal work programs to employ millions of men during the Great Depression, women were often discriminated against. (The Library of Congress.)

suggested, would ultimately undo any efforts of long-term recovery. As it turned out work relief never reached more than 40 percent of the unemployed and spending limitations always constrained the further expansion of programs into more permanent agencies. New Dealers seldom escaped the conception that relief was temporary and that recovery was just around the corner. They, like everyone else, underestimated both the depth of the Depression and the massive spending required to "prime the pump" of the economy. It was not until the late 1930s that the extent of the situation became more obvious. By then congressional conservatism began stripping the New Deal of its strength. By 1939, for example, Roosevelt was no longer able to ask for the large budgets for work relief he was able to secure in 1935 and 1937. By 1940 Congress put caps on the number of people who could be employed by the WPA. The British economist John Maynard Keynes met with Roosevelt in Washington, DC, in 1934 and urged the President to spend more on relief, even to consider deficit spending. This, Keynes insisted, was the only way to stimulate the economy. But always wary of spending deficits, Roosevelt could not imagine that it would require the massive spending and deficit financing at the level World War II eventually produced to conquer the Depression. It was also difficult to expect Congress to approve the type of budgets Keynes suggested was necessary.

It was easy in hindsight for critics to accuse the New Deal for not instituting larger spending programs for relief than it did. No satisfactory theory existed, however, on the relationship between money, employment, and spending until the late 1930s. Just as many economists at the time were expounding a return to the limited budgets of the Hoover years. Critics sometimes also underestimated the external constraints on the New Deal. For example, no federal system existed to undertake massive relief in an economic emergency when Roosevelt took office. Government action characterized by the New Deal simply did not exist before 1933. The size and relative efficiency of the administrative structure that sprung up almost overnight was inconceivable in 1929. Balanced against the strong forces of localism and entrenched conservative leadership in Congress, the creation of relief programs was even more impressive. In a country historically suspicious of centralized authority, hostility to big government and political constraints on central planning were formidable. Perhaps what is most amazing was that the New Deal relief programs reached as many as 40 percent of the unemployed. The programs clearly made a significant impact. Federal public work programs prevented the Depression from getting worse and even initiated a modest recovery. Workers received very real benefits of food and money allowing them to survive.

Local Perspectives

Local perspectives around the nation were quite varied and the way localities dealt with the growing federal presence varied according to the region, state, and county. It frequently depended on the local culture, political system and power structure. This diversity owed to the fact that culturally America was much less homogenous during the 1930s than in later times. For example expenditures on New Deal programs in Colorado were greater than any other Western state. In the end, however, the impact on political reorganization, its force as a Democratic state, was minimal. Why this occurred is a very complex question having much to do with cultural perceptions of the New Deal in the West. Virginia, on the other hand, had historically been a strongly Democratic state but probably no state in the union received the New Deal with less hospitality than there. This had largely to do with the New Deal's threat to the political power structure and Southern social order. Massachusetts received the New Deal warmly but Democrats could not capitalize on the inroads made, due to the pre-New Deal weakness of Democratic Party organization in the state. The impact of the New Deal in different regions varied considerably and this remained a topic much studied by later historians. Generally, however, the federal government was, on some level, a threat to local power. This threat did not always show itself in direct confrontations between state and federal officials, although this did happen. Mostly it was a matter of New Deal electoral majorities eroding a local political power base. Newcomers could challenge long-standing state or county politicians by allying themselves with the New Deal work relief programs.

An important factor was that the federal government was not that significant a presence before the New Deal in most states. State governments had firm control of their areas and state politicians could be quite powerful. Senator Burton K. Wheeler of Montana, who became disenchanted with the New Deal by the late 1930s, thought of Roosevelt as nothing more than a powerful regional leader like himself, and said so. Even federal courts had relatively little jurisdiction over the states except perhaps when it came to navigable waters and issuing injunctions to stop labor union activity. There were no federal agencies that affected states or localities to any significant degree other than Port Authorities dealing with international commerce, military bases, or agencies managing Native American reservations.

Impact

To many Americans the most obvious impact of the New Deal work relief programs stem from the lasting results of the projects themselves. The accomplishments of the Public Works Administration are still with us today—the Grand Coulee and Bonneville Dams, the Queens Midtown Tunnel, the Triborough Bridge, and the All American Canal are a few of the more well known of 34,000 projects. The PWA also began a federal housing program institutionalized by the Federal Housing Act of 1938, which served as a forerunner for the modern Department of Housing and Urban Development. The CCC, the FERA, the CWA, and the NYA all had equally impressive accomplishments. Roads, bridges, and reservoirs built by these agencies were still used all over the country into the twenty-first century. In the case of the CWA, it also laid the groundwork for the massive work relief program under the Works Progress Administration.

Changing Attitudes

Perhaps the most lasting impact, however, was the changing attitude that Americans developed toward both the government and the unemployed. For the first time Americans looked to the federal government for direct relief. Despite the New Deals' ultimate failure to achieve pre-1929 employment levels, the scale of the enterprise of federal work relief was not only unprecedented but also never equaled since. Millions of people were put back to work and, although national economic recovery was not fully achieved until the early 1940s, the relief programs did help families survive.

For all the faults of the relief organizations under the New Deal, it is also important to consider the immense scale of administration required. The New Deal and its relief agencies launched the modern administrative state. Americans gained a new sense of the possibilities of the federal government. When dealing with unemployment, every presidential administration since Truman has in some way come under the New Deal's shadow.

Changing Role of Government

The Harry Truman and Dwight Eisenhower administrations undertook new federal programs, including the National Defense Education Act. Increased federal grants for vocational training re-trained the work force for unemployment caused by technological displacement. The John F. Kennedy administration launched the Area Redevelopment Act of 1961 and the Accelerated Public Works Act of 1962. These were much smaller versions of the PWA placed in depressed areas. Lyndon

More About...

Woody Guthrie and the Great Dams of the Columbia River

The building of the Bonneville and Grand Coulee dams undoubtedly stand as two of the most impressive human engineering achievements in the history of the world. Less known, however, are the political difficulties that almost prevented the dams from being built. Not everyone in the Pacific Northwest thought the Bonneville Dam, which was the first of the giant dams on the Columbia, was such a good idea. There had been talk about building a dam during the 1920s but a bitter debate ensued over where on the Columbia it should be located.

In 1933 Roosevelt chose the location of the Grand Coulee Dam at the head of a large coulee in the scablands of central Washington. Few people living in the area, however, wanted a high dam. Even when the Bonneville Dam in the Columbia River Gorge east of Portland, Oregon, was completed four years later, the Spokane Chamber of Commerce in northeastern Washington still opposed public rather than private power.

The situation worsened when the Grand Coulee Dam was completed in 1941. Calling the idea a "socialist boondoggle," because the Bonneville Power Administration was organized as a public company run by the federal government as opposed to a private corporation as utility companies had been in the past, voters throughout the Northwest rejected the idea of switching their electrical lines to the Bonneville Power Administration that could now provide near limitless electricity from both dams on the Columbia. "Boondoggling" was a term widely used in the 1930s to criticize the New Deal relief projects as useless, "make-work" programs. The word rapidly came to embrace a broader meaning by newspapers and the public to mean pointless, unnecessary, or wasteful work created by the government to occupy individuals. It also came to be used to describe misuse of public funds for private benefit. The Bonneville Power Administration (BPA) had a tough public relations job on its hands. How was it going to convince the people of Oregon and Washington the advantages of public power?

A lanky, 28-year-old singer/songwriter who had spent a good deal of time riding the rails searching for jobs in the early 1930s and worked for a few years as a radio personality in Hollywood seemed hardly the person to hire as the Bonneville Power Administration's "information consultant" to deal with the problem. But Woody Guthrie, who desperately needed a job, strummed and sang for an hour on a May morning in 1941. He impressed the BPA director so much that the director gave him a contract to write songs that would make people in the Pacific Northwest appreciate the work of the BPA and the value of public power.

Guthrie began his efforts on May 13, beginning one of the most productive periods of songwriting in his life. In one month he wrote 26 songs for the BPA. Guthrie's songs soon became popular and were given radio airtime. He portrayed the dams as among the greatest achievements ever contemplated by humanity and triumphs of the workingman.

Many later folk singers, including Bob Dylan, Joni Mitchell, and Bruce Springsteen, consider Woody Guthrie to be a source of great inspiration, and today Woody Guthrie is revered as one of America's greatest balladeers.

Johnson's "War on Poverty" modeled itself after the New Deal, at least in ideology. Unfortunately the Job Corps and Neighborhood Youth Corps provided only limited work opportunities for young people and were not much of a comparison to the scale of the NYA or CCC. Nevertheless, support for a large-scale federal employment program never disappeared.

In 1970 Congressional Democrats passed the most ambitious work program since the New Deal under the Employment and Training Opportunities Act. The act provided $9.5 billion to create 310,000 jobs over three years. President Richard Nixon, however, did not believe in WPA-type programs that create federally funded projects to employ the jobless, and he vetoed the bill. A recession in 1971 did prompt Nixon to support a watered-down version of the bill through the Public Employment Program under the Emergency Employment Act of 1971. Like the CWA it was conceived as a temporary measure but once again it barely approached the scale of the New Deal program. At its peak in 1933 the CWA employed four million people. The Emergency Employment Act only provided jobs for 185,000 at its peak in 1972, and hardly made a dent in the six percent unemployment that year.

Clearly all of these programs pale in comparison to the size of the CWA or WPA, but each has been compared to the New Deal. The factor that has remained constant over time is an expectation on the part of the American people that unemployment is a problem that can and should be addressed by the federal government.

The Unemployed

Americans also changed their views about the unemployed during the 1930s. No longer were the unemployed seen as individuals with character flaws or as failures. Instead they were perceived as unwilling casualties of a modern industrial economy. Images of the worker in the paintings and murals of the 1930s depicted heroic men and women. Though sometimes at the mercy of a ruthless industrial order, their achievements in building the country and the character they showed could never be challenged or taken away. The public recognized that the effects of economic depression, like a disease, could strike anyone and a much greater compassion for the unemployed and the poor evolved.

A poignant reminder of the compassion of the New Deal toward the unemployed can be grasped from the words of the New Dealers themselves. On June 27, 1936, President Franklin D. Roosevelt accepted the Democratic nomination for President for a second term (reprinted in Franklin Roosevelt's *The Public Papers and Addresses of Franklin D. Roosevelt, Vol. V.,* p. 230). In his acceptance speech he told the assembly,

> Governments can err, Presidents do make mistakes, but the immortal Gandhi tells us that divine justice weighs the sins of the cold-blooded and the sins of the warm-hearted in different scales. Better the occasional fault of a government that lives in the spirit of charity than the consistent omission of a government that lives in the ice of its own indifference.

Notable People

Robert Fechner (1876–1939). Robert Fechner's six years as director of the Civilian Conservation Corps was actually the culmination of a career as a labor leader and early life as an adventurer. Born in Chattanooga, Tennessee, on March 22, 1876, Fechner attended public schools in Macon and Griffin, Georgia, until the age of fifteen. After leaving school he got a job as a vendor on trains and somehow managed to fit in a few months training at the Georgia Institute of Technology. At sixteen he became a machinist's apprentice for the Georgia Central Railroad and at twenty he left the United States to work in mines in Mexico and both Central and South America. Fechner returned to Georgia sometime in the late 1890s and soon involved himself in labor union activities. In 1913 he became the executive officer of the International Association of Machinists where he remained until 1933. Roosevelt had met Fechner in Washington during World War I when Roosevelt was the assistant Secretary of the Navy and Fechner was serving as an advisor on labor policy to President Wilson. In the summer of 1917 Fechner demonstrated great negotiating skill in settling the Boston and Maine Railroad strike and by the 1920s was well known as a labor advocate.

When Roosevelt first launched the Civilian Conservation Corps, he encountered considerable opposition from the American Federation of Labor fearing that the Corps would undercut gains of union workers. Roosevelt decided he needed a labor leader to head the agency in order to counter this opposition and chose Fechner for the job. Fechner proved an able administrator and his years as head of the CCC were generally successful. Still, as the New Deal's most visible agency, the CCC was criticized for spending too much money and for initially rejecting an education plan, which Fechner later accepted. The most vocal criticism was leveled against Fechner in the late 1930s when he refused to allow military training in what he considered a fundamentally civilian program. After several months of ill health, Fechner died in December 1939.

Harry Hopkins (1890–1946). Harry Lloyd Hopkins, a gangly, chain-smoking workaholic was, in many respects, the prototypical New Dealer. He seemed to embody in his complex personality the many apparent contradictions of the New Deal itself. Hopkins was willing to use immense federal power to bring about recovery, but shared a distrust of a permanent welfare state. Hopkins played one of the most important roles in guiding the unprecedented expansion of the federal bureaucracy, while having misgivings about bureaucratic routine.

As in his public life, there also seemed to be contradictions in his own personality. Hopkins' commitment to government service was tireless, yet he often joked about health problems from overwork. He was painstaking in tracking and managing the funds of the federal agencies under him, but spent a good deal of his own money at the races and died with scarcely any savings. Though not trained as a professional social worker, he eventually came to represent the pinnacle of the profession.

In fact Hopkins' early career in social work uniquely prepared him for his later career in the New Deal and World War II. Raised in Iowa by deeply religious parents, he attended Grinnell College at a time when it was heavily influenced by the Christian reformism of the Social Gospel Movement filling him with ideals of social reform. After graduation he moved to the lower eastside of New York, was quickly introduced to the diversity of turn-of-the-century American urban life, and worked at the Christadora House, a social settlement center. He married Ethel Gross, a Jewish immigrant, and moved rapidly into the network of the city's social reformers.

In 1913 Hopkins began working for one of New York's largest private welfare agencies, the Association for Improving the Condition of the Poor. Within a short period of time he was selected to head its new Employment Bureau. During the recession of 1914–15 Hopkins pioneered the use of a work relief program at the Bronx Zoo. He became an expert and advocate on "widow's pensions," a social insurance program for single women that would be the predecessor of Social Security.

In 1915 Hopkins was appointed Executive Secretary of the city's Bureau of Child Welfare, the agency that administered the program. He stayed until America's entrance into World War I, whereupon he resigned to join the Red Cross as the assistant director of "civilian relief" in the Southern Division in New Orleans. He had a caseload of over 200,000 families of servicemen. He remained in New Orleans with the Red Cross until 1923 when he finally returned to New York to become the director of the New York Tuberculosis Association. Hopkins stayed at the helm of the Association until the early years of the Depression when Governor Roosevelt asked him to head New York's Temporary Emergency Relief Association.

John Maynard Keynes (1883–1949). John Maynard Keynes was a British economist whose work ultimately had a profound influence on United States economic policy. Born in 1883 in Cambridge, England, Keynes went on to have a brilliant career as a student at King's College, Cambridge. He spent two years in the India Office in London where he wrote a book on Indian currency and finance. He was given the editorship of the Economic Journal as a result of the book's positive reception.

In 1918 Keynes went to Versailles to assist in the peace negotiations after World War I, where he protested the imposition of war reparations on Germany and felt compelled to resign his post as deputy for the Chancellor of the Exchequer. He immediately wrote *The Economic Consequences of the Peace* (1919). His conclusions about the imminent failure of the Versailles Peace Treaty gave him an international reputation. During the 1920s Keynes accumulated a small fortune as a speculator on the international securities markets. He wrote a few influential books on the theory of money, criticizing the preoccupation with the gold standard.

John Maynard Keynes, a British economist who advanced the theory that government spending was the cure for the Depression. *(UPI/Corbis-Bettmann. Reproduced by permission.)*

When the Depression turned the economic world upside down, Keynes focused his attention on studying its causes. His greatest influence came when he published *The General Theory of Employment, Interest and Money* in 1936. The theory he advanced was that contrary to classical economic theory, which assumed that the invisible hand of the market would eventually restore to balance any economic downturn, modern industrial economies could decline indefinitely. Declines in production, employment, and income were so interrelated that each could reinforce the other in a downward spiral. The strategy to offset this event, according to Keynes, would be government spending during periods of depression. For a sick economy this was the only way employment and investment could be revived.

By the late 1940s Keynes' theory was generally accepted by most industrialized countries. It was not until the 1970s that his *General Theory* came to be questioned.

Aubrey Williams (1890–1965). Aubrey Williams was born in Springville, Alabama, in 1890 but spent most of his childhood living in extreme poverty in Birmingham. So poor was his family that he only attended one year of elementary school before he was taken out to work as a "cash boy" in a local supermarket. His childhood memories were of always being hungry and the uncertainties of living with the day-to-day grind of poverty. He also experienced firsthand the town's discriminatory treatment of its black population.

At an early age Williams concluded that discrimination against black Americans in the South was an outrage. Poverty, he believed, was the region's largest problem, and racial prejudice only reinforced a social order that sustained poverty. It was a profoundly deep realization for a young, white Southern boy to make in turn-of-the-century Birmingham. His beliefs were bolstered by an equally profound commitment to social justice that he absorbed through his religious mother and two ministers who filled him with the social gospel.

Williams went to France during World War I as a Red Cross volunteer, but later resigned to join the French Foreign Legion. After returning to the United States he became involved in social work. In 1922 Williams was selected to be the executive secretary of the Wisconsin Conference of Social Work, an organization dedicated to preventing delinquency, poverty, and child neglect. He argued that social workers must draft model legislation and that work relief was the only respectable form of public assistance.

When the Depression came, Williams went to work for the Reconstruction Finance Corporation in Texas and Mississippi. When the new administration arrived in 1933, Harry Hopkins appointed Williams to be his deputy in both the FERA and CWA. The two of them developed a very good working relationship that lasted throughout the New Deal. Williams believed that the New Deal could bring far-reaching reforms to America, including reform in racial relations. He was often outspoken in his insistence that blacks be given their fair share of assistance. He alienated many Southern politicians as a result, but Roosevelt never reprimanded him for his statements.

In 1935 Williams was selected to head the National Youth Administration (NYA) where he served as an able administrator until 1943. He made sure no discrimination existed within the NYA. Throughout his tenure as director, Williams continued to be outspoken on matters of race and politics. At times he could be unabashedly partisan, reminding relief workers to vote for the New Deal.

Occasionally his outspoken views were a political liability to Roosevelt. They were not, however, enough to keep him from being appointed to draft the legislation for the Fair Employment Practices Committee in 1941. The resulting bill ended employment discrimination in defense industries.

Williams spent the last twenty years of his life after World War II speaking out against racial discrimination. He was called before the House Un-American Activities Committee in 1954 for speaking against the Committee and was accused of being a communist for his civil rights activities with the Southern Conference Education Fund. This ultimately damaged Williams' publishing business and he became increasingly disillusioned at the politics of the post-war South. Though somewhat embittered, this only intensified his commitment to social justice.

During the late 1950s and early 1960s Williams continued to speak out against the systematic denial of civil rights to Southern blacks. Together with E.D. Nixon, he became instrumental in organizing the Montgomery bus boycott. Williams died in 1965, having lived long enough to witness the passage of the Civil Rights Act. The anger that poverty instilled in him as a youth never subsided nor did his commitment to social justice.

Primary Sources

Receiving Aid

Hank Oettinger grew up in Wisconsin and worked in a printing office until he was laid off in 1931. He remained unemployed for two years. Most people in his county were unemployed. Oettinger reminisced to Studs Terkel about his experiences in ... (from Terkel, *An Oral History of the Great Depression,* p. 115).

> I can remember the first week of the CWA checks. It was on a Friday. That night everybody had gotten his check. The first check a lot of them had in three years. Everybody was celebrating. It was like a festival in some old European city. Prohibition had been repealed, of course. You'd walk from tavern to tavern and see people buying ponies of beer and sharing it. They had the whole family out. It was a warm night as I remember. Everybody was so happy, you'd think they got a big dividend from Xerox.
>
> I never saw such a change of attitude. Instead of walking around feeling dreary and looking sorrowful, everybody was joyous. Like a feast day. They were toasting each other. They had money in their pockets for the first

time. If Roosevelt had run for President the next day, he'd have gone in by a hundred percent.

The Fight against Unemployment

C.B. (Beanie) Baldwin was an assistant to Henry Wallace, Secretary of Agriculture. Baldwin served in Roosevelt's administration the entire time, from 1933 to 1945. He remembered the following about Harry Hopkins and the fight against unemployment, which had increased to 16 million by 1933 (from Terkel, *An Oral History of the Great Depression,* p. 256).

> Hopkins persuaded the President that the situation was so desperate that everybody in the country who wanted a job had to have a job. Even with very low pay. Almost overnight, he set up the Civil Works Administration.
>
> Harry was really a sloppy administrator. Ickes [Secretary of Interior] was a very careful guy. Hopkins was impatient and he knew you had to have something to eat on. He was the kind of guy that seldom wrote a letter. He'd just call and say, 'Send a million dollars to Arkansas and five million to New York. People are in need.'
>
> They set up this CWA very hurriedly... Any guy could just walk into the county office—they were set up all over the county—and get a job. Leaf raking, cleaning up libraries, painting the town hall... Within a period of sixty days, four million people were put to work.
>
> There was no real scandal in this thing, but it lent itself to all the reactionary criticisms that it couldn't be well managed. With our mores, you just can't dump $20,000 into a county in the Ozarks and say: put people to work. That's contrary to everything our political establishment was brought up to believe. This lasted only six months. Roosevelt and Hopkins had to end it. They weren't able to get Congressional support to continue.
>
> Roosevelt won another appropriation—three billion—through an omnibus (general) bill. This brought on another ruckus. Ickes thought it should go for public works: Grand Coulee Dam, Bonneville, projects of this type. They're slow to get under way—wonderful, but they take time. Hopkins thought people should be put to work immediately, even though it might not be done very efficiently.

Suggested Research Topics

- Describe which you think would be more useful to the unemployed today, public works programs or better worker education for re-training? Why?
- Research what the CCC, the PWA, the NYA or WPA did in your area during the 1930s? What youth work programs exist in your area today?
- How do you think people feel about the unemployed today? Is it a serious problem or are most unemployed out of work only temporarily?
- Imagine being unemployed during the Depression. What could you do to make a living? If there were no jobs where you lived, and you had no money, would you be willing to travel across the country by sneaking aboard a freight train and getting off where there might be jobs?
- If you were the local director of the Civilian Conservation Corps in your area, what worthwhile building or conservation projects would you design? What sort of training would it be important to give young people?

Bibliography

Sources

Blumberg, Barbara. *The New Deal and the Unemployed: The View from New York City.* Lewisburg, PA: Bucknell University Press, 1979.

Charles, Searle F. *Minister of Relief: Harry Hopkins and the Depression.* Syracuse, NY: Syracuse University Press, 1963.

Patterson, James T. *America's Struggle Against Poverty, 1900–1980.* Cambridge, MA: Harvard University Press, 1986.

Salmond, John A. *The Civilian Conservation Corps, 1933–1942: A New Deal Case Study.* Durham, NC: Duke University Press, 1967.

———. *A Southern Rebel: The Life and Times of Aubrey Williams, 1890—1965.* Chapel Hill: University of North Carolina Press, 1983.

Schwartz, Bonnie Fox. *The Civil Works Administration, 1933–1934: The Business of Emergency Employment in the New Deal.* Princeton, NJ: Princeton University Press, 1984.

Terkel, Studs. *Hard Times: An Oral History of the Great Depression.* New York: Pantheon Books, 1970, 1986.

Further Reading

Adams, Henry H. *Harry Hopkins: A Biography.* New York: G.P. Putnam's Sons, 1977.

Bernstein, Irving. *Turbulent Years: A History of the American Worker, 1933—1941.* Boston: Houghton Mifflin, 1970.

———. *The Lean Years: A History of the American Worker, 1920–1933.* Boston: Houghton Mifflin, 1960.

Watkins, T.H. *Righteous Pilgrim: The Life and Times of Harold L. Ickes.* New York: Henry Holt, 1990.

See Also

Civilian Conservation Corps; New Deal (First, and Its Critics); New Deal (Second); Reconstruction Finance Corporation; Works Progress Administration

Escapism and Leisure Time

1929-1941

Introduction

The United States is known internationally for its popular culture. Easy access to multi-channel television, video games, video, DVD, the World Wide Web, movies, magazines, radio, live music, recorded music, books, and other such amusements and entertainment are taken for granted. It is important, however, to recognize that this access to popular culture, and the leisure time needed to enjoy it, is relatively recent. Most people living at the beginning of the twentieth century were more concerned with the day-to-day matters of survival and had little leisure time. As a result, amusements were relatively limited and especially cherished.

During the first two decades of the twentieth century, industrialization, new technologies, labor unions, and population movement to the cities began to contribute to an improved quality of life for most people. Survival, for many, became less time consuming. With more money, a higher standard of living, and amenities to make life easier, people found themselves with more free time on their hands. The increased leisure time contributed to unprecedented growth in amusement activities and other forms of popular culture.

Significantly, people living at the time of the Great Depression may have only been the first or second generation in their families to experience leisure time and the options it afforded. Despite the economic devastation of the 1930s, people were not to forego what they had so recently come to take for granted. In fact, popular culture—and the amusements and entertainment associated with it—may have been crucial to public well being during the period. Attending movies, listening to the radio, dancing to live music, and reading cheap magazines or books containing sensational or gruesome material, popularly known as pulp fiction, allowed people to escape from the uncertainties, anxieties, and loss of self esteem associated with the Depression years.

Living during the Great Depression is closely associated with the popular culture of the time. Unlike other industries in the 1930s, many of the entertainment industries responsible for creating and distributing popular culture thrived and evolved. In the case of radio and movies this period is considered a "golden age." Since so many people were unemployed during the Depression and had no other options, they sought for ways to fill their time. Due to lack of funds, they turned to cheap and easy entertainment. Furthermore, much of what we enjoy today as popular culture can be traced to roots in the Great Depression years.

Chronology:

1929: The Great Depression begins.

1930: The Movie Production (Hays) Code agreement on self-censorship is adopted.

1932: Vaudeville disappears; jigsaw puzzles are mass-produced for the first time.

1932: Prohibition is repealed; movies become the most popular form of entertainment.

1934: Eastman Kodak introduces the Baby Brownie snapshot camera, which sells for $1.

June 19, 1934: The Federal Communications Act is passed resulting in the Federal Communications Commission (FCC).

1935: Introduction of sound on film movie cameras spurs rise in home movie making; NBC and CBS radio networks both enjoy large numbers of local affiliates.

1937: Walt Disney Pictures releases *Snow White and the Seven Dwarfs* as a feature length animated cartoon.

1938: Pocket Books introduces Queens Paperback books.

1938: Superman emerges as a comic book hero.

October 30, 1938: Orson Welles' Mercury Theater radio production of "War of the Worlds" creates a national panic.

April 30, 1939: New York World's Fair opens in Flushing Meadow.

Issue Summary

In 1938 social science researchers hypothesized that unemployment leads to emotional instability. These studies seemed to indicate that the longer a person was unemployed, the more likely his or her personality would become fatalistic and distressed. In an attempt to escape from this psychological state, it was speculated that people were turning to popular forms of entertainment such as the movies, radio, or reading. Such speculation is not unreasonable given studies that show children will play even during the worst of times. The fact that very few popular culture forms dealt with the realities of the Great Depression in any explicit way further supports popular culture as a vehicle of escape. Using pop culture to escape emotional stress can also be supported through the generally accepted psychological idea of "flow."

Flow is that point within any activity when you lose your sense of self and become one with whatever you are doing. With the complete absorption in an activity, time disappears, along with the sense of self and all that it might have been feeling prior to absorption. It is plausible that becoming absorbed in an off the wall comedy, a radio adventure, melodramatic pulps, or dancing to the Lindy Hop would provide relief from the uncertainties associated with everyday life.

Entrepreneurs, investors, and popular culture promoters exploited the public's desperate desire to escape by continually creating, distributing and promoting radio shows, movies, print media, fads, sporting events and the like for an eager audience. This creativity was simultaneously stimulated by technological developments, which allowed for the mass distribution and consumption of what was being created. Hearing a piece of favorite music by a particular orchestra was no longer dependent upon being near a concert or dance hall. Technological advances allowed music to be available coast to coast over network radio. The same was also true of sporting events. Technology associated with the motion picture allowed the nation to sit

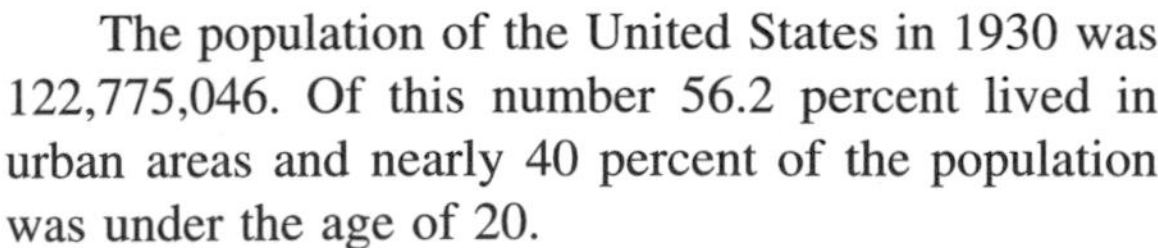

At a Glance
Quick Facts

The population of the United States in 1930 was 122,775,046. Of this number 56.2 percent lived in urban areas and nearly 40 percent of the population was under the age of 20.

In 1935 there were approximately 25 million automobiles in the United States. The American Automobile Association estimated that 25 percent of driving was for pleasure.

In 1930, 11 million people could be accommodated in movie theaters with yearly attendance close to the national population. In 1931 there were an estimated 22,731 movie theaters in the United States.

The 1930 census indicated that 12,078,345 families, or 40 percent of the population, had radios.

In 1930 attendance at professional baseball games numbered 10,185,000 while players in amateur leagues numbered 241,766.

In 1930 there were 30,000 miniature golf courses.

Between September 1932 and March 1933, 10 million jigsaw puzzles were purchased per week with total purchases amounting to 100 million for the period.

In 1933 because of the depressed economy Babe Ruth's pay was cut from $75,000 to $52,000 for the year.

The 1939 New York World's Fair cost $150 million dollars and was located on 1,216 acres in Flushing Meadows, Queens. The Grounds were planted with ten thousand trees and one million tulips from Holland. One thousand five hundred exhibits were contained in three hundred buildings on 65 miles of paved roads.

Swing music rescued the recording industry. In 1932 just 10 million records had been sold in the United States. By 1939, however, that number would grow to 50 million.

Radio serials mirrored pulp fiction genres; in 1940 soap operas made up 60 percent of daytime radio programming.

The growth in mass production of records was reflected in 1939 by the presence of 225,000 jukeboxes and 13 million records sold that year.

---

together in movie theaters across the country and enjoy the common experience of watching their favorite actors play compelling roles in fascinating stories.

The technologies associated with mass production and distribution of products, such as assembly line production, would stimulate the mass consumption in virtually all cultural forms. The benefits of mass production and distribution meant a greater audience for the goods, and trends could sweep the nation, rather than remain local or regional phenomena. For the first time in the nation's history the United States could claim an American culture. The resulting wide appeal of music, drama, dance, literature, and moving pictures was based on the commercialization and mass distribution of these cultural forms, and it gave the individuals something to relate to and share as a nation.

Leisure in the United States 1929–1941

Just prior to the Great Depression the relationship of culture to democracy was most evident in "the democratization of entertainment." Prices were low and forms of entertainment were readily available and accessible. The country was participating in leisure time activities because of an ever-increasing standard of living coupled with new technologies supporting participation in a variety of cultural forms. The Great Depression, however, brought, for the first time to many, forced leisure, as the standard of living collapsed due to unemployment, underemployment, and wage reductions. Forced leisure meant that, due to lack of employment and lack of money to support activities like vacations and such, many people had no choice but to fill their time with activities traditionally considered leisure. Unemployment and reduced standards of living compromised peoples' self esteem and social status. At this point probably many used readily available and economically accessible forms of entertainment and other leisure time activities to escape from the psychologically painful, stressful, and demanding realities of everyday life.

Nine years into the Great Depression the National Recreation Association completed a study of five thousand people asking them to name the recreational activities in which they participated the most. Among the most frequently mentioned activities were reading newspapers, magazines, and books; listening to the radio; going to the movies; visiting or entertaining; motoring; swimming; writing letters; conversation; card parties; picnicking; going to the theater; attending parties and socials; hiking; family parties; tennis; and serious study.

It was apparent from this list that the economic situation in the United States was definitely influencing the type of entertainment and other types of leisure time activities in which children, youth, and adults were participating. Many of the activities on this list were available for free or at low cost. For this reason, the 1930s are sometimes referred to as the "nickel and dime decade."

The National Recreation Association list of activities is best understood by considering it within the context of the breadth of popular culture available in the United States during the Great Depression as well as public preferences for popular cultural forms during the period. Popular culture during the Great Depression has been categorized as fads, radio, print media, the movies, popular music, sports, and miscellany.

Fads

Numerous public fads emerged during the Great Depression. Many were short lived and have since disappeared from popular culture such as dancing "The Big Apple" dance steps. Others continue to periodically capture the public's imagination either in their original form, such as miniature golf and jigsaw puzzles, or as translated into newer technological formats. It is also interesting to note that Great Depression era fads were centered both in the home as well as in the public sphere.

Some fads transcended age groups with participants being children and youth as well as adults. For example, just prior to the Great Depression bicycling and roller-skating were primarily activities for children. During the Great Depression, however, both became popular with adults. Bicycling in particular had not been considered an adult pastime since the 1890s, when it first became trendy. Parlor games such as bridge and board games enjoyed an unprecedented popularity and in 1931 alone five hundred thousand people were enrolled in bridge courses. An estimated twenty million were playing the game including children as young as 11. Monopoly was mass marketed by Parker Brothers in 1935, and by 1937 six million games had been sold.

From 1932 to 1933 children, youth, and adults were all infatuated with jigsaw puzzles. Prior to this time jigsaw puzzles were expensive and thus not accessible to most people. Once they could be mass-produced through die cutting, however, they could be marketed very cheaply. In an attempt to generate more interest in them, jigsaw puzzles were given away as incentives for buying products such as toothpaste or over the counter medications. Images appearing on jigsaw puzzles included landscapes, scenes from history, artwork, movie stars, and even personal portraits. At the height of the fad for working jigsaw puzzles they moved beyond the home and family to became the focus of clubs and parties.

Some fads were associated with get rich quick schemes. For example millions of chain letters began to circulate requesting that sums of money be sent to people appearing at the top of the chain. Lotteries and sweepstakes also became more popular and accepted by the general public. In 1930 thousands of Americans entered the Irish Sweepstakes. By 1933 four hundred thousand Americans were participating and hoping to win the $150,000 prize. By 1936 an estimated $1 billion was sent abroad for such purposes.

Endurance manias also became popular during the Great Depression. Tree sitters, egg eaters, pie eaters, goldfish swallowers, phone booth crammers, and the like attracted local, regional, and national attention because people were intrigued by how long someone could sit, how much a person could eat, or how many people a space could hold. The public also enjoyed bicycle marathons and roller derbies. It was not unusual for roller derby teams to skate four thousand miles in 35 days.

Some of these endurance contests provided both a public spectacle and an income for the participants. Couples were attracted to dance marathons by prize money and free refreshments. In the beginning the dancing was lively and the audience tried to guess who would ultimately become the winners. The earlier contests would last several days, the later contests for several months. Sometimes known as "pageants of fatigue" or "the dance of death" economically desperate contestants would do anything necessary to remain the last ones standing in the contest. Fifteen-minute intervals per hour were allowed for rest and refreshment and, frequently, a sprint or walk-a-thon was staged with the slowest contestants being removed from the contest. Contestants pushed themselves beyond the normal boundaries of exhaustion and some deaths were reported.

Amateur photographers captured many of these fads for family photo albums. Snapshot photography became popular with the release of the $1 Baby Brownie camera by Eastman Kodak in 1934. Some families also documented their activities in 16 mm and 8 mm home movies. It was even possible, beginning in 1935, to make a home movie with sound.

Radio

The 1930s are often referred to as the "golden age" of radio. This label resulted from the rapid proliferation of radio listeners coupled with the quality and breadth of programming. Shortly after the stock market crash of 1929, radio, unlike newspapers, was able to increase revenue from advertising. Radio could more easily reach far larger audiences than individual local newspapers. At the beginning of the decade the United States census reported that 12 million of the nation's 30 million households had a radio. By the end of the decade 80 percent of the population had a radio, a figure that included over two million car radios. In 1934, in response to the growth in the number of radio stations and radio networks, the United States Congress passed the Communications Act resulting in the Federal Communications Commission (FCC).

As numbers of listeners grew, so too did the breadth of programming. Radio listeners could choose from an array of offerings on a daily basis that included music, news, comedy, drama, variety, women's shows, children's shows, and sports.

Music All types of music, both live and recorded, could be heard on the radio. Listeners could tune into dance orchestras led by Guy Lombardo and Paul Whiteman. Popular vocalists included Rudy Vallee and Kate Smith. The former was known for singing through a megaphone and the latter for her rendition of "God Bless America." The crooner Bing Crosby also made his radio debut in 1931.

Jazz and swing enthusiasts could listen to the orchestras and artistry of Duke Ellington, Artie Shaw, Tommy Dorsey, Gene Krupa, Benny Goodman, Glenn Miller, and Louis Armstrong, or vocal stylists such as Ella Fitzgerald and the Andrews Sisters. Country or "hillbilly" music was plentiful, performed by singing cowboys like Gene Autry or heard in the live broadcasts from the Grand Ole Opry in Nashville. For classical music enthusiasts there were contralto Vaughn DeLeath, known as the "First Lady of Radio," Arturo Toscanini conducting the NBC Symphony Orchestra, and George Gerswhin, hosting his own show.

Songs, now considered pop standards, heard on the radio during the 1930s included "As Time Goes By," "Love Letters in the Sand," "I Only Have Eyes for You," and "Santa Claus is Coming to Town." Fans could buy magazines, usually with a favorite singing star on the cover that contained the words to their favorite pop songs. In 1939 announcers began to be paired with recorded music to become known as "disc jockeys." They paired music with comedy routines, news, community notices, and fielded listener requests.

News Radio did offer listeners a number of daily news programs. Some of these programs presented news as information, but also entertainment. One example of news as entertainment was "The March of Time." This news and entertainment program dramatized news stories from "Time" magazine on a weekly basis. Celebrity news and gossip was also popular. At times a news story heard on the radio would attract national attention. One example was the 1937 broadcast as live report (actually it was taped) by Herb Morrison of the crash and burning of the German airship, the Hindenberg. Morrison was heard coast-to-coast giving a detailed and emotional description of the fiery crash at the Naval Air Station in Lakehurst, New Jersey.

Comedy Numerous radio shows on air during the Depression were comedic. Probably the most notorious and controversial was "Amos 'n' Andy." The show focused on the misadventures of two black American men, played by white actors, seeking their fortune in the city. The show was immensely popular; for example a survey of farmers in 42 states ranked it as their number one show. It was so popular that movie theaters piped in episodes into theater lobbies so that people would not stay home to listen to it instead of attending a movie. Many people, including large numbers of black Americans, however, considered the show racist and offensive. At one point a petition was circulated to have the show removed from the air. Seven hundred and fifty thousand people signed but the effort was futile as the highly popular show's ratings soared.

Humor associated with ethnic groups was generally a popular radio staple. Vaudevillian and Jewish humorist, Eddie Cantor, was a huge success on the radio. So too was the show "The Goldberg's" starring Gertrude Berg. These shows played off stereotypes people held about Jewish peoples and culture. Less controversial were shows like "Lum" and "Fibber McGee and Molly" that dealt with issues more common to the mainstream white Protestant society. They did not exploit minorities to such a degree.

Drama Like comedy, drama was also popular. Exemplary was the CBS Mercury Theater on the Air. Although only run between 1938 and 1940, it epito-

Tommy Dorsey's dance orchestra became one of the most popular swing bands during the Depression.
(American Stock/Archive Photos, Inc. Reproduced by permission.)

mized the way in which drama could be translated from the stage into a sound only environment. The Mercury Theater also attracted notable actors of the time. The "Mercury Players" included Martin Gabel, Ray Collins, Joseph Cotton, and Agnes Moorehead among others. Such actors as Orson Welles and Basil Rathbone augmented the players. Productions included "Dracula," "Treasure Island," "A Tale of Two Cities," "The Immortal Sherlock Holmes," and the "War of the Worlds." Of these the most famous is "War of the Worlds." Orson Welles, Frank Readick, and Bill Herz's acting in this production about an invasion of earth by aliens was believed by some to be real. Panic and pandemonium ensued in some locations.

Another form of radio drama that emerged during the Great Depression was the soap opera. Notable examples include "The Romance of Helen Trent" on CBS and "Guiding Light" on NBC.

Variety As vaudeville waned in popularity, many of its stars moved on to radio. Some hosted variety shows while others became regular guests on such broadcasts. Comedian W.C. Fields, now known primarily for his movie comedies, debuted on the radio in 1937. Crooner Rudy Vallee hosted a variety show, as did ventriloquist Edgar Bergen and his puppet Charlie McCarthy. McCarthy, the puppet, received top billing, and the show premiered in 1937 as the "Charlie McCarthy Show."

Special Interest Programs A number of radio programs appealed to specific audiences; for example women, sports fans, and children. First Lady Eleanor Roosevelt was a regular contributor to radio broadcasts that focused on women's issues and contributions. Numerous radio programs addressed cooking, housekeeping, child-rearing, fashion, and other domestic arts. Children could listen to a radio version of the comic strip "Little Orphan Annie." There were also quiz shows for children. Mayor Fiorello LaGuardia of New York City also read the daily newspaper comic strips over the air.

Sports Radio is credited with maintaining a public interest in sports during the Great Depression with virtually all types of sporting events receiving airtime. Sports were first broadcast on the radio in 1920. The first sporting event to be broadcast was a baseball game between the Pittsburgh Pirates and the Pittsburgh Corsairs (Corsairs won eight to five). Radio sportscasting during the Great Depression has been likened to poetry. Sportscasters created play-by-play descriptions of games that people could only hear. It was not unusual for sportscasters to employ sound effects to heighten the experience for listeners; tapping a wood block for the sound of a bat or hiring a group of actors to provide cheering. Sportscasters also became linked to certain catch phrases like "Holy Cow," "Going, Going, Gone," or "How sweet it is." Common use of all of the phrases would persist in American culture throughout the twentieth century.

The Movies

Movies were the most popular form of commercial entertainment during the Great Depression. In the early 1930s there were an estimated 23,000 theaters seating 11 million people. Attendance was almost equal to the population of the United States. A multitude of movie fan clubs existed across the country and autographed pictures of movie stars were a popular collectable.

The 1930s are sometimes referred to as the "Golden Age" of movie making because of the quantity, quality, and breadth of the films being made, as well as the quality of the actors appearing in them. Twenty-two movies, either released or in production from this period, are on the American Film Institute's (AFI) list of the one hundred greatest films produced between 1915 and 2000. At least 34 of the stars listed among the 50 greatest screen legends appeared in films during the 1930s. No other decade is as well represented.

Movie theater owners used a variety of strategies to keep people coming through their doors during the Great Depression. One strategy was to create a hierarchy of theaters so that a film might premier in a first run theater, be bumped to a second run theater to make way for a new release, and then be bumped again to a third run theater. In this way a film could be kept in circulation for a longer period of time before disappearing from the nation's screens. Another strategy used by theater owners was to initiate what would become known as "Bank Night." Bank Nights occurred on those days of the week when attendance was usually low, with tickets becoming part of a lottery for prize money. At one point five thousand theaters were distributing $1 million per week on Bank Night. Some theaters initiated "Dish Night," where moviegoers received a piece of china. Over a period of many months of movie attendance an entire set of dishes could be collected.

Movie Themes The popularity of films during the Great Depression is usually associated with people desiring an escape from the economic brutality of everyday life. In support of this belief is the fact that very few films from the period deal with the Great Depression in a realistic way. One notable exception is the *Grapes of Wrath* (1940), directed by John Ford and starring Henry Fonda, based on John Steinbeck's novel about economic refugees. Another is *Sullivan's Travels* (1941) directed by Prestin Sturges and starring Joel McCrea and Veronica Lake, which tells the story of a movie director trying to find out how the Great Depression affected the impoverished. More typical for the period were movies associated with genres such as gangster, comedy, animated features, musicals, westerns, horror, melodramas, costume dramas, thrillers, and literary dramas.

The Gangster Genre Gangster films were often inspired by headlines in the nation's newspapers. Such films cost little to produce and contained lots of action. *Doorway to Hell* (1930) directed by Archie Mayo, *Little Caesar* (1930) directed by Mervyn LeRoy, and *The Public Enemy* (1931) directed by William Wellman are all Depression era movies that fall within this genre. In *Little Caesar* Edward G. Robinson plays a

Moviegoers wait for tickets outside of a theater in Chicago, Illinois, in 1941. Movies were the most popular form of commercial entertainment during the Great Depression. (The Library of Congress.)

small-time hood and killer who becomes head of a mob. Like most gangster movies from the period, gunfights, killings, robberies, and other forms of mayhem entertained audiences. Like many of the films associated with this genre, Robinson's character dies at the end of the movie under circumstances that communicate some larger moral lesson.

Comedy Comedies were of several types. Some had sophisticated plots and characters and have come to be known as "screwball" comedies while others contained more slapstick. Another type of comedy featured "child" stars.

Mr. Smith goes to Washington (1939) starring James Stewart and Jean Arthur and directed by Frank Capra was a typical screwball comedy. Stewart's character finds himself a member of the United State Senate. This movie is serious in its presentation of democratic ideals, but comedic in the situations encountered by a freshman senator. Many screwball comedies were

Shirley Temple was the most popular child star during the Depression years. Children and adults alike flocked to her movies. *(Corbis-Bettmann. Reproduced by permission.)*

set in palatial surroundings with wealthy, but zany characters. Notable examples include *Bringing Up Baby,* (1938) directed by Howard Hawks and starring Cary Grant and Katherine Hepburn; *Topper,* (1937) directed by Norman Mcleod and starring Cary Grant and Constance Bennett; and *It Happened One Night,* (1934) directed by Frank Capra and starring Claudette Colbert and Clark Gable.

Comedies featuring the Marx Brothers are typical of those that used slapstick. For example, *A Night at the Opera* (1935) directed by Sam Wood concentrated on the hijinks of Groucho Marx as an opera promoter attempting to con a wealthy patron played by Margaret Dumont. Like all Marx Brothers films this one combines very funny one-liners with hilarious physical routines. Other Marx Brother classics include *Animal Crackers* (1930) directed by Victor Herman and *Duck Soup* (1933) directed by Leo McCarey. Charlie Chaplin who became famous for his physical comedy during the 1920s became known during the Great Depression for using physical comedy to bring an audience's attention to important social issues. For example in *Modern Times* (1936) directed by Chaplin, Chaplin played a character struggling with industrialization and new technology.

A number of child stars emerged during the Great Depression around whom comedies were developed. These stars included Mickey Rooney, Judy Garland, and Shirley Temple. Audiences for these films were both children and adults. Shirley Temple was by far the most popular of these stars, appearing in numerous, very profitable films, such as *Little Miss Marker* (1934) directed by Alexander Hall, *Captain January* (1936) directed by David Butler, and *Heidi* (1937) directed by Allan Dwan.

Animated Features During the Great Depression movie audiences were usually treated to a feature length film of around ninety minutes coupled with previews of coming attractions, a "newsreel," an adventure "serial," comedy short, and/or an animated short subject or cartoon. The Walt Disney Studio gained prominence for creating animated short subjects with characters like Mickey and Mini Mouse, Donald Duck, Goofy, and Pluto. Beginning with the *Three Little Pigs* in 1933 and continuing with *Snow White and the Seven Dwarfs* (1937) and *Fantasia* (1940) the studio pioneered animated feature length films. The Disney studio also pioneered the development of merchandise and social clubs associated with its releases. Audiences for these animated features were both children and adults.

Musicals Extravagantly staged filmed musicals were another popular genre during the Great Depression. Such movies concentrated on elaborate dance sequences, compelling melodies, fabulous costumes, and thin story lines. *42nd Street* (1933) directed by Lloyd Bacon and starring Warner Baxter and Ruby Keeler included dance sequences choreographed by Busby Berkeley that are a combination of dance movements and elaborate cinematography. Set on Broadway, movie audiences' emotions are manipulated by a plot in which an understudy to a narcissistic dancer is able to take center stage, become an immediate star, and save the Broadway musical from folding. "42nd Street" was so successful that it was followed up in 1933 with "Gold Diggers of 1933" also directed by Mervyn LeRoy. Song standards such as "We're In the Money," "Pettin' in the Park," and "Brother Can You Spare a Dime" were featured within another Broadway oriented plot.

The enormously popular dancing team of Fred Astaire and Ginger Rogers became famous for movie musicals such as "Top Hat" (1935), directed by Mark Sandrich. "The Wizard of Oz" (1939) directed by Victor Fleming and starring former child star Judy Garland, Margaret Hamilton, Ray Bolger, Bert Lahr, and

Jack Haley, whom are all representative of the movie musical genre.

Westerns Numerous movies during the Great Depression were set in the American west. *Stagecoach* (1939) directed by John Ford and starring John Wayne epitomizes the genre. The plot revolves around passengers traveling by stage during hostilities between Apaches and European American settlers. This film is a classic for many reasons including its use of placing stock characters such as a dance hall girl, drunken doctor, pregnant woman, a gambler, a banker, and an outlaw together under dramatic circumstances.

Horror The Great Depression years set a standard for horror films that has yet to be eclipsed. *Frankenstein* (1931) and *Bride of Frankenstein* (1935) directed by James Whale; *Freaks* (1932) and *Dracula* (1931) directed by Todd Browning; and *King Kong* (1933) directed by Merian C. Cooper continue to be seen on late night television, on video, and during repertory film festivals. Boris Karloff's Frankenstein and Bela Lugosi's Dracula caused terror in their audiences and have come to symbolize the visual image of these monsters. Few movie monsters today communicate the violence, compassion, eroticism, and pathos of *King Kong*. Fay Wray's scream, while held in the monster's grip, chilled and thrilled American audiences.

Melodrama Actors like Bette Davis, Joan Crawford, and Joan Fontaine became know for appearing in melodramas or what are sometimes referred to derogatorily as "weepies" or "handkerchief" films. In these movies characters having to live though a series of adverse and tragic circumstances heightens the drama. Typical is *Dark Victory* (1939) directed by Edmund Goulding and starring Bette Davis. In this film Davis' character faces blindness and a brain tumor. She also falls in love with her doctor and then learns that she has one year to live. She is ultimately able to make peace with her circumstances and die with dignity.

Costume Dramas and Swashbucklers *Gone with the Wind* (1939) directed by George Cukor, Victor Fleming, and Sam Wood, and starring Vivian Leigh and Clark Gable epitomizes this Depression era genre. *Gone with the Wind* is continually shown on television and is periodically re-released to theaters in restored copies. It regularly appears on lists of the best film of all times. There were many other notable costume dramas and swashbucklers, however, produced during the period.

Boris Karloff stars as Frankenstein, in the 1931 film, Frankenstein. *The Great Depression years set a standard for horror films that has yet to be eclipsed.* (The Kobal Collection. Reproduced by permission.)

Swashbucklers are those movies that are often set among pirates and knights and which include melodrama coupled with sword play and/or cannon fire. *Captain Blood* (1935) directed by Michael Curtiz and starring Errol Flynn is typical. The plot involves a wrongfully convicted doctor who becomes a slave and then a pirate. After a series of battle scenes between ships and sword fights, Flynn's character regains his honor and wins the hand of his true love. Also typical of the genre is *Mutiny on the Bounty* (1935) directed by Frank Lloyd and starring Clark Gable and Charles Laughten. This movie combines elements of the costume drama and the swashbuckler. The plot revolves around the hardships endured by the crew of the H.M.S. Bounty in 1789 under the captaincy of Captain Bligh and the eventual mutiny of its crew.

Thrillers Alfred Hitchcock emerged as a master director of thrillers during the Great Depression, with *The 39 Steps* (1935) as one of his masterpieces. The plot focuses on murder, mistaken identity, a mysterious woman, and an international spy ring. Another example of this genre is *The Maltese Falcon* (1941) directed by John Huston and starring Humphrey Bogart and Mary Astor. Like many thrillers it featured a private detective, a sinister atmosphere, mounting tension, and a convoluted and purposefully confusing plot. Such detective stories are referred to as "film noir" for their dark and moody atmospheres.

Literary Adaptations During the Great Depression numerous literary classics were adapted for the screen. These classics included Eugene O'Neill's "Anna Christie" (1930) directed by Clarence Brown; Louisa May Alcott's "Little Women" (1933) directed by George Cukor; "David Copperfield" (1935) directed by George Cukor; and Shakespeare's "A Midsummer Night's Dream" (1935) directed by Max Reinhardt.

At times movies associated with this genre might also be exemplary of another. For example James Whale directed "The Invisible Man" (1933) but earned fame for his direction of the horror films "Frankenstein" and "Bride of Frankenstein." He used his skills to execute horror in the service of H.G. Welles' classic story of a man who makes himself irreversibly invisible, becomes insane, and terrorizes the citizens of a small town.

Print Media

We know from Depression era surveys that reading fiction and non-fiction was a popular pastime of the period. Readers searching for escapist literature had a vast array of materials to choose from, including "pulps;" comic strips and comic books; general interest magazines; and fiction.

Pulps For 10¢ readers could buy a cheaply produced periodical containing lurid stories about such superheroes as Doc Savage, The Shadow, the Lone Ranger, Phantom Detective, The Ghost, The Whisperer, Sheena Queen of the Jungle, and Ki-Gor, King of the Jungle. Primarily read by youth, these periodicals were filled with mystery and adventure taking place in exotic locations with good triumphing over evil. Locations could include the American west as in the case of the Lone Ranger or the tropics as in the case of Doc Savage and Sheena. Parents and schoolteachers did not always approve of such escapist literature, believing that it lacked literary merit and appealed to baser instincts.

Comic Strips, Comic Books, and Little Big Books Comic strips first began appearing in the nation's newspapers towards the close of the nineteenth century. During the Depression, strips and comic books began to feature characters very much like those found in the pulps. Readers could enjoy the capers of "Dick Tracy," the jungle adventures of "Tarzan," the heroics of "Prince Valiant," the domestic comedy of "Blondie," and the superheroics of "Superman," "Batman," and "Wonder Woman." Expertly drawn, with great attention paid to rendering the human figure in action, these strips and books captivated both children and adults with action oriented adventures. Good always triumphed over evil, but not without the heroes or characters being first put to the test and facing down certain death or domestic chaos. Comic strips and books were both criticized regularly for their violence, slapstick, and political leanings. For example, Daddy Warbucks in the comic strip "Little Orphan Annie" was regularly singled out for representing corporate greed.

Closely related to comic strips and comic books were Little Big Books. They were inexpensive and similar in content to comic books and strips, however, their stories were usually presented in a narrative format with pictures supporting the text. Little Big Books had a unique dimension of one inch thick by four inches by four and one half inches.

Magazines Magazines were available to a broad range of interests and frequently responded and supported other forms of escapism like the movies, sports, or radio. Some magazines targeted a specific gender. For example romance-oriented magazines like "Modern Romance," "True Story," and "Secrets" were confession-oriented publications marketed to women. Women audiences also purchased movie-oriented publications like "Modern Screen," "Movies," and "Movie Life." Men were more likely to read magazines about sports or the male lifestyle. Two such publications that are still in print, but which originated in the 1930s are "Sports Illustrated" and "Esquire." Men also tended to read crime-oriented periodicals such as "True Detective Mysteries" and "Official Detective Stories." "Photography" and "Modern Photography" stimulated the fad for photography during the Great Depression. The 1930s was also the era in which photojournalism magazines like "Life" and "Look" premiered.

Fiction As in film, numerous genres dominated the market for escapist fiction during the Great Depression. Raymond Chandler gained popularity for mystery thrillers such as *The Big Sleep* (1939) and *Farewell My Lovely* (1940). Writing within the same genre was Dashiell Hammett, known for *The Maltese Falcon* (1930) and *The Thin Man* (1934). The popularity of these books ultimately resulted into all four being made into movies.

Historical novels during this period are exemplified by Margarett Mitchell's *Gone with the Wind*

(1936), which was also adopted for the screen. Edna Ferber also created notable historical novels such as *Cimarron* (1930). Readers attracted to what were considered exotic locations turned to Pearl Buck and Louis Bromfield. Buck's *The Good Earth* (1931), was set in China and Bromfield's *The Rains Came* (1937) was set in India.

Popular Music

The Depression era may be one of the very first periods in American history so closely associated with popular music that it almost serves as a soundtrack for the times. Despite the fact that the recording industry was in a free fall, people were able to continue consuming popular music through live shows, radios, and movies. As a result jazz, in the form of "swing" became mainstream and country western music emerged as a combination of folk sounds from Appalachia and other parts of the south. Singers like Woody Guthrie used folk music as a way to vocalize the nation's troubles.

Dancing was one of many forms of entertainment used to escape everyday doldrums during the Great Depression. (©Bettmann/Corbis. Reproduced by permission.)

Swing Popular music during the Great Depression was dominated by "swing." Swing, a form of jazz, was so pervasive that it is considered by many to define the era. Swing, somewhat less improvisational than modern jazz, incorporated written arrangements, emphasized solos, and included danceable rhythms. Rhythms were freely borrowed, particularly from African rhythms.

Swing bands were larger than jazz ensembles and became know as "big bands," including saxophones, trumpets, trombones, clarinets, guitars, a keyboard, bass and drums. Notable big bands included those of Duke Ellington, Count Basie, Benny Goodman, Lionel Hampton, Glenn Miller, Tommy Dorsey, and Artie Shaw, among many others. Typically a "stand up" vocalist or two would also accompany a big band. One of the most notable was Frank Sinatra who began his singing career in 1936 but became a national celebrity in 1940 when he joined the Tommy Dorsey Orchestra.

Big bands played in dance halls across the country with names like the "Aragon" in Chicago, the "Alcazar" in Baltimore, and the "Ali Baba" in Oakland. Big band musicians, particularly bandleaders and vocalists, received the same kind of admiration and public attention as movie stars and sports heroes.

Swing was so pervasive during the Great Depression that it could be heard simultaneously on the radio, live in dancehalls, on records, on jukeboxes, and in the movies. Swing was also associated with dances such as the Lindy Hop or jitterbug, the Big Apple, the Shag, and the Suzy Q. All of these dances emphasized a series of basic steps, some improvisation, and high physicality including aerial moves. Swing permeated the culture to such an extent that it even had its own slang and clothing styles, such as the "zoot suit" worn by black and Mexican American men.

Music critics during the Great Depression found in swing a musical equivalent to New Deal progressivism. In this regard swing has been credited with introducing mainstream American culture to black American music for the first time. Most bands, however, were not integrated; with black American bands playing one circuit and white American bands playing another. Bandleader Benny Goodman's decision to add Charlie Christian, a black American musician, to his band in 1936 was an extraordinary and controversial decision on his part.

Folk and Country Music Folk and country music also enjoyed some popularity during the Great Depression. Shortly after the onset of the Depression, Woody Guthrie began to write new lyrics to old folk songs and periodically played live on local radio. Woody Guthrie's songs appealed to listeners because they often focused on trying to get by with little or nothing and life as a hobo. Guthrie's best-known song from this era is "This Land is Your Land."

Joe Louis, shown here in 1936, won the world heavy weight boxing championship in 1937. With the win Louis became a symbol of black power, during a time when many blacks felt powerless.

(Corbis-Bettmann. Reproduced by permission.)

Beginning in the early 1920s it was possible to turn on the radio in the southern United States and listen to "barn dances" with "hillbilly" music. Commercial recording companies began recording such music for sale shortly afterwards. Jimmie Rogers, credited with being one of the first and finest country western singers made his first recordings in 1927. Because of the popularity of country western music, the film industry began to make movies that featured singing cowboys. Throughout the Depression Gene Autry, Roy Rogers, and Tex Ritters' cowboy crooning was heard not only in the United States, but also in Europe. When record sales plummeted during this period, because people didn't have the funds to buy the records, country western music could still be heard on the radio. It was during this period that Nashville, Tennessee's Grand Ole Opry was broadcast coast to coast for the first time.

Sports

Sporting events and athletes grew to be immensely popular during the Great Depression. This occurred as a result of new technological advances such as the radio, changes in the ways that some sports were played, and people's inclination to personally identify with particular teams and athletes. In combination these factors contributed to sports being a major form of escapism during this period.

In the early 1930s the rule changes in college football allowed for more passing and thus a more exciting and unpredictable game. College football games were also broadcast on the radio for the first time. The growing popularity of football during this period is evidenced in the proliferation of bowl games. At one point during the Great Depression college teams were playing one another in the Rose, Orange, Sun, Sugar, Cotton, Eastern, and Coal bowls. Also bringing public attention to college football was the creation of the Knute Rockne Trophy and the Heisman Trophy. Pro football also gained in popularity, which is traceable to radio broadcasts, rule changes encouraging passing, and a slimmer football that allowed for greater passing distances.

Baseball adapted to the nation's depressed economy by also allowing games to be broadcast on the radio and by holding games at night. Players like Babe Ruth also helped to attract national attention. Little League baseball originated in the 1930s as one response to the growing popularity of baseball.

During the Great Depression basketball, golf, tennis, and boxing also had their fans. Again a fan base would often grow because of the popularity of a particular athlete. For boxing it was Joe Louis, the "Brown Bomber" and his capturing of the world heavy weight championship over James J. Braddock in 1937. Louis became a representative of black America in popular culture and gained international acclaim when he defeated German championship boxer Max Schmeling in 1938. The victory to many represented the supremacy of American democracy over Nazi Germany.

The United States hosted both the summer and winter Olympics of 1932. During the summer games Babe Didrikson Zaharias came to public attention for her ability to excel in multiple sports. It was the 1936 Olympic Games in Berlin, however, that galvanized the nation. This was particularly true because of the success of black American athlete Jesse Owens in numerous track and field events. His superior athleticism, coupled with a simultaneous shattering of Adolf Hitler's propaganda regarding Nordic superiority, captured national and international attention.

Leisure in Difficult Times

People entered the Great Depression years with an acquaintance with leisure time and a predisposition to enjoy it through a variety of pursuits. Myriad forms of inexpensive entertainment were available to the general population. People were not prepared, however, for the economic devastation resulting from the Great Depression and the forced leisure that many would experience as a result. Given the nation's severe economic downturn it is remarkable that the Depression years were ones in which popular culture was sustained, and in many cases thrived. This was probably possible, in part, because of people's desire to escape from the stress associated with economic instability coupled with technological developments commercialized for entertainment purposes.

At a Glance

Escape by Travel

Many people during the Great Depression found escape by getting into their cars and driving. Sometimes they had no idea where they would end up or where they wanted to go—they just got into their cars and drove. As the Dust Bowl of the plains of America drove some people West, others were forced to move on due to lack of employment, loss of home, or in search of "the good life." If a car was unavailable, many took to hitchhiking or riding the rails. An estimated 250,000 of those riding the rails were youth, some as young as 13. Called "boxcar boys and girls," they shared the same dangers and hardships experienced by the adults riding the rails at the same time.

Contributing Forces

Leisure in the United States 1900–1929

The United States entered the twentieth century as the world's leading economy. This economy resulted from the industrialization of the nation that began during the nineteenth century. This industrialization was also resulting in more and larger cities. In 1900 fully 40 percent of the seventy six million total population of the United States population was living in urban areas. This was an increase of 25 percent from only 50 years before.

A higher standard of living for the majority did not initially result from industrialization. In the beginning a very small percentage of the population controlled the largest amount of capital. Workers labored long hours for little pay. The average workweek at the beginning of the century was 60.2 hours per week and weekly salaries of ten dollars were not unusual. It is not surprising that these conditions resulted in the unionization of labor. Unions are organizations formed by workers that bargain with the employer for better pay and working conditions.

With unionization, working conditions and the standard of living improved and for the first time in the nation's history large numbers of people found that they had leisure time. This development, particularly in the growing urban areas, was coupled with new technologies such as automobiles and radios. People had more information about leisure time options and the ease with which to participate. Soon entrepreneurs began to realize that money could be made by providing people with leisure time alternatives. This realization resulted in the commercialization of leisure.

Popular pastimes during the first three decades of the twentieth century included theatrical forms such as vaudeville and burlesque as well as short silent movies. Amusement parks proliferated and exhibit halls featured shows about sports, pets, and transportation. Baseball became "the national pastime" and the World Series began in 1903. Prizefighting captured the public imagination. People also began to document their lives through snapshot photography. People sang and listened to music at church socials and community sings. Pianos and phonographs became affordable. A national American culture began to be formed through such shared pastimes.

By the 1920s discussion began to rise around what culture should be within the United States. Much of this discussion centered on the relationship of culture

In 1935 the American Automobile Association estimated that 25 percent of driving was for pleasure. *(Courtesy of American Automobile Association. Used with permission.)*

to democracy. Some argued that democracy encourages business entrepreneurs and the wealthy to greatly influence the public toward participation in cultural activities, including leisure time activities, that they believed to be best for the "common good." Not surprisingly this common good was often closely associated with economic gain through the commercialization of culture. Others, however, believed that all people contribute to the definition of culture within a democracy, including the entrepreneur and the common citizen. The resulting variations contribute positively toward a unique national identity. They felt confident that over the long term culture for the common good in a democracy would more likely come from contributions of the many rather than only a few. Therefore commercialization of culture and leisure can dominate society's view of culture but does not always necessarily do so.

A Demand for Escapism Rises

The 1920s had been a decade of unprecedented prosperity. Suddenly beginning with the stock market crash of October 1929, leisure time took a different course. As the Great Depression swept across the nation leisure became a byproduct of joblessness. Certain forms of leisure began to serve different purposes including providing an escape from the economic problems. By 1933 unemployment reached a scale never experienced before. The sudden collapse of the nation's banking system and dramatic decline in industrial production were very distressing to people trying to cope with it all. Various forms of escapism were taken by the jobless, those who still had work but at reduced incomes, and the youth.

Though the precise level of unemployment was difficult to estimate, for the month of March 1933, when the Depression was near its worst, the federal government estimated that over 15 million people were jobless. It was estimated that almost a third of the workforce was out of work. Many families in the rural areas were abandoning their farms and youth were riding the rails in search of employment and to get away from the harsh realities of home. The demand for escapism had never been greater in U.S. history.

Perspectives

National and Local

The story of escapist culture during the Great Depression is very much a national story rooted in popular culture, mass production, mass distribution, and mass consumption experienced by the great majority of citizens on the local level. Because the population of the United States was continuing to become more urban during this period, the spread of popular cultural forms was easily achieved. It is important, however, to remember that despite the growth of urban areas, large numbers of Americans lived relatively isolated lives in rural areas. Some of these people were only infrequent visitors to those urban centers where dances were held, movies were seen, and printed material was purchased. Until the Rural Electrification Act of 1935 great parts of the United States were without electricity and thus without easy access to the radio. In addition, because of crop failures in various parts of the country and/or discriminatory rural labor practices, there were Americans who were living in abject poverty that could never afford to participate in the popular culture with which the country was obsessed.

Ultimately, there is no consensus that the popular culture of the 1930s was totally escapist despite its emphasis on humor, melodrama, craziness, and blatant exhibitionism. For example, scholars are not in agreement about the actual messages conveyed by American movies during the 1930s. Some scholars see the movies as advocating traditional ideas about individualism, success, consumerism, and progress. Others see the movies of this period as projecting fantasies about the past based on American myths and values such as simplicity and community life. The movies projected an ideal of what people thought America represented. These perceptions provided a sense of security colored by what people wanted to believe as much or more than what they actually experienced. The case can also be made that while most popular films were often comedic and superficial, some films did address important social issues such as the transformation of the United States from a farming (agrarian) society to a more urban one. Gangster films have been singled out as helping Americans to master their new environment and make sense of, and control, the social facts they were encountering in their daily lives.

Other scholars see the popular culture of the 1930s as reflective of socio-economic class tensions during the period. Despite the Great Depression there were many people in the United States who amassed a great deal of wealth. Thanks to mass communication, this wealth and the lifestyles it afforded were not hidden from public view. Class differences were very much on the minds of people, particularly on the part of those struggling to get by on a day-to-day basis. On the one hand the country was being urged to unify in the face of economic instability and hardship, while on the other hand there were clearly have and have nots. Screwball comedies on film and radio, with their emphasis on wealthy and zany characters, made manifest some of the resentment felt towards the rich by making them appear as buffoons. Or take a radio program like the enormously popular, but racially problematic comedy "Amos n' Andy." On the surface this show appealed to its listeners' sense of humor. They were probably also appreciative, however, of the main characters' attempts to get by during harsh and difficult times.

A conclusion about the purpose of popular culture during the Great Depression can probably be found somewhere in the middle. Certainly the popular culture

More About...

The New York World's Fair

The New York World's Fair opened on April 30, 1939. Fairgrounds were located on what once had been a dump in Flushing Meadows, Queens, but now were dotted with buildings housing national and international commercial exhibits. Auto companies, insurance agencies, candy companies, camera companies, meat packers, and tire manufacturers were among those represented. The National Cash Register Company's exhibit was housed in a pavilion with a giant cash register on the roof. Civic associations such as the Boy Scouts as well as cultural exhibits from around the world were also present.

The fair was conceptualized and created to encourage people to look to the future, particularly in relation to democracy and technology. In this regard fairgoers could look at exhibits of futuristic automobiles, television sets, and robots. Fairgoers could also partake of more traditional fair activities such as sideshows, thrill rides, and agricultural exhibits. Amusements included an archery range, Ferris wheels, bowling alleys, and a parachute jump sponsored by Lifesaver candy. For adults there were beer and champagne gardens.

The centerpiece for the World's Fair was a seven hundred foot needle-like Trylon and a two hundred foot Perisphere marking a site for freedom of assembly. President Roosevelt, Albert Einstein, and the King and Queen of England were among the over forty million people who attended.

being consumed was immensely entertaining and potentially escapist. We should not, however, let that quality interfere with a careful analysis of the content of the entertainment. A careful study of the popular culture consumed by citizens of the United States during the Great Depression is likely to continue to reveal a citizenry engaged with the very important issues of the time. The best summation may have come from the period's movie producers and directors who believed "that it had been they who had staved off revolution, because they had worked to make people happy. They had achieved a careful, artful transformation of social anger and stress into laughter and shared experience." (Brinkley, *Culture and Politics in the Great Depression,* 1998, p.10)

International Popular Culture

The 1930s were a politically turbulent time in most parts of the world. Americans, when not concerned with their own personal well-being, were probably most concerned with the political changes in Europe and the European sphere of influence and vice versa. Fascism was prevailing within the governments of Italy and Germany. Spain was in civil war with Fascists also prevailing there. In France, the Popular Front was gaining popularity and would take control of the government in 1936. Great Britain's colonialism was being challenged, particularly in India.

Technology was also stimulating the growth of popular culture in Great Britain and Western Europe. Britain, France, Germany, and Italy all had movie industries. In Germany and Italy the films produced supported a nationalistic agenda. The case of France is interesting because rather than movies becoming escapist during a time of social upheaval they tended to concentrate on a socially realist perspective mirroring the eagerly anticipated changes hoped for from the Popular Front. Britain and the United States film communities were closely aligned, with numbers of filmmakers and actors from Britain coming to the United States to work. Among many notable examples include James Whale, director of "Frankenstein" and Vivian Leigh, star of "Gone With the Wind."

As the 1930s progressed parts of Europe became more and more fascinated with American popular culture. For example in March 1939 Duke Ellington and his Orchestra played in France to great critical and popular acclaim. The Orchestra was also well received in Belgium, the Netherlands, and Denmark. German youth were also entranced by American swing. Nazi soldiers, however, would not allow Ellington and his entourage to disembark from their train because of policies barring "foreign blacks" from Germany and because they saw jazz as "Nigger-Jew" music.

Impact

The Great Depression era was a period of severe economic instability coupled with a national obsessive infatuation with popular culture. Evidence suggests that this infatuation was reinforced and stimulated by forced leisure and people's desire to escape from the daily stress of living with economic uncertainty. To only think in these terms, however, about the surge in popular culture during the Great Depression would be simplistic. It is also important to recognize the role of new technologies, corporate entrepreneurship, and aggressive marketing campaigns as a part of what encouraged and shaped popular culture during this period. It is equally important to look beyond the amusing and entertaining quality of the culture of the period to find and identify those values, attitudes, and beliefs embedded within the movies, radio, print material, fads, and the like that were capturing people's attention. Also important is to consider what the impact of this period has been on subsequent generations.

One very obvious point of impact is the way that people have come to think about the Great Depression era. Given the apparent superficial character of much of the popular culture consumed by the public, coupled with the fact that much of this popular culture failed to portray the realities of the Great Depression, it is not surprising that we see the people of the era as fearful and anxious; wanting to escape the stress of everyday life. This very one-dimensional view does not encourage us to know that many citizens were thoroughly immersed in the most important issues of the day. To only know the Great Depression through a superficial look at its popular culture is to deny national, regional, and local conversations that were taking place around reshaping the nation economically and politically towards a more equitable and democratic society. Ignored also is the collective dialogue that was taking place about the United States and its role in the world.

Also of concern is to what extent the nation remains obsessively infatuated with popular culture and the possible ramifications of this obsession. Arguments can be made that the Great Depression era heralded an even greater infatuation with amusements and entertainment continuing to the present. Neal Gabler in his book *Life The Movie: How Entertainment Conquered Reality,* (1998) argues that entertainment now pervades all aspects of American life to such an extent that it has become the most powerful agent of social change. He compares it to a kind of cancer that promotes simple narratives built on sex, scandal, gossip, and action promoting neat and tidy resolutions.

More About...
Youth Culture

The games and activities of children and youth during the Great Depression are a perfect example of appropriating objects at hand for playful purposes. Many children and youth could not expect their parents to provide them with toys or games. Instead, children had to find their own means of accessing creative, imaginative and fun activities. Following are examples of some of the more popular childhood pastimes of the era.

Jacks

Jacks were played in a group, each participant would take turns seeing how far they could continue scooping up the small, star-shaped, metal "jacks" on a single bounce and catch of a rubber ball. Players progressed from 'onesies,' 'twosies,' 'threesies,' etc. The winner was the first person to successfully scoop up all the jacks. Variations included "around the world," where the player would scoop the jacks and circle the ball with his or her hand and catch it before it bounced again.

Jumprope

Jumprope was a favorite during the Depression since the only equipment needed was one or two lengths of rope and a couple of friends. As today, the singsong rhymes that accompanied each jump were an integral part of the activity. Pantomime and acting out the words to the rhymes was also a part of the jump rope routine.

Card Games

Gin Rummy, Old Maid, and the more sophisticated Canasta and Bridge were ways to spend an afternoon. All you needed was a deck of cards and a few friends.

Paper Dolls

As cutouts from magazines, or as original creations, girls of the Depression spent hours creating, designing, and cutting out clothes for their paper dolls. The dolls from magazines were often of famous movie stars of the era including Shirley Temple and Judy Garland. Some children created their own paper dolls by cutting out pictures from catalogs and magazines.

Kick the Can

All that was needed for this game was a large soup, vegetable, or fruit tin can. Kick the Can involved maneuverability, endurance, and a space in which to run and hide. Kick the Can was a neighborhood game involving as many children and youth as wanted to participate. Teams were picked and the game was played similar to a rough game of soccer.

Imaginary Play

There was also imaginary play, when children would dream and pretend of better lives, fairy tales, and riches. Sometimes they just imagined an escape to a better life.

A more positive legacy of the period may be that popular culture allowed the United States to become a more integrated society. For example, the enormous popularity of swing allowed for more interactive relations between black American and European American communities. At least one scholar has argued that American popular culture is far more pluralistic, dynamic, and tolerant than United States legal and political culture. The Great Depression also was an era in which folk music became popularized as large numbers of people simultaneously learned of its ability to communicate the hardships of daily life and as a musical form able to contain a political purpose. This legacy was first fully realized during the protests by young people during the 1960s.

Finally, the Great Depression era, with its surging popular culture, encouraged distinctions between what was then considered to be high art (i. e. painting, sculpture, classical music, theater, ballet) and low art (i.e. movies, jazz, pulp fiction, the jitterbug) to begin disintegrating. Few would make the argument that films like Orson Welles' *Citizen Kane* (1941) with its innovative cinematic techniques and socially critical screenplay or a jazz composition by Duke Ellington are in any way inferior to those other creations called art. This change in attitude about popular culture would allow artists like Andy Warhol during the 1960s to unabashedly draw subject matter from popular culture and to break down barriers between high and low culture once and for all.

Notable People

Because of huge numbers of celebrities that accompanied popular culture during the Great Depression it is difficult to single out a few notable people from the time. The following selections are merely representative of the types of contributions made during the period.

James Algar (1912–1998). James Algar was one of the principle animators for Walt Disney Studio's *Snow White and the Seven Dwarfs.* Originally trained as a journalist, he came to Disney in 1934. Following his work on *Snow White* he became Animation Director at the studio.

Jack Cooper (1888–1970). Jack Cooper was the first black American disk jockey on the radio. He bought time from WSBC in Chicago around 1931. He is also known for the production of the "All Negro Hour" radio variety shows.

Vaughn DeLeath (1894–1943). Vaughn DeLeath emerged in early radio as a woman who could sing without destroying radio power tubes. She did this by perfecting a lullaby like singing style that would become known as "crooning." Billed as the "First Lady of Radio" and later as "The Original Radio Girl" she was imitated by many including Kate Smith. DeLeath was also a radio manager and producer and in 1930 Vaughn appeared on early television.

Ella Fitzgerald (1917–1996). A jazz singer, Fitzgerald joined the Chick Webb orchestra in 1935 and made her first recording that year. Her first major hit came only three years later in 1938. Fitzgerald stayed with the band until it broke up in 1942. She then had a spectacular solo career for the next 50 years and was regarded as the "First Lady of Song." Fitzgerald's greatest fame came in the 1950s when she won 12 Grammy Awards for her various recordings.

Benny Goodman (1909–1986). Goodman was a clarinetist who made his first recording with the Ben Pollack jazz band in 1926. After moving to New York City from Chicago in 1929 he formed his own orchestra in 1933. Goodman's orchestra became the most popular swing band in the United States and introduced mainstream America to jazz. By later in the 1930s he performed in smaller jazz trios and quartets, some of the first racially integrated jazz groups. He performed steadily through the 1950s before reducing his number of performances. Goodman was widely noted for his fast rhythm, enthusiasm, and improvisation.

Woody Guthrie (1912–1967). Throughout the Depression Woody Guthrie wrote songs inspired by the Dust Bowl and his intermittent life as a hobo. In 1934 Guthrie was hired by the Bonneville Power Administration (BPA) to spend a month in Portland, Oregon, putting into song the damming of the Columbia River to bring electricity to areas of the Northwest. In 1937 he moved to California to pursue a country music career by teaming with his cousin, Jack Guthrie, on a radio show on KFVD-Hollywood where he was able to sing his Dust Bowl ballads live. In 1939 Guthrie moved to New York to be an active part of the socialist movement. Guthrie performed with Bess Lomax on occasion who was the sister of Alan Lomax, one of the first ethnographers of American folk music. Alan recorded Guthrie on several occasions at the Library of Congress. RCA Victor released Guthrie's first album, "Dust Bowl Ballads," in 1940. Guthrie's most famous song is "This Land is Your Land," a song that protests the private ownership of land, hunger, and poverty.

E.Y. "Yip" Harburg (1898–1981). Yip Harburg wrote the song "Brother Can you Spare a Dime" (1932) that combined popular ballad with a social protest song. ("Once I built a Railroad, I made it run, I made it run against time...now it's done, Buddy can you spare a dime.") Harburg worked for Universal and Warner films throughout the Depression. Harburg also penned "Over the Rainbow" from the film *The Wizard of Oz,* winning an Oscar for this song.

John Lomax (1867–1948). In 1933 John Lomax began his work in the Library of Congress as the curator of the American Folksong. Throughout the 1930s John and his son, Alan, traveled the South and Southwest recording folk music. While recording prison songs in Louisiana, the two discovered Leadbelly who went on to become a successful recording artist. The two also recorded Woody Guthrie.

The Mills Brothers. The Mills Brothers were the first black Americans to have a show on network radio. They were signed to the CBS radio network in 1930. The Mills Brothers consisted of John Jr. (1910–1936), Herbert (1912–1989), Harry F. (1913–1982), and Donald F. (b. 1915). Born in Piqua, Ohio, the Mills brothers were the sons of a barbershop quartet member father and a light opera singer mother. The brothers sang locally until 1928 when they went on the radio in Cincinnati, Ohio. Duke Ellington is credited with helping them gain national attention by introducing them to a New York record label. While in New York they signed with CBS radio. Mills Brothers hits include "Tiger Rag," "Goodbye Blues," and "Lazy River." In 1931 *Radio Digest* named the Mills Brothers the "vocal find of 1931."

Billy Strayhorn (1915–1967). Billy Strayhorn joined the Duke Ellington Orchestra in 1938 as an arranger and pianist. With a background in classical music and jazz, Strayhorn came to the attention of Ellington as the composer of "Lush Life." From 1938 until his death he was a close collaborator with Ellington who described him as "my listener, my most dependable appraiser [and] critic."

Mae West (1888–1980). Mae West first emerged as a child vaudeville star known for doing comedy. As an adult she brought her knowledge of comedy to the theater and the movies as a playwright, screenwriter, and actor. West made her film debut in 1932 in *Night after Night.* Her risqué dialogue, bejeweled appearance, and independence made her attractive to movie audiences. These same characteristics, however, made her a target of censorship under the Hays Act. During the Great Depression years she made nine films, five of which she received a writer's credit for, one of which was *Diamond Lil* is one of the most famous.

Primary Sources

Radio

On May 6, 1937, the German airship the Hindenburg crashed and burned at the Lakehurst Naval Station, killing 36 passengers and crew. The next day Herb Morrison's commentary during the crash was heard over the radio, as if live, to a captivated and horrified nation (as quoted in Michael Macdonald Mooney. *The Hindenburg.* New York: Dodd, Mead, 1972, p. 148).

> It's crashing. It's crashing terrible. Oh, my get out of the way, please. It's bursting into flames. And it's falling on the mooring mast. All the folks agree this is terrible, one of the worst catastrophes on the world. Oh, the flames, four or five hundred feet in the sky, it's a terrific crash ladies and gentlemen. The smoke and the flames now and the frame is crashing to the ground, not quite to the mooring mast. Oh, the humanity and all the passengers.

The Movies

William Hays' comments on the importance of film to national morale and education during the Great Depression are reprinted in Andrew Bergman's *We're in the Money: Depression America and its Films* (1992). William Hays was the head of the Hays Commission, which developed a moral code that guided what images were appropriate for including in movies.

> No medium has contributed more greatly than the film to the maintenance of the national morale during a period featured by revolution, riot and political turmoil in other countries. It has been the mission of the screen, without ignoring the serious social problems of the day, to reflect aspirations, optimism, and kindly humor in its entertainment.

The Hays Commission's code was not without its critics, however, and film producer David O. Selznick argued with William Hays over the inclusion of a memorable line he considered critical to a movie he was producing at the time, *Gone With the Wind.* Selznick addressed Hays on October 29, 1939 (quoted in David Colbert, *Eyewitness to America,* 1998, pp. 455–456).

> As you probably know, the punch line of *Gone With the Wind*, the one bit of dialogue which forever establishes the future relationship between Scarlett and Rhett, is, "Frankly, my dear, I don't give a damn."...
>
> Under the [Hays] code, Joe Breen in unable to give me permission to use this sentence because it contains the word "damn," a word specifically forbidden by the code....
>
> I do not feel that your giving me permission to use "damn" in this one sentence will open the floodgates and allow every gangster picture to be peppered with "damn"s from end to end. I do believe, however, that if you were to permit our using this dramatic word in its rightfully dramatic place, in a line that is known and remembered by millions of readers, it would establish a helpful precedent... which would give... discretionary powers to allow the use of certain harmless oaths... whenever... they are not prejudicial to public morals.

Greatest Pleasure

Al Cunningham was a youth growing up during the Great Depression. In 1999, at the age of 73, Cunningham's recollections were recorded adding to the oral history of the period. He recalled his experiences in escapism in an article titled "How I Came to Love the Classics" (as quoted on the *Reel Classics* website http://www.reelclassics.com/Articles/Statements/alcunningham.htm).

> Movies were one of my greatest pleasures and I would try to go every weekend, although that was seldom possible. It wasn't often that my folks were able to come up with the price of a ticket (ten cents), so I had to be creative and find other ways to find the money. Hunting for returnable soda bottles in order to get refunds was one of my methods. Another was searching the gutters along the curbs of the busy shopping areas.
>
> Sometimes the only way I could get to see a movie was to sneak in. My best bet was at a certain theater about five miles from home ... Unfortunately, my only pair of shoes had holes in the soles, which were bigger than the size of quarters. Even though I would cut out pieces of cardboard and place them inside my shoes, the long hike would wear through them long before my journey had

ended. Seldom was the time when my feet weren't cut or blistered. A bloody foot wasn't all too unusual, but hiking to see a good movie was well worth it.

Many of the neighborhood theaters in those days would give away dishes. One night each week would be "Dish Night," and every lady in attendance would receive a free dish with the price of admission. Each week a different dish was available and by returning week after week, you could eventually collect a complete set ...

There were the days when many of the great classic films were made and I was there to enjoy their debut n the silver screen. As a young boy I recall enjoying most every type of movie Hollywood produced including westerns, musicals and adventure films.

Suggested Research Topics

- Compare and contrast the movie genres common during the Great Depression with those genres common today. Speculate on the reasons why some have continued while others have disappeared. Speculate on what movie genres will be unique to the first decade of the twenty first century.
- For the most part, popular culture during the Great Depression ignored the social realities of the period. This has been attributed to peoples' desire to escape from the painful realities of the period. To what extent does popular culture attend to the social realities of today? Do you believe that there is a link between economic downturn and how people choose to amuse themselves?
- The focus of this text has been primarily on public figures. Discover those notable people who ran the companies and industries responsible for creating and distributing popular culture, but who may not have been known to the general public.
- It has been proposed that entertainment now pervades American life. Look at an area of social concern that is of interest to you. Discover to what extent the social issue is addressed by the popular entertainment. If it is addressed by entertainment, do you see that as a positive, negative or neutral influence?

Bibliography

Sources

Brinkley, Alan. *Culture and Politics in the Great Depression.* Waco, TX: Baylor University, 1998.

Csikszentmihalyi, Mihaly. *Flow: The Psychology of Optimal Experience.* New York: Harper Collins, 1991.

Cullen, Jim. *The Art of Democracy: A Concise History of Popular Culture in the United States.* New York: Monthly Review Press, 1996.

Dickstein, Morris, "Depression Culture: The Dream of Mobility." In Bill Mullen and Sherry Lee Linkon, eds. *Radical Revisions: Rereading 1930s Culture.* Urbana: University of Illinois, 1996.

Gabler, Neal. *Life the Movie: How Entertainment Conquered Reality.* New York: Knopf, 1998.

Gregory, James N. *American Exodus: the Dust Bowl Migration and Okie Culture in California.* New York: Oxford University Press, 1989.

"Halper's History of the Radio," [cited June 21, 2001] available from the World Wide Web at http://www.old-time.com/halper/index.html

Hamilton, Marybeth. *When I'm Bad, I'm Better: Mae West, Sex, and American Entertainment.* Berkeley: University of California Press, 1997.

Hardy, Phil and David Laing, eds. *The Faber Companion to 20th Century Popular Music.* Boston: Faber and Faber, 1991.

Hitchcock, H. Wiley, ed. *The New Grove Dictionary of American Music. V. II and v 15.* New York: MacMillan Press Limited, 1986.

Kammen, Michael. *American Culture American Tastes: Social Change and the 20th Century.* New York: Knopf, 1999.

Kingsbury, Paul, ed. *The Encyclopedia of County Music.* New York: Oxford University Press, 1998.

Larkin, Colin, ed. *The Encyclopedia of Popular Music. v 1.* New York: Muze UK ltd, 1999.

Mullen, Bill, and Sherry Lee Linkon, eds. *Radical Revisions: Rereading 1930s Culture.* Urbana: University of Illinois Press, 1996.

"Radio Sportscasting," [cited June 21, 2001] available from the World Wide Web at http://www.americansportscasters.com/radio-how.html

Santelli, Robert and Emily Davidson, eds. *Hard Travellin': The Life and Legacy of Woody Guthrie.* Hanover, NH: University Press of New England, 1999.

Stowe, David W. *Swing Changes: Big Band Jazz in New Deal America.* Cambridge: Harvard University Press, 1994.

Further Reading

"American Film Institute," [cited June 21, 2001] available from the World Wide Web at http://www.afionline.org/cover/main.html

Bergman Andrew. *We're in the Money: Depression America and its Films.* Chicago: Ivan Dee, 1992.

Best, Gary Dean. *The Nickel and Dime Decade: American Popular Culture during the 1930s.* Westport, CN: Praeger, 1993.

Guthrie, Woody. *Dust Bowl Ballads.* New York: Folkways Records, 1964.

"Jazz: A Film by Ken Burns," [cited June 21, 2001] available from the World Wide Web at http://www.pbs.org/jazz/

Time-Life Books. *This Fabulous Century: 1930–1940.* New York: Time-Life Books, 1969.

Uys, Errol Lincoln. *Riding the Rails: Teenagers on the Move during the Great Depression.* New York: TV Books, 2000.

Various. *Brother Can You Spare a Dime: American Song During the Great Depression.* New World Records, 1977.

See Also

Crime; Ethnic Relations; Everyday Life; Hollywood; Interwar Era; Radio; World's Fairs

Ethnic Relations

1929-1941

Introduction

"When we moved to California, we would work after school. Sometimes we wouldn't go. 'Following the crops,' we missed much school. Trying to get enough money to stay alive the following winter, the whole family picking apricots, walnuts, prunes." This comment was from farm labor organizer Cesar Chavez on remembering his youth during the Great Depression. His family became migrant farm laborers in California after losing their home in Arizona (in Terkel, *An Oral History of the Great Depression.* p. 54).

With the rapid pace of industrialization following the Civil War (1861–1865), life in the United States offered a promise of economic opportunity and financial security found in few other places in the world. In the late-nineteenth century and early-twentieth century thousands had moved to the United States from foreign lands, which were previously little represented in U.S. society. By the 1920s the United States had become the home of increasing numbers of social groups distinguished by their race, nationality, language, or cultural traditions.

These groups, known as ethnic groups or ethnic minorities, added complexity to a society long dominated by Americans whose ancestry lied primarily in western and northern Europe. Ethnic minorities may differ from racial minorities since race is often more narrowly based on skin color. Ethnicity may be based purely on cultural traditions including language, but it often includes skin color as well. For example, people immigrating from Germany or Russia or Scandinavia may all have the physical features similar to Anglo Americans, but belong to their ethnic group based on cultural heritage. In the United States people are commonly considered members of ethnic groups regardless of their U.S. citizenship status.

Among those arriving in the United States in the late-nineteenth and early-twentieth centuries were many people from Mexico and Asia. Because they differed in skin color, culture, and language from mainstream U.S. society, Mexican citizens (Nationals) and Mexican Americans as well as Asians and Asian Americans were treated similarly despite differing legal status. They did not readily blend in and were given few opportunities to do so. Ethnic groups arriving from various regions of Europe including Italy, Ireland, and Germany were not as severely discriminated against. Black Americans and American Indians have histories of relations with the U.S. government that are significantly different than those of the Mexican and Asian immigrant populations and are each addressed in other entries in this volume.

Until the twentieth century, the increasing ethnic diversity posed few social and political problems in the United States. However with the abrupt downturn in the U.S. economy in 1929, ethnic groups, particularly those from Mexico and Asia, quickly became scapegoats for the growing social and economic problems the United States faced.

Highly restrictive immigration laws passed beginning in 1882 had largely stopped the flow of peoples from Asia into the United States, while those who were already in the United States faced severe discrimination and exclusion from mainstream society. This exclusion led to even more isolated ethnic communities of Asian Americans. As a result Chinese and Japanese populations in the United States had stopped growing by the late 1920s.

With Asian Americans largely isolated from U.S. society by the 1930s, Mexican Americans became a major target of government action during the Great Depression. They presented an easy target since most Mexican Americans were farm laborers, a type of job which was not protected by federal or state laws. As the Great Depression set in they saw farm wages fall dramatically, if they were able to keep a job at all. Farm workers making average daily wages of $2.55 in 1930 were only making $1.40 a day in 1933 and some laborers were only making 15¢ an hour. Many returned to Mexico to seek out employment there, while others were forcefully sent to Mexico during the 1930s. Mexican Americans became the target of one of the largest mass removal efforts ever promoted by the U.S. government, as well as state governments, particularly California's. For many continuing to work as field laborers, conditions were often deplorable. Efforts to organize and seek better working conditions gained momentum, but the agricultural industry, including growers, aggressively fought such efforts. As the Great Depression continued Mexican Americans received little relief and fewer work opportunities.

The overall effect of the Depression was that Asian Americans became even more isolated from U.S. society and the movement of Mexican laborers northward to the United States during the previous several decades temporarily reversed. The California Mexican population declined for the first time in 80 years. During the period of years between 1929 and 1937 the Mexican American population in the United States decreased by over a third. Though the forced reduction in population

Chronology:

1882: Chinese Exclusion Act prohibits Chinese immigration causing a decline in the population of Chinese Americans.

1924: Congress passes the National Origins Quota (Immigration) Act to drastically limit immigration into the United States, particularly immigrants from all Asian countries except the Philippines.

1929: Federal and local law authorities begin to conduct raids on Mexican American communities seeking to deport illegal aliens and even U.S. citizens who had insufficient proof of citizenship. The raids continue for several years.

1933: President Franklin D. Roosevelt combines the two federal bureaus handling immigration and naturalization matters into one agency, the Immigration and Naturalization Service (INS).

1934: Congress passes legislation granting the Philippines independence by 1945, but also greatly restricting Filipino immigration.

1943: The United States reaches an agreement with Mexico to establish the Bracero Program encouraging Mexican workers to once again enter the United States to take agricultural jobs in support of the war effort.

had little effect on ending the Great Depression, it did greatly alter the ethnic makeup of the nation's farm labor force, particularly in California. The return migration to Mexico also devastated the lives of many immigrants and citizens and greatly set back the Mexican American communities in the United States. All people of Mexican descent were subjected to constant fear of forced removal throughout the Great Depression.

Issue Summary

As the nineteenth century progressed, the United States became more ethnically diverse. Foreigners who came to stay, called immigrants, arrived from distant overseas nations as well as from countries in North and South America. Immigrants arrived both legally, through established official entry locations, and illegally through more secretive means. Before becoming a U.S. citizen, both legal and illegal immigrants are known as aliens, who can become citizens through the naturalization process. This process involves satisfying several requirements including being a legal resident for five years, being literate in English, and having a good behavior record. The U.S. government can legally evict, or deport aliens, sending them back to their country of origin after federal proceedings. A specific cause must exist, however, for deporting those legally in the country. Prior to deporting an individual U.S. authorities must notify a foreign official from the country involved, known as a foreign consul, of U.S. intentions to send the person to their country. Aliens can also be sent or forced back to their country of national origin through other means in addition to deportation. This more general process is often referred to as repatriation. Repatriation is the return of individuals to their place of origin, or ancestry, which can include the formal process of deportation or less formal processes such as voluntary decisions to return.

The Great Depression dramatically changed ethnic relations in America. During earlier economic boom times members of ethnic groups had filled the demand for low-wage, unskilled workers. In addition to the many immigrants and their children who were U.S. citizens by birth or naturalization, six million aliens, legal and illegal, also resided in the United States at the onset of the Great Depression. The demand for ethnic minorities to fill labor positions suddenly ended as U.S. economic conditions deteriorated and they were no longer wanted by the economically-dominant white society.

In place of a demand for immigrants, a groundswell against ethnic groups erupted. Mexican Americans, Chinese Americans, Japanese Americans, and other ethnic groups were considered part of the national problem. Many believed the Depression was dragging on because "foreigners" were taking jobs away from white Americans. The "foreigners" were also accused of depleting government relief funds by receiving welfare payments. Many minorities were deprived of work opportunities, some faced government deportation programs involving mass roundups, and others faced violence and intimidation. Deportation was part of a massive repatriation effort that sent several hundred thousand people, some U.S. citizens, out of the country. Most aliens remained culturally isolated and had not intermingled with U.S. society. A large number did not speak English and did not understand the economic factors driving deportation. Many felt resistance was useless and passively complied with U.S. demands to leave. They often fully expected to eventually return. Few wanted to leave.

Immigration issues rose in prominence during the 1930s, garnering greater attention from public officials more than any time before. Existing immigration laws which favored some ethnic groups over others, such as the Chinese Exclusion Act of 1924, were more tightly enforced and immigration officials were given broader powers to issue arrest warrants and detain aliens.

Mexican Americans

Mexican and Mexican American workers were under high demand by U.S. businesses during the economic boom years of the 1920s. Over one million new immigrants came from Mexico between 1900 and 1930 to take advantage of the growing U.S. economy. Most worked in the agricultural fields of California and the Southwest settling into Mexican American communities for the long term. Their goals were often to save up enough money to move back to Mexico and purchase farmland or establish a business. Growing numbers were also finding work in mines and then manufacturing by the 1920s. When the Great Depression arrived, however, and jobs became more scarce, discrimination against Mexican Americans greatly escalated.

Deportation to Mexico A forceful expression of the anti-minority sentiment that grew in the 1930s was an increased effort to deport illegal aliens and this action was particularly aimed at Mexicans. As long as the business community needed workers the issue of illegal aliens had little urgency, but when jobs disappeared and competition for wages with non-minorities grew, the public sought to deport illegal aliens.

Deportation efforts started within the agricultural industry as it struggled through the 1920s. A U.S. fed-

More About...

Immigration and Naturalization Service (INS)

The Immigration and Naturalization Service (INS) located within the U.S. Department of Justice administers all laws regarding admission, restriction, deportation, and naturalization of aliens. The modern version of the agency was born in 1933 under President Franklin Roosevelt. Roosevelt issued an executive order combining the functions of two agencies that had separately dealt with immigration and naturalization.

During the first hundred years of U.S. history state governments were largely left to regulate admission of aliens. Congress had passed a federal law about immigration as early as 1819, however, it was more concerned with keeping statistics on immigration than regulating it. With New York being the main port of entry for people from foreign nations, the New York State Board of Commissioners of Emigration carried most of the burden. Finally in 1876 the U.S. Supreme Court ruled that only the federal government had authority to regulate immigration and state laws and regulation on the subject were deemed unconstitutional. After several years of debate, Congress passed the Immigration Act of 1882, which assigned enforcement of immigration laws to the Department of Treasury. By 1891 the federal government assumed total control over immigration matters.

How and who should oversee immigration within the government remained unsettled for years. In 1903 immigration responsibility was transferred to the newly created Department of Commerce and Labor. The bureau was expanded in 1906 to also include naturalization matters and renamed the Bureau of Immigration and Naturalization. The following year the Immigration Act of 1907 brought all other immigration matters under the Bureau, yet uncertainty of how to best address immigration persisted. Only seven years after combining immigration and naturalization functions into one agency Congress separated them once again into two bureaus in 1913.

Immigration increased as an issue in the mid-1920s as the U.S. Border Patrol was established. Concerns over immigration became expressed in the 1924 Immigration Act that placed strong restrictions on immigration. In 1933 Roosevelt reunited the two bureaus once again, this time into the INS. The agency became very active during the Great Depression years leading into World War II. By 1940 with war prospects growing, Roosevelt transferred INS from the Department of Labor to the Department of Justice. Then the agency focused more on national security rather than economic issues as it did during the Great Depression. Since World War II the INS patrols U.S. borders, reviews applicants for naturalization, and faces complex immigration issues that gained momentum again in the 1990s.

---

eral deportation campaign against Mexican workers was launched in the Lower Rio Grande Valley of Texas in 1929. During that year alone 17,600 Mexicans were sent back to Mexico. The deportation program spread nationwide and Mexican aliens were deported daily through the early years of the Great Depression. For example, in August 1931 over 1,500 aliens were deported followed by 1,700 in September.

Federal agents brought militaristic strategies to the deportation program. Raids and roundups by immigration agents, called *levas* or *razzias* by the Mexican Americans, in California's Mexican communities began in 1930. The agents wielded considerable legal power and rounded up federal agents, county sheriffs, and local police to participate. Anyone who looked Mexican, including U.S. citizens of Mexican ancestry, and were legal or illegal immigrants were subject to being picked up and taken into custody during street sweeps. Mass arrests were made in public places without warrants or particular reason (show of probable cause). Besides street sweeps, agents would go door-to-door without warrants demanding proof of legal residency. Those unable to satisfactorily produce official papers to the agents were taken to jail.

To satisfy the white business community, on behalf of President Herbert Hoover (served 1929–1933), Secretary of Labor William N. Doak focused on labor strikes involving minorities. Farm strikes in California became a key target to seeking out illegal aliens. The roundup and arrest of aliens while they were on strike served as warning to others who would strike. The business community was pleased by this assistance by the government officials in resolving their labor issues and keeping minorities at bay.

Evidence of racial harassment by government agents was also widespread. Reports and complaints were common about beatings, rough treatment, and verbal abuse. Given no opportunity to post bail for release from jail, the gathered individuals were held until the next deportation bus, ship, or train was available. As intended these governmental *razzias* created chaos and a climate of fear across the nation in Mexican communities. Many, including U.S. citizens of Mexican ancestry, lived in constant fear that they would be next. A large number of Mexican immigrants chose to leave on their own accord and returned to Mexico as a result.

One of the more infamous *razzias* was La Placita raid in Los Angeles, which was conducted on February 26, 1931. Agents sealed off and then swept through a city park that was popular among the Mexican American population. The orchestrated sweep resulted in about 30 Mexicans, five Chinese, and one Japanese being detained.

Deportation efforts continued under President Franklin D. Roosevelt (served 1933–1945). As part of the New Deal reorganization of government, in 1933 President Roosevelt combined the two agencies charged with immigration and naturalization matters into one agency, the Immigration and Naturalization Service (INS, see sidebar). During the time period of August 1933 to May 1934, 1,279 Mexicans were deported.

Supposedly aliens had legal protections against such arbitrary deportation efforts. If a person could prove they had legally resided in the United States continuously for five years they could not be deported without the government showing specific cause. Officials, however, often overlooked this legal requirement. Also, in addition to not having warrants, the mandate to notify foreign consuls before deportation of individuals was frequently ignored. Very often Mexican consuls only learned about the deportation after the person had already left the United States; therefore they had little opportunity to become involved. Furthermore, many Mexicans had little knowledge of U.S. immigration and deportation laws. Detainees could only see lawyers with approval of the immigration officials. Usually they could not have access to a lawyer since U.S. deportation officers did not consider deportation hearings to be formal judicial proceedings. A lawyer would normally only be involved if the INS decision to deport was formally appealed and the case went to court.

Such U.S. deportation practices during Hoover's term of office were the subject of an official inquiry. The National Commission on Law Observance and Enforcement, otherwise known as the Wickersham Commission, issued a report denouncing such government tactics. However, Secretary Doak denied all charges and successfully appealed for public support and as a result, little was changed.

Other Repatriation Efforts Besides deportation other efforts to repatriate Mexican Americans also began. Unlike deportation that is a formal federal matter, more general repatriation efforts were made by local law enforcement and private organizations. Unlike the militaristic and legal nature of deportation, repatriation relied more on intimidation and enticements, such as the allure of free transportation to Mexico. However due to its magnitude this type of repatriation took a good deal of logistical planning.

Among the organizations strongly supporting repatriation were labor unions such as the American Federation of Labor (AFL) and "patriotic" organizations such as the America for Americans Club. Repatriation became a highly organized effort, which focused largely on Mexican American populations in large cities from California to the Midwest. The effects were sweeping and as a result some Mexican American communities disappeared altogether.

In response to the pressures, immigrants left for Mexico through various means of transportation. Trains, cars, buses, trucks, and ships streamed southward in the early 1930s toward Mexico, while the poorest journeyed on foot. Shiploads of 500 or 600 people would leave Southern California ports for destinations in Mexico, many using any available space on the open decks or in empty hulls. Trains, capable of cheaply carrying hundreds of repatriates, became the most common means of travel and boxcars and cattle cars were also often used. Others journeyed in overloaded cars and trucks traveling over dangerous roads. Most immigrants left the United States with expectations of someday returning when economic conditions improved and they returned to Mexican communities, which were already living in poverty before the Depression. Many repatriates joined family members to work in the fields for food. Most Mexican authorities were displeased to see more hungry citizens arrive and were angry with the rough treatment Mexican citizens and Mexican Americans in the United States received.

Repatriation efforts slowed after 1932, after the period between 1929 and 1932, when 365,000 people left for Mexico. Approximately 75,000 Mexicans were repatriated from Los Angeles area alone. From 1933 to 1937 only 90,000 left the United States for Mexico.

The house and yard of a Mexican family living in San Antonio, Texas, in March 1939. People of Mexican descent were subjected to constant fear of forced removal during the early years of the Great Depression.

(The Library of Congress.)

Economic Hardships of the Depression Many resisted repatriation and avoided deportation. By the 1930s a generation had grown up in the Mexican American communities with no personal attachments to Mexico. The communities were the only home they knew and they had no intention of moving. Those remaining in the United States suffered from the Great Depression's economic woes and unemployment rates in Mexican communities averaged 50 percent. Access to public works projects for any minority was limited.

As many were leaving, far fewer were entering the United States. The lack of job opportunities, in addition to U.S. immigration policies discouraged many legal and illegal aliens from entering the country. From 1925 to 1929 2,474,500 Mexican immigrants had entered the country. Between 1930 and 1934 only 1,216,396 entries were recorded. Those admitted in the 1930s were mostly Mexicans joining family members already settled in the United States.

The wages of agricultural workers sharply dropped from a monthly income of almost $61 in 1930 to $30 in 1933, or from $2.55 a day down to $1.40 a day. Some workers were earning only 15 ¢ an hour for their labor. Faced with racial discrimination, low pay, and poor working and living conditions, Mexican American farm laborers increased efforts begun in the late 1920s to organize unions. In 1933 the Mexican Farm Labor Union led a widespread strike in southern California demanding a minimum wage of 25¢ per hour. Some concessions were gained by the strike. The Confederation of Mexican Farmers and Workers Unions (Confederacion de Uniones de Campesinos y Obreros Mexicanos—CUCOM) became the most active farmworker union in California. CUCOM had 10,000 members by 1935. However, organized strikes and union activity between 1933 and 1939 were often met with threats and violence from the growers. Throughout the decade numerous strikes involving Mexicans and Mexican Americans occurred in cotton and celery fields of California, the pecan industry in Texas, coal mines in New Mexico, and the steel industry of Chicago. The strikers often met strong resistance. For example, California growers would hire men as strikebreakers to physically intimidate the strikers. Such frequent violent reactions by the growers clearly discouraged many workers from participating in strikes.

Mexican American women became active as well, in industrial unions. With many Mexican women working as seamstresses in the garment industry, Rosa Pesotta became a well-known labor organizer

Immigration to the United States, 1891-1950
in thousands

Period	Asia	Britain	Germany	Mexico
1891-1900	75	272	505	15
1901-1910	324	526	341	50
1911-1920	247	341	144	219
1921-1930	112	330	412	459
1931-1940	16	29	114	22
1941-1950	37	132	227	61

Nearly 460,000 people from Mexico immigrated to the United States form 1921 to 1930. Only 22,000 immigrated in the next decade. (The Gale Group.)

for the International Ladies' Garment Workers' Union (ILGWU). A massive strike in 1933 brought garment production in Los Angeles to a stop. The strikers prevailed as workers received a new contract containing increased wages.

Asian Americans

Chinese Americans By the 1920s the Chinese population in the United States was in decline due to stiff legal restrictions on immigration provided by the 1924 Chinese Exclusion Act prohibiting Asian entry into the country. The construction and farm work that had drawn Chinese males to the United States, primarily in the Far West region, throughout the last half of the nineteenth century was no longer available.

Throughout the Great Depression the Chinese Exclusion Act remained firmly in place. In fact many Chinese returned to China because of the poor job opportunities and rampant discrimination in the United States. This out-migration led to a significant Chinese American population decline. In California the Chinese American population, comprising over 9 percent of the state's population in 1860, fell below 1 percent by the end of the Great Depression. Aging and declining in number, the remnant Chinese American society was a largely bachelor society surviving under severe strain by the early 1930s. Chinese Americans experienced severe discrimination and were largely excluded from mainstream U.S. society. With the steady loss of agricultural employment throughout the 1920s and 1930s they increasingly turned to the big cities for social and economic survival. In 1910 slightly less than half of Chinese Americans lived in cities. By 1940 the figure had risen to just over 70 percent. A third of those living in large cities congregated in San Francisco through the Great Depression. Ethnic enclaves within the cities, known as Chinatowns, provided a major support system for daily Chinese American life.

Like other minorities, Chinese Americans did not benefit from New Deal programs to the extent that white society did. Because of past severe discrimination, many Chinese Americans feared U.S. authorities and had little knowledge of relief programs available. Consequently, having little assistance, they endured great hardships living in crowded, unsanitary conditions without basic necessities. Some communities were exceptions. For instance Chinese Americans found relief in San Francisco where the Chinese Six Companies organized federal relief. Over 13 percent of the Chinese population in San Francisco was on economic relief by October 1933, a higher percentage than the general population. In other cities, where no such organizations existed, far fewer Chinese Americans received aid.

Overall the Great Depression continued the exclusion of Chinese Americans from U.S. society and restricting them to low paying labor jobs. Ironically during this time many Chinese Americans who remained in the country acclimated themselves more to mainstream American life. Following World War II, Chinese Americans would play increasingly more prominent roles in the worlds of science, economics, and politics in the latter half of the twentieth century.

Japanese Americans Unlike Chinese Americans who persistently filled low paying labor needs, by the 1930s, Japanese Americans, whose population was also highly concentrated on the West Coast, had achieved a lower middle-class economic status. These gains in status were set back during the Depression because Japanese Americans faced increased discrimination and segregation from white society. White America had great difficulty accepting Asians as equals particularly during bad economic times. With jobs increasingly scarce some Japanese Americans immigrated back to Japan, but most stayed. For example Seattle's Japanese population decreased from 8,500 to 7,500 in the late 1930s.

Those Japanese Americans remaining in the United States primarily found employment in agriculture, forestry, commercial fishing, and wholesale and retail businesses. Most businesses that employed Japanese Americans were Japanese-owned. Even Japanese-grown crops were primarily marketed by Japanese-owned small businesses during the 1930s. As conditions worsened for farm laborers during the Great Depression the Japanese Farm Laborers Association became involved in a series of agricultural strikes in Southern California

Most Japanese Americans found employment in agriculture, forestry, commercial fishing, and wholesale and retail businesses during the Depression. These Japanese agricultural workers are packing broccoli near Guadalupe, California in 1937. (The Library of Congress.)

in 1936. Japanese American business leaders, however, including members of the Japanese Chamber of Commerce, joined with the white establishment to quickly counter the workers' efforts.

Those that left for Japan were largely those who had been born in Japan. As a result by the end of the 1930s, U.S.-born Japanese Americans had come of age and began to equal the number of foreign-born Japanese Americans. As a result, the Japanese American population was becoming increasingly Americanized.

Filipino Americans Legislation on immigration passed during the New Deal era served to further restrict Asian entry into the country. Following the U.S. conquest of the Philippines in 1898, all Filipinos became American nationals. Exempt from the 1924 immigration ban on Asians, they remained free to enter the United States. The first substantial Filipino immigration began in 1907 with over 2,300 arriving in Hawaii to work in the sugar cane fields by 1910. At that time only four hundred Filipinos were in the U.S. mainland. In the 1920s labor conflicts led most Filipinos to relocate to California in search of work. By 1930 over 30,000 Filipinos were working in California, primarily as migrant workers.

As with Mexican migrant workers, racism during the Great Depression heightened as the competition for work with non-minorities increased. By 1934 the open privilege of immigrating to the United States was changed dramatically. Congress passsed the Tydings-McDuffie Independence Act granting the Philippines independence from U.S. control by 1945. The act immediately withdrew free access to the States and established a very restrictive Filipino immigration policy. Congress even made available public funding to assist Filipino Americans living in the United States to return to the Phillipines.

Support Organizations

During the difficult times of the Great Depression, grassroots organizations began appearing to assist ethnic groups living in the United States. For Mexican Americans these included the Latin American Club in Phoenix, the Mexican American Political Club in East Chicago, and the League of United Latin American Citizens (LULAC) in Texas. These organizations pursued political action to gain improved economic opportunities. LULAC expanded to various parts of the nation and became active in civil rights issues on behalf of Mexican Americans.

More About...

Traditional Craft Revival in New Mexico

Prior to the 1930s the U.S. government had done little toward integrating Mexican immigrants and Mexican Americans into U.S. society or helping preserve their heritage. Through the leadership of local New Mexico officials, some New Deal programs sought to preserve Mexican cultural heritage through works programs. They also sought to make Mexican American communities more economically "efficient."

Various New Deal programs, such as the Works Progress Administration (WPA) and the Federal Emergency Relief Administration (FERA), brought teachers to Mexican American communities. Included were arts and crafts experts, English teachers, and health and nutrition specialists. They created demonstration gardens, taught home canning techniques, brought hot lunch programs to school children, and operated nursery schools. Vocational and adult education classes were also offered in spinning and weaving, ironwork, tinwork, leather working, and furniture making.

In the town of Taos, a craft vocational school opened in September 1933. Spanish ornamental ironwork was first taught with woodworking, weaving, leatherwork, and tinwork later added. Being an area of limited industrial potential, the economic goal was to attract tourism. As a result of these educational programs, a cottage crafts industry grew in New Mexico.

Efforts to record and preserve Mexican American lifestyle began through work relief projects under the Public Works of Art Project (PWAP) in December 1933. The program was aimed at unemployed artists, writers, and musicians. For example the PWAP hired 51 artists, many of them American Indian and Mexican American, to decorate New Mexico public buildings. These activities increased through the WPA's Federal Art Project, Federal Writers Project, and Federal Music Project. The Federal Art Project promoted the painting of murals on public buildings, sculptures, and other artwork and a Hispanic arts and crafts revival resulted. Two Hispanic New Mexico artists emerged "discovered" from these programs, Petrocino Barela and Juan Sanchez.

The Federal Music Project recruited local musicians to transcribe, revive, and record Hispanic musical heritage. Music education programs sponsored songfests and folk festivals. A Mexican American "Song and Game Book" was published in 1942 describing the songs as the oldest folk music in America. Similarly the Federal Writers' Project collected Mexican folklore including customs, legends, folk beliefs, and oral histories. The New Mexico efforts to focus New Deal programs toward Mexican Americans as well as American Indians represented a unique approach and highlighted the flexibility local authorities had in shaping New Deal programs in their states.

Due to the fact that Japanese Americans were economically and socially isolated within their own communities throughout the Great Depression, social clubs, church groups, and athletic leagues were formed to provide mutual support. In San Francisco Japanese Americans gathered forming a Japantown. It became the site for the national headquarters of the Japanese American Citizens League (JACL). The JACL, established in 1930, became a key organization for the younger Japanese generation growing up in America during the Depression. It stressed Americanization of Japanese Americans and exercise of their civil rights. Other more traditional organizations known as *ken-jin* groups served both economic and social functions. The groups provided apprenticeships in certain trades or financial aid to persons in need.

The New Deal and Mexican Americans

The administration of President Franklin Roosevelt attempted to bring more humane governmental policies to all Americans. Roosevelt introduced the New Deal, which was a combination of diverse economic and social programs designed to bring economic relief to those affected by the Great Depression. Regarding deportation, for example, after 1934 the number of Mexicans deported decreased by 50 percent. Some New Deal programs served to bring minority youth more into Anglo culture. The Civilian Conservation Corps (CCC) and the National Youth Administration (NYA) employed not only black but many Mexican American youth as well. The CCC provided outdoor jobs for males between ages 18 and 25 in soil erosion control, tree planting, fighting forest

Families such as this one living in Amalia, New Mexico benefited from New Deal programs like the WPA and NYA. Many of these programs were designed to document and preserve traditional music, art, folklore, and social customs. (The Library of Congress.)

fires, and many other similar activities. The enrollees received $30 a month with $25 of it required to go back to their homes. New Mexico CCC camps contained up to 95 percent Mexican American youth. The NYA provided work-study for students between the ages of 16 and 24 including work in school laboratories, libraries, and as teacher aides. The two programs also trained youth in farming, home economics, and how to live on small plots of land. But the CCC and NYA were not much help to many migrant workers because they often did not have a permanent address, a standard requirement of the programs. Similarly, the New Deal's primary agricultural reform program operated by the Agricultural Adjustment Administration (AAA) was aimed at helping farm operators not farm laborers.

In some parts of the country New Deal work programs went further to benefit ethnic groups. They involved the recording of cultural traditions and even sought to restore some traditions that had been lost. These programs were aimed at documenting and preserving traditional music, art, folklore, and social customs. A key example of these types of programs took place in Northern New Mexico, an area heavily settled by Mexican Americans. The Works Progress Administration (WPA) and the NYA taught classes in such subjects as traditional Mexican craft woodworking. Many who became highly respected artists later in the twentieth century learned their crafts in New Deal's WPA classes, or were taught or influenced by those who were.

Economic improvement of rural ethnic communities was also a concern. A few programs sought to revive native arts and crafts that could be sold to bring in revenue to assist the development of cottage industries in rural communities. Conservation measures meant to revive small subsistence farming, promoted nationally by the Roosevelt administration, were introduced to the small Mexican American farm operators of the Southwest. The WPA also brought teachers and schools to many ethnic communities that did not have them before in order to foster long-term economic improvement through education. These efforts also included popular hot lunch programs.

Though New Deal programs did make efforts to help the economic situation of Mexican Americans, the long-term economic gains were scant. Poverty of Mexican Americans and their dependence on the larger society continued through the remainder of the twentieth century. Some Mexican Americans were displeased with the New Deal and saw the New Dealers as taking an unwanted special protective relationship over them, like a parent to a child. The bureaucrats were telling the residents what they needed rather than letting them decide what might be best to improve their communities. This was much like the government's treatment of American Indians throughout the nineteenth century. This parental-like relationship with Mexican American groups was perhaps at its peak during the New Deal as government officials attempted to "correct" what they considered economically inefficient social customs of ethnic groups. For example the high value placed on family ties often kept individuals in high unemployment areas and overrode opportunities to gain employment available in other parts of the country.

It was during the 1930s that Mexican American George I. Sanchez wrote the classic study, *Forgotten People: A Study of New Mexicans.* The study supported efforts to retain cultural distinctiveness and urged Mexican Americans to resist complete assimilation (blending) into white American culture. Sanchez focused on maintaining cultural pluralism—different cultural groups maintaining their traditional values and their own autonomy while still participating within a larger society.

Ironically the "whitening" of the farm labor force resulting from deporting and repatriating Mexicans and the population decline of Asians led to rising concerns over the hardships faced by farm laborers. The public and government were not as concerned when it was primarily ethnic groups working in such deplorable conditions. But with a greater percentage of white laborers, state and federal programs were created to address the needs of farm workers. A national labor union of agricultural workers was also established. In California the State Emergency Relief Administration established the Division of Rural Rehabilitation in 1934. These federal and state programs also served to benefit the ethnic minority workers still employed in the fields.

Recovery from the Great Depression

As with other segments of society, World War II mobilization brought new job opportunities as well as military service to ethnic group members. The war ended the deportation/repatriation era as the demand for Mexican labor increased once more. The doors were not opened, however, to other ethnic groups. Many attempting to flee the spread of Nazism were denied entrance to the United States in the late 1930s and early 1940s. Following the attack on U.S. military bases at Pearl Harbor, over 100,000 Japanese Americans were forced to leave their jobs and homes and were taken to detention camps as a national security measure and were not released until late 1944. In contrast, World War II dramatically improved Chinese American's position in U.S. society since China served as a military ally in the war against Japan.

Contributing Forces

A Land of Immigrants

Settlement of North America came in waves with peoples generally arriving from different parts of the world at different times. After thousands of years of American Indian settlement explorers and colonists began arriving in earnest in the seventeenth century largely from Western and Northern Europe. Soon came black slaves transported from Africa.

In 1787 the U.S. Constitution paid little attention to ethnic relations and immigration matters. Those of

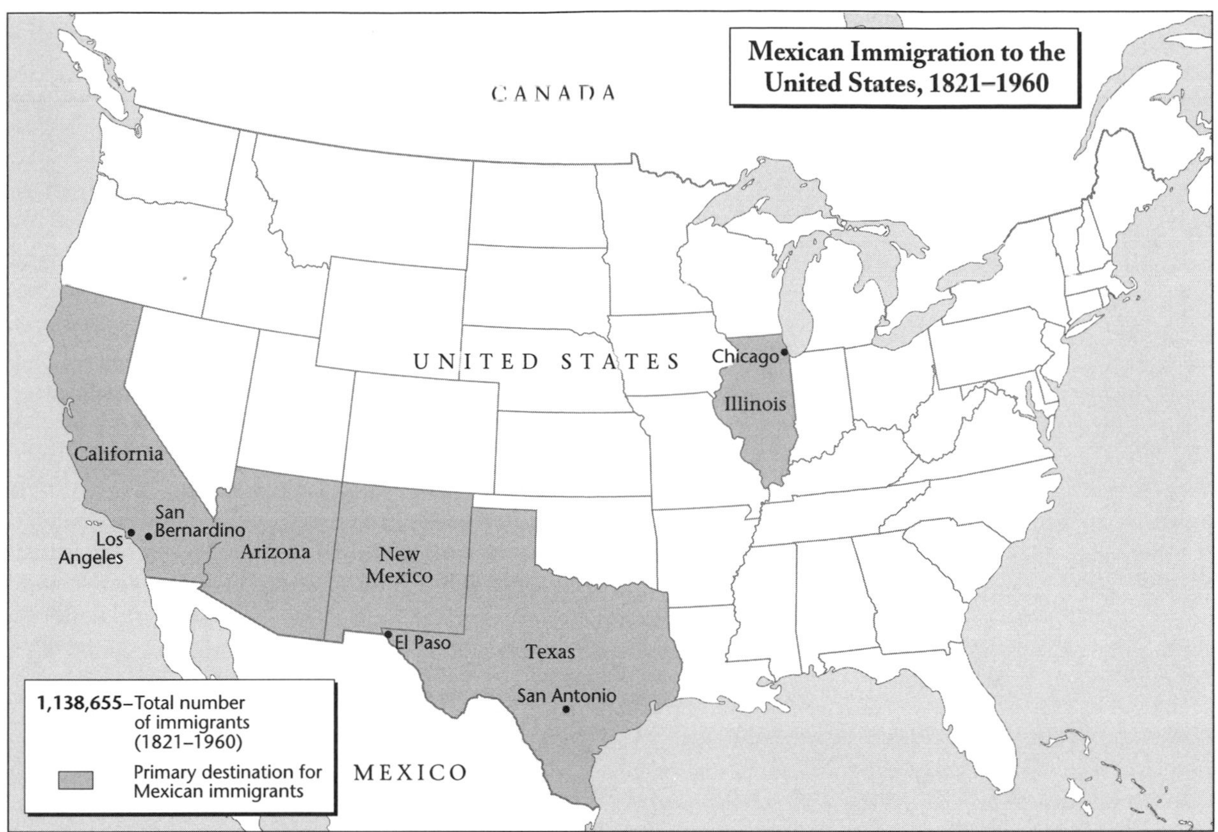

Map of states and cities in the United States that were primary destinations of Mexican immigrants from 1821 to 1960. (The Gale Group.)

Anglo-Saxon descent who controlled the early institutions of the United States saw little threat to their control of power. The Naturalization Act, passed by the first U.S. Congress in 1790, had very liberal citizenship requirements for immigrants who were primarily white Europeans at the time. Soon concerns over increasing numbers of refugees from European conflicts brought greater attention to immigration. Congress amended (revised) the act several times through the 1790s raising naturalization requirements from two to 14 years. Finally in 1800 Congress settled on a five-year residency requirement that stood through the next two centuries. Congress took no further major action on immigrant matters for the next eight decades until the 1880s.

Immigration began increasing after 1840 resulting in millions of immigrants settling in the United States by the 1920s. Before 1883 approximately 85 percent of immigrants were from northern and western Europe including Ireland, Britain, and Germany. This led to few concerns because their backgrounds and traditions were largely the same as those who founded the nation. Then immigrants from Southern and Eastern Europe began arriving in larger numbers, raising greater issues over ethnic relations. European immigrants, who were primarily unskilled industrial laborers, stayed largely in the East. Asians who began to arrive in large numbers by 1849 found work in mines and agriculture on the West Coast. Mexican Americans were largely located in the Southwest including California.

Most immigrants came for a common purpose, economic improvement. Many were impoverished and poorly educated and the rapid industrial and agricultural growth of the United States between the 1850s and 1920s offered them opportunities that could not be found in their homeland. Approximately 25 million immigrants arrived between the 1880s and 1920s as U.S. industry was rapidly expanding and needed additional workers. Some came hoping to gain skills, save up some money, and then return home with an improved economic and social position.

A Mexican cotton picker in San Joaquin Valley, California, in 1936. Many Mexican laborers were forced to return to Mexico by the U.S. government, as well as state governments. (The Library of Congress.)

Substantial hostility against immigrants arose in the United States in the second half of the nineteenth century, particularly toward newly arrived peoples who looked, talked, or acted different from the mainstream. Congress, which has exclusive constitutional power to regulate immigration, began passing laws restricting entrance of new immigrants in 1875.

By the 1930s the manner in which these ethnic groups viewed each other was fairly well established. Skin color, language, appearance, religion, and customs distinguished groups from one another.

Growth of Mexican American Population

In the U.S. Southwest Mexican Americans have a long history. In some respects they are the oldest immigrant (or ethnic) group in the United States. The first Mexican Americans were those Mexican citizens living in the northern parts of Mexico that were annexed by the United States between 1836 and 1853. The annexation of Texas (1845), the Treaty of Guadalupe Hidalgo ending the Mexican War (1848), and Gadsden Purchase (1853) took an immense area away from Mexico and added it to the United States. When the United States acquired these areas stretching from Texas to California, it also acquired approximately 80,000 Mexican colonists. They had earlier migrated from interior Mexico to its northern frontier joining the long resident American Indian population. The expansive area was sparsely settled by Mexican colonies and for years following U.S. acquisition the border between Mexico and the United States remained indistinct, with resident groups continuing free movement between the two countries.

Increasing economic opportunities through the late nineteenth century began enticing many more Mexicans to journey north. First the discovery of gold in California in 1848 attracted numerous Mexican miners from Sonora and other parts of Mexico to the California gold fields. Next, expansion of railroad lines into the Southwest in the 1880s brought great changes within the region. Mines and farms grew within easy reach of the new rail lines. These developments increased the demand for labor beyond what the small population already residing in the region could provide. Approximately 127,000 Mexicans came to the Southwest in the 1880s and 1890s as the region's economy grew. By 1900 the rail system had integrated Texas, New Mexico, Arizona, California, and northern Mexico allowing the Mexican population to gradually expand throughout the Southwest. Many moved to the cotton farms of Texas and sugar beet farms of Colorado after 1900.

Adaptation to American life proved difficult with almost all Mexican immigrants living in poverty, coming from the lower class of Mexico to join existing communities. Both the new immigrants and the long-time U.S. residents faced similar problems of ethnic discrimination.

The start of the Mexican Revolution in 1910 triggered a major 20-year increase in immigration. Mexican citizens were fleeing the military draft, persecution, violence, and a declining economy as Mexico began implementing major economic reforms, forcing many small farmers off their land. This time middle-class families were also immigrating. In addition, the restrictions established by Congress against further Asian immigration led U.S. employers to look more to Mexican workers to fill vacant jobs. Mexicans were favored because they were considered as more readily accepting of low wages and poor working conditions, and less likely to protest, than some Asians and whites. World War I created further demand for Mexican immigrant laborers and opened up more jobs in other regions of the United States. By 1915 Mexican Americans and Mexican immigrants were settling in Kansas City and Chicago. Travel was much easier and movement between the two countries was no longer limited to the immediate border area.

A white backlash against the growing number of Mexican immigrants increased. The American public viewed both Mexican Americans and aliens from Mexico as foreigners regardless of how long they had lived in the United States or their citizenship status. Congress passed the Immigration Act of 1917 requiring literacy tests and placing an eight-dollar tax on each immigrant, known as a head tax. Literacy tests were designed to assess the immigrant's understanding of the English language and immigration agents used the tests at border crossings. Those who did not pass were forced to return to the country they had left. American businesses, needing workers, found the head tax too exorbitant and thus the official demand for alien workers declined while efforts to bring in aliens illegally grew. Though the 1917 bill was aimed at southern and eastern Europeans, Mexicans felt its effects because the illiteracy rate in some Mexican areas was 85 percent. Business owners, however, pressured Congress to ease some requirements of Mexican agricultural workers, as they relied heavily on Mexican labor. Nevertheless, the restrictions, particularly the head tax, remained stiff leading to greater unauthorized immigration.

An economic recession in the early 1920s in the United States triggered an early wave of "repatriation" of unemployed workers journeying back to Mexico. This period quickly passed, however, and U.S. economic expansion of the 1920s brought more Mexican laborers northward. Besides agriculture and mining, now Mexicans increasingly found work in manufacturing and Mexican immigrant communities in the United States expanded further. As with earlier immigrants, most immigrants arriving in the 1910s and 1920s intended to return to Mexico after working in the United States for a while. Immigrants would try to make enough money in the United States so they could return and set up a small business or buy some good farmland. These immigrants maintained a strong emotional attachment to their home regions. In their new country, however, they faced racial discrimination, poverty, poor housing, police brutality, menial labor jobs, and general social rejection.

Job demands for Mexican laborers continued growing during the 1920s despite strong opposition from anti-immigrant advocates. For example Congress passed the National Origins Quota Act of 1924 but agricultural and mining businesses were able to convince Congress to exclude Mexicans and other Latin Americans from its restrictions. As a result over one million Mexican immigrants came to the United States between 1900 and 1930, mostly to become agricultural workers in the Southwest.

Asian Immigration

In the latter half of the nineteenth century immigrants arrived in the United States from various Asian nations including China, Japan, Korea, and the Philippines.

Chinese Americans played a significant role in developing the economy of the Western United States. Significant immigration of Chinese began with the discovery of gold in California in 1848 and it continued with the building of the transcontinental railroad during the 1860s and agricultural labor needs in the 1870s. Soon these California growers came to rely primarily on Chinese laborers to harvest their crops. Chinese also were responsible for the construction of hundreds of miles of levees in central California, converting marshes into farmland. By 1882 almost 300,000 Chinese were known to have entered the United States, however, never more than 125,000 Chinese were actually in the United States at any given time. Many returned to China permanently to rejoin families or temporarily to visit. Of these immigrants over 90 percent were adult males seeking labor jobs and many came from the same Kwangtung province of China. Consequently, these traditional Chinese clan associations served as support groups in the new social settings. The clans provided protection and mutual aid to Chinese who faced harsh conditions in the United States under severe discrimination. Ties to the home villages in China remained strong and many returned home to visit every few years and sent much of their earnings to their families.

By the late 1870s a strong anti-Chinese sentiment had grown, culminating in anti-Chinese demonstrations in California. Many believed the Chinese lowered wages causing the American standard of living to decline. They also accused Chinese of not assimilating into U.S. society causing further suspicion and mistrust among white Americans. Despite the relatively low numbers of Chinese aliens present, a fear of massive Chinese immigration gripped the United States.

With these fears and concerns rising among the general population, Congress passed the Chinese Exclusion Act of 1882 that focused primarily on laborers. This act was the first effort by the U.S. government to restrict immigration from particular countries. An 1888 act expanded the prohibition to all Chinese, not just Chinese laborers, and the 1892 Geary Act called for deportation of those Chinese aliens in the country illegally. With anti-Chinese sentiments remaining high, riots broke out in 1893 in California's San Joaquin Valley. Given the restrictions and public attitudes, the number of Chinese in the United States declined to a low of 60,000 in 1920. With the exclusion of Japanese, Asian people became the only ethnic group in U.S. history to be totally excluded from new entries.

Shortly after passage of the Chinese exclusion law stopping most Chinese immigration, Japanese immigration picked up. This immigration occurred on the West Coast as well as in Hawaii. Whereas Chinese immigration came primarily from a small part of the Kwangtung province of China, Japanese immigrants came from various parts of Japan. Only 10,000 Japanese lived in California in 1900 but the number began growing as 24,000 Japanese immigrated there between 1900 and 1910, most of which came looking for agricultural work. In addition several thousand Koreans and Asian Indians came to California between 1905 and 1917. Unlike the Chinese, Japanese began buying farmland and becoming growers themselves. During this time public pressure grew to limit Japanese immigration just as it had Chinese, but many in Congress viewed Japan as a more modernized nation than China. As a result no immigration laws restricting Japanese were passed during the early years of Japanese immigration. However, as Japanese gained property and provided strong competition with white businesses, pressure mounted to limit the number of Japanese in the United States as well. With continued public pressure, an agreement between the United States and Japan was reached in 1907 to limit immigration of laborers.

Finally Japanese immigration, like Chinese immigration, became prohibited by the sweeping Immigration Act of 1924. The act established ethnic limitations (known as "national origins quotas") on entering the United States. A quota is the number of people allowed entry into the United States each year from a particular area. The quotas favored northern and western Europe the most, and Asia the least. The 1924 law essentially banned all Asian immigrants except those from the Philippines, as it was then under U.S. control.

Perspectives

Resentment in the United States Against Minorities

Resentment against immigrants and citizens of ethnic minorities was rampant in the 1930s. Labor wanted to get the Mexican Americans and other ethnic groups out of the way. They resented that Mexican Americans worked for lower wages than union members and were often preferred by employers because of their industriousness and loyalty. Of course the Mexican Americans would have preferred higher wages but were happy to get any work at all. They came to be considered "part of the problem" during the Great Depression with the continuing economic decline in the United States. Solutions raised included prohibiting entry to the United States of more ethnic group members, deporting and repatriating those already in the country to supposedly free up more job opportunities, and decrease the number of "foreigners" on government welfare rolls. For ethnic minorities, it was a period of little economic opportunity, rampant discrimination, and often violence. What few economic and social gains had been made in earlier years were largely wiped out.

International Relations Affected

The further tightening of immigration laws and deportation of ethnic minorities strained international relations with other countries. Mexico took measures to cut back doing business with U.S. companies and was reluctant to enter into later immigration agreements. Many in foreign nations saw the United States as preaching democracy and equality on one hand and being outwardly discriminatory in daily life. Sensitive to this criticism the United States decreased the number of deportation raids after 1931. In the same vein of thought U.S. officials decided to back off on deportation raids in Southern California with the arrival of the Los Angeles Summer Olympic Games in 1932, wishing to avoid bad publicity at such a time.

Impact

Lasting Impact of the New Deal

Despite the various cultural projects and activities implemented in such places as New Mexico in the 1930s as part of the New Deal, little evidence of them existed in the late twentieth century. In addition farm and rangeland conservation remained a key issue among Mexican American farmers. Agricultural production had actually declined in some areas of the Southwest and village cottage industries promoted by the New Deal in some areas largely disappeared. Mexican Americans were still poor and had limited employment opportunities. Approximately 27 percent of residents in 16 New Mexico counties heavily occupied by Hispanics received food stamps or other forms

Curtis "Buzzie" Dall, President Roosevelt's grandson, shakes hands with Flying Higher, a young Blackfeet chieftan near Glacier National Park in Montana. (AP/Wide World Photos. Reproduced by permission.)

of public assistance in the 1990s. This area gained government attention again as part of the 1960s War on Poverty programs. What the New Deal programs did achieve for many was introduce the English language, teach business matters, provide a formal education for the first time, construct school buildings and roads, as well as provide Mexicans with a renewed sense of ethnic identity. Unfortunately World War II cut short much of the cultural and economic gains made by the New Deal programs.

The Great Depression posed major implications on the ethnic mix of the United States population and the relations between ethnic groups and the dominant society. The number of aliens in the United States decreased owing in part to increased human rights violations and a decline in economic opportunities. These trends changed following the Depression as the doors to immigration began to open again, however, anti-alien sentiment still persisted toward the end of the century.

A Decline of Immigrants

One implication of the Great Depression was the entry into the United States of far fewer people than before. Prior to the Depression, from 1921 to 1930, total immigration into the United States was 4.1 million persons. Almost 2.5 million came from Europe and 1.5 million from other nations of the Americas, primarily Mexico and Latin America and immigration from Asia was prohibited, particularly after 1924. In contrast, during the Great Depression years of 1931 to 1940 the number of immigrants from Europe fell below 350,000. The number rose to 621,000 in the 1940s and 955,000 from 1951 to 1957. The number of Mexican and Asian aliens within the United States actually declined. Besides immigration restrictions, this flow out of the United States was due to deportation and repatriation policies and simply because many sought better economic opportunities elsewhere. Other implications involved human rights violations and declining job opportunities. All of these trends largely reversed after World War II.

Human Rights Violations

Efforts to deport and repatriate Mexican immigrants and Mexican Americans by the federal and local governments involved significant violations of their legal rights. Despite this issue, the general public largely encouraged the activity. U.S. authorities did not see Mexican immigrants or Mexican Americans as permanent members of U.S. society. For example, of those expelled in the 1930s without specific legal cause, 60 percent were children born in the United States, which made them legal U.S. citizens even if their parents were not. Consequently the United States was arbitrarily expelling U.S. citizens without cause.

Such sweeping violations of human rights triggered by widespread suspicions, fear, and ethnic hostility was to occur once again a short time later. From 1942 to 1944 during World War II Japanese Americans were taken en masse from their homes on the West Coast and placed in long-term internment camps. The U.S. Army rounded up both citizens and non-citizens with the backing of President Roosevelt and Congress. Much like the Mexican Americans in the previous decade, the Japanese Americans were forced to leave jobs and sell their homes and belongings with only days notice. As a result many suffered major economic losses. Also like Mexican aliens during repatriation, authorities transported the Japanese Americans by train or bus, this time to makeshift and unsanitary detention camps in hot and dry desert areas of the American West. Such inhospitable conditions combined with inadequate food set the stage for widespread disease. The camps were often greatly overcrowded with no privacy. A total of 112,000 Japanese Americans were detained of which 70,000 were U.S. citizens. Finally in December 1944, long after the threat of Japanese invasion had ended, they were freed.

Mexican American Economics

Declining job opportunities coupled with U.S. efforts to force "foreigners" out of the country led to almost a 50 percent decline in the Mexican population during the 1930s. Such a loss of population and income posed dramatic effects on Mexican American communities. The social and economic development of Mexican American communities established in previous decades was particularly affected and some communities dissipated altogether. With so many Mexican Americans repatriated and deported, those Mexican American businessmen not expelled themselves saw their businesses decline substantially because of fewer customers. The decline of these communities posed far more consequences for the Mexican American population than any other impact in the twentieth century, even more than the illegal immigrant issues of the 1980s and 1990s.

With U.S. mobilization efforts for World War II, demand for workers increased again. Through an agreement between the U.S. and Mexican governments, a temporary farm worker program was established called the Bracero Program, bracero meaning manual laborer. Not wanting to see another era of repatriation occur again in the future the Mexican government was at first hesitant to agree to increased immigration from Mexico to the United States. The program, which lasted from 1943 until 1964, allowed U.S. labor agents into Mexico to recruit thousands of workers. Those recruited received contracts to work in the United States, usually in agricultural communities and railroad camps. Some braceros stayed in the United States after the program ended while others came back to the United States later after initially returning to Mexico. The state of Texas, where anti-Mexican sentiment remained strong from the 1930s, chose not to participate.

End of Race Quotas

With China becoming a U.S. ally against Japan in World War II, Congress repealed the 1882 Chinese Exclusion Act in 1943. This marked the beginning of the end of using ethnic factors to regulate immigration and naturalization. Quotas on the number of immigrants allowed to enter the country remained tight though. Further improvement in policy toward ethnic groups, however, came in the following years as the hostilities of the 1930s melted away to some degree. The privilege of naturalization was extended to Filipinos in 1946 though immigration of new Fil-

More About...

Census 2000

U.S. society at the beginning of the twenty-first century looked very different from the Depression years. The 2000 census highlighted an ever-growing ethnic diversity in the United States resulting from waves of new immigration, both legal and illegal. The category of Hispanic Americans combined Mexican Americans with Spanish-speaking peoples from other Latin American nations, particularly Cuba and Puerto Rico. Hispanic Americans increased through the 1990s at a 58 percent rate for the decade. More than half of Hispanic Americans were from Mexico, as they outnumbered all other Hispanic groups. In Los Angeles County Hispanics composed 44 percent of the population and in New Mexico 42 percent of the state population was Hispanic. Nationally they had become equal in number to black Americans whose population had increased 21 percent from the 1990 to 2000. Both groups each had over 35 million individuals and each constituted 12.5 percent of the U.S. population. It was anticipated the two groups would increasingly share political and economic issues in the twenty-first century. Even more dramatically Asian Americans increased 74 percent from 1990 to 2000 to almost 12 million persons and American Indians increased 92 percent to over three million. In comparison, the white population increased over five percent to 198 million from 1990 to 2000. In addition to increased numbers, ethnic groups were much more broadly spread across America than in the 1930s. For example the greatest Asian growth was not on the West Coast as previously but on the East Coast, especially in New York City. Hispanic populations were growing in places like Georgia and Iowa where none existed in the 1930s.

The Hispanic population at the beginning of the twenty-first century was itself increasingly diverse. Spanish-speaking peoples came from over 20 nations in the Western Hemisphere that primarily had descendents of Spain and Portugal. They represented many different cultures and traditions yet shared common traits of language, Roman Catholic religious tradition, and a strong sense of family and community. Despite the diversity of origins, Hispanics were largely arriving from poor countries and taking jobs in low-paying, labor-intensive industries as they did earlier in the twentieth century. Nonetheless, Hispanic culture was affecting U.S. society more than ever including food, music, and marketing. In May 2001 President George W. Bush began having his weekly Saturday radio addresses to the nation translated into Spanish, recognizing the growing Hispanic political clout.

The diversity within the Asian/Pacific American population increased also. They were arriving from East Asia including Japan and China, Southeast Asia, and the Asian Subcontinent. They represented many languages, ethnic backgrounds, and religious traditions.

---

ipinos was prohibited. The Nationality Act of 1952, known as the McCarran Act, simplified the national origins consideration of potential immigrants. The 1952 act based the annual quota from all countries on a flat one-sixth of one percent of the population as recorded in the 1920 census.

Major change in policy came with the 1965 Immigration Act, which abolished national origin quotas. In their place, the act established hemispheric quotas, which were still substantial. For example, until 1965 no limitations applied to the Western Hemisphere. The act set an annual limitation of 120,000. The eastern hemisphere was set at 170,000 annually with a limit of 20,000 from any one country. Those who benefited most from the new act were Asians. The Asian American population, which rose modestly from 250,000 in 1940 to 900,000 in 1960, skyrocketed to 3.5 million in 1980 and 7.3 million in 1990 aided by a high birthrate as well. Asian Americans became the fastest growing immigrant group in the Untied States. They also experienced a dramatic rise in image and status.

Anti-Immigrant Mood of the Late-Twentieth Century

Through the remainder of the twentieth century the United States continued to be a nation of immigrants as the 2000 census reflected. The resulting cultural pluralism was increasingly recognized but fears and concerns over ethnic groups, rampant in the 1930s, increased again. Concerns focused on job competition and lowered wages due to Mexican workers. Congress provided greater support to INS border patrols in catching illegal

William Doak, who was appointed as secretary of labor by Herbert Hoover, actively sought to deport hundreds of thousands of Mexican illegal immigrants. Doak saw the deportations as the solution to opening up more jobs for American workers. *(AP/Wide World Photos. Reproduced by permission.)*

aliens and sealing off borders. By the late 1970s the government was catching over one million illegal aliens each year and the border between the United States and Mexico became a controversial issue between the two nations. Because of poor economic conditions within Mexico and the willingness of U.S. businesses to hire illegal aliens, the flow continued despite increased INS efforts. In 1986 in a renewed effort at slowing illegal immigration Congress passed the Immigration Reform and Control Act (IRCA). The act placed the burden on U.S. employers not to hire illegal aliens and it also allowed many existing illegal aliens a chance to gain legal status. Despite the act, the illegal immigration issue continues to grow and remains a major issue at the beginning of the twenty-first century.

Notable People

Cesar Estrada Chavez (1927–1993). Cesar Chavez, most noted as the leader of the United Farm Workers of America labor union in the 1960s, grew up during the Great Depression. At the age of six, he and his family packed their belongings in a wagon and moved off of the long-held family property in North Gila Valley near Yuma, Arizona. They lost the property when a bank would not approve much-needed loans. Apparently, as they later discovered, others had wanted the land. Two years later they packed again, this time heading to California to find migrant work where they moved from farm to farm harvesting crops. In an eight-year period young Chavez attended 37 schools. At times the family would only make $5 for an entire week of work and at one time they lived under a bridge. Chavez gained national attention in 1965 when members of his union working in the California vineyards supported striking Filipino farm workers against California grape growers. Chavez became an effective and widely recognized spokesman for the poor.

William N. Doak (1882–1933). Doak was Secretary of Labor under President Herbert Hoover and brought with him a strong anti-Mexican bias as he set an arbitrary figure of 400,000 illegal Mexican immigrants to be deported. Doak was eager to gain labor support for Hoover as well as to the business community who strongly backed Hoover. The reason being that labor wanted aliens removed from the United States job market to open up jobs for white Americans. Doak firmly believed that if aliens were sent back to Mexico plenty of jobs would be available for others and the Great Depression would finally come to an end.

Pedro J. Gonzalez (?–?). In addition to targeting the common laborer for deportation, U.S. immigration agents also focused on social activists of ethnic groups. Authorities labeled the activists as communists or radicals and targeted them for deportation. One such person who attracted their interest was Pedro J. Gonzalez. Gonzalez was a folk singer and radio idol in Los Angeles who had a morning radio program called "Los Madrugadores." He became Los Angeles' first Spanish-speaking disc jockey. He came to the United States from Mexico in 1924 and later became a U.S. citizen. An advocate for social justice, Gonzalez used his radio program in the early 1930s to denounce U.S. policies that discriminated against Mexican Americans. Branded a radical by U.S. authorities, Gonzalez found himself falsely accused of felony charges, then convicted, and finally deported. Through his tangles with authorities, he became a hero to many Mexican Americans and a symbol of Mexican cultural pride. Gonzalez was later the subject of highly acclaimed documentaries produced by Cinewest for KPBS in San Diego, "Ballad of an Unsung Hero" in 1983 (30 minutes) and "Break of Dawn" in 1989 (100 minutes).

John Steinbeck (1902–1968). A famed American novelist, John Steinbeck received the Nobel Prize for literature in 1962. He was best known for his books addressing the plight of farm workers during the Great Depression. *The Grapes of Wrath,* published in 1939, was about the desperate situation of migrant California farm workers.

Steinbeck was born in the key agricultural area of Salinas, California, where Mexican and Mexican American farm laborers were prevalent. His first book to gain widespread popularity was *Tortilla Flat* (1935), a story of Mexican Americans. His next novel, *In Dubious Battle* (1936), was much more serious, focusing on striking agricultural laborers. His *Of Mice and Men* (1937) also centered on migrant laborers. *Grapes of Wrath* won Steinbeck a Pulitzer Prize and a National Book Award and was made into an award winning Hollywood movie in 1940.

Charles P. Visel (?–?). Visel was director of the Los Angeles Citizens' Committee on Coordination of Unemployment Relief. Like U.S. Labor Secretary Doak, Visel believed California's economic problems would be solved with mass removal of Mexicans. In 1930 and 1931 Visel organized deportation and repatriation efforts to remove Mexicans from California. He relied on local police, federal immigration authorities, and private organizations to conduct deportation raids and spread fear in the Mexican American communities.

Primary Sources

Support in Chinatowns

The following remarks were made by a Chinatown resident in the mid-1920s. It reflects increasing reliance on the largely self-contained ethnic communities located within large, mostly white communities. The ethnic enclaves became even more important in maintaining a quality of life for immigrants during the Great Depression as job opportunities and discrimination escalated (quoted in Daniels, *Asian America: Chinese and Japanese in the United States Since 1850,* 1988, p. 70).

> Most of us can live a warmer, freer and a more human life among our relatives and friends than among strangers ... Chinese relations with the population outside Chinatown are likely to be cold, formal, and commercial. It is only in Chinatown that a Chinese immigrant has society, friends and relatives who share his dreams and hopes, his hardships, and adventures. Here he can tell a joke and make everybody laugh with him; here he may hear folktales told which create the illusion that Chinatown is really China.

Deportation of Mexican Americans

The following quote describes the actions of federal immigration agents in the early 1930s to deport aliens. Maria Luna, eyewitness to an INS raid in the San Fernando Valley of Southern California, made the observations. It was published in the Spanish-speaking *La Opinion,* February 22, 1931, and reproduced in Francisco Balderrama and Raymond Rodriguez's *Decade of Betrayal: Mexican Repatriation in the 1930s* (1995, p. 56).

> It [the San Fernando raid] was for us the day of judgment. The *marciales,* deputy sheriffs, arrived in late afternoon when the men were returning home from working in the lemon groves. They started arresting people and holding them ... The deputies rode around the neighborhood with their sirens wailing and advising people to surrender themselves to the authorities. They barricaded all the exits to the community so that no one could escape. Some men showed up at the ball court with their suitcases so they could at least have a change of clothes en route. There were so many arrestees, the fronton was not large enough to hold all the prisoners. We the women cried, the children screamed, others ran hither and yon with the deputies in hot pursuit yelling at them that their time had come and to surrender.

Anti-Immigration Fever

A loud voice in the U.S. Congress against ethnic groups, Congressman Martin Dies of Texas, sponsored numerous immigration bills in the mid-1930s. To support his views, he wrote an article published in *The Saturday Evening Post* (April 20, 1935) entitled "The Immigration Crisis." In it he claimed that unemployment problems would not exist if the 20 million immigrants allowed in the United States since 1880 had been denied entry in the first place. The article catered to the racial fears and prejudices of the general public.

> The total white population found in the United States by the first census of 1790, was 3,172,444. It was all English-speaking save for the little island of Pennsylvania Dutch, and for the French and Spanish on the frontiers. It was practically homogeneous, with similar political, institutional and cultural traditions. It was this homogeneous race hat produced an extraordinary group of men of talent and ability ... at the Convention of 1787 at Philadelphia ...
>
> From the conclusion of the war between the states until the beginning of the World War, the great alien invasion of the United States took place ... [B]etween 1890 and 1910 more than 8,000,000 immigrants reached our shores from Southern and Eastern Europe ... [as a result of an] unwise and destructive [immigration] policy ... If our nation had awakened ... to the perils of its immigration policy and promptly excluded the 20,000,000 or more of aliens that have since joined the competitive ranks of labor, agriculture and business, it is reasonable to believe that the unemployment problem

would never have assumed such serious and unprecedented proportions in this country. In fact, it is not improbably that a labor surplus would not have been known in our generation ... A serious mistake had been made when the quota [of the 1924 Immigration Act] was not applied to the Western Hemisphere ... especially Mexico ... I am advised by the Federal Emergency Relief Administration that according to their estimate ... 6,400,000 aliens are deriving their livelihood from employment in this country that would otherwise [go] to American citizens ... [The new bill] which I introduced ... will further restrict immigration by reducing the existing quotas 60 per cent and apply them to countries of this hemisphere.

Suggested Research Topics

- From novels set in the Great Depression, concentrate on the unique struggles experienced by people of various cultures in the United States. Write a diary of day to day problems facing an immigrant family that seeks food and jobs during the Great Depression, and finding support from others in the ethnic community. How do these experiences possibly differ from white American experiences in the Great Depression?
- Trace the life of Cesar Chavez through the Great Depression and afterward including the founding of the United Farm Workers of America. What influences did he draw from his childhood in the Great Depression?
- Why were ethnic groups treated with particular hostility during the Great Depression? In good times why did white workers not want jobs that ethnic workers took?

Bibliography

Sources

Balderrama, Francisco E., and Raymond Rodriguez. *Decade of Betrayal: Mexican Repatriation in the 1930s.* Albuquerque: University of New Mexico Press, 1995.

Daniels, Roger. *Asian America: Chinese and Japanese in the United States Since 1850.* Seattle: University of Washington Press, 1988.

———. *Coming to America: A History of Immigration and Ethnicity in American Life.* New York: HarperCollins, 1990.

Daniels, Roger, and Otis L. Graham, eds. *Debating American Immigration, 1882–Present.* Lanham, MD: Rowman & Littlefield Publishers, 2001.

Hutchinson, Edward P. *Legislative History of American Immigration Policy, 1798–1965.* Philadelphia, PA: University of Pennsylvania Press, 1981.

Rodriguez, Clara E. *Changing Race: Latinos, the Census, and the History of Ethnicity in United States.* New York: New York University Press, 2000.

Terkel, Studs. *An Oral History of the Great Depression.* New York: Pantheon Books, 1986.

Further Reading

"Ancestors in the Americas," [cited February 19, 2002] available from the World Wide Web at: http://www.pbs.org/ancestorsinthe americas/

Asian American Oral History Site, [cited February 19, 2002] available from the World Wide Web at: http://www.itp.berkeley .edu/~asam150/index.html.

Divine, Robert A. *American Immigration Policy, 1924–1952.* New York: Da Capo Press, 1972.

Immigration and Naturalization Service (INS), [cited February 19, 2002] available from the World Wide Web at: http://www.ins.gov.

Levinson, David, and Melvin Ember, eds. *American Immigrant Cultures: Builders of a Nation.* New York: Simon & Schuster Macmillan, 1997.

Reid, Jesse T. *It Happened in Taos.* Albuquerque, NM: The University of New Mexico Press, 1946.

Uchida, Yoshiko. *A Jar of Dreams.* New York: Atheneum, 1981.

———. *The Best Bad Thing.* New York: Aladdin Books, 1986.

———. *The Happiest Ending.* New York: Atheneum, 1985.

See Also

American Indians; Black Americans; Farm Relief

Everyday Life

1929-1941

Introduction

In the face of the suffering caused by the Great Depression, the family remained a source of strength for most Americans. Nevertheless, the economic bad times did affect the lifestyles of all but the very wealthy. Almost everyone saw their income decrease but likewise the prices of goods decreased. Those of the working class, middle class, and upper middle class fortunate enough to keep their jobs carried on with life as close to normal as they could. Families devised various ways to "cut corners," "make do," and "keep up appearances." To "cut corners," clothing could be sewn at home. To "make do," a pot roast could be stretched to last in several creative meals. Painting the outside of a home or shopping at nice secondhand dress shops would help "keep up appearances." Likewise, farm families who did not lose their farms relied on thrift, conservation, gardens, and strong family ties to see them through.

Effects of the Depression on the family structure included postponed marriages, fewer babies, youths staying home longer, and combining households to aid needy relatives. Still the strain of economic pressures broke some families apart.

Americans most susceptible to hard times were black Americans, the elderly, those in areas where factories shut down, farmers caught in Dust Bowl areas, and those in coal-mining regions. All were marginally poor before the Depression—barely making ends meet. The country's overall economic difficulties left them to struggle for survival amid poverty, hunger, and illness.

Chronology:

1930: The number of miles of paved roads in the United States reaches 695,000.

1930: Glamorized by movies, cigarette production reaches 124 billion, up from only 9.7 billion in 1910.

1931: Sales of glass jars for preserving food at home increases dramatically.

1933: The number of marriages declines 40 percent from the 1920s level.

May 27, 1933: On the south side of Chicago the Century of Progress World's Fair opens.

December 5, 1933: The prohibition of the sale of alcoholic beverages, in effect since 1920, ends.

May 28, 1934: The Dionne quintuplets are born in Canada.

1935: Bingo begins in movie houses and quickly becomes popular.

1935: People buy 20 million Monopoly games in one week.

1935: Krueger Beer of Newton, New Jersey, introduces the first canned beer.

1937: People listen to radio an average of 4.5 hours a day.

October 31, 1938: Orson Welles broadcasts "Invasion from Mars" and panics listeners who think Martians have landed in New Jersey.

1939: Eleanor Roosevelt resigns from the Daughters of the American Revolution in protest of their refusal to allow black opera singer Marian Anderson to perform in Constitution Hall.

1939: The Golden Gate International Exposition opens in San Francisco, and the New York World's Fair opens in New York City.

Issue Summary

Employed—The Fortunate Americans

While 25 percent of the American labor force was unemployed during the Great Depression, 75 percent maintained at least some kind of an income. Some managed to do quite well. Although several hundred thousand businesses went under, some two million endured, providing products and services. Those fortunate enough to maintain income, although it almost always was lower than before the 1929 stock market crash, carried on with life as close to normal as possible. Especially in thousands of small towns, the traditions of community life ran deep and endured. Families held to their normal values and stressed the importance of family unity.

In the midst of the Depression what did it mean to be a "middle-income family?" How did they modify their lives to survive the Depression? Could they still own homes and cars? Was there any leisure time, and if so, how did they fill it? What did families do for fun? Did they ever take vacations? How did the young adults in their late teens and early twenties deal with the availability of so few jobs? The answers to these questions piece together the picture of life led by a majority of Americans in the 1930s.

The Middle Class

From 1935 to 1936 the median family income was $1,160. An annual wage of $1,000 or more placed a family in the middle-income range. The middle-income family did not have a surplus of income but did have a fairly comfortable standard of living. Before the onset of the Depression in the fall of 1929, the term "standard of living" had come to mean not just adequate food, housing, and clothing but anything families were unwilling to go without. After the Depression, at least for the first half of the 1930s, standard of living again referred to the basics of food, shelter, and clothing, since the means to achieve more than the basics had declined. These basic necessities absorbed at least three-quarters of a household budget. Luxuries played a very small part in the life of most families. Nevertheless, people of middle incomes clung to the idea that certain material goods and lifestyles that had become important to them would again eventually be attainable.

An upper-middle-class family's income began at about $2,500. In the mid-1930s, only 12 percent of families were in this bracket. In 1929, before the crash, 29 percent of American families were in the affluent range. To illustrate the decline, between 1929 and 1933, the incomes of affluent doctors and lawyers dropped as much as 40 percent. Although severely tested, the upper middle class did their best to maintain a refined standard of living. Shaken by their friends who had lost all, most lived with the fear of being next. Nevertheless, the great majority labored to "keep up appearances." T.H. Watkins reports in his book, *The*

Hungry Years (1999, pp. 104–105), that although expectations lowered they, "simply refused to abandon the values by which they defined themselves." Their concessions included riding the subways, smoking cheaper cigars, and the women learning to cook once they had given up servants. Secondhand dress shops were reborn, and when some especially smart and stylish clothes came in the word was spread quickly through groups who were in the "know."

Many families, especially in the middle- to upper-middle income groups, made a conscious attempt to plan their expenditures in response to wage reductions or employment changes. Special budgeting sections appeared in women's magazines. Women wrote personal accounts of their budgeting for the articles. The magazines even ran contests for the perfect budgets.

The middle- and upper-income families were able to maintain a relatively comfortable standard of living because many of the necessities of life—especially food—showed striking decreases in costs. Another way to maintain the standard of living was to have a second income in the household.

Average Family Budget, 1935

Income	Amount, $
Average annual income	$1,348
Expenses	
Food and alcoholic beverages	472
Housing, utilities, furnishings, etc.	456
Clothing	136
Automobile purchase and maintenance	73
Medical care	53
Recreation, reading, tobacco	72
Taxes	5
Miscellaneous expenses	5
Total Expenses	**$1,272**

There was little room for error in spending for the average family during 1935. (The Gale Group.)

An Extra Wage Earner

Many families maintained a middle- to upper-middle income by having additional family members employed. The presence of more than one wage earner in the family greatly impacted a family's standard of living. At low income levels, under $800, fewer than one in five families had an extra wage earner. Almost one out of four families in the $800 to $1,600 range had an extra wage earner. Even higher ratios of families with extra wage earners occurred above the $1,600 per year level. In the early 1930s, children between 14 and 18 years of age often provided the extra income. By the end of the 1930s, it was most likely the married housewives making an economic contribution through paid employment rather than children under the age of 18.

Married Working Women

Increased participation of married women in the labor force depended on a variety of developments and needs including dramatically decreased child labor, relative economic need, and the availability of jobs. A prime motivator, particularly at the middle and upper income levels was the desire to provide "extras" such as education of children or payment on a house.

The number of married women in the labor force increased by 52 percent in the 1930s. By 1940 over four million married women worked for pay, but this still represented only 15 percent of all married women. Many housewives simply found it impossible to run a household and work. Over 80 percent reported spending 48 hours or more on household chores alone.

Married working women were often criticized for taking jobs that could have gone to an unemployed man. Women managed to hold on to certain positions when advocates of women's employment stressed that some occupations were especially suited to women. Such jobs included clerical positions, beauty salon managers, dental hygienists, nurses, and occupational therapists. Women did not have to compete with men for these jobs.

Corner-Cutting and Making Do

Family expectations with respect to standard of living remained high, but the means to maintain their expectations declined. The most logical way for a family to adapt to Depression conditions was to adopt a lower standard of living. The ability to do this rested on several factors such as actual family income, the family's material needs, and the skills of the family consumer manager—frequently the woman. Making ends meet involved corner-cutting, "making do," sometimes going without, and shifting around various payments. Families commonly curtailed expenses by growing and canning food that used to be bought at a store, making their own clothing, and holding on to an aging car. Some adults went to the doctor and dentist less to avoid paying for those services. By taking care of their own necessities rather than purchasing services, families maintained their standard of living.

The middle class mom prided herself on "making do" when feeding her family. If very careful, a woman could feed a family of six on five dollars a week. She

The middle class mom prided herself on "making do" when feeding her family. She relied on basic foodstuffs to stretch meal portions. *(The Library of Congress.)*

relied on the basic foodstuffs in her pantry such as flour, cornmeal, and sugar or corn syrup. Meat came from the local butcher. Sending the children to the butcher for 25¢ worth of round steak could amply supply enough meat for a filling stew. Mothers could make a pot roast last an entire week—reincarnated each day as something different such as meat loaf and soup. Meals were stretched with gravy, potatoes, macaroni, and homemade bread. Vegetable gardens sprang up in backyards and vacant city lots. Women did their own canning, pickling, and preserving. A colorful array of jars on the pantry shelves lent reassurance to the whole family through winter months.

Families shared all they could with the less fortunate. Frequently, struggling families were invited to Sunday dinner. If a homeless person knocked at the back door they were given food, clothing, and even—at times—a place to sleep. Assistance and kindness towards others was a hallmark of families in the 1930s.

Most women were adequately skilled in sewing. Exciting hours were spent in picking out dress patterns from pattern catalogues. With pattern and material in hand, their foot-operated treadle sewing machine whirred until a garment was completed. Very few clothes were store bought. If the soles of a pair of shoes began to wear through, cardboard was inserted to prolong their life.

During the 1920s new labor-saving household devices had been the rage, but by the 1930s few could afford these luxuries. As a result, sales of washing machines, percolators for coffee, vacuum cleaners, toasters, and electric mixers plummeted.

Automobiles

By 1930 the middle and upper middle classes were likely to own automobiles. Roughly 26 million cars were on the road by 1930. Even in the worst years of the Depression, anyone who owned a vehicle, including those at the lower end of the middle class and farming families, were reluctant to give up driving. In the first half of the 1930s, however, most families put off purchasing a new car and kept driving the old. By 1933 car manufacturers began tempting families with streamlined models sporting beautiful curved lines. The box-like chassis that sat above the axle was eliminated. The new models were rounded, had steel roofs, and came in colors other than black. Engines, trunks, and bumpers molded into one whole unit, and cars had increased horsepower. Nevertheless, holding to strict budgets, people continued to resist temptation and drove their old cars longer and longer. Someone in the family likely took care of oil changes, patching tires, and doing whatever they could to keep the car running.

The automobile repair industry, which took care of the more difficult repairs, actually grew during the Depression. As economic conditions and confidence improved by 1936, purchases of the new, sleeker cars resumed. Buying on credit became one way to avoid paying the entire cash amount of the purchase up front. By 1937 the number of cars on the road had increased to 29 million.

Home Ownership

Middle- and upper-middle-class urban families in the 1930s tended to own their own homes, usually located in a suburb at the edge of a city. Houses of the bungalow style, with one-and-a-half stories, two bedrooms, one bath, living room, dining room, and kitchen were very popular. Homes of the Colonial Revival or Dutch Colonial styles were popular in the east. In western states, neighborhoods had Spanish style houses with low-pitched red tile roofs and stucco exteriors. Most of the homes had been built and purchased in the 1920s. Most homes in cities and suburbs were electrified. In the difficult economic times, a popular way to "keep up appearances" was to paint the outside of the family home.

Americans continued to drive their cars even at the height of the Depression. From 1930 to 1937, three million more cars were added to the road. *(Courtesy of American Automobile Association. Used with permission.)*

Perhaps the biggest middle-class Depression fear was loss of the family home. With downturns in income many families fell behind in their house payments. By the middle of 1933, those people behind in payments turned to the newly established Home Owners' Loan Corporation (HOLC) or, by 1934, to another new agency, the Federal Housing Administration (FHA). Through both the HOLC and FHA, home loans were refinanced. Refinancing set up new payment terms that families could meet. By 1936 the HOLC alone had refinanced 992,531 home loans, allowing millions of Americans to stay in their homes.

News Sources

How did people learn of the day's news? The major source of news for most Depression-era families was newspapers, due primarily to their inexpensiveness. The *New York Times* cost two cents. Newspapers reported the latest in politics and sports, and kept track of the lives of Hollywood and high society celebrities. Headlines, big and bold, announced the major news story of each Depression day. Newsboys delivered papers to homes. Being a news delivery boy was a proud job for young boys as they could contribute to the family income.

Newspaper publishers could be depended on to put out special editions if a big story broke. Boys sold the special editions on street corners, calling out the familiar "Extra! Extra! Read all about it!" and pocketing still more change.

Newsreels—short motion pictures of current events—had become a major news source by the 1930s. Introduced in the late 1890s, they first were shown in music halls between performances and then gained great popularity in the new motion picture theaters by the 1920s. "The March of Time" was introduced in 1935. It combined filmed news with interviews. The public would frequently go to the movies to learn what was happening in the world.

Another news source was the radio. In fact, the radio quickly became a center of family life during leisure time.

Leisure Time

Those who maintained their steady jobs generally worked a five-day week with two days off. To fill leisure time, people looked to life's free pleasures. Dropping unaffordable club memberships, they turned to listening to the radio, playing games,

Children participate in a pie eating contest at a 4-H Club fair in Cimarron, Kansas in 1939. Families looked to fill their leisure time with affordable entertainment during the Great Depression. (The Library of Congress.)

stamp collecting, and visiting with neighbors on front porches. Board games, such as Monopoly (invented in 1933) were extremely popular. In Monopoly people could wheel and deal in real estate even if in reality the house payment was a struggle.

Card games were a popular way to spend an afternoon or evening. Adults would invite friends over for Canasta or Bridge. Children loved to play Old Maid. Baseball was the most popular sport of the day. Going to the movies, having family picnics, going to church and church socials, attending bingo parties, playing miniature golf, enjoying a soda at the corner drug store, and dancing were all popular stepping-out activities.

Radio and Movies

The radio and movie industries provided an exciting escape from the worries of Depression living. The sale of radios increased from 10 million sold at the beginning of the 1930s to around 30 million at the end of the decade. Almost 90 percent of American households owned a radio. Just as popular as radio were the movies. Once a week around 65 percent of the population found the movie ticket, which cost 25 cents or less, affordable, even necessary. The United States had over fifteen thousand movie theaters, more than the number of banks and twice the number of hotels. The 1930s proved to be a golden age for radio and motion picture industries.

The typical family spent hours in the living room each evening listening to their favorite programs. The big rounded radio was a window to adventure, comedy, music, romance, and news. Americans stayed glued to their radios when President Roosevelt gave a "fireside chat," explaining what was happening in Washington, DC, to ease the Depression.

Families gathered together after supper for such programs as the comedy *Amos 'n' Andy* that aired from 7:00 to 7:15 PM each weekend evening. Another favorite comedy program was that of husband and wife team George Burns and Gracie Allen, airing at 8:00 PM on Monday. Ventriloquist Edgar Bergen and his wooden dummy Charlie McCarthy provided hours of laughter on the *Chase and Sanborn Hour,* Sundays at 8:00 PM Just before the *Chase and Sanborn Hour,* there was a thirty-minute segment featuring Ozzie Nelson and Harriet Hilliard, who quickly became the famous Ozzie and Harriet Nelson, one of America's first families of entertainment.

Many favorite shows opened with a standard line that people eagerly awaited. At the start of her variety show, singer Kate Smith belted out, "Hello everybody" at 8:00 PM every Thursday night. Variety shows drew loyal audiences. *Kraft Music Hall* was popular with Bing Crosby crooning over the airwaves at 10:00 PM Thursdays. A great success of the mid-1930s was *Major Edward Bowes Original Amateur Hour.* Comedians Fred Allen and Jack Benny entertained with their original wit. If you didn't go to the movies Saturday night you stayed home and listened to *Your Hit Parade* on the radio.

Popular news broadcasters of the day were H.V. Kaltenborn and Lowell Thomas. Radio also bought sports into people's living rooms. Americans could listen to army-navy football games, boxing title fights, horse racing, tennis matches, the 1932 Winter Olympics from Lake Placid, New York, and the World Series. Fearing no one would come to the park, however, baseball teams in the early 1930s resisted broadcasting games. As early as 1931, golfer Bobby Jones had a radio program on which he handed out golf tips.

Daytime broadcasts were aimed at target audiences. The first woman's service program to go national in the 1920s was the Betty Crocker Cooking School of the Air. Betty gave out recipes and suggested ways to "make do" in the home throughout the 1930s. The U.S. Department of Agriculture broadcast a daily 15-minute home economics program coast to coast. A female voice known as Aunt Sammy anchored the program. As housewives washed clothes they could listen to soap operas such as "Guiding Light."

One of the most memorable radio programs of all time aired on the night before Halloween, October 30, 1938. The broadcast—a dramatization of H.G. Wells novel *War of the Worlds*—was intended as a simulation of a real news broadcast. It was so realistic, however, that people thought the play about Martians landing in New Jersey and devastating the countryside was real. Many Americans, especially those in New Jersey and New York, panicked, packing up their children and possessions in preparation to evacuate and calling newspapers and police stations to find out where they should go to avoid the Martian attack. The reaction of the public was a testament to the realism of Welles's broadcast and to the mindset of a nation that was worried about the possibility of another world war. CBS had to issue repeated assurances that the play was entirely fictional and promised not to broadcast any more "news" programs like "War of the Worlds."

All through the Depression, Americans lined up in front of the movie theaters. Many of the 1930s films featuring glamorous stars offered pure escape focusing on romance, good times and wealth. Mae West, a curvaceous blonde, earned $480,000 a year. Fred Astaire and Ginger Rogers became America's favorite dance partners and starred in the first of ten romantic musical comedies, *Flying Down to Rio* (1933). The extravagant musical *Gold Diggers of 1933* introduced the song "We're in the Money."

Comedies and gangster films were very popular. The most famous comedians were the Marx Brothers, Charlie Chaplain, and W.C. Fields. Gangster films with stars such as Edward G. Robinson and James Cagney included *Little Caesar* (1930) and *The Public Enemy* (1931). By 1935 the gangsters were surrendering to government agents as depicted in another Cagney film, *G-Men.*

Depression-saddened Americans cheered up when the kind-hearted people won out over greedy individuals in *Mr. Deeds Goes to Town* (1936). Walt Disney's first full-length animated fantasy, *Snow White and the Seven Dwarfs,* fascinated audiences in 1937. Perhaps two of the biggest stars of the 1930s were child stars Shirley Temple and Mickey Rooney. Mothers all across the nation would dress their little girls and curl their hair into ringlets for Shirley Temple look-alike contests. Two enduring classics of the silver screen premiered in 1939, *Gone with the Wind* and *The Wizard of Oz.*

At a Glance

Miniature Golf

Garnet Carter of Lookout, Tennessee, had an entrepreneurial idea—golf for the whole family played on a series of small courses. In 1929 he built the Tom Thumb Golf Course, and miniature golf was born. Later that summer he went to Miami to build a course there. Miniature golf was a huge instant success, and by 1930 roadside courses appeared in many areas. The owner provided putters and balls and created imaginative course designs with an array of obstacles to challenge balls heading for the cup. It became quite the rage to stop at a roadside course for a game. For a time some optimists actually suggested the miniature golf industry might lift the United States out of the Great Depression.

Going to the movies became a way of life for most Americans during the Great Depression. Close to 100 million people per week visited the movies by 1929–1930. (The Library of Congress.)

The lives of the movie stars were everyday topics of conversation. Newspapers and magazines followed their every move. Even people in the poorest families were likely to know the latest "doings" of their favorite star.

Some movie houses had a platform at the front which rose up out of the orchestra pit. On the platforms were musicians, perhaps one playing an organ or an entire band. People packed these movie houses and waited in great anticipation for the platform to rise.

Swing Bands

Swing became the dance craze for the mid- and late 1930s. Swing evolved from jazz played by black groups in the 1920s. Jazz was characterized by a driving beat and improvised solos. In the early 1930s, most white Americans had only heard the sedate orchestra versions of jazz. In 1934 Benny Goodman decided to form a band and take it across country playing real jazz. He was disappointed in his reception, as the 24-year-old's band was reduced to playing tame dance music by the time it arrived in California. At the end of an evening's performance in Hollywood at the Palomar Ballroom, however, Goodman told his band to swing out. The crowd went wild and the swing craze swept into mainstream American culture.

Older adults still preferred the tamer orchestral big bands or "sweet" bands, but young adults and teens adopted swing bands. The hard-driving beats conjured up dance steps such as the raucous Big Apple that became a national craze. Even Depression years could not suppress the energy of youth as they danced their troubles away to the likes of Louis Armstrong, Tommy Dorsey, Jimmy Dorsey, Glenn Miller, Artie Shaw, Count Basie, and Duke Ellington. A whole vocabulary called jive talk emerged to accompany swing.

The Dance Marathon

One of the more unusual types of music and dance entertainment in America was the dance marathon. Dance marathons began as fads but evolved into a bizarre way to make money both for the participants and the dance hall owners. Couples—a male and female team such as brother and sister, father and daughter, mother and son, or boyfriend and girlfriend—competed against other couples. Contest rules required the couple to be in motion on the dance floor 45 minutes of every hour, day and night. The couple who lasted the longest won the monetary first prize.

Ringside seats and balconies for spectators surrounded the dance floor.

The first dance marathon contest in America was held in 1910 but attracted few interested spectators. The real craze began in the spring of 1923 and spread to big cities across the nation in only a few weeks. The zany early marathons evolved into endurance dances lasting months. The dance for money often became a dehumanizing spectacle of exhaustion, sometimes with tragic results. In 1935 Horace McCoy wrote a novel titled *They Shoot Horses, Don't They?* about dance marathons as an exploitative form of entertainment, featuring a participant who dies at the end. A movie adaptation of the book starring Jane Fonda was made in 1969.

"Leapin' Lizards"

What did Depression kids do for fun? Besides leisure time activities with families and spending hours at the movies on Saturday afternoon, children lived in the world of heroes and heroines brought to them in the media of the day. The world of these characters remained always cheery or exciting, often much preferred to the rather drab days of the Depression.

"Leapin' lizards" was a favorite saying of a red-headed moppet of comic strips and radio, Little Orphan Annie. She and her dog, Sandy, entertained throughout the Depression. Children poured over her comic strips in the newspapers and by mail joined her secret society. She also came into their homes through radio. Annie was actually quite conservative politically. She had undying faith in regular old capitalism which pleased many Depression-frightened parents. Through Annie, cartoonist Harold Gray expressed his pro-business, anti-labor, and anti-liberal politician stances. Her famous philosophy was "Ya hafta earn what ya get." Children, however, were simply interested in her exploits and decoding the secret messages from the radio program *Adventure Time with Little Orphan Annie* with the help of badges and decoders that they would receive for sending in Ovaltine labels (Ovaltine was the sponsor of the radio show) and nominal amounts of money.

Science fiction hero Flash Gordon appeared in comics, books, and movie house cartoons. Gordon was frequently left in a precarious position, such as hanging from a cliff, to ensure children would be back the next week to see what happened. As Americans became increasingly uneasy about the emerging Asian Continent, Gordon always triumphed over Ming the Merciless from Mongo. Jack Armstrong, football hero of Hudson High, came over the radio waves encouraging children to love America and have "hearts of gold." If they did they would conquer meanness and have the world's riches.

The character of Tarzan came on the scene in 1914. Tarzan was once an orphaned boy in Africa who had grown into an agile jungle man. By the end of the 1930s, he could be found in 21 novels, 16 movies, comic strips, and on the radio. Behind the western straight-shooting character Tom Mix was a real western movie stunt man. His radio show began in 1933, but previously he had been in numerous action films and the comics. Other super heroes of mega-fame were science fiction character Buck Rogers and hard-nosed detective Dick Tracy.

Two favorite real-life little girls were English princesses Elizabeth and Margaret Rose. It was easy for little girls to forget their homemade Depression clothes when dressing dolls of the princesses in paper finery. Perhaps the sunniest of all the heroes and heroines was another real-life girl, Shirley Temple. Besides her many movies, merchandisers created Shirley Temple dolls,

More About...

Jive Talk

Depression or not, to be hip in the late 1930s you had to speak jive. Jive was spoken fast, loud, and sassy. Hip teens and young adults knew the following words (adapted from *Our American Century, Hard Times: The 30s,* p. 144):

Alligator: follower of swing
Canary: a female singer
Cats: musicians in the swing band
Cuttin' a rug: dancing to swing
Disc or swing platter: a recording
Hepcat: a fan who knows all about swing
Ickie: a person who doesn't understand swing
In the groove: feeling the beat of swing
Jitterbug: dancing to swing
Kicking out: dancing fast and free
Licorice stick: clarinet
Long hair: dull, one who likes symphonic music over swing
Skin beater: drummer
Sweet: music good only for tame dancing

trunks of doll clothes, and books. What all of these characters had in common was their theme—clean living will bring unlimited rewards. This message seemed very important to Depression-weary children.

After school and during long summer days, another favorite activity of children was designing, building, and playing with homemade toys. All that was needed to build a scooter was a scrap piece of 2 x 4 lumber, an orange crate, and a dismantled roller skate for wheels. The scooters would take children on wild rides down city or country hills. Skateboards were built out of a board and roller skate. Racer airplanes were built using wood and glue. Although boys grew into men, many never outgrew their love of flying the planes. Kites were also popular everywhere. All that was needed to create one was newspaper, flour paste glue, and string from the big ball that mom always had on hand.

Children also enjoyed outdoor activities of all sorts. Sandlot baseball was the favorite sport. A game called "king of the mountain" occupied many hours. It was an exciting game where boys would climb up the steepest hill, pushing each other down until only one was left—the king. Jacks, jump rope, and kick-the-can were also favorite activities. If a swimming hole was available, it was a place to cool off and have a grand time.

Vacations

As the Depression wore on, few Americans could afford vacations in Europe, but they could hit the open road in their automobiles. They could camp along the way and see the United States. Gasoline prices were lower, and the road seemed to be the quickest way to escape the hard times and recreate. Businesses sprung up along the roads to service all the tourists.

Campgrounds and motor courts appeared across the nation, first in California, Texas, and Florida. The motor courts had the luxury of indoor plumbing and private bathrooms. Howard Johnson opened a chain of roadside restaurants. Big Boy restaurants offered Americans hamburgers and fries. Roadside culture became a permanent feature of American life. The only families to still travel freely abroad were the very wealthy, who seemed to have voted not to participate in the Depression.

The Very Rich

As the Depression dragged on, the lives of all but the most wealthy Americans were affected in some way. Generally, the very wealthy had financial roots in the industrial empires begun in the nineteenth century rather than in the 1920s stock speculation. It was the quickly accumulated wealth of the 1920s that had vanished in the early years of the Depression—not the wealth of the industrial giants. Although not unaware of those struggling mightily under the weight of the Depression, the lives of the very rich went on pretty much as usual. The sacrifices they did make seemed shallow. T.H. Watkins reports in his book, *The Hungry Years* (1999, p. 106), that in the early spring of 1932, John P. Morgan Jr., banker, decided to not sail his yacht believing "it is both wiser and kinder not to flaunt such luxurious amusement in the face of the public."

Local newspapers and tabloids were diligent in their coverage of the very rich, and generally even the destitute likely knew many details of the lives of the wealthy. Favorite events to cover were the débutante balls. Débutante balls were extravagant parties thrown by the very rich each year to introduce their daughters to high society and advertise their eligibility for marriage. Balls cost between $10,000 and $100,000, and families tried to outdo one another. Débutantes, wearing beautiful fashionable gowns attended dances almost nightly from late November until January. Champagne, fresh flowers, elegant table settings, sumptuous food, and extravagant stage sets all pointed to conspicuous consumption. The débutante's new clothes alone could add up to $10,000. Popular magazines such as *Life* and *Saturday Evening Post* published pictures of the affairs for the public to view and possibly imagine that they too could be a part of the parties. As they had done for decades, New York's upper tier, such as the Vanderbilts, Belmonts, and Harrimans, continued their stylish summers in Newport, Rhode Island, with croquet on the lawns, cocktails, swimming, and sailing, oblivious to the world outside.

A problem that had greatly troubled the very rich during the 1920s was the servant problem. After World War I (1914–1918), fewer individuals were willing to work for the low wages coupled with long, irregular hours. As the Depression reached its lowest ebb in 1932, the servant pool grew dramatically. Women would work for as little as $4 a month and board. A gardener could be hired in Los Angeles for $1 a week. The easing of the servant problem greatly pleased the rich as they hated to abandon any part of their privileged lifestyle.

Café Society

Trend setters for young people by the mid- and late 1930s were the celebrities of the so-called Café Society. Out of the darkest days of the Depression, as the country hit rock bottom, high society found its way out. The old New York speakeasies of prohibition days when the sale of alcohol beverage was illegal had

A débutante and her escort enjoy a snack of doughnuts and coffee at a ball in the late 1930s. Despite the economic difficulties of the Depression, many of the very wealthy still maintained their lifestyles, which included attending lavish debutante balls. (AP/Wide World Photos. Reproduced by permission.)

transformed into trendy restaurants such as the Stork Club, El Morocco, and the Colony. Occupying tables at these establishments were an energy-charged, glittering social set.

Women from families such as Chicago's Marshall Fields, Boston's Kennedys, and New York's Vanderbilts rivaled the Hollywood stars to be the most fashionable and glamorous. Reigning glamour girl of the set in the late 1930s was Brenda Frazier, an heiress due to inherit four million dollars at age 21. She would dine and dance the night away with various handsome beaus. Brenda was an extraordinary beauty with black hair, penciled eyebrows, pale skin, and red, red lipstick. She started a national fad with the strapless evening gown. Tabloids and newspaper social columnists reported her every move. She became the idealized woman of the

A bustling street view of 42nd Street and 5th Avenue in New York City on April 20, 1935. Many of the nation's wealthiest Americans lived in or near New York City during the Great Depression. (AP/Wide World Photos. Reproduced by permission.)

decade. Young women and girls across the country attempted to imitate her look and style.

Throughout the United States, in smaller towns and in cities, Americans who had managed to stay in the middle and upper middle class mimicked the Café Society. Young people pledged social clubs with names such as the Sub-Debs and Stardusters. The clubs entertained with teas, luncheons, picnics, and many dances. Protocol always included formal invitations and local newspaper coverage of every detail, including descriptions of flowers, dresses, table settings and, of course, the complete guest list. Within these social circles, especially in the later 1930s, the Depression ills seemed to have been overcome. One area, however, where the Depression's consequences would last for lifetimes was family relationships—babies, marriage, and divorce.

Effects on the Family—Babies, Marriage, and Divorce

The Great Depression put severe strain on family relationships. While some families grew closer in the face of adversity, others broke apart.

Hard times forced couples to postpone marriage. The marriage rate in 1929 was 10.14 marriages per 1,000 persons. By 1932 it dropped to 7.87 per 1,000 persons. Among those aged 25 to 35, the number of women who had never been married in 1935 was 30 percent higher compared to women of the same age group in 1930. Prolonged engagements were also common.

Birthrates dropped during the early years of the Depression. Many couples had fewer children or put off having children rather than bring them into the uncertain climate of the Depression. The birthrate, long declining, hit a low point in 1933 when only 75.7 of every 1,000 women of childbearing age gave birth. One-quarter of all women in the United States in their 20s during the Depression did not bear children.

Divorce rates dropped in the 1930s because people could not afford the costs of an official divorce. Between 1930 and 1935, 170,000 fewer divorces occurred than would have been predicted had 1920s divorce rates continued. Men just simply walked away. Unemployed men who had been dependable and self-respecting workers now took to the streets in search of jobs. A few weeks or months were endurable, but as the time period stretched to one or more years and families suffered, some men became so discouraged that they left and never went back. As husbands left their families without divorcing their wives, there were more than 1.5 million married women living apart from their husbands by 1940. Compared to 12 percent in 1930, 15 percent of all households were headed by females in 1940. As the Depression continued through the decade, the divorce rate did begin to increase and by 1940 was above the 1920s divorce levels.

Needy relatives stretched thin the resources of families. Single people in their late teens and early twenties and sometimes even young married couples lived with parents, resulting in crowded quarters and tensions. There was a lack of privacy, and young people often disliked close parental supervision.

Who Stayed Together?

The unemployment of the husband sometimes led to the wife taking a job outside the home. Even if it did not, a husband's unemployment always brought changes to the family relationships. The man's continual presence in the home might contribute to his loss of status. If the provider role in his family was his key to importance within the family, unemployment was devastating. On the other hand, if the father's role was primarily based on love and respect, the family often showed a remarkable stability in the face of unemployment. The attitudes of both husband and wife affected the family's adaptation. Companionship marriages where couples shared activities, mutual interests, work, and chores held together the best.

The Depression broke apart some families but others stayed close. The well-organized family, even if severely affected, tended to continue as a unit. The initially disorganized families became further fractured and often did not survive. An organized, adaptable family could accept a lower standard of living without losing its togetherness.

Youth

The Depression was terribly hard on young people aged 16 to 20. More than 200,000 youth left home in the 1930s looking for better opportunities. Those who stayed home learned to lower expectations. More stayed in high school. In 1930 less than one-half of youth aged 14 to 18 attended high school, but by 1940 three-quarters of that age group were in school. Those who did not continue on to college generally had a great deal of difficulty finding a job. It could take several years of job hunting to finally find work. Young people therefore remained dependent on their families longer in the 1930s than they had in the 1920s.

College

Those youth that could go on to college usually were on strict budgets, took part-time work—often at the college—and viewed their education as serious business. The college generation of the early 1930s was much less of a "rah-rah anything goes" group than the college students of the 1920s. They largely got on with the business of earning a degree. Campuses became involved with the social and political issues of the times. Students at UCLA and other large universities demonstrated for more involvement in administrative affairs. Liberal and communist groups were very active. Students of the 1930s, however, also found time to play. Football, fraternities, and other social clubs were popular diversions. Drinking and sexual promiscuity among students worried deans and parents alike as it had in the 1920s during prohibition. In 1935 a new campus craze emerged. Lothrop Withington, Jr., a freshman at Harvard, swallowed a live goldfish on a bet. Three days later another young man at Franklin and Marshall College downed three goldfish. The race was on to see who could swallow the most. Reportedly, in 1938, an M.I.T. student swallowed 42 in succession.

The Depression's Most Susceptible Victims

While 25 percent of the national workforce overall was unemployed, national unemployment of black Americans stood at 48 percent, much higher in some cities, especially in the south. The unemployment rate among blacks in Memphis, Tennessee, was 75 percent and in Charleston, South Carolina, was 70 percent.

While for some middle-class white families the Depression was an inconvenience or at worst a disruption of their usual daily life, for already poor black Americans and the elderly the Depression turned into a struggle for survival. Likewise, Mexican Americans and American Indians faced a harsh existence during the Depression.

Black Americans

Over 75 percent of black Americans lived in the South, where the conditions of their Depression life were very difficult. Most had always lived in extreme poverty, and the widespread economic plunge had only made life more miserable. Eighty percent were agricultural laborers and worked as hired hands, sharecroppers, or tenant farmers. Tenant farming is a system of farm work where the families supply their own tools but rent the farmland for cash. Sharecropping is a system of farm work where a landlord supplies the tools and land to be farmed. Both tenant farming and sharecropping requires the family to give a part of the crops to the landlord. Tenant farmers and sharecroppers work all spring and summer to have something left over to live on in the fall. More than likely after rents, sharecropping fees, grocery bills, and doctor bills were paid, little or nothing was left. This meant there was no money to live on all winter. In early spring owners would advance the families $10 a month for seed and to live on. That was $10 for a family of perhaps eight or more. For picking cotton a hired hand might be paid as low as twenty cents for one hundred pounds. For a 14-hour day a hand might make only 60¢.

Most rural black American families lived in housing that could only be described as shacks which had no windows or screens, little furniture, dirt floors, and no sanitation or running water. Bathing was done in a tin tub, making personal cleanliness difficult to achieve. Most lived on a diet of corn bread, greens from the garden, hominy grits (corn), salt pork, and molasses. Malnutrition was common. Most women faced childbirth without a doctor or midwife because they could neither pay medical fees nor find transportation into town. In the early 1930s, black women died in childbirth at almost twice the rate of white women. Their children were more than twice as likely to die before reaching one year of age than were those of whites. If children attended school at all it was generally in one-room substandard structures that families in the community had banded together to build. Parents hoped their children could get enough education to read, write, and "figure" so as not to get cheated. Rural high schools for black students in the South were all but nonexistent. There were technical high schools for blacks in some southern cities. With no power, few connections, little education, and being surrounded by the racist activities of terrorist organizations such as the Ku Klux Klan, blacks kept to themselves, did not protest, and did their best to live.

Approximately three million blacks lived in northern cities and were not much better off than those in the South. The Works Progress Administration estimated a family of four needed $800 a year just to survive, but those employed blacks generally earned much less, often less than $500 a year. Industrial jobs that blacks held in the 1920s, such as coal mining and construction, became all but nonexistent in the 1930s. Traditional jobs such as chauffeurs, maids, cooks, elevator operators, door hops, garbage collectors, and hospital attendants disappeared as the middle and upper middle class saw their salaries decline. By 1933 many of these same white Americans realized they could rehire household help, either black or white, for pitiful wages. Four dollars a week for long, unpredictable hours was common.

The Depression years also saw an increase in racial violence against black Americans by unemployed whites competing for the same jobs. Black Americans were often intimidated into quitting.

Northern urban blacks fared no better than southern blacks when it came to housing. Blacks, along with poor urban whites, were crowded into tiny apartments. Buildings that once housed sixty families now were crammed with two hundred families. Landlords accomplished this by dividing a six-room apartment into six tiny "kitchenettes," each with a single bed, refrigerator and hot plate. All six families shared a single bathroom. The previous six-room apartment had brought in $50 a month, but the same space subdivided into six kitchenettes brought $142 a month. Landlords' profits soared.

If families failed to pay their rent, a city official would show up to evict the tenants, putting all their belongings out on the street. In Caroline Bird's memoir of the Depression, *The Invisible Scar,* she noted, "Eviction was so common that children in a Philadel-

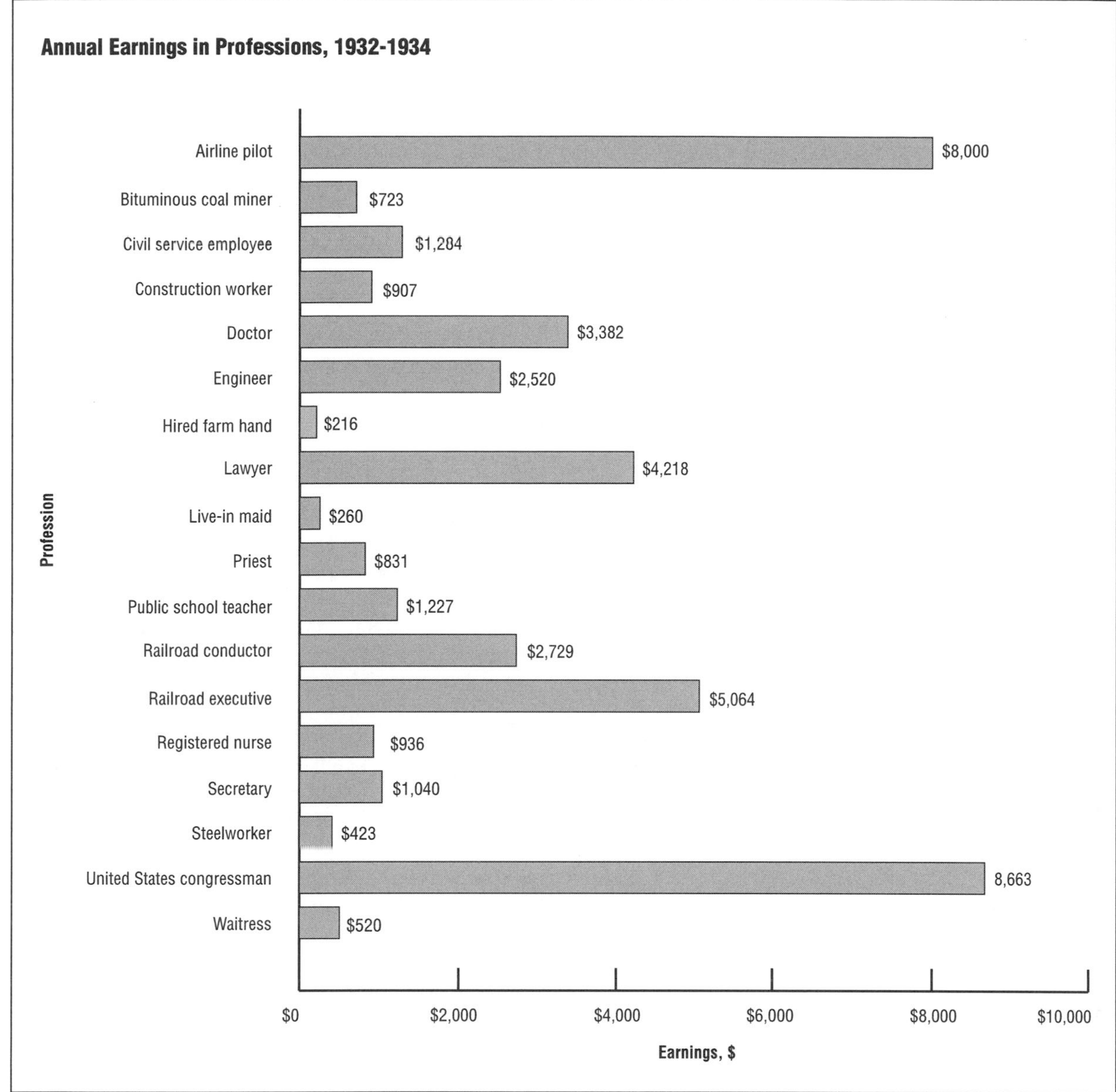

Hired farm hands earned the lowest annual pay, at only $216 per year. U.S. Congressmen made the most. *(The Gale Group.)*

phia day care center made a game of it. They would pile all the doll furniture up first in one corner and then in another" (1966, p. 34). Nevertheless, neighborhood networks were created in the buildings, and eviction protests developed in some cities, namely New York, Baltimore, and as far away as Sioux City, Iowa. Men and women, greatly outnumbering officials, would gather, march to an eviction site, put all the tenants' belongings back into the apartment and thereby buy two or three months of time before officials showed up again.

As in the South, malnutrition and diet-related diseases such as rickets and pellagra were common. Although many vacant lots were turned into gardens, many inner-city families still had no access to any garden vegetables. Children would wait at the back door of the butchers for chicken feet or bones—anything for a watery soup. Restaurant garbage was scrounged through daily. Schools recognized that many children were suffering from malnutrition. An estimated one-fifth of children living in New York City were malnourished.

As a consequence of the poverty, just as in the middle-class families experiencing unemployment, poor families broke apart under the strain. Lack of a steady job left men devoid of their role as breadwinner and authority figure. Because of desertion or premature death, it is estimated that as many as 50 percent of black American urban families were without a husband and father. Many mothers both worked outside the home and cared for children and all domestic duties.

Overall, public relief programs helped many more whites than blacks. Before 1933 relief agencies often turned blacks away or gave them much less than they gave white families. President Roosevelt, inaugurated in March 1933, attempted to correct some of the inequalities with his New Deal programs. By 1935 almost 30 percent of black families received some sort of aid, and in some cities 50 percent were receiving aid. Roosevelt became very popular with black Americans.

Elderly Americans

During the early years of the twentieth century, more and more Americans over 65 years of age lived in cities. As had younger people, they had followed the growing job market in urban factories and other industrial jobs. As they aged they could no longer keep up with the rigorous physical demands of such jobs. Before industrialization extended farm families cared for the aging, but urban elderly workers had no such extended family care. Most had no pensions, and social security payments did not exist. When they lost their job, they quickly fell into poverty, living off their meager savings. By the end of the 1920s, it was estimated 50 percent of the elderly lived at the poverty level.

For many older Americans the Depression became a nightmare when numerous banks failed between 1929 and 1933. Some elderly lost all of their savings and were left with nothing. Others saw their incomes disappear with the stock market crash. Often, the few pension plans that existed with companies were poorly planned and collapsed. Twenty-eight states offered state-funded pension programs, but most paid very little, between $7 and $30 a month. Proud older Americans—often loyal employees all their lives—were forced to turn to relatives and friends who were also struggling or to private charities. Dignity and self-respect were lost. Many elderly neither had adequate food nor housing and were forced to move in with relatives, usually their children.

The Homeless

The Depression forced many thousands of the poorest to leave their homes and travel the country looking for work or eventually giving up. The nomads included single men who had left their families; young adult males leaving families in search of a better life; rural families uprooted by the 1935 and 1936 Dust Bowl storms which affected eight mid-western states from Texas and Oklahoma to Montana and the Dakotas; and tenant and farm laborers. Many headed for California to work as migrant farm workers. Transportation included hitchhiking, jumping on a freight train boxcar, or piling in an old car for the journey. While on the road getting enough to eat was very difficult. People asked for handouts at backdoors in towns along the way, found an occasional meal at a mission or shelter in bigger cities, or stole from farmers or shopkeepers rather than starve. Single drifters often slept on the ground and ate in "jungle" campsites along the railroads. When subfreezing temperatures hit, people did not have adequate clothing or overcoats. Many developed severe health problems and suffered from malnutrition. Deaths from pneumonia and tuberculosis were common. Those hopping on and off moving boxcars often were injured or killed.

Once the destitute travelers arrived in California or Oregon, life did not improve much. Some found jobs on farms, in canneries, or picking fruit and vegetables up and down the west coast. Some applied for relief, and many resorted to begging. Cities and towns could barely care for their own poor and offered little in the way of housing. Shantytowns known as "Hoovervilles" sprung up on vacant land, so called because of the derision in which President Herbert Hoover (served 1929–1933) was held by many in the public, who saw him as responsible for their Depression woes. Despite his search to alleviate the harsh economic situation, Hoover held fast to his opposition of granting money to feed hungry Americans. He referred to direct relief as the "dole." Calling the shacks, often made of scraps of wood, cardboard, or tin—any material that could be found or pulled from the rivers, "Hoovervilles" was an effective insult to the president.

Indeed, a scornful vocabulary evolved using Hoover's name. "Hoover blankets" were old newspapers. "Hoover flags" referred to empty pocket linings turned inside out. Jackrabbits caught for food in the country were "Hoover hogs." Broken down cars moving only with the help of mules were "Hoover wagons."

The residents of Hoovervilles shopped for their food at the local dumps and in the garbage of restaurants. Many lived in tents, cooking outside. Families crowded into the shacks or tents and had no water or sinks. One toilet would serve many. Garbage was tossed on the ground. Children paid a terrible price. They were malnourished, sick, had no schooling, and had been pulled away from all familiar surroundings. In the worst years of the Depression (1930–1933), increased numbers of children were placed in orphanages by parents who could no longer support them. The number of children entering orphanages increased by 50 percent between 1930 and 1931.

Contributing Forces

The Depression came at the culmination of several decades of unprecedented prosperity—decades in which many families were making the important and nearly irreversible adaptation to a mass consumption society. The 1920s were marked by the new material culture—the automobile, the lure of new time-saving devices such as washing machines; fashionable clothes in store windows; the freedom of youth; the rage for jazz, radio and movies; and the intrusion of school and community affairs into the life of the family. All had occurred since the late nineteenth century and with the new materialism, the growing sense that people lacked control over those changes within their own family grew. Family breakdowns due to the pressure of changing values increasingly concerned social scientists.

Family expectations with respect to the standard of living were high. Perhaps more than anything else, owning a car represented the American dream. Through the 1920s car makers came out with new models every year and for every size pocketbook. Car manufacturers encouraged consumers to trade their year-old model in and to trade up; that is, buy a more expensive model each year. The number of gasoline stations rapidly increased. Standard Oil went from 12 stations in 1920 to one thousand stations in 1929. When the Depression hit in 1929 Americans found they had lots of reliable cars that with good care could keep on running.

The 1920s were a time of spending. Shopping was a national pastime. A revolution in merchandising was establishing fast-growing chain stores across the nation. The chain stores offered a broad selection, lower prices than "mom and pop" stores, and convenience for the housewife. Lerner Dress Shops grew from six stores in 1920 to 133 stores in 1929. In that same time period, Woolworth enlarged from 1,111 stores to 1,825 stores, J.C. Penney from 312 to 1,395, and Western Auto Supply from three to 54 stores. The 1920s ushered in commercial advertising. Products were described in flashy color ads in national magazines. General Electric refrigerators, Listerine mouthwash, Coca-Cola, Palmolive soap, and cigarette companies all pushed their products via advertisements. Magazines and newspapers received a majority of their revenue from advertising by 1925. Grocery store chains such as A & P, Safeway, and Piggly Wiggly sprang up nationwide. The power of buying soared for millions. Wives of construction laborers could afford store-bought food products, silk stockings, and fashionable dresses.

No group exemplified the excitement and gusto of the 1920s more than young adults. Girls cut their hair to the ear level in a style called the "bob" and hemmed dresses as high as the knees. Raccoon coats and peek-a-boo hats completed the dress of the fashionable young lady. These "flappers" could dance the night away doing the shimmy, black bottom, and Charleston. Born in black American communities, the jazz craze swept the country. More and more young men owned cars and parked them at city overlooks and dark roads to "neck" with girlfriends. Morals liberalized. A hip topic was physician and psychoanalyst Sigmund Freud's views on sexual complexities.

Reaching the mass market in the 1920s, radio sales rose. In 1922, sixty thousand families owned radios, and by 1930 13,750,000 did so. Fictional characters Little Orphan Annie and Tarzan were created in the 1920s and their adventures aired through the radio waves. Going to the movies also became a way of life for most Americans. Sets were magnificent in this fantasy world where adventure and sex dominated the screen. By 1927 "talkies" arrived, adding even more inducement. By 1929–30 close to 100 million people went to the movies weekly.

The pleasure loving, self-gratification society did not reach into all homes. Many farming families already feeling the pinch of low prices for their products had likely rarely bought a store-made dress, didn't know who Freud was, had only seen flappers in magazines and the movies, knew little of jazz, and went to church faithfully. Most of their life was untouched by the extravagance of the 1920s. For these reasons, farming families not devastated by the Dust Bowl or set adrift from their tenant or sharecropping farms probably weathered the Depression as well as any group.

By the early 1930s, family values and lifestyles for all but the most wealthy would be altered. How well people adjusted to lower incomes and a reduced standard of living determined their lifestyle of the 1930s and whether or not their family life survived.

More About...

Women's Fashion

Between the stock market crash of 1929 to the beginning of the New Deal in 1933, fashions for the American women changed dramatically, replacing the short straight lines of the 1920s. Hemlines plummeted just as the market had. By 1930 evening dresses touched the ground. By 1933 the hemlines of everyday dresses reached halfway between the knees and shoes. The flat-busted straight dresses of the 1920s gave way to curvaceous, womanly outfits. Lingerie of the 1930s followed suit. Hats were likely to be small, perky, and resting on the top of the head. The tight helmet hat of the 1920s was definitely out.

Those who could afford store-bought dresses could view examples of them in store windows adorning lifelike mannequins or in various catalogues. The Depression triggered a return to simple fabrics and design. Cost became a prime consideration in dress design, from material to cut out to decoration. The dominant look for women's everyday dress was a simple printed dress made of synthetic material, reasonably priced, and easy to accessorize. Women used hats, a "pocketbook," gloves, and jewelry to help change the look of rather plain outfits. The dresses reflected the nation's quieter, more somber mood as compared to the high-spirited flapper look of the 1920s. By 1934 the bright practical dresses served the hard times and the new working women well. Dresses made of polka-dot material were very cheery and popular. The typical cost of a practical dress was $4.50. Those many thrifty-minded women who sewed their own clothes took their ideas of styles from the store windows and catalogues.

By 1940 the hemline of the everyday dress had changed again—upward to just below the knee. Hemlines would continue to rise and fall through the 1960s, causing women to purchase new wardrobes frequently to keep fashionable and sustain the income of the garment industry. Sometime in the mid-1970s, hems became less important with length left up to the individual.

Perspectives

Optimism

Even after the stock market crash in 1929, most Americans wanted to believe President Hoover (served 1929–1933) that everything was basically all right. The American optimism continued for a time. Immediately after the crash, most people resumed going about their everyday business. As the months, then years, began to drag by with little improvement, some still clung to their optimism, but many others turned highly pessimistic.

Pessimism

Those individuals who had lost their jobs began to believe that they would not be able to find work. Many became highly pessimistic, as it was most difficult to be optimistic when you were hungry. Some people were so demoralized by the hard times that they lost their will to survive. Between 1928 and 1932, the suicide rate rose by nearly 30 percent. Also, three times as many people were admitted to state mental hospitals than in previous years.

Pride

The working class, middle class, and upper middle class were steeped in the American work ethic and self-reliance. When these Americans found themselves unemployed or with greatly lowered wages, the psychological impact of the Great Depression became apparent. These once-proud individuals were deeply embarrassed by the situation in which they and their families found themselves. If they sought relief, they often begged that their request for help be kept confidential. They always pointed out how long and hard they had worked. They stressed they did not want charity, but were only asking to borrow money for a time. Riots or protests rarely broke out, for the men and women of the Depression ultimately blamed themselves for their predicament.

Older Americans

Having been employed all their lives, older Americans were bitter that the Depression had taken all the joy from their last years. Up to 50 percent of Americans 65 years and older lived in poverty and in fear that necessary medical care would not be available to them. They often thought of themselves as the forgotten men and women of the Depression.

Hope

When Roosevelt came into power and started offering programs for the poor, people for the first time had hope. Black and white Americans came to nearly worship the new president. They were glued to his fireside chats, soaking in his confidence. Most would have followed him anywhere. When the Works Progress Administration (WPA) and Civilian Conservation Corps (CCC) camps became organized, even many drifters went back home because they qualified for help in their own states.

Individuals often thought of the Roosevelts as parental figures. They frequently wrote letters for help directly to the Roosevelts. It was not unusual for writers to offer cherished possessions as security for loans they requested from the Roosevelts.

Middle Class Who Stayed Put

Middle-class Americans continued to believe that hard work, thrift, and self-reliance would bring them through. Tomorrow was bound to be a better day. Families spent a lot of time with each other. They were always willing to lend a helping hand or share with less fortunate families. It was also very important to "keep up appearances." They might paint the outside of their house, make their own clothes or shop for nice secondhand clothes found at thrift stores, and attend social gatherings in homes or churches.

Affluent

The very affluent or wealthy continued to believe people should work for whatever they got. They believed people on relief were lazy and incompetent and lacked the virtue of thrift. Although the suffering of other American families made them nervous or uneasy, they carried on with their lives of privilege with rarely any alteration.

Differences Between Men and Women

Unemployed men were more affected by their situation than their wives. Women could continue their rounds of cooking, cleaning, and mending, while men often seemed helpless when their routine was disrupted. Some unemployed men helped with housework, and companion marriages developed. Others, however, deeply resented doing "women's chores" and felt an acute loss of self-esteem.

Married Working Women

For most white Americans, a working wife was a stigma on the husband and families. Although a George Gallup Poll showed that 805 of the men surveyed did not want their wives to work for pay, for many it was an economic necessity. Married working women were often criticized for taking jobs away from men. In a 1936 Gallup Poll, 82 percent of the respondents agreed married women should not work if their husbands had jobs. Interestingly, black families did not share the white value system. Black Americans had a much higher proportion than whites of married women in the labor force at all economic levels. It had long been accepted in black American culture that married black women worked outside the home as a necessity to make ends meet.

At a Glance

The Dionne Quintuplets

A sensational Canadian news story broke in 1934 that captured the interest of Depression Americans. In the backwoods town of Callander, Ontario, on May 28, Mrs. Ovida Dionne gave birth to five baby girls. The babies were identical quintuplets whose combined birth weight was under ten pounds. A country doctor, Allen Roy Dafoe, delivered the girls, who were named Annette, Cecile, Emilie, Marie, and Yvonne.

When their survival seemed assured, newspaper men, movie men, advertising agents, and tourists began arriving in Callander. For the quintuplets' protection, they were made wards of the King and had fourteen individuals on their payroll. By the ages of four, they already owned $600,000 in government bonds earned through movie contracts and fees. The town of Callander received up to three thousand visitors—eight thousand on weekends—to visit the Dafoe Nursery. Americans eagerly followed their development throughout the 1930s, and they were a popular topic of household conversation.

Impact

The stigma of poverty remained with many people for the rest of their lives. The memories of scrimping

Four women work together on assembling a jigsaw puzzle in the packing room of a Cleveland puzzle manufacturer. Jigsaw puzzles became a popular, inexpensive way to pass the time during the Depression. (AP/Wide World Photos. Reproduced by permission.)

and going without never really disappeared. Likewise, for many, even if they themselves were not devastated, the Depression pictures of starving and homeless families left indelible impressions. The fear persisted that it could happen again, and they might then be the homeless. Hence, achieving financial security and then maintaining that security became the foremost goal of many Americans. People developed habits of saving and thrift that saw them through the 1930s and into the dark days of World War II (1939–1945). When food was rationed in World War II, Americans quickly adjusted. They had practiced doing with less for the entire decade prior to the war. So-called "victory gardens" appeared in backyards and city vacant lots just as in the 1930s. Married women worked outside the home in factories supporting the war effort. After the war most returned to raising children and taking care of domestic duties, but many enjoyed the partnership style of marriage that had evolved in the 1930s. Marriage partners shared more duties and enjoyed activities together. Married women working outside the home, however, would not gain wide acceptance until the late 1960s and 1970s.

Following World War II, the United States as a whole experienced unprecedented prosperity through the second half of the twentieth century. Nevertheless, many of those who lived through the Depression held tightly onto all possessions with the rationale that you never knew when times would turn bad and something you needed would not be available.

The Depression-era "psyche" also contributed to the infamous generation gap experienced by young people and their parents in the late 1960s and 1970s. Having lived only in times of plenty, many young people of those decades questioned the strong emphasis of their parents on money and possessions. That emphasis seemed to have been more lasting than the helping and sharing attitudes of the 1930s. When young people decried their parents' materialism, many older Depression-era Americans were baffled. The resulting "generation gap" loomed wide and for many families never closed.

At a Glance

"Jigs"

By 1934 over 3,500,000 jigsaw puzzles were in the hands of Americans. Whether the attraction was solving a problem or not having to worry about the more serious matters of the day, people diligently worked over the puzzles. Puzzles consisting of hundreds or thousands of irregular-shaped little pieces lay on a table waiting to be fitted together into a single picture.

At first, puzzles were expensive wood cuts, but a New England entrepreneur began cutting puzzles from heavy cardboard. These more affordable jigsaws sold from ten cents up to a few dollars for a thousand-piece colossal puzzle. By 1934 they could be found at newsstands, drugstores, toy departments with adult games, and shops where books and stationery were sold. Throughout the 1930s solving jigsaw puzzles remained a favorite national pastime.

Notable People

Louis Armstrong (1901?–1971). Born in New Orleans, Armstrong learned to play the cornet as a teenager and played in local jazz clubs. Even at this early age, Armstrong's natural ability, unique style, and passionate playing caught attention. He moved to Chicago in 1922 to play with Joe "King" Oliver, a premier horn player from New Orleans who had moved north. In 1924 Armstrong joined the Fletcher Henderson big band in New York City. He became a trumpet player and innovative soloist. Returning to Chicago, he went on to become the premier trumpeter in jazz. His influence in the jazz world was unmatched. His early recordings are classics: "Hot Five," the "Hot Seven," and the "Savoy Ballroom Five." Recordings that rank as the greatest in jazz include "Cornet Chop Suey," "West End Blues," and "Potato Head Blues."

Hattie Carnegie (1889–1956). Hattie Carnegie was one of the most well-respected and popular dress designers of the 1930s. She began as a milliner (hat maker) with a shop on East Tenth Street in New York City. Although never learning to sew herself, she began designing dresses. She believed in simple but beautiful clothes and soon was the talk of the fashionable women of New York. Carnegie's original designer clothes were too expensive for most Americans, but were copied by other designers and produced at lower prices. Carnegie herself soon designed an inexpensive line of ready-to-wear clothing that she allowed some department stores to carry. Her influence was extensive over both designer and everyday clothing.

Lilly Daché (1913–1990). Lilly Daché was the most well known milliner of the 1930s. By 1940, 47 department stores sold her hats for $25 apiece. Daché opened her own shop producing forty to fifty hats a day in the late 1920s, and by the early 1930s moved into her own building. Daché's hats, which were produced utilizing a wide range of fabrics and design, usually had brims tilted to the side. She made hats for many Hollywood stars. Police often had to be called to her hat sales as customers fought over the hats.

Lou Gehrig (1903–1941). In 1931, following the great Babe Ruth, Lou Gehrig had become the captain and symbol of the New York Yankees. Baseball was the favorite American sport during the Depression, and Gehrig became a baseball hero. He hit four home runs in one game on June 3, 1932. In 1934 he won baseball's triple crown and was awarded his second MVP in 1936. He played in 2,130 consecutive games, earning the name "the Iron Horse." Gehrig died in 1941 of a degenerative muscle disease—Amyotrophic Lateral Sclerosis—that now bears his name.

Benny Goodman (1909–1986). Benny Goodman, known as the "King of Swing," introduced swing to America in 1935. Swing was a form of jazz. His recording, "The Music Goes 'Round and 'Round," fueled the swing rage. Goodman quickly gained a national, then an international, reputation as a clarinetist and swing bandleader.

Eleanor Roosevelt (1884–1962). Eleanor Roosevelt, wife of President Franklin Roosevelt, was viewed as a champion of the American people. She worked tirelessly for women's rights in the work place, supported civil rights for black Americans, and lent a compassionate ear to working class families and the unemployed. She was a chief advisor to the President and frequently helped him devise political policies.

Franklin Delano Roosevelt (1882–1945). President Franklin D. Roosevelt instilled confidence in the American people mired in a deep Depression. Families eagerly gathered around the radio for his regular "fireside chats," through which he reported the whys and wherefores of his numerous programs. As he established his New Deal agencies, many people began to regain hope that the future would take a turn for the better.

Lowell Thomas (1892–1981). Lowell Thomas made his radio debut in 1930 as a news reader. After the first six months, Thomas was heard only on NBC until 1947. He had a strong voice without a trace of an accent and presented balanced political commentary in his nightly broadcast. In 1939 Thomas broadcast NBC's first televised news program.

Primary Sources

A Middle Class Family Lifestyle in the Great Depression

Cabell Phillips' in his book *From the Crash to the Blitz: 1929–39,* (1969, pp. 416–417) relates the following account of a close-up view of a middle-class family's lifestyle in the 1930s. The author was a lifetime friend of the couple described. The subject's names are fictitious:

John and Mary, in their mid-twenties, married in 1930. John's salary was $50 a week and they moved into a nice furnished one-bedroom apartment in a large mid-western city. The following year John's company collapsed and he lost his job. He and Mary moved to a single "light housekeeping" room with a tiny icebox in a clothes closet, a two burner gas stove, and a shared bath at the end of the hall. The room was in an old brownstone near the slums and rented for $7 a week in advance. After a year of unsuccessful job hunting John and Mary decided to move back east into John's parents' home. John traveled back by freight train and Mary took what belongings were left and traveled east by bus.

> We moved in on my family at just about the time that my father's business failed. My brother and his wife moved in too; it seemed that everybody we knew was doubling up the same way . . . Our house was a modest one in a modest neighborhood. It had eight rooms, one bath, and a tiny yard, but six people and three families crowded it physically and emotionally. In-laws were never meant to live together. Every so often we had to draw up a truce.
>
> The economics of our existence for the next year are still vague in my mind. My father was cleaned out when his business failed, but he managed a few months later to get a job with a former competitor at about $30 a week. My brother picked up a few dollars from time to time . . . I did about as well peddling brushes, magazine subscriptions, and what-not door to door, and as a part-time helper in a warehouse. My first regular job came late in 1933 when the NRA 30-hour week caused one of the local papers to hire a couple of extra reporters. The pay was $15 a week, which was $2.50 less than the warehouse offered me to go on full time. It was a hard choice to make but I opted for the newspaper.
>
> Out of our combined resources we had to pay something on the mortgage, taxes, insurance, and so forth. Our food budget for the entire household was $15 a week, and that took a lot of scrounging and corner-cutting. . . . There were no labor-saving gadgets in our house. Bread was toasted in the gas oven, dishes were washed in the sink, housecleaning was done with a broom or carpet sweeper, the ice man delivered a 50-pound cake of ice every other day to the ponderous refrigerator . . . After the gas heater blew up one summer we had to fire up the coal furnace twice a week to get water for baths and dishwashing. This made the house unbearable for hours.
>
> There was one car in the family, a six-year old Hupmobile with chronically weak tires. We didn't dare take it on trips out of town . . . .
>
> My parents kept up their church attendance, and we went along occasionally to keep them happy. My parents had never been more than moderately well off but the experience of suddenly finding themselves "poor as church mice," as my mother put it, was hard for them to take. It was a blow to their faith and to their pride, and they tended to withdraw and to brood. It was less of a spiritual wrench to the younger members of the family; for them it was more a cause of exasperation and an occasional outburst of nerves. In our natural optimism we were sure that there was a way out of the trap and that sooner or later we would find it. Most of the friends in our age group felt the same way, and it created an extra bond of intimacy.

There was a lot of visiting back and forth in the evenings, games of pennyante poker, monopoly, and bridge, sampling the newly legal beer and whiskey, going on picnics, discovering golf at a nearby country club which had opened its course to all-comers at one dollar greens fee. And we spent hours in noisy confabulation, most of it off the top of our heads, about politics, morality, philosophy, and the frustrations and occasional joys of job hunting. But we weren't depressed, really; we all had a sort of insouciant optimism—things couldn't get any worse, they could only get better—and we managed to enjoy ourselves in the way young people always do.

Things began to break a little better for Mary and me in 1936. We moved into our own apartment but continued to help out our parents financially. We were still "poor as church mice" and living pretty shakily with borrowed furniture, make-do clothes, and an awesome pile of debts. But I was now making $25 a week and Mary was making about $15. We felt that the trap which had held up for five years had at least been sprung, and, as it turned out, it had.

Growing Up in Rural Texas

Rita Van Amber, in *Stories and Recipes of the Great Depression of the 1930s, Vol. II,* (pp. 6–7) shares the memories of George Stockard of Eau Claire, Wisconsin, when he was growing up in rural East Texas:

> We were a large family; at times sixteen sat around the table. That included aunts and cousins brought in to Grandma's house when we learned they had no food or money. I was sixteen years old.
>
> This was Texas, 80 miles east of Dallas. It was 1931 when the depression really hit. Oil wells had stopped operating because prices of consumer goods had dropped out of sight.
>
> We lived on a farm and raised and sold cotton, peanuts, and all kinds of fruits and vegetables. We had our own cattle for beef and milk, plus hogs for butchering and to sell as well. There was lots of waste out there for the hogs to fatten up on. But we didn't have electricity then and ice had to be shipped in. It was a valued commodity, especially in the warm season which we had a lot of. . . .
>
> Jobs were unheard of, and when the drought hit we were lucky to be able to raise some of our food for our accumulated family.
>
> Women made everything out of flour sacks from the Hackers Best flour mills. Yukon flour was popular, but the ink didn't wash well. When the girls strolled by with new skirts on we called them "Yukon Queens." They wore "prairie skirts," and when the wind blew it did all sorts of flirty things with them.
>
> Our parents had to learn to be inventive and make do and passed these qualities on to their kids. We actually had a lot of fun. We'd work incredibly hard to figure out how to make a toy and then scrounge to find the scraps of material to build it. We made the Paddle & Wheel. A syrup-can lid provided the wheel and a stick and handle made a toy you never tired of playing with, going up and down the dusty roads and fields. The stick horse, of course, never went out of vogue especially for the smaller ones who couldn't keep up with some of our big toys. The Flying Jenny was something else. The biggest we made was a true to life merry-go-round. Crude and rough, but it went around and was made to last. Our wagons had wheels cut from logs. Big boys had to do the cutting, but we all had wagons for play and for our chores. And we had the swimming hole. Boys stepped out of their overalls and jumped in and the girls came after, put on the overall and jumped in, too. It was wonderful through all the hot weather. No electricity meant no air conditioning and no refrigeration. Ice was scarce.

Hoovervilles

The following is a description of a shantytown, or Hooverville, located in Knoxville, Tennessee, as recounted by Fan Flanigan. This selection was collected by team members of a Federal Writers Project of the Works Progress Administration and compiled into a 1939 book, *These Are Our Lives* (pp. 372–373):

> As much sand and gravel as they is about here, you wouldn't hardly think nothing would grow. But it does. Every house down here, they's a spot for a garden near it if them that lives in it ain't too trifling to put it in. We have plenty of corn and 'taters and cucumbers and tomatoes in season. We shares with them that ain't got any if they's been down on their luck. I has flowers, too. Them seeds over there in the drying box is every one of them flower seeds. I save them from one year to the next. . . .
>
> It's all right here . . . and I like it pretty fair as long as the river don't start acting up. We don't have no rent to pay, jest sort of squat here betwixt the railroad tracks and the water and build our places out of what we can git off the dump and the wood we can ketch floating down the river. Me and mammy been here sence [sic] nineteen and thirty-two, that hard old year . . . .
>
> You kind of grow to like this place. . . You'd like any place, though, if you live in it long enough, I reckon. A rich man up to Knoxville give this whole strip betwixt the bridges for poor folks to build they houses on. Them that come first taken the pick of what they was here. Ma done that. She come right after Pop died. We use to live in that biggest house over there. My brother'in'law lives there now. Him and Sis had sech a flock of children you couldn't stretch a leg without tromping on one. So me and Mammy moved out. This one room here we has is fair size and plenty for us. Mammy owns that brother-in-law house. She don't own a stick of this one.
>
> When you git your claim that rich man don't care what you make your house of. But the's one thing about it, the outside, I mean the roof, is got to be tin. That's the law. No way to put out a fire in Shanty Town. So it's tin roofs here or you can't put up a house.

The Upper Crust

The most wealthy families in the United States seemed to have gone through the Depression relatively unscathed. The daughters of those privileged families, débutantes, were young women being introduced in high society. The débutante's ball was the parent's lavish way of making the announcement that their daughter had reached marriageable age. In New York society, two hundred or more débutantes were introduced each year. In addition to her own ball, each débutante was expected to attend many other balls, luncheons, and teas. The December 1930 issue of *Fortune* magazine, in a short article titled "The $3,000,000 Machine" (pp. 96, 98), reports on the average cost of a ball and on the average débutante clothes allowance. Remember these figures are in 1930 dollars:

> With these expenditures the ball should be paid for unless late in the evening a guest happens to throw a potted palm at a mirror. But that is rare. Thus, taking an approximate average of the...figures, we find that a débutante's ball cost:

Ballroom	$500
Music	1,350
Supper	3,000
Entertainment	500
Cigarettes	200
Mineral water	250
Champagne	2,000
Tips	400
Flowers	2,500
Invitations	800
(Total)	$11,500

> Which can probably be made less, which can, but very easily, be made more ...
>
> There remains the matter of clothes. The average débutante allowance is $200 a month, and the time during which she buys clothes is from September to March, which would give her $1,400 for clothes if she didn't have to pay for taxis. However, the parents provide and will usually give the offspring an evening wrap, three best evening dresses, and a fur coat. Most girls wear $7.00 or $8.00 hats and cheap evening slippers, satin-dyed and with buckles that can go from one pair to the next. It must be remembered that débutantes dance continuously and that no matter how gallant the swain, he is prone to step on her toes. The débutante's evening wardrobe will probably consist of four good evening dresses ($150–$250), four others for lesser occasions ($100), one new evening coat with fur, and one old one. And it is quite all right to wear the same dress twice in the same week, but *never* should one wear it on consecutive nights. Your débutante can dress on $4,000 and be very smart, and there is no reason why she cannot meet the situation with $3,000. Be it said, however, that the above statements are anathema to most of New York's smartest shops. Bergdorf Goodman, for instance, cannot imagine the débutante who does not spend at least $10,000 on her clothes...

This was a large sum of money as $10,000 in 1930s dollars would be equal to more than $100,000 in 2000 dollars.

Suggested Research Topics

- What pressures did the American family experience during the Great Depression? Were there fewer births, marriages, divorces? If so, explain likely reasons.
- What groups of Americans had their lifestyles severely affected? Which groups fared better? Are there any groups whose lifestyle went unaffected?
- Make a list of persons who students know that lived during the Depression. Decide on which person to interview. Develop questions ahead of time. Tape record the interview and later transcribe the recording into notes. Share this oral history with the class.

Bibliography

Sources

Bergman, Andrew. *We're in the Money: Depression America and Its Films.* New York: New York University Press, 1971.

Bird, Caroline. *The Invisible Scar.* New York: David McKay Company, Inc., 1966.

Britten, Loretta, and Sarah Brash, eds. *Hard Times: The 30s.* Alexandria, VA: Time-Life Books, 1998.

Cott, Nancy F., ed. *No Small Courage: A History of Women in the United States.* New York: Oxford University Press, 2000.

Federal Writers Project. *These Are Our Lives.* Chapel Hill: The University of North Carolina Press, 1939.

Hewes, Joseph M., and Elizabeth I. Nybakken, eds. *American Families: A Research Guide and Historical Handbook.* Westport, CN: Greenwood Press, 1991.

McElvaine, Robert S. *Down & Out in the Great Depression: Letters from the "Forgotten Man."* Chapel Hill: The University of North Carolina Press, 1983.

Phillips, Cabell. *From the Crash to the Blitz: 1929–39.* New York: The Macmillan Company, 1969.

Thacker, Emily. *Recipes & Remembrances of the Great Depression.* Canton, OH: Tresco Publishers, 1993.

Van Amber, Rita, ed. *Stories and Recipes of the Great Depression of the 1930's.* Neenah, WI: Van Amber Publishers, 1993.

Washburne, Carolyn Kott. *America in the 20th Century, 1930–39.* North Bellmore, NY: Marshall Cavendish Corp., 1995.

Watkins, T.H. *The Hungry Years: A Narrative History of the Great Depression in America.* New York: Henry Holt and Company, 1999.

Further Reading

Bondi, Victor, ed. *American Decades: 1930–39.* Detroit, MI: Gale Research, Inc., 1995.

Britten, Loretta, and Paul Mathless, eds. *The Jazz Age: The 20s.* Alexandria, VA: Time-Life Books, 1998.

Calabria, Frank M. *Dance of the Sleepwalkers: The Dance Marathon Fad.* Bowling Green, OH: Bowling Green State University Popular Press, 1993.

Danzer, Gerald A., J. Jorge Klor de Alva, Louis E. Wilson, and Nancy Woloch. *The Americans: Reconstruction Through the 20th Century.* Boston: McDougal Littell, 1999.

McCoy, Horace. *They Shoot Horses, Don't They?* New York: Avon Books, 1935.

McDonnell, Janet. *America in the 20th Century, 1920–29.* North Bellmore, NY: Marshall Cavendish Corp., 1995.

Peduzzi, Kelli. *America in the 20th Century, 1940–49.* North Bellmore, NY: Marshall Cavendish Corp., 1995.

Rogers, Agnes. *I Remember Distinctly: A Family Album of the American People 1918–41.* New York: Harper & Brothers Publishers, 1947.

Winslow, Susan. *Brother, Can You Spare a Dime? America From the Wall Street Crash to Pearl Harbor, An Illustrated Documentary.* New York: Paddington Press, LTD, 1976.

See Also

Black Americans; Dust Bowl; Education; Ethnic Relations; Food; Hollywood; Housing; Public Health; Riding the Rails; Social Security

Glossary, Bibliography, & Master Index

Glossary

A

abstinence: a deliberate self denial of alcoholic beverages; an individual who does not drink any liquor is abstaining from liquor.

abstract expressionism: art that seeks to portray emotions, responses, and feelings rather than objects in their actual likeness.

absurd: something ridiculous or unreasonable.

academic freedom: freedom to teach without interference or unwanted influence by another group or government.

Academy Awards: annual awards granted by the Academy of Motion Pictures for outstanding acting, directing, script writing, musical scoring, service, and creative contributions to the film industry.

adaptation: something that is remade into a new form, as in a play being an adaptation of a short story.

administration: the art or science of managing public affairs. Public administration is the function of the executive branch of government and is the procedure by which laws are carried out and enforced. In the United States, the president is the head of the executive branch, which includes an advisory staff and many agencies and departments.

affiliate: a firm closely connected to another.

agribusiness: an industry involved in farming operations on a large scale. May include producing, processing, storing, and distributing crops as well as manufacturing and distributing farm equipment.

alien: foreign-born person who has not been naturalized to become a U.S. citizen. Federal immigration laws determine if a person is an alien.

Allies: nations or states that form an association to further their common interests. The United States' partners against Germany during World War II (1939–1945) are often known collectively as "The Allies" and include Great Britain and Russia. (*See also* Axis powers)

allottee: the legal owner of a specific parcel of land, held in trust by the federal government for a minimum of 25 years under the provisions of the General Allotment Act of 1887. An allottee has an allotment, a specific portion of a reservation that was held apart from other tribal lands for that person's use or the benefit of his or her descendents.

allotment: the parcel of land granted to an individual that was taken out of a tribe's communal land base known as a reservation. While allotments dated to colonial times, they became a major part of national Indian policy in the General Allotment Act of 1887.

AM: amplitude modulation, the first type of radio transmission, characterized by considerable static interference.

amendment: changes or additions to an official document. In the United States government, constitutional amendments refer to changes in the Constitution. Such amendments are rare and may be proposed only by a two-thirds vote of both houses of Congress or by a convention called by

Congress at the request of two-thirds of the state legislators.

American Federation of Labor (AFL): a national organization of craft unions that sought to give voice to the concerns primarily of skilled workers.

amortized: the payment of a loan by stable monthly payments which include both principle and interest over a period of time, resulting in a declining principle balance and repayment in full by the end of the loan period.

anarchism: a belief that no forms of government authority are necessary and that society should be based on the cooperative and free association of individuals and groups.

animated cartoon: a motion picture made from a series of drawings simulating motion by means of slight progressive changes in the drawings.

anti-Semitism: hateful sentiment or hostile activities towards Jews; racial or religious intolerance.

antitrust: opposing large combinations of businesses that may limit economic competition.

Anti-Trust Acts: federal and state laws to protect economic trade and combat discrimination between companies, price fixing, and monopolies.

appraisal: to set a value of a property by the estimate of an authorized person.

appropriations: Funds for specific government and public purposes as determined by legislation.

Aquacade: a program of lights, music, and synchronized swimming developed by Billy Rose for the 1939 New York World's Fair.

area coverage: a system of electrical service designed to serve all possible customers in a given area rather than only those customers pre-selected on the basis of their projected consumption or ability to pay.

assets: total value of everything owned by, and owed to, a business. A bank's assets include its physical building and equipment, the loans it has made on which interest is owed, stock owned in the Federal Reserve System, government bonds it owns, money in the bank's vaults, and money deposited in other banks.

assimilation: a minority group's adoption of the beliefs and ways of life of the dominant culture.

Axis powers: The countries aligned against the Allied nations in World War II (1939–1945). The term originally applied to Nazi Germany and Fascist Italy (Rome-Berlin Axis), and later extended to include Japan. (*See also* Allies)

B

B-Movie (B-Picture, B-Film): cheaply produced movies usually following a simple formula and intended to serve as the second film in a "double bill," the showing of two movies for one theater admission.

bank holiday: a day or series of days in which banks are legally closed to correct financial problems.

bank runs: occurred when worried depositors, fearing about the stability of a bank, rushed to the bank to withdraw their deposits.

benefits: financial aid in time of sickness, old age, or unemployment.

bill: a proposed law. In the United States bills may be drawn up by anyone, including the president or citizen groups, but they must be introduced in Congress by a senator or representative.

bipartisan: cooperation between the two major political parties; for example, Republican and Democratic.

bond: a type of loan, such as savings bonds, issued by the government to finance public needs that cost more than existing funds can pay for. The government agrees to pay lenders back the initial cost of the bond, plus interest.

budget deficit: occurs when money spent by the government or other organization is more than money coming in.

bureau: a working unit of a department or agency with specific functions.

bureaucracy: an administrative system, especially of government agencies, that handles day-to-day business and carries out policies.

Burlesque: a type of variety show that focuses on musical acts and skits with sexual overtones.

business cycle: an economic cycle usually comprised of recession, recovery, growth, and decline.

buying on margin: a fairly common practice in the 1920s when investors purchased stock on credit, speculating on its increase in value. They planned to pay their loans back with the money they anticipated making. Such risks sometimes proved disastrous.

bootlegger: a person who illegally transports liquor; an individual who produces or distributes liquor illegally; smuggler.

bootlegging: the illegal manufacture or distribution of alcoholic products.

boycott: refusal of a group of persons to buy goods or services from a business until the business meets their demands.

bribery: giving gifts of money or property in return for specific favors.

broker: a person who brings a buyer and a seller together and charges a fee for assisting in the exchange of goods or services. A stockbroker brings together sellers and buyers of stocks and bonds.

budget deficit: refers to a government spending more than it receives through revenues and other means; it must rely on borrowing of money thus creating a debt.

C

cabinet: a group of advisors. In the federal government the cabinet is made up of advisors who offer assistance to the president. Each president determines the make up and role of their cabinets, although most include the heads of major departments such as State, Treasury, and Justice, and the vice president.

capital: money invested in a business; capital in banking terms includes the bank's stockholders' investments; additional money invested by the bank owners; any earnings still in the bank that have not been divided up; funds for taxes, expansion, and interest on accounts. Capital is the amount banks owe its owners.

capitalism: an economic system where goods are owned by private businesses and price, production, and distribution is decided privately, based on competition in a free market.

cartel: a combination of producers of any product joined together to control its production, sale, and price so as to obtain monopoly and restrict competition in any particular industry or commodity.

CCC: the Civilian Conservation Corps, a make-work agency for men aged 18 to 25 which operated between 1933 and 1942 and worked on numerous projects on public lands across the U.S. and its territories.

CCC-LEM: the Civilian Conservation Corps, Local Experienced Men, consisting initially of older, local laborers with special skills in carpentry, blacksmithing, auto mechanics, and other trades who came in to teach CCC enrollees.

CCC-ID: units of the Civilian Conservation Corps-Indian Division, staffed with American Indian recruits working on reservation projects.

cells: transparent celluloid on which sketches of animation are traced, inked, and painted.

charter: legal authorization from a federal or state agency to carry out business. To be chartered, a bank must have sufficient capital, competent management, deposit insurance, and a commitment to the local community.

child-centered: hands-on learning with children actively participating in an activity such as counting with blocks or piecing together a puzzle of the United States. This type of learning is a departure from traditional highly structured learning where a teacher tells children information or children read information from a book and repeat it.

cinematographer: the person in charge of camera work during the production of a movie.

civil liberties: freedom of speech, freedom of the press, freedom from discrimination, and other right guaranteed by the U.S. Constitution that place limits on governmental powers.

civil rights: civil liberties that belong to an individual.

civil service: a term describing the system employing people in non-military government jobs. The system is based on merit classifications.

clause: a section or paragraph of a legal document, such as a specific part of the U.S. Constitution.

clergy: ordained as religious priests, pastors, or ministers.

coalition: an alliance between political or special interest groups forged to pursue shared interests and agendas.

collateral: something of value that a borrower agrees to hand over to the lender if the borrower fails to repay the loan. The pledged item protects the lender from loss.

collective bargaining: the negotiations between workers who are members of a union and their employer for the purpose of deciding upon such issues as fair wages and work-day hours.

collectivism: shared ownership of goods by all members of a group; a political or economic system where production and distribution are decided collectively.

colonialism: a foreign policy in which a nation exercises its control over residents of foreign countries.

commerce: exchanging, selling, or trading goods on a large scale involving transporting goods from one place to another.

Commerce Clause: a provision of the U.S. Constitution that gives Congress the exclusive power to regulate economic trade between states and with foreign countries.

commercial bank: national or state bank, owned by stockholders whose activities include demand deposits, savings deposits, and personal and business loans. Many commercial banks also provide trust services, foreign money exchange, and international banking.

commercialism: to manage a business for profit; sometimes used in referring to excessive emphasis on profit.

committee: a group of individuals charged by a higher authority with a specific purpose such as investigation, review, reporting, or determining action.

commodities: any moveable item of commerce subject to sale.

communism: a theory calling for the elimination of private property so that goods are owned in common and, in theory, available to all; a system of government where a single party controls all aspects of society such as the official ideology of United Soviet Social Republic (USSR) from 1917 until 1990.

Communist Party, U.S.A. (CPUSA): a U.S. political party promoting the political and economic teaching of German political philosopher Karl Marx that grew rapidly in membership during the 1930s.

company union: a worker organization formed by a company commonly requiring membership of all employees to prevent their joining a national labor union.

compulsory: something that is required.

"conchies": an abbreviation identifying conscientious objectors who declined to serve in the military when drafted but who took alternative duty at Public Service Camps (former CCC camps) from 1941 to 1947.

congregation: an assembly of persons gathered as a religious community.

Congress: the term used to describe the combined Senate and House of Representatives.

Congress of Industrial Organizations (CIO): a labor organization formed in 1935 initially as the Committee on Industrial Organization within the AFL. The CIO was founded on broad-based industrial unionization rather than specialized crafts or skills like the AFL.

conscientious objector: a person who refuses to serve in the military because of personal beliefs. In the United States a person cannot refuse to serve, but Congress has allowed conscientious objectors to participate in non-combat duty or complete an exemption process on religious grounds. This exemption does not include objection for political, sociological, philosophical, or personal reasons, although the Supreme Court has upheld some requests for exemption based on these grounds if they are held with the fervor of religious beliefs.

conservation: the planned management of natural resources, such as soil and forests.

conservative: politically referring to one who normally believes in a limited government role in social and economic matters and maintenance of long-standing social traditions; conservative thought in education often stresses traditional basic subject matter and methods of teaching.

consumer: a person who buys or uses economic goods.

contour plowing: to till a sloping hillside following the same elevation back and forth, rather than up and down the hill, to prevent water erosion from rains.

cooperative: a private, nonprofit enterprise, locally owned and managed by the members it serves, and incorporated (established as a legal entity that can hold property or be subject to law suits) under State law.

corporatism: a system in which companies are organized into a cooperative arrangement that is recognized by the government and granted exemptions from antitrust laws in exchange for observing certain controls.

correspondent: an individual who communicates news or commentary to a newspaper, magazine, radio, or television station for publication or broadcast.

counterculture: a culture with values that run counter to those of established society.

credit: loan; agreement by which something of value is given in exchange for a promise to repay something of equal value; an advance of cash or a product, such as a car, in exchange for a promise to pay a specific sum in the future.

cultural democracy: the concept of cultural democracy comprises a set of related commitments: protecting and promoting cultural diversity, and the right to culture for everyone in our society and around the world; encouraging active participation in community cultural life; enabling people to participate in policy decisions that affect the quality of our cultural lives; and assuring fair and equitable access to cultural resources and support.

curator: an individual in charge of the care and supervision of a museum.

curriculum: courses of study offered by educational institutions such as English, social studies, and mathematics.

D

dailies: newspapers published everyday.

débutante ball: extravagant parties thrown by the very wealthy to introduce their daughters to high society and advertise their eligibility for marriage.

default: failure to meet the payment terms of a legal contract such as failure to make loan payments in repayment of a home loan; the lender may then begin foreclosure proceedings to recoup his loses.

deficit: the amount by which spending exceeds income over a given period.

deficit spending: a government spending more money than it receives in through taxes and other sources by borrowing.

demand deposits: checking accounts.

democracy: a form of government in which the power lies in the hands of the people, who can govern directly, or indirectly by electing representatives.

democratic: relating to the broad masses of people and promoting social equality and rule by majority.

Democratic Party: one of the two major political parties in the United States that evolved from the Democratic-Republican group that supported Thomas Jefferson. In the twentieth century, the Democratic Party has generally stood for freer trade, more international commitments, greater government regulations, and social programs. Traditionally considered more liberal than the Republican Party.

denomination: a religious organization with local congregations united together under a name and set of specific beliefs under one legal and administrative body.

department: an administrative unit with responsibility for a broad area of an organization's operations. Federal departments include Labor, Interior, Health and Human Services, and Defense.

dependent: persons who must rely on another for their livelihood. Generally applied to children 18 years and younger. The term can also refer to a person 62 years old or older.

deportation: expulsion of an alien from the United States.

deposit insurance: government-regulated protection for interest-bearing deposits, such as savings accounts, to protect the depositor from failure of the banking institution.

depression: a period of economic decline usually marked by an increase in unemployment.

desegregation: to end the legally enforced separation of races.

devaluation: to reduce the value of a nation's currency relative to other nations' currencies; often by lowering its gold equivalency.

disarmament: to reduce the amount of military arms a nation controls that can be used to attack or for defense.

divest: something of value that a person must give up. For example, the Banking Act of 1933 required officers of banks to divest themselves of any loans granted to them by their own banks to avoid a conflict of interest. Bankers could no longer be accused of using their depositors' money for their own, sometimes risky, investments.

Dixiecrat: southern Democrats who bolted from the party during the 1948 presidential campaign because of President Harry Truman's support of civil rights issues, as well as their opposition to a growing federal government by supporting strong state governments.

doctrine: a principle of law established in past decisions.

documentary still photograph: a photographic image in black-and-white or color that is realistic, factual, and useful as a historic document.

dole: when a needy person or family receives a handout from the government in the form of money, food, or vouchers from the government for support, it is referred to as "going on the dole." Though rarely used in the United States anymore, it is still commonly used in Britain.

double bill: showing two movies for one admission to a theater, usually with a main feature and a B-Movie.

dramatization: acting out events that actually happened, as in the events surrounding the negotiations were dramatized for television.

drug trafficking: buying or selling illegal drugs, the drug racket.

drys: people who supported Prohibition.

dual banking: the system of banking in the United States that consists of national banks and state banks. National banks are chartered and supervised by the Office of Comptroller of the Currency in the Treasury Department. State banks are chartered and supervised by state banking authorities.

due process of law: a basic constitutional guarantee that laws are reasonable and not arbitrary and their affects are well considered when developed; also guarantees that all legal proceedings will be fair and that a person will be given notice and an opportunity to speak before government acts to take their life, liberties, or property.

durable goods: goods that are not consumed or destroyed when used, often repeatedly for a number of years. Examples include armored tanks, ships, airplanes, and machinery.

E

electric power grid: a system for distributing electricity, interconnecting electric power plants and end users and comprising such equipment as power lines, poles, transformers, and substations.

electrification: the process or event in which a house, farm, industry, or locality is connected to an electric power source.

embezzle: for a person legally entrusted with funds to steal some for his or her own benefit. Embezzlers typically work in banks or other business institutions where they have access to funds.

End Poverty In California (EPIC): Upton Sinclair's proposal to pay everyone over the age of 60 a pension of $50 a month. He also urged that unemployed be put to work to produce necessities of life.

entrepreneur: an individual willing to try new approaches, who takes the risks of organizing and managing new enterprises.

EPIC Tax: Upton Sinclair's proposal in 1934 in California to charge a tax on property assessed at greater than $100,000 in value and use the income to fund the Central Valley Project of irrigation and agriculture to combat the Great Depression.

epidemiology: the branch of medicine dealing with the incidence and prevalence of disease in large populations and with detection of the source and cause of epidemics.

equal protection: a constitutional guarantee that no person or class of persons will be denied the same protection of the laws in their lives, liberty, property, or pursuit of happiness as other people in similar circumstances.

ethnic group: a large number of people considered a group based on shared racial, tribal, national, linguistic, religious, or cultural background.

exchange rate: a key part of international trade in which a rate guides how much one kind of currency can purchase another currency; can be either set by free international market or fixed by governments.

executive order: a rule or regulation issued by the president or a governor that has the effect of law. Executive orders are limited to those that implement provisions of the Constitution, treaties, and regulations governing administrative agencies.

ex-officio: members of a committee determined solely because of the office they hold.

exports: goods shipped to another nation for trade.

extender: foodstuffs to be added to dishes to stretch the meal, make the meal portions seem bigger, and feed more people. Common depression extenders were potatoes, onions, macaroni and spaghetti, rice, breads, and garden vegetables.

extortion: gaining another's property, money, or favors by use of threats of violence, disruption, or disclosure. For example, a crime group visits a shopkeeper and demands protection money. If the shopkeeper does not pay, the group may strike at him or his property until the shopkeeper does pay or is forced out of business.

extras: people hired to act in a group scene in a motion picture; background actors.

F

fascism: an ideology that focuses on nationalism or race as a uniting factor. Fascism first arose in Italy and Germany in the 1920s and 1930s, where it was characterized by government dictatorship, militarism, and racism.

federal: relating to the central government of a nation rather than to individual states.

federal aid: funds collected by the federal government (generally through taxes) and distributed to states for a variety of reasons including education and disaster relief.

federal budget: The annual financial plan of the United States government including all sources and amounts of income and items and amounts of expenditure. The federal budget must be approved by Congress and the president.

federalist: one who supports a strong central government as opposed to those favoring most governmental powers residing with the states and a weak federal government. It was the name of an early political party in the United States.

Federal Reserve System: a system of 12 Federal Reserve banks, a board of governors appointed by the president and state banks that apply for membership that hold money reserves for the banks in their region.

feminism: organized activity seeking political, social, and economic equality of the sexes.

filibuster: a means of obstructing progress in a legislative assembly by a legislator or group of legislators holding the floor for a prolonged period of time to prevent action on a proposed bill.

FM: frequency modulation, a type of radio transmission discovered in the 1930s but not routinely used until later, characterized by a clear, precise transmission.

forced leisure: due to unemployment during the Great Depression a person had lots of time and little choice but to pursue activities traditionally considered as leisure pursuits.

foreclosure: the process in which a bank that loaned money to a customer to purchase property takes over the property when customer fails to make payments. For example, farmers who failed to keep up with payments would have their farm loan foreclosed, thereby losing their property.

Fourteenth Amendment: one of three amendments to the Constitution passed shortly after the Civil War; this amendment guarantees the same legal rights and privileges of the Constitution to all citizens by guaranteeing that state laws cannot deprive any person of life, liberty, or property without due process of law and equal protection of the laws.

fraud: illegal misrepresentation or hiding the truth to obtain property, money, business, or political advantage.

free silver: rallying cry of the People's Party in the 1890s and the Liberty Party in 1932, promoting the increase in silver coinage and the greater amount in circulation per capita.

G

genre: refers to a type or classification. For example, "thrillers" as a movie genre; science fiction as a literary genre.

gold standard: a monetary system in which a nation's unit of money is set as equal to a given weight of gold. For example, one ounce of gold equals $300.

Grange: a rural social and educational organization through which farmers combated the power of railroads and utility companies in the early twentieth century.

grant: money provided by a government or organization to an individual or group for a specific purpose. For example, the federal government makes education grants to students for college expenses and to states to improve schools.

grassroots: political organizing at the most fundamental level of society—among the people.

Grazing Service: a federal agency established after passage of the Taylor Grazing Act (June 28, 1934) to bring federal management to more than 150 million acres of public lands, located mostly in the West. This agency supervised CCC activities in many areas. The Grazing Service merged with the U.S. General Land Office (GLO) in 1946 to become the Bureau of Land Management (BLM).

Great Depression: period in U.S. history from 1929 until the early 1940s when the economy was so poor that many banks and businesses failed and millions of people lost their jobs and their homes. Business problems were combined with a severe drought that ruined many farms and contributed to the economic disaster.

Great Society: term used by Lyndon Johnson during his presidential administration (1963–1969) to describe his vision of the United States as a land without prejudice or poverty, that would be possible by implementing his series of social programs.

Gross Domestic Product (GDP): a measure of the market value of all goods and services produced within the boundaries of a nation, regardless of asset ownership. Unlike gross national product, GDP excludes receipts from that nation's business operations in foreign countries, as well as the share of reinvested earnings in foreign affiliates of domestic corporations.

Gross National Product: total value of all goods and services produced by the nation's economy.

grounds: there exist reasons sufficient to justify some form of legal relief.

H

hierarchy: leadership or ruling structure of clergy organized into rank.

hooch: alcoholic beverages that are made or acquired illegally and are frequently of inferior quality.

holding company: a company or corporation whose only purpose or function is to own another company or corporation.

Hollywood: a section of Los Angles, California, at the base of the Santa Monica Mountains where several film producers established studios to make movies in the first half of the twentieth century.

House of Representatives: one of the two bodies with specific functions that make up the legislative branch of the United States government. Each state is allocated representatives based on population. (*See also* Congress; Senate)

housing starts: the number of residential building construction projects begun during a specific period of time, usually a month.

humanitarian: a person who works for social reform and is concerned about the welfare of people.

hydroelectric power: to generate electricity from the energy of swift flowing streams or waterfalls.

I

icon: an image, picture, or logo that becomes closely associated with a particular event, belief, or organization.

immigration: the legal or illegal entry of foreigners into a country intending to remain permanently and become citizens.

income distribution: the portion of annual earnings or accumulated wealth held by members of a society. The poor have low incomes, while the wealthy usually have high incomes and a resultant growing accumulation of assets.

independent: a voter who does not belong to any political party and votes for individual candidates regardless of their party affiliation.

indoctrinate: to instruct so as to instill a particular point of view.

indolent: a person not working because of laziness.

industrialism: to change an area or economy from agricultural to industrial production.

infrastructure: permanent developments to support a community's economy such as roads, buildings, and bridges.

inflation: a sharp increase in prices for goods and services decreasing the value of currency.

injunction: a judicial order that requires someone to stop or avoid certain actions that might harm the legal rights of another.

inoculate: to inject or implant a vaccine, microorganism, antibody, or antigen into the body in order to protect against, treat, or study a disease.

installment buying: purchasing commodities on credit and, having taken possession of the item, paying for it with a fairly high rate of interest over months or even years. The system encouraged those without savings to buy unwisely.

integration: to unite different races together into equal participation in society.

internationalism: a government policy of cooperation with other nations.

interest: money paid to a lender for use of his money.

interest rate: a percentage of money borrowed that must be paid back in addition to the sum of the original loan for the privilege of being able to borrow.

interventionism: a governmental policy of becoming involved in political matters of another nation.

invalidate: to determine that a law does not have sufficient legal justification to be enforceable; therefore it is no longer valid.

isolationism: opposition to economic or political alliances with other nations.

J

Jim Crow laws: state laws and ordinances primarily created in the South, requiring the separation of races in almost every aspect of public life. Jim Crow laws lasted from the late nineteenth century to the middle of the twentieth century. The laws were powerful barriers to legal and social equality.

journalism: written description of newsworthy events or presentation of facts designed to be published in a newspaper, magazine, or delivered vocally over radio or television.

judicial restraint: for courts not to interfere with what would more properly be the role of a legislature or the executive branch to decide the wisdom of a particular law.

judiciary: relating to the courts and legal system.

jurisdiction: the geographic area over which legal authority extends, such as the legal jurisdiction of a city police force.

juvenile delinquency: criminal behavior of children or young teens.

K

Keynesian economics: the theory of economist John Keynes that advocates government spending and economic recovery programs to promote spending and increase employment.

L

labor market: the people available for employment.

labor racketeering: corrupt activities between labor unions and organized crime. Members of criminal groups position themselves in places of authority within a labor union. Once inside they use funds such as pension and health funds to their own advantage.

labor union: a group of organized workers who negotiate with management to secure or improve their rights, benefits, and working conditions as employees.

laissez faire: a political doctrine that opposed governmental interference in economic affairs except for the minimum necessary to protect property rights and for safety.

lard: hog fat obtained by rendering down the fat deposits that exist between the flesh and the skin and around internal organs of the pig.

laundered money: transferring huge sums of illegally obtained money through banks or businesses with large cash flows until the original source of the money is untraceable.

lay people: membership of a religious faith who are not clergy; the general membership; also referred to as laity.

League of Nations: the forerunner of the United Nations, envisioned by its originator, Woodrow Wilson, as a forum where countries could resolve their differences without resorting to war and promoted economic and social cooperation.

leftist: a term used to describe individuals whose beliefs are on the "left" side of the political spectrum, constituting more liberal views. Often used derogatorily.

legislation: measures that are intended to become law after approval by legislative bodies.

liabilities: what a person owes to others. A bank's liabilities include checking and savings account deposits, investment of stockholders, funds for taxes and expansion, interest to be paid to depositors on their accounts, and earnings not yet divided among the stock holders.

liberal: politically referring to one who commonly emphasizes government protection of individual liberties and supports government social and economic reforms and regulation of business to encourage competition; liberal thought in education is often associated with new methods of teaching or nontraditional subject matter.

liquidate: to convert property into cash by selling it.

liquidity: being able to meet the demands of depositors to withdraw funds and to meet the needs of borrowers for credit (loans) or cash. Liquid assets include cash on hand and securities that can be sold quickly for cash.

loan sharking: loaning money at exorbitantly high interest rates and using threats to receive repayment.

lump-sum payment: one time only payment.

***lumpenproletariat*:** those on the very bottom of the social scale described in the *Communist Manifesto* as "social scum."

M

Mafia: organized crime syndicate concerned with power and profit. The term originated in Italy some six centuries ago from the slogan: *Morte Alla Francia Italia anela!* ("Death to the French is Italy's cry.")

mafioso: member or members of the Mafia. Plural form is mafiosi.

"making do": creating filling and tasty meals with limited ingredients, with foods at hand or those readily available. Typical "making do" foods were flour, cornmeal, lard, eggs, potatoes, and onions.

maldistribution: a substantially uneven distribution of income or wealth to such an extent that it can cause general economic problems.

mandate: an authorization to act given by a political electorate to its representative.

margin call: when a creditor, who has loaned money, calls for immediate payment of the amount due.

Marxism: the theories—political, economic, and social—of Karl Marx, calling for class struggle to establish the proletariat (work class) as the ruling class, with the goal of eventually establishing a classless society.

means test: a battery of questions about a person's financial, employment, and residential history used to determine eligibility for charity or financial assistance.

mechanization: the increasing use of gas or diesel powered machinery such as tractors, harvesters, and combines; often replacing human or animal labor and introducing greater efficiency in growing and harvesting farm crops.

mediation: the intervention of an unbiased party to settle differences between two other disputing parties; any attempt to act as a go-between in order to reconcile a problem.

Mobilization: to assemble war materials and manpower and make ready for war.

melodrama: movies, sometimes referred to as "weepies," focused on characters living through a series of adverse and tragic circumstances. A character with a terminal illness is a frequently used plot.

Memorial Day Massacre: a 1937 Steel Workers' Organizing Committee strike in Chicago at the Republic steel mill of U.S. Steel that led to the deaths of ten workers and 30 others wounded by police.

minimum wage: the wage established by law as the lowest amount to be paid to workers in particular jobs.

minstrel shows: stage performances of black American traditional melodies and jokes performed by white actors impersonating blacks, including having their faces blacked.

moderation: acting in a responsible, restrained manner, avoiding excessive behaviors.

modernism: the cultural expression of Western society including the United States since the late nineteenth century, primarily as expressed in literature and visual designs.

modernist art: modernist art may be defined by its self-conscious interest in experimentation with the materials and creative processes of each individual art medium. Freed from representing objects as they actually exist, Modernist artists have tended to stress the subjective uniqueness of their own particular visions.

monopoly: when only one seller of a product, or a combination of sellers, exists who can set his own price.

moonshiner: maker or seller of illegal liquor.

moratorium: a legally authorized period of delay in performing some legal obligation; a waiting period set by an authority; a suspension of activity.

mortgage: normally involves a long-term real estate loan; the borrower gives the bank a mortgage in return for the right to use the property. The borrower agrees to make regular payments to the lender until the mortgage is paid up.

movie star: an actor or actress groomed for celebrity status by a movie production studio.

muckraking: a type of journalism that exposes the misdeeds and corruption in American business and politics of a prominent individual.

munitions: war supplies, particularly ammunition and weapons.

mutual fund: an investment company that invests the money of its shareholders in a diversified group of securities.

N

National Labor Relations Board: a board created in 1935 by the National Labor Relations Act to assist employees in the free selection of representative organizations (unions) to deal with employers, to prevent unfair labor practices, and to see that employers bargained in good faith.

National Union for Social Justice (NUSJ): an organization founded in 1935 by Father Charles Coughlin, the "Radio Priest" of Royal Oak, Michigan, who began a strong lobbying effort to influence Congress on the course of the New Deal.

nationalism: a strong loyalty to one's own nation above all others.

naturalization: the process in which an alien can apply to become a U.S. citizen. Requirements include five years of legal residence, literacy in English, and a record of good behavior.

Nazism: a political philosophy based on extreme nationalism, racism, and military expansion; dominated Germany from 1933 to 1945.

neutrality: policy of not becoming involved in war between two other nations.

New Deal: the name given to Franklin Roosevelt's plan to save the nation from the devastating effects of the Great Depression. His programs included direct aid to citizens and a variety of employment and public works opportunities sponsored by the federal government.

nickelodeon: an early movie theater, usually charging a nickel for admission.

non-durable goods: goods that are consumed or destroyed when used. Examples include chemicals, paper, rubber, textile, apparels, and foods.

O

old-age insurance: assurance of cash payments, generally made monthly, to retired workers' pensions.

oral history: the memories of an event or time, captured in the words of the person who lived it.

organized crime: a specialized form of crime with two major characteristics: organized into loosely or rigidly structured networks of gangs with certain territorial boundaries; the networks with rigid structures have bosses and a centralized management; and devoted to producing, protecting, and distributing illegal goods and services.

P

pacifism: opposed to armed conflict or war to settle disputes.

papal encyclical: an official letter from the Pope stating the Catholic Church's position on timely social issues and offering guidance for Catholic living.

parish: a local area or community of the members of a church.

partisan: adhering to a particular political party.

patron: a wealthy or influential supporter of an artist.

patronage: the power of public officials to make appointments to government jobs or grant other favors to their supporters, or the distribution of such jobs or favors.

pension(s): money given to an employee when they retire from a company. Pensions can be funded by the government, an employer, or through employee contributions.

philanthropy: humanitarian gifts to be distributed for the welfare of the fellow man.

photojournalism: emerged in the 1930s as a special filed of print communications. Magazines, newspapers, and movie newsreels tapped talented photographers to document labor, rural and urban settings, nature, warfare, and other subjects.

Photo-Secession: an informal society and a movement among photographers in the United States founded in 1903 by Alfred Stieglitz. The movement pursued pictorial photography and high aesthetic standards.

pictorial photography: using the camera to create artwork and moving photography outside of the studio. The techniques included soft-focus, manipulation of the negative and print in the dark room, and production of photographs to mimic paintings, watercolors, and other works of art.

pluralism: a situation in a nation when diverse ethnic, racial, or social groups participate in a common political and economic system.

pogrom: planned massacres of groups of people as the massacres experienced by the Jewish people.

pope: the bishop of Rome and head of the worldwide Roman Catholic Church.

pocket veto: a means by which the president of the United States can prevent a bill passed by Congress from becoming law by delaying the signing of the bill within the 10-day time limit required by the Constitution while the Congress is not in session. In contrast should the president fail to sign the bill while the Congress is in session, it would automatically become law.

Ponzi scheme: a fraud racket in which innocent profit-seeking investors pay their money only to discover the company has few assets and no potential to make a profit. Most such schemes collapsed with a few investors running off with the money of many unhappy people.

popular culture: popular culture consists of expressive forms widely available in society. Such forms include, but are not limited to, theater, television, festivals, architecture, furniture, film, the Internet, books, magazines, toys, clothing, travel souvenirs, music, dance, and body customization. Popular culture can also include folk culture and most of what is thought of as elite culture (i.e. the fine arts).

Popular Front: at the direction of the communist leadership in the Soviet Union, the Communist Party, USA, waged strong opposition from 1935 to 1939 against fascism. Part of its strategy was to support the New Deal and President Roosevelt.

populist: to represent the concerns of common people in political matters.

preference hiring: to legally favor members of a particular racial or ethnic group over other people in hiring for work.

protectionism: adoption of policies that protect a nation's economy from foreign competition.

price supports: a government financial aid program for farmers in which commodity prices are set at a certain level at or above current market values. If the market value is less than the set value, the government will pay the farmer the difference. Usually price supports are combined with limitations on production and with the storing of surpluses.

principal: the actual amount of money loaned that must be repaid.

private sector: business not subsidized or directed by the government.

progressive: one who believes in political change, especially social improvement through government programs.

progressive education: educational approach based on child-centered activities that involve hands-on learning in contrast to the highly structured traditional classroom setting focused on memorization.

prohibition: legal prevention of the manufacture, sale, or distribution of alcoholic beverages. The goal of Prohibition is partial or total abstinence from alcoholic drinks. Prohibition officially began on January 16, 1920, when the Eighteenth Amendment took effect, and ended December 5, 1933, when the amendment was repealed.

***proletariat*:** a low social or economic group of society generally referring to the working class who must sell their labor to earn a living.

protestant work ethic: a code of morals based on the principles of thrift, discipline, hard work, and individualism.

public utility: a business that provides an essential public service, such as electricity, and is government regulated.

public works: government funded projects that are intended to benefit the public such as libraries, government buildings, public roads, and hydropower dams.

pump priming: an economic theory as applied by the New Dealers that if enough people received paychecks once again, that they would once again buy goods and services, and the economy would eventually come back into balance.

Q

quotas: the number of people of a certain kind, such as a race or nation, allowed to legally immigrate into a country.

R

racketeering: engaging in a pattern of criminal offenses. Examples of racketeering include gambling, robbery, loan sharking, drug trafficking, pornography, murder, prostitution, money laundering, kidnapping, extortion, fraud, counterfeiting, obstruction of justice, and many more.

ratify: approve.

reactionary: a strongly conservative response or a strong resistance to change.

receiver: a device, such as part of a radio, that receives incoming signals and translates them into something perceptible, such as sound.

recession: an economic slowdown of relatively short duration. During a recession, unemployment rises and purchasing power drops temporarily.

reconversion: to change something, such as industry production, back to what it was before its more recent changes.

refinance: arrange new loan terms so that regular payments can be more affordable. This usually involves adjustment of the interest rate and the length of the repayment period.

regionalism: an artistic movement primarily associated with the 1920s and 1930s in which artists chose to represent facets of American rural and urban life.

relief: when a needy person or family receives money, food, or vouchers from the government for support. This term is not commonly used in the United States anymore, it is currently called welfare.

render: to cook and thereby melt out fat from fatty animal tissue. The cooked fat is then put into a press and the lard squeezed out The remaining product is called crackling.

reorganization: refers to the Indian Reorganization Act of 1934 and a major shift in federal policy toward American Indians during the New Deal. Under Reorganization, the federal government encouraged native arts and crafts, tribalism, and protection of native lands and resources.

repatriation: return to the country of origin.

republic: a government in which political power is primarily held by the citizens who vote for elected officials to represent them.

Republican Party: one of the two major political parties in the United States. The Republican Party emerged in the 1850s as an antislavery party. In the twentieth century, the Republican Party represents conservative fiscal and social policies and advocates a more limited role for federal government.

retrenchment: cutting of expenses from budgets; school retrenchment of the 1930s also included cutbacks in instruction, teacher salaries, number of teachers, and resulted in larger class size.

rhetoric: the use of language effectively toward influencing the conduct of others.

rumrunner: an individual bringing illegal liquor across a border; rumrunners often use boats and sometimes airplanes for the illegal transportation.

S

scabs: non-union laborers brought in to replace striking laborers.

screwball comedy: comedies with sophisticated plots and characters.

scrip: coupons or certificates, usually paper, issued as substitutes for cash in retail establishments to be used for goods and services. The coupons are assigned a specific value and are used as temporary money.

securities: stocks and bonds.

securities loan: a bank loan that uses stocks or bonds as collateral; or a bank's loan to a stockbroker.

segregation: maintaining a separation of the races, normally in public facilities such as restaurants, hotels, theaters, and other public places.

seminary: an institution of higher learning for the religious training for ministers, priests, or rabbis.

Senate: one of the two bodies with specific functions that make up the legislative branch of the United States government. Each state is allocated two senators. (*See also* Congress; House of Representatives)

sensationalism: arousing interest or emotions with shocking, exaggerated treatments and presentation of the news.

separate but equal: an early Supreme Court doctrine established in 1897 held that racial segregation in public facilities did not violate equal protection of the law if equal facilities are available.

separation of powers: the constitutional division of responsibilities between the three independent branches of government—executive, judicial, and legislative.

serial drama: a drama that takes place over a series of episodes, such as a soap opera.

Share-Our-Wealth Plan: Huey Long, senator from Louisiana, promoted the idea of wealth distribution by heavy government taxation of the rich and guaranteeing every family an average wage of $2,000 to $3,000 per year. This concept was carried starting in 1935 by the Share-Our-Wealth Society.

sharecroppers: farm workers who worked the land of a landowner and often could keep half the value of their crops; for the other half they received from the landowner land to farm, housing, fuel, seed, tools, and other necessities in return for part of the crops raised.

shyster: a slick, smart movie character, usually portraying a lawyer, politician, or newspaperman, who was professionally unscrupulous in their dealings.

silver screen: nickname for motion pictures based on the color of the projection screen in a theater where images of adventure and romance entertained viewers.

sit-down strike: a strike where workers remain in the workplace but decline to work. This action effectively blocked the employer from replacing them with other workers. The Supreme Court outlawed this practice in 1939.

slapstick: films employing comedy and farce to entertain viewers.

slums: severely overcrowded urban areas characterized by the most extreme conditions of poverty, dilapidated housing, and crime-ridden neighborhoods.

soap opera: a drama that takes place over a series of episodes. Takes its name from the early sponsorship of radio serial dramas by soap manufacturers.

social insurance: a broad term referring to government sponsored social welfare programs of old age assistance and old age pensions, unemployment supports, worker's compensation, and healthcare programs. The term has two elements: (1) the social element meaning its programs applied to groups not just individual self-interests;

and, (2) the insurance principle under which people are protected in some way against a risk.

social legislation: a bill or legislative proposal sent to Congress which addresses social issues such as old age assistance, pensions, unemployment supports, worker's compensation, and healthcare programs.

social reconstructionism: a more radical form of progressive education; calls for the establishment of a new, more equitable social order accomplished through instruction by teachers in the schools.

Social Security: a public program that provides economic aid and social welfare for individuals and their families through social insurance or assistance. In the United States, Social Security was passed into law in 1935, as a life and disability insurance and old age pension for workers. It is paid for by employers, employees, and the government.

socialism: various political and economic theories calling for collective ownership and administration either by the people or government of the means of production and distribution of goods; sometimes thought of an in-between step between capitalism and communism.

speakeasy: a place where alcoholic beverages were sold illegally during Prohibition; patrons gained admission by giving a simple password, thus the name "speakeasy."

speculation: high risk investments such as buying stocks and/or bonds in hopes of realizing a large profit.

stalemate: a situation in which the two sides in a contest are evenly matched and neither is able to win.

standard of living: basic necessities of food, clothing, and shelter, plus any other conveniences or luxuries the family is unwilling to do without.

stock: certificate of ownership in a company also known as shares.

stock market: a market where shares of stock, or certificates of ownership in a company, are bought and sold.

strike: a labor stoppage where workers, usually through the action of their union, refuse to work until management addresses their complaints or requests about wages, hours, working conditions, and benefits.

strip plowing or strip cropping: to till an agricultural field in strips leaving untilled areas between the tilled strips.

studio system: operating between 1930 and 1945 to produce over 7,500 feature films, eight "studios" or major companies dominated film production, distribution, and exhibition. Studios not only made films, they owned theaters that projected their products. They also secured exclusive contracts with actors and actresses.

substantive due process of law: pertaining to the purpose of the act such as limitations put on someone.

suburb: a community on the outskirts, but within commuting distance, of a city.

suburbanization: to create suburbs around a central city.

suffrage: the right to vote especially in a political election.

survivors' insurance: monthly cash benefits paid to the surviving family members of a worker who has died. Survivors may include the wife, dependent children under eighteen years of age, and a dependent parent age 62 or older.

swashbuckler: movies generally set among pirates and knights with melodrama, sword play, and cannon fire.

swing: a type of rhythm driven jazz that became very popular during the depression era. Like other forms of jazz, swing incorporates improvisation. Swing is also associated with "big bands" of sixteen musicians or more. Vocalists were also associated with swing and big bands. The term swing is often credited to Duke Ellington and the 1932 song "It Don't Mean a Thing (if it ain't got that swing);" the dance craze of the mid- to late 1930s.

syndicate: an association or network of groups of individuals who cooperate to carry out activities of an enterprise. The groups may be formal or informal and may carry out legal or illegal activities.

syndicated: to sell a piece or column written by one journalist to many newspapers across the country for publication at the same time. The column is generally signed by the author.

synthetic: something made by artificially combining components, unlike a process which occurs naturally.

T

talkie: a motion picture with sound accompaniment.

tariff: a tax on items imported, often in the form of duties or customs. It is intended to make foreign-made goods more expensive than goods made in the United States.

tenant farming: an agricultural system in which farmers rented farmland and provided their own tools. They received two-thirds to three-fourths of the value of their crops. Often they purchased tools, clothing, and food with loans against crops they expected to grow the following season. The landlord kept records and computed earnings.

tenement: large housing structures containing apartment dwellings that barely meet or do not meet minimum standards of sanitation and comfort.

tenure: an assurance of job stability.

temperance: the use of alcoholic beverages in moderation or abstinence from their use.

terracing: changing a sloped hillside into a series of flat planting areas.

totalitarianism: a political system in which the government exercises complete control over its citizens.

Townsend Plan: proposal of Dr. Francis E. Townsend of Long Beach, CA., in 1933, calling for the federal government to give a pension of $200 a month to every U.S. citizen on the condition that the money be spent within 30 days.

Townsendites: advocates of the Townsend Plan who pressed hard for their version of old-age pension benefits between 1933 and 1940.

***Townsend Weekly*:** a publication of the supporters of the Townsend Plan which articulated their views and discontent with the Social Security Act.

transcription show: in early radio, a show that was recorded on disc for distribution to radio stations for later transmission.

transients: a person traveling around, usually in search of work.

transmitter: a device that generates a carrier wave encapsulating a signal derived from speech or music or other sources, and radiates the results from an antenna.

trespass: to unlawfully enter the land of another person.

tribalism: maintaining the social integrity of a traditional Indian tribe through support of its customs and beliefs.

trilogy: a series of three artistic works such as three musical pieces or books.

trust: the fiduciary (legal and monetary) responsibility of the federal government is known as trust or "trust responsibility." This concept was guaranteed by treaties and supported by the findings of the U.S. Supreme Court in the case of *Cherokee Nation v. Georgia* (1831). The trust responsibility compels the federal government to act in the best interest of tribes when setting policy or passing laws.

trustee: one to whom property is entrusted to be administered for the benefit of another, or one of a number of persons appointed to manage the affairs of an institution.

U

unconstitutional: to determine that a federal or state law is not in agreement with the Constitution.

underworld: the world of organized crime.

underwrite: to guarantee financial support of a company or program, assuming financial responsibility.

unemployment insurance: cash payments made for a certain period of time to a worker who involuntarily loses their job. The worker must be able and willing to work when a new job is available.

unionism: a belief in the right of workers to organize and bargain collectively with employers over work conditions.

urban: relating to a city.

urbanization: people moving from farms and small rural communities to large cities.

V

vaccine: any preparation introduced into the body to prevent a disease by stimulating antibodies against it.

vagrant: a person wandering about with no permanent address and no visible or permanent means of financial support.

variety show: a form of entertainment, usually consisting of a series of acts, such as songs, comedy, and dances.

Vaudeville: emerged out of burlesque in the early twentieth century for family audiences. Vaudeville consists of musical acts, short plays, comedy acts, and skits. Vaudeville, unable to compete with the movies, virtually disappeared in the early 1930s with many vaudeville theaters converted to movie houses.

venereal disease: contagious disease acquired through sexual intercourse.

ventriloquist: the art of projecting one's voice, often into a wooden dummy. A form of entertainment that includes a dialogue between the dummy and the ventriloquist.

vivisection: the action of cutting into or dissecting a living body; the practice of subjecting living animals to cutting operations in order to advance physiological and pathological knowledge.

volunteer: carrying out a service out of one's own free will and without payment for the action.

W

Wall Street: the location in New York City of the New York Stock Exchange.

welfare: when a needy person or family receives money, food, or vouchers from the government for support. Traditionally called "going on the dole," or relief.

welfare-to-work: term used in the late twentieth century in the United States to describe programs that seek to move welfare recipients from welfare to private employment.

western: a film genre which became popular in the 1930s and despite some criticism remained popular through the years.

wets: those who opposed Prohibition.

wildcat strike: a locally organized work stoppage, not necessarily endorsed by a labor union, to try to achieve worker goals.

workers' compensation: programs designed to provide cash benefits and medical care to workers who sustain a work-related illness or injury.

work relief: when the government provides a needy person with a paying job instead of simply giving them money for support. Different from the current term, welfare-to-work, in that the "work" in work relief is on a government-sponsored project; the "work" in welfare-to-work is in the private sector. The term is not commonly used anymore in the United States.

Y

yardstick: in a sense like a real yardstick, a standard by which to measure. As used by Franklin D. Roosevelt, the term refers to a government program or agency set up to perform a task normally done by private industry in order to assess whether that private industry is charging a fair price for its services.

yellow dog contract: a signed agreement in which an employee promises not to join a labor union.

yellow journalism: an extreme form of sensationalism taking real life events and twisting and turning stories to catch the public's attention. Stories are not only exaggerated but misrepresented.

Young Communist League: An organization focused on teenagers and Americans in their twenties promoting the philosophy and politics of the Communist Party, USA; active in the 1920s and 1930s.

Z

Zionism: the movement to established a national homeland for the Jewish people in Palestine.

General Bibliography

This bibliography contains a list of sources, including books, periodicals, novels, and websites, that will assist the reader in pursuing additional information about the topics contained in this volume.

Books

Adams, Henry H. *Harry Hopkins: A Biography.* New York: G.P. Putnam's Sons, 1977.

Agee, James, and Walker Evans. *Let Us Now Praise Famous Men: Three Tenant Families.* Boston: Houghton Mifflin Co., 2000.

Altmeyer, Arthur J. *The Formative Years of Social Security.* Madison: The University of Wisconsin Press, 1968.

Andersen, Kristi. *The Creation of a Democratic Majority, 1928–1936.* Chicago: University of Chicago Press, 1979.

Anderson, James D. *The Education of Blacks in the South, 1860–1935.* Chapel Hill: University of North Carolina Press, 1988.

Appel, Benjamin. *The People Talk: American Voices from the Great Depression.* New York: Simon & Schuster, 1982.

Balderrama, Francisco E., and Raymond Rodríguez. *Decade of Betrayal: Mexican Repatriation in the 1930s.* Albuquerque: University of New Mexico Press, 1995.

Barber, William J. *Designs within Disorder: Franklin D. Roosevelt, the Economists, and the Shaping of American Economic Policy, 1933–1945.* New York: Cambridge University Press, 1996.

———. *From New Era to New Deal: Herbert Hoover, the Economists, and American Economic Policy, 1921–1933.* New York: Cambridge University Press, 1985.

Bauman, John F., and Thomas H. Goode. *In the Eye of the Great Depression: New Deal Reporters and the Agony of the American People.* DeKalb: Northern Illinois University Press, 1988.

Bentley, Joanne. *Hallie Flanagan: A Life in the American Theatre.* New York: Alfred A. Knopf, 1988.

Bergman, Andrew. *We're in the Money: Depression America and Its Films.* New York: New York University Press, 1971.

Bernstein, Irving. *A Caring Society: The New Deal, the Worker, and the Great Depression.* Boston: Houghton Mifflin Co., 1985.

———. *Turbulent Years: A History of the American Worker, 1933–1941.* Boston: Houghton Mifflin Co., 1970.

Best, Gary D. *The Critical Press and the New Deal: The Press Versus Presidential Power, 1933–1938.* Westport: Praeger, 1993.

Bindas, Kenneth J. *All of This Music Belongs to the Nation: The WPA's Federal Music Project and American Society.* Knoxville: University of Tennessee Press, 1995.

Black, Gregory D. *Hollywood Censored: Morality Codes, Catholics, and the Movies.* New York: Cambridge University Press, 1994.

Bloomfield, Maxwell H. *Peaceful Revolution: Constitutional Change and American Culture from Progressivism to the New Deal.* Cambridge, MA: Harvard University Press, 2000.

Brinkley, Alan. *Culture and Politics in the Great Depression.* Waco, TX: Markham Press Fund, 1999.

———. *The End of Reform: New Deal Liberalism in Recession and War.* New York: Alfred A. Knopf, 1995.

———. *Voices of Protest: Huey Long, Father Coughlin, and the Great Depression.* New York: Knopf, 1982.

Brown, Lorraine, and John O'Connor. *Free, Adult, Uncensored: The Living History of the Federal Theatre Project.* Washington, DC: New Republic Books, 1978.

Brown, Robert J. *Manipulating the Ether: The Power of Broadcast Radio in Thirties America.* Jefferson, NC: McFarland & Co., 1998.

Buhite, Russell D., and David W. Levy, eds. *FDR's Fireside Chats.* Norman: University of Oklahoma Press, 1992.

Burns, Helen M. *The American Banking Community and New Deal Banking Reforms.* Westport: Greenwood Press, 1974.

Bustard, Bruce I. *A New Deal for the Arts.* Seattle: University of Washington Press, 1997.

Caldwell, Erskine, and Margaret Bourke-White. *You Have Seen Their Faces (1937).* New York: Derbibooks, 1975.

Ciment, James. *Encyclopedia of the Great Depression and New Deal.* Armonk: M.E. Sharpe, Inc., 2001.

Clarke, Jeanne N. *Roosevelt's Warriors: Harold L. Ickes and the New Deal.* Baltimore: Johns Hopkins University Press, 1996.

Clavin, Patricia. *The Failure of Economic Diplomacy: Britain, Germany, France and the United States, 1931–36.* New York: St. Martin's Press, 1996.

Cole, Olen, R., Jr. *The African American Experience in the Civilian Conservation Corps.* Gainesville: University Press of Florida, 1999.

Cole, Wayne S. *Roosevelt and the Isolationists, 1932–1945.* Lincoln: University of Nebraska Press, 1983.

Conkin, Paul Keith *The New Deal.* Arlington Heights: Harlan Davidson, 1992.

Cook, Blanche W. *Eleanor Roosevelt: Vol. 2, The Defining Years, 1933–1938.* New York: Penguin, 2000.

Crouse, Joan M. *The Homeless Transient in the Great Depression: New York State, 1929–1941.* Albany: State University of New York Press, 1986.

Cushman, Barry. *Rethinking the New Deal Court: The Structure of a Constitutional Revolution.* New York: Oxford University Press, 1998.

Davis, Kenneth S. *FDR: The New Deal Years, 1933–1937.* New York: Random House, 1986.

DeNoon, Christopher. *Posters of the WPA.* Los Angeles: Wheatley Press, 1987.

Dickinson, Matthew J. *Bitter Harvest: FDR, Presidential Power, and the Growth of the Presidential Branch.* New York: Cambridge University Press, 1997.

Dubofsky, Melvyn. *Hard Work: The Making of Labor History.* Urbana: University of Illinois Press, 2000.

Dubofsky, Melvin, and Stephen Burnwood, eds. *Women and Minorities During the Great Depression.* New York: Garland Publishing, 1990.

Edsforth, Ronald. *The New Deal: America's Response to the Great Depression.* Malden, MA: Blackwell Publishers, 2000.

Eliot, Thomas H. *Recollections of the New Deal: When the People Mattered.* Boston: Northeastern University Press, 1992.

Fausold, Martin L. *The Presidency of Herbert C. Hoover.* Lawrence: University Press of Kansas, 1985.

Federal Writers Project. *These Are Our Lives.* New York: W.W. Norton & Company, Inc., 1939.

Fine, Sidney. *Sit-Down: The General Motors Strike of 1936–1937.* Ann Arbor: University of Michigan Press, 1969.

Flanagan, Hallie. *Arena: The Story of the Federal Theatre.* New York: Duell, Sloan and Pearce, 1940.

Flynn, George Q. *American Catholics and the Roosevelt Presidency, 1932–1936.* Lexington: University Press of Kentucky, 1968.

Fraser, Steve, and Gary Gerstle, eds. *The Rise and Fall of the New Deal Order, 1930–1980.* Princeton: Princeton University Press, 1989.

Freidel, Frank. *Franklin D. Roosevelt: Launching the New Deal.* Boston: Little, Brown, 1973.

———. *Franklin D. Roosevelt: A Rendezvous with Destiny.* New York: Little, Brown & Co., 1990.

French, Warren, Ed. *A Companion to the "The Grapes of Wrath."* New York: Penguin Books, 1989.

Fried, Albert. *FDR and His Enemies.* New York: Palgrave, 1999.

Galbraith, John Kenneth. *The Great Crash, 1929.* Boston: Houghton Mifflin Company, 1997.

Gall, Gilbert J. *Pursuing Justice: Lee Pressman, the New Deal, and the CIO.* Albany: State University of New York Press, 1999.

Graham, Maury, and Robert J. Hemming. *Tales of the Iron Road: My Life as King of the Hobos.* New York: Paragon House, 1990.

Greenberg, Cheryl Lynn. *"Or Does It Explode?": Harlem in the Great Depression.* New York: Oxford University Press, 1991.

Gregory, James N. *American Exodus: The Dust Bowl Migration and Okie Culture in California.* New York: Oxford University Press, 1989.

Guerin-Gonzales, Camille. *Mexican Workers and American Dreams: Immigration, Repatriation, and California Farm Labor, 1900–1939.* New Brunswick: Rutgers University Press, 1994.

Hall, Thomas E., and J. David Ferguson. *The Great Depression: An International Disaster of Perverse Economic Policies.* Ann Arbor: University of Michigan Press, 1998.

Hamilton, David E. *From New Day to New Deal: American Farm Policy from Hoover to Roosevelt, 1928–1933.* Chapel Hill: University of North Carolina Press, 1991.

Harris, Jonathan. *Federal Art and National Culture: The Politics of Identity in New Deal America.* New York: Cambridge University Press, 1995.

Hastings, Robert J. *A Nickel's Worth of Skim Milk: A Boy's View of the Great Depression.* Carbondale: Southern Illinois University Press, 1986.

Healey, Dorothy, and Maurice Isserman. *Dorothy Healy Remembers: A Life in the Communist Party.* New York: Oxford University Press, 1990.

Hill, Edwin G. *In the Shadow of the Mountain: The Spirit of the CCC.* Pullman, WA: Washington State University Press, 1990.

Himmelberg, Robert F. *The Origins of the National Recovery Administration.* New York: Fordham University Press, 1976.

Hockett, Jeffrey D. *New Deal Justice: The Constitutional Jurisprudence of Hugo L. Black, Felix Frankfurter, and Robert H. Jackson.* Lanham: Rowman & Littlefield Publishers, 1996.

Horan, James D. *The Desperate Years: A Pictorial History of the Thirties.* New York: Bonanza Books, 1962.

Hurt, Douglas. *American Agriculture: A Brief History.* Ames: Iowa State University Press, 1994.

Hurt, R. Douglas. *The Dust Bowl: An Agricultural and Social History.* Chicago: Nelson-Hall, 1981.

Ickes, Harold L. *The Secret Diary of Harold L. Ickes: The First Thousand Days, 1933–1936; The Inside Struggle, 1936–1939; The Lowering Clouds, 1939–1941.* 3 vols. New York: Simon & Schuster, 1952–54.

Jeansonne, Glen. *Messiah of the Masses: Huey P. Long and the Great Depression.* New York: HarperCollins College Publishers, 1993.

Jellison, Charles A. *Tomatoes Were Cheaper: Tales from the Thirties.* Syracuse, NY: Syracuse University Press, 1977.

Jonas, Manfred. *Isolationism in America, 1935–1941.* Ithaca: Cornell University Press, 1966.

Kalfatovic, Martin R. *The New Deal Fine Arts Projects: A Bibliography, 1933–1992.* Metuchen: Scarecrow Press, 1994.

Kennedy, David M. *Freedom From Fear: The American People in Depression and War, 1929–1945.* New York: Oxford University Press, 1999.

Kindleberger, Charles P. *The World in Depression, 1929–1939.* Berkeley: University of California Press, 1986.

Kirby, John B. *Black Americans in the Roosevelt Era: Liberalism and Race.* Knoxville: University of Tennessee Press, 1980.

Klein, Maury. *Rainbow's End, The Crash of 1929.* New York: Oxford University Press, 2001.

Kornbluh, Joyce L. *A New Deal for Workers' Education: The Workers' Service Program, 1933–1942.* Urbana: University of Illinois Press, 1987.

Lacy, Leslie A. *The Soil Soldiers: The Civilian Conservation Corps in the Great Depression.* Radnor: Chilton Book Company, 1976.

Leuchtenberg, William E. *The FDR Years: On Roosevelt and His Legacy.* New York: Columbia University Press, 1995.

———. *Franklin D. Roosevelt and the New Deal, 1932–1940.* New York: Harper & Row, 1963.

———. *New Deal and Global War.* New York: Time-Life Books, 1964.

Lindley, Betty, and Ernest K. Lindley. *A New Deal for Youth: The Story of the National Youth Administration.* New York: Viking, 1938.

Long, Huey P. *Every Man a King: The Autobiography of Huey P. Long.* New Orleans: National Book Company, Inc., 1933.

Low, Ann Marie. *Dust Bowl Diary.* Lincoln: University of Nebraska Press, 1984.

Lowitt, Richard. *The New Deal and the West.* Bloomington: Indiana University Press, 1984.

Lubov, Roy. *The Struggle for Social Security, 1900–1935.* 2nd ed. Pittsburgh: University of Pittsburgh Press, 1986.

Maidment, Richard A. *The Judicial Response to the New Deal.* New York: Manchester University Press, 1991.

Martin, George. *Madam Secretary: Frances Perkins.* Boston: Houghton Mifflin, 1976.

McElvaine, Robert S. *The Great Depression: America, 1929–1941.* New York: Times Books, 1993.

McJimsey, George. *Harry Hopkins: Ally of the Poor and Defender of Democracy.* Cambridge: Harvard University Press, 1983.

———. *The Presidency of Franklin Delano Roosevelt.* Lawrence: University of Kansas Press, 2000.

Meltzer, Milton. *Brother, Can You Spare a Dime? The Great Depression, 1929–1933.* New York: New American Library, 1977.

———. *Driven From the Land: The Story of the Dust Bowl.* New York: Benchmark Books, 2000.

Melzer, Richard. *Coming of Age in the Great Depression: The Civilian Conservation Corps in New Mexico.* Las Cruces: Yucca Tree Press, 2000.

Mettler, Suzanne. *Dividing Citizens: Gender and Federalism in New Deal Public Policy.* Ithaca: Cornell University Press, 1998.

Milner, E.R. *The Lives and Times of Bonnie and Clyde.* Carbondale, IL: Southern Illinois University Press, 1996.

Moley, Raymond, and Eliot A. Rosen. *The First New Deal.* New York: Harcourt, Brace & World, Inc., 1966.

Nye, David E. *Electrifying America: Social Meanings of a New Technology.* Cambridge: The MIT Press, 1990.

Ohl, John K. *Hugh S. Johnson and the New Deal.* De Kally: Northern Illinois University Press, 1985.

Olson, James S., ed. *Historical Dictionary of the 1920s: From World War I to the New Deal, 1919–1933.* Westport: Greenwood, 1988.

———, ed. *Historical Dictionary of the New Deal: From Inauguration to Preparation for War.* Westport: Greenwood, 1985.

———. *Saving Capitalism: The Reconstruction Finance Corporation and the New Deal, 1933–1940.* Princeton: Princeton University Press, 1988.

Parker, Stamford. *FDR: The Words That Reshaped America.* New York: Quill, 2000.

Parrish, Michael E. *Anxious Decades: America in Prosperity and Depression, 1920–1941.* New York: W.W. Norton, 1992.

———. *Securities Regulation and the New Deal.* New Haven: Yale University Press, 1970.

Perkins, Frances. *The Roosevelt I Knew.* New York: The Viking Press, 1946.

Perkins, Van L. *Crisis in Agriculture: The Agricultural Adjustment Administration and the New Deal, 1933.* Berkeley: University of California Press, 1969.

Philip, Kenneth R. *John Collier's Crusade for Indian Reform, 1920–1954.* Tucson: University of Arizona Press, 1977.

Phillips, Cabell. *From the Crash to the Blitz, 1929–1939.* New York: Macmillan, 1969.

Potter, Claire Bond. *War on Crime: Bandits, G-Men, and the Politics of Mass Culture.* New Brunswick, NJ: Rutgers University Press, 1998.

Powers, Richard Gid. *G-Men, Hoover's FBI in American Popular Culture.* Carbondale: Southern Illinois University Press, 1983.

Radford, Gail. *Modern Housing for America: Policy Struggles in the New Deal Era.* Chicago: University of Chicago Press, 1996.

Reagan, Patrick D. *Designing a New America: The Origins of New Deal Planning, 1890–1943.* Amherst: University of Massachusetts Press, 1999.

Reiman, Richard A. *The New Deal and American Youth: Ideas and Ideals in a Depression Decade.* Athens: University of Georgia Press, 1992.

Reisler, Mark. *By the Sweat of Their Brow: Mexican Immigrant Labor in the United States, 1900–1940.* Westport, CN: Greenwood Press, 1976.

Rogers, Agnes. *I Remember Distinctly: A Family Album of the American People, 1918–1941.* New York: Harper & Brothers Publishers, 1947.

Roosevelt, Eleanor. *The Autobiography of Eleanor Roosevelt.* New York: Da Capo Press, 2000.

———. *The Autobiography of Eleanor Roosevelt.* New York: Harper and Brothers Publishers, 1958.

Roosevelt, Franklin D. *The Public Papers and Addresses of Franklin D. Roosevelt.* 5 vols. New York: Random House, 1938-1950.

Rose, Nancy E. *Put to Work: Relief Programs in the Great Depression.* New York: Monthly Review Press, 1994.

Rothermund, Dietmar. *The Global Impact of the Great Depression, 1929–1939.* New York: Routledge, 1996.

Rozell, Mark J., and William D. Pederson. *FDR and the Modern Presidency: Leadership and Legacy.* Westport, CN: Praeger, 1997.

Ruth, David E. *Inventing the Public Enemy: The Gangster in American Culture, 1918–1934.* Chicago: University of Chicago Press, 1996.

Rutland, Richard A. *A Boyhood in the Dust Bowl, 1926–1934.* Boulder: University Press of Colorado, 1997.

———. *The Democrats: From Jefferson to Clinton.* Columbia: University of Missouri Press, 1995.

Salmond, John A. *The Civilian Conservation Corps, 1933–1942: A New Deal Case Study.* Durham: Duke University Press, 1967.

Schieber, Sylvester J., and John B. Shoven. *The Real Deal: The History and Future of Social Security.* New Haven: Yale University Press, 1999.

Schlesinger, Arthur M., Jr. *The Coming of the New Deal: The Age of Roosevelt.* Boston: Houghton Mifflin Company, 1988.

Schwartz, Jordan A. *The New Dealers: Power Politics in the Age of Roosevelt.* New York: Alfred A. Knopf, 1993.

Sennett, Ted. *This Fabulous Century: The Thirties.* New York: Time-Life Books, 1967.

Shindo, Charles J. *Dust Bowl Migrants in the American Imagination.* Lawrence: University Press of Kansas, 1997.

Sitkoff, Harvard. *A New Deal for Blacks: The Emergence of Civil Rights as a National Issue, the Depression Years.* New York: Oxford University Press, 1978.

Skidelsky, Robert. *John Maynard Keynes: The Economist as Saviour, 1920–1937.* New York: Viking Penguin, 1994.

Smith, Page. *Redeeming the Time: A People's History of the 1920s and the New Deal.* 8 vols. New York: Penguin, 1987.

Smith, Wendy. *Real Life: The Group Theatre and America, 1931–1940.* New York: Knopf, 1990.

Sobel, Robert. *The Great Bull Market: Wall Street in the 1920s.* New York: Norton, 1968.

Sternsher, Bernard. *Rexford Tugwell and the New Deal.* New Brunswick Rutgers University Press, 1964.

Stevens, J .E. *Hoover Dam: An American Adventure.* Norman: University of Oklahoma Press, 1988.

Storrs, Landon R.Y. *Civilizing Capitalism: The National Consumers' League, Women's Activism, and Labor Standards in the New Deal Era.* Chapel Hill: University of North Carolina Press, 2000.

Svobida, Lawrence. *Farming in the Dust Bowl.* University Press of Kansas, 1986.

Swados, Harvey, ed. *The American Writers and the Great Depression.* New York: Bobbs-Merrill Company, Inc., 1966.

Swain, Martha H. *Ellen S. Woodward: New Deal Advocate for Women.* Jackson: University Press of Mississippi, 1995.

Szostak, Rick. *Technological Innovation and the Great Depression.* Boulder: Westview Press, 1995.

Terkel, Studs. *Hard Times: An Oral History of the Great Depression.* New York: Pantheon Books, 1986.

Thompson, Kathleen, and Hilary MacAustin, eds. *Children of the Depression.* Bloomington: Indiana University Press, 2001.

Tobey, Ronald C. *Technology as Freedom: The New Deal and the Electrical Modernization of the American Home.* Berkeley: University of California Press, 1996.

Toland, John. *The Dillinger Days.* New York: Da Capo Press, 1995.

Tugwell, R. G. *The Brain Trust.* New York: Viking Press, 1968.

Tyack, David, Robert Lowe, and Elisabeth Hansot. *Public Schools in Hard Times: The Great Depression and Recent Years.* Cambridge: Harvard University Press, 1984.

Uys, Errol Lincoln. *Riding the Rails: Teenagers on the Move During the Great Depression.* New York: TV Books, 2000.

Ware, Susan. *Beyond Suffrage: Women and the New Deal.* Cambridge: Harvard University Press, 1981.

———. *Partner and I: Molly Deson, Feminism, and New Deal Politics.* New Haven: Yale University Press, 1987.

Watkins, T. H. *The Hungry Years: A Narrative History of the Great Depression in America.* New York: Henry Holt and Company, 1999.

———. *Righteous Pilgrim: The Life and Times of Harold L. Ickes, 1874–1952.* New York: Henry Holt & Co., 1990.

Wicker, Elmus. *The Banking Panics of the Great Depression.* New York: Cambridge University Press, 1996.

Wigginton, Eliot, ed. *Refuse to Stand Silently By: An Oral History of Grass Roots Social Activism in America, 1921–1964.* New York: Doubleday, 1992.

Winfield, Betty H. *FDR and the News Media.* New York: Columbia University Press, 1994.

Winslow, Susan. *Brother, Can You Spare a Dime? America From the Wall Street Crash to Pearl Harbor: An Illustrated Documentary.* New York: Paddington Press, 1979.

Worster, Donald. *Dust Bowl: The Southern Plaines in the 1930s.* New York: Oxford University Press ,1982.

Zieger, Robert H. *The CIO, 1930–1935.* Chapel Hill: University of North Carolina Press, 1995.

Periodicals

Adamic, Louis. "John L. Lewis's Push to Power," *Forum,* March 1937.

Amberson, W.R. "The New Deal for Share-Croppers," *Nation,* February 13, 1935.

Ballantine, A.A. "When All the Banks Closed," *Harvard Business Review,* March 1948.

Berle, A.A., Jr. "What's Behind the Recovery Laws," *Scribner's,* September 1933.

Broun, Heywood. "Labor and the Liberals," *Nation,* May 1, 1935.

Cannon, Brian Q. "Power Relations: Western Rural Electric Cooperatives and the New Deal," *Western Historical Quarterly,* vol. 31, Number 2 (2000).

Childs, M.W. "The President's Best Friend," *Saturday Evening Post,* April 26, 1941.

Cole, Olen, Jr. "The African-American Experience in the Civilian Conservation Corps," *Western Historical Quarterly,* vol. 31, no. 4 (2000).

Daniels, Jonathan. "Three Men in a Valley," *New Republic,* August 17, 1938.

Don Passos, John. "Washington: The Big Tent," *New Republic,* March 14, 1934.

Epstein, Abraham. "Social Security Under the New Deal," *Nation,* September 4, 1935.

Fleck, Robert K. "Population, Land, Economic Conditions, and the Allocation of New Deal Spending," *Explorations in Economic History,* Volume 38, Number 2 (2001).

Flynn, J.T. "The New Capitalism," *Collier's,* March 18, 1933.

Fogel, Jared A., and Robert L. Stevens. "The Cavas Mirror: Painting as Politics in the New Deal," *Magazine of History,* vol. 16, no. 1 (2001).

Garraty, John A. "Unemployment During the Great Depression," *Labor History,* Spring 1976.

Hirsch, Arnold R. "'Containment' on the Homefront: Race and Federal Housing Policy From the New Deal to the Cold War," *Journal of Urban History,* vol. 26, no. 2 (2000).

Hopkins, Harry L. "Beyond Relief," *New York Times Magazine,* August 19, 1934.

Ickes, Harold L. "My Twelve Years with F.D.R.," *Saturday Evening Post,* June 12, 1948.

Lord, Russell. "Madame Secretary," *The New Yorker,* September 2 and 9, 1933.

McCormick, Anne O'Hare. "The Great Dam of Controversy," *New York Times Magazine,* April 20, 1930.

McWilliams, Carey. "A Man, a Place, and a Time: John Steinbeck and the Long Agony of the Great Valley in an Age of Depression, Oppression, and Hope," *The American West,* May 1970.

Metzer, Richard. "Coming of Age in the Great Depression: The Civilian Conservation Corps Experience in New Mexico, 1933–1942," *Western Historical Quarterly,* vol. 32, no. 3 (2001).

Morgenthau, Henry, Jr. "The Paradox of Poverty and Plenty," *Collier's,* October 25, 1947.

Naison, Mark D. "Communism and Black Nationalism in the Depression: The Case of Harlem," *Journal of Ethnic Studies,* Summer 1974.

Nelson, Daniel. "Origins of the Sit-Down Era: Worker Militancy and Innovation in the Rubber Industry, 1934–1938," *Labor History,* Spring 1982.

Ohanian, Lee E. "Why Did Productivity Fall So Much During the Great Depression?," *American Economic Review,* vol. 91, no. 2 (2001).

Perkins, Frances. "Eight Years as Madame Secretary," *Fortune,* September 1941.

Poe, J.C. "The Morgan-Lilienthal Feud," *Nation,* October 3, 1936.

Pringle, H.F. "The President," *The New Yorker,* June 16–23, 1934.

Richberg, Donald. "The Future of the NRA," *Fortune,* October 1934.

Sherwood, Robert E. "Harry Hopkins," *Fortune,* July 1935.

Shover, John L., ed. "Depression Letters From American Farmers," *Agricultural History,* July 1962.

Stevens, Robert L., and Jared A. Fogel. "Images of the Great Depression: A Photogrpahic Essay," *Magazine of History,* vol. 16, no. 1 (2001).

Summers, Mary. "The New Deal Farm Programs: Looking for Reconstruction in American Agriculture," *Agricultural History,* vol. 74, no. 2 (2000).

Swing, R.G. "Father Coughlin," *Nation,* January 2, 1935.

Swing, R.G. "The Purge at the AAA," *Nation,* February 20, 1935.

Tugwell, Rexford. "The Price Also Rises," *Fortune,* January 1934.

Tugwell, Rexford. "America Takes Hold of Its Destiny," *Today,* April 28, 1934.

Webbink, Paul. "Unemployment in the United States, 1930–40," *American Economic Review,* February 1941.

White, Edward G. "The Constitution and the New Deal," *Journal of Interdisciplinary History,* vol. 32, no. 2 (2001).

Novels

Adamic, Louis. *My America (1938).* New York: Da Capo Press, 1976.

Caldwell, Erskine. *Tobacco Road.* Thorndike, ME: G.K. Hall, 1995.

Cantwell, Robert. *The Land of Plenty.* Carbondale: Southern Illinois University Press, 1971.

Dos Passos, John. *U.S.A.* New York: Penguin Books, 1996.

Farrell, James T. *Studs Lonigan: A Trilogy.* New York: The Modern Library, 1938.

Hurston, Zora Neale. *Their Eyes Were Watching God (1937).* New York: Harper & Row, 1990.

Lee, Harper *To Kill a Mockingbird.* Philadelphia: Chelsea House Publishers, 1998.

Steinbeck, John. *The Grapes of Wrath.* New York: The Viking Press, 1939.

Wright, Richard. *Uncle Tom's Children.* New York: The World Publishing Company, 1938.

———. *Native Son.* New York: Harper & Row, 1940.

Websites

Bonneville Power Administration. http://www.bpa.gov

Civilian Conservation Corps Alumni. http://www.cccalumni.org

Franklin D. Roosevelt Library and Museum. http://www.fdrlibrary.marist.edu

Roosvelt University. Center for New Deal Studies. http://www.roosevelt.edu/newdeal.htm

Library of Congress. American Memory. http://memory.loc.gov/ammem/fsowhome.html

New Deal Network. http://newdeal.feri.org

Riding the Rails. The American Experience. Public Broadcast System. Website: http://www.pbs.org/wgbh/amex/rails/

Social Security Administration. http://www.ssa.gov

Tennessee Valley Authority. http://www.tva.gov

Index

Bold page numbers indicate a primary article about a topic. Italic page numbers indicate illustrations. Tables and charts are indicated by a t *following the page number. The index is sorted in word-by-word order.*

A

B

C

D

Index

F

Index

G

H

I

J

K

L

Index

O

P

Index

Q

R

T

U

V

W

Y

Z

Index